General Principles of EU Law and European Private Law

EUROPEAN MONOGRAPHS

In the European Monographs series this book, *General Principles of EU Law and European Private Law* is the eighty-fourth title. The titles published in this series are listed at the end of this volume.

General Principles of EU Law and European Private Law

Edited by

Ulf Bernitz
Xavier Groussot
Felix Schulyok

Wolters Kluwer
Law & Business

Published by:
Kluwer Law International
PO Box 316
2400 AH Alphen aan den Rijn
The Netherlands
Website: www.kluwerlaw.com

Sold and distributed in North, Central and South America by:
Aspen Publishers, Inc.
7201 McKinney Circle
Frederick, MD 21704
United States of America
Email: customer.service@aspenpublishers.com

Sold and distributed in all other countries by:
Turpin Distribution Services Ltd
Stratton Business Park
Pegasus Drive, Biggleswade
Bedfordshire SG18 8TQ
United Kingdom
Email: kluwerlaw@turpin-distribution.com

Printed on acid-free paper.

ISBN 978-90-411-4683-0

Printed and Bound by CPI Group (UK) Ltd, Croydon, CR0 4YY.

List of Editors and Contributors

Helene Andersson is currently a Doctoral Candidate at Stockholm University, after having worked in private practice for twelve years, specializing in competition law. In her research she focuses on the enforcement of EU Competition rules from a fundamental rights perspective. She published a number of articles in journals such as the ECLR, Concurrences and the GCLR (Global Competition Litigation Review).

Joxerramon Bengoetxea (Ph.D. Edinburgh) is professor titular of Jurisprudence and Sociology of Law in the University of the Basque Country where he coordinates the ehuGune project on interaction between Academia and Civil Society in current social issues and teaches EU law and Comparative Legal Cultures. He is actively involved with the International Institute for the Sociology of Law at Oñati and the Centre of Excellence on Foundations of European Law and Polity of the University of Helsinki.

Ulf Bernitz is Professor of European Law at Stockholm University. He is also a fellow of St Hilda's College, Oxford and Director of the Oxford/Stockholm Venture in European Law. He has published an extensive amount of works in the field, as well as in civil law. He is former chair and currently a member of the Swedish Network for European Legal Studies, chair of the Swedish Association of European Law and a former President of FIDE.

Guido Comparato is a post-doctoral researcher at the European University Institute in Florence in the framework of the research project 'European Regulatory Private Law: the transformation of European private law from autonomy to functionalism in competition and regulation'. He was a doctoral researcher at the Centre for the Study of European Contract Law at the University of Amsterdam from 2008 until 2012 in the framework of the research project 'National resistance against the Europeanization of private law'. Bachelor and Master of Laws from the University of Ferrara, Italy (2005 and 2008). Current research interests include private law theory and European private law.

Wouter Devroe is full professor of law at KU Leuven and professor of Competition law at Maastricht University. He previously clerked at the ECJ and is a member of the Belgian national competition authority. Publications and legal practice focus on national and EU economic and competition law. He co-manages the 'Ius commune casebooks for the common law of Europe' (www.casebooks.eu). As an attorney (Brussels Bar, Allen & Overy LLP) he pleads before national and EU authorities and courts (a.o. in Cases C-45/08 *Spector*, C-439/08 *VEBIC* and C-17/10 *Toshiba*).

Ian S. Forrester QC LLD practises European law with White & Case in Brussels. Admitted: Faculty of Advocates (the Scottish Bar) (1972), New York State Bar (1977), English Bar (1996), Brussels Bar (1998). Appointed Queen's Counsel (1988), Visiting Professor (1991), Honorary Professor and Honorary Doctor of Laws (2009), Glasgow University. Arbitrator under the rules of the ICC and ICSID. Master of the Bench, Middle Temple. Head of White & Case's worldwide pro bono practice. Academic teacher and author of some 100 articles or chapters on European legal and policy topics, in particular competition, customs, dumping, pharmaceuticals, sport, the precautionary principle, and human rights. From 2009 to 2013, has published several articles on due process in competition cases. Has participated in many competition cases before the European Courts, European Commission and national courts and agencies, including *Government of Gibraltar v. Council*; *Magill*; *Bosman*; *Microsoft*; *IMS*; *Pfizer Animal Health*; *Glaxo Spain*; *Syfait et al. v. GlaxoSmithKline*; *Les Laboratoires Servier*; *A and Others v. National Blood Authority*; *Halcor*.

Xavier Groussot is professor of EU Law at Lund University and guest professor at the European College of Paris (Université Panthéon-Assas, Paris II). His fields of research are related to EU constitutional law, free movement and procedural law.

Arthur Hartkamp obtained his Doctorate at the University of Amsterdam in 1971 after studies in law in Amsterdam, Munich and Rome. He worked previously in the Civil Code Revision Office, Dutch Ministry of Justice (1974–1989) and was Advocate General and Procureur-General at the Supreme Court of The Netherlands (1986–2006). He is Professor of European Private Law, Radboud Universtiy Nijmengen (2006 to date) and first Vice-President of UNIDROIT. Arthur Hartkamp is author of a treatise in several volumes on the Dutch Law of Obligations (8 editions) and of (*inter alia*) *European Law and National Private Law. Effect of EU Law and Human Rights Law on Legal relationships between Individuals* (Kluwer 2012).

Marijn W Hesselink is Professor of European Private Law and Director of the Centre for the Study of European Contract Law at the University of Amsterdam. He studied law at the University of Amsterdam and Panthéon-Assas (Paris II) and obtained his doctorate at the University of Utrecht. He is an editor of the *European Review of Contract Law* and a member of the European Commission's expert group on European contract law. He is also a deputy justice at the Court of Appeal in Amsterdam.

Dorota Leczykiewicz is Leverhulme Trust Early Career Fellow in the Faculty of Law and a Fellow of Trinity College, University of Oxford. Her research interests include EU fundamental rights, comparative private law and the EU law of remedies. She is the author of 'Horizontal Application of the Charter of Fundamental Rights' (2013) 38 European Law Review 479, '"Where Angels Fear to Tread": The EU Law of Remedies and Codification of European Private Law' (2012) 8 European Review of Contract Law 47, and '"Effective Judicial Protection" of Human Rights after Lisbon: Should National Courts Be Empowered to Review EU Secondary Law?' (2010) 35 European Law Review 326.

Robert van Mastrigt (B.A. (Hons.)) is a LL.M. student in the Master Programme European Law of Utrecht University. After he obtained his Bachelor degree in Law with honours (cum laude) he was one of the few students who were selected for the honours programme of the Master European Law.

Hans-W. Micklitz is Professor for Economic Law at the European University Institute since 2007, since 2012 Head of Department, and Jean Monnet Chair of Private Law and European Economic Law at the University of Bamberg, Germany, on leave. He is holder of an ERC Grant 2011–2016 on European Regulatory Private Law. His main field of activities are European Law, European Private and Consumer Law.

Peter Oliver is a Legal Advisor in the European Commission. He worked as *référéndaire* for Advocate General Slynn from 1983 to 1986. He holds a Ph.D. from Cambridge University and is a Visiting Professor at the Université Libre de Bruxelles. He is the author of over sixty-five publications on EU law, including 'Free Movement of Goods in the European Union' (5th ed., Hart Publishing, 2010). He is currently working on a book entitled 'The Fundamental Rights of Corporations' (Hart Publishing).

Juha Raitio is Professor of European Law at the University of Helsinki, Finland. Previously he has worked as a Professor of European law at the University of Joensuu. He has written various books and articles in the field of EU law and legal theory. For example, his monograph 'The Principle of Legal Certainty in EC Law' (2003) has been published by Kluwer Academic Publishers' Law and Philosophy series. Currently his main research interest relates to Internal Market Law as well as EU Constitutional law. He is President of the Finnish European Law Association and Member of the Steering Group in the Nordic Network for European Legal Studies.

Norbert Reich is Emeritus professor of German and European Civil and Economic Law at the University of Bremen. He is now a visiting professor at the University of Groningen/NL and has held similar prior positions at Montpellier, Lucerne, Keele/UK, Tartu/Estonia, Vilnius/Lithuania. He was Rector of the Riga Graduate School of Law from 2001–2004 and Fernard Braudel Senior Fellow at the EUI Florence in 2009. Main publications: (with Hans Micklitz and Peter Rott) Understanding EU Consumer Law, 2009; Understanding EU Internal Market Law, 3rd ed. 2013 forthcoming.

Marek Safjan, born 1949; Doctor of Law (University of Warsaw, 1980); habilitated Doctor in Legal Science (University of Warsaw, 1990); Professor of Law (1998); Director of the Civil Law Institute of the University of Warsaw (1992–1996); Vice-Rector of the University of Warsaw (1994–1997); Secretary General of the Polish Section of the Henri Capitant Association of Friends of French Legal Culture (1994–1998); representative of Poland on the Bioethics Committee of the Council of Europe (1991-1997); Judge (1997–1998), then President (1998–2006), of the Constitutional Court; member (since 1994) and Vice-President (since 2010) of the International Academy of Comparative Law, member of the International Association of Law, Ethics and Science (since 1995), member of the Helsinki Committee in Poland; member of the Polish Academy of Arts and Sciences; Pro Merito Medal conferred by the Secretary General of the Council of Europe (2007); author of a very large number of publications in the fields of civil law, medical law and European law; Doctor honoris causa of the European University Institute (2012); Judge at the Court of Justice of the European Union since 7 October 2009.

Felix Schulyok is currently Ph.D. candidate at Copenhagen University, after having studied law at Vienna University (Mag.iur. in Austrian law) and Lund University (LL.M. in European Business Law). In his current research he focuses on the scope of application of EU law, especially EU fundamental rights, and questions of horizontal effects, as well as on EU Citizenship. He published a number of articles on different questions of EU law, ranging from VAT law over Trade Mark law to EU Citizenship and EU fundamental rights.

Carla Sieburgh is professor of Private law, in particular the influences of European Law on national private law (Radboud University Nijmegen, 2003). She has degrees in both medicine and law. After having obtained her doctorate in law (2000, cum laude) she was until 2003 law clerk of the Procureur-Général at the Supreme Court of The

Netherlands. Since 2001 she is also part time Alternate Judge in the Amsterdam Court of Appeal. Since 2010, she is a member of the Royal Netherlands Academy of Arts and Sciences. Her most significant field of research is the confrontation and interaction of European law and private law and the growing influence of Europe on private law. One of her current research projects is the Ius Commune Casebook on Horizontal effects of primary EU law. See for a short impression *Juridical pioneering/Fast facts*, video with introduction to field of research, November 2011, http://www.youtube.com/watch?v=r2jx6Io-vkA.

Ingeborg Simonsson is one of Sweden's leading experts in competition law. She is a judge in the Stockholm City Court, and Ph.D. and associate professor in competition law at Stockholm University. Her previous work experience includes several years in private practice and five years as a full time academic.

John Temple Lang is Professor of law at Trinity College Dublin, and Senior Visiting Research Fellow at Oxford University. He was a Director at the Directorate General Competition of the European Commission from 1989 to 2000 and before that worked in the Legal Service of the European Commission, and in private practice. He has an LL.D. degree from Trinity College Dublin, and an honorary doctorate in law from the University of Lund. He has published a book and more than 300 articles, mostly on European law, and has appeared in many cases before the European Courts. In 2000 he joined Cleary Gottlieb Steen & Hamilton LLP in Brussels.

Takis Tridimas is the Sir John Lubbock Professor of Banking Law at the Centre for Commercial Law Studies, Queen Mary University of London. He is also the Nancy A. Patterson Distinguished Faculty Scholar and Professor at Pennsylvania State University. He is a barrister at Matrix Chambers. He is the author of numerous publications including *The General Principles of EU Law* (2nd Ed., Oxford, 2006). He has acted as advisor to EU institutions and public and private organizations. He was senior legal adviser to the EU Presidency (2003) and Chairman of the Committee set up by the EU Council of Ministers to draft the Treaty of Accession of 2003.

Sybe de Vries (Ph.D.) is the Jean Monnet Chair in EU Single Market Law & Fundamental Rights at the Europa Institute, Utrecht University. In 2006, he obtained his Ph.D. at Utrecht University for his dissertation 'Tensions within the Internal Market – The Functioning of the Internal Market and the Development of Horizontal and Flanking Policies'. In 2010 he was a visiting researcher at the Institute of European and Comparative Law of the University of Oxford. His research has focused on the protection of fundamental rights within the EU internal market. He has authored and co-authored a number of articles in law journals and books in the field of European law and public economic law. He was the co-editor of the book *The protection of fundamental rights in the EU After Lisbon,* Oxford: Hart Publishing, 2013 (with S. Weatherill and U. Bernitz).

Angela Ward is a référendaire in the Cabinet of Advocate General Niilo Jääskinen at the Court of Justice of the European Union. Prior to joining the Court she was in practice in the Bars of England and Wales and Ireland, specialising in EU law and Human Rights. She has held several academic posts, and is currently a Visiting Professor at Birkbeck College, University of London. She is a founding editor of the Cambridge Yearbook of European Legal Studies, and is the author of around thirty publications on EU Law, including 'Judicial Review and the Rights of Private Parties in EU Law' (OUP, 2007).

Summary of Contents

Table of Contents

Part IV: Competition Law and General Principles

Preface

This volume on the General Principles of EU Law and European Private Law deals with an area of European law of particular complexity and ever growing importance. Due to their nature, the general principles offer a more or less unlimited field for legal studies, at the same time as they play a rapidly increasing role in legal practice. The first volume on General Principles of EC Law was published in the year 2000, based on an international conference held in Malmö, Sweden in 1999. The second volume, General Principles of EC Law in a Process of Development, based on a conference in Stockholm in 2007, was published in 2008. They dealt primarily with general principles from the perspective of human rights and administrative law. Both volumes have been very well received and are often cited; the first volume has been sold out.

This third volume has another focus, namely the role of general principles in the ongoing development of European private law. The vision behind the volume, its main structure and core features of its eighteen articles are presented by the editors in an introductory chapter. The other chapters are centered around four main themes: the methodology in the elaboration of private law principles within union law, the constitutionalization of private autonomy, horizontal direct effect of general principles and the role of general principles in competition law. As an overriding conclusion, there is reason to stress the colossal potential and impact of the EU Charter of Fundamental Rights in relations between private parties. Like the previous volumes, the contributions in the book also demonstrate the fundamental role of the general principles in the successive creation of a *jus commune europaeum*.

As a platform for the preparation of this book, The Swedish Network for European Legal Studies organized in Lidingö, just outside Stockholm, in 8–9 November 2012, an international conference on the subject. Invited as speakers were a mixture of eminent and well known experts, many of whom had taken part already in the previous general principles conferences, and a selection of younger scholars in the field. We had two days of most fruitful exchange of ideas based on excellent papers. Although this volume is based on a selection of the papers presented at the conference, all papers have been rewritten and edited extensively before publication.

The object of the Swedish Network for European Legal Studies (Snels) is to establish an independent forum that will allow researchers to meet, discuss and open up new paths of investigation within the field of European law, on national and European level. The Network, funded by public means allocated by the Swedish Parliament, arranges conferences, symposia and seminars and actively supports the publishing of research material. More information about the Network can be found at www.snef.se

I wish to thank my co-organizers and co-editors Xavier Groussot, Professor of European Law at Lund University and doctoral candidate in European law Felix Schulyok, Copenhagen University for all their intellectual efforts in preparing the project. Felix has been instrumental also in the more practical parts of the process and its successful completion. We also wish to thank Professor Antonina Bakardjieva Engelbrekt, Professor of European Law at Stockholm University and chair of the Network for the strong support of the project offered by the Network.

Ulf Bernitz
Professor of European Law at Stockholm University

Vision, Essence and Narratives of General Principles and European Private Law: An Introduction

Ulf Bernitz, Xavier Groussot & Felix Schulyok

This introductory essay presents, first, the pre-conference vision and ideas of the organizers on the issues and questions to be discussed at the conference. Second, it systematizes and discusses the essence and narratives of the papers presented at the conference. Finally, it concludes with opening the debate on the enormous potential of the EU Charter of Fundamental Rights (hereinafter 'the Charter' or 'CFR') when it comes to relations between private parties.

I THE VISION

General principles in European law have been widely debated in the last decade. During the two conferences on general principles held in Malmö (1999) and Stockholm (2007), general principles of law were mainly discussed from the perspective of human rights and administrative law. General principles of law, however, are essential to the development of European Private Law.

In fact, there are traces of general principles emerging in EU law, which can affect the private law sphere. All private relations have a public law component. First of all, overriding general principles will, of course, affect the private law sphere when issues like proportionality and legal expectations arise. The question is though whether there are any more specific principles of EU law, which have such an impact? What come to mind would be principles of law established by the Union courts, which in a very general way affect or regulate relations between private parties – rather than just being motivated by general welfare interest. Not legislative enactments, but judge-made principles. The right to property is, for example, already an established principle. One would also think of the freedom to contract, *pacta sunt servanda* or good faith. They are examples of general principles in private law, which could qualify as such general principles – if it can be established that they have been pronounced on by the EU courts. But have the courts made statements, which specifically relate to them or to the private law sphere in general?

[A] Issue 1: Methodology

It appears to us that the issues of methodology and legal theory have been addressed to an insufficient degree in relation to general principles of private law. What is the methodology (if any) of the CJEU in discovering general principles of private law? Could the human rights methodology based often on a comparative approach ('the evaluative approach') be used as a source of inspiration? Is there a role to play for the EU Charter of Fundamental Rights? Are there other sources of inspiration better fitted for European private law? What is the relationship between constitutional principles and private law principles in EU law? What is the impact of the *Audiolux* and *NCC Danmark* cases on the understanding of general principles of law? Is there a hierarchy between private law and public law principles? Ought we to talk about general principles of European private law?

[B] Issue 2: Horizontal Effect

Another issue proposed by the organizers to be discussed during the conference was the horizontal effect of EU law rights from a private law perspective. Advocate General Bot opined in *Kücükdeveci,* that 'given the ever increasing intervention of Community law in relations between private persons, the Court will ... be inevitably confronted with other situations which raise the question of the right to rely, in proceedings between private persons' on EU fundamental rights. The Case C-70/10 *Scarlet Extended* offers, in that sense, a recent illustration of the horizontal effect of intellectual property rights. What is the status of horizontal effect in EU law? What are the rights boasting such a nature in EU Law? Is there a future for 'increased' horizontal effect in EU law after the entry into force of the EU Charter of Fundamental Rights? Horizontal effect also inevitably leads to the question of liability and damages. The *Laval* saga constitutes a perfect illustration. The Swedish Labour court afforded horizontal damages in *Laval* on the basis of, *inter alia*, Case C-94/07 *Raccanelli.* Still, it is rather unclear, to say the least, and contentious what criteria of assessment should be used in the context of damages between private parties for breach of EU law.

[C] Issue 3: Private Law and General Principles of EU Law

The third broad issue envisioned by the organizers of the conference concerned the classical relationship between private law and general principles of EU law, to be debated in light of recent jurisprudential developments and the entry into force of the EU Charter of Fundamental Rights. It is now well known that the general principles constitute effective tools for the European judge reviewing acts of the Union institutions or of the Member States which have an impact on the private law context. The rights of defence, which are backed by general principles of EU law, are often an issue in competition law proceedings. Likewise, the general principle of effective judicial protection is extensively used in the field of civil remedies. Looking at the recent CJEU case law, it appears that the respect of the rights of defence in competition law proceeding constitutes a burning issue. This is even more true if we place it in the broader context of the accession of the EU to the European Convention of Human Rights. The Grand Chamber in Case C-17/10 *Toshiba Corporation* from 14 February 2012 reflects this growing concern. In this case, the Court had to deal with the difficult application of the *ne bis in idem* principle in competition law.

[D] Concluding Remarks

It is clear that the scope of the 2012 conference was intended to be very broad since it covered both the very existence of general principles of private law and the relationship between private law and general principles of EU law. This approach was in our view necessary in order both to understand the divide, or lack thereof, between private and public law in the EU legal order and to shape an EU methodology which is rendered unavoidable by the growing heterogeneity of the legal sources. This broad scope was also reflected in the discussions at the conference and the contributions to this book, which in some sense went beyond the three issues defined by the organizers before the conference to be the basis of the discussions and can rather be grouped into four narratives, as will be outlined below.

II ESSENCE AND NARRATIVES OF GENERAL PRINCIPLES AND EUROPEAN PRIVATE LAW

This book enshrines eighteen papers delivered at the conference in plenary sessions or within the three working groups, which were set up according to the three broad issues envisioned by the organizers before the conference as outlined above. We have, however, considered that the papers may be classified into four main narratives, which highlight the core issues related to general principles and European private law. The first group of papers (Hesselink, Bengoetxea and Temple Lang) concerns issues of methodology and theory in the elaboration of new general principles of law. The second group of papers (Comparato & Micklitz, Safjan and Leczykiewicz) deals with the constitutionalization of private autonomy. The third group of papers (Hartkamp, Raitio, Tridimas, Sieburgh, De Vries & Van Mastrigt, Oliver, Reich and Ward) concerns the broad issue of horizontal direct effect viewed in the light of different (conceptual, sectoral and remedial) perspectives. The fourth group (Forrester, Andersson, Simonsson and Devroe) considers the relationship between general principles of EU law and competition law. In the following sections the essence of these four narratives will be presented.

[A] First Narrative: Methodology in the Elaboration of Private Law Principles

It is important to keep in mind as a starting point that it is not an easy task to define the general principles of EU law. In that respect, we think it is appropriate to refer to AG Mazak in the *Masdar* Case.[1] According to the Advocate General, '... [A]s is generally the case with general principles of law as a legal source, until there is settled case-law on the matter discussing the concrete content of such a principle can be very much like discussing the shape of a ghost'.[2] The CJEU has started to rely on the concept of general principles of civil law in cases like *Société Thermale, Messner, Hamilton* and *E-Fritz.*[3] As expressed by Hesselink, although it is not entirely clear what exactly the Court means by (general) private law principles,[4] the wording adopted by the Court nevertheless seems to have been a deliberate choice. The specific principles that have been indicated, so far, by the Court as (general) principles of civil law, include, in particular, the principles of the binding force of contract, of good faith, and of unjust enrichment.

During the Stockholm conference and in the contributions of this anthology, many speakers/authors have developed their views in relation to the methodology in elaborating private law principles. In his paper ('Private law principles, pluralism and perfectionism'), Hesselink addresses the question of whether state endorsed general principles of private law can ever be legitimate in the presence of a plurality of values and principles that people regard as fundamental for their lives and for their interaction with each other as the central question of his paper. In particular, he focuses on the potential normative challenges to the Court's and the European Commission's sets of private law principles. These normative challenges have in common that they share the modernist project of grounding political institutions in reasonable principles. For Hesselink, as long as we remain cautious and remain subject to a firm commitment to a common political conception of the right, the quest for general private law principles is perfectly legitimate. There is no contradiction in seeking to find general private law principles in a pluralist world.

Bengoetxea in his contribution ('General Legal Principles Navigating Space and Time') considers that the history of European legal culture shows principles travelling across frontiers and systems and settling down, sedimenting, to form specific (national) *legal institutions*. This process is still taking place and the discussion on the models of Europe depends very much on tracing back the travels and itineraries of ideas (including very importantly general principles of law) and predicting their new destinations. Who are the main players redefining such legal cultural heritage? Will

1. Case C-47/07 P *Masdar* [2008] ECR I-9761, para. 45.
2. *Ibid.*, para. 45.
3. The main examples include Case C-277/05, *Société thermale d'Eugénie-les-Bains v. Ministère de l'Économie, des Finances et de l'Industrie* [2007] ECR I-06415; Case C-412/06, *Annelore Hamilton v. Volksbank Filder eG* [2008] ECR I-02383; Case C-489/07 *Pia Messner v. Firma Stefan Krüger* [2009] ECR I-07315; Case C-215/08, *E. Friz GmbH v. Carsten von der Heyden* [2010] ECR I-02947.
4. For an attempt at clarification, see Martijn W. Hesselink, 'The general principles of civil law: their nature, roles and legitimacy', in Dorota Leczykiewicz & Stephen Weatherill (eds) *The Involvement of EU Law in Private Law Relationships* (Oxford: Hart Publishing, forthcoming).

they follow an inclusive, dialectical and participatory approach or will they yield to market forces, elites, or powers that be? Ultimately for Bengoetxea the question is not so much whether one can formulate normative ideas into a general principle of law but rather whether this principle will carry acceptability and consensus, and this depends not so much on calling it a 'principle', even though principles do carry a positive charge just for the term's sake, but on moral, political and ultimately religious or cultural-ideologically bounded conceptions of the person or the self, factors of the audience and the actors that have to make the decision. That these factors will be at play when a given court analyses concrete cases is undeniable. But the way the Court of Justice, for instance and more clearly so than the US Supreme Court, deals with them does show a tendency to rely on seemingly neutral *ideology-free* principles in order to avoid having to appear to be making decisions based on more personal views and inclinations, on preferences.

John Temple Lang ('Emerging European General Principles in Private Law') provides us with an intellectual framework for general principles in private law, and suggests to us potential general principles since there is scope for developing 'General Principles' in private law. According to him, not all those suggested may ultimately be accepted as general principles, but there are a number of principles that are important enough to be considered by the European Courts. For Temple Lang, the General Principle that seems most relevant in private law is the duty of sincere cooperation of national authorities with the objectives of the EU and the EEA under Article 4(3) TEU and Article 3 EEA. This duty obliges national courts to provide 'effective' protection in a wide variety of situations for rights given by EU and EEA law, including private rights. However, criteria are needed to identify circumstances in which national courts should not allow private parties to waive their rights under EU law. Importantly for the author, the Charter has enormous potential that has not yet been realized under the Convention.

[B] Second Narrative: The Constitutionalization of Private Autonomy

The constitutionalization of private autonomy constitutes the second narrative and, to put it concisely, reflects the clash between the different and opposite goals in European law (or European Policies) and private law. Notably, the concept of private autonomy may gain in weight and importance due the entry into force of the Charter, which incorporates provisions clearly anchored in such a concept, as can, for example, be seen in its Article 16. If this is true, it means that private autonomy can be used to counter-balance EU policies or the so-called 'regulated autonomy' in horizontal situations and may thus help to shift the balance towards the individual in certain circumstances. The Charter appears here as a perfect tool to challenge the 'Marketization of private autonomy' (a term coined by Comparato and Micklitz in their paper) and perhaps opens the path to a new test that could be employed by the CJEU (see in this respect the contributions of Leczykiewicz and Sieburgh on horizontal direct effect) to restore the balance between specific general interests (e.g., fundamental freedoms) and individual autonomy. This second narrative can be related both to the issues of methodology and horizontal direct effect.

In their contribution ('Regulated Autonomy between Market Freedoms and Fundamental Rights in the Case-Law of the CJEU'), Comparato and Micklitz describe how the principle of private autonomy can undergo a process of 'constitutionalisation', specifically in the context of the European legal system, and what this means for the substance of the principle.[5] The premise of this contribution is that, although several principles at the European level are drawn from the national legal orders, the alleged constitutionalization of private autonomy at the European level does not coincide with the mere supranational recognition of the same principle which is already enshrined in national constitutions. Autonomy in the European order, which can be termed as regulated autonomy, can be better described as an instrument to conform individual behaviour for the purpose of achieving the policy objectives of the European Union. To a certain extent, constitutionalised autonomy in the EU differs from the traditional understanding of autonomy as a constitutional legal principle which has been proposed in the literature and case law of the highest national courts.

For judge Safjan ('European Law *versus* Private Law: Transformation or Deformation of the Paradigm?'), the influence of European law is visible not only in specific solutions adopted in private law, but also in the methodology that imposes a certain style of legal interpretation which must ensure the co-existence of various systems. Safjan in his essay goes into the specific feature of European private law, which is related to the fact that the mechanisms of European private law are dominated by the goals to which the European Union aspires as a separate, autonomous legal and political body. By contrast, the starting point for the regulatory instruments of classical private law is an individual and his or her autonomy; while the starting point for the European regulatory instruments in the sphere of private law are specific general interests represented by the European Union, among them the protection of fundamental freedoms and general principles on which the European legal order is based. For Safjan, even if the change of the private law paradigm should be inevitable, he strongly believes that it should consist in a transformation and not deformation of its fundamental mission of expressing individual interests, in order to satisfy the goals related to the construction of the common legal area. The evolution of European private law, taking place over recent decades, should not lead to a questioning of the goals and the fundamental mission of private law.

Dorota Leczykiewicz in her paper ('Fundamental Rights: In Search of Social Justice or Private Autonomy in EU Law?') argues that until recently fundamental rights were in horizontal situations mainly used to achieve greater social justice rather than to enhance private autonomy, yet in more recent case law parties increasingly rely on Article 16 CFR as a (limited) guarantee of private autonomy, the protection of which can be a legitimate aim to limit the full effectiveness of Directives and public (and EU) as well as private regulation in general. With regard to the relationship between the

5. According to Comparato and Micklitz, 'This is not the place to discuss what constitutionalisation at the EU level means. For the sake of the argument it suffices to equate constitutionalisation with the existence of a higher legal order which shapes the contours of the private legal order'.

fundamental freedoms and private autonomy, she states that these situations are rather to be seen as triangular (public regulation as a restriction). She analyses the question in how far and how Articles 15 & 16 of the Charter can be relied upon in horizontal situations in order to protect private autonomy, mainly by discussing the judgments in *Scarlet Extended* (also *Promusicae*), *Netlog* and *TV2 Danmark*, and concludes that largely thanks to Article 16 CFR private actors can enjoy more explicitly the protection of their autonomy. She questions whether also Directives outside the field of intellectual property law (which obviously restrict economic freedom), like those guaranteeing equal treatment, will in the future be interpreted by the Court not only in the light of social fundamental rights but also in the light of Article 16 of the Charter.

[C] Third Narrative: Horizontal Direct Effect

The third narrative concerns the analysis of Horizontal Direct Effect. The different contributions can be linked to three types of analysis: a conceptual analysis of horizontal direct effect, a sectoral analysis of horizontal direct effect (i.e., related to specific EU instruments/areas such as the economic freedoms, the Charter or merely Article 16 of the Charter); and an analysis of horizontal direct effect in connection to remedies and the principle of effectiveness.

For Hartkamp ('The Concept of (Direct and Indirect) Horizontal Effect of EU Law. The Terminology of European Law Scholars and of Private Law Scholars Compared'), the concepts of direct and indirect effect and of vertical and horizontal effect have been coined in the doctrine of European law. To those studying the effects of European law on private law the definitions used by scholars of European law are not always clear. For a private lawyer to be able to describe the different effects of European law on private law it is necessary to analyse the differences more in detail than, apparently, is customary in the professional literature on European law. According to Hartkamp, it is not the intention of his paper to embark upon a discussion of the nature of the difference(s) between public law and private law or on exact definitions of the two. Speaking about private law he refers to general private law which comprises *i.a.* contract law, tort law, the law of restitution (unjust enrichment) and property law. For clarity's sake and in order to avoid misunderstandings he only considers relationships between private individuals, although of course in a number of jurisdictions private law extends to (some) relationships between private individuals and public authorities, e.g., unlawful acts or undue payments.

Raitio ('The Expectation of Legal Certainty and Horizontal Effect of EU law') puts the case law of the CJEU into the context of recent Nordic conceptions of legal certainty, such as Gustafsson's idea of social acceptability and moral acceptability in the context of substantive legal certainty or his own, consisting of a threefold conception of legal certainty, namely formal, factual and substantive (corresponding to legal positivism, legal realism and natural law, respectively). As an example of early case law he discusses *Defrenne II* and finds that the aspect of the case limiting its temporal effects takes the demands of factual legal certainty (or social acceptability) into account in a well-balanced way, however, that the Court normally with regard to the question of temporal effects relied on the more predictable formal legal certainty. With regard to recent case law (such as *Mangold, Kücükdeveci, Ruiz Zambrano, Dereci* and *Dominguez*), his hypothesis is that if the Court would be inclined to rely more on fundamental rights arguments its interpretation would become more teleological, but that it has not been willing to 'run wild' and stayed more with its traditional systematic interpretation. He opposes an ultra-teleological interpretation of EU law, as he is of the opinion that if courts settle for casuism and neglect a systematic interpretation, the coherence of the legal system will be hampered.

In 'Horizontal effect of general principles: Bold Rulings and Fine Distinctions', Takis Tridimas considers that the distinction between direct and indirect horizontality lies mostly in the formal reasoning that underpins each form of horizontality and less in their effects. Direct and indirect horizontality can best be viewed as different sides of the same coin. For Tridimas, the horizontal effect of a general principle may be justified for many reasons. It may be necessitated on functional grounds where a private entity exercises de facto public power or a power traditionally reserved to the state. It may be justified because of the value that the principle incorporates. It may be said, for example, that the prohibition of discrimination on grounds of race or gender are of such constitutional value that they should trump the principle of private autonomy and bind both public and private actors. In the absence of direct horizontality, however, it is not clear that EU law places national courts under a general duty not to enforce any private law obligations which run counter to general principles, beyond the duty of consistent interpretation. Tridimas concludes that the indirect horizontality of the general principles of law and the Charter is wide. However, the case law as it stands does not go as far as to require in all circumstances that national rules which fall within the scope of EU law and are incompatible with the general principles or the Charter must be set aside.

Sieburgh ('General Principles and the Charter in private law relationships. Constructive and critical input from private law') believes that, besides the classic analysis of the effects that EU law has, as coming from above (supranational law), on private law (top-down approach to research), it is also necessary to analyse what she calls the bottom-up effects (bottom-up approach), raising basically the question that given the effects that EU law has on private law, what are the expected reactions from private law actors and how will they use EU law. She argues that individuals will always seek all existing possibilities and arguments to support their case and will, therefore, also use fundamental rights arguments in horizontal situations. She exemplifies this by pointing to the use of fundamental rights arguments to justify restrictions to fundamental freedoms, the justification of anti-competitive agreements (Article 101), and the moulding of EU law remedies of *private law origin* by balancing mutual aims (e.g., the passing-on defence).

Sybe de Vries and Robert van Mastrigt discuss in their paper ('The horizontal direct effect of the four freedoms: From a hodgepodge of cases to a seamless web of judicial protection in the EU Single Market?') the case law on horizontal effects of the four freedoms and give three strands of argumentation when it comes to the rationale behind such effects. (1) *Effet utile*, (2) a certain dominance of one of the parties (*Ferlini, Angonese, Raccanelli*) and (3) the underlying principle of non-discrimination (which is, as, the 'fundamental rights-twist', the reason for the horizontal application in *Angonese* and *Raccanelli*). They further discuss the implications of accepting such horizontal effects, spanning from the effects on private autonomy (which according to them should not be seen as absolute and should, therefore, not be a reason against horizontal effects from the outset), the questions of liability for breaches (also *Laval* style of liability questions), the convergence between free movement and competition law and the problems with the justifications for restrictions that individuals might face. They also point to the possible extension of legislative competence (or competence creep) for the Union through the horizontal application of fundamental freedoms (as, e.g., with regard to roaming costs for mobile phones, which can be seen as a restriction of free movement, which in turn can justify legislative measures by the Union). The article shows the shortcomings of alternatives to horizontal effects (consistent interpretation). According to the authors *full* horizontal effect should be reserved for discriminatory measures (*Angonese*) (fundamental rights-twist), otherwise a limited horizontal effect is to be preferred, taking factors such as the collectiveness of the rules, the dominant position of one of the parties, the de facto regulatory power of a party or the fact that (e.g., in a similar situation as the 'Buy Irish' campaign) the measure draws on nationalism and ethnicity that could strongly influence consumers into account. However, the purchasing choices of an individual undertaking should not be caught by, e.g., Article 34 TFEU.

Peter Oliver ('The Freedom to conduct a business under Article 16 of the Charter') focuses on the analysis of a specific provision of the EU Charter of Fundamental Rights. According to him, the right to freely conduct a business should (now) only be based on the Charter and not (also) on the General Principle, however, the pre-Lisbon case law should now be relevant for the Charter right. He analyses the relevant case law and argues that claims based on what is now Article 16 CFR were never successful (except *Scarlet Extended*, which, however, was mainly decided on the basis that the required injunction would be disproportionate; he states that this was a perhaps unique case in which the Court expressly held a measure to be in breach of Article 16 CFR, albeit not read in isolation, but with Union legislation and submits that *ABNA* should also be regarded as a case in which an argument based on freedom to conduct a business was successful, however also this case was decided on the basis of proportionality). The reason for this low success rate is to be found in the fact that the right is closely related to the right to property. Also claims based on that right are almost always rejected by the Court, which is partly due to the broad exceptions that the ECtHR accepts as justifications for its limitation under the ECHR. Furthermore, cases in which the freedom to conduct a business is threatened are often solved on the basis of other grounds, such as equality, legitimate expectations or fundamental freedoms. However, he submits that Article 16 of the Charter nevertheless has an important role to play, as it has to be taken into account by all authorities, and especially also the Union legislature. Thus, the direct application of Article 16 CFR seems to be reserved for extreme cases, which he welcomes.

Norbert Reich ('The Principle of Effectiveness and EU Private Law') enters into the application of the principles of effectiveness in EU Law. He distinguishes between three different functions and approaches of the effectiveness principle in EU law, namely (1) the elimination rule (the traditional understanding limiting national procedural autonomy in the sense that it eliminates restrictions *to* protection, but does not create remedies *for* protection), (2) the hermeneutical use of the principle (i.e., use as interpretative principle, e.g., with regard to the Air-Passenger Regulation and the Court's interpretation that it can only be effective if also passengers who were suffering from a 'long delay' are treated like those whose flights are cancelled) and (3) the remedial principle ('upgrading' of national remedies to make them sufficient for the protection of Union rights; see also Article 19(1) TEU). Linking rights to remedies should, thus, be done by a hybridization approach: The applicable national remedy has to be identified, then it needs to be measured against the eliminatory principles of effectiveness and equivalence and if the result is unsatisfactory as providing 'insufficient remedies' it has to be 'upgraded' to meet the required EU standards. The result is a *hybrid*, as it takes elements of national law in the limits of procedural autonomy as well as effectiveness in its different functions into account. Effective remedies relate to both, substance (e.g., compensation, restitution, avoidance of a contract term) and procedure (standing, injunctions, time-limits).

Angela Ward ('Remedies under the Charter in disputes arising in private law') points out that the Charter does not lay down any rules about the legal sanctions that should be available in cases of breaches of rights contained in it. Yet, she argues that the established case law by the Court on effective judicial protection (equivalent and effective protection) and Article 47 CFR do have significant potential for certain Charter rights to be enforceable horizontally. She also puts special emphasis on Article 47 (also in combination with Article 19(1) TEU), which, according to her, has horizontal effects by virtue of its content.

[D] Fourth Narrative: Competition Law and General Principles

Ian Forrester ('From Regulation 17/62 to Article 52 of the Charter of Fundamental Rights') traces the different phases of procedural rules applicable to decisions by DG Competition in competition cases and contrasts the present situation with the applicable fundamental rights standards under the ECHR (and ECtHR case law) and the Charter. He comes to the conclusion that the procedures are not sufficient as competition fines have to be qualified as criminal penalties, meaning that the procedure would have to live up to the requirements under Article 6 ECHR, which they do not. He makes several suggestions of how to solve these problems (or at least make them less grave), by, e.g., separating the persons investigating from the decision-maker, upgrading the importance of the hearing or upgrading the role of the hearing officer. He also points to the problem of the sometimes low intensity of review carried out by the General Court and the CJEU (in his submission especially inappropriate when it comes to the review of the level of fines imposed). He concludes that the case law of the ECtHR is not clear (with regard to the required level of judicial review under Article 6 ECHR and whether 'full' judicial review can remedy procedural shortcomings at the first instance), that the case law from Luxembourg is inadequate to satisfy Article 6 ECHR in all cases and that the Commission's decision-making regime in competition cases is 'deeply inadequate'. He hopes that this will be changed in the future or that the decisions will at least be exposed to scrutiny from the ECtHR.

Helene Andersson ('Judicial Review after *Menarini*') is concerned with the question of the standard of judicial review required in competition law from the standpoint of fundamental rights. She analyses case law from the ECtHR (*Menarini*), the EFTA Court and the CJEU on the question whether the standard of review lives up to the requirements under the ECHR and the Charter. This analysis takes *Menarini* as its starting point (the ECHR being the minimum standard) and comes to the conclusion that the ECtHR in this case gave the term 'full jurisdiction' a more narrow meaning for administrative as compared to hardcore criminal proceedings (she terms this new required standard a 'good enough standard' of review and points at the *in casu* assessment of the review). Turning to the CJEU she argues that the required standard for review that the General Court has to carry out with regard to levels of fines imposed by the Commission is, in general, somewhat stricter now following the judgments in *KME* and *Chalkor* (it is not allowed anymore to apply a 'manifest error test'), but that the Court in these cases in the end was satisfied with the General Court's assessment. Thus, also here there is an *in casu* assessment and she concludes that the level of review appears, in the light of the judgment in *Menarini*, in line with the requirements of the ECHR (which appears to be contrary to Forrester's assessment). Yet, she raises the question whether the EU system should be satisfied with this 'good enough standard', or whether it should merely regard this as the minimum and should actually go beyond it, guaranteeing a higher level of protection (i.e., a more intense review). This could especially be necessary as fines imposed on EU level might also have severe consequences for the individuals involved on the Member State level (Member States might even have the power to send individuals to prison) and that this might also lead to problems with *ne bis in idem*.

Judge Simonsson ('Data Mirroring during Dawn-Raids: Right to Judicial Review') critically anlaysed the so-called Data Mirroring in light of the right to judicial review. When competition authorities carry out investigations and inspections, the practice has spread in recent years of making extensive copies of contents of computers or servers. This is sometimes referred to as mirroring. The competition authority brings back the mirror image to its own premises in order to analyse it extensively with the help of forensic software. This type of indexing and searching can take anything from a few days to several months. Companies subjected to mirroring will ask themselves whether they can challenge the practice before a court. For judicial review, there must be access to court. In addition, the standard of legal review must be sufficient to allow for a real review. The thesis put forward in the paper is that there is a right to judicial review under EU law and in the Member States pursuant to the ECHR of decisions authorizing mirroring of data. Such judicial review must meet the standards set by the CJEU and, at least in Member States, by the ECtHR in *Primagaz, Canal Plus* and *Robathin*.

Finally, Devroe ('How General Should General Principles Be? Ne Bis In Idem in EU Competition Law') argued that EU law has never safeguarded the *ne bis in idem* principle better than today. In addition to General Principles developed in the case law by the CJEU and the ECHR, the principle is now also enshrined in the Convention Implementing the Schengen Agreement (the CISA) and in Article 50 the Charter, which has become a binding legal instrument since the entry into force of the Lisbon Treaty. Furthermore, the Charter and the Lisbon Treaty have linked EU law more closely than ever before to the ECHR, as interpreted by the ECtHR. However, the words contrast sharply with the simple observation that in practice no one has so far been able to successfully raise a *ne bis in idem* argument in a competition law case before the General Court or CJEU. The argument is regularly raised but the ECJ systematically rejects it. In his essay Devroe deals first with the traditional case law of the European courts on *ne bis in idem*. He then highlights the evolutions in EU and ECHR law which might have altered the traditional jurisprudence. Subsequently, the CJEU's *Toshiba* judgment is analysed and critically appraised. In this judgment, the Court had to decide which impact these evolutions had on its existing restrictive interpretation of *ne bis in idem* in competition matters. It ruled that nothing should change, so that the *ne bis in idem* principle is now interpreted differently in competition law and certain other areas of the law. It is also striking that the reference to the ECHR, present in the older case law, is no longer present in *Toshiba*.

III CONCLUSION: THE IMPACT OF THE CHARTER ON PRIVATE PARTIES

To conclude, we would like to stress the colossal potential and impact of the EU Charter of Fundamental Rights in relation between private parties. With the entry into force of the Lisbon Treaty, the EU Charter of Fundamental Rights has finally become a legally binding document of primary law, a core element of the Union's legal order and the starting point for the CJEU judge for assessing the compatibility of EU or Member State measures with EU fundamental rights.[6] But what is the impact of this Charter as to the relationship between private parties?

Many have argued using a textual interpretation of Article 51 CFR that the Charter does not apply in relation to private parties.[7] Yet, it appears to us that Article 51 is rather concerned with the material scope of the Charter and not its personal scope, or in other words, that it is concerned with the question which situations are covered by EU fundamental rights and confirms the case law by the Court pre-Lisbon to the effect that EU fundamental rights are applicable whenever a situation falls under the material scope of Union law,[8] but that it is not concerned with the question as to the Charter's possible horizontal effects.[9] Furthermore, it should be pointed out that 'the need to

6. For a general overview on the impact of the Lisbon Treaty as regards fundamental rights protection in the EU, see e.g. X. Groussot and L. Pech, 'Fundamental Rights Protection in the EU post Lisbon Treaty', *Foundation Robert Schuman Policy Paper*, European Issue no. 173, 14 June 2010. Concerning the use of the Charter as a starting point in EU adjudication, see e.g., Opinion of AG Bot in Case C-108/10 *Ivana Skattolon* [2011] nyr.
7. See e.g. Opinion of AG Trstenjak in Case C-282/10 *Dominguez* [2011] nyr, paras 80-83.
8. See for a recent interpretation of the Court of Article 51 CFR concerning the question of the material scope of EU fundamental rights Case C-617/10 *Åkerberg Fransson* [2013] nyr, paras 17-21.
9. See in this regard C. Ladenburger, 'Artikel 51 Anwendungsbereich', in P. Tettinger & K. Stern (eds), *Kölner Gemeinschaftskommentar zur Europäischen Grundrechte-Charter* (München, C.H.

protect the rights and freedoms of others' is explicitly mentioned in Article 52(1) CFR, which concerns limitations on rights laid down in the Charter.[10] This provision reflects, in our view, the position that the Charter (and in particular its economic fundamental rights such as Articles 15, 16 and 17) may be applied in horizontal situations and can be used as the fundamental cause of a civil proceeding brought by a private party against another one.

Section 2 of the Charter and particularly Articles 15, 16 and 17 embody the so-called economic fundamental rights, respectively the right to engage in work and to pursue a freely chosen or accepted occupation, the freedom to conduct business and the right to property. Interestingly, for example in the *Sky Österreich* case delivered in 2013,[11] the Grand Chamber of the CJEU has shown its willingness to give wide interpretation to these rights, in this particular case by interpreting the freedom to conduct business as including the freedom to contract. These rights are not absolute and have been previously recognized as general principles of EU law by the CJEU. They are also closely connected to the economic freedoms enshrined within the TFEU. Similarly to the economic freedoms, they may be relied on by individuals in horizontal situations. After the entry into force of the Lisbon Treaty, many cases have come before the CJEU with the main aim to interpret the scope of Articles 15, 16 and 17 Charter. These cases involve private parties and deal with the interpretation of EU secondary legislation (having horizontal effect) in light of the Charter or/and the conflict of fundamental rights (two conflicting economic rights or/and one economic right used as a derogation from a fundamental right).

For instance in *Scarlet Extended* (2011), *Netlog* (2012), *TV2 Denmark* (2012), *Denise McDonagh v. Ryanair* (2013) and *Parkwood Leisure* (AG Opinion delivered in 2013) the horizontal application of EU law between private parties is closely related to the so-called economic fundamental rights enshrine in section 2 of the Charter. These cases concern the balancing of fundamental rights related to the interpretation of EU secondary legislation.

In *Scarlet Extended*,[12] the CJEU had to decide on the scope of application of Article 52(1) of the Charter, particularly whether an injunction could fall under the first condition defined in this Article, namely that of being 'provided for by law'.[13] This condition is necessary to accept a limitation on the exercise of a right defined in the Charter.[14] In the present circumstances, the injunction would have restricted the right

Beck 2006), Artikel 51 Rz. 11, who also points out that the possibility of horizontal effects of the Charter was not discussed at the Convention which that the Charter.

10. In this regard one should also recall recital 6 to the Charter, according to which '(e)njoyment of these rights entails *responsibilities and duties with regard to other persons*, to the human community and to future generations' (emphasis added).
11. Case C-283/11 *Sky Österreich GmbH v. Österreichischer Rundfunk*, Judgment of the Court (Grand Chamber) of 22 January 2013.
12. Case C-70/10 *Scarlet Extended v. SABAM* [2011] nyr.
13. It is worth noting that Article 52(1) of the Charter is identically worded as Articles 8(2) and 10(2) of the ECHR.
14. The Charter states, in well-known terms, the conditions to which any limitation on the exercise of the rights and freedoms which it recognises are subject, just as the ECHR defines the circumstances in which, *inter alia*, any interference in the right to a private life or any restriction on freedom of expression may be considered lawful.

to conduct a business (Article 16 CFR) of an ISP by requiring the installation of a filtering system, which would have involved the monitoring of all electronic communications made through its network in the interests of the holders of intellectual property rights (as protected by Article 17(2) CFR).

In the *Denise McDonagh* case (2013),[15] Ryanair claimed that the obligation to provide care to passengers imposed on air carriers in circumstances such as those at issue in the main proceedings has the effect of depriving air carriers of part of the fruits of their labour and of their investments. Referring to the doctrine of the reconciliation of rights and the need to strike a fair balance between fundamental rights, the CJEU balanced Articles 16 and 17 of the Charter with Article 38 Charter which seeks to ensure a high level of protection for consumers, including air passengers, in European Union policies. The CJEU held that Regulation No 261/2004 must be considered to comply with the requirement intended to reconcile the various fundamental rights involved and strike a fair balance between them and therefore, the provisions of the regulation did not breach Articles 16 and 17 of the Charter.[16]

More recently, in *Parkwood Leisure*,[17] concerning another horizontal situation (employer/employee) arising at the national level, the UK Supreme Court asked in essence whether a finding that dynamic clauses referring to collective agreements are compatible with Directive 2001/23 and might, in any event, be in breach of EU fundamental rights.[18] For the Advocate General the matter should be considered in light of Article 16 of the Charter since, after the transfer of the undertaking, Parkwood has no means of being represented at all on the NJC. The restriction of rights suffered by Parkwood derives not from being obliged to join an organization (that would be a matter to be dealt with by Article 12 of the Charter) but from the fact that it is required to take on obligations that were undertaken pursuant to agreements over which it is not capable to exercise any influence. Interestingly the Advocate General went into the history of the freedom to conduct business and its close link with the right to property.[19] The AG concluded that Article 16 of the Charter of Fundamental Rights of the European Union does not prevent national legislation that requires the transferee of an undertaking to accept the existing and future terms and conditions agreed by a collective bargaining body, provided that the requirement is not unconditional and irreversible. The transfer of dynamic clause is therefore viewed in light of Article 16 CFR and it will be for the national court to assess, pursuant to national law, whether the requirement is in fact unconditional and irreversible in nature.[20]

15. Case C-12/11 *Denise McDonagh v. Ryanair* [2013] nyr.
16. *Ibid.*, paras 63-64.
17. Case C-426/11 *Mark Alemo-Herron v. Parkwood Leisure*, AG Cruz-Villalón Opinion delivered on 19 February 2013.
18. These dynamic clauses require the transferee of an undertaking to accept the existing and future terms and conditions agreed by a collective bargaining body. The transfer of the clause means that the transferee, in this case Parkwood, is bound by such terms and conditions as are agreed, now and in the future, by the NJC.
19. *Ibid.*, paras 48-50.
20. *Ibid.*, para. 58.

Another line of cases concerns questions as to the validity of EU secondary legislation in proceedings between private parties. For instance, in *Interseroh,*[21] the CJEU had to deal with the protection of business secrets, which is also constitutionally protected by the German Basic Law, and had to assess whether this right restricts the scope of Article 18(1) of Regulation No 1013/2006. The Court ruled that even if the obligation to disclose the name of the waste producer to the consignee of a shipment of waste were to constitute a breach of the protection of the business secrets of intermediary dealers, that could not have the consequence of restricting the scope of a provision of secondary law that is clear and unconditional. As put by the Court of Justice, in those circumstances, any unjustified breach of the protection of business secrets, assuming it were established, would not be such as to limit the scope of Article 18 of Regulation No 1013/2006, but rather to call into question the validity of that provision.[22]

Two other cases, *Association Kokopelli*[23] and *Sky Österreich,*[24] as discussed by Dorota Leczykiewicz in this book, are also of importance. *Association Kokopelli* concerned a dispute between two competitors. The claimant sought compensation for loss it had suffered due to the defendant's marketing of vegetable seeds which were excluded from circulation by a Directive. In its defence the defendant argued that the relevant provision of the Directive was invalid because it violated Article 34 TFEU and the principle of proportionality and also its freedom to conduct a business. *Sky Österreich* was another case where the validity of a Directive had direct consequences for a private dispute. Sky had acquired exclusive rights to broadcast Europa League matches. Under the Broadcasting Directive, as amended in 2007, Sky was required to allow broadcasters, for the purpose of short news reports, to use short extracts from the matches to which it had exclusive rights at a compensation not exceeding the additional costs in providing access.

In addition, the horizontal application of free movement of goods through the use of the doctrine of regulatory bodies as developed in *Bosman*[25] and *Laval*[26] has been recognized by the CJEU in *Fra.bo.*[27] This means that in the future, the Charter may be relied on in private proceedings in this context. In *Fra.bo*, the CJEU confirms its line of reasoning in *Bosman* and *Laval* in relation to Article 34 TFEU (ex Article 28 EC). More precisely, it considered that the free movement of goods applies to standardization and

21. Case C-1/11 *Interseroh v. SAM* [2012] nyr. The reference has been made in proceedings between Interseroh Scrap and Metals Trading GmbH ('Interseroh'), a dealer specialising in steel and metal scrap, and Sonderabfall-Management-Gesellschaft Rheinland-Pfalz mbH (SAM) ('SAM'), to which Land Rheinland-Pfalz has entrusted *inter alia* the supervision of specific waste streams in Land Rheinland-Pfalz, concerning the details to be given in the document contained in Annex VII to Regulation No 1013/2006 ('the shipment document').
22. The national court has not, however, asked the Court of Justice to rule on the validity of Article 18 of Regulation No 1013/2006, or even expressed any doubt in that regard, and the Court does not have sufficient facts before it to enable it to assess the validity of that provision.
23. Case C-59/11 *Association Kokopelli v. Graines Baumaux SAS*, opinion of 19 January 2012.
24. Case C-283/11 *Sky Österreich GmbH v. Österreichischer Rundfunk*, Judgment of the Court (Grand Chamber) of 22 January 2013.
25. Case C-415/93 *Bosman* [1995] ECR I-4921.
26. Case C-341/05 *Laval* [2007] ECR I-11767.
27. Case C-171/11 *Fra.bo* [2012] nyr.

certification activities of a private law body in Germany (the DVGW).[28] *In casu*, the CJEU had to determine in the light of the legislative and regulatory context in which the DVGW operates, whether the activities of a private law body has the effect of giving rise to restrictions on the free movement of goods in the same manner as do measures imposed by the State. First, the Court considered that the German legislature had established that products certified by this private law body are compliant with national legislation. Second, it observed that the body offers the only possibility for obtaining a compliance certificate for such products.[29] Third, it emphasized that in practice, the lack of certification by this body places a considerable restriction on the marketing of the products concerned on the German market since almost all German consumers purchase copper fittings certified by the DVGW. In light of those three elements, it is clear for the CJEU that the DVGW, by virtue of its authority to certify the products, in reality holds the power to regulate the entry into the German market of products such as the copper fittings at issue in the main proceedings, with the effect of Article 34 TFEU being applicable to it even though it is a private law body.[30] It appears to us that the fact that following *Fra.bo* also Article 34 TFEU can have (limited) horizontal effects means that now regulatory bodies, such as the DVGW in the case, will be able to rely on the Charter in order to (try to) justify restrictions so the free movement of goods, such as was established by cases such as *Laval* and *Viking Line*.[31]

In the end, looking at the recent CJEU case law, it is possible to establish at the present stage four main situations in which the EU Charter of Fundamental Rights can be relied upon in horizontal situations falling within the scope of EU law:

(1) The situation of interpretation of EU Secondary legislation involving balancing of rights at the national level (*Scarlet* Situation, see, e.g., also *Denise McDonagh, Parkwood Leisure*).
(2) The situation of validity of EU secondary legislation arising at the national level in a proceeding involving private parties (*Interseroh* Situation, see, e.g., also *Association Kokopelli* and *Sky Österreich*).
(3) The use of the Charter by regulatory bodies in derogating from one of the economic freedoms (*Fra.Bo* Situation).
(4) The use of the Charter in horizontal situations to challenge national legislation or/and private law contracts (*Mangold*[32] Situation), which are contrary to

28. This body is a non-profit, private-law body whose activities are not financed by Germany. Moreover, the State has no decisive influence over the DVGW's standardisation and certification activities, although some of its members are public bodies.
29. Except for a procedure involving an expert with the task of verifying the products compliance, which, however, is only of little or no practical use. (See para. 29 of the judgment).
30. *Ibid.*, paras 27-31.
31. Case C-438/05 *Viking* [2007] ECR I-10779. Arguably, these cases, in which the Court held that fundamental rights can be a justification for derogating from fundamental freedoms with the result that the applicable fundamental rights will have to be balanced against the free movement rights, are based on earlier case law such as Case C-112/00 *Schmidberger* [2003] ECR I-5659 and Case C-36/02 *Omega* [2004] ECR I-9609.
32. Case C-144/04 *Mangold* [2005] ECR I-9981.

mandatory provisions of EU law, e.g., Article 21 or 47 EU Charter of Fundamental Rights.

The national courts have evidently an essential role to play in the application of the CFR in horizontal situations falling within the scope of EU law. Authors like Temple Lang and Tridimas have clearly pointed out this aspect in their contributions. However, criteria are needed to identify circumstances in which national courts should not allow private parties to waive their rights under EU law. When is there an EU obligation and what is the extent of this obligation? In absence of direct horizontality, it is not obvious that EU law puts national courts under a general duty not to enforce any private law obligations which run counter to general principles, beyond the duty of consistent interpretation. As argued by Tridimas in his contribution, relying on the seminal judgment of the US Supreme Court in *Shelley v. Kraemer*,[33] even though general principles and Charter rights may not bind individuals directly, national courts have an obligation to enforce them in the exercise of their state powers.[34] It should also be kept in mind that the material scope of application of the Charter is broader than that of general principles of EU law established by the CJEU in its case law pre-Lisbon. When one adds this to the more highly visible nature of the Charter, one cannot exclude that claimants and their counsels may not seek on a more regular basis to test the applicability of the Charter's rights before national courts in the context of 'horizontal' litigations, provided that the matter falls within the scope of EU law. Ultimately, it appears to us that the EU Charter of Fundamental Rights is a key factor for the construction of a harmonious and Common European private law space.

33. 334 U.S. 1 (1948).
34. According to Tridimas in this book, '(i)n the context of the free movement of goods, the Court has held private agreement may under no circumstances derogate from mandatory provisions of the Treaty on the free movement of goods (Case 58/80 *Dansk Supermarked v. Imerco* [1981] ECR 181, para. 17). If that is the case in relation to the free movement of goods, it is also *a fortiori* in relation to fundamental rights as enshrined in the Charter or the general principles of EU law, such as the right not to be discriminated against on grounds of race or ethnic origin. This view is also supported by the *Mangold* line of case law'.

Part I: Methodology in the Elaboration of Private Law Principles

CHAPTER 1

Private Law Principles, Pluralism and Perfectionism

Martijn W. Hesselink[*]

§1.01 THE QUEST FOR GENERAL PRINCIPLES IN A PLURALIST WORLD

It is a well known characteristic of our society today that different people hold different world views, ideals and values. This is true for our national societies and probably even more so with regard to our European society.[1] Some people believe in one ultimate value, such as devotion to God, be it in a Roman Catholic, Muslim or other version. Others adhere to several values and ideals at the same time and struggle in balancing them when trying to decide how to act in concrete situations. It may well be that some of the different understandings that people have concerning what matters in life turn out to be incommensurable in the sense that there does not appear to be a common standard by which they could be compared (other than the nominal standard that they are all conceptions of a good human life).[2]

Values and ideas about how a life should be lived may provide moral guidance to people in many different contexts. A fairly obvious context in which someone may wish to rely on her moral principles is the political context, i.e., in relation to the questions of how our society should be organized, what aims the state should pursue and for which purposes it can make legitimate use of its power. In political debates or

* This chapter was presented at the 'International Conference on General Principles of EU Law and European Private Law', 8-9 November 2012, at Stockholm.

1. The existence of a European people (*demos*, *Volk*) is contested (see e.g. the German constitutional court in *BVerfGE* 123, 267 (the Lisbon judgment). However, the existence of a European *society*, at least in the most usual sense in which this concept is used, seems undeniable to me.
2. Charles Taylor, 'The diversity of goods', in: Amartya Sen & Bernard Williams (eds), *Utilitarianism and beyond*, 129-144 (Cambridge: Cambridge University Press, 1982).

in the voting booth many people are guided by their moral convictions. They wish to see their values, ideals and, more generally, their conception of what makes a good society, reflected in governmental action. In particular, they may wish the laws to correspond to their values. Someone who would enforce his vision of the good through legal rules, even if others reject that view, is called a perfectionist.[3]

One specific sector where people may seek their values and ideals to obtain some legal expression is the making of private law. There exist many different theories that present private law as the expression of one single value. Sometimes, these monist theories are intended merely as statements of an ideal private law. However, usually they are presented as the best way of making sense of the private law that we actually have in our own society today. Moreover, often it is also argued that our existing private law should be interpreted, and where possible even reformed, in line with the suggested underlying principle or value. Thus, some theorists argue that ideally private law should be based on commutative (or corrective) justice.[4] Others claim that contract law should be regarded and interpreted as an expression of Kantian autonomy.[5] Still others have advocated human welfare (or economic efficiency) as the true basis of all governmental action including private law making.[6] In sum, today there exists a rich variety of private law theories which usually are monistic in that they claim private law to be based (ideally) on one ultimate value. Most of these private law theories, although not necessarily entirely convincing, are perfectly reasonable. We could call this the fact of reasonable private law pluralism.

More generally, private law thinking, theoretical and practical, is usually based on the idea (largely unexpressed) that there somehow exist some general (or even universal) truths with regard to private law questions, that private law therefore is not contingent and that its interpretation and further development is not a matter of mere choice but should be guided by its underlying principles. Thus, private law thinking has traditionally been based on the idea that it is the task of all those who contribute to the making and further development of private law (judges, legislators and professors, as the case may be) to try to find its best possible interpretation. The dispute is then about what the true principles are.[7]

3. See F.H. Buckley, *Perfectionism*, 13 Supreme Court Economic Review 133-163, 135 (2005), who usefully distinguishes, in this regard, between self-regarding private perfectionism (or paternalism) and other-regarding public perfectionism.
4. For two very different versions of private law as commutative justice, see James Gordley, *Foundations of Private Law. Property, Tort, Contract, Unjust Enrichment* (Oxford: Oxford University Press, 2006) and Ernest J. Weinrib, *The Idea of Private Law* (Cambridge, Massachusetts: Harvard University Press, 1995).
5. See, as recent examples, e.g. Jürgen Basedow, *Freedom of Contract in the European Union*, 16 ERPL 901-923 (2008), and Hannes Unberath, *Die Vertragsverletzung* (Tübingen: Mohr Siebeck, 2007).
6. See e.g. Louis Kaplow & Steven Shavell, *Fairness versus Welfare* (Cambridge, Massachusetts: Harvard University Press, 2002) and Horst Eidenmüller, *Effizienz als Rechtsprinzip* (Tübingen: Mohr Siebeck, 2005).
7. We could call this legal (or more specifically: private law) perfectionism. Legal perfectionism, which strives for the law's perfection, should be distinguished from moral perfectionism, which aims at human perfection, and which will be discussed below.

In a series of recent cases, the Court of Justice of the European Union (CJEU) referred to general principles of civil law.[8] Although it is not entirely clear what exactly the Court means by (general) private law principles,[9] the wording adopted by the Court nevertheless seems to have been a deliberate choice. The specific principles that have been indicated, so far, by the Court as (general) principles of civil law, include, in particular, the principles of the binding force of contract, of good faith, and of unjust enrichment.

The Court's reference to general principles of civil law can be placed in the wider context of a search for post-national principles of private law. In this respect, an early example in modern times was Schlesinger's common core project that aimed at elaborating, for the realm of private law, 'general principles of the law recognised by civilised nations' in the sense of Article 38(1) (c) Statute of the International Court of Justice.[10] More recent prominent examples include the UNIDROIT Principles of International Commercial Contracts and the Lando Commission's Principles of European Contract Law.[11] Moreover, when the European Commission commissioned a 'common frame of reference' (CFR), it indicated that this CFR should 'first set out common fundamental principles of contract law'.[12] And such a set of four 'underlying principles' (i.e., the principles of freedom, security, justice and efficiency) was indeed delivered in the DCFR.[13] The Unidroit Principles, PECL and DCFR became the main sources of inspiration for the drafters of the European Commission's proposal for a Common European Sales Law (CESL),[14] which, in its turn, also contains a 'general principles' section, this time with three general principles – the principles of freedom

8. The main examples include Case C-277/05, *Société thermale d'Eugénie-les-Bains v. Ministère de l'Économie, des Finances et de l'Industrie* [2007] ECR I-06415; Case C-412/06, *Annelore Hamilton v. Volksbank Filder eG* [2008] ECR I-02383; Case C-489/07 *Pia Messner v. Firma Stefan Krüger* [2009] ECR I-07315; Case C-215/08, *E. Friz GmbH v. Carsten von der Heyden* [2010] ECR I-02947.
9. For an attempt at clarification, see Martijn W. Hesselink, 'The general principles of civil law: their nature, roles and legitimacy', in: Dorota Leczykiewicz & Stephen Weatherill (eds.) *The Involvement of EU Law in Private Law Relationships* (Oxford: Hart Publishing, forthcoming).
10. See Rudolf B. Schlesinger, *Research on the General Principles of Law Recognized by Civilized Nations*, 51 American Journal of International Law 734 (1957) and Rudolf B. Schlesinger (ed.), *Formation of contracts; A study of the common core of legal systems* (New York, 1968).
11. UNIDROIT Principles of International Commercial Contracts Rome (Rome: Unidroit, 2010); Hugh Beale and Ole Lando (eds.), *Principles of European Contract Law, Parts I and II, Prepared by The Commission on European Contract Law* (The Hague: Kluwer Law International, 2000); Ole Lando, Eric Clive, André Prüm and Reinhard Zimmermann (eds.), *Principles of European Contract Law Part III* (The Hague: Kluwer Law International, 2003).
12. Communication from the Commission to the European Parliament and the Council: European contract Law and the revision of the *acquis*: the way forward, COM(2004) 651 final, 12.
13. Christian von Bar et al. (eds.), *Principles, Definitions and Model Rules of European Private Law; Draft Common Frame of Reference (DCFR); Outline Edition* p. 37ff (Munich: Sellier, 2009). On the remarkable difference between the principles contained in the Interim Outline (2008) and in the Outline edition (2009) of the DCFR, see Martijn W. Hesselink, 'If you don't like our principles we have others. On core values and underlying principles in European private law: a critical discussion of the new 'Principles' section in the draft CFR', in: Roger Brownsword, Hans-W. Micklitz, Leone Niglia, Stephen Weatherill (eds.), *The Foundations of European Private Law* 59-71 (Oxford: Hart Publishing, 2011).
14. Proposal for a regulation of the European Parliament and of the Council on a Common European Sales Law, COM(2011) 635 final.

of contract, good faith and fair dealing, and cooperation – which are meant to guide both the behaviour of the contracting parties and the interpretation of the CESL.[15]

The European law makers' quest for general principles is, on the one hand, fully in line with the attempt by theorists to explain and justify contract law in terms of fundamental principles and underlying values. On the other hand, however, we also saw that there exists a rich variety of accounts of what would amount to the ideal private law. These accounts are often inspired by (or can easily be explained in terms of) well-established theories of moral philosophy, such as deontological, consequentialist and virtue-oriented theories. Moreover, from both the private law theory debate and the broader debates in political and moral philosophy we know that discussions concerning fundamental principles, however serious, respectful and open-minded they may be, are not likely to make the disagreement go away. If anything, in the realm of values and principles, positions tend to be strengthened rather than weakened by theoretical and practical discussions.[16] Given this state of affairs, i.e., given what Rawls has called the 'fact of reasonable pluralism',[17] the question arises whether it is legitimate for European lawmakers to canonize a set of private or contract law principles as 'general principles'. Should state institutions not be neutral when it comes to fundamental principles and ultimate values? By endorsing one specific, controversial set of principles does not the state disrespect people adhering to other principles? If private law is the *constitution civile* of our society,[18] does not the state then create in-groups and out-groups when it announces that from now on these are the general principles which should guide the interpretation of European private law and the behaviour of private parties *vis-à-vis* each other? Or is there a legitimate way for the European institutions to promulgate and apply a set of general principles of private law in spite of the existence of a variety of different, often incommensurable ideas concerning the fundamental principles of private law and the general principles by which a good life should be lived?

That question, i.e., the question of whether state endorsed general principles of private law can ever be legitimate in the presence of a plurality of values and principles that people regard as fundamental for their lives and for their interaction with each other, will be the central question addressed in this paper. In particular, I will focus here on three potential normative challenges to the CJEUs and the European Commission's sets of private law principles. The three normative challenges have in common that they share the modernist project of grounding political institutions in reasonable principles.[19] The first challenge comes from the liberal perfectionist argument for an internally pluralist private law, an idea which is, of course, diametrically opposed to

15. Arts 1-3 address the parties, but Art. 4 indicates that the CESL 'is to be interpreted autonomously and in accordance with its objectives and *the principles underlying it*' (emphasis added).
16. See Charles Larmore, *The morals of modernity* 168 (Cambridge: Cambridge University Press, 1996).
17. John Rawls, *Political Liberalism*, expanded edition 4 (New York: Columbia University Press 2005).
18. Jean Carbonnier, 'Le Code civil', in: P. Nora (ed.), *Les lieux de mémoire* vol. II, 293-315 (Paris: Gallimard, 1986).
19. The critique from Teubner and his followers, if I understand it correctly, positions itself as external to (or beyond) the modern project. See the path-breaking, G. Teubner, "Global

the idea of general principles. The second possible normative threat to the legitimacy of general principles of private law endorsed by the European law making institutions comes from political liberalism. The argument that I will address is that if these general principles are to be understood as political principles of private law, they should be sufficiently neutral. Thirdly, I will consider the Habermasian argument that lawmakers proposing such legal principles must provide good reasons for them that are acceptable to all those who will be affected by them. Having established that none of these challenges gives a fatal blow to the project of formulating general principles of European private law I will discuss the suggestion in the opposite direction, that even a perfectionist European code of principles could be a legitimate project for European law makers to pursue. I will conclude that there is nothing inherently contradictory in seeking to find general private law principles in a pluralist world and that, as long we remain cautious in a number of respects – the four important lessons to be learned in this regard from political theory -, the quest for general private law principles can be perfectly legitimate.

§1.02 STRUCTURAL PLURALISM

One response to the fact that people hold different views, sometimes radically opposed and often incommensurable, of how we should live our lives, individually and in society, is to regard it as the state's main task to actively promote individual freedom so that people can live and organize their own lives in accordance with their own conceptions of the good life. This is what liberal perfectionists advocate. Given that there are many values and that in many cases to adhere to one value cannot be said to be more reasonable than adherence to another one, the best the state can do, they argue, is to abstain altogether from choosing for one ideal or reaching some compromise between several of them.[20] Instead, the government should promote liberty. Isaiah Berlin underlined, in particular, the importance of 'negative' liberty, i.e., liberty as non-interference by the state.[21] Joseph Raz, in contrast, emphasizes the task of the state in making possible a broad and diverse range of valuable ways of living for people to choose from.[22]

In a recent series of papers, Hanoch Dagan has applied this idea to private law.[23] Dagan argues for what he calls 'structural pluralism' in private law. The idea is that private law should not be understood any longer as being based on one guiding principle or one fundamental value or idea (such as promise, efficiency or corrective

---

Bukowina': Legal Pluralism in the World Society', in: Gunther Teubner (ed.), *Global Law Without a State* 3-28 (Dartmouth, 1997).

20. Isaiah Berlin, 'The Pursuit of the Ideal', in: Isaiah Berlin, *The Crooked Timber of Humanity: Chapters in the History of Ideas* 11-29 (ed. Henry Hardy) (London: Pimlico, 2003).
21. Isaiah Berlin, 'Two concepts of liberty', in: Isaiah Berlin, *Liberty* 166-217 (ed. Henry Hardy) (Oxford: OUP, 2002).
22. Joseph Raz, *The morality of freedom* (Oxford: Clarendon Press, 1986).
23. See, in particular, Hanoch Dagan, 'Autonomy, pluralism, and contract law theory', *Law and Contemporary Problems,* forthcoming; Hanoch Dagan, *Pluralism and perfectionism in private law,* 112 Columbia Law Review 1409-1446 (2012); Hanoch Dagan, *Private law pluralism and the rule of law,* available http://ssrn.com/abstract=2131372.

justice) but rather as a rich mosaic of different doctrines, each of which supports a valuable practice of social interaction, and each with its own underlying principles, which may therefore differ from one doctrine to another.[24] Dagan's theory is a direct attack on the idea of general private, property, contract and tort laws, and on the related general theories of property, contract and tort law. Clearly, if pertinent, this critique would also severely question the desirability of fundamental or general principles of the kind that the CJEU and the European Commission have recently recognized or proposed (and indeed of projects like the PECL and the Unidroit principles).

As said, Dagan's theory has an explicit normative basis in the political philosophy of Joseph Raz. The central idea in this philosophy is that people should be the authors of their own lives and that the state should facilitate such self-authorship by making available a sufficiently broad range of valuable and attractive alternative ways of life to choose from.[25] The theory therefore is both pluralist in that it assumes that there are many different, incompatible and indeed incommensurable, ultimate values, and perfectionist in that it claims that it is better for anyone to be the author of one's own life than to 'drift through life' without ever making any real choices,[26] and that the state should actively support self-authorship, even for those citizens who do not believe in it, by making and keeping available an adequate range of good ways to live.[27]

The fact that Dagan's theory is based explicitly on Raz's perfectionist version of liberalism makes it vulnerable to the critique that is generally addressed to Raz's and other types of perfectionist liberalism, by the proponents of political liberalism. I will discuss the theory of political liberalism in more detail below. For now it suffices to point out that political liberals take the same idea of value pluralism as their starting point but apply it also to perfectionist liberalism. They argue, convincingly in my view, that the precept of state neutrality should extend not only to monistic moral theories but also to the theory of moral pluralism. The claim that people should be regarded as the authors of their own lives is wholly unacceptable to many people, for example, as Nussbaum points out, to those who believe that God is the ultimate author of their lives, or for those, as Larmore underlines, who are convinced that our choices in life are shaped, at least in part, by the society we grew up in and that an unencumbered self who chooses between different attractive life paths does not in fact exist. Whatever their precise merits, such anti-liberal-perfectionist claims are not prima facie so unreasonable that the state should simply disregard them. Therefore, if the state would endorse a form of perfectionist liberalism, i.e., a liberalism that regards individual freedom as the ultimate value to be promoted by the state, then it would choose between different controversial conceptions of the good life and thus would create out-groups of people who do not regard their lives, their allegiances and their ultimate

24. For a similar approach, see Roy Kreitner, *On the New Pluralism in Contract Theory*, 45 Suffolk University Law Review 915-933 (2012).
25. Raz, note 22 above, 373.
26. *Ibid.*, 370.
27. See Raz, note 22 above, 424ff.

values as something entirely for themselves to choose. In other words, liberal perfectionism becomes part of the problem of how to find a moral basis for living together in a society where people hold different but equally reasonable conceptions of the good life, instead of solving that problem.[28]

Moreover, apart from its moral foundation Dagan's specific theory of structural pluralism is problematic, at least for contract law, also in other respects.[29] As said, Dagan's main claim is that different contract law doctrines are governed by different principles. However, it is important to realize that he understands 'doctrines' in a somewhat unusual way. He is not proposing, say, utilitarian rules on formation of contract, a Catholic doctrine of invalidity, and a libertarian doctrine of privity of contract. In the context of property law, Dagan understands 'doctrines' as different types of proprietary entitlement; his argument is that, for example, intellectual property rights and different types of condominium such as 'common interest communities' should not necessarily be governed all (entirely) by the same principles. Similarly, what Dagan means by different doctrines in the context of contract law are, in fact, different types of specific contracts which should be governed (partly) by different principles. What structural pluralism in contract law boils down to, then, is a retreat from general contract law and a return to specific contracts. If taken seriously, this approach would bring us back to Roman law or to the *ius commune* as it existed before general principles of private law were developed, first as natural law and subsequently as the law of reason, culminating in the private law codifications.[30]

There is no doubt that the scholarly rationalism that inspired the twentieth century's codifications often went too far, at the expense of realism and user-friendliness. The best example of exasperated rationalism is, of course, the concept of a juridical act (*Rechtsgeschäft*), the crowning glory of *Begriffsjurisprudenz*, which became a central organizing category determining the structure of many twentieth century civil codes, in particular the German *Bürgerliches Gesetzbuch* (1900), the Portuguese *Código Civil* (1967) and the Dutch *Burgerlijk Wetboek* (1992). Although it is true that a contract, a last will, the act of transferring title in an immoveable, the recognition of a child, the dismissal of an employee, and the foundation of a company, to mention only a few examples of juridical acts, have something in common – i.e., that they all are the result of declarations of intent, be they unilateral, bilateral or multilateral -, but they are also – and even primarily – very different. Therefore, dedicating a separate section in the most general part of the civil code (as in Book 1 *BGB*, Book 3 *BW*, Book 1 *Código Civil* and Book 2 DCFR, respectively) to juridical acts and declarations of intent, leads to such an extreme degree of abstraction that, from the normative point of view, it seems pointless (because there are hardly any common principles by which these diverse acts should be governed) or even wrong (because it

28. See Larmore, note 16 above, ch. 7, especially with regard to Berlin, and Martha C. Nussbaum, *Perfectionist Liberalism and Political Liberalism*, Philosophy & Public Affairs 39, no. 1 (2011), especially with regard to Raz.
29. It may be different for property law in relation to which Dagan first developed and articulated his theory.
30. See F. Wieacker, *A history of private law in Europe* Part 4 (Oxford: Oxford University Press, 1995).

misleadingly suggests that the principle of party autonomy is of paramount importance for all these diverse acts) while from the practical point of view it is extremely user-unfriendly. This explains why it was one of the main tasks of the European Commission's expert group to turn the DCFR into a more user-friendly set of rules (i.e., one with fewer levels of abstraction).[31]

Nevertheless, it remains a sound principle of legislative economy to avoid useless repetitions. When setting up a law of contract – when drafting, say, a civil code or a common frame of reference – it makes sense to follow a bottom-up approach, starting from specific recurrent contract types, to draft specific rules appropriate for these specific contractual relationships (sales, service, lease, insurance, franchise contracts etc.), and then to see whether, for certain subjects, the resulting rules for each of these contract types are different or actually identical, and only insofar as the latter is the case to opt for general contract law rules. This legislative approach naturally leads to a structure with rules having different degrees of generality, e.g., specific consumer sales law, general sales law, general contract law, general law of obligations, and sometimes general law of juridical acts. That is, of course, exactly how the modern civil codes were drafted. It was also the drafting method explicitly adopted by the drafters of the DCFR. As said, often legislators (and the academics who do the actual drafting) go too far in seeking perfectly rational structures, but this does not mean that it would amount to progress if in the next civil code the book on contracts would consist only of endless chapters dedicated to specific contracts.

Dagan is certainly right that not all contracts should be governed by the same general principles and only by those most general principles. However, a contract law where insurance contracts are governed by extensive disclosure duties and where franchise or joint-venture contracts are governed by intense duties to cooperate, is fully compatible with the existence of a regime of general contract law which is applicable, on the basis of the *lex specialis derogat legi generali* principle, to those aspects of those specific contracts that are not specifically regulated by specific (and often different) principles. In particular, this does not exclude that all types of contracts, subject to certain mandatory rules which may, for example, contain compulsory terms, should be governed by the principle of freedom of contract and that their performance should be governed by the principle of good faith and fair dealing. Like cases must be treated alike and to abandon general contract law altogether, be it in legislative practice or in contract theory, would amount to throwing the baby out with the bathwater.

There is another important dimension to this. The historical development of general contract law had two distinctive traits. It is true that it led to a reduced importance and relevance of the various specifically regulated ('nominate') contract

31. See Commission Decision of 26 April 2010 setting up the Expert Group on a Common Frame of Reference in the area of European contract law, 2010/233/EU, *OJ* 27.4.2010, L105/109. For severe critique of the DCFR's structure, in particular the concept of juridical act, See e.g. Ole Lando, *The Structure and the Legal Values of the Common Frame of Reference*, ERCL 245-256 (2007); Reiner Schulze & Thomas Wilhelmsson, *From the Draft Common frame of Reference towards European Contract Law Rules*, 4 ERCL 154 (2008); Hugh Collins, *Review*, Modern Law Review 840-844 (2008); Martijn W. Hesselink, *The Common Frame of Reference as a source of European private law* 83 Tulane Law review 4 919-971 (2009).

types, each with its own set of specific rules, obligations and remedies. However, from the normative perspective much more important was the recognition, in medieval canon law, of the binding force of innominate contracts (*pacta sunt servanda*).[32] From the perspective of liberty as self-authorship this was crucial. It was no longer the state courts that decided on a limited set of contract types that the parties should try to mould their relationships into. Henceforward, subject to the public policy control for illegality and immorality of the contract (or its causa), the law would enforce any kind of contract that the parties freely agreed to.[33] Therefore, a true liberal should certainly be concerned with making sure that the contracting parties had sufficiently attractive alternative options – in other words: should assure substantive freedom of contract -, but, apart from that, the state should not limit the options by forcing or even nudging them into certain contract types. It is a well known fact that the presence in civil codes of certain types of (nominate) contracts, with their own sets of rules, makes courts become suspicious of untypical (innominate) contracts.[34] Such a 'normalisation' effect (Foucault) may endanger pluralism and autonomy, given the fact that the decision to which contract type a contract belongs (the classification of contracts) remains reserved to the courts. In other words, if there is only specific contract law it is the legislator who decides on the shape and (political) colour of the available boxes and courts decide in which box a certain relationship belongs, while with a vibrant general contract law the parties can freely (in a substantive sense – that remains an important limit, from a liberal perspective) decide for themselves what their favourite boxes should look like.

As a last point of criticism, the sole focus of Dagan's structural pluralism on certain contract types, as an expression of Razian liberal perfectionism, seems rather arbitrary given the very diverse ways in which contracts and contractual relationships can differ from each other. We might just as well distinguish contracts along a variety of other axes, e.g., business to business versus business-to-consumer contracts, gratuitous contracts versus contracts for consideration, long-term versus discrete contracts, aleatory versus commutative contracts et cetera. Therefore, either we must make a choice among these different criteria for distinction, which seems arbitrary, or the result will be a very complex matrix, with dozens of distinct contract types, each with their different sets of rules. Not only would that, contrary to what Dagan maintains, be likely to undermine legal certainty; it would also inevitably lead to rather formal legal disputes and to litigation on classification rather than on the contextualized interpretations of general rules of contract law. The key question in a contract would become whether the contract belongs in this rather than in another box. That hardly would amount to progress.

32. Reinhard Zimmermann, *The Law of Obligations: Roman foundations of the civilian tradition* 537-545 (Oxford: Oxford University Press, 1996).

33. See explicitly Art. 1322, para. 2, Italian civil code: 'Le parti possono anche concludere contratti che non appartengano ai tipi aventi una disciplina particolare, purché siano diretti a realizzare interessi meritevoli di tutela secondo l'ordinamento giuridico.'

34. See M.W. Hesselink, *Non-Mandatory Rules in European Contract Law*, 1 ERCL 43-84 (2005), with further references.

Therefore, the familiar organization of contract law consisting of a combination of general and specific contract law, as expressed in the structure of most civil codes and all text books and commentaries on contract law,[35] seems to be rather ideal from a Razian liberal point of view. Similarly, the structure of the DCFR (apart from its excessive conceptualism) might also be attractive from Dagan's perspective. That 'code' even has an innovative structure where service contracts are subdivided into a first set of general rules on services (in addition to the general rules of contract law) plus specific sets of rules for a variety of types of services (i.e., construction, processing, storage, design, information and advice, and treatment), all this on top of the other specifically regulated non-service contracts, i.e., sales, lease of goods, mandate, commercial agency, franchise and distributorship, loan contracts, personal security, and donation.[36] These are too many layers of abstraction, in my view, because it makes the code become insufficiently user-friendly, but the basic idea of general plus specific contract law is not a bad one. The underlying philosophy of such a structure is based on the values of autonomy and equality. In principle, the parties are free to shape their own legal relationships. However, like cases should be treated alike, while for certain types of unbalanced relationships the state will dictate part of the terms. In conclusion, also from a liberal perfectionist perspective general rules and principles of private law would seem to be nothing to be worried about as long as they are combined with more specific principles for specific contracts which should have priority on account of the *lex specialis* principle.

Still, there is something important that we should retain from Dagan's normative analysis, i.e., a certain scepticism towards private law principles which are too general and too abstract. Today, contractual relationships are so diverse that, without important qualification by certain more specific principles for more specific situations, they may indeed risk becoming inappropriately limitative of diversity. This may also be true specifically for the general principles that the European law makers have formulated so far. Of course, the concept of 'general principles' in itself suggests that there is room also for more specific principles, but until these are formulated, in the meantime the general principles apply without qualification. From this perspective a sweeping, programmatic principle of freedom of contract, especially when understood in a formal sense, may indeed be worrying, from the perspective of those who care for the true, substantive autonomy of individuals. It has indeed been argued in the literature that the CJEUs principles are too general, abstract and unqualified and that instead we need principles of an intermediate level of abstraction.[37]

35. The exception are, of course, the common law countries.
36. On the 'functional approach' that inspired this structure see, Marco B.M. Loos, 'Service contracts', in: Arthur S. Hartkamp et al. (eds.) *Towards a European Civil Code* 757-786 (Alphen aan de Rijn: Kluwer Law International, 2011). The structure was criticised severely by F. Faust, H.C. Grigoleit, N. Jansen, G. Wagner and R. Zimmermann, *The Common Frame of Reference for European Private Law—Policy Choices and Codification Problems*, Oxford J Legal Studies 28 (4) 659-708 (2008).
37. Jürgen Basedow, *The Court of Justice and Private Law: Vacillations, General Principles and the Architecture of the European Judiciary* 18 ERPL 443-474 (2010).

§1.03 POLITICAL PRINCIPLES OF PRIVATE LAW

Another potential challenge to the legitimacy of general principles of private law of the kind developed by the CJEU and contained in the CESL-proposal, comes from political liberalism. Political liberals reject all forms of state perfectionism including liberal perfectionism (which is committed to moral pluralism and is therefore incompatible with moral monism, a category of convictions that political liberalism explicitly aims to keep on board) and advocate neutrality as the proper response by the state to the fact of reasonable pluralism.[38] Are European general principles of private law compatible with the neutral state?

Political liberals reject the endorsement by the state of any conception of the good life – be they perfectionist or non-perfectionist, such as welfarism – for both practical and, in particular, moral reasons. A practical problem with a state that promotes a certain conception of the good is that the ultimate ends that will be pursued by the state and the fundamental values that the society will be based on, will constantly depend on the balance of power of the day. Given the often contradicting and sometimes mutually exclusive values that people have, the government and legislation that is inspired by sectarian values is, therefore, likely to remain unstable perennially. In addition to this practical difficulty, there is a more fundamental problem. If the majority of the day, with the help of the power of the state, seeks to impose its values on others who hold different, maybe diametrically opposed values, then the former fail to respect the latter as moral persons. A state that takes sides creates in- and out-groups.[39] For example, a European Union based on Christian values to be expressed in a preamble to the Constitution would have made atheist and Muslim Europeans feel like second-rate citizens,[40] just as much as State schools which teach pupils that faith, religion and allegiance to communities are entirely a matter of individual choice would fail to show equal respect to a variety of communities holding beliefs that differ from liberal perfectionism.

It is a distinct characteristic of our modern time that we have become aware of the fact that many different views of how a human life should be lived, even if they are not our own, seem nevertheless prima facie reasonable to us. This is what Rawls called 'the fact of reasonable pluralism'.[41] Moreover, we have learned (at least since the major religious conflicts) that discussion will not make the disagreement go away. If anything, an exchange of arguments will exacerbate and entrench disagreements on matters of principle. The moral requirement of the respect for other people and their values strongly suggests that the state should remain neutral with regard to ultimate

38. See Charles E. Larmore, *Patterns of moral complexity* (Cambridge: Cambridge University Press, 1987), esp ch 3 and 5. Not only political liberals but also certain comprehensive liberals regard state neutrality as the core of liberalism. See, in particular, Ronald Dworkin, *A Matter of Principle* (Oxford: Clarendon Press, 1985), 192 ff).
39. Nussbaum, see note 28 above.
40. Not only Pope John Paul II, but also German Chancellor Angela Merkel, in 2006, stressed the need for the European constitution to refer to 'our Christian values'. (*The Guardian*, 29 August 2006 - see http://www.guardian.co.uk/world/2006/aug/29/germany.eu).
41. Rawls, see note 17 above, 36.

values and conceptions of the good life, at least to the extent that these different doctrines are reasonable in the sense that they themselves are not disrespectful of the human dignity of others. Theories of political liberalism seek to promote state neutrality in this sense by proposing political principles that everyone could reasonably agree to whatever their more comprehensive moral doctrines, values and ideals.

The idea is to find a limited set of principles that the main institutions of society should correspond to. These 'political principles' should be principles that everyone in a given society could agree to, whatever their conception of the good life, not as a matter of compromise or trade-off between irreconcilable general doctrines or world views, but rather as the part that otherwise diverse doctrines have in common, as a matter of 'overlapping consensus', as Rawls put it.[42] These political principles should still be moral principles but obviously they should be based on a common, core morality shared as much as possible by everyone in the given society (be based, in other words, on a 'thin' conception of the good). Moreover, not all types of state action have to be justified by these principles, only the main institutions. These political principles may therefore also be regarded as constitutional principles.

A controversial question is what part of contract law, if any, should be directly affected by these principles?[43] Principles of political association are principles that address us in our capacity of political subjects, i.e., as citizens.[44] In contrast, private law principles do not address us in our capacity as citizens. We are involved in a contractual relationship or engaged in a dispute before a civil court, not as citizens but as private individuals. Indeed, private law and its principles also apply to non-citizens. When we invoke private law we are not seeking any political role. On the other hand, however, private law is also constitutive of our society. In particular, it is uncontroversial today that contract law plays an important role in distributing welfare and life chances.[45] And with privatization and the reduction of the welfare state the degree to which, for important aspects of their lives, people depend on contracts and, hence, on contract law, has only increased. Therefore, any political principles must also address the roles and tasks of private law and it must, at least minimally, address its normative content. This suggests that we should seek certain political principles, also in relation to the relationships that are governed by private law. Another important reason for regarding the legal rules applicable to contractual relationships as being at least partly included in the basic structure of society in the political liberal sense, is that contract

42. John Rawls, 'The idea of overlapping consensus' (1987), in: John Rawls, *Collected papers* 421-448 (ed. Samuel Freeman (Cambridge, Massachusetts: Harvard University Press, 1999).
43. See K.A. Kordana & D.H. Tabachnick, *Rawls and Contract Law*, 73 George Washington Law Review 598-632 (2005); Lyn Tjon Soei Len, 'European Contract Law and the Capabilities Approach: On Distributive Responsibility for Contract Law' in: Niels Weidtmann, Yanti Martina Hölzchen, Bilal Hawa (eds.), *The Capability Approach on Social Order* 132-148 (Münster: LIT Verlag, 2012); Josse Klijnsma, 'Contract law as fairness' (forthcoming).
44. Cf. Charles Larmore, *The Autonomy of Morality* 140 (Cambridge: Cambridge University Press, 2008), who refers to 'political liberalism's distinction between *homme* and *citoyen*' (emphasis in original). See also Martha C. Nussbaum, *Creating Capabilities: The Human Development Approach* 90 (Cambridge Massachusetts, and London: Belknap Press, 2011).
45. See Anthony T. Kronman, *Contract Law and Distributive Justice*, 89 Yale Law Journal 472 (1980).

law provides the basis for the enforcement of contracts with the help of state power. The state enforcement of contractual obligations and other private law claims is ultimately about seizing someone's property with the help of the state's monopoly forces (Weber).[46] To the extent that contract enforcement thus involves the exercise of state power it must be assured that this use of state power is legitimate. In other words, private law should be subject (directly or indirectly, via the constitution – see below) to political principles, not only because of its distributive role (which is undeniable) but also (and maybe primarily) because of its coercive nature. That is why contract law, at least its most basic principles, requires political legitimation.[47]

At first sight, this seems to suggest that any general principles of private law adopted or recognized by the European Union should be neutral. In other words, it seems that the general principles of private law adopted by the European law making institutions in order to be legitimate should be of such a nature that they could be acceptable as *political* principles of private law, i.e., as principles on which an overlapping consensus could be reached, and which could be included, as a 'module', in the more general conceptions of the good life that people in Europe have, and thus should be compatible with their reasonable ultimate values and ideals.

Are the 'general principles of civil law' recognized by the CJEU and the 'general principles' contained in the European Commission's proposal for a regulation on a common European sales law indeed so neutral and uncontroversial that they are easily acceptable as political principles of private law for the European polity? That seems doubtful. Especially the principle of freedom of contract and the principle of good faith and fair dealing seem to be rather controversial principles that may fit well within certain world views but are much less well compatible with certain other reasonable conceptions of the good.

The principle of good faith and fair dealing requires a certain degree of virtuous conduct of buyers and sellers on the European market. In the CESL-proposal 'good faith and fair dealing' is defined as 'a standard of conduct characterized by honesty, openness and consideration for the interests of the other party to the transaction or relationship in question'. Although formulated as a standard of conduct the principle might be perceived also as seeking to implement a certain idea of human perfection, independently of the moral conceptions that the parties affected by it themselves might hold. In any case, even if it is not a perfectionist principle, within the context of the European polity the good faith principle can hardly count as neutral, since it is a well known fact that it is rejected by the Member States whose private law is based on the common law, i.e., England and Ireland. It is true that the principle of good faith and fair dealing in the CESL is meant to have a more limited role than the one it obtained, in the

46. This illustrated dramatically by the recent Spanish cases where families who, as a result of the economic crisis, can no longer pay their mortgages and, as a consequence, are expulsed from their homes by banks that even hold 'executive titles'. See the Opinion of Advocate General Kokott in Case C-415/11 Aziz [2012].
47. The point is even more obvious if private law is understood as addressing, not private parties but courts, as rules which determine what use the state can make of its powers in relation to disputes between private parties.

course of the twentieth Century, in many civil law systems (in particular Germany),[48] but it has already been argued that its role should be limited still further, to only a 'shield' function (i.e., no longer also a 'sword' function) exactly because of its controversial nature.[49] Similarly, the recognition by the CJEU in its *Messner* judgment of the principle of good faith as one of the 'principles of civil law' has also been criticized.[50] In sum, it is not self-evident that the principle of good faith and fair dealing counts as a non-controversial principle that could be accepted in an overlapping consensus as one of the fundamental principles that European private law should be based on. Rather, it seems, the endorsement of the controversial principle of good faith and fair dealing as a fundamental principle of European private law would risk making common lawyers feel like an out-group.

Freedom of contract and party autonomy, on the other hand, are closely related to the controversial comprehensive doctrine of liberal perfectionism as developed by Kant, Mill, Berlin and Raz, among others. Therefore, its endorsement by the European legislator as a general principle does not seem to be that neutral either. Recital thirty to the proposed regulation reads as follows: 'Freedom of contract should be the guiding principle underlying the Common European Sales Law. Party autonomy should be restricted only where and to the extent that this is indispensable, in particular for reasons of consumer protection. (...)' Apart from the fact that the definite article used in this phrase ('*the* guiding principle') seems to be in contradiction with the presence of not one but three general principles,[51] it places the burden of justificatory proof wholly on those in Europe who would favour a more limited role for freedom of contract and party autonomy (in sales law or generally). This seems disrespectful of those European citizens who do not regard private autonomy and individualism as prime values. In any case, the principle, and the role attributed to it by the recital, are certainly not uncontroversial. Indeed, it was a similar phrase in the European Commission's Action Plan that inspired the Manifesto which gave rise, almost a decade ago, to the debate on social justice in European contract law.[52] In other words, also the endorsement of freedom of contract as 'the guiding principle' for European sales law is bound to create an out-group of Europeans holding entirely reasonable (i.e., non-extremist) ideals and values.

It could, of course, be argued that the principle of freedom of contract and the principle of good faith and fair dealing are opposing principles and by endorsing one principle and its counter-principle European private law would have a neutral basis after all. Although it is true that the principle of good faith has traditionally been embraced by the political left while the principle of freedom of contract has been

48. See the proposal, note 14 above, recital 31.
49. Statement of the European Law Institute on the Proposal for a Regulation on a Common European Sales Law COM(2011) 635 final.
50. Stephen Weatherill, *The 'principles of civil law' as a basis for interpreting the legislative acquis*, 6 ERCL 74-85, 84 (2010).
51. Or is there a conceptual difference between the guiding principle and the general principles?
52. *A More Coherent European Contract Law, an Action Plan*, Brussels, 12.2.2003, COM(2003) 68 final, 62. Study Group on Social Justice in European Private Law, *Social Justice in European Contract Law: a Manifesto*, 16 European Law Journal 653-674 (2004).

advocated chiefly by the right,[53] the left/right distinction is merely one among many relevant dimensions along which Europeans are likely to differ when it comes to the aims and values of private law.[54] Moreover, for political liberals, as we saw, a political compromise is not sufficient. For a set of principles to count as political principles of private law *each* of the principles should be ones that could be accepted by citizens with different general commitments and values in life, as a matter of overlapping consensus.

How, then, to address the political liberal charge to the Court's and the Commission's principles of civil law, of inadequacy as political principles for their seeming lack of neutrality? There are at least three possible responses.

First, it could be argued that political liberalism is not meant for post-national constellations like the European Union. Rawls' political liberalism is notoriously weak on transnational issues.[55] However, that would not be a very satisfactory response since it would leave us with no determinate answer to the important question of the legitimacy of the European Union and its institutions. There would be no basis for determining whether some of the EU's institutions, including possibly private law institutions, should be regarded as unjust. It is for this reason that others have extended the Rawlsian project beyond the 'closed community' (Rawls' own expression for the society that his theory is meant to model) of the nation state.[56] Moreover, Larmore is quite outspoken about the fact that the whole point of political liberalism is that it should be neutral with regard to different senses of belonging (i.e., what he calls the 'Romantic views, stretching from Herder to today's communitarians). So, if we assume for now that we must also apply the idea of political liberalism directly to the European Union as at least one of the relevant societies that people in Europe belong to,[57] this means that we still have to answer the question as to whether the endorsement of general principles of private law by European law making institutions is acceptable if we regard state neutrality as the political basis for a diverse society.

53. See Christophe Jamin, *Une brève histoire politique des interprétations de l'article 1134 du code civil*, 178 Dalloz 901-907 (2002); Martijn W. Hesselink, *CFR & Social Justice* 49 (Munich: Sellier, 2008).
54. On this dimension see, in particular, Duncan Kennedy, *The Political Stakes in 'Merely Technical' Issues of Contract Law*, 10 *ERPL* 7–28 (2002).
55. See Martha C. Nussbaum, *Beyond the Social Contract: Capabilities and Global Justice. An Olaf Palme Lecture, delivered in Oxford on 19 June 2003*, Oxford Development Studies, Vol. 32, No. 1, 3-18, 6 March 2004: 'But the gravest problem with the analogy [between the national and the international 'original position'] is its assumption of the self-sufficiency of states. In designing principles at the first stage, the society is assumed to be 'a closed system isolated from other societies'. ... This is so far from being true of the world in which we live that it seems most unhelpful. Rawls's structure has no room even for a supranational political/economic structure such as that of the EU, far less for the complex interdependencies that characterize the world as a whole.'
56. See Martha C. Nussbaum, *Frontiers of Justice*, chapters 4 and 5 (Harvard: Belknap, 2006), and Thomas W. Pogge, *Realizing Rawls* Part 3, especially p. 247, on the 'deep contingency' of nationality (Ithaca and London: Cornell University Press, 1989).
57. On the relevance of multiple identities and senses of belonging for determining the limits of the relevant polity, see Martijn W. Hesselink, 'How many systems of private law are there in Europe? On plural legal sources, multiple identities and the unity of law', in Leone Niglia (ed.), *Pluralism and European private law* (Oxford: Hart Publishing, forthcoming).

A second response would consist of the claim that the three principles are sufficiently neutral after all. How do we know whether they are? As said, the political principles are meant to be neutral, but they should still be moral principles, not normatively empty ones. In their work, Larmore, Rawls, and Nussbaum proposed different content for them. Larmore is not very specific with regard to the content of political principles beyond the two norms of rational dialogue and equal respect.[58] Those are not very determinate requirements. They seem to leave open, at least in theory, the possibility that principles such as the ones on good faith and freedom of contract could be compatible with state neutrality. On the other hand, however, Larmore also argues that 'forcing people to comply with principles of conduct' – which seems to be exactly what the good faith principle does – 'is to treat them as a means'.[59] Nussbaum proposes her capabilities approach as the content of political justice.[60] It seems doubtful that the principles of freedom of contract and good faith and fair dealing could easily pass the test of the capabilities approach without important qualification. Capabilities impairing consequences of freedom of contract (including such consequences for third parties),[61] which may well occur especially if freedom of contract is understood in a more formal sense, seem to be inadmissible in Nussbaum's approach, if freedom of contract is to be understood as a political principle. Similarly, neither the principle of freedom of contract nor the principle of good faith and fair dealing are certain, at such a general level, to always favour the least privileged, as required by Rawls' difference principle,[62] which, from a Rawlsian perspective, would put the legitimacy of both these principles as political principles of private law into serious doubt.[63] But are they political principles?

Indeed, a third response could be that the general principles of civil or contract law should not be regarded as political principles (or as being directly subject to political principles), after all, but rather as principles having a lower, non-constitutional, status of ordinary private law principles which exempts them from the requirement of state neutrality. Larmore, Rawls and Nussbaum agree that only the basic structure of society is directly answerable to the political principles, such as Rawls' principles of justice and Nussbaum's capabilities approach. Larmore writes:

> One point to note immediately is that this requirement of neutrality applies primarily to the fundamental, that is, constitutional, principles of political association, which fix the basic rights and duties of citizens. Such a political order may and generally will assign non-constitutional decisions to less demanding rules, and notably to majority voting.[64]

58. Larmore, see note 16 above, 134.
59. *Ibid.*, 137.
60. Martha C. Nussbaum, see note 44 above, 89.
61. See Tjon Soei Len, note 43.
62. See Klijnsma, see note 43.
63. Both for Rawls and for Nussbaum, what seems to matter are outcomes. Of course, we do not know yet to what extent the EU's general private law principles are actually going to decide cases and, in particular, whether these principles will actually become the basis for decisions that violate the difference principle or undermine people's capabilities.
64. Larmore, note 16.

It could be argued, then, that, in the national context, private law rules and principles are subject to the constitution, while EU private law is subject to the founding treaties and to the 'general principles of EU law' which, as unwritten primary law, have the same, constitutional status as the treaties, but - insofar as they comply with the constitution - are not themselves directly subject to the political principles and to the requirement of state neutrality because that would unduly elevate these ordinary principles of private law to a constitutional status which they do not have (and which the principles of political justice do not require them to have). The argument would then be that the general principles of civil law have the mere status of unwritten secondary EU law,[65] and would, as such, be fully subject to the Treaties and to the principles of primary EU law (just like national private law is fully subject to the national constitution). The fact for rules and principles of European private law of being subject, as secondary EU law, to primary EU law (and for national rules and principles of private law to the national constitution) would include, of course, the horizontal effect of certain provisions and principles of EU law (and of the national constitution, respectively). Those horizontal effects (their existence and modalities) would then indeed be subject to the neutral political principles on which a society would agree in an overlapping consensus. However, within those constitutional limits (i.e., the constitutional limits required by the political principles) the ordinary private law legislator (and the same would apply, of course, for criminal law, administrative law and other fields) would be free to shape private law principles, through majority voting, without the risk of them being unjust, for example, in the sense of Rawls' two principles of justice.[66] To put it differently, the argument would be that Rawls does not require that social justice flow from private law principles in a strict sense. If private law principles are subject to constitutional principles that is fine, as long as the rules and principles of the constitution do not violate the principles of justice.[67] This interpretation seems plausible both for the general principles in the CESL-proposal and for the CJEU's general principles of civil law. For the former, this follows from the simple fact that the principles of freedom of contract, good faith and fair dealing and cooperation are contained in a proposal for a regulation and therefore, at least formally, aspire to no higher status or more general scope than that of secondary EU law (which is subject to primary EU law, which, according to political liberalism, in turn, would be answerable to the political principles) and within the same limited substantive and personal scope of sales and related contracts for cross-border B2C and B2SME contracts that parties have voluntarily opted into.[68] As to the latter, I have argued elsewhere that a European constitutional status for the CJEU's general principles of civil law is neither

65. See Hesselink, note 9.
66. This seems to match also with Kumm's idea of private law as applied constitutional law. See Mattias Kumm, *Who is Afraid of the Total Constitution? Constitutional Rights and Principles and the Constitutionalization of Private Law*, 7 German Law Journal, 341-369, 359 (2006).
67. The situation seems to be different in countries, like the US, where the horizontal effect of constitutional rights is less well developed.
68. However, it is argued sometimes that Art. 16 of the Charter on the freedom to conduct a business, constitutionalises the freedom of contract. Cf *Charter of Fundamental Rights of the European Union, Explanations relating to the complete text of the Charter*, 34 (December 2000).

plausible (as a matter of positive law) nor desirable; they are best regarded – within the realm of EU law – (primarily) as unwritten secondary EU law.[69]

The conclusion, therefore, seems to be that the general private law principles under discussion here could be compatible with the political liberal requirement of state neutrality because they are not likely to belong to the 'constitutional essentials' (Rawls) that are subject to political principles in relation to which an overlapping consensus is sought (nor are they themselves such principles), but rather as principles of ordinary private law or – in the EU context – of secondary EU law. Having said that, the fact that neither the principle of freedom of contract nor the principle of good faith can be regarded as neutral and uncontroversial gives us reason for caution. State neutrality is not a question of either or but rather a matter of degree. Therefore, to the extent that general principles of civil law are more controversial or sectarian they become more problematic as state enforced principles.

§1.04 THE INCLUSION OF THE OTHER

A third and final challenge to the legitimacy of general principles of private law as recently adopted and proposed by European law makers comes from Habermasean thought. Habermas supports the neutrality of the state with regard to world views, including religious views, and explicitly endorses the project of political liberalism (albeit in a modified, republican form) as the proper response to the fact of pluralism.[70] However, he differs from Rawls and Larmore in his foundational emphasis on the democratic process.[71]

The core of Habermas' political and legal philosophy is the idea of the co-originality of private and public autonomy, and of fundamental rights and democracy, which in turn, is based on the fundamental (Kantian) idea that for the legitimacy of law – be it public or private law – it is indispensable that those who are the addressees of the norms could at the same time regard themselves also as their authors.[72] There is no democracy unless people have equal fundamental rights and there is only collective self-determination when individuals are autonomous. Ultimately, all political principles and rights therefore derive from collective self-legislation; there are no pre-democratic rights or principles.

It is from this perspective of inclusive and deliberative democracy that the project of European principles of private law, both in the Commission's and, especially, in the CJEU's version, seems to be particularly vulnerable. Although for Habermas also, the

69. In the same sense, Arthur S. Hartkamp, *The General Principles of EU Law and Private Law*, 75 RabelsZ, 241-259, 257 (2011).
70. See Jürgen Habermas, *Zwischen Naturalismus und Religion* ch 4 ('Vorpolitische Grundlagen des demokratischen Rechtsstaates?') (Frankfurt: Suhrkamp, 2005).
71. See the famous debate between Habermas and Rawls (Jürgen Habermas, *Reconciliation through the public use of reason: remarks on John Rawls' Political Liberalism*, Journal of Philosophy 109-131 (1995); John Rawls, *Reply to Habermas*, Journal of Political Philosophy 132-180 (1995)), on which see also Larmore, note 44, ch 6 ('The Moral Basis of Political Liberalism').
72. Jürgen Habermas, *Faktizität und Geltung; Beiträge zur Diskurstheorie des Rechts und des demokratischen Rechtsstaats* (5th ed., Frankfurt: Suhrkamp, 1997); Jürgen Habermas, *Die Einbeziehung des Anderen: Studien zur politischen Theorie* (Frankfurt: Suhrkamp, 1996).

reference point is the constitution – understood in a substantive sense as the basic political principles that associated citizens give themselves -,[73] and although he regards any democratic debate as always ultimately a debate about the proper understanding of the constitution,[74] he draws no categorical distinction, with regard to legitimacy requirements, between the constitution and ordinary laws, in the sense that all laws, including private law, are only legitimate to the extent that the addressees can regard themselves also as their authors.

The CJEU's recognition of general principles of civil law, however, has so far been entirely apodictic. The Court has given no reasons for their adoption. This is particularly troubling since, without any further clarification, the background, scope and implications of these principles are far from being self-evident. Indeed, as said, they are rather controversial. Therefore, it is not at all certain that an inclusive debate on European principles of private law would have led to the same outcome.

It is important to emphasize that from a Habermasian perspective the idea of European (as opposed to national) principles of private law is not per se illegitimate. The European Union, which belongs to the European citizens and the European nations,[75] can decide in a democratic process to give itself private law principles.

Moreover, it is also not the case that from the Habermasian point of view the CJEU itself lacks legitimacy as a lawmaker.[76] It is not required for the legitimacy of private law principles that they actually were the outcome of an inclusive and deliberative democratic process. What is of crucial importance, however, is that they could have been the outcome of such a process.

Also the European Commission gives no reasons why its three principles should be the general principles that guide the interpretation of the CESL. However, the Commission's proposal is, of course, only the beginning of the formal legislative process. Therefore, in this case there is still ample room for good reasons to enter the debate and to inform the deliberation. On the other hand, however, we also know how much a proposal can already frame a political debate. It is, therefore, important for the European Parliament to be fully aware of how contingent the proposed general principles actually are. Every earlier version of the present text (i.e., the DCFR Interim Outline Edition, the DCFR Outline Edition, and the Expert Group Feasibility Study) contained partly different general principles than the current CESL-proposal does. The fact that these principles change overnight, from one text to another, does not reinforce their credentials as neutral principles. Rather, it suggests that they are politically controversial, as indeed they are. There is, therefore, no reason to think that the three principles that are now proposed are somehow self-evidently fundamental European principles of contract law. Nor is it inevitable that there should be a limited set of general principles spelled out at the beginning of a common Europe sales law, that should guide its interpretation. A CESL limited to rules would not at all be unthinkable.

---

73. Habermas, *Zwischen Naturalismus und Religion*, 108.
74. *Ibid.*, 110.
75. See Jürgen Habermas, *Zur Verfassung Europas: Ein Essay* (Frankfurt: Suhrkamp, 2011).
76. Contrast Scharpf's sharp criticism of the *Mangold* and *Viking Line* rulings. See Fritz W. Scharpf, *Legitimacy in the Multilevel European Polity*, European Political Science Review 173–204 (2009).

Indeed, arguably the provisions on the freedom of contract, the duty of good faith and the duty to cooperate are best understood as being at least also rules (with exceptions), not only principles (with a dimension of weight, to be balanced).

Having said that, like the liberal perfectionist and the political liberal critiques, also the Habermasian critique does not in itself delegitimize the project of formulating general principles of European private law.

§1.05 A PERFECTIONIST CODE OF PRINCIPLES

If the elaboration by European lawmakers of general private law principles is not in itself illegitimate, does this then also mean, we might ask, that even the determination of perfectionist European private law principles might be a legitimate project for them to pursue?

Hugh Collins has argued that private law has traditionally relied on rationalist perfectionism in making its claims for achieving justice and that private law perfectionism is compatible with a pluralist society. He writes:[77]

> My suggestion is that national private law systems in Europe share in common this strong commitment towards a perfectionist style of reasoning in order to secure social justice in the sense of well-being. This underlying perfectionist approach may be expressed in a number of overlapping ways, including respect for rights, the need for a coherence of principles and a requirement of rational justification for all the distinctions drawn by legal materials. Legal systems may differ in how they express the perfectionist approach, but the basic idea of promoting well-being through rational examination of principles provides a common core.

It is fully compatible with this common 'rationalist perfectionist' tradition, according to Collins, to strive for what he calls 'a common code of principles'. As he puts it:

> That legal culture has always been dominated by the perfectionist strand in its moral and legal reasoning, which is part of the common heritage of private law systems throughout Europe. The project for a European Civil Code, conceived as a code of principles that articulate this perfectionist argumentation regarding well-being, builds on what the national legal systems share in common rather than seeking to destroy their traditional identities.

If we define perfectionism as a commitment to the objective truth of one world view, which should guide the actions of individuals and of the state, including its law,[78] then it is not clear that indeed private law has been committed to that mode of thinking, at least not since the idea of natural law was abandoned. Admittedly, in the debate about private law participants have argued in terms of the specific values and ideals they are committed to and which they wish to see expressed in private law. However, arguing that private law rules should promote the common good of Europeans is not the same

---

77. Hugh Collins, *The European Civil Code: The Way Forward* 165 (Cambridge: Cambridge University Press, 2008).
78. Steven Wall, 'Perfectionism in Moral and Political Philosophy', Edward N. Zalta (ed.),*The Stanford Encyclopedia of Philosophy* <http://plato.stanford.edu/archives/win2012/entries/perfectionism-moral/>.

as arguing that through private law the state should make us become better Europeans (or better persons). There is a difference between rules of just conduct for the Internal Market or a rational system of contract law rules, on the one hand, and a system of contract law that seeks to contribute to making us better persons as defined by some objectively true, state endorsed standard. A truly perfectionist private law would be a private law which tells us what kind of persons we should be, for example that we should become autonomous persons or virtuous persons. It is not clear that this is what we should want. Indeed, in light of what we saw above there is good reason to think that such a strongly moralistic private law would actually be illegitimate.[79]

Having said that, in relation to human practices such as law categorical and rigid distinctions do not usually further our understanding. So too is the question of private law perfectionism and its legitimacy clearly a matter of degree. While comprehensive, thick and sectarian private law perfectionism would be highly problematic, a more localized and thinner perfectionism would not only be less objectionable but is actually quite familiar. It is not clear that private law thinking committed to finding rational answers to legal questions implies an exclusive commitment to a specific moral conception of man,[80] but if it does, a private law perfectionism drawing primarily on the virtue of rationality would in any case remain relatively thin. And while it is true that the duty of good faith and fair dealing, the doctrine of unfair exploitation (defined, in Article 51 CESL, as exploiting the other party's situation by taking an excessive benefit or unfair advantage) and the invalidity of contracts on the ground of immorality are indeed expressions of a thicker private law perfectionism, they also remain specific and local inroads into an otherwise relatively neutral branch of the law. Indeed, the existing instances of perfectionism in contract law may well have been so uncontroversial exactly because they are localized (i.e., prominent only in certain doctrines) or thin (limited to a commitment to rationality) and, in any case, with limited effects in that the public enforcement of moral principles through contract law will never go beyond cases where the parties themselves seek the state's aid for the enforcement of their voluntary agreements. In the words of Buckley, 'In deliberating over whether to enforce a contract, we are not asked to choose between moral tyranny and the destruction of society. The stakes are lower than that, all around.'[81] However, deliberating over general principles of private law would be a different story: the stakes would be considerably higher. Contract law perfectionism should remain thin and localized. Therefore, a set of foundational principles of European contract law aspiring to legitimacy had better not be perfectionist.

79. Of course, as said, good faith and freedom of contract can also be argued for in non-perfectionist terms, although, as said also, that still leaves open the question whether they are sufficiently neutral.
80. Indeed, as we saw, rational dialogue is one of Larmore's two proposed political principles. Critical, Nussbaum, see note 28, who argues that political liberalism should also try to keep irrational doctrines, such as the Christian dogma of the Trinity, on board.
81. *Ibid.*, 163.

§1.06 LEGITIMATE PRIVATE LAW PRINCIPLES

Just as private law, arguably, may be regarded as applied constitutional law, so too may we regard private law theory as applied political theory. This paper has addressed the legitimacy of general principles of private law as they have been formulated recently by the CJEU and the European Commission. There are four specific lessons to be learned from the theories we have seen. The first one concerns the level of generality. Perhaps the quest should not be for very general and abstract principles with a very broad scope, but rather for principles of an intermediate level of abstraction and a limited scope, which could explain and bring coherence to a set of rules, a legal doctrine, but not to the whole law of contract. Private law principles which are too general and sweeping would risk neglecting the need for internal diversification within private law. Secondly, maybe these private law principles should be situated on the non-constitutional level of ordinary private law, subject to the constitution (including its horizontal effect) – which, for example, could 'colour' or 'concretise' and substantiate the concept of freedom of contract with constitutional principles where the private lawyers' reading risks to become too formal, after the famous example of the German *Bundesverfassungsgericht* in the *Bürgschaft* case[82] – which in turn must be compatible, in order to be legitimate, with the political principles of justice that the society (in this case the EU polity) has given itself. Thirdly, the European Court of Justice, although an institution that is not in itself a less legitimate lawmaker than the legislator, when it comes to private law principles, nevertheless has a much stronger duty than the legislator explicitly to explain itself and to provide good reasons for adopting general principles of civil law and for choosing certain principles, especially if these principles happen to be controversial, either from a comparative law point of view or along any of the other axes (left/right, progressive/conservative, young/old etc.) along which European citizens and European Member States may differ. Finally, there is no legitimate place for perfectionism in the deliberation on fundamental European private law principles; any private law perfectionism should be either local (in specific doctrines like unfair exploitation) or thin (limited to values like rationality).

So, there is reason for caution. It may well be that the application of certain private law principles could lead, in certain contexts, to the violation of the difference principle or to capability deprivation.[83] Or the principle of good morals, as a test for immoral contracts, may be lead to state coercion in the name of sectarian (e.g., Christian) values. Or, to give yet another example, the call for coherence may have the effect, in certain cases or generally, of removing certain principles and values from the table. We should not be convinced too easily that the outcome of the ordinary law making process remains securely within the limits of an existing overlapping consensus concerning constitutional principles, or that all addressees of the principles could equally regard themselves as their authors. We must be careful in assuring that the debate on the nature of private law has been sufficiently inclusive. The overlapping

82. *BVerfGE* 89, 214, *NJW* 1994, 36.
83. See, respectively, Klijnsma, above, and Tjon Soei Len, above.

consensus may exist merely among experts.[84] And it may well be that the division of labour between those who shape private law and those who passively accept the expert's views cannot be explained easily by good reasons, especially if it turns out that the life and world views of those who are at the core of the decision-making process differ from those at the periphery. A permissive consensus is not the same as an overlapping consensus. And as Habermas reminds us, experts have no privileged status in the political debate on private law principles.[85] There is always a risk that a limited section of society with easy access to the private law making process will push, with the best of intentions (the common good of Europeans), its own normative agenda (which by no means needs to be very radical; it may just not be neutral in the sense of uncontroversial) via general private law principles to be enforced by the state. We should be particularly cautious, as we saw, when proposed principles do not seem prima facie neutral and if principles are formulated in a very general way, because it may well be that the permissive consensus is not in fact an overlapping consensus that would be the outcome of a deliberative and inclusive debate.

However, if we keep these caveats in mind there is nothing wrong with seeking the best possible private law principles. As long as we remain cautious in all these respects, the quest for general private law principles is perfectly legitimate. There is no contradiction in seeking to find general private law principles in a pluralist world. As long as the pursuit of the common good of Europeans in private law matters is not undertaken in the name of creating good Europeans and remains subject to a firm commitment to a common political conception of the right, then there is nothing illegitimate in seeking to find convincing general principles of private law.

84. However, this is equally true for the opposition. The strongest opposition against the Europeanization of private law, for example in Germany and the United Kingdom, seems to be no less elite driven than the pro-Europeanization argument.
85. Jürgen Habermas, *Between Facts and Norms: Contributions to a Discourse Theory of Law and Democracy* 395 (Cambridge: Polity Press, 1996).

CHAPTER 2

General Legal Principles Navigating Space and Time

*Joxerramon Bengoetxea**

§2.01 INTRODUCTION

Amongst the factors contributing to the integration of European legal cultures we find general legal principles and basic values of practical reason. Intuitively, in a rough sense, we can distinguish general principles and values, but it seems difficult to define principles without a reference to the values they embody. Both go beyond the written sources or instruments, i.e., the texts and provisions found in provisions (sections or articles) of positive law, adopted and applied within and across European legal orders (of the EU, of its Member States, of the Council of Europe). These provisions contain detailed norms that regulate rights and duties, remedies and procedures, institutions and organs, private persons and relationships, and so on. But how do principles and values interact and operate in relation to such legal orders? Principles or values influence legal orders through various dynamics like sedimentation, reception, transplants, harmonization, cross-fertilization, dissemination. They also operate by bridging, diachronically, the horizon between the normative premises or starting points of those legal systems and the objectives or *teloi* that they pursue.

* Research for this chapter has been carried out with funding and in the framework provided by *project der2010-19715* on fundamental rights after the Lisbon Treaty (subprogram juri of the Spanish del Ministry for Science and Innovation) and also in the framework of *Grupo de Investigación consolidada* GIC07/86 and UFI 11/05 both on European integration. The chapter builds upon lectures delivered in Copenhagen in the fall of 2008, in a seminar in the University of Glasgow in January 2009, in a Ph.D. seminar at the University of Milan in May 2010. Heartfelt thanks to all those who contributed with comments in these lectures.

I suggest grouping these dynamic processes under an encompassing idea: the flow, circulation, *trade,*[1] movement, navigation of principles and ask myself generally how principles travel across normative systems within and into the EU. I will do this by (1) summing up the humble corpus of knowledge I have so far amassed concerning general principles (of EU law and in relation to European private law) and then (2) relating this knowledge to one example brought from the general principle of self-determination, as a test-case for other general principles. The point I shall try to make relies on a distinction between system-bound, rule-based rights and duties and free floating principle-based rights and duties, drawing some provisional conclusions from this distinction. This seems to be necessary if we refer to the general principles of European Union as related to, but different from, the rules and principles of European *private* law. Next, (3) I shall try to identify two components of European Legal Culture, the determination of Europe and legal cultures. Five theoretical features of general legal principles are then sorted out (4) as they function in legal discourse and characterize legal culture at the European Court of Justice. The paper concludes (5) by asking some questions concerning the agenda setting around these principles.

§2.02 THE THEORY OF GENERAL PRINCIPLES OF (EU) LAW, IN A NUTSHELL

There are two analytical approaches that I would want to pursue in order to sketch a core of a theory of general principles: (a) a lexical approach that considers the meaning – reference and intension – of each of the terms of the expression 'general principles of EU law' and (b) a systemic approach. The two dimensions common to both approaches will give us hints on the major difficulties of our subject. While the ontology of general principles is deeply problematic and inherently contested, an understanding of their function in legal discourse – gap filling, aid to interpretation and validity review – is less contentious. The pragmatic dimension of general principles of EU law somehow makes up for their dodgy pedigree:

(a) On the expression 'general principles of law' we need to think further about each of its components: 'principles', 'general', 'of', 'EU law':

- As regards *principles*, the reference is to initial sources, to grounds or foundations, to basic, original or primordial norms, to axioms, to premises, to origins, starting points or beginnings: *principia*.
- *Generality* relates to comprehensiveness, to reach, to amplitude of normative scope, to diversity of objects and is in contradistinction with concreteness or specificity, but needs distinguishing also from universality or universalizability, the opposite of which is not concreteness but individuality. The difference is that a normative statement can be

1. Justice Holmes already talked about a far reaching trade in legal ideas (dissenting opinion in *Abrams v. US*, 1919, 250 US, 616, 630).

more or less general but it cannot be more or less universalizable; it either is universal or not.

- But more revealing as regards ontology is the preposition 'of': *of* law, not necessarily *in* law nor *on* or *about* law. This seems to imply that the principles are legal without necessarily having to be located at the source material *in* the sources of law; that they are legal at a level – higher, deeper or parallel – where we reflect on or about the law and find principles in the process of reflection. The principles are indistinctly of law, not about law, they are not principles of legal theory, philosophy or methodology. But Jurisprudence helps in finding them out from the law.
- Likewise, the 'law' referred to seems to point to an agreed, observable reference, a shared concept of law, which allows the juristic community to refer to and identify such level of law and assume a common understanding, a reference or base language upon which principles are predicated or from which they are abstracted, as explained in point (iii). One would need to apply this reference not just to any law, an ideally universal, perhaps cross-cultural understanding of 'law' as natural lawyers would want it, but rather to the law of the EU. Before the Lisbon Treaty came into force, from a formal point of view the EU 'existed' without a legal personality. One talked more strictly and formally about EC *law*. After Lisbon, this is an easier task. EU law is composed of so many layers that it becomes difficult to comprehend.
- The reference to *European law* used by the Conference conveners in the expression 'General Principles of EU law and *European* Private Law' is much more difficult: not only because the reference European is always controversial, but also because all those layers get immediately superseded (Member State or national private laws, EU private law, European third countries private law ...). We cannot really commit ourselves yet to the ontology of general principles of European private law when learned speakers at the Conference (Hartkamp,[2] Sieburgh[3]) warned that general principles of European private law might not be general principles of EU law. This could mean that such principles of European private law do exist but that they are either independent from or lower than those of EU law, or it could mean that they do not exist, or that they may exist but no agreement is found as to which they are. So what about private law of the EU (generated by the EU) or private law in the EU (generated either in the EU or in the national legal orders)?There is no area or domain of EU law that comes pre-identified, labelled and categorized as 'private'. Perhaps talk of private law is the product of legal dogmatics or legal science, perhaps it is only an approximation, a hermeneutic pre-understanding. Can *private* be contrasted or compared

2. See contribution in this book, Chapter 7.
3. See contribution in this book, Chapter 10.

to other domains like *public*? Can both categories be abandoned altogether as confusing categories brought from our domestic, provincial conceptual toolkits? Or is the private/public distinction[4] based on any real difference between the types of legal norms that we tend to classify as private – a family resemblance based on personal autonomy of the will – and those we place in the public domain – a family resemblance orbiting around authority and imperium. The private public distinction is itself blurry because the boundaries are blurry as Hans Micklitz aptly observed in the course of the Conference, but when analysing EU law and fine tuning, the dichotomy is of little value because the private law has a public, interpersonal, inter-connectedness dimension.[5] Common to the private and the public dimension is their social dimension and the existence of a public interest.

(b) From a slightly different, systemic approach that analyses norms in their systemic relations and context, I try to sum key features about general principles:

- Generality and universalizability: all principles tend to be general, or at least rather general as compared to rules, although Hesselink[6] warned us in his presentation against making them too general. Both rules and principles can be more or less general, although principles are usually more general than rules, but still both rules and principles are equally universalizable.
- Principles are *normative*, they are a special type of norm that lacks a normative consequence (apodosis). They have a dimension of weight (*D!*) because they are considered important, fundamental, constitutional, overriding. It is this structure that distinguishes principles from rules, which do have specific apodosis (the structure $p \rightarrow q$). Principles contain evaluations with no concrete legal results (no q) or consequences, whereas rules provide for concrete results (q), although they may contain evaluations as well. Precisely because rules have this structure with concrete consequences, they can be quite resistant to the defeating influence of principles, and retain their concrete consequences.
- Following from this structure, when principles are used to fill a gap, they do not, they cannot, provide for the solution, (because they have no consequence, q) whereas rules applied by analogy ($p' \rightarrow q$) provide for the result, for the legal consequence. This has to be postulated by the

4. On the distinction see Constanze Semmelmann, 'Theoretical Reflections on the Public-Private Distinction and their Traces in European Union Law', *Oñati Socio-legal Series*, Vol 2, No 4 (2012).
5. Claudio Michelon, 'On the Necessarily Public Character of Law' University of Edinburgh School of Law Working Paper Series No 2010/35, also in C McCorkindale, G. Clunie, H Psarras and C Michelon (eds) *The Public in Law*, Ashgate 2011.
6. At his presentation power point in the Conference, see also his contribution in this book, Chapter 4.

decision-maker in a discretionary act, which means solving gaps by recourse to principles is always a creative or norm-making activity involving leeway, because the principle contains no specific legal solution (apodosis), but it is the interpreter that 'finds' this solution.

- When controlling or reviewing the validity of another norm, of a concrete rule, the principle need not be applied to the case and need not provide with any specific result or consequence, but it may lead to declare the invalidity of a rule if the apodosis or consequence of the rule clearly goes against the higher and overriding value proclaimed by the principle or, for example, if the rule leads to a discrimination on grounds of nationality.
- Rules are always, and principles are often, formulated in the normative text, in the written sources of the law, but principles need not be. Even when principles are written in the law, e.g., incorporated into the Charter of Fundamental Rights,[7] the formulation of the principle is subsequent to a perceived pre-textual or pre-canonical existence as a normative idea which can be formulated in different ways, and the written format is less important than the idea behind it; on the other hand rules that are not formulated in the source provisions do not exist in EU law.
- Rules lose their validity when they are annulled by other superior or posterior rules, they can cease to exist, but it sounds counter-intuitive to annul or delete principles. Principles do not die, nor are they born; even when they become positivized, i.e., formulated in the positive law, they do not cease to exist. The way a principle fades away is by no longer being applied in deliberations of practical reason, or in the interpretation and application of the law. In this sense they resemble custom, which ceases to exist gradually by desuetude.
- Principles make most sense when applied in legal reasoning, in practical discourse, in the interpretation and application of the law in hard cases where the law applicable to the dispute before the jurisdiction is not clearly governed by straightforward rules of law or where the application of such rules gives rise to contending but seemingly plausible interpretations. Principles enter into play when rules are shown to be insufficient. A useful metaphor can be brought from playing cards and card games: general principles can be seen as jokers to combine with a set of rules when some concrete rule is missing in a given case (gaps in the law) and, as Dworkin suggested in his Taking Rights Seriously,[8] some fundamental general principles containing rights work

7. For a contrary view, in the Conference Peter Oliver, relying on Clemens Ladenburger, FIDE 2012 Report on 'Protection of Fundamental Rights Post-Lisbon'p. 5, and implicitly following Okham's razor, claimed that principles superseded by the Charter somehow lost their legal relevance. The situation would otherwise be one of over complexity.
8. Ronald Dworkin, 'Rights as Trumps' in J. Waldron (ed) *Theories of Rights*, Oxford, 1984.

as trump cards when offsetting the application of specific rules that contradict them.

- General principles are inherently contested and the contestation often comes from competing principles, as can be seen in cases like *Grogan,*[9] *Grant,*[10] *Carpenter,*[11] *Schmidberger*[12] or *Omega*[13] to name but a few. But the Court deals with general principles as if they were neutral. Courts will try to give the impression that they have a rule of recognition for principles, and that they have clear criteria on their operation and impact. Courts do not want to be seen as making decisions based on personal preferences.
- While there is nothing wrong with having preferences, it is perhaps insincere to deny them or hide them under a forced neutrality of principle. This is perhaps the trouble with principle. They are contentious and contested and often have to be weighed and balanced when deciding their extent and scope, their reach and intension; some are more dialectical than others.
- On the other hand, a rule applies uncontested or does not apply at all. Rules are normally readily applicable but principles have to be modulated, adjusted and elaborated. Rules derive their validity from hierarchically higher rules, or from the constitution, but principles are difficult to rank in hierarchical relationships. They might be more or less general, but their validity is not all or nothing, it is gradual and dialectical.

And yet, even on the basis of this knowledge, which could be approximating us to a rule of recognition, it is still difficult to define and identify the general principles of EU law. Precisely for the reason set out, even if one were to find a canonical reference to the principles in the positive law, or even a list of such principles, this would not necessarily settle their ambivalent ontology. A directive might make reference to an idea or a norm as a 'general principle' but that does not necessarily turn it into a 'general principle of EU law'. It may lack relevance, or rather the Court might consider that it lacks a sufficiently constitutional status.[14] Ultimately the ECJ becomes the guardian of the rule of recognition, but since this rule of recognition is not always clear

9. Case C-159/90, *SPUC v. Grogan* [1991] ECR 4685.
10. Case C-249/96, *Grant v. South West Trains LTD* [1998] ECR I-621.
11. Case C-60/00, *Mary Carpenter v. Secretary of State for the Home Department* [2002] ECR I-6279.
12. Case C-112/00, *Schmidberger* [2003] ECR I-5659.
13. Case C-36/02, *Omega Spielhallen* [2004] ECR I-9609.
14. Case C-101/08, *Audiolux SA e.a. v. Groupe Bruxelles Lambert SA (GBL) and Others* [2009] ECR I-9823 and C-174/08, *NCC Construction Danmark A/S v. Skatteministeriet* [2009] ECR I-10567. In these cases secondary EU law makes reference to a general principle like minority shareholder protection or equality of shareholders, or neutrality of taxation. However in spite of this apparent pedigree or recognition, the ECJ has not allowed them to operate as 'general principles of EU law' beyond their specific company law or tax law affiliation; in other words, they may be general but not general enough to inspire the whole of EU legal order. The Court could have taken them to be manifestations of more general principles of EU law like equality

and is even blurry or indeterminate at times, the ECJ appears to be oracular and apodictic. In order to decide on their existence, it is futile to look for any list of general principles; one can only analyse, case-by-case, the contexts of application in which general principles of EU law are invoked by parties and successfully resorted to before the Court or where the Court refuses to rely on them or denies their existence. In terms of Jurisprudence, the approach to the ontology of general principles of EU law is neither positivist nor naturalist; it is realist, even at the Court.

§2.03 A TEST-CASE FOR GENERAL PRINCIPLES: THE PRINCIPLE OF SELF-DETERMINATION

In 2008, I addressed a think tank, *Alkartasuna Fundazioa*, in a special symposium held in Bilbao to analyse the Scottish Executive's White Paper of 2007: *A Conversation*,[15] and the issue of self-determination. The *Conversation* calls the Scots to engage in a debate on the best institutional options for Scotland's national status: preserving the current devolution arrangement, intensifying devolution to new areas and competences or relative independence, i.e., creating a new Member State within the EU while remaining part of the Crown and Commonwealth. This process will materialize in the referendum on Scottish independence of 2014.[16] The option of independence in Europe opens up the whole (unresolved) issue of internal enlargement and whether and on what terms Scotland would retain its member-statehood; an issue of utmost legal and constitutional interest. But this was not my focus.

I explored the possible differences between the *principle* and the *right* to self-determination. This was no easy task. The principle of self-determination refers to a broad range of ideas based on the value of autonomy of groups and/or individuals to decide on basic issues concerning their identity, their status, their view of the 'common good' or their relations with other individuals and other groups. The same guiding principle of autonomy can be found behind individual determination, identity or preference (e.g., sexual determination), behind worker's self-managing cooperatives and workers councils, or behind peoples right to self-determination. In each concrete normative system this principle will receive its own normative development into more concrete norms, which will specify the conditions under which the right to self-determination of an individual or a group might be said to exist and how it can be practised.

As regards peoples' self-determination, it is a universally accepted principle of law and politics: the freedom of a recognized people within a given territory and State, to decide on how they want to be governed and on their constitutional status. The translation of this principle into normative systems becomes a complex task with

and neutrality or impartiality, and then given them greater impact in reviewing or at least conform-interpreting secondary EU law, but it chose to limit their scope.

15. See the relevant documents in the website, www.anationalconversation.com.
16. On this issue see Michael Keating, 'Rethinking Sovereignty. Independence-lite, Devolution-max and National Accommodation', *REAF* 16, 2012, 9-29.

definitions and criteria for determining which groups may legitimately claim self-determination, to what extent and under what conditions. Each system contains norms providing with a different response or includes a procedure whereby a State institution is authorized to determine such conditions by way of norm-making or norm interpretation. The principle has received concrete formulation in the system of public international law, and/or in the different constitutional laws of established states and the right of self-determination thus becomes a rule-based right in a given legal system.

Likewise, the principle might be developed in political theories and ideologies. The proclamation of the right to self-determination of a certain people, e.g., the Basque people, in several political manifestos (political system) or even in the declarations of the Basque Parliament (soft law) might not be accepted by the (hierarchically superior) Spanish constitution (legal system) because each system regulates the right differently, even where these different normative systems claim to be respectful to the principle of self-determination. This contradiction has been dealt with by the Spanish Constitutional Court, by restricting the status of people, the *demos*, to the totality of Spain and denying it to any other groups within Spain (STC 11-09-2008). For the time being, this argument of authority settles the issue from the point of view internal to the Spanish legal system. It does not settle the issue for the normative (political) system shared by Basque national parties and movements, but denied by other political agents like the Spanish national parties. Each normative system has its own criteria of validity and there is no absolute overarching system finally settling the issues for all normative systems.

It is only according to the concrete normative system that we can identify the extent of the right to self-determination. One needs to examine each normative system in order to analyse how the principle is actually regulated. It is uncontested that rule-based rights are system-relative and institutional; they do not exist independently of the systems of norms that regulate them – material and procedural rules. But does the same predicament apply to principles?

What enlightenment can we draw from this test-case and how can we extrapolate this to other test-cases? In my review of Conference convener Xavier Groussot's *General Principles* I wrote the following:

> general legal principles travel from local legal cultures through a comparative European legal culture (e.g. or to the Strasburg Human Rights culture) into the Luxembourg Court's legal culture and then travel back to national judiciaries in a cross-fertilization of principles or, if one wants to put it in other terms, of shared assumptions generating shared normative conclusions. Indeed, contributions in this field from the legal traditions of the different Member States – like proportionality from French and German law, legitimate interest and procedural rule of law mainly from British (Common) law or transparency, access to documents and open administration from the Nordic countries, have made it into the assumptions

> made by the Court of Justice of the EC and together with other principles like proportionality and non-discrimination, travelled back in all directions.[17]

A similar point was made, as I later found out, by Sally Engle Merry who advocates an approach based on a 'legal realism that recognizes the way ideas and norms travel and are adopted around the world'.[18] Surely these norms include general principles of law.

To the extent that general principles are shared assumptions generating shared, i.e., interpersonal normative expectations and claims, it might very well be that they are not bound to concrete normative systems, that they are not system-relative in the way rule-based rights are. Could it then be that principles can be detached from the specific detailed rules of any system and acquire a capacity to travel on their own across different normative systems? The principle of self-determination, freedom and self-rule has become an attractive idea ever since the Declaration of Independence of the US[19] and influencing the French Revolution and then the 'liberation' of Latin American countries, and it has travelled into International Law, once again through US influence in the *Wilsonian* doctrine followed by the League of Nations. From there it moved to the Charter of the UN, to the process of decolonization and the rhetoric of, often violent, national liberation movements, to the two major UN Human Rights Covenants from 1966 and to the Constitutions of some States. Recently it led to the restructuring of Eastern and Central European states, including Germany, from the Baltic to the Balkans and, through judicial interpretation and legislation, to the constitutional system of Canada and Québec, and then it adopted a new secession-oriented reconstruction in the Kosovo unilateral declaration of independence of 2008 and the opinion of the ICJ of 22 July 2010 to the effect that international law contains no 'prohibition on declarations of independence', the issue of recognition being a political one. At different moments the principle of self-determination has inspired and influenced all sorts of normative systems – political movements, legal systems, international law. The principle of self-determination does not always require complex theoretical developments. Sometimes it can be put into practice simply on the basis of an underlying consensus on the part of the actors involved. Thus Greenland exercised the right in a referendum of 25 November 2008 in a very calm and serene mood which has gone almost unnoticed in European, let alone, wider circles.

The principle adopts different forms and conditions of application in each system as it is transformed into a rule-based and procedurally conditioned right of that system, but the sources of inspiration, the basic values and normative ideas underpinning peoples' self-determination are often shared across the systems, and they will interact with other normative ideas generating normative expectations, i.e., with other principles against which they will be offset and balanced: individual freedom, state stability

17. 'Review Essay of Xavier Groussot, General Principles of Community Law', in 45 *Common Market Law Review*: pp. 1279-1303, 2008. Groussot's monumental thesis, (Europa Law Publishing, Groningen 2006), shows how general principles have travelled up and down creating a ius commune Europaeum.
18. 'New Legal Realism and the Ethnography of Transnational Law', 31 *Law and Social Enquiry* (2006), pp. 975-95, at p. 975.
19. Itself influenced by Locke, by the Scottish Enlightenment and by the political theory of Montesquieu.

and status quo, the protection of minorities but the need for minorities themselves to respect individual self-determination, ... Thus, during the Cold War, the communist block balanced the principle of peoples' self-determination against their freedom from want – rather than against individual self-determination or cultural or religious minority rights – and this led to an economic version of peoples' self-determination, a right not to be exploited by neo-colonial powers and to preserve their natural resources. This is where principles are interacting with many other ideas and becoming thick, acquiring substance. They are being offset and balanced against other normative principles like individual freedoms, state integrity, minority protection.

The difference between principles and rule-based rights in the example of self-determination can be extended to other principles, and to General Principles of Law. Take personal freedom, autonomy, *volonté individuelle*, which is related to individual self-determination, itself related to other general principles of practical reason like equality or equal respect and dignity, but also personal responsibility and general duty of respect for others considering them as equally autonomous. This is a very general principle that can be concretized through specific rights in a given normative system like freedom of movement and of residence in the legal order of the EU, or in some, not all, state constitutions like the freedom of opinion, of thought, of expression, the freedom to the pursuit of happiness or the freedom from economic want, from hunger and cold, or in the civil codes and legislations of states, like the freedom of contract. There is a strong normative impact behind this set of autonomy-related principles, not least the Kantian golden rule, or the Smithian categorical imperative.[20]

Or take more contested principles possibly deriving from personal responsibility like 'consumer protection', 'polluter pays', 'the right to pure water or clean air', 'animal welfare'. Some of these can be derived from some legislations and constitutions of the Member States and perhaps even from the EU Treaties (including the Charter of Fundamental Rights), but their nature and status is essentially contested and their universal validity is debatable. However they all encompass values that originate in normative spheres of practical reason like personal responsibility in morality, group ethics, union and social rights politics, ecology, and in some cases they make it to the law as general principles or even as more concrete norms. When sufficient consensus builds around a principle like 'equality between men and women' in a given region then the general principle will acquire a greater normative impact and will be more readily transplantable to other normative systems. But possible derivations from this consensus of sexual equality like 'father's right to paternity leave', 'father's duty of care towards a teenage child', or 'the right to marry someone of the same-sex', originate fundamental dissent, even if they get positivised or constitutionalised.

Other principles might have developed in more legal-institutional and procedural contexts like 'estoppel' or 'bona fide', the duty to motivate decisions, or effectiveness of remedies, and can be even more specific to some forms of law, but some of these encompass values that make their way to other contexts of practical reason. Each of

20. The late Neil MacCormick, *Practical Reason in Law and Morality* OUP 2009, brilliantly conflated Kantian fundamentalism and Smithian sentiments.

these can be seen as general principles, themselves concretized in more specific, but still general, principles and in rights recognized and duties imposed, all regulated in greater detail by the rules of different normative (legal) systems, with different conditions and consequences.

General principles of law differ from legal rules and institutions because principles express values and (shared) assumptions generating shared normative expectations and broad claims. Principles acquire a sort of lightness when they are detached from the specific rules defining the holders of the rights, the extent of the obligations, the scope of application and procedural conditions for their claims. By being detached and light but still retaining a normative appeal, they travel rather well. There is a dialectical tension between the less system-bound principle-based rights and the more system-determined rule-based rights; and the interactions will be many and complex. But, as Otto Kahn-Freund once explained,[21] deeply engrained legal ideologies (combining sets of principles) may pose a limit to transplantation and travel and we cannot take for granted that principles, even less so, specific rules and institutions, are per se transplantable, as the social and political context of the law, its resistances, have to be taken into account. Imagine the resistances from some legal cultures to consider the EU Charter's 'right of workers to paid vacation' as a general principle of law. Cultural resistances, deep ideological dissent and technical resistances like specific legal rules with very concrete and definite results are crucial in understanding why sometimes some general principles do not travel so well: they clash with other deeply engrained principles

§2.04 RULE-BASED RIGHTS AND PRINCIPLE RIGHTS

The differences between principles and rights are difficult to perceive, because they are not always clear and, indeed, in theories like that of Ronald Dworkin,[22] rights often derive from principles, but the concrete recognition of rights and their consequences require detailed rules and procedures in given normative systems. The distinction would then be one between rights contained in principles and rule-based rights. Formally speaking, it is possible to distinguish a principle from a rule, when the latter is conceived as a type of norm provided with concrete consequences that apply to the conditionals it foresees. As we saw in section §2.02, the rule has a binary conditional structure (protasis→apodosis, p→q, if *p* then *q*) with a detailed set of conditionals to which a consequence attaches with a deontic operator –must, may, may not. The consequence would be the existence and/or invokeability of a right in specific circumstances, or the application of another rule with further specific consequences. As we also saw, principles do not foresee detailed consequences: they are a special type of norm that limit themselves to affirming values[23] (**x!**: *x* is *valuable*).

21. *Chorley Lecture*, 'On Uses and Misuses of Comparative Law', 1973. His debate with Alan Watson, who stressed the feasibility of transplants, is a classic. Eric Stein (*Un Nuovo Diritto per l'Europa*, Milano 1991, 79-97) also had interesting things to add on this debate.
22. See mainly *Taking Rights Seriously* (London, 1978) and *A Matter of Principle* (Oxford 1985).
23. I am aware there is little agreement in legal theoretical literature on the concepts of rules and principles. In *How To Do Things With Rules*, Twining and Miers (London 1999, p. 124), for

Principles are purely deontic charges like ought, should, may, ought not, should not, they state the desirability of recognizing rights or of imposing obligations, but in order to know whether and to what extent, when and exactly how a right or an obligation is contemplated in a system, and to what effect, concrete rules – substantive and procedural – are necessary to derive any normative consequence and if there is a gap, norms will have to be found.

Perhaps we can advance that principles are normative ideas containing rights or obligations and expressing values and expectations. As such, they operate mostly as sources of normative systems, not only of laws and legal systems, but also of other systems of practical reason in the philosophical realm – political morality, ethics, perhaps even aesthetics. These sources are normative ideas that might be generated through different dynamic processes: sedimentation[24] from detailed rules of the system, reception of ideas from other normative systems existing in the same society or in other societies, attempts at harmonization of ideas found in different normative systems, cross-fertilization of ideas from different ideologies, and dissemination, 'colonisation' to other systems. We can try to represent the dynamics of these processes and phenomena with the help of arrows. Most of these concepts represent processes, except for transplants, which are to be seen more properly as the items that are 'traded', and transformed in those processes.

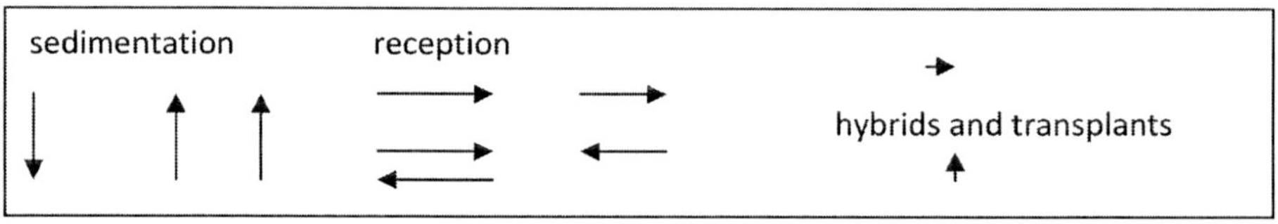

When relating these processes to legal orders, we come across general *legal* principles. General principles *of law* are general principles of practical reason that play a special role as a source of law and/or as an aid to the interpretation of legal norms and/or as a parameter to review the validity and applicability of a given rule of a legal order. General principles of law are very important, fundamental elements of a legal culture that articulate views or ideas about the sources of the law, the structure and features of the legal order, the relationship between legal norms, about what it means to make law, and to apply law, about the limits of interpretation and the role of different institutions, about the values that are to be preserved and enhanced, and also about some of the main values that govern social relationships between individuals,

instance hold that in a 'broad sense, 'rule' is a term for the genus of which precepts, regulations, conventions, principles, and guiding standards are species'. This broad sense of rule is what I suggest replacing with the term norm, also valid for other spheres of practical reason, e.g. see R.M. Hare, *Moral Thinking*, Oxford, 1981. The issue is controversial to the extreme in Jurisprudence as a discipline.

24. I draw the term sedimentation from Kaarlo Tuori: 'The voluntas of the legislator engenders surface-level turbulences, which are calmed down by the ratio sedimented into the law's deeper layers', lecture given at the Oñati Institute, 26-3-2006. Voluntas could refer to the concrete rules, and ratio, to the principles, but this would be my interpretation of Tuori's idea of multilayered legal culture. See his *Ratio and Voluntas*, Ashgate, 2011.

between groups and individuals and between groups, individuals and the wider institutionally organized society (the state or a state-like form). Four dimensions of general principles of law can be sorted out:

(1) General *constitutional* Principles as constitutional features of a legal order whether or not they are explicitly formulated in any of its written norms, or as certain norms of a legal order that formulate its general aims or have a fundamental character.
(2) Principles as basic *generalizations* or sedimentations obtained from existing rules of the system or to refer to the logical consequences or rather upward inductions of a group of norms of the legal order (this is the way in which many textbooks of law use the term in Western legal cultures, the principles governing certain institutions like the family, contract, tort, legislation).
(3) General *comparative* Principles as supra- or trans-systemic features obtained by induction and comparison of different legal systems or of different domains of the law (administrative, private, procedure, criminal justice system).
(4) General Principles of *Law and Justice* as natural laws or ideas of practical reason based on criteria of justice, equity, morality.

It is probably in this last sense, that general principles of law are pictured as elements of a *thick* legal integration, incorporating moral, economic and political values. Ideas like freedom, self-determination, dignity of the person, children's rights, equality between the sexes, reverse discrimination, affirmative action, state liability for damages, fair competition, most-favoured nation, polluter pays, unfair terms, etc. can all be seen as normative ideas that capture the minds and practical reasoning of different actors in different societies and cultures. The feature of principles as normative ideas makes this circulation easier. They are light, they are not bound to the concrete canon formulations. Because principles are not bound by specific canons and formulae, because they do not depend on the very specific and detailed conditions behind each of the elements in the $p \rightarrow q$ structure of rules, but simply posit certain ideas as being normatively desirable, they can be easily detached from their contingencies and peculiarities. They become ideas and as such are easily abstracted and uplifted. Seen from this angle, the legal system would be feeding from independent sources, general principles, containing ideas that travel between normative systems, other laws, politics, ethics and even wider systems of belief, i.e., economic thought, religion, traditional knowledge; in short, from ideology and culture. The study of legal cultures and diffusion would therefore need to pay greater attention to principles. Let us now take these ideas to the context of European integration.

§2.05 GENERAL PRINCIPLES OF A EUROPEAN LEGAL CULTURE

The idea of a European legal culture is elastic and has different possible meanings, most of which will be vague and ambiguous. In one understanding, it will relate, amongst other visions, to a certain *idea or concept* of Europe and to a given *concept of law* as legal culture, rather than the law of any particular legal system of a state. Having an idea of Europe, and of legal Europe or European law is not necessarily the same as a concrete project of Europe or a concrete phase of European integration, now materialized in transitional *EU*, i.e., EU according to Lisbon, which has spanned from EU-15 to EU-25 and EU-27, and very soon EU-27+.

But European law and legal culture could also refer to the laws and legal traditions of any of the European nations, or to common legal traditions, or to attempts at finding – through comparative law methods – and developing normative harmonization, common frames of reference, or mutual recognition techniques, common standards in particular areas of law like consumer law, family law, contract law, private law generally. This could even extend to the law of the EEA,[25] which incorporates some, but not all, general principles of EU law, and also to the soft and hard law emanating from the Council of Europe, sharing important general principles of fundamental rights and freedoms with the EU, or to principles that would encapsulate from an even more general level all of these together, as when the jurisprudence of the Court of Justice first, and the EU Constitutional documents like the Charter, later, referred to fundamental rights principles following from the European Convention and the common constitutional traditions of the Member States.[26] These general principles have not faded away simply because they have been constitutionalised in the Charter.

Another strategy for identifying European legal culture could give up the attempts to find common principles and shared understandings and stress the divergences, diversity and plurality inherent in Europe, the amazing plurality within and across such a small territory. Private law, understood in its social group or subcultural-societal dimension underlining inter-connectedness, is a key instrument and guarantee of legal and cultural plurality. Disparity, complexity and the recognition and awareness of this mosaic of legal orders, together with the attempt to develop rules of conflict based on shared principles like those embodied in the Brussels and Rome Conventions and in choice of laws principles,[27] is perhaps just as important as the search for common and unifying norms, and for the reduction of complexity.[28]

25. See, very significantly, on the principles of legal certainty and the duty to state legal reasoning, the judgment of the EFTA Court of 8 October 2012 in Joined Cases E-10/11 and E-11/11, *Hurtigruten ASA and Norway v. EFTA Surveillance Authority*, paras 252, 261-262 and 280-283.
26. Echoing, perhaps, Art. 38(1,c) of the Statue of the International Court of Justice, which refers to the 'general principles of law recognised by civilised nations'. The reference has at least two readings: a) they are those principles that *the* civilised nations recognise, the recognition mints the principle or b) nations are civilised to the extent and insofar as they recognise these principles. The principles are pre-existent and their recognition makes the nations civilised. The absence of the article *the* in English is significant.
27. An interesting application of choice of law techniques to multicultural challenges to the law in context of the feminist post-essentialist cultural debate can be found in Karen Knop, Ralf Michaels and Annelise Riles, 'From Multiculturalism to Technique: Feminism, Culture and the Conflict of Laws Style' 64 *Stanford Law Review*, 3, March 2012.
28. I would not hereby want to minimise the relevance and desirability of reducing complexity in a sense inspired by a better understanding and knowledge of the law by the citizens, a priority which Hans Micklitz rightly emphasized during the Conference. However, agreement on normative standards that enhance legal protection for individuals might help in the search for

One possible approach to understanding the concept of legal Europe which seems to be presupposed in the Conference title on European private law is an open-ended geographical or even *geopolitical* concept of Europe. Other thicker concepts will introduce criteria from *history*, or rather from interpretations of it, picking special moments of a purportedly common legal heritage - Roman Law, the rediscovery and reception of Roman Law and Canon Law, the Renaissance, the birth of the European city and the *lex mercatoria*, the Enlightenment[29] and its impact on criminal law and rational procedure, the French revolution with the birth of modern administrative law, the social democratic waves, the rise of the welfare systems and labour law, all these historical episodes would lead to a special European way of law.[30] Religious criteria - *cuius regio*, tolerance - can also be brought in from the Wars of religion at the origin of many European nation-states, and from the French Revolution. Could European legal culture perhaps involve a special *European laic culture* (still to be) developed in culturally *Christian* democracies, conceiving the Christianity of subsidiarity as a residual unity and identity factor, still compatible with actual religious, cultural and ideological pluralism and atheism or is this an attempt to reintroduce culturally hegemonic principles? In any case, the impact of this historical diversion raises not only the image of the title of this contribution of general principles (of practical reason) travelling in time, but also the issue that will be discussed below on the setting of principle agendas. Again, the issue of reducing plurality and complexity, rethinking the central role of state authority and state institutions in that role is very much linked to principles, but there are no value-neutral agendas.

Allow me a parenthesis to engage in yet another historical digression about the *diffusion of principles*. Much of the history of European legal culture has involved principles travelling across frontiers and settling down to form specific (national) legal institutions. This process is still taking place and the discussion on the models of Europe depends very much on tracing back the travels and itineraries of ideas (including very importantly general principles of law) and predicting their new destinations. Culture and legal culture has been travelling with Humanity, probably from Neolithic times; it is no specific feature of globalization. What's specifically modern is the speed with which principles travel and are assimilated but also the speed in which they fade and are forgotten. Neo-liberalism as an ideological current and the so-called Washington consensus carried with them very rapidly a host of principles associated with capital freedom, absolute right to property, and labour deregulation that were influential in many legal systems, also in the EU deregulation-friendly approaches to the free movement of capital and of financial investments. Likewise the post 9/11 counterterrorist wave brought along a host of other principles associated with risk and security adopted in many international and national laws and in so many airports around the world, and the European Arrest Warrant is partly a product of this trend. But counter-hegemony, sub-alternity, is also possible: we have seen the

---

those overarching general principles or criteria that guide us through fragmented and complex, sometimes superseding, legal instruments.

29. See Tvetan Todorov, *L'Esprit des Lumières*, Paris, 2006.
30. See V. Gessner and D. Nelken, *European Ways of Law*, Hart 2007.

so-called Arab Spring, the Icelandic popular empowerment or the Occupy movement and the general principles of practical reason they invoke are not alien to the historical sketch above. Are we now in Europe approaching a new phase where new principles like accountability, solidarity, sustainability, equal access, collective and individual self-determination will travel freely and inspire new institutions? Will this lead for instance to reaffirm procedural Human Rights in the fight against terror as in the *Kadi*[31] case and to rethink neo-liberal views of property and of the freedom to provide services? It will largely depend on whose voices are heard, a point we shall come back to below.

Political and ideological criteria are perhaps more 'controllable' although just as debatable as the historical and religious ones. The accession criteria to join the EU were defined in the June 1993 Conclusions of the Copenhagen European Council:

> Membership [of the EU] requires that the candidate country has achieved stability of institutions guaranteeing democracy, the rule of law, human rights and respect for and, protection of minorities, the existence of a functioning market economy as well as the capacity to cope with competitive pressure and market forces within the Union. Membership presupposes the candidate's ability to take on the obligations of membership including adherence to the aims of political, economic and monetary union.

If we take these criteria to be aspirations rather than conditions, perhaps they do reveal important aspects of the concept of Europe understood as the project EU. Note that the legal criteria in the list are not really predominant. The Union is political, economic and monetary, not 'legal', but law is seen at the same time as an instrument that will help bring about (political) democracy and (economic) market conditions and stability of institutions; while at the same time ensure the rule of law, human rights, and the implementation of the acquis communautaire. General principles of law are in this sense also in the service of those more fundamental and even more general principles of practical reason encompassing values and ideologies. In this sense, principles of private law are not necessarily general principles of EU law, but there is still an important sense in which they connect with those general principles of practical reason since they rely upon values like autonomy, responsibility, sociability and inter-connectedness, respect for the autonomy and dignity of others, general duty of care. There is an overall link between the principles of practical reason, to the extent that the isolation of the purely private or purely legal dimension in the understanding and hermeneutic construction of the general principles of law is too formalistic.

The second element is the *concept of law* underlying European legal culture. I follow the late Sir Neil MacCormick[32] in suggesting we conceive of law as institutional normative order, but this is, again, more a theoretical reconstruction than a description of legal culture or the conceptions of jurists: to what extent have we now learnt to view law as pure institutional fact, freed from the category of the nation-state and its

31. Joined Cases C-402/05 P and C-415/05 P, *Kadi and Al Barakaat* [2008] ECR I-6351.
32. Neil MacCormick, *Institutions of Law*, Oxford 2007. In my view this has been, to date, the most valuable contribution to a comprehensive theoretical, yet critical, analysis of modern law and its branches valid throughout the different 'families of law' in the European tradition.

authority? To what extent do we still stick to formalism and legal positivism and to the sources thesis as the way to approach legal questions of validity, identity and effects, neglecting plurality, dissent, or relative pluralism? And to what extent does legal positivism require the idea of a legal order or a legal system? If European legal culture draws from elements other than the sources identifiable in official rules of recognition, what should those elements be?

Some see European legal culture reflected in broader principles and ideas, not necessarily identified with any particular source. Others see it in the (legal and other) cultures, including the social and political background of the legal elites, the judges and officials operating with those sources, especially in supra- and transnational institutions like the European Courts (the Luxembourg courts and the Strasburg court), the Commission and the European Parliament function as channels of legal cultural integration. Principles are again key elements of this process to the extent that the normative interpretations of these European institutions seek *integrity and coherence.*[33] But they also risk shunning complexity insofar as it reflects diversity. Principles function in this sense as convenient sources, especially in the integration of the system by filling in the gaps, and as hermeneutic devices ensuring purposeful interpretation ensuring '*adherence to the aims of political, economic and monetary union*'.[34] It seems to me that principles are ultimately in the service of coherence, but there are limits to the desirability of coherence, especially when this is understood as uniformity.

These two discourses – a multi-layered, complex idea of Europe inspiring several principles and an idea of law for European integration, or if you prefer, integration as coherence and legal system as regulative ideal – conflate in the European Courts. But the resulting scheme might ignore many other normative phenomena taking place in Europe and it would be too restricted a view of European legal culture to believe that it is exhausted by the jurisprudence of these courts. Legal pluralism cannot be reduced to constitutional pluralism, since the latter is a matter of authority, whereas the former is a matter of rule-following and rule-recognition and of persons following different types of norms and finding the autonomy of private law a convenient practical discourse.

§2.06 PRINCIPLES AND AGENDA SETTING

The major *functions* of general legal principles are, as *sources of norms,* to fill gaps and to aid in reconciling antinomies and, *as hermeneutic devices,* to aid to interpretation. In either case, they always involve evaluations about what is acceptable or desirable in law, and they do so allowing for maximum discretion; since invoking a general principle that is commonly shared works as an argument of authority. In the first case, they will integrate and provide system-qualities to the legal order, by generalizing and

33. In a joint paper with Neil MacCormick and Leonor Moral Soriano, we discussed the relation between the Dworkinian notion of integrity and the European value of integration: 'Integration and Integrity in the Legal Reasoning of the European Court of Justice', *The European Court of Justice*, Gráinne de Búrca and J.H.H. Weiler (eds), Oxford 2001.
34. See the conclusions of the Copenhagen European Council above.

simplifying its more concrete and detailed rules, by giving it a sense of direction and ranking of importance; in the second, they will contribute to the development of a style of reasoning from general clauses and purposes which will be seen as rather coherent since the reasons for certain interpretations will be *principled* and authoritative, almost fair rather than random, capricious or excessively idiosyncratic:

> [I]t is therefore not only the legitimacy of the Court's jurisprudence but the very credibility of the European Union as a 'community based on the rule of law' which is at stake if the use of general principles is perceived as an arbitrary exercise of judicial law-making rather than a rational process guided by a transparent and consistent methodology.[35]

To develop criteria that secure the rationality of this process of reasoning from principles requires an understanding of key theoretical features of the general principles of law and of sociological factors involved in their use or abuse. But given that their ontology is hugely problematic, this rational methodology is really a rational reconstruction.

When principles are used to fill a gap or lacuna in the law, they do not, they cannot, provide for the solution if we understand by solution a legal consequence foreseen by a legal rule (with an antecedent –protasis – and a consequent – apodosis).[36] The reason is that principles are special norms that contain no specific solution. The solution has to be given by the decision-maker in a discretionary act by postulating the existence of a legal rule, which implies that solving gaps by recourse to principles – assuming there would be agreement on their existence and relevance – is always a creative or norm-making activity, a reconstruction, because a principle is made to operate as a rule.[37]

When controlling or reviewing the validity of another legal norm, of a concrete rule or even of another principle considered to be defeasible, the prevailing principle need not be applied to the case and need not provide with any specific result. It can simply operate to set aside the incompatible norm and the decision-maker has discretion to decide which norm (which rule) applies to the case. The situation can be redefined as a legal gap; or a different rule has to be found and constructed to govern the case. We are assuming that *non-liquet* – another travelling principle partly related to *iura novit curia* – is not an option once we find ourselves in a relevant jurisdiction, within a legally relevant question – *ratione materiae* and *ratione personae*. By using some version of Latin, I also hint at the notion that legal principles travel in language forms, ideally in lingua franca formulae or brocards, as they did well before the term 'globalisation' was invented.

Principles often are, but need not be, formulated in the normative text, in the written sources of the law, but even in those cases where principles are expressed in

35. Matthias Herdegen: 'General Principles of EU Law – The Methodological Challenge', in *General Principles of European Community Law in a Process of Development*, Kluwer, 2008. pp. 349–361.
36. See my joint paper with Ola Wiklund, 'General Constitutional Principles of Community Law', in Ulf Bernitz and Joakim Nergelius (eds) *General Principles of European Community Law*, Kluwer International, The Hague 2000.
37. The apodosis or legal result is not provided by the principle, but rather by the interpreter.

legal provisions, their textual formulation is considered to be subsequent to their perceived pre-textual existence as a *normative idea,* which could be formulated in different ways. The written format, the formula, is less important than the idea behind it. It might be a useful, nemotechnic formula to capture the complex meaning. It will be the underlying idea that gets to travel rather than the specific formulation it might receive in one document, say the European Convention of Human Rights, or in another, say the Charter. But if the formula is catchy and felicitous, as in many brocards, it might easily sediment into the legal culture. There is an interesting interaction between written and unwritten principles: the textual formulation seems to be dependent on a pre-existing idea of the principle.

At any rate, principles only acquire normative meaning when they are applied in legal reasoning as elements of a given practical discourse, in the interpretation and application of the law in hard cases where the law applicable to the dispute before the jurisdiction is not clearly governed by straightforward rules of law or where the application of such rules gives rise to contending interpretations, all seemingly plausible.

Finally, general principles are inherently contentious, interpretative and contested and often have to be weighed and balanced when deciding their extent and scope, their reach and intension. The debate might then be whether principles exist independently of any partisan agenda, and what they are used for.

Ultimately the question is not so much whether one can formulate normative ideas into a general principle of law but rather whether this principle will carry acceptability and consensus, and this depends not so much on calling it a 'principle', even though principles do carry a positive charge just for the term's sake, but on moral, political and ultimately religious or cultural-ideologically bounded conceptions of the person or the self, factors of the audience and the actors that have to make the decision. That these factors will be at play when a given court analyses concrete cases is undeniable. But the way the Court of Justice, for instance and more clearly so than the US Supreme Court, deals with them does show a tendency to rely on seemingly neutral *ideology-free* principles in order to avoid having to appear to be making decisions based on more personal views and inclinations, on preferences.[38] In reality they are following interpersonal preferences but giving the impression that they are relying on readily available sources. While there is nothing wrong with having preferences, it is perhaps insincere to deny them or hide them under a forced neutrality of principle. Here is the rub. One of the merits of Dworkin was to show that the debate was also one of political morality about the extent of rights. Perhaps his shortcoming was not to see that the great debates and divides are not confined exclusively to disputes about rights, but extend to other normative items.

If 'principles don't fall from heaven, except, perhaps, in a very metaphorical sense',[39] but rather are the result of given agendas, the question might be to enquire

38. One only has to think of cases before the Court of Justice like *Grogan* (case C-159/90, [1991] ECR I-4605), *Grant* (case C-249/96 [1998] ECR I-621), *Carpenter* (case C-60/00 [2002] ECR I-6279) or *Omega* (case C-36/02, [2004] ECR I-9609) to name but a few.
39. T. Koopmans, 'Judicial Activism and Procedural Law, *ERPL* 1993, 67-81, at p. 78.

into the dynamics of that agenda setting: What topics are considered worthy of attention and what are the priorities? Who is in charge of transforming, translating or interpreting normative views into legal principles? Who are the guardians of that European legal heritage? Are they going to follow an inclusive, dialectical and participatory methodology in doing so or will this be left for the dominant but invisible market forces to determine? Whose views do those guardians listen to? Whose inputs and opinions are dominant when elaborating those views, inclinations and preferences inherent to general legal principles? Who are the main players redefining such European legal culture? Whose voices are being heard? Again, I have more questions than answers.

The key question in agenda setting is whether the influential views of the elite and hegemons, of powerful stakeholders or of privileged interlocutors, the views that make up a socially constructed 'normality' or Faktizität[40] can be compensated by other voices, views, aspirations, claims, criticisms like those of civil rights movements, consumers, NGOs, academics, scientists, researchers, intellectuals, artists acting as counter-hegemonic agents.[41]

40. Jürgen Habermas, *Between Facts and Norms*, Cambridge, Massachussets 1996.
41. Boaventura de Sousa Santos and César Rodriguez Garavito (eds), *Law and Globalisation From Below, Towards a Cosmopolitan Legality*, Cambridge 2005.

CHAPTER 3

Emerging European General Principles in Private Law

John Temple Lang

§3.01 INTRODUCTION

The general legal principles that are usually regarded as the 'General Principles' of EU law (proportionality, legal certainly, legitimate expectations, legality, and so on) developed primarily as rules of public law, and they affect private rights only indirectly.

'General Principles', in the sense in which the phrase is used here, have four kinds of consequences.[1] (For clarity, the phrase 'General Principles' is used here with capital initial letters). First, they are principles of interpretation of EU measures or of national legislation in the sphere of EU law, which lead courts applying EU law to adopt or to avoid particular interpretations. In this respect they are essentially presumptions. Second, they are 'constitutional'[2] requirements that override EU or national measures in the sphere of EU law, and can invalidate or prohibit them to the extent that the measures infringe the General Principles in question. In this second respect, they have essentially the same status as the EU Treaties, although they are or were originally largely judge-made law. As far as national measures of EU Member States are concerned, the General Principles apply where the States are 'implementing' EU law, under Article 51 of the Charter of Fundamental Rights.[3] However, the General Principles also seem to apply when a Member State is regulating rights given by EU

1. Advocate General Trstenjak, in Case C-282/10, *Dominguez v. Centre informatique*, [2012] n.y.r. (judgment dated January 24, 2012), paras 91-144. At para. 126 she said *'in the light of this case-law the direct application of fundamental rights in the form of general principles in relationships between private individuals cannot be ruled out in principle'*. See Hesselink, The General Principles of Civil Law – Their Nature, Roles and Legitimacy, Amsterdam Law School Legal Studies Research Paper No. 2011-14.
2. Case C-174/08, *NCC Danmark*, [2009] ECR I-10567.
3. E.g. Case C-107/97, *Rombi and Arkopharma*, [2000] ECR I-3367, para. 65.

law,[4] which would not naturally be described as 'implementing' EU law. The better view is that the Charter applies, and therefore presumably the General Principles, whenever EU law applies.[5] Third, General Principles are legal rules infringement of which may give rise to a duty to pay compensation. Fourth, in some circumstances General Principles 'fill gaps' in the EU legal order and provide answers to questions not otherwise provided. Principles may do this even if they are not overriding or 'constitutional'. It is natural that in a wholly new kind of legal order gaps in the existing rules will be encountered, and solutions must be found that are consistent with broader legal principles. It follows that new General Principles may need to be developed or found, in particular in less developed areas of EU law.

A General Principle, in the sense in which I have tried to use the phrase, is not necessarily binding on private parties, unless of course it has been implemented by a national or EU measure which is binding on them.

A General Principle may be subject to exceptions. For example, the General Principle against discrimination on the grounds of age, set out in the Charter, is subject to derogations set out in Directive 2000/78/EC. But all such derogations must be interpreted strictly[6] and they must be authorized by EU law and not merely by national law. Confusingly, some limited derogations are permitted even if the Charter provision stating the General Principle appears to be in absolute terms, such as Article 21, which prohibits discrimination. (The explanation is that discrimination is unjustified difference in treatment, and apparent derogations say when there is justification).

Under the European Convention on Human Rights, there are some rights that are unqualified, and States may not opt out of them or derogate from them. Others are subject to certain express and limited qualifications, because they need to be regulated or reconciled with the rights of others.

It seems that a General Principle may have derogations or exceptions imposed by directives, but that a principle has not got 'constitutional' or overriding status (except perhaps in very clear or extreme cases) if it could be applied only after it was embodied in or implemented by secondary legislation, that is, if it is not precise enough by itself to have direct effects in national courts.

I have avoided using the phrase 'General Principles' for principles that, however important, are not overriding or obligatory. If the phrase is applied to principles merely because they are important and broad in their application, without having any other characteristics, the phrase becomes less useful. General Principles that are overriding are by definition important, so they need to be identified whenever possible. I also suggest that it is less useful to use the phrase General Principles for policies or principles (such as protection of minority shareholders or fiscal neutrality) which need to be implemented by secondary legislation and which rarely if ever can have direct

---

4. Case C-12/86, *Demirel v. Stadt Schwäbisch Gmund*, [1987] ECR 3719; Case C-260/89, *ERT*, [1991] ECR I-2925.
5. Lenaerts & Gutierrez-Fons, The Constitutional Allocation of Powers and General Principles of EU Law, 47 Common Market L. Rev (2010) 1629. See for clarification of this point also Case C-617/10, *Åkerberg*, n.y.r. (judgment dated February 26, 2013), paras 17-21.
6. Advocate General Sharpston in Case C-152/11, *Odar v. Baxter Deutschland*, Opinion dated 12[Th] July 2012 para. 57.

effect. A principle that is justiciable only when implemented by legislation can in itself have little practical effect.

These overriding or 'constitutional' principles should be clear enough to comply with the general principle of legal certainty, which requires rules of law to be clear enough to allow private parties, if necessary having taken legal advice, to know their rights and obligations under EU law. It is not always clear when e.g., the proportionality principle has been infringed, because that may be a matter of degree, and largely dependent on facts. That degree of uncertainty cannot be avoided. But the legal certainty principle means that the content of a General Principle must be clear *in any circumstances in which it clearly applies*. It cannot otherwise have direct effect in national courts. Therefore, when it was argued that there is a General Principle that minority shareholders in companies should be protected, the Court rejected the argument, since it was considered impossible to identify any general rule saying clearly how or how far or in what circumstances they were to be protected.[7] A degree of uncertainty about *when* a General Principle applies is apparently acceptable.

It is important to try to identify new or emerging General Principles, because they may apply in situations that have not previously come before the EU Courts or the EFTA Court. New General Principles are particularly likely to develop in connection with Police and Judicial Cooperation (not discussed here), and in connection with private law. If a supposed General Principle can be shown to be derived from the Charter of Fundamental Rights or the European Convention on Human Rights, it automatically overrides inconsistent measures, and it is not necessary to show that it is already established in a body of national law precedents. General Principles are rules of law. They are not matters of discretion. *'To remit the maintenance of constitutional right to the region of judicial discretion is to shift the foundations of freedom from the rock to the sand'*.[8]

Because this paper is concerned with trying to identify new or emerging General Principles, it is necessary to look at a broad and many-faceted subject from as many different viewpoints as possible. If the result is that no clear overall picture emerges, it

7. Case C-101/08, *Audiolux*, [2009] ECR I-9823. Cp. Case C-249/96, *Grant*, [1998] ECR I-621; Case C-267/06, *Maruko*, [2008] ECR I-1757. In Case 155/79, *AM & S Europe*, [1982] ECR 1575, the Court found that there was a principle that clearly protected legal advice from disclosure, even though the reasons for the rule, and the precise scope of it, differed in different Member States. In spite of the *Audiolux* judgment, there may be specific General Principles prohibiting certain specific kinds of ill-treatment of minority shareholders. 'General Principles' are not necessarily broad principles, and principles that do not generally impose broad duties on private parties may do so in extreme or unusually clear cases.

It seems likely that even if a principle or policy is too imprecise to be applied generally by national courts, it may in some clear or extreme cases be capable of having direct effects.

However, in Case C-174/08, *NCC Danmark*, [2009] ECR I-10507 the Court referred to *Audiolux* as if it were a general principle, but one which requires secondary legislation to give effect to it. See also Case C-284/11, *EMS Bulgaria Transport*, [2012] ECR. I-, July 12, 2012.

See the important conclusions of Advocate General Trstenjak in Case C-282/10, *Dominguez v. Centre informatique*, [2012] n.y.r., (judgment dated January 24, 2012) in particular paras 135-141 (the right to paid annual leave is not precise enough to apply between private parties).

8. Lord Shaw, in *Scott v. Scott*, [1913] A.C. 417 at 477.

can only be said that there is no such picture, and no established taxonomy of General Principles, in the present state of the law. The law is still developing.

§3.02 THE SOURCES AND CHARACTERISTICS OF GENERAL PRINCIPLES

The first General Principles to be developed by the European Court of Justice were the principles of proportionality and legal certainty, including the principle of legitimate expectations. These were derived or induced from national administrative law in the original six Member States, and primarily from German law. The principles of equivalence and effectiveness were the logical implications of the Court's conclusion that national courts have duties to protect rights given or guaranteed by EU law. Other principles were derived from the European Convention on Human Rights. The principle that official action must always have an identifiable legal basis is a consequence of the broad principle of the rule of law[9] in a democracy (and is essential for judicial review): there are no 'inherent' or prerogative powers of European institutions under EU or EEA law. More recently the principle of good administration seems likely to obtain the status of a General Principle, at least in situations in which the specific consequences of it, such as the requirement of care, objectivity, and record-keeping, are clear and precise enough. But these sources do not help very much to identify potential sources of General Principles of private law.

General Principles have 'constitutional' status even if they are not stated expressly in the EU Treaties, the European Economic Area Agreement, the Charter of Fundamental Rights, or the European Convention on Human Rights.[10] 'Constitutional'

9. For some references to the 'rule of law' under the EU Treaties, see Case 57/86, *Greece v. Commission (export credit)*, [1988] ECR 2875, para. 10; Joined Cases C-402/05 P and C-415/05 P, *Kadi and Al Barakaat Foundation*, [2008] ECR I-6351, para. 281; Case C-335/09 P, *Poland v. Commission*, [2012] n.y.r., para. 48, (June 26, 2012); Case C-336/09 P, *Poland v. Commission*, [2012] n.y.r., para. 36, (June 26, 2012); Case C-533/10, *CIVAD*, [2012] n.y.r., para. 30, (June 14, 2012); Case C-145/10, *Painer*, [2011] n.y.r., para. 113, (December 1, 2011); Case C-407/08 P, *Knauf Gips*, [2010] n.y.r., para. 44, (June 29, 2010); Case C-550/09, *E and F*, [2010] n.y.r., para. 44, (June 29, 2010).

   These cases mostly concern the right to judicial review of official action, on which there is a great deal of case-law. Some of the cases are listed in Temple Lang, The Duty of National Courts to Provide Access to Justice in the EEA, in EFTA Court (ed.), Judicial Protection in the European Economic Area (2012, Stuttgart) 100-137, at 116. See Article 6, TEU.

10. In Case C-174/08, *NCC Danmark*, [2009] ECR I-10567, the Court said that the principle of fiscal neutrality is a fundamental principle underlying the common system of value added tax which is intended to reflect the principle of equal treatment. That principle 'has constitutional status' although it needed to be implemented by directives.

   In retrospect it is rather surprising that it took so long for it to be realised that the European Institutions must be bound by the Convention. All of the Member States were bound by the Convention, and therefore they could not, separately or together, set up any European institutions that were not subject to the Convention. So the Court's recognition that the Convention was, in effect, a part of EU law was not 'judicial activism'. The delay in recognizing this seems to have been partly due to the fear that if it were accepted clearly that the Convention applied, the Court would be subject to review by the European Court of Human Rights. It was also due to the assumption that since EU law was mostly economic law, human rights issues would not arise.

status means that they can override secondary EU legislation and national law (in the sphere of EU/EEA law). They are principles with a broad application. They are mostly directly applicable, since they may need to be applied by national courts even if they may be implemented by directives. (The principle of sincere cooperation under Article 4(3) TEU, which is usually regarded as a General Principle,[11] and which obliges national courts to give 'effective' protection to EU law rights, is not necessarily directly applicable, because in every case it involves a *renvoi* to some other rule of EU law, and it is directly applicable only if the other rule is directly applicable).

No clear tests of 'constitutional' status for a principle have been stated, except of course when the principle is stated in or clearly derived from the Charter or one of the Treaties. Presumably the tests concern the undoubted and unqualified nature of the supposed principle, its presumed permanence, whether any breach of it would be widely considered unreasonable and unjust, whether it is widely accepted and applied, and whether it appears to provide sound solutions in a wide variety of situations. There is a moral or ethical reason for all General Principles.[12] It may not be a precise criterion, but one test of a General Principle is whether it would generally be considered seriously unjust or unfair, in a democracy subject to the rule of law, if it were not the law. Once understood, a General Principle is unquestionable. But it is also important not to adopt General Principles which are likely to have unintended consequences. A directive, without more, cannot be the legal basis of a General Principle binding on private parties.[13]

The General Principles that were originally recognized, proportionality and legal certainty, were never seriously questioned and were always recognized as overriding secondary measures, at least in clear cases. They were considered to have a moral basis, as the Charter is.

In Case C-415/93, *Bosman*, [1995] ECR I-4921 Advocate General Lenz argued that free movement of workers was a fundamental right (para. 203) and the Court took the same view (para. 129).

11. Skouris, The Principle of Procedural Autonomy and the Duty of Loyal Cooperation of National Judges under Article 10 EC, in Andenas and Fairgrieve (eds.), Tom Bingham and the Transformation of the Law (2009, Oxford) 493-507. Temple Lang, The Development by the Court of Justice of the Duties of Cooperation of National Authorities and Community Institutions under Article 10 EC, in 31 Fordham International Law Journal (2008) 1483-1532; General Report, The Duties of Co-operation of National Authorities and Courts and the Community Institutions, Fédération Internationale pour le Droit Européen (FIDE), XIX Congress (Helsinki, 2000) vol. I, 373-426 and vol. IV, 65-72; Temple Lang, Article 10 EC – the most important General Principle of Community Law, in Bernitz, Nergelius & Cardner (eds.), General Principles of EC Law in a Process of Development (2008, Wolters Kluwer) 75-113; Temple Lang, The Duties of Cooperation of National Courts under European Union Law – Principles and Unresolved Issues, in Sharpe (ed.), Lincoln's Inn Lectures on European Law and Human Rights (2012) 33-88.
12. See Case C-36/02, *Omega Spielhallen*, [2004] ECR I-9609, paras 33-39 on human dignity and fundamental rights, and Opinion of Advocate General Stix-Hackl; paras 74-94.
13. In Case C-282/10, *Dominguez*, [2012] n.y.r., (24 January 2012) the Court said that '*the entitlement of every worker to paid annual leave must be regarded as a particularly important principle of European Union social law from which there can be no derogations.*' The Court did not, however, say that the Directive 2003/88/EC on the organization of working time created obligations for private parties. Obligations for private parties may be based on the Treaty, including the Charter, but not on a directive.

The most important differences between rights based on the Charter and rights based on the Convention are that Charter rights apply only in the sphere of EU law (however exactly that may be defined), and that questions about the interpretation of the Charter can be referred to the Court of Justice under Article 267 TFEU. Strictly speaking, the Charter does not apply in the EEA, but the Convention does. Only questions about the Convention can be brought before the Court of Human Rights in Strasbourg. In principle, a case should not go to Strasbourg until other remedies have been exhausted, and that will usually involve a hearing in the European Court of Justice, if EU law applies.

General Principles are *leges generales*, both in the sense that they apply to a wide range of situations and in the sense that they are often implemented, embodied in or replaced in practice by specific, more precise, legislative or treaty measures. Implementing measures may confirm, but cannot take away, the status of a General Principle.

General Principles are not absolute, and may be limited or modified by other principles or policies. For example, there is undoubtedly a General Principle that private parties injured by breaches of EU law have a right to compensation (the *Francovich*, *Crehan v. Courage*, and *Manfredi* judgments, discussed below). Claims for compensation must be brought in national courts, and national courts have a duty under Article 4(3) TEU to provide 'effective' protection for the rights claimed. In the ordinary way that would oblige the courts to order disclosure of evidence needed to make the claim.[14] However, this duty could be, and perhaps as a result of case law already is, limited by the need to balance the EU competition policy interest in encouraging applications for immunity and leniency.[15]

§3.03 'GENERAL PRINCIPLES' AND PRIVATE LAW: 'HORIZONTAL DIRECT EFFECT'

In the sphere of private law, a number of specific and basic rules of procedural fairness and justice, derived from or accepted by national procedural rules, many of which could probably be based ultimately on the requirement in the Charter and the Convention for a 'fair hearing', seem to be useful sources of 'General Principles'. Some of these rules are discussed below, without necessarily claiming that all of them yet deserve the status of 'General Principles'. Although these rules are narrower in scope than the usually recognized General Principles, they seem to be absolute enough and clear enough to have the same status, in particular insofar as they are required for a 'fair hearing'. The best known and most striking of these principles is legal professional privilege, which is certainly a General Principle, although it has so far arisen in EU law only in connection with competition law.

14. Case C-526/04, *Laboratoires Boiron*, [2006] ECR I-7529, paras 33-39.
15. Case C-360/09, *Pfleiderer*, [2011] n.y.r., (14 June 2011); Case E-8/12, *DB Schenker v. EFTA Surveillance Authority*, [2012].

As the EFTA Court said in *Fokus Bank*,[16] the provision in the EEA Agreement prohibiting discrimination 'requires equal treatment... not only concerning substantive rights, but also with regard to procedural rights insofar as procedural rights are prerequisite to the protection of substantive rights'.

In the sphere of private law, General Principles have a rather different character from the General Principles that deal with the relations between private parties and the State. In relations between private parties, conflicting interests and rights may be balanced and reconciled in a variety of different ways. Since General Principles are intended to be simple, precise and absolute, so that they can have direct effects, there are relatively few of them that apply as between private parties, and those that do apply seem all to be narrower in scope than the broad principles of proportionality and legal certainty. Indeed, some of what are said to be General Principles, such as the principle of judicial economy, can be achieved in so many different ways in different circumstances that they should perhaps be described as policies rather than principles, although specific practical consequences can be deduced from them in particular situations. In this, of course, General Principles in private law are not unique: the principle of proportionality, and the duty of sincere cooperation of national authorities under Article 4(3), are both broad and apparently imprecise in the abstract, although many concrete practical consequences have been derived from them.

In addition, although private litigants are more likely to be equally matched than private parties are when dealing with the State, some General Principles in private law are concerned with ensuring that in litigation one party is not allowed to take unfair advantage of the other, and that parties should not be prevented from claiming their rights, or obliged to claim them in unnecessarily complex or inconvenient or difficult ways. Equality before the law may be too general and vague to be a General Principle in the sense in which that phrase is used here, but it is of fundamental importance.[17]

§3.04 NATIONAL COURTS' DUTY OF SINCERE COOPERATION AND THE EFFECTIVENESS PRINCIPLE

Broadly, the well known General Principles have effects on private rights in several ways.

The principle of 'effectiveness' requires national courts and other national authorities to give 'effective' protection to rights given by EU law. This duty to give effective protection results from what is now Article 4(3) TEU, the principle that requires 'sincere cooperation' from national authorities with the institutions and policies of the EU. 'Effective' protection must be given both against national authorities and, when appropriate, EU institutions, and against private parties if they infringe or interfere with rights given by EU law. Effective protection includes the right to a fair hearing.

16. Case E-1/04, *Fokus Bank*, [2004] EFTA Court Report 11.
17. Sedley, Ashes and Sparks: Essays on Law and Justice (2011, Cambridge) ch. 35.

The principle of effectiveness therefore obliges Member States, in particular national courts, to give injunctions or compensation when duties imposed on private parties by EU law are infringed, at least if the duties are considered to have been imposed in part for the protection of an identifiable class of private parties, even when the duties are primarily imposed for the protection of the general interests of society or the EU.

The principle of effectiveness also obliges Member States to prevent private interference with rights given or protected by EU law, even when the rights in question (e.g., the right to free movement of goods or freedom of establishment and services) are primarily regarded as rights against Member States rather than as rights against private parties.

Both these obligations are discussed below.

The duty of 'sincere cooperation' also gives rise to a rather different obligation, that requires national courts, when applying national legislation that is said to give effect to EU directives (and apparently to other rules of EU law that are not directly applicable), to interpret the legislation if possible in such a way as to carry out the obligations of the Member State in question under the directive or other rule, even if that is not the normal interpretation of the legislation. This is the *Marleasing* principle.[18] This obligation of national courts applies even between private parties: it is not limited, as is the principle of indirect effect of directives, to situations in which a private party is relying on the directive against the Member State or a State authority.

Another principle, which it is convenient to regard as a 'General Principle', says that when what are essentially regulatory powers under public law have been delegated to or made exercisable by private bodies, they have the same obligations, in particular the obligation not to discriminate and the obligation not to restrict the fundamental freedoms, as public authorities and Member States themselves.[19]

§3.05 THE EUROPEAN ECONOMIC AREA

All the well recognized General Principles, in the sphere in which EEA law applies, are part of EEA law. In that sphere they are therefore part of the private law of EEA States in the same way as and to the same extent as in the EU States. Article 3 of the EEA Agreement corresponds to Article 4(3) TEU. However, although the European Convention on Human Rights is part of EEA law, the Charter of Fundamental Rights is not. This

18. Case C-106/89, *Marleasing*, [1990] ECR I-4135; Joined Cases C-397/01 to C-403/01, *Pfeiffer*, [2004] ECR I-8835; see however Case C-168/95, *Arcaro*, [1996] ECR I-4705; Case C-456/98, *Centrosfeel v. Adipol*, [2000] ECR I-6007; Case C-555/07, *Kücükdeveci*, [2010] ECR I-365; Case E-18/11, *Irish Bank Resolution Corporation v. KaupThing Bank*, [2012] EFTA Court Report.
19. Case 36/74, *Walrave v. Union Cycliste Internationale*, [1974] ECR 1405, para. 17; Case C-415/93, *Union Royale Belge des Sociétés de Football Association and others v. Bosman*, [1995] ECR I-4921, paras 83-84; Case 43/75, *Defrenne v. Sabena*, [1976] ECR 455, paras 31, 39; Case C-281/98, *Angonese*, [2000] ECR I-4139, paras 34-35; Case C-411/98, *Ferlini*, [2000] ECR I-8081; Case C-309/99, *Wouters v. Nederlandse Orde van Advocaten*, [2002] ECR I-1577, para. 120. Council Directive 2000/78/EC Article 18 allows Member States to entrust 'the social partners' with the implementation of the Directive 'as regards provisions concerning collective agreements'. See Case C-171/11, *Fra.bo v. DVGW*, [2012] n.y.r., (July 12, 2012) (private law certification body).

means that if it is suggested that EEA law includes a rule or principle that is stated in the Charter but not stated expressly in the Convention, the EFTA Court may need to carry out what is essentially a comparative law analysis of the constitutional traditions of the EU and EEA States to see whether the supposed rule is found there. If it is, it is one of the fundamental rights included in EU and EEA law, in accordance with the case law of the Court of Justice, and of the EFTA Court itself.[20] However, as the Charter is itself largely based on the constitutional traditions of the EU Member States, the fact that a given rule is found in the Charter is prima facie evidence that it is part of their constitutional traditions. If this argument is accepted, the comparative law analysis might be comparatively simple to carry out.

§3.06 GENERAL PRINCIPLES IN THE CASE LAW OF THE FOUR EUROPEAN COURTS

General Principles are to be found in the case law of the General Court and the EFTA Court, as well as in the judgments of the European Court of Human Rights and of the European Court of Justice. They are also to be found in the judgments of national courts. None of the sources of General Principles may safely be disregarded. General Principles are principles that are most likely to be the subject of judicial dialogue. Lawyers appearing before all four European Courts must expect that judges will look at the case law of all of them when appropriate. It is important not to look only at the case law of one Court, even if it is the Court that you are appearing in.

The Court of Justice is likely to become more important, in the context of the present paper, because it is the Court which ultimately determines the interpretation of the Charter, because national courts can refer questions to it under Article 267, and because it is more likely than the Court of Human Rights be concerned with private law.

§3.07 THIS PAPER

The rest of this paper discusses the following accepted or possible General Principles:

- Directly applicable General Principles dealing with private rights and obligations, the prohibitions of discrimination on the basis of sex, age and of nationality.
- A possible General Principle on the consequences of infringements of directives.
- The General Principle of 'effectiveness'.
- A possible General Principle that duties imposed by EU public law on private parties may be enforced by private parties if that is necessary for 'effectiveness'.

20. Case E-2/03, *Asgeirsson*, [2003] EFTA Court Report 185, para. 23; Case E-4/11, *Clauder*, [2011] EFTA Court Report 216, para. 49; Case E-15/10, *Posten Norge*, [2012] EFTA Court Report – para. 85.

- A General Principle limiting the freedom to waive fundamental rights.
- General Principles of procedure based on the right to a 'fair hearing within a reasonable time'.
- Possible General Principles of private law when there is a consensus of national laws on a given issue.
- General Principles protecting collective rights and rights of vulnerable individuals.
- General Principles concerning the protection of rights given by the Charter.

§3.08 GENERAL PRINCIPLES OF EU LAW BINDING PRIVATE PARTIES AS WELL AS MEMBER STATES: THE *ANGONESE* AND *DEFRENNE* JUDGMENTS ON DISCRIMINATION

Certain provisions of EU Treaty law, although expressed to bind Member States, also impose obligations on private parties. These are in particular the principles against discrimination between the sexes, and against discrimination on the grounds of nationality.

Article 18 TFEU says:

> Within the scope of application of the Treaties and without prejudice to any special provisions contained therein, any discrimination on grounds of nationality shall be prohibited.

Article 21 of the Charter says:

> Any discrimination based on any ground such as sex, race, colour, ethnic or social origin, genetic features, language, religion or belief, political or any other opinion, membership of a national minority, property, birth, disability, age or sexual orientation shall be prohibited. Within the scope of application of the Treaties and without prejudice to any of their specific provisions, any discrimination on the grounds of nationality shall be prohibited.

This Article in the Charter raises several issues:

- To what extent does it apply to different kinds of discrimination by private parties?
- What justifications are possible for particular kinds of different treatment by private parties?

The Directive establishing a general framework for equal treatment in employment[21] set out to give practical answers to these questions, in connection with religion and belief, disability, age or sexual orientation. Differences might be objectively justified by a legitimate aim if the means used are appropriate and necessary. There are already Directives on equal pay for men and women, and on equal treatment of persons of

21. Council Directive 2000/78/EC, O.J. No. 303/16, December 2, 2000. See generally Bell, Anti-Discrimination Law and the European Union (2002, Oxford University Press).

different racial or ethnic origin.[22] But it is the Treaty, and not merely the Directives, which prohibits discrimination, and which has direct effects.

In *Angonese*[23] the Court ruled that the prohibition in the Treaty of discrimination on the grounds of nationality applies to conditions of employment fixed by private persons. Specifically, the Treaty prevents an employer from obliging candidates for recruitment to prove their linguistic knowledge exclusively by one particular diploma issued only in one province of a Member State (in the case in question, Bolzano or South Tyrol). The Court pointed out that the Treaty prohibition is in general terms and is not specifically addressed to Member States. It applies to all rules aimed at regulating in a collective manner employment and the provision of services, including acts of associations or organizations not governed by public law. In *Defrenne*[24] in 1976 the Court had held that the Treaty provision on equal pay for women was 'mandatory in nature', and therefore that it applied equally to all agreements intended to regulate paid labour collectively, as well as to contracts between individuals. 'Consequently' the Court said in *Angonese*, the prohibition on discrimination on grounds of nationality '...must be regarded as applying to private persons as well'. The employer in the case was a private banking undertaking, and not a public authority. The requirement for the diploma was based on the National Collective Agreement for Savings Banks, which authorized savings banks to fix their selection criteria, but which did not authorize or require any particular requirements.

In *Mangold,*[25] a case involving national legislation, the Court said that the sole purpose of Directive 2000/78 is:

> to lay down a general framework for combating discrimination on the ground of religion or belief, disability, age or sexual orientation, the source of the actual principle underlying the prohibition of those forms of discrimination being found... in various international instruments and in the constitutional traditions common to the Member States. The principle of non-discrimination on grounds of age must thus be regarded as a general principle of Community law.

In *Kücükdevici*[26] the Court again confirmed that the prohibition of discrimination on grounds of age is a general principle of EU law.

Several comments need to be made about the *Angonese* judgment.

First, it goes further than rules aimed at regulating employment 'in a collective manner'. The specific discriminatory feature of the bank's recruitment conditions was its own idea, and not the result of anything in the National Collective Agreement. Its importance is not limited to trade associations or trade unions or federations of

22. Directive 2000/43/EC, O.J. No. L. 180, July 19, 2000.
23. Case C-281/98, *Angonese*, [2000] ECR I-4139; Case C-411/98, *Ferlini*, [2000] ECR I-8081; see Öberg, The Doctrine of Horizontal Direct Effect in EC Law and The Case of Angonese, (Stockholm University, 2007); Dashwood, *Viking* and *Laval*: Issues of Horizontal Direct Effect, 10 Cambridge Year Book of European Legal Studies 525 (2007-2008); Krenn, A Missing Piece in the Horizontal Effect 'Jigsaw': Horizontal Direct Effect and the Free Movement of Goods, 49 Common Market Law Review (2012) 177-216.
24. Case 43/75, *Defrenne v. Sabena*, [1976] ECR 455, para. 31.
25. Case C-144/04, *Mangold v. Helm*, [2005] ECR I-9981, paras 74-75.
26. Case C-555/07, *Kücükdeveci*, [2010] ECR I-365.

industry. Nor, as in the *Mangold* case, was the Court dealing with national legislation. In *Raccanelli*[27] the Court confirmed that the prohibition of discrimination based on nationality applies to private law associations (in that case, the Max Planck Institute). This prohibition has direct effects on private parties, unlike most provisions of the Charter.[28]

Second, the judgment can be effectively applied only when the employer is so unwise as to state its discriminatory policy explicitly. If nothing had been said, and the employer had chosen or rejected a candidate without saying why, any improper preference would have been difficult if not impossible to prove. The provisions of Directive 2000/78 on a general framework for equal treatment concerning 'indirect discrimination' are intended to deal with this, and to regulate the burden of proof.

Third, since the prohibition on discrimination applies to private employers, they must in theory have the same rights to derogate from the principle of free movement of workers as are available to Member States (public policy, public security, public health). But these derogations are designed to deal with official action, not private behaviour (as was acknowledged in *Bosman*[29]). Private employers, who are not subject to any democratic constraints, should not take it on themselves to discriminate in the supposed interests of the general public. If they do claim to do so, they must expect to have to disclose their internal memoranda fully, in the light of *Laboratoires Boiron*.[30]

Fourth, as Tridimas says 'as a general rule, the liability of private parties for breach of Community law, precisely because of its private law nature, is much more dependent on national rules of remedies than the liability of public authorities where the Court is more confident to lay down the parameters'.[31] Nevertheless, if a breach of European law by a private party has been proved, the claim for a remedy must be subject to the same European principles of equivalence and effectiveness as claims against Member State authorities.

Fifth, the principle stated in *Angonese* may apply in connection with the right of establishment and freedom to provide services, as well as in connection with employment.

Sixth, the prohibition of discrimination applies also to discrimination by private parties on the basis of race and age, as well as nationality.[32] Article 21 of the Charter

27. Case C-94/07, *Raccanelli v. Max-Planck-Gesellschaft zur Förderung der Wissenshaften*, [2008] ECR I-5939, para. 46.
28. Advocate General Trstenjak, in Case C-282/10, *Dominguez v. Centre informatique*, [2012] n.y.r., (judgment dated January 24, 2012). She said that in *Kücükdeveci 'The Court expanded the principle of primacy of EU law over national law to cover so-called 'horizontal relationships''*, but said that this was not due to directives but to the general principles of non-discrimination and equal treatment (para. 146). *'The distinctive feature of prohibitions on discrimination is that their substantive core is essentially identical at both primary and secondary – law levels'* (para. 162). The *Domínguez* case concerned the right to paid annual leave, which the Court seems to have considered as a general right not dependent on Directive 2003/88/EC, although needing to be dealt with in national legislation.
29. Case C-415/93, *Union Royal Belge de Sociétés de Football v. Bosman*, [1995] ECR I-4921, para. 86.
30. Case C-526/04; *Laboratoires Boiron*, [2006] ECR I-7529.
31. Tridimas, The General Principles of EU Law (2nd ed., 2006, Oxford) p. 545.
32. Case C-144/04, *Mangold*, [2005] ECR I-9981, para. 75; Case C-555/07, *Kücükdeveci*, [2010] ECR I-365, para. 20; Council Directive 2000/78/EC of 27 November 2000 establishing a general

specifically mentions age, as well as other unlawful grounds for discrimination. But there are, and must necessarily be, different exceptions to the prohibitions on the different kinds of discrimination.

Seventh, the longest-established and most important Treaty prohibition of discrimination on the basis of sex, applied in *Defrenne*, needed to be supplemented by a directive to make it work satisfactorily in practice. But national laws on discrimination have not been fully harmonized, so cases may still need to be decided by reference to the Charter.[33] The Charter imposes duties on private parties, although directives do not.

Eighth, the claimant may be able to recover compensation (for its own benefit) and also to get an injunction, which might benefit other individuals as well as the claimant himself, or which might protect the single market. This would be particularly important if the discrimination seemed likely to be repeated, or was one of a number of similar cases.

It will be seen that although the facts of the *Angonese* case concerned the special linguistic situation in Bolzano, the implications are wider.

[A] The Need for a Limiting Principle for Individual Discrimination Cases

A claimant for compensation must prove the amount of loss suffered, and show that it was due to the illegal discrimination. He also needs to prove that the infringement was 'serious' for some reason. Some such requirement is needed to provide a limiting principle and to prevent litigation over the prejudices of individual employers against individual employees, however unreasonable the prejudices may be. An isolated case of discrimination by a single private employer is not likely to cause significant loss. But discrimination would be illegal if for some reason it had wider effects on the single market, for example if it were one of a number of similar cases, or by a large employer.

§3.09 EU LAW PRINCIPLES APPLYING TO PRIVATE RIGHTS AND OBLIGATIONS UNDER DIRECTIVES

In general, directives themselves impose no obligations on private parties (except indirectly as a result of the *Marleasing* principle[34]). Any obligations imposed on private parties are the result of the national measures implementing, or said to implement, the directives. However, several questions arise.

---

framework for equal treatment in employment and occupation, O.J. No. L. 303/16, 2000; Advocate General Kokott, in Case C-550/07 P, *Akzo Nobel Chemicals*, [2010] ECR I-8301, para. 96.

33. See Case E-9/11, *EFTA Surveillance Authority v. Norway (Financial Services Institutions)*, [2012] EFTA Court Report, July 16, 2012, para. 78.

34. Case C-106/89, *Marleasing*, [1990] ECR I-4135; Joined Cases C-397/01 to C-403/01, *Pfeiffer*, [2004] ECR I-8835.

First, Member States, when they implement a directive, are bound by general principles of EU law, and in particular by the principle of proportionality.[35] That means that if a directive requires Member States to prohibit or regulate certain conduct, the States may not impose unnecessarily or unjustifiably severe penalties on private parties which infringe the implementing measures. If the penalties were fines or other consequences under public law, the infringing party could challenge the penalties. However, the situation is more complicated if the implementing measures lay down consequences, in particular for awarding compensation in favour of private parties, which are said to be disproportionate and unjustified, either in general or in the specific circumstances of a particular claim. In this situation, the private party claiming compensation is not responsible for the implementing measures, and cannot be said to be taking advantage of its own wrong (the main basis for the effects of directives against a State). It would seem absurd, and contrary to the principle of effective protection for EU law rights, to say that the private party can claim in full all the compensation allowed by the national measures, and that the infringing party may then recover from the State whatever proportion of the compensation is excessive. It would be much more rational and efficient to say that the private claimant can recover only whatever compensation is allowed by the principle of proportionality, because its claim, being in fact based on EU law, must be subject to the conditions and limits imposed by EU law, even though formally it is relying on national measures. The right to compensation must be subject not only to the terms of the directive, but also to all the other rules of EU law.

The next question concerns the position if the national measures implementing the directive do not limit the amount of compensation, but it is said to be excessive in the circumstances that have arisen in a specific case. This has arisen in a so far unreported case under the EU directive on collective redundancies. It was argued, on behalf of former employees, that as a result of a breach of the legislation implementing the directive, they were entitled to be paid wages and salaries as if they were still employed, without any limit on the number of years for which they should be paid. If there had been nothing in the national law preventing such an unlimited claim, it is suggested that EU law would have prevented it. The application of the General Principle of proportionality cannot depend on whether the excessive compensation results from the express terms of national legislation implementing the directive or from the supposed fact that the national law simply fails to limit the compensation. Similar issues might arise if the national law provided punitive or exemplary damages.

In short, it is suggested that General Principles of law apply as between private parties, to national measures governing the implementation of directives, as well as between a private party and the State.

35. Tridimas, The General Principles of EU Law (2nd ed., 2006, Oxford) chapter 5; Council Directive 2000/78/EC, Article 17 ('sanctions.... may comprise the payment of compensation to the victim, must be effective, proportionate and dissuasive').

§3.10 THE GENERAL PRINCIPLES OF EQUIVALENT AND EFFECTIVE PROTECTION FOR RIGHTS GIVEN BY EU LAW

The well known principles that national courts must give protection for rights under EU law that is 'equivalent' to that given to corresponding rights under national law, and that is 'effective' to protect the rights in question, apply as between private parties. In all cases it may be necessary to say precisely what the EU law right is, and in some cases it may be necessary to define precisely what obligation is imposed on the private party, since that may not correspond precisely to the claimant's claim. Under the equivalence principle, it is necessary to identify the corresponding national law right.

The effectiveness principle is more important, but its implications may be less clear. It necessitates not only defining the scope and terms of the rights and duties involved, but defining what remedies are needed to provide 'effective' protection for those rights. One of the basic questions about 'effective' protection, discussed below, is whether a party who has suffered loss has a right to sue on its own behalf, or whether it must depend on official actions to defend its interests.

§3.11 WHEN CAN A PRIVATE PARTY RELY AGAINST ANOTHER PRIVATE PARTY ON AN EU LAW RULE THAT IS PRIMARILY TO PROTECT THE PUBLIC INTEREST?

This part of this paper considers the question how far there is a General Principle that duties imposed on private parties as a result of EU law can be enforced by other private parties. When for example can a competitor or other interested party obtain a remedy in a national court against a company that infringes EU measures that are primarily designed to protect the general welfare and consumers' interests? The cases require careful analysis. Unlike discrimination cases, the questions have not been dealt with by directives. The underlying question is when EU rights are protected 'effectively'. Remember that duties can be imposed on private parties by the Charter or the Treaty or by Regulations, but not by Directives.

[A] Private Enforcement of Competition Rules

As is well known, this question arose under EU competition rules in *Crehan v. Courage*.[36] All tenants of the Courage brewery were obliged to buy beer only from Courage, and Mr Crehan argued that this exclusivity was contrary to what is now Article 101. The national court did not know whether the Article could protect parties to illegal agreements, and said that under UK national law one party to an illegal agreement cannot claim damages from the other party. Advocate General Mischo considered that a party to an agreement that is contrary to Article 101 may rely on that

36. Case C-453/99, *Crehan v. Courage*, [2001] ECR I-6297. The quotations are from paras 19, 20 and 23 of the judgment.

illegality, to claim compensation, and not merely to argue that the agreement is void under Article 101(2).

The Court said that:

> Just as it imposes burdens on individuals, Community law is also intended to give rise to rights which become part of their legal assets. Those rights arise not only where they are expressly granted by the Treaty but also by virtue of obligations which the Treaty imposes in a clearly defined manner both on individuals and on the Member States and the Community institutions.

What is now Article 101 'constitutes a fundamental provision which is essential for the accomplishment of the tasks entrusted to the Community and, in particular, for the functioning of the internal market'. Articles 101–102 'produce direct effects in relations between individuals and create rights for the individuals concerned which the national courts must safeguard'. So any individual can rely on a breach of Article 101 even where he is a party to the unlawful contract. National courts must ensure that these rules take full effect and must protect the rights which they confer on individuals. The full effectiveness and the practical effect of Article 101 would be put at risk if it were not open to any individual to claim damages for loss caused by an unlawful contract. Actions for damages make a significant contribution to maintaining effective competition. However, a claimant's claim against another party to an unlawful agreement may fail if it has 'significant responsibility' for the distortion of competition.

This was strong language, but it appeared to apply only to Treaty provisions '*fundamental*' for the functioning of the internal market, and which expressly made void the illegal provisions of agreements. As Advocate General Mischo said (paragraph 22), since agreements prohibited by Article 101 are void, they could not be allowed to obstruct a claim by an injured party. It was not obvious that the same principles would apply to EU regulations (as distinct from Treaty provisions) that are not '*fundamental*' and which say nothing about the civil or commercial law consequences of infringement.

The Court confirmed the *Crehan* judgment in *Manfredi*.[37] 'Any individual can claim compensation for the harm suffered where there is a causal relationship between that harm and an agreement or practice prohibited under Article [101]'.

Although the Court did not need to discuss the question in either *Crehan* or *Manfredi*, it is necessary to decide what interests of a complainant are protected by competition law, and whether it is those interests that are affected by the infringement.[38] An 'effective' remedy is needed only if an identifiable EU law right has been infringed. EU competition law protects buyers' and suppliers' interests against exploitative abuses (excessive prices and imposition of unreasonably onerous terms). It also,

37. Case C-295/04, *Manfredi*, [2006] ECR I-6619, para. 61.
38. Since 2003 there is an anomalous situation in relation to interim measures under EU competition procedures. Though private parties may sue for loss caused by breaches of Articles 101-102, the Commission under Regulation 1/2003 Article 8 now accepts no obligation to adopt interim measures to protect them. This seems to be due only to the Commission's long-standing reluctance to use its powers to adopt interim measures. For interim protection private parties must rely on national courts.

in effect, protects competitors against exclusionary abuses, such as conduct that prevents competitors getting access to important technology, raw materials, or buyers. But it is less obvious, for example, that if an exclusive purchasing obligation is illegal because it prevents a competitor from selling to the purchaser in question, the purchaser is also protected against having to pay more to the exclusive supplier than it would have paid to the competitor. In *Crehan* the Court assumed that the purchaser could be protected in this way, but the question was not considered. (The question arose later in the national court). Such issues can arise in a variety of situations. The claimant's loss must be caused by an infringement of competition law, not merely by some conduct linked to an infringement. A car ferry company may not be refused access to a harbour from which to operate, but it has no right to acquire part of the harbour, which might be more profitable. Under Article 101 a user of a patent may not be refused a licence from a patent pool on reasonable and non-discriminatory terms, but it has no right to insist on joining the pool.

This is obvious in 'pay for delay' cases. If a pharmaceutical company makes an agreement to resolve a patent dispute with a producer of generic medicines under which the latter is paid and keeps its product off the market, consumers may perhaps be harmed, but the generic company could hardly complain that it is suffering loss because of the restrictive bargain that it made (although it could argue that the agreement was invalid under Article 101(2)).[39]

[B] Fruiticola: Competitors' Rights to Enforce Regulations

This kind of question arose again in the case of *Munoz and Fruiticola*.[40] The measure in question was the quality standard for fruit under the EU Regulation on the common organization of the market in fruit and vegetables. There was a national public authority which had power to end the infringement in question. The question sent to the Court of Justice was whether the legal duties under the Regulation could be enforced by a national court at the request of a substantial grower within the EU of the fruit concerned.

Advocate General Geelhoed, in a careful and thorough Opinion, said that the question transcends the specific issues of the organization of the fruit and vegetables market. (The infringement was the failure to give the correct name of the variety of grapes on the label). He said that there was harm to an interest that the Regulation was designed to protect, because it was intended to protect both dealers and consumers from products of unsatisfactory quality (including incorrect labelling). It was to protect fair trading, and not only to safeguard consumers' interests. Regulations have direct effects, and provisions of regulations often protect several interests. Although 'there

39. Temple Lang, Current European Competition Law Questions for Pharmaceutical companies, in Baudenbacher (ed.), Current Developments in European and International Competition Law: 16Th St Gallen International Competition Law Forum (2010) 79-111.
40. Case C-253/00, *Munoz and Fruiticola*, [2002] ECR I-7289; Case C-59/11, *Kokopelli v. Baumaux*, [2012] n.y.r., (July 12, 2012) (unfair competition). For a case of what was said to be unfair competition that did not involve consumer protection, see Case 58/80, *Dansk Supermarked v. Imerco*, [1981] ECR 181.

must be a link between the interest on which the person concerned is relying and the protection afforded by a provision of a regulation' (paragraph 47), the requirements do not need to be too strict. Under Article 10 EC (now Article 4(3) TEU) Member States are obliged to ensure enforcement of regulations. The fact that the national authorities had decided not to take action did not give the defendant the right to infringe the rule and cause loss to a third party. The Commission and the Advocate General said that this was analogous to the position under EU competition law. 'Civil enforcement ensures the full effectiveness of Community law' so 'Community law requires there to be a right of action under the national legal order' (paragraph 66). National law may require the complainant to show an actual economic interest that is protected by the regulation and that differentiates it from other economic operators, and may require other procedures to be tried first.

The Court gave a short, clear judgment. Regulations confer rights on individuals which national courts have a duty to protect. National courts must ensure that regulations take full effect. The full effectiveness of the quality standards requires it to be possible to enforce obligations under the Regulation by proceedings by a trader against a competitor. The possibility of such proceedings strengthens the practical working of the rules on quality standards. It helps to discourage practices which distort competition. Such proceedings are particularly suited to contribute substantially to ensuring fair trading and transparency of markets.

This judgment shows that if an EU regulation includes precise rules that protect the economic interest of the claimant, at least if the position of the claimant has some special feature that differentiates it from other companies in the market, it may have a right to an injunction or damages, or both, if loss is caused. That is relatively uncontroversial. The two more surprising features of the *Fruiticola* judgment are that the Regulation was interpreted as protecting the interests of competitors against sale of incorrectly labelled or unlabelled products (a question of the interpretation of the Regulation in question), and that it was assumed that the claimants had a special interest sufficient to differentiate them from other fruit producers and distributors (a question of law and fact, so not decided by the Court). Incorrect or incomplete labelling, unless positively misleading, is not normally regarded as unfair competition. The defendants' conduct had resulted in the same variety of grape being sold under several different names, which reduced the transparency of the market and affected distribution. It was more obvious in the *Crehan* case that everyone has a right to be protected against loss caused by breach of EU competition rules, and that if loss is caused to the claimant, the causal link is specific enough. It would be easier to see that fruit distributors would have a right to be protected against e.g., sales of sub-standard products at 'dumped' prices, especially if competition between the claimant and the defendant was particularly close or direct, so that the defendant's actions reduced the claimant's sales. Competition might be close or direct because both parties sold goods or offered services in the same locality, or because they sold exactly the same kind of products or services to the same buyers, or perhaps because the defendant operated on such a large scale that it affected all its competitors.

Perhaps these features of the *Fruiticola* judgment, which suggest a strict rule of liability for defendants, should be regarded as so unusual that they explain why the judgment does not seem to have given rise to many other similar claims. The question was referred by a national court, so the Court of Justice could not make a finding of fact that the claimants' interests were sufficiently different to justify their claim. The Advocate General had drawn the analogy with State aids law. Competitors are able to challenge a decision allowing a State aid if they are sufficiently and particularly affected by the aid.[41] Not every competitor has a right to bring proceedings to enforce an EU regulation on quality standards. The judgment does not say precisely in what circumstances a claimant has standing to sue, and presumably the circumstances would not necessarily be the same under all EU Regulations. The terms of the Regulations, and the interests protected by the Regulations, would not necessarily be the same, and the extent and nature of the effect of the infringement on the claimant might be significantly different.

It will be seen that similar questions may arise under EU measures imposing obligations on e.g., banks, energy companies, insurance companies, and credit rating agencies, at least if the supervisory bodies are ineffective.

[C] Unilever Italia: Private Reliance on Failure to Comply with Public Law

In *Unilever Italia*[42] the State had failed to notify to the Commission a new national measure on labelling. The failure was contrary to the Directive requiring the Commission to be informed of all measures capable of creating technical barriers to trade. The question before the Court arose from a dispute between private parties, and was whether the measure could be relied on as a justification for refusal to pay for goods that were not labelled as the measure required. The Court said that the measure, because it had not been notified, was 'inapplicable'. The directive on technical barriers to trade 'is designed, by means of preventive control, to protect freedom of movement for goods, which is one of the foundations of the Community'. The aim of the directive was not merely to inform the Commission, but also to eliminate or restrict obstacles to trade. In *CIA Security*[43] the Court had held that failure to notify a technical measure made it unenforceable against individuals, and that individuals could rely on this as a defence in proceedings brought by public authorities in national courts. In *CIA Security* the Court also said that the effectiveness of preventive control would be greater if breach of the obligation to notify made the technical measure inapplicable to individuals. The question in *Unilever Italia*, therefore, was whether the 'inapplicability' could also be invoked in civil proceedings between private parties concerning contractual rights and obligations. The finding of inapplicability in *CIA Security* was made in proceedings between competing undertakings based on national law prohibiting unfair trading. There was no reason to treat the contractual dispute in *Unilever Italia* differently from the dispute involving unfair trading in *CIA Security*. Unlawfully

41. Case 169/84, *Cofaz*, [1986] ECR 391; Case C-106/989, *Comité d'entreprise de la société française de production*, [2000] ECR I-3659.
42. Case C-443/98, *Unilever Italia*, [2000] ECR I-7535.
43. Case C-194/94, *CIA Security*, [1996] ECR I-2201.

adopted technical measures should not be allowed to hinder the use or marketing of products that do not conform to those measures. The inapplicability of the measure in *Unilever Italia* could therefore be relied on.

In the *Unilever* case the State's failure to fulfil its obligations meant that the measure could not be used as a reason for not paying for goods, since the only objection to the goods was their failure to comply with the unlawful measure. The measure was not only in breach of the State's obligations (and so could have been relied on in litigation against the State), but was, in effect, void for all purposes. The Directive imposed no duty on private parties, but prevented them from relying on the national law.

In *Unilever,* as in *Fruiticola* and the competition cases, the Court supplemented its other reasons by saying that the right of private parties to rely on the EU rule would make it more effective. That is always true, but it does not seem to be a sufficient reason for concluding that any particular rule can be enforced by or relied on in a private claim. It would hardly be correct to suggest that every rule of EU law may be enforced by private rights of action, or that every competitor has a right to sue for infringements.

§3.12 *WELLS V. SECRETARY OF STATE FOR TRANSPORT*: EFFECT ON THIRD PARTIES OF FAILURE TO CARRY OUT AN ENVIRONMENTAL IMPACT ASSESSMENT

In *Wells,*[44] the EU environmental impact assessment directive required an assessment to be made before official permission was given for re-opening of a quarry, but the assessment had not been carried out at the right time. The Court held that mere adverse effects on the rights of third parties do not justify preventing an individual from relying on the directive against the national authorities, which should have made the assessment. The authorities were obliged, under Article 4(3) TEU, to correct or nullify the unlawful consequences of the breach of the directive. This might mean revoking or suspending the permission improperly given, to allow an assessment to be carried out, or if the claimant agreed, payment of compensation. The proceedings were between Mrs Wells and the State, so she was not relying on the directive against the owners of the quarry, which she could not have done directly.

Advocate General Leger had been very clear. Having said that Mrs Wells was entitled to rely on the directive in proceedings against the State, he went on (paragraph 63):

> The corollary of that entitlement conferred on individuals is the duty of the Member States, laid down by Article 10 EC, [now Article 4(3) TEU] to take all appropriate measures, whether general or particular, to ensure fulfilment of the obligations on them under Community law. Among these is the obligation to nullify the unlawful consequences of a breach of Community law. That law is binding on all the authorities of Member States, including judicial authorities. It

44. Case C-201/02, *R. (Wells) v. Secretary of State for Transport,* [2004] ECR I-723. Cp. Case C-290/03, *R. (Ex p. Barker) v. London Borough of Bromley,* [2006] ECR I-3949.

> has been consistently held that the national courts, whose task it is to apply the provisions of Community law in areas within their jurisdiction, must ensure that those rules take full effect and must protect the rights which they confer on individuals. The national court must therefore set aside any measure of national law preventing Community rules from having full force and effect. That obligation is owed in light of the principles of direct effect and of precedence of Community law.

In the *World Wildlife Fund* case,[45] another case under the environmental impact assessment directive, the ECJ said that where the discretion permitted by the directive has been exceeded by the national legislative or administrative authorities, individuals may rely on the directive against the national authorities, and have national rules or measures incompatible with the directive set aside. The Court said:

> As regards the right of individuals to rely on a directive and of the national court to take it into consideration, the Court has already held that it would be incompatible with the binding effect conferred on directives by Article 189 of the EC Treaty (now Article 249 EC) for the possibility for those concerned to rely on the obligation which directives impose to be excluded in principle. Particularly where the Community authorities have, by directive, imposed on Member States the obligation to pursue a particular course of conduct, the effectiveness of such an act would be diminished if individuals were prevented from relying on it in legal proceedings and if national courts were prevented from taking it into consideration as a matter of Community law in determining whether the national legislature, in exercising its choice as to the form and methods for implementing the directive, had kept within the limits of its discretion set out in the directive.

A directive can be relied on only against the State or a State body, and cannot be used directly against another private party. But EU law does not say what kinds of private parties may rely on directives against the State. If national law allowed only a narrow category of claimants to invoke a directive, that would be contrary to the principle of effectiveness. For example, neighbours are clearly entitled to rely on the environmental impact directive, but it is not clear how far environmental protection organizations have a right under EU law to do so, although they are more likely to be able to ensure effective protection than neighbours might be.

The judgment in *Bund für Umwelt und Naturschutz Deutschland* clarifies this.[46] The Environmental Impact Assessment Directive 85/337/EEC gives non-governmental organizations promoting environmental protection a right to rely in court on infringement of a rule of EU environmental law. This includes the right to rely on the Directive 92/43/EC on the conservation of natural habitats 'even where, on the ground that the rules relied on protect only the interests of the general public and not the interests of individuals, national procedural law does not permit this'.[47]

45. Case C-435/97, *World Wildlife Fund*, [1999] ECR I-5613, para. 69; Case C-115/09, *Bund für Umwelt und Naturschutz Deutschland*, [2011] n.y.r., (May 12, 2011) (environmental protection organisations). Cp. Case C-321/959, *Greenpeace v. Commission*, [1998] ECR I-1651; Case C-240/09, *Lesoochranárske*, [2011] n.y.r., (Aarhus Convention on environmental matters).
46. Case C-115/09, *Bund für Umwelt und Naturschutz Deutschland*, [2011] n.y.r., (May 12, 2011).
47. Para. 59 and operative part.

Again, the Directives imposed no duties on private parties, but affected their rights indirectly.

§3.13 THE *FRENCH FARMERS'* CASE AND *SCHMIDBERGER*: THE DUTY OF STATES TO PROTECT PRIVATE RIGHTS AGAINST INTERFERENCE BY OTHER PRIVATE PARTIES

The Commission brought proceedings against France, for failure to protect free movement of goods from interference by French farmers protesting against imports of agricultural products. The Treaty provisions on free movement of goods are addressed to Member States, are directly applicable, and protect free movement from interference by State authorities. But the French farmers had carried on a systematic campaign of blocking roads and destroying imports, and the French authorities had done little or nothing to prevent them.

The Court of Justice[48] held that the French authorities had a legal duty under what is now Article 4(3) TEU to prevent the rights of importers from being interfered with. National authorities have duties to protect rights given by EU law, when necessary even against other private parties. The importers were, therefore, indirectly relying on EU fundamental freedoms, which benefit both consumers in general and importers in particular. They had to rely on their rights against the French State: although the relevant rules of EU law were directly applicable, they could not have obtained effective injunctions against an amorphous group of farmers.

In *X and Y v. Netherlands*[49] the European Court of Human Rights held that the State infringed the European Convention on Human Rights because Dutch criminal law did not make it criminal to commit a sexual assault on a mentally handicapped young woman. (It was accepted that the civil remedy was ineffective). This infringed the right of privacy of the woman, which involved positive obligations requiring adoption of State measures to ensure respect for private life even in the sphere of the relations of the individuals between themselves. In another case, more like the *French Farmers'* case, *Plattform 'Arzte fur das Leben' v. Austria*,[50] the Court of Human Rights held that a State must take reasonable and appropriate measures to protect demonstrators from interference with their right to assemble freely, when the interference was coming from other private parties.

In *Schmidberger*,[51] the Court of Justice held that Austria had not infringed its obligations to allow free movement of goods, although movement along one important route had been temporarily blocked by an environmental protest, which was duly authorized, peaceful and properly conducted. The demonstrators were legitimately exercising their rights of freedom of expression and assembly, so their fundamental

48. Case C-265/95, *Commission v. France*, [1997] ECR I-6959; see now Regulation 2679/98 on the Functioning of the internal market in relation to free movement of goods, O.J. No. L. 337/8, 1998.
49. *X and Y v. Netherlands*, A 91 (1985); 8 EHRR 235.
50. *Plattform 'Arzte fur das Leben' v. Austria* No. 10126/82 DR65 (1985).
51. Case C-112/00, *Schmidberger* [2003] ECR I-5659; cp. *R. v. Chief Constable of Sussex ex parte International Traders' Ferry*, [1999] 2 A.C. 418.

rights had to be weighed against traders' rights to move goods freely. The Court distinguished the *French Farmers'* case on several grounds. The Austrian demonstrators had asked for and received authorization; only one road was blocked, on only one occasion, and for only thirty hours; they were exercising a fundamental right, and were concerned with the environment and not trying to interfere with movement of goods; the authorities and the demonstrators had cooperated to minimize inconvenience; no general climate of insecurity had been created. A ban on the demonstration would have been an excessive and unacceptable interference with the demonstrators' right to express their opinions peacefully. The legitimate aims of the demonstration could not have been achieved by measures restricting trade less.

The *Schmidberger* case is important because it shows how apparently conflicting fundamental rights may be reconciled by reasonable behaviour by the public authorities and by both sides. Unreasonable behaviour should reduce the rights of the parties behaving badly.

§3.14 *VIKING LINE* AND *LAVAL*: PRIVATE PARTIES INTERFERING WITH FREEDOM OF ESTABLISHMENT AND SERVICES

Like the Treaty rules on free movement of goods, the Treaty provisions on freedom to provide services and freedom of establishment create individual rights that may be claimed, in appropriate cases, against private parties. In *International Transport Workers' Federation v. Viking Line*,[52] the ECJ confirmed that collective action by a trade union trying to prevent an enterprise from exercising its right of establishment may be contrary to Article 49 TFEU. That Article confers rights on a private enterprise that may be relied on against a trade union. The restriction on the right of establishment can be justified by some overriding reason of public interest, such as the protection of workers, but only if it is suitable for ensuring the attainment of the legitimate objective pursued and does not go beyond what is necessary to achieve that objective.

In *Laval*[53] the question asked by the national court was whether the Treaty and an EU directive on minimum rates of pay prevent collective action by a trade union to force a provider of services to enter into a collective agreement to give rates of pay more favourable to workers than those resulting from the relevant legislation. The ECJ confirmed that Article 56 TFEU (as it now is) on freedom of services confers enforceable rights on individual employers, which national courts must protect. Compliance with Article 56 is required even in the case of rules that are not public or statutory in nature but are designed to regulate collectively the provision of services.

A related question has arisen, but does not seem to have been authoritatively decided. If a trade union agreed with e.g., a harbour company that the union would not allow any of its members to work for a competing enterprise, the agreement would not

52. Case C-438/05, *Viking Line* [2007] ECR I-10779, paras 56-58, 66.
53. Case C-341/05, *Laval* [2007] ECR I-11767. See Flynn, The Protection of Workers' Rights and the Freedom of movement: Compatible objectives in the EU Legal order? A Critical Analysis of the Laval and Rüffert judgments of the ECJ, 16 Irish Journal of European Law (2009) 159-194.

come under Article 101 TFEU because an agreement with a trade union is not an agreement with an 'enterprise'. But the agreement would restrict competition, and would interfere with the freedom of competitors to compete and would restrict freedom of establishment. The agreement might also create or strengthen a dominant position of the company making the agreement. It seems clear that competitors could have the agreement declared illegal, on the grounds that it was contrary to the rules on freedom of establishment. If the agreements demanded by the trade unions in *Viking Line* and *Laval* had been made, they might have been illegal, not under Article 101, but because they would have been contrary to the freedoms guaranteed by internal market rules.

The result is therefore that whether trade unions are regarded in any particular case as collectively regulating provision of services or as private parties interfering with fundamental freedoms, they are subject to essentially the same rules under the Treaty.

§3.15 DIRECTIVES, DIRECTLY APPLICABLE RULES AND THE EFFECTIVENESS PRINCIPLE

Where the relevant EU law rule is directly applicable, whether it is a Treaty provision or a Regulation, private parties may be sued for infringement, as in *Fruiticola, Crehan, Manfredi, Viking Line* and *Laval*. If the rule is not directly applicable, a private claimant may indirectly be able to achieve similar results against another private party by making a claim against the State for infringement of its obligations, as in *Wells*, or by relying on the unlawfulness or inapplicability of a national measure interfering with the claimant's rights, as in *Unilever*, or by relying on the principle stated in *Marleasing*.[54] If the national measures implementing a directive create a private right of action, of course that right may be exercised. But clearly the case law with the most potential for development for claims against private parties is that concerning directly applicable rules, whatever their legal basis.

The case law suggests that the ECJ increasingly tends to interpret directly applicable EU rules as conferring rights on private procedural parties, both by interpreting the rules in question in that way, and by stressing that private rights make EU rules more effective. There may be a presumption or a general policy in favour of such interpretations in order to make rules effective, unless official enforcement can be relied on.[55] The ECJ has repeatedly emphasized that Regulations (but not directives except insofar as they have direct effects) create rights and duties for private parties.

---

54. Case C-106/89, *Marleasing*, [1990] ECR I-4135. This principle applies in litigation between private parties, as well as litigation involving State bodies, if a directive is relevant but may not have been fully implemented.

55. The Court has always recognised the importance of private parties' rights to sue. In Case 26/62, *Van Gend en Loos*, [1963] ECR 1 at p.13 the Court said '*the vigilance of individuals concerned to protect their rights amounts to an effective supervision*' (page 13); Case C-453/99, *Crehan v. Courage*, [2001] ECR I-6297, paras 26-27.

If, on the correct interpretation of a directive or regulation, private claimants have a right to sue, any national measures taking away that right would be contrary to EU law. A national measure giving a right to sue would be permissible even if the EU measure did not itself give such a right. If the EU measure does not answer the question, Member States, and national courts, are free to decide, subject to the principles of equivalence and effectiveness.

Whether any particular rule of EU law creates such rights depends, of course, on the terms and interpretation of that rule, and in particular on what the preamble says about the purposes of the relevant measure. It may be important to know whether, if the claimant succeeded, it would benefit only itself, or also the general interests of the public. That suggests that a claimant might be more likely to get an injunction than to obtain damages, a suggestion that would be important if it proved to be correct. It also suggests that a claimant should be able to get damages only if it has a right to an injunction, since it would be regarded, in effect, as bringing the case on behalf of the public, as well as on its own behalf. A national court considering such a claim might want to know why the authority responsible for applying the regulation in question had not thought it necessary or appropriate to enforce it, in case there was a specific reason why it should not be enforced.

EU regulations are not the only kind of legislation in which the legislator has failed to make it clear whether it is intended to create private rights and to give what is in effect an action for breach of statutory duty. Examples of similar failures by national legislatures could be given. Sometimes this failure may be due to failure to foresee the question. More often it seems to be due to unwillingness or inability to decide what policy should be adopted to answer the question. Whatever the explanation may be in any particular case, it is poor legislative drafting, both in EU measures and in national legislation, because it leads to uncertainty, and to litigation. If effective enforcement depends on, or would benefit significantly from, private rights, then that should be made clear. If private rights are thought undesirable for some identifiable reason, that should be said. If the legislators do not know what they intend, in most cases that shows that they have not fully considered their policy. EU legislation is not always thoroughly thought out. It should make it clear when private rights are being created.

If the European Court of Justice concludes that an EU rule will not be effectively enforced unless there are private claims, the case law suggests that it will allow them. That raises another question. Suppose that the rule would be effectively enforced in some Member States without private claims being allowed, but would not be effectively enforced in others? Since the Court in general considers that Member States must enforce EU rules effectively, but have a discretion about how to do so, it would be reasonable to conclude that there would be a right to bring private claims in Member States where the rule in question would not otherwise be enforced adequately. This apparently odd result, that there would be a right in some Member States but not in others, would be logically correct, because the right would not be based on the substantive EU rule itself (which would be the same everywhere), but on the duty of Member States to ensure effective enforcement, which can be ensured in different ways by different States. The conclusion is important because public authorities and official enforcement work much better in some Member States than in others. The Court has found it increasingly necessary to look at how national procedures actually work.[56] But the Court would be reluctant to rule that a private party could make a claim in one Member State because the public authorities in *that* State were not enforcing the law.

56. E.g., Case C-129/00, *Commission v. Italy*, [2003] ECR I-14637; Case C-496/04, *Slob v. Productschap Zuivel*, [2006] ECR I-8257, Opinion of Advocate General Sharpston, paras 50-51.

So the Court is likely to say that private enforcement is legitimate in all Member States if it is needed in some. The Court has always said that EU law concepts must be interpreted in the same way everywhere.[57]

§3.16 WHO CAN SUE AND WHAT ARE THE ALTERNATIVES?

If the measure creates rights of this kind for private parties, the remaining question is whether they are conferred on and exercisable by every private party within their terms, or whether they can be exercised only by parties which have a special position of some kind. Again, this may depend on the terms of the EU measure. Treaty provisions may confer rights more widely than provisions of Regulations, either because of the formal status of the Treaty, or because its provisions are more generally applicable and more fundamental for the EU legal order. Clearly, if a claimant would have standing to sue to enforce the corresponding national law rule, the principle of equivalence means that it also has standing to enforce the EU law rule. But the application of the principle of effectiveness, though probably more important, is less clear. Effectiveness means different things in different situations.

Presumably the following considerations are relevant in the light of the principle of effectiveness. What other means of enforcing the EU law rule against private parties are available? Has the claimant used them, and why have they not proved sufficient? Is the alternative remedy available as of right, or is it discretionary, or dependant on the exercise of prosecutors' discretion or the availability of official resources? What reasons, if any, has the enforcing authority given for not acting? Is the remedy that could have been given sufficient to prevent the claimant from suffering loss? Is the claimant in a special position in some respect, or merely one of many parties in the same situation, or is this a test case? Has it suffered greater loss than others, or is it more vulnerable for some reason? Are there countervailing rights, such as those of the workers in *Viking Line*, which must be weighed against the rights of the claimant? Is the situation complained of continuing or likely to occur again? Does it involve a deliberate effort to deny the claimant's rights, as in *French Farmers*, or are they interfered with only incidentally and to a limited extent, as in *Schmidhuber*, or are they already at least partially protected, as they were by the police in *International Trader's Ferry*?[58] Is there any special reason why the national court should defer to the enforcement authority, and does that authority regard enforcement as undesirable, or merely as unnecessary? Is there a relevant rule of national law which is incompatible with the principle of effectiveness and so should not be applied? How great is the loss suffered by the claimant? Does the enforcement authority believe that it has adequate resources for effective enforcement, and if it does, why has it not used them? If the authority has procedures for handling complaints, are they satisfactory? Has the claimant any remedy for the enforcement authority's failure to act? (Can it for example

57. Case C-174/08, *NCC Danmark*, [2009] ECR I-10567, October 29, para. 24.
58. *R. v. Chief Constable of Sussex, ex parte International Traders' Ferry*, [1999] 2 A.C. 418.

recover compensation from the authority itself?). Has the authority begun to act, and then delayed indefinitely, or made only ineffective gestures?

It is not likely that a private claimant should be able to sue *only* if the enforcement authority was insufficiently active. Even an active authority may not work fast enough to prevent all damage to private interests, and a party which has suffered loss might claim to recover it even if no criticism could be made of official enforcement. The Court would not regard a private claim as necessarily implying a criticism of the national authorities. So whether the rule would be effectively enforced if there was no private right to sue is not the only question. Private parties may sue to enforce Articles 101–102 TFEU and State aid rules although both are enforced by the Commission, and Articles 101–102 are enforced by national competition authorities as well. The key question is therefore whether a private right of action is needed to protect private rights. Put that way, it seems likely that it is needed in many cases.

It is the duty of each national court to ensure that directly applicable rules of EU law are effective, so if the national court considers that whatever national authority is responsible for enforcement has insufficient resources or is ineffective for some other reason, it should tend to allow private proceedings. This might be particularly important on the area of environmental protection, because many environmental protection bodies have insufficient resources, although most EU environment measures are directives, not regulations.

In the case of a directive, the national court has a duty to interpret the *whole* body of national laws if possible so as to be consistent with the directive, under the principle stated in *Marleasing*. The national court must therefore decide, as in the case of a regulation, whether the EU measure should be interpreted as protecting individual rights and therefore providing for private claims. If it should be interpreted in this way, the national court should allow private claims, even if national measures do not envisage them explicitly. The *Marleasing* principle obliges the national court to use available procedures to achieve effectively the result required by the directive, as well as interpreting the substantive national law so as to be consistent with the directive. (Whether this is best described as the *Marleasing* principle or the effectiveness principle, or both, probably does not matter very much in most cases). The difference may be that a directive is less likely than a regulation to provide a clear answer to the question whether private claims should be allowed. However, a national court in all cases has a duty to ensure that a directive is effectively enforced, and it may therefore need to consider whether the national measures implementing or available to implement the directive are effective, or need to be supplemented by private claims.

Clearly not every citizen has a right to bring proceedings to enforce every rule of EU law. But the question of who may sue is in practice probably primarily a question of the evidence showing that the infringement caused clear and substantial harm to a protected interest, rather than a question of formal legal standing to sue. If a claimant can show substantial harm, actual or potential, it should be allowed to sue. If it cannot, it cannot get either damages or an injunction anyway. In most cases standing to sue should depend primarily on proof of direct and significant harm, rather than depending on the nuances of interpretation of the EU measure in question, if the legislature's intention was not made clear.

Although not directly relevant, the judgment of the Court of Justice in the *Chernobyl* case[59] should be recalled here. The Court said that the Parliament should be able to sue, although the Treaty had not at that time given it standing to do so, because otherwise there would be no way in which its rights would be protected. That case involved the *'institutional balance'* created by the Treaties, and the undoubted right of the Parliament under the Treaty to be consulted. But one would expect the Court in other cases to say robustly that if a right can only be protected effectively in one way, that way must be permissible.

It seems reasonable, in the light of the case law summarized here, to say that there is a General Principle that rights given or guaranteed by EU law must be effectively protected against private parties as well as against Member States and the EU Institutions, and that effective protection may necessitate private enforcement. The European Commission considers that private enforcement of competition law is desirable, although it has not taken measures to promote it, because of the fear of discouraging leniency applications. The Court of Justice has always said that private claims are useful to ensure respect for European law.[60]

National authorities have duties under Article 4(3) TEU to enforce EU rules when appropriate. Private parties normally have no way of obliging the authorities to carry out these duties, and have no way of obliging the European Commission to bring proceedings against the Member State concerned to make it carry out its duties. Proceedings by one Member State against another are very rare. Proceedings in national courts, brought against its competitors by a private party suffering loss as a result of under-enforcement, might be the only available remedy.

To sum up, therefore:

- An EU Regulation primarily intended to protect the public or general interest may also protect interests of competitors and other private parties, such as the interest in 'fair competition'.
- If the measure is infringed and the infringement causes harm to a protected interest of a private party, that party may have a right to an injunction, damages, or both.
- The claimant may need to show that it is in a special position in some respect that differentiates it from other competitors.
- The right of a private party to an injunction or damages is particularly likely to arise if the EU measure in question would not be effectively enforced unless the right was recognized, or if the claimant would suffer significant loss unless it was allowed to sue.
- There seems to be an emerging General Principle that there is at least a presumption of a right under EU Regulations to an effective remedy for private parties and against private parties, if necessary.

59. Case C-77/88, *European Parliament v. Council (Chernobyl)*, [1990] ECR I-2041.
60. Case 26/62, *Van Gend en Loos*, [1963] ECR 1 at p.13.

- In the case of a directive, specific provisions may give a right to private parties against the State, even if the national law does not give them standing to sue.

§3.17 CONSUMERS AND ENVIRONMENTAL ORGANIZATIONS

The next question that arises is when a consumer has a right to sue for damages. At first sight this seems simple: a consumer is usually presumed to have a right to sue for loss caused by a breach of an EU measure, since most EU measures are designed directly or indirectly to protect the interests of consumers, and most such measures make this clear enough. The infringement must be shown to have harmed an interest that is protected by the measure in question. There is normally no need to prove that the consumer is in a special position of any kind if the claim is for damages. A special need might have to be proved if an injunction is claimed. The consumer normally does not need to show that the effectiveness of the measure depends on private claims for damages being available.

There may be questions about causation. A customer of a bank may suffer loss if it reduces its rate of interest on deposits, and it may have been forced to do this because it has lost money on unauthorized investments. But the customer's loss is unlikely to be directly related to the improper investment, and the customer is not likely to be in a special position of any kind.

However, these comments do not apply to EU environmental measures, infringements of which often cause indirect losses. It is suggested that there is an emerging General Principle that environmental organizations should be able to sue. Supervisory authorities cannot always be relied on, and litigation by organizations is more likely to be effective than litigation by individuals.

Also, if national procedural rules allow a private party to challenge a national measure on the grounds that it is contrary to EU law, the national court may of course decide the case,[61] and the result may have substantial consequences for other private parties. It is suggested, below, that a private party may have a right to a declaration of its rights under European law against another private party, if its rights cannot be effectively protected otherwise.

§3.18 THE GENERAL PRINCIPLE AGAINST CONTRACTS LIMITING THE FREEDOM TO CLAIM EU LAW RIGHTS FOR THE FUTURE

National courts should annul or disregard some kinds of contracts by which one party gives up, for the future, its rights under EU law, the Charter, or the Convention, or makes it unreasonably difficult to claim those rights, or penalizes their assertion. But not all rules of EU law are obligatory or 'overriding' rules which cannot be waived or set aside by contract. Only a few EU law rules have so far been identified as rules of

61. See e.g. Case C-60/05, *WWF Italia v. Regime Lombardia*, [2006] ECR I-5083.

'public policy', and there will certainly be others. Criteria are needed. One criterion to identify EU law rights that cannot be validly waived or surrendered for the future may be whether the private party seeking to exercise its rights is also indirectly protecting the public interest, or the interests of third parties who have not waived their rights. Other possible criteria are that such a contract should be binding only where the parties were in substantially equal negotiating positions, where there was some identifiable reason why the usual rule was considered inappropriate for both parties, and it was proportionate to modify it or set it aside to the extent agreed upon. It is not easy to think of cases in which these requirements would be fulfilled in the case of an obligatory rule such as the rule requiring equal pay for men and women, if indeed they can ever be. But if the relevant rules are not clear in particular circumstances, the parties may agree on how they should be interpreted and applied for the future, so that they work more smoothly. Good faith settlement, compromise, or arbitration of genuine disputes arising from the past are of course permissible, and General Principles should facilitate them.

A contract by which a buyer agrees to buy exclusively from a dominant company is invalid (to the extent of the illegal exclusivity) if it would involve an abuse of a dominant position contrary to Article 102 TFEU. This is because a contract which is illegal for this reason is contrary to the interests of rival suppliers, and to the public interest. If the exclusive buying obligation was justified by the fact that it was needed to make the dominant supplier's investment in extra capacity profitable, that would be the reason why the usual rule would be inappropriate. Similarly, it would probably be unlawful for a company to agree that it would be treated in such a way that it could be discriminated against by a dominant company, unless there was a clear reason for the special treatment. (e.g., a fixed price long-term contract may prove to be favourable or unfavourable for the buyer, depending on how the market develops.)

If a patent licence says that the licensee loses its licence if it challenges the validity of the patents licensed, that is reasonable, because the licensee should not be allowed to have the benefit of the licence while he argues simultaneously that he does not need it. But the licence should not say that the licence is terminated if the licensee challenges the validity of *other* patents, or if he asserts his own patent rights against the licensor. Contracts should not unduly restrict rights given under patent law, or penalize their exercise, because it is in the public interest that they should be exercisable. There may be a General Principle of reciprocity in such situations, and there is probably a General Principle that a party's rights should not be restricted by contract if it is in the public interest for them to be exercised.

The European Commission has objected to clauses in settlements of competition cases by which a complainant gives up its right to complain about future actions of the other party, or promises not to provide evidence to the Commission unless it is legally required to do so.

§3.19 AGREEMENTS THAT ARE CONTRARY TO EU LAW

There is probably a General Principle that illegal contracts are not enforceable, and may be void. However, the terms of this Principle are not clear, because national laws on these issues differ, and because the Principle would apply to such a wide range of different circumstances.[62] This supposed General Principle would be open to the same objection as the supposed principle protecting minority shareholders in *Audiolux*,[63] that it was impossible to identify a consensus on precise terms or consequences resulting from the principle.

Article 4(3) TEU presumably prohibits any agreement by which one company agrees to pay a Commission competition fine imposed on a second company, since that would take away the deterrent effect on the company fined.[64] However, if the company fined has been sold, the buyer may have a right to be indemnified by the seller if the unlawful conduct occurred before the sale, and the liability had not been disclosed to the buyer.

One other example under EU law concerns agreements made by dominant companies that constitute or are based on abuse of a dominant position. The Commission's practice has been to order the dominant company concerned to re-negotiate the agreements.[65] That is necessary if it would not be possible or satisfactory simply to declare particular clauses to be invalid. This is the result of the Principle that the parties should as far as possible be put in the position in which they would have been if no infringement had occurred.

§3.20 A 'FAIR HEARING' AND GENERAL PRINCIPLES THAT ARE BASIC RULES OF PROCEDURAL JUSTICE

The Charter and the Convention both require a 'fair hearing within a reasonable time'. The Charter applies to everyone whose rights and freedoms are guaranteed by the law of the Union, and Article 47 gives a right to an effective remedy. The Convention applies to everyone, 'in the determination of his civil rights and obligations'. The Charter says that it must be interpreted and applied so as to give at least as much protection to fundamental rights, in the sphere of EU law, as is given by the Convention. The requirement of a 'fair hearing' under those two treaties and the requirement of 'effective protection' under the case law of the Court of Justice overlap and usually lead to the same conclusions. A hearing would not be 'fair' unless it could lead to effective protection of the rights being claimed, if the claim is successful. These requirements apply to litigation between private parties as well as litigation between a

62. See e.g. Case 58/80, *Dansk Supermarked v. Imerco*, [1981] ECR 18; Case C-126/97, *EcoSwiss ChinaTime v. Benetton*, [1999] ECR I-3055; Cauffman, The Impact of Voidness for Infringement of Article 101 TFEU on Related Contracts, 8 European Competition Journal (2012) 95-122.
63. Case C-101/08, *Audiolux v. Groupe Bruxelles Lambert*, [2009] ECR I-9823.
64. See Case C-429/07, *X BV*, [2009] ECR I-4833.
65. O'Donoghue & Padilla, The Law and Economics of Article 82 EC [2006, Elgar] ch.15.

private party and the State. All of these principles may override, when appropriate, the normal principle of national procedural autonomy.

As already mentioned, the best known procedural General Principles concern legal professional privilege[66] and the right to obtain legal advice in confidence, and the rights of the defence, recognized in Article 41 of the Charter, and in much case law.

The General Principle of 'equality of arms', usually thought of in connection between private parties and State authorities, is also applicable in litigation between private parties, if circumstances such as availability of evidence or commercial pressure create a serious imbalance between litigants[67] which the court can correct.

Although not all the rules set out below have been the subject of judgments of the European Courts, it seems that these treaty provisions give rise to the following rules, among others. If these rules are valid, it is clear that not all of their implications have yet been seen everywhere. They all seem relevant to private law issues.

(1) Certain rules of EU law are a matter of public policy which must be automatically applied by national courts[68] on their own initiative. These include the Treaty competition rules, Articles 101–102 TFEU. Presumably they also include the provisions of the Charter of Fundamental Rights. Public policy is a General Principle, although it is not usually described as such.

(2) There is a principle or policy of 'judicial economy', which requires that court cases should be arranged as far as possible so as to avoid delay, expense, unnecessary complications, duplication or multiplication of proceedings, and transfers of cases between courts. Seriously inconvenient and unnecessary procedural steps are contrary to this principle. As far as possible all the issues arising in a case should be decided, in the first instance, in the same court, which can then decide the issues in whatever order seems best to determine the case efficiently. This principle is based

66. Case C-155/79, *A M & S Europe*, [1982] ECR 1575; Case C-550/07 P; *Akzo Nobel Chemicals*, [2010] ECR I-8301. Advocate General Trstenjak in Case C-282/10, *Dominguez v. Centre informatique*, [2012] n.y.r., (judgment dated January 24, 2012) discussed *'the procedural rights which are equivalent to fundamental rights and which, as general principles of the rule of law, have been elevated to the status of constitutional law in the European Union'* (para. 95). The Opinion mentioned *'principles which are not alien to contract law such as the general principle pacta sunt servanda or the principle of rebus sic stantibus'* (para. 96).

67. On equality of arms, see Joined Cases C-201/09, *Aalborg and others*, [2004] ECR I-123, paras 100-106; Case C-521/09 P, *Elf Aquitaine*, [2011] n.y.r., para. 59; Case C-404/10 P, *Editions Odile Jacob*, [2012] n.y.r., para. 132; Case T-23/99, *LR AF 1998*, [2002] ECR II-1705, para. 171.

At least in cases of clear inequality of arms, a national court may have a duty to ask the Commission to explain a conflict between its conclusions and those of a national court: Temple Lang, Inntrepreneur and the Duties of National Courts under Article 10 EC, 5 Competition Law Journal (2006) 231-235.

68. Case C-126/97, *Eco Swiss*, [1999] ECR I-3055, paras 39-40; Joined Cases C-295/04 to C-298/04, *Manfredi*, [2006] ECR I-6619, para. 31; Joined Cases C-341/06 P and C-342/06 P, *Chronopost v. UFEX*, [2008] ECR I-4777, paras 46,48.

Compare Case C-7/98, *Krombach v. Bamberski*, [2000] ECR I-1935 (national rules of public policy).

on the Charter and Convention requirement of a hearing 'within a reasonable time', which is an obligation imposed on the judicial system as a whole, and not only on individual courts.

This means for example that a national court applying EU or EEA law should not be obliged to adjourn a case to allow another court (in practice, usually a constitutional court) to determine whether national legislation is contrary to EU or EEA law. The *Simmenthal*[69] judgment confirmed this. There should be no unnecessary preconditions imposed on claims under EU law. The duty of national courts of final appeal to refer questions to the European Court of Justice under Article 267 TFEU is justified by the duty to try to ensure uniform application of EU law, and a result binding on national courts throughout the EU. (There is what seems to be a corresponding obligation under the European Economic Area Agreement, in spite of a slight difference in language).[70] The power (not an obligation) of lower courts in certain States to refer questions or to 'state a case' for a ruling by higher national courts is a way of obtaining a final result sooner. So these apparent exceptions in fact promote economy of procedures and reduce litigation in the longer term. But judicial economy is perhaps better described as a policy with some limited direct effects in specific circumstances, rather than as a General Principle. This is because, like the protection of minority shareholders in *Audiolux* and the principle of fiscal neutrality in *NCC Danmark*, judicial economy is not precise enough, and can be promoted or ensured in too many different ways, to have direct effects except in unusual or extreme cases. In such cases, Article 4(3) TEU would oblige a national court to find the most satisfactory solution available, or to avoid clearly unnecessary duplication of proceedings.

A right to a fair hearing 'within a reasonable time' may, depending on the circumstances, give a right to interim measures, whether an injunction or a right to payment of a proportion of the compensation, if liability is clear. EU law requires national courts to give 'effective' remedies, and a remedy may need to be given promptly if it is to be effective.[71] Interim measures are particularly likely to be necessary in States where court proceedings are particularly slow, as they are in certain EU Member States. The principle of national procedural autonomy is not a justification for breach of the right to a hearing within a reasonable time. This is so in particular in family law cases in which long delays are extremely undesirable even if the best solution is finally reached.

The principle or policy of judicial economy (and the General Principle in favour of settlement of litigation) also means that a court in a competition

69. Case 106/77, *Simmenthal*, [1978] ECR 629.
70. Case E-18/11, *Irish Bank Resolution Corporation v. Kaupthing Bank*, [2012] EFTA Court Report. Temple Lang, The Duty of National Courts to Provide Access to Justice in the EEA, in EFTA Court (ed.), Judicial Protection in the European Economic Area (2012) 100-135.
71. Case C-213/89, *Ex parte Factortame*, [1990] ECR I-2433.

law case involving the settlement of a patent claim should not decide how a patent court would have decided the claim if it had not been settled, or how likely it is that the claim would have succeeded. To decide that, the competition court would need to consider *all* the evidence that would have been before the patent court. In effect, it would re-litigate the patent case. So judicial economy, though certainly not a precise or directly applicable principle in all circumstances, may have specific practical effects.

It seems that national courts should be very much aware of the need to minimize litigation throughout Europe (and not merely in their own courts) and to ensure that reasonable and fair results overall are arrived at, however specifically the litigation may have developed. Contacts between judges, which should be reported to the parties, may even be appropriate. Duplication and splitting of legal proceedings should be avoided, as well as conflicting judgments.

(3) A judgment should not be given against a party if the justification for the judgment depends on the final result of proceedings, including proceedings in another court, which have not yet been concluded.

This means, for example, that an injunction should not be granted to enforce a patent right before the validity of the patent has been determined. A claim for compensation should not be decided until the validity of a counterclaim has been determined. A judgment should not be based on legislation if it has not yet been held to be constitutional, or compatible with EU law, if these issues have been raised in court.

(4) A party claiming legal rights must comply with all the conditions necessary to make the claim lawful.

This means that a private party may not claim the benefits of the situation without accepting the obligations. Similarly, a Member State that claims the right to regulate gambling activities in order to limit gambling addiction and to protect vulnerable gamblers may not at the same time allow or encourage unregulated advertisements of gambling opportunities or prizes.[72]

This also means, among other things, that the owner of a patent who is under a legal obligation to licence the patent on fair, reasonable and non-discriminatory (FRAND) terms may not get an injunction against a willing and creditworthy licensee unless the owner is offering a licence on terms that are accepted as, or have been determined to be, fair, reasonable and non-discriminatory. If the patent owner is a member of a patent pool and Article 101 requires the members to licence essential patents on FRAND terms, it cannot be allowed to seek an injunction without offering those terms, because its failure to offer them would infringe Article 101.[73]

72. See e.g. Case C-243/01, *Gambelli*, [2003] ECR I-13031.
73. Temple Lang, Commonly accepted errors and misunderstandings in European Competition law – Abuse of dominance, and patent licensing, in Baudenbacher (ed.), Current Developments in Competition Law, 19Th St. Gallen International Competition Law Forum 2012.

An injunction would simply be a means of putting pressure on the user to pay a higher rate of royalty than might be justified.

(5) A party may not be allowed to take advantage of its own wrong.
This is the principle underlying the right of a private party to rely on a binding but unimplemented directive against State authorities of the State that has failed to carry out the directive. The principle applies as between private parties in many situations.
There is also a General Principle of 'legality', the essence of which is that unlawful acts must not be allowed to have legal effects, either for the party responsible for the unlawful act or for others. This may be regarded as a broader version of the principle that a party may not rely on or take advantage of its own (or another's) wrongful act.
In *LR AF* the General Court said that there is '... the principle of legality, according to which a person may not rely, in support of his claim, on an unlawful act committed in favour of a third party'.[74]
In *P & O European Ferries (Vizcaya)*[75] the Court said that this principle is 'intended to prevent unlawful acts from giving rise to effects in the common market'.
In *SGL Tokai Carbon*[76] the Court said that 'even if the Commission had improperly favoured UCAR by not increasing its fine, the aggravating nature of SGL's conduct would not be affected. SGL cannot legitimately... rely to its advantage on any unlawful treatment of UCAR'.

(6) A party cannot be required to give up one legal right in order to obtain another unrelated right to which it is entitled.
A party should, for example, not be required to give up its right to challenge the validity of a patent as a condition of obtaining a compulsory licence of the same patent. A party that has validly obtained a public contract cannot be required, as a condition of being allowed to carry out the contract, to give up its claim for repayment of tax unlawfully imposed on it. A party should not be required to make a disputed tax payment in order to apply for or obtain a licence or a public contract. An insured party should not be forced, in order to obtain its insurance payment, to promise to pay the insurance company *more* than it recovers in litigation.
This principle applies in particular where there is a public interest in the result, as there is when the validity of a patent is challenged.

(7) A party should not be allowed to achieve indirectly a result that it could not legally obtain directly.
For example a woman who validly asserted her right to equal pay, or to maternity leave, could not lawfully be penalized by being refused an

74. Case T-23/99, *LR AF*, [2002] ECR II-1705, para. 367. See also Case 134/84, *Williams v. Court of Auditors*, [1985] ECR 2225, para. 14; Case C-188/83, *Witte v. Parliament*, [1984] ECR 3465, para. 15; Case T-68/04, *SGL*, [2008] ECR II-2511, paras 119, 136; Case T-308/04, *Cascades*, [1998] ECR II-925, para. 259; Case C-297/98, *SCA Holding*, [2000] ECR I-10,101, para. 160.
75. Joined Cases T-116/01, *P & O Ferries (Vizcaya)*, [2003] ECR II-2957, para. 206.
76. Case T-68/04, *SGL*, [2008] II-2511.

appropriate reference letter when she moved to another employment.[77] Companies that make an unlawful agreement to divide markets, contrary to what is now Article 101, are not allowed to create a trademark and use it to obtain the same result.[78] If a binding agreement to limit retail prices would be unlawful, a supposedly 'non-binding' agreement would be unlawful if it were enforced by commercial measures. A private party that makes a competition law complaint against a dominant enterprise, or that chooses to compete vigorously, must not suffer reprisals as a warning or penalty for having done so. Courts should protect litigants and witnesses from reprisals.[79] These rules are based on the principle of effectiveness under Article 4(3) TEU.

(8) The rights of the defence give each party the right to know all the evidence and arguments against it, and to answer them fully.
The rights of the defence, which are clearly the subject of a General Principle, mean, in my view, that each party should have the right to question the witnesses giving evidence against it. A hearing cannot be considered 'fair' if evidence given by witnesses cannot be effectively rebutted, and it may not be possible to rebut evidence without questioning the witnesses who gave it. This would imply, if it is correct, that in this respect a 'fair' hearing may need to be adversarial rather than inquisitorial.[80] It probably also implies that in cartel cases defendants have a right to see each other's pleadings.

(9) Legal professional privilege has been accepted by the Court of Justice in the context of investigations by the European Commission under EU competition law.[81] This is based on the fundamental right, in a democracy based on the rule of law, to obtain legal advice in confidence without creating evidence that might be used later against the party seeking the advice. In the House of Lords in England Lord Hoffmann described privilege as a 'fundamental human right'.[82] This description has been cited with approval in a number of subsequent cases. There is no justification for the suggestion that privilege only applies to advice on the subject of competition law. It must apply to legal advice on all kinds of legal questions. The nature of the later private claim for damages or of the later investigation

77. Case C-185/97, *Coote v. Granada Hospitality*, [1998] ECR I-5199. Compare the definition of 'indirect discrimination' in Article 2(2)(b) of Directive 2000/78/EC establishing a general framework for equal treatment in employment, and Article 11 on victimization, and see *DH v. Czech Republic*, ECtHR judgment dated 13 November 2007 (application No. 57325/00).
78. Cases 56 and 58/64, *Consten & Grundig*, [1966] ECR 299.
79. Temple Lang, Reprisals and overreaction by Dominant companies as an Anticompetitive Abuse under Article 82(b), 29 European Competition Law Review (2008) 11-15.
80. Harris, O'Boyle & Warbrick, Law of the European Convention on Human Rights (2nd ed., 2009) p. 253.
81. Case 155/79, *A M & S Europe*, [1982] ECR 1575; Case C-550/07 P, *Akzo Nobel*, [2010] ECR I-8301.
82. *R. (Morgan Grenfell & Co Ltd) v. Special Commissioners of Income Tax* [2003] 1 AC 563 at 606.

cannot alter the scope of the privilege, which arises when the legal advice is requested and given.

(10) The burden of proof imposed on a party must not be greater than the nature of the case requires, and must not be so great that it cannot in practice be fulfilled.
This principle is important in cases in which national measures have been designed to make it almost impossible for private parties to reclaim taxes improperly imposed on them by EU Member States.[83] But the principle is important also in private law. It is particularly important when one party is asked to prove matters that are primarily within the knowledge of the other party, or when a presumption is said to be rebuttable.

(11) Where it is said that different treatment is justified by different circumstances, it is not legitimate to differentiate in practice in favour of parties which are acting unlawfully.
This is certainly a principle of public law. But it would also apply to e.g., the discriminatory policies of a dominant enterprise. It may perhaps be regarded as an aspect of the principle of 'legality', mentioned above. It would be relevant to discrimination in recruitment by an employer, if it e.g., discriminated in favour of illegal immigrants.

(12) 'Off the record' or 'without prejudice' efforts to avoid or settle disputes should not be used against the party which made them. This principle is necessary in order to encourage settlements and to minimize litigation.[84]

(13) There should also be a principle that a party that is directly affected by the result of a procedure should have a right to be fully informed, to intervene and to be heard. For example, both the beneficiary of a supposed State aid and the beneficiaries' competitors, although private parties, should have a right to get the key documents and a formal opportunity to comment on them, in Commission State aid cases. These rights have not yet been recognized, because the procedure is regarded as involving only the Commission and the State concerned. (The Commission is proposing to reform the State aid procedure). The principle that a party directly affected by the result must have a right to intervene is well recognized in other situations, and is surely a General Principle applicable in many kinds of procedures. As a minimum, a party that would have a right to challenge the result should have a right to intervene effectively in the initial or administrative procedure, after having seen the relevant documents. The right to intervene must be a right to intervene at the right time. A limited right to intervene later is not an adequate substitute.
It is true that in infringement cases under Article 258 TFEU and Article 31 of the EFTA Court Agreement private parties have no right to intervene.

83. Case 199/82, *San Giorgio*, [1983] ECR 3595; Case C-90/09 P, *General Quimica*, [2011] n.y.r., conclusions of Advocate General Mazak, para. 34; Case C-521/09 P, *Elf Aquitaine*, [2011] n.y.r., (September 29, 2011), paras 59, 62.
84. See Joined Cases C-317/08, *Alassini*, [2010] ECR I-2213.

This is said to be justified, first, by saying that in infringement cases the issues involved are broader than the interests of any individual private party, and that there are not usually identifiable private parties primarily concerned by the result. It is said that such issues should if possible be solved diplomatically. The second justification is that a private party directly concerned has the alternative of bringing proceedings in a national court. But the arguments are not entirely convincing.
This Principle also suggests that amicus curiae submissions, at least from representative organizations, should be allowed more often than they are at present.

(14) A party which is in sole possession of important evidence should be required to produce it. Therefore a party that is in a position to show that its conduct is not discriminatory should disclose the evidence, rather than trying to put the burden of proof on the other parties. An owner of a process patent should not be forced to prove that it is infringed, if that cannot be detected by analysing the defendant's product.

§3.21 A RIGHT TO CLAIM RIGHTS UNDER EUROPEAN LAW

(1) European law gives private parties a right, in substance, to go to court to ask for a finding or a declaration that a national measure is contrary to EU law, without it being necessary to infringe the measure and risk prosecution and penalties.[85] I suggest that there is also a General Principle that a private party has a right to go to a national court to ask for a declaration of his or her rights under EU law, against another private party.[86] Such a procedural right is necessary in order to give 'effective' protection to private law rights under EU law, and national courts have a duty under Article 4(3) TEU to provide effective protection.

(2) There is also a need for a General Principle giving private parties claiming rights under EU law or the Charter, if they cannot assert their rights directly against other private parties, the right to bring proceedings against the State to require it to use its existing powers to protect the rights in question.[87] (This question is discussed below).

(3) EU law does not give a right to punitive or exemplary damages, or to compensation exceeding the loss suffered as a result of the infringement of

85. Case C-432, *Unibet*, [2007] ECR I-2271; Case C-279/09, *DEB*, [2010] ECR I-13849 (right to legal aid and the right to effective judicial protection).
86. See Directive 2000/78/EC establishing a general framework for equal treatment in employment, O.J. No. L. 303/16, December 2, 2000, Articles 9–11.
87. See *R. v. Chief Constable of Sussex, ex parte International Traders' Ferry*, [1999] 2 A.C. 418; Case C-112/00, *Schmidberger*, [2003] ECR I-5659. In *Byrne v. Ireland*, [1972] I.R. 241, Walsh J. said '*Where the people by the Constitution create rights against the State or impose duties on the State, a remedy to enforce these must be deemed to be also available*': *Meskell v. C.I.E.*, [1973] I.R. 121.

EU law rights,[88] even in the case of breach of an EU rule of public policy such as competition law. Punishment, as distinct from payment of compensation, should result only from fines. If EU prohibits punitive damages (which is not yet clear) that would be due to the proportionality principle, and the duty to seek uniform application of EU law.

(4) There must be a General Principle obliging national courts to avoid arriving at conclusions that would involve unjustifiably different results for different companies in the same or closely related cases, in particular if they are not all before the national court dealing with the case. In a case in which it was argued that the claimants should be awarded 'exemplary' (i.e., punitive) and not merely compensatory damages, the English High Court said, in a 'follow on' claim for compensation for breach of Article 101,[89] that it would introduce undesirable differences between national courts if the English courts would award punitive damages when other courts do not do so. This can be regarded as a General Principle resulting from the duty under Article 4(3) TEU to try to ensure uniform application of EU law, or at least not knowingly to bring about a situation in which the results will not be uniform. This creates a private right to a uniform result, although a right which is clearly not simple or absolute.

(5) A General Principle should be recognized to facilitate arbitration on European law questions, and alternative dispute resolution, both of which should be encouraged when the parties consider that there are more efficient or more satisfactory methods of dealing with disputes. If this is accepted, it might lead to reconsideration of the case law of the Court of Justice, and in particular to the old ruling in *Nordsee*[90] that an arbitrator may not refer a question of European law to the Court under Article 267. That judgment now seems contrary to the principle of judicial economy.[91]

88. Joined Cases C-295/04 to C-298/04, *Manfredi*, [2006] ECR I-6619; *Devenish Nutrition v. Sanofi-Aventis*, [2007] EWHC 2394(Ch.), (English High Court); *Crehan v. Inntrepreneur*, [2004] 3EGLR 128.
89. *Devenish Nutrition v. Sanofi-Aventis*, [2007] EWHC 2394 (Ch.) at paras 68-69. On interim measures in national courts, see Case C-465/93, *Atlanta*, [1995] ECR I-3761.
90. Case 102/81, *Nordsee v. Reederei Mond*, [1982] ECR 1095.
91. Temple Lang, Precedents and Judicial Dialogue in European Union Law, Present and Future, in Bandenbacher and Planzer (eds.), International Dispute Resolution: The Role of Precedent, (2011, German Law Publishers Stuttgart) 141-174 at pp. 170-172; Temple Lang, The Duty of National Courts to provide Access to Justice in the EEA, in EFTA Court (ed.), Judicial Protection in the European Economic Area (2012, German Law Publishers, Stuttgart) 100-135 at pp. 121-123.

§3.22 THE PRINCIPLE OF CONSULTATION IN LABOUR LAW

In *Dunnett*[92] the General Court held that a provision in the staff rules of the European Investment Bank 'merely enshrines a General Principle common to the laws of Member States... under a general principle of Employment law, an employer can unilaterally withdraw a financial advantage which he has freely granted to his employees on a continuous basis only after consultation of those employees or their representatives.' Although 'such consultation must be such as to have an influence on the substance of the measure adopted',[93] it does not give employees a right to co-decision or a veto. As it is essentially a procedural right, it may not be an overriding General Principle. It is not clear how effectively courts could enforce a mere right to consultation, and General Principles need to be effectively enforceable. So it is mentioned here for completeness.

§3.23 A NEW KIND OF 'GENERAL PRINCIPLES' IN PRIVATE LAW, BASED ON THE CONSENSUS OF NATIONAL COURTS

It is suggested here that courts should recognize a new kind of 'General Principle' which would be particularly appropriate in private law. Where national law is not clear, and in particular where the question is one that has recently arisen in many countries, courts should see if there is any clear sign of a consensus emerging among national courts in other countries. It is not suggested that courts should invent new Principles, but they should search carefully to see whether there is a solution that seems to be the best one, and whether there is something approaching a consensus to that effect. Courts should induce principles from particular cases, and make a consensus explicit if one exists.[94]

Such a practical comparative law approach is necessary for several reasons. Increasing numbers of people change their countries of residence, and the inconvenience of having different solutions under different national laws is greater than it ever was. There are important minorities and immigrant communities in many European States. Traditional private international rules do not solve these problems. New legal problems arise in many countries as a result of new technology, in particular new medical technology, to which existing laws provide no obvious solutions, and if some national courts have considered the issues carefully, their findings should be preferred unless there are strong reasons for differing from them. Most States now are multicultural, and courts may have to decide how far to protect or restrict traditions of immigrant communities. Many national courts can learn from the analyses carried out by courts in other countries, and not only from e.g., the European Court of Human Rights. National courts, faced with wholly new problems, may be tempted to decide the

92. Case T-192/99, *Dunnett and others v. European Investment Bank*, [2001] ECR II-813, paras 85-6, 89-90.
93. *Ibid.*, para. 90.
94. See Lord Bingham, There is a World Elsewhere: The Changing Perspectives of English Law, in Bingham, The Business of Judging (2000, Oxford) 87-102 and 41 International and Comparative Law Quarterly (1992) 513-529: Bingham, Widening Horizons (2010, Cambridge).

issues on purely technical grounds, or on the basis of rules of national law applicable to other circumstances, rather than trying to find the best and most widely-applicable solution. Courts should also recognize that the lawyers appearing before them have not necessarily had an opportunity to consider what courts elsewhere have said about these issues, which may be valuable. This is especially likely if the lawyer is representing an individual without much money, or is providing legal aid under rules that limit the amount of time that can be spent on research on the law in other jurisdictions. The case law in most countries is concerned with the rights of individuals, and not enough attention has so far been given to protecting the collective rights of groups or communities.

Principles identified and expressed in this way might be of two kinds. If derived from the Charter or Convention, they would override other laws. If identified only from national case law, they would not necessarily take precedence over existing national law rules, if there were any such rules. The mere fact that there seems to be a consensus would not be enough to make it overriding and 'constitutional'. But the Charter is in many respects merely a summary and synthesis of the most important rules derived from national case law, and it is therefore legitimate and necessary to look at the relevant case law of as many States as possible, even if it pre-dates the Charter, or is not expressly stated to be based on it. Fundamental rights and General Principles of law can certainly be found in national case law if it is carefully studied.

If this comparative law approach were accepted openly, it is clear that the Convention and the Charter would be among the most important sources of these General Principles. The idea of European Union citizenship would also be useful. The case law of the Court of Justice on questions of 'equality' in the broadest sense, would be valuable.[95] The Convention and the Charter are usually thought of as providing protection for individuals against State power. It has not yet been fully realized that they are also the basis for protecting individuals against private parties, and protecting communities against excessive interference by other non-State groups.

It will be seen that many of the principles that might be recognized in this way are at least in part moral or ethical principles. Insofar as this is so, it should help to make them more widely understood and accepted. Some of them will be based on the fundamental idea of democracy, that every individual is valuable and important and should be respected, and that every individual should have as much liberty as possible consistent with the rights of others. If general agreement on these principles can be reached in a multicultural Europe, it would help to give Europeans a sense of what 'European' law can achieve.

It is therefore suggested that if a national court finds that there is a well-considered consensus of the national courts of other States that a legal question should be answered in a particular way, even if the answer is not the same as that (if any) given previously by its own national law, the court should consider carefully whether it should accept the consensus, and it should do so unless there are strong reasons to the contrary.

95. Tridimas, The General Principles of EU Law, (2nd ed., 2006, Oxford) ch. 2.

§3.24 SOME POSSIBLE NEWLY RECOGNIZED PRIVATE LAW GENERAL PRINCIPLES: VULNERABLE INDIVIDUALS, DIVERSITY, AND COLLECTIVE RIGHTS

Some possible General Principles in private law are suggested below.

As far as the rights of individuals are concerned, there is surely now a General Principle of private law to the effect that in family law cases solutions must always be sought that are as far as possible in the best interests of the children. This principle is stated in the Charter (Article 24) and in the Convention (Article 8). It is embodied in the Brussels II A Regulation.[96] It is stated in the U.N. Convention on the Rights of the Child 1989.[97] It must also apply outside the sphere of public law. More generally, there must surely be a General Principle saying that courts must always seek to protect unrepresented but interested third parties, and in particular third parties who are vulnerable for some reason, or who can be subjected to social pressure from which courts cannot easily protect them. The duty of courts to consider the interests of unrepresented third parties may be especially important in interim measures cases, and when large numbers of claimants with small claims are involved.

It seems reasonable to say that there is, or should be, a General Principle favouring keeping families together, and respecting identifiable communities and collective cultural traditions. European lawyers should be ready to look at the laws of the Ottoman empire, which used the concept of a 'millah', an identifiable partly self-governing community not necessarily based on a particular locality. Laws in various non-European countries include provisions applying only to followers of specified religions. Legislation in Northern Ireland has developed and used the idea of two identifiable communities in the same geographical area.[98] Article 2 of TEU says

96. Regulation 2201/2001 on Jurisdiction and Recognition and Enforcement of judgments in Matrimonial Matters and Matters of Parental Responsibility, [2003] O.J. No.L.338/1. The Regulation does not include clauses suggested by the Commission, giving the child a right to be heard, and a right to maintain, on a regular basis, a personal relationship and direct contact with both parents, unless this is contrary to the child's interests. See Case C-400/10 PPU, *J. MCB v. L.E.*, [2010] ECR I-8965, October 5, 2010; Case C-296/10, *Purrucker*, [2010] ECR I-11163, para. 68.

97. See also Case C.244/06, *Dynamic Medien*, [2008] ECR I-505; Hague Convention on the Civil Aspects of Child Abduction: *Neulinger v. Switzerland*, [2001] 1 FLR 122; *Re E (Children)*, [2011] 2 WLR 1326.

98. See Directive 2000/78/EC establishing a general framework for equal treatment in employment and occupation, O.J. No. L.303/16, December 2, 2000 Article 15. Case C-274/96, *Bickel and Franz*, [1998] ECR I-7650 (a case involving positive discrimination); Council of Europe, Framework Convention for the Protection of National Minorities, European Treaty Series, No. 157; Weber, Individual Rights and Group Rights in the European Community's Approach to Minority Languages, 17 Duke Journal of Comparative and International Law 361-413 (2007); Hofman, National Minorities and European Community Law, 2 Baltic Year Book of International Law 159-174 (2002); Palermo, The Use of Minority Languages: Recent Developments in EC law and judgments of the ECJ, 8 Maastricht Journal of European and Comparative Law (2001) 299-318; Pollak (ed.), A Citizens' Enquiry – the Opsahl Report on Northern Ireland, by Opsahl, Gallagher and others (1993, Lilliput, Dublin) ch. 5, 10; Ahmed, The Impact of EU Law on Minority Rights (2011, Hart, Oxford).

See generally Lord Bingham, Law in a Pluralist Society, in Bingham, The Business of Judging (2000, Oxford) 103-115.

that the EU is founded on *'respect for human rights, including the rights of persons belonging to minorities'*. Article 19 of the Charter already recognizes one collective right, the right of groups or communities not to be expelled from a Member State: *'Collective expulsions are prohibited'*.

It will be seen immediately that General Principles on collective rights of these kinds may be controversial. The point being made here is not that any particular solution should be adopted in connection with e.g., the rights of women and children, or of particular groups. What is being suggested is that courts in many countries are now unavoidably facing similar problems involving issues of collective rights and freedoms, and that this should be said frankly, and the best solutions should be sought wherever they can be found.

One aim of developing and making explicit such General Principles would be to clarify and protect the rights of communities to maintain their traditions, on condition that they do not infringe the rights of other communities, and on condition that they do not involve unacceptable oppression of individuals who may be vulnerable, perhaps precisely because of those traditions.

Any principle on these lines will involve not only deciding how far it is necessary to interfere with community practices and traditions, as it clearly is necessary to e.g., stop forced marriage, 'honour killings', suttee (ritual burning of widows), and female genital mutilation, but also how to reconcile conflicting traditions. A commemorative or patriotic parade of one community may be considered offensive or triumphalist by another. A national parade by one community should not necessarily be expected to include representatives of a group which is not considered part of the community in question. A triumphalist parade may be legitimate, but not through an area where the residents have very different ideas. In particular, individuals who dislike or disagree with one tradition should not be allowed to prevent supporters of that tradition from expressing it. The Sikh turban and the Jewish yarmulke are religious symbols or emblems which do no harm to individuals who are not members of those communities. It is important in a multicultural democracy that individuals and communities should not be prevented from wearing their symbols or following their traditions merely because other individuals dislike them or disagree with them. Bigotry and prejudice should not be the basis for legal rules, and bigots, whether secular or religious, should not be allowed to prevent others from practising their religions openly. Professed liberals are often intolerant of those who they disagree with. Unexpressed prejudices must not be allowed to influence the law. It is unfortunately relevant that 'it is hard to think of an area, in recent years, where the [Strasbourg] Court's jurisprudence has provoked as much unfavourable comment as that of religious dress'.[99]

It may be said that developing General Principles in this way will occasionally lead to conflicts between competing or mutually incompatible fundamental rights. To the extent to that this is so, the conflicts will arise anyway. They will not be caused or made more difficult by recognizing them, and they will not be avoided by pretending that they are not there. Conflicts or supposed conflicts between fundamental rights in

99. Harris, O'Boyle & Warbrick, Law of the European Convention on Human Rights (2nd ed., 2009) 438.

the economic sphere have already come before the European Court of Justice, e.g., in *Schmidberger,*[100] and in *Scarlet Extended*[101] and in connection with the right of privacy in the Court of Human Rights in *Von Hannover.*[102] They may have to be resolved by the courts, and it is obviously desirable that as far as possible they should be resolved in the same way everywhere, and on the basis of the fullest and most careful consideration. European courts should have a policy favouring similar solutions, even in areas of private law not harmonized at EU/EEA level.

If collective rights are recognized, there will need to be procedures for claiming them, by injunctions or declarations, either at the request of any individual member of the group in question, or at the request of a representative organization. Litigation would be minimized, and better-considered results arrived at, if representative bodies were allowed to bring any legal proceedings that may be necessary. A General Principle saying when representation or group actions are admissible may be needed, bearing in mind that not all the individuals in a large group may have the same interest.[103]

§3.25 IS THERE A GENERAL PRINCIPLE IMPOSING A DUTY ON PRIVATE PARTIES NOT TO INTERFERE WITH THE RIGHTS OF OTHERS UNDER THE CONVENTION AND THE CHARTER?

Article 51 of the Charter says that its provisions 'are addressed to the institutions, bodies, offices and agencies of the Union with due regard for the principle of subsidiarity and to the Member States only when they are implementing Union law'. However, the fact that the Charter is 'addressed' to the EU Institutions and to Member States does not mean that the Charter imposes no obligations indirectly on private parties. The Charter is addressed to States and EU Institutions because they have much greater powers than private parties have. The Charter, like Regulations but unlike Directives, can impose legal duties directly on private parties. Since everyone has rights under the Charter, everyone may have duties. The question, in relation to each provision of the Charter, is whether it is unconditional and precise enough to have direct effects.

Article 17 of the Convention says:

> Nothing in this Convention may be interpreted as implying for any State, group or person any right to engage in any activity or perform any act aimed at the destruction of any of the rights and freedoms set for on herein or at their limitation to a greater extent than is provided for in the Convention.

In other words, no private party has a right to take any action 'aimed at destruction' of the benefits of the Convention. 'Aimed at' presumably includes action objectively likely to have the prohibited results. But this provision, though important, does not

100. Case C-112/00, *Schmidberger*, [2003] ECR I-5659.
101. Case C-70/10, *Scarlet Extended*, [2011] n.y.r., (November 24, 2011).
102. *Von Hannover* [I] (application no. 59320/00), June 24, 2004.
103. *Emerald Supplies v. British Airways*, Court of Appeal, England, EWCA Civ. 1284; Zuckerman, Civil Procedure-Principles of Practice (2nd ed., 2006) section 12–22.

imply a general obligation on all private parties to respect all the rights of others under the Convention. 'Destruction' is a strong word, and the Article seems to be primarily intended to prevent extremist or totalitarian groups from seeking to rely on the Convention or to have Convention rights removed generally or widely.

There is a general question under private law: in what circumstances is there a duty on private parties to avoid interfering with rights given by the Convention and the Charter? (The situation under other rules of EU law has been considered above). In many cases, of course, the issue does not arise, because the interference is contrary to long established rules of private law or criminal law, and there is no need for an injured party to rely on any international agreement.

This general question gives rise to several specific issues:

- Is the Charter or the Convention directly applicable in the national law of the State in question?

  They may be directly applicable because the State is monist, or because they have been received into national law by national legislation, (which leads in practice to substantially the same result, because once the Convention has been received into national law, the legislation could hardly be repealed). The Austrian Constitutional Court in a judgment on 14 March 2012 declared that the Charter is an integral part of the Austrian constitutional order, as is the Convention. If it were clear that a provision of the Charter is not directly applicable, it could not impose obligations on private parties.
- Is the relevant provision of the Charter or Convention one which imposes binding obligations on private parties, or does it bind only the State?
- If the provision binds private parties, does the infringement need to be particularly serious before it becomes enforceable by other private parties?
- Where there are national laws not explicitly based on the Charter governing relations between private parties, how far should the Charter be used to interpret the national laws to determine their rights and duties?
- If a provision in the Charter or Convention binds only the State (or is not effectively enforceable against private parties for some reason), how far has the State an enforceable legal obligation to protect the rights of the parties whose rights are being infringed against the actions of other private parties?[104]
- Have the parties who are said to be infringing the Convention or Charter a fundamental right of their own that justifies limiting the rights of the claimants?

It is convenient to consider these questions under the Charter, for several reasons, although similar issues arise under the Convention. First, there are several rights given by the Charter but not given (at least, not expressly) by the Convention. Second, the

104. Harris, O'Boyle & Warbrick, Law of the European Convention on Human Rights (2nd ed., 2009) pp. 389 ff.

Charter must be interpreted so as to give at least as much protection to fundamental rights as the Convention. Third, under the Convention private rights may be asserted directly only against States, while controversies between private parties may come before national courts and questions under the Charter can be referred, if appropriate, to the Court of Justice under Article 267 TFEU.

The Charter applies only where the EU Member States are 'implementing' EU law. There is no corresponding limitation on the scope of the Convention. Apparently this means that as between private parties the Charter is applicable only when some rules of EU law are applicable. The obligations of private parties under the Charter could never be broader than the obligations of Member States, and clearly in many areas are narrower. However, if the Charter does apply to the Member State because it is *'implementing'* Union law (or if the State is regulating rights given by EU law), then it seems that the only other question is whether the relevant provision of the Charter imposes obligations on private parties.

§3.26 WHEN DOES THE CHARTER IMPOSE LEGAL OBLIGATIONS ON PRIVATE PARTIES?

Even if it is thought that some provisions of the Charter impose legal duties on private parties, it is clear that not all its provisions do so, since some Articles could not be infringed by individuals or companies not exercising State powers. It is therefore necessary to consider each Article separately.

At first sight, one would expect certain clauses to be binding on private parties, for example:

- the prohibition on making the human body and its parts as such a source of financial gain, and the prohibition of the reproductive cloning of human beings (Article 3);
- the prohibition of servitude and forced labour (Article 5);
- the right to the protection of personal data (Article 8);
- the right to freedom of religion (Article 10);
- freedom of assembly and of association (Article 12);
- the rights of the child (Article 24);
- the right to protection against unjustified dismissal (Article 30);
- prohibition of child labour and protection of young people at work (Article 32).

On the other hand, it would be more surprising to find that some other provisions were intended directly to impose legally enforceable obligations on private parties. Some provisions expressly say that the rights conferred are exercisable in accordance with national law (e.g., the right to conscientious objection, under Article 10; the freedom to conduct a business, under Article 16; workers' right to information, under Article 27 and to collective bargaining, under Article 28). If those rights involved duties for other private parties, they would be the results of national legislation, not of the Charter itself.

This suggests that one would expect there to be certain criteria for distinguishing duties imposed directly on private parties:

- Duties stated in clear general terms, which do not seem to be subject to exceptions (or which are subject only to strictly limited exceptions), and infringement of which would be serious and shocking, are more likely to be binding on private parties, and not merely on national authorities and the EU Institutions.
- Rights that need to be recognized primarily by other private parties are more likely to give rise to duties on those parties, and not merely on the State. These include the right to privacy,[105] secrecy of correspondence, and the right to education. The difficulty of these rights is that they are not absolute.

On the other hand:

- Where the practical exercise of the rights is subject to a wide national discretion, the Charter provisions cannot be directly applicable; each State must legislate or reconcile or deal with the issues in some way.
- Many of the Charter rights are not clear and precise enough to be directly applied and enforced by national courts, except perhaps in extreme cases.
- Rights expressed to be regulated by national law or practices are presumably not binding on private parties, since they need to be clarified and made specific. These Charter provisions are, at most, analogous to directives.
- Rights that need to be balanced against the rights and interests of others are probably not binding on private parties, but need to be implemented in detail by national legislation, and procedures provided for regulating them.

(These four categories of course overlap).

It will be seen that these questions are the converse of those arising in e.g., *Fruiticola*.[106] In *Fruiticola* there was a clear duty imposed by law, and the question was whether the law gave claimants a private right to enforce the duty directly. In cases under the Charter, there are clear rights against the State given by law, and the question is whether the Charter imposes obligations on private parties as well as obligations on States.

If a provision of the Charter creates obligations directly for private parties, it is suggested that there must be a requirement that the obligation should be enforceable only if the infringement of the corresponding right is serious. The rule that States are liable only for 'serious' infringements of EU law[107] is intended to recognize that States have a wide discretion in many respects and that they should not be obliged to pay small amounts of compensation if they accidentally impose trivial inconvenience. If a

105. See *Campbell v. Mirror Group Newspapers*, [2004] A.C. 457.
106. Case C-253/00, *Muñoz and Fruiticola*, [2002] ECR I-7289.
107. Joined Cases C-46/93 and 48/93, *Brasserie du Pêcheur* and *Ex parte Factortame (No.3)*, [1996] ECR I-1029, especially at para. 45

private party does something that constitutes a breach of another's fundamental rights, there is no such consideration. However, there must be a *de minimis* rule in this context. It is not clear what should limiting principles there may be: is it the effect on the internal market that matters, or the effect on the private rights of the claimant?[108] On either view, discrimination by one individual employer against one potential employee does not prevent the employee obtaining a job from another employer, and does not affect the internal market. Interference by private parties with rights given by the Charter should lead to an injunction or compensation only if it is serious.

§3.27 THE CHARTER SHOULD BE USED TO INTERPRET NATIONAL LAWS

It seems clear that where there are national laws governing rights given or guaranteed by the Charter, the provisions of the Charter should be used to interpret the national rules, even if the rules are not expressed to have been adopted to implement the Charter. There would be no justification for distinguishing between the rare national laws expressly based on the Charter (there are not many of them yet), and the very many rules of national law which are the inspiration for the Charter. The Charter should be used to guide the interpretation of all the national laws and practices envisaged by the terms of the Charter itself, just as those national laws should be used to interpret the Charter. The relationship between the Charter and national law is a two-way street.[109]

EU law already requires national courts to interpret national laws if possible so as to make them consistent with EU directives, and this rule applies in litigation between private parties.[110] In the United Kingdom, the Human Rights Act 1998 requires the courts to interpret national law as far as possible in accordance with the Act. It therefore seems reasonable to suggest that national laws that protect or regulate rights of the kinds given by the Charter or the Convention (even if the laws were adopted before the Charter, or were not originally adopted for that purpose) should be interpreted if possible so as to give effect to those rights. If this is accepted, it is an important General Principle, both in public law and private law.

108. Case C-110/05, *Commission v. Italy*, [2009] ECR I-519.

109. Lenaerts and Gutierrez-Fons, The Constitutional Allocation of Powers and General Principles of EU Law, 47 Common Market Law Review (2010) 1629-1669. Case C-400/10 PPU, *J.McB. v. L E*, [2010] ECR I-8965, October 5, 2010, paras 49-64 (use of Charter to interpret a Regulation, ECJ followed a judgment of the European Court of Human Rights).

110. Case C-106/89, *Marleasing*, [1990] ECR I-4135; Joined Cases C-397/01 to C-403/01, *Pfeiffer*, [2004] ECR I-8835; Case E-18/11, *Irish Bank Resolution Corporation v. KaupThing*, [2012] EFTA Court Report.

§3.28 IF A PROVISION IN THE CHARTER BINDS ONLY THE STATE, WHEN HAS THE STATE AN ENFORCEABLE LEGAL OBLIGATION TO PROTECT THE RIGHTS OF THE PARTIES WHOSE RIGHTS ARE BEING INFRINGED AGAINST THE ACTIONS OF OTHER PRIVATE PARTIES?

If the rights of a private party under the Charter or Convention are infringed, the party injured may claim compensation from the State, in the Court of Human Rights if necessary. But if the rights have been infringed by another private party, it would be quicker and more efficient if the injured party could enforce its rights directly against the other private party, or if the State would enforce the right against those responsible for the infringement.

It seems that no Member State has yet adopted comprehensive legislation obliging private parties to respect the rights under the Charter or the Convention of those protected by these treaties. This is understandable since, as explained above, many of the provisions of the Charter are not clear and precise enough to be directly applicable in national courts. The Commission has not yet proposed Directives designed to implement the Charter, even in specific areas.

The result is that although the State always has a duty to pay compensation, it can take action against a private party infringing a right under the Charter only in unusual circumstances. The Charter does not seem to give a State any additional powers to enforce its provisions against private parties. Such powers can only be given by national legislation, or as the result of duties imposed by Article 4(3) TEU or, possibly, Article 3 EEA. If the Charter does not impose an obligation directly on private parties, the citizen whose rights are infringed has to sue the State and may be able to get the real infringer before a national court only indirectly and in circumstances that are always not likely to arise.

Article 4(3) TEU (formerly Article 10 EC) obliges the national authorities of EU Member States to take appropriate measures to ensure fulfilment of the obligations arising out of the Treaties. This presumably means that they have a duty, when necessary, to use their *existing* powers to enforce the Charter, not only against State authorities but also against private parties interfering with Charter rights. Since there was a legal duty to protect free movement of goods in the *French farmers* case,[111] there must *a fortiori* be a duty to defend rights given by the Charter if they are significantly interfered with. This duty must arise in particular if the private parties whose rights are affected are not able, for whatever reason, to defend themselves directly by legal proceedings against those interfering with their rights. In most cases in which private parties interfere with the rights of others under the Charter, the interference is contrary to some existing rule of national law, and there is no need to argue that the Charter imposes obligations directly on private citizens, although it may do so. But the State may be obliged to use all its existing powers to provide an effective remedy, even if the

111. Case C-265/95, *Commission v. France*, [1997] ECR I-6959. See Regulation 2679/98 on the Functioning of the internal market in relation to free movement of goods, O.J. No. L. 337/8, 1998.

Charter gives it no additional powers. It would be more efficient if there were a General Principle that private parties are able to bring proceedings against the State in national courts, to oblige the State to protect their rights or to compensate them for loss caused by an infringement of the Charter[112] rather than suing the State in the Court of Human Rights and (if successful) getting compensation years later.

§3.29 CONFLICTING FUNDAMENTAL PRIVATE RIGHTS

The Charter says nothing expressly about situations in which fundamental rights under the Charter are, or appear to be, in conflict, or to need to be reconciled. This kind of situation can arise when rights of private parties conflict, e.g., when the right to freedom of the press conflicts with the right to personal privacy,[113] or when the right to protection of intellectual property rights conflicts with the right of internet companies to run their businesses (*Scarlet Extended*[114]) or when the right of the natural father of a child conflicts with the rights of the mother and foster parents.[115] *Viking Line,*[116] discussed above, involved a conflict between the rights of a trade union to collective action and the right of establishment.

Cases involving apparently conflicting rights are likely to become increasingly important in private law. The most serious issues will not concern e.g., tyrannical fathers and victimized children or aggressive children and vulnerable parents, but interference with privacy by powerful and unscrupulous media, or with public health by polluters.

112. A private party must be able to claim compensation from an EU Member State if the State itself infringes its rights under the Charter, on the principle of State responsibility stated in Joined Cases C-6 and C-9/90, *Francovich v. Italy*, [1991] ECR I-5537. If the Charter imposes a duty on private parties which the injured party is unable to enforce for some reason but which the State could have enforced, the injured party should be able to obtain compensation from the State. The European Courts of Human Rights in *Otto-Preminger-Institut v. Austria*, [1994] ECHR 26 said at para. 49 '*whoever exercises the rights and freedoms enshrined in the first paragraph of [Article 10] undertakes 'duties and responsibilities'. Amongst them – in the context of religious opinions and beliefs – may legitimately be included an obligation to avoid as far as possible expressions that are gratuitously offensive to others and thus an infringement of their rights, and which therefore do not contribute to any form of public debate capable of furthering progress in human affairs. This being so, is a matter of principle it may be considered necessary in certain democratic societies to sanction or even prevent improper attacks on objects of religious veneration …*'.
113. BVerfG 15 Dec 1999; EC t HR *Von Hannover* [I], (application no. 59320/00) of June 24, 2004; *Campbell v. Mirror Group Newspapers*, [2004] A.C. 457.
114. Case C-70/10, *Scarlet Extended*, [2011] n.y.r., (November 24, 2011).
115. ECtHR, *Görgülü* (application No. 74969/01) 24 February 1999; BVerfG, Beschluss v 14-10 2004 – 2 BvR 1481/04, para. 56. See also Case C-438/05, *International Transport Workers Federation v. Viking Line*, [2007] ECR I-10779, discussed above. See Besselink, The Protection of Fundamental Rights post-Lisbon: The Interaction between the EU Charter of Fundamental Rights, the European Convention on Human Rights (ECHR) and National Constitutions, General Report for the Congress of FIDE, the Fédération International pour le Droit European 2012, Tallinn, pp. 17-24.
116. Case C-438/05, *International Transport Workers' Federation v. Viking Line*, [2007] ECR I-10779, paras 45, 52-55, 79.

It is usual, when considering these kinds of situations, to say that courts must 'balance' the competing rights in some way.[117] But is it less usual to suggest useful general criteria saying how this should be done. However, certain things can be said:

- When balancing competing rights, it is particularly useful and important to see what courts in other States have done when similar issues came before them. This is useful even where the States are allowed to exercise a wide discretion, and where the State concerned may consider that its circumstances are different from those elsewhere.
- Not all rights are equally strong or equally important, and some rights can be limited or restricted without being taken away, while others are not open to being compromised: they are either given or denied, in any particular situation.
- The European Court of Human Rights has allowed States a wide margin of discretion in how they reconcile competing or conflicting rights, e.g., in connection with voluntary abortion, although one would expect that the right to life would be a very 'strong' and strictly protected right.[118] This is understandable and indeed necessary on questions on which there are big differences between national laws and policies.
- The balance may need to be struck in the light of the facts of the particular case, and in particular with regard to whether the exercise by the opposing parties of their respective rights was reasonable and moderate, or unusual or exaggerated, and whether a conflict could have been avoided or minimized by the actions of one or both parties. In other words, subjective as well as objective elements may be involved, and unusual circumstances may need to be taken into account. The relative importance of the interests protected by the conflicting rights, in the circumstances of each case, must be weighed against one another. (Was the intrusion on personal privacy justified by any public interest concern?). Presumably there is a General Principle that rights under the Charter should be exercised as far as possible to avoid interfering with the Charter rights of others, and that unnecessary or disproportionate interference with the rights of others is likely to be illegal. Legitimate rights may be improperly exercised. There must also be a General Principle that both parties should cooperate with any public authorities which may be even-handedly trying to avoid or minimize conflict or to reconcile rights, as in *Schmidberger*.[119] If one party is infringing other national law rules, its conduct is not likely to be legitimate under the Charter, unless those rules are themselves contrary to the Charter.

117. See Heim, When Rights conflict, in Ligere (ed.), Lincoln's Inn Lectures on European Law and Human Rights (2010) 23-37. For a valuable discussion, see Alexy, A Theory of Constitutional Rights (2002, Oxford), (primarily discussing German law, saying that principles require objectives to be realized to the greatest extent legally and factually possible).
118. Harris, O'Boyle & Warbrick, Law of the European Convention on Human Rights (2nd ed., 2009, Oxford) 53-56.
119. Case C-112/00, *Schmidberger*, [2003] ECR I-5659.

- In cases in which three rights are involved (as in the *Görgülü* case, the rights of the father, the rights of the child, and the rights of the mother and the adoptive family), it is particularly important to reconcile the interests involved as sensitively as possible, and it is not likely that any precise general rule would be suitable in all cases.
- In balancing economic and social objectives, it is necessary to see e.g., whether the jobs or conditions of employment of workers are really jeopardized or under serious threat, whether the action taken went further than necessary to attain a legitimate objective, and whether less restrictive measures could have been used.[120] In short, the principle of proportionality is applied to private actions.

More generally, cases making it necessary to balance competing fundamental rights are not suitable for direct effects, since much may depend on the special circumstances and the behaviour of the parties and their willingness, if any, to compromise.

§3.30 IN AREAS WHERE STATES HAVE A WIDE DISCRETION, HOW MUCH SCOPE IS THERE FOR DEVELOPING GENERAL PRINCIPLES IN PRIVATE LAW?

In areas where States have a wide discretion and exercise it in different ways, the rights and obligations of private parties are governed by national law, and only in extreme or unusual cases by the Charter. This seems to mean that in these areas there will be little scope for private law General Principles to emerge from the case law under the Charter, unless they are derived or induced from a consensus of national case law.

However, this does not mean that there is little scope for trying to identify and develop principles by studying the case law of national courts in other States. Even in areas where the results are different, the considerations weighed against one another are likely to be similar. The experience of one State is likely to be useful in another. The more experience is looked at, the better, in particular when assessing the possible implications of particular policies.

§3.31 CONCLUSION

Courts should be on the watch to see if General Principles apply. It is desirable for cases to be decided on the basis of General Principles whenever appropriate, because this reduces the tendency to decide cases on the basis of their special facts, which leads to more frequent litigation and less harmonized results. Recognizing General Principles also leads gradually to more harmonized legal rules, and to filling the gaps in the European legal structure.

120. Case C-438/05, *International Transport Workers' Federation v. Viking Line*, [2007] ECR I-10779, paras 80-90.

General Principles of law are moral principles. Like fundamental rights, they are fundamental ethical principles applied to legal issues. That makes it important that lawyers should identify as many of them as we can. It also means that they are part of the concept of Europe on which we should try to get peoples of all religions and traditions to agree. They are part of the European tradition and the European ideal.

Europe, and the European Union and the European Economic Area, are more diverse than, for example, the U.S.A. So Europe needs to do more to protect and manage its diversity. For this purpose also, General Principles are useful, and necessary.

In this paper efforts have been made to suggest an intellectual framework for General Principles in private law, and to suggest potential General Principles. Not all those suggested may ultimately be accepted, but there are a number that are important enough to be considered by the European Courts. The Charter has enormous potential that has not yet been realized under the Convention.

Part II: The Constitutionalization of Private Autonomy

CHAPTER 4

Regulated Autonomy between Market Freedoms and Fundamental Rights in the Case Law of the CJEU

*Guido Comparato & Hans-W. Micklitz**

§4.01 THE CONSTITUTIONAL DIMENSION OF GENERAL PRINCIPLES

Some of the general principles of private law can be considered to be fundamental enough to be distinctive not only of a legal system, but even more basically of economic and social orders. If this is true, it is legitimate to ask whether such principles should be given a particular position in a ranking of the fundamental values of a society – those which, expressed in legal concepts, have been often laid down in national constitutions. In this light, even some principles of private law have been considered to be important enough to be placed in a hierarchically higher position than other legal rules, and have, therefore, been vested with a constitutional status in different national contexts and based on different philosophical and economic considerations. This is in particular the case for the principle of private autonomy, which, in its traditional understanding, embodies the freedom of individuals to determine their legal relationships according to their free will. As such, the principle can be considered an expression of a constitutionally guaranteed human freedom, but it also comprehends more specific manifestations of that liberty, such as economic freedom and freedom of contract, whose link to basic human rights may be more difficult to establish and which have occasionally been considered to be covered by different provisions of national 'economic constitutions'. Expressing the individual's autonomy to freely organize their

* This chapter was written within the framework of the research project 'European Regulatory Private Law: the Transformation of European Private Law from Autonomy to Functionalism in Competition and Regulation' at the European University Institute and has benefited from discussions within the research group. The usual disclaimer applies.

social and economic life, private autonomy – together with the recognition of private property – is the foundation of a free market economy. But this link to a certain political and economic ideology is already a hint to the fact that behind the generic definition of private autonomy lurks a wide range of understandings, ideologies and designs.

The purpose of this contribution is to describe how the principle of private autonomy can undergo a process of 'constitutionalization', specifically in the context of the European legal system, and what this means for the substance of the principle.[1] The premise of this contribution is that, although several principles at the European level are drawn from the national orders, the supposed constitutionalization of private autonomy at the European level does not coincide with the mere supranational recognition of the same principle which is already enshrined in national constitutions. Autonomy in the European order, which can be termed as regulated autonomy, can be better described as an instrument to conform individual behaviour for the purpose of achieving the policy objectives of the European Union and which involves both an extension and a compression of individual economic freedom.[2] Therefore – this is our argument – constitutionalized autonomy in the EU differs from the traditional national understanding of autonomy as a constitutional legal principle which has been proposed in the literature and case law of the highest national courts.

To highlight the particular character of Europeanized regulated autonomy, it will be necessary to look at the contents and borders of the private autonomy principle in the EU legal order and, particularly, in the jurisprudence of its Court of Justice. In the course of this analysis, it will also emerge that, while autonomy has traditionally been considered the core of general contract law, the most important and innovative developments concerning private autonomy do not affect the core areas of traditional contract law, but are rather taking place in the increasingly significant peripheral areas of private law such as transport, telecommunication, which so far remain widely out of the research interests of private lawyers and the law on the information society, where the ECJ has taken the lead. In order to outline the contours of this regulated autonomy, our contribution will start with placing the private autonomy discourse into the broader frame of the so called '*general principles on private law*', one of the most recent 'inventions' of the ECJ. This part should be understood as our way of setting the scene to trigger a debate on private autonomy in EU law. The next three parts suggest a certain path in the development of private autonomy, starting from the marketization of private autonomy over the balancing of marketization against fundamental rights which are enshrined in the steadily growing areas of Europeanized policies, until the on-going process of fragmentation. We will start by analysing the relationship between autonomy and the market freedoms, which on the one hand extend the limits of autonomy but on the other hand use that concept to achieve the objective of the

1. This is not the place to discuss what constitutionalization at the EU level means. For the sake of the argument it suffices to equate constitutionalization with the existence of a higher legal order which shapes the contours of the private legal order.
2. In a more theoretical perspective Ch. Schmid, *Die Instrumentalisierung des Privatrechts durch die Europäische Union, Privatrecht und Privatrechtskonzeption in der Entwicklung der Europäischen Rechtsverfassung* (Baden-Baden, Nomos, 2010); still relevant the ground breaking analysis of the ECJ case law, E. Steindorff, *EG-Vertrag und Privatrecht* (Baden-Baden, Nomos, 1996).

common market. This is what we call *marketization of autonomy*. In a next step we will look at how the marketization of autonomy triggered a process of balancing economic freedoms against fundamental rights. This was made possible by the extension of competences under the various Treaty amendments which triggered the Europeanization of ever more areas of policy and, finally, at the new innovative and telling case law of the Court on the 'information society', which seems to be paradigmatic for what we term fragmentation. More research is needed in other areas of European law, such as regulated markets, but astonishingly also in consumer law[3] (less so in employment law and anti-discrimination law[4]) in order to find out to what extent European private autonomy is not only regulated but also fragmented. It will remain for the future to deepen our knowledge on regulated autonomy in fragmented markets before we may investigate the relationship between fragmented concepts of autonomy and possible ways to find a genuine concept of European private autonomy, which cuts across the different areas of private law. This will also imply the need to elaborate on the differences between the national and the European understanding. Again this short contribution does not allow for developing the argument, it is simply suggested that such a difference between national and European concepts exist.

We put emphasis on cases before the CJEU. Much has been written on private autonomy as part of the European legal order, but only few contributions really go into the case-law of the CJEU. We have applied two different sets of criteria in the selection of the cases. The first is based on screening the case-law to find out whether and to what extent the CJEU is using autonomy, freedom of contract and the related concept of freedom to do business in its reasoning. Here we relied on previous research not least undertaken by Arthur Hartkamp complemented by our own research along the same line. The second is the significance of the cases for the establishment of private autonomy in the European economic constitution in its interplay with fundamental and social rights. Our bottom-up approach led us to discover the new battlefield of information society, which is usually left to intellectual property right lawyers despite its strong impact on the concept of private autonomy as such. Another area, which we did not invest into, is certainly consumer law, where the recent economic crisis seems to have triggered a number of preliminary references prompted by consumers who are over-indebted or have even lost their homes. Here the 'constitutionalization' is less visible and less explicit than in IP law, as will be demonstrated. Our assumption is that

---

3. Most of the research of the last ten years analyses the impact of national constitutional law on private and consumer law, see, with further references, C.-W. Canaris, *Grundrechte und Privatrecht. Eine Zwischenbilanz* (Berlin, de Gruyter, 1999); O. Cherednychenko, *Fundamental rights, contract law and the protection of the weaker party. A comparative analysis of the constitutionalisation of contract law, with emphasis on risky financial transactions* (Munich, Sellier, 2007); Ch. Mak, *Fundamental rights in European contract law. A comparison of the impact of fundamental rights on contractual relationships in Germany, the Netherlands, Italy and England* (Alphen aan den Rijn, Kluwer, 2008); G. Brüggermeier, A. Colombi Ciacchi, G. Comandé (ed) *Fundamental Rights and Private Law in the European Union. Volume I and II* (Cambridge, University Press, 2010).
4. See the contributions in R. Schulze, *Non-Discrimination in European Private Law* (Munich, Mohr Siebeck, 2011)

regulated private autonomy in consumer law bears particular characteristics of regulated private autonomy, which neither fits into nation state categories of constitutionalization nor into regulated autonomy as reconstructed in the case law of the information society. For the time being and without touching upon the field of consumer law, we will limit ourselves to discussing one of the most outspoken cases of the CJEU in that field - *Mohammed Aziz* - in order to demonstrate how the marketization of autonomy faces more and more resistance from a fundamental rights perspective.

§4.02 PRIVATE AUTONOMY AS A GENERAL AND A CONSTITUTIONAL PRINCIPLE OF EUROPEAN PRIVATE LAW

The principle of private autonomy characterizes the vast majority of European private law systems. Although it primarily relates to the more general concept of self-determination, when it is linked to contract law the principle essentially stands for freedom of contract.[5] The possibility to enter into agreements, the freedom to determine the subjects with whom contracts can be concluded and the contents of those agreements are in a way included in the very notion of a contract as an agreement expressing the free wills of two parties. Even the academic plans to codify or to achieve a compilation of the principles of European contract law would acknowledge a pivotal place to private autonomy among the principles of private law. The Draft Common Frame of Reference directly links the principle to the overarching principle of freedom, which is qualified as one of the 'underlying principles' of the project.[6] Therefore, it appears that private autonomy already represents a principle of European contract law, although it is strongly limited by the increasing interventions of the EU in contract law.

The question remains whether it also has a constitutional status in the European Union legal order, similar to what has been established in national law by various national courts. Those who sustain the constitutional dimension of autonomy at the national level seem convinced of this:[7] after all, it seems difficult in light of the *Solange-II* doctrine to accept that there can be a fundamental principle which is part of

5. For this reason and given the multiple interpretations that can be given of those concepts in different context, in this paper the terms private autonomy and freedom of contract will be employed interchangeably.
6. For a critical assessment see M.W. Hesselink, 'If You Don't Like our Principles We Have Others. On Core Values and Underlying Principles in European Private Law: A Critical Discussion of the New 'Principles' Section in the Draft Common Frame of Reference', in *The Foundations of European Private Law*, R. Brownsword, H.-W. Micklitz, L. Niglia, S. Weatherill (ed.) (Oxford, Hart Publishing, 2011) 59; M.W. Hesselink, Ch. Mak, J.W. Rutgers, *Constitutional Aspects of European Private Law. Freedoms, Rights and Social Justice in the Draft Common Frame of Reference*, CSECL Working Paper 2009/05.
7. D. Coester-Waltjen, 'Constitutional Aspects of Party Autonomy and Its Limits – The Perspective of Law' in *Party Autonomy and the role of Information in the Internal Market*, S. Grundmann, W. Kerber, S. Weatherill (eds) (Berlin, Walter de Gruyter, 2001) 41, 42, referring in particular to the case *Rau v. BALM (Berlin-Butter)* of 1987 which spoke of the freedom to pursue a trade or profession as a general principle of Community law.

national constitutions but not also of the European constitutional order.[8] It is consistent to assume that precisely because of the high number of mandatory rules in European contract law the existence of private autonomy as an overarching implicit principle can be presumed.[9] But even if this proves the existence of a general principle of autonomy, it would still be insufficient to infer the *constitutional* nature of that principle, since mandatory rules do not prove the existence of a constitutionalized freedom of contract any more than censorship proves the existence of freedom of expression. The constitutionalization of a principle must mean something more than just the rhetorical recognition of the important role of that principle, as it imposes a burden to justify any limitation to it by reference to other constitutional principles. As to what this concretely means, the recently discovered 'general principles of private law' do not provide an answer.

[A] The CJEU General Principles of Private Law

Private autonomy too can be identified in the series of general principles of private law which have been more or less explicitly mentioned by the Court of Justice, and which have already triggered an extensive doctrinal discussion in Europe.[10] The recognition of the existence of those general principles mainly occurred in the well known cases of *Société thermal*,[11] *Hamilton*,[12] *Messner*,[13] *Friz*.[14] In those circumstances, the Court referred in particular to principles such as the binding force of a contract, discharge by performance, good faith and unjust enrichment. Freedom of contract was not explicitly mentioned in those decisions, but the Court had already had an occasion to articulate this principle in several other cases. For example, in *Werhof*,[15] a case concerning the effects of collective agreements on the relations between employee, transferor and transferee of a business, the CJEU already expressed that 'a contract is characterized by the principle of freedom of the parties to arrange their own affairs',[16] and that, 'as a rule',[17] a contract cannot be made binding on a third party, although European

8. *See* C.-W. Canaris, 'Verfassungs- und europarechtliche Aspekte der Vertragsfreiheit in der Privatrechtsgesellschaft', in *Wege und Verfahren des Verfassungslebens. Festschrift für Peter Lerche*, P. Baudura and R. Scholz (eds) (Munich, Beck, 1993) 887-888.
9. H.-W. Micklitz, 'A Comment on Party Autonomy and Consumer Regulation in the European Community - A Plea for Consistency', in *Party Autonomy and the role of Information in the Internal Market*, S. Grundmann, W. Kerber, S. Weatherill (eds) (Berlin, Walter de Gruyter, 2001) 197, 199.
10. S. Weatherill, *The "principles of civil law" as a basis for interpreting the legislative acquis*, 6(1) European Review of Contract Law (2010) 74; A.S. Hartkamp, *The General Principles of EU Law and Private Law*, 75 RabelsZ 241 (2011); M.W. Hesselink, 'The General Principles of Civil Law: their Nature, Roles and Legitimacy' in *The Involvement of EU Law in Private Law Relationships*, D. Leczykiewicz and S. Weatherill (eds) (Oxford, Hart Publishing, 2012).
11. *Société thermale d'Eugénie-les-Bains v. Ministère de l'Économie, des Finances et de l'Industrie*, 2007 I-06415, C-277/05 (18/7/2007).
12. *Annelore Hamilton v. Volksbank Filder eG*, 2008 I-02383, C-412/06 (10/4/2008).
13. *Pia Messner v. Firma Stefan Krüger*, 2009 I-07315, C-489/07 (3/9/2009).
14. *E. Friz GmbH v. Carsten von der Heyden*, 2010 I-02947, C-215/08 (15/4/2010).
15. *Hans Werhof v. Freeway Traffic Systems GmbH & Co. KG*, 2006 I-02397, C-499/04 (9/3/2006).
16. *Werhof*, para. 23.
17. *Werhof*, para. 23.

legislation may occasionally derogate from that principle in order to avoid the erosion of the rights of workers. However, a reference made to the principle certainly does not amount to constitutionalization of private autonomy. The case was also about the impact of general principles of Community law and fundamental rights on private law relations, but the Court rather focussed on a different fundamental principle to support its decision, namely freedom of association and even more particularly on the other side of the coin of that freedom, namely the freedom *not* to associate.[18] This case may already be considered to be indicative of a certain tendency in an understanding of autonomy primarily as individual autonomy, downplaying its possible collective dimension, but also of the tendency to employ fundamental rights such as the freedom of (non-)association to support particular interpretative solutions. The possible use of fundamental rights to support particular judicial decisions in private law matters will be discussed further in the next sections.

However, freedom of contract is not absolute and can be restricted by EU law. As early as in the case of *Spain v. Commission*, the Court stated that 'the right of parties to amend contracts concluded by them is based on the principle of contractual freedom and cannot, therefore, be limited in the absence of Community rules imposing specific restrictions in that regard'.[19] In *Harms*, the Court stated even more clearly that 'although a contract is characterized by the principle of freedom of the parties to arrange their own affairs, according to which, in particular, parties are free to enter into obligations with each other, limitations on freedom of contract may none the less arise from the applicable European Union rules'.[20] Neither the general principles of private law nor the few cases in which the CJEU refers to private autonomy or freedom of contract provide a clear message on whether private autonomy has turned into a constitutional principle. What remains is the reference to the Treaty being understood by the CJEU as a genuine legal order first and later as a constitutional charter.

[B] Autonomy and the Four Freedoms

The fundamental freedoms of the EU – free movement of goods, capital, services and people – were read in particular by German scholars as an acknowledgment at the highest level of the freedom to conclude contracts, to transfer capital and goods, to provide services and so on – indeed, of private autonomy beyond the borders of national legal orders.[21] Due to the supremacy of the EU legal order – this is the argument – national legal orders cannot, except in exceptional circumstances, limit those freedoms. Privateautonomy receives a quasi-constitutional status since national rules of a lower level cannot derogate from it. From this point of view, the economic

18. *Werhof*, para. 33.
19. *Kingdom of Spain v. Commission of the European Communities*, 1999 I-06571, Case C-240/97 (5/10/1999) para. 99.
20. *Arnold und Johann Harms als Gesellschaft bürgerlichen Rechts v. Freerk Heidinga*, 2010 I-04431, C-434/08 (20/5/2010) para. 36.
21. P.-C. Müller-Graff, 'Basic Freedoms – Extending Party Autonomy across Borders' in *Party Autonomy and the role of Information in the Internal Market*, S. Grundmann, W. Kerber, S. Weatherill (eds) (Berlin, Walter de Gruyter, 2001) 133-150.

constitution of the EU would very likely resemble the ideal of an ordo-liberal constitution: private autonomy receives protection at the highest level and intrusions in the private law society are only justified by the goal of ensuring competition.[22] Significantly, the rules on competition were indeed the first provisions of the Treaties which had direct horizontal effect on private relations.

In countries such as Germany the legal basis which offered a constitutional anchor for private autonomy was in particular personal freedom, which gives a more 'political' flavour to the principle. A comparable development took place in France as well,[23] where the constitutional status of that principle, after having been denied for quite a long time, was eventually derived directly from Article 4 of the *Déclaration des Droits de l'Homme et du Citoyen* of 1789, which acknowledges the general personal freedom. Autonomy is apparently considered something more prominent than just an element of the 'economic constitution' and is rather considered part of the political or (as the German Constitutional Court held later)[24] the social constitution of the State. The legal framework of the European Communities, on the other hand, at least initially entirely built on economic grounds, autonomously offered just an 'economic constitution'. Therefore autonomy can be interpreted as an exclusively economic principle, which is crystallized in the 'freedom to conduct a business'[25] rather than in personal freedoms as it has usually been suggested in the already mentioned national contexts. In *Jean Neu* the Court recognized that the 'freedom to pursue a trade or profession, which ... forms part of the general principles of Community law, includes, as a specific expression of that freedom, the freedom to choose whom to do business with',[26] a prerogative which is traditionally seen as one of the core aspects of freedom of contract.

However, freedom of trade, later qualified as freedom to conduct a business, appears to be at the same time a narrower and a broader category than private autonomy – on the one hand it is limited to the economic sphere, on the other hand it extends beyond purely private law relationships and affects more fundamentally the very relationship between the citizen and the administration. Freedom to trade seems to encompass private autonomy in its both dimensions, the enabling and the restricting.

The latest stage of that development was the inclusion of the principle as developed by the Court into the Charter of Fundamental Rights, which eventually entered into force with the Treaty of Lisbon.[27] While the Charter does not make any

22. On ordo-liberalism and competition law in Europe see, among others, D.J. Gerber, *Law and Competition in Twentieth Century Europe. Protecting Prometheus* (Clarendon, Oxford, 1998) 232 ff.
23. J.-C. Bonichot, 'Constitution et contrats en droit français' in *Nouveaux défis du droit des contrats en France et en Europe*, G. Mäsch, D. Mazeaud, R. Schulze (eds.) (Munich, Sellier, 2009) 104.
24. BVerfG NJW 1994, 36.
25. On the freedom to conduct a business, see also the contributions in this book of D. Leczykiewicz, Chapter 6 and P. Oliver, Chapter 12.
26. *Jean Neu and others v. Secrétaire d'Etat à l'Agriculture et à la Viticulture*, 1991 I-03617, joined cases C-90/90 and C-91/90 (10/7/1991) para. 13.
27. Article 16, *Freedom to conduct a business*, quite humbly states that 'The freedom to conduct a business in accordance with Union law and national laws and practices is recognised'.

explicit reference to private autonomy as a self-standing constitutional right,[28] in *Sky Österreich* the European Court has most recently explicitly recognized that the freedom to conduct a business covers freedom of contract[29] and in particular the freedoms to choose with whom to do business and to determine the price of a service.[30] Only the circumstances of the case tell the whole story. Freedom of contract is meant to enlarge the freedoms of audio-visual users against the interests of the broadcaster who might have an interest in restricting access to information. *Sky Österreich* demonstrates the double nature of autonomy, enabling and restricting at the same time. Whilst one might argue that this logic is intrinsic to the fact that enlarging the freedom of one party necessarily implies restricting the one of the other party, in the EU context autonomy gains a different meaning. It cannot be disconnected from the internal market, from the freedom to do business across borders.

§4.03 THE MARKETIZATION OF AUTONOMY

Economic operators in the Member States complained already from the 1960s that the interventions of the European Communities, setting standards of production and access to the market, infringed on their freedoms to perform their businesses, to freely determine the amount of the production and to choose the parties with whom to conclude contracts. It is quite evident that some of the traditional understandings of autonomy were being altered by regulatory interventions. This was in particular the case in the judgments in which private autonomy got a first constitutional recognition through the channel of freedom of trade, and more specifically in the cases of *Internationale Handelsgesellschaft*,[31] *Nold*,[32] *Eridania*,[33] *Hauer*.[34] In particular *Internationale Handelsgesellschaft* and *Nold* are regarded as the important judgments which, after *Stauder*,[35] fostered the process of recognition of fundamental principles as part of the European legal order. Since then, private autonomy, in its European guise of freedom of trade, freedom to choose and practise a trade or profession, and later the freedom to conduct a business, has been listed among those principles. However, while the Court recognized the existence of a general principle of freedom to conduct a business, it accepted at the same time that strong constraints could be imposed on that freedom. In an historical phase in which national judges faced problems recognizing

28. In this respect, the Charter of Fundamental Rights has followed the tradition of national constitutions which, after the Weimar Constitution, have preferred not codifying the principle arguably for political reasons, see C. Castronovo, *Autonomia Privata e Costituzione Europea*, 1 Europa e diritto privato 29, 30 (2005).
29. *Sky Österreich GmbH v. Österreichischer Rundfunk*, Case C-283/11 (22/1/2013) para. 42.
30. *Sky Österreich*, para. 43.
31. *Internationale Handelsgesellschaft mbH v. Einfuhr- und Vorratsstelle für Getreide und Futtermittel*, 1970 01125, Case C-11/70 (17/12/1970).
32. *J. Nold, Kohlen- und Baustoffgroßhandlung v. Commission of the European Communities*, 1974 00491, Case C-4/73 (14/5/1974).
33. *SpA Eridania-Zuccherifici nazionali and SpA Società Italiana per l'Industria degli Zuccheri v. Minister of Agriculture and Forestry, Minister for Industry, Trade and Craft Trades, and SpA Zuccherifici Meridionali*, 1979 02749, Case C-230/78 (27/9/1979).
34. *Liselotte Hauer v. Land Rheinland-Pfalz*, 1979 03727, Case C-44/79 (13/12/1979).
35. *Erich Stauder v. City of Ulm – Sozialamt*, 1969 00419, Case C-29/69 (12/11/1969).

the idea of supremacy of EC law and tried to conquer European legislation declaring it to be contrary to principles of national constitutional law (among which the freedom of trade and the right of property), European judges were almost forced to acknowledge that those constitutional principles also formed part of the European legal framework, recognizing their constitutional status but at the same time having to justify limitations on them. The jurisprudence inaugurated by *Internationale Handelsgesellschaft* and *Nold* remained constant through decades, and was followed in *Rau v. BALM*,[36] *Hauptzollamt Gronau*,[37] *Jean Neu, Kühn*,[38] *Germany v. Council*,[39] *Wintersekt*,[40] *SAM Schiffahrt/Heinz*,[41] *Metronome Musik*,[42] and most recently in *Weintor*,[43] and *Kokopelli*.[44] Accordingly the economic freedom of trade is a fundamental right which is protected in the European legal order. However, it is not absolute and can be limited by proportionate measures meant to achieve a legitimate goal of the European Communities. It suffices to refer to a number of key cases to explain that process.

[A] *Nold*

In the *Nold* case, a German undertaking complained of a violation of its economic freedom protected in Articles 2(1) (personal freedom, considered as protecting private autonomy) and 14 (property) of the German Constitution. After the merging of two mining companies into a new one whose terms of business had to be authorized by the European institutions, a decision by the European Commission approved the new terms despite the fact that they were more restrictive than the previous terms. The right of coal dealers to qualify for direct purchase from Ruhrkohle AG was made dependent on the conclusion of a two-year contract of a given minimum quantity of Ruhr coal a year. Nold, an undertaking which had been active in that business for more than a century, brought an action to the Court claiming that the decision of the European Commission was, among other things, discriminatory and against the 'freedom of trade and the need to ensure that individuals have the means to realize their capabilities to the full'.[45] The Court rejected the first claim of discrimination and considered, in more detail, the second claim concerning an alleged violation of fundamental rights. This second claim of Nold was rejected too since, as the Advocate General had explained, if

36. *Walter Rau Lebensmittelwerke and others v. Bundesanstalt für landwirtschaftliche Marktordnung*, 1987 02289, Case C-133/85 (21/5/1987).
37. *Hermann Schräder HS Kraftfutter GmbH & Co. KG v. Hauptzollamt Gronau*, 1989 02237, Case C-265/87 (11/7/1989).
38. *Ralf-Herbert Kühn v. Landwirtschaftskammer Weser-Ems*, 1992 I-00035, Case C-177/90 (10/1/1992).
39. *Federal Republic of Germany v. Council of the European Union*, 1994 I-04973, Case C-280/93 (5/10/1994).
40. *SMW Winzersekt GmbH v. Land Rheinland-Pfalz*, 1994 I-05555, Case C-306/93 (13/12/1994).
41. *SAM Schiffahrt GmbH and Heinz Stapf v. Bundesrepublik Deutschland*, 1997 I-04475, joined cases C-248/95 and C-249/95 (17/7/1997).
42. *Metronome Musik GmbH v. Music Point Hokamp GmbH*, 1998 I-01953, Case C-200/96 (28/4/1998).
43. *Deutsches Weintor eG v. Land Rheinland-Pfalz*, Case C-544/10 (6/9/2012).
44. *Association Kokopelli v. Graines Baumaux SAS*, Case C-59/11 (12/7/2012).
45. Opinion of Advocate General Trabucchi, Case C-4/73 (28/3/1974) 513.

this argument were correct, the European administration would have no power at all to authorize terms of business. Therefore, on a closer look, the company adopted a classical view of private autonomy as a negative freedom against the State, which meant that the imposition of requirements by the European Commission would intrude on the freedom of the individuals to pursue their own constitutionally protected interests.

The Court, following its Advocate General, was clear in rejecting this interpretation and defended the authority of the European legal order to organize the economy. Advocate General Trabucchi explained the meaning of constitutionalization, highlighting that constitutionalization cannot amount to a simple tool to prevent regulation: 'Recognition by the Constitution does not mean that the subject matter is no longer subject to any rules, but that the rules must be inspired and limited by an effective and essential recognition of the principles'.[46] This certainly does not mean that freedom of trade does not exist and that the economy is planned in the European legal order. On the contrary, the European judges laid down the reason to justify restrictions of freedom of trade. This argument became widespread and was almost literally followed in all successive judgments of the Court: after recalling that fundamental rights are part of the general principles of law which are binding in European law, the European judges considered that even:

> if rights of ownership are protected by the constitutional laws of all the Member States and if similar guarantees are given in respect of their right freely to choose and practice their trade or profession, the rights thereby guaranteed, far from constituting unfettered prerogatives, must be viewed in the light of the social function of the property and activities protected thereunder. For this reason, rights of this nature are protected by law subject always to limitations laid down in accordance with the public interest. Within the community legal order it likewise seems legitimate that these rights should, if necessary, be subject to certain limits justified by the overall objectives pursued by the Community, on condition that the substance of these rights is left untouched.[47]

The need to balance the right to property and the right to freely choose and practise a profession with the social function of economic activities confirms how European fundamental rights are drawn from their counterparts in national constitutions, where indeed – at least in the most progressive of them – the social function of property and private enterprise was already acknowledged and used to justify the constitutionality of State intervention in the economy. At the same time, the Court added a new element which is distinctive of the European system: private autonomy in the European legal order can also be constrained, within limits, to pursue the overall objectives of the Community, in particular the building of a well-functioning common market. However, a well-functioning common market necessarily requires freedom of trade, so that a balance between the opposite exigencies has to be found too.

Again, this point is developed in the Opinion of Advocate General Trabucchi:

46. Opinion of Advocate General Trabucchi, Case C-4/73 (28/3/1974) 514.
47. *Nold*, para. 14.

> Such important limitations are justified by the general interest in the proper functioning of the common market; this is not the only consideration; one must regard these limitations as established for the purpose of supporting the other fundamental criterion relating to the safeguarding of the essential right to trade. Even though they fetter the initiative of private individuals, limitations on direct access to supplies from the coal producers can in turn contribute to well-ordered economic, commercial and productive activities ... and they can therefore stimulate the competition existing between coal and other sources of energy.[48]

In order to fully understand the conceptual foundations of the judgment, it seems useful to quote what the Advocate General wrote in a famous handbook on Italian private law several years before:

> Il sistema seguito dal diritto vigente in tema di rapporti privati risente ancora indubbiamente della concezione dominante nel secolo scorso che aveva combattuto ogni restrizione legale o sociale; è stato detto appunto che l'autonomia contrattuale costituisce uno dei trofei della più generale vittoria dell'individualismo. Ma oggi la situazione è ben diversa dal tempo in cui alla legge, quale espressione della vita sociale, era riconosciuto il solo compito di porre i limiti estremi da rispettare nel libero giuoco degli interessi e delle volontà. L'esperienza ci mette ogni giorno più a contatto con profonde modificazioni del mondo giuridico e ci convince che nello studio del contenuto contrattuale il concetto puro di autonomia dev'essere sottoposto a revisione.[49]

The market-steering function of the European interpretation of autonomy also appears in the judgment: the Court states that the economic disadvantages claimed by the applicant are not the result of the contested decision of the Commission but rather of economic change, which the applicant had to tackle simply by acknowledging the situation and by carrying out the necessary adaptations.[50]

The purpose to create a European common market impacts on private law relations and proves the hybrid nature of the European communities. The Court extended the application of the economic freedoms to private subjects, binding a continuously increasing number of private subjects who exercise some regulatory functions in the internal market. The most advanced position in this sense was expressed by the Advocate General in the highly debated *Viking*[51] case, in which he stated that 'the rules on freedom of movement apply directly to any private action that is capable of effectively restricting others from exercising their right to freedom of movement', although 'there seems to be no simple answer' to the question as to how one should determine what is an effective restriction.[52]

48. Opinion of Advocate General Trabucchi, Case C-4/73 (28/3/1974) 514, 515.
49. A. Trabucchi, *Istituzioni di diritto civile* (Padova, Cedam, 1960) 632.
50. *Nold*, para. 16.
51. *International Transport Workers' Federation and Finnish Seamen's Union v. Viking Line ABP and OÜ Viking Line Eesti*, 2007 I-10779, Case C-438/05 (11/12/2007).
52. Opinion of Advocate General Poiares Maduro, Case C-438/05 (23/5/2007) para. 43.

[B] *Hauer*

After the specification that the substance of the rights must be left untouched, the Court opened the door to an evaluation of the admissibility of limitations to the principles on the basis of a test of proportionality, comparable to the one usually performed by constitutional courts to test the constitutionality of legislation which restricts fundamental rights. In this sense, functionalized private autonomy has to be treated like any other constitutional principle, which occasionally has to be balanced with other and contrasting principles. Such a proportionality test was already performed in the *Haue*r case in 1979.

Confronted with the claim that European regulations prohibiting the planting of certain types of vines breached the principles of ownership and freedom of trade established in the German constitution, the Court firstly recognized that this kind of measures already existed in all Member States in conformity with their constitutional orders. Nevertheless, the Court admitted that this reality would not in itself be sufficient to declare the European regulations valid. It held that it was necessary to verify whether any limitations were proportionate and justified by the need to pursue the objectives of the Communities. As the Court said, 'it is therefore necessary to identify the aim pursued by the disputed regulation and to determine whether there exists a reasonable relationship between the measures provided for by the regulation and the aim pursued by the Community in this case'.[53] At the end of the judgment, the limitations to the right of property and freedom of trade posed by the European regulations were considered proportionate since they were only temporary measures justified by the need to achieve the general objectives of the Communities. Among these objectives, the 'common organization of the market' clearly had a pivotal role since, as the Advocate General also pointed out,[54] the European regulations at stake were meant to adjust the productive potential to the requirements of the market. Because of this objective, the Advocate General also rejected the submission, advanced by the applicants, that this position would be incompatible with that of the German Constitutional Court, which had considered similar types of interventions to be unconstitutional. After all, the limitations which had been imposed by German law and which had been rejected by the constitutional court of that country were meant to ensure certain quality standards in the wine production. This was, as the Advocate General affirmed, quite a different and more limited objective from the one of stabilizing the market at a particular moment of time which was pursued by the European regulations. This was 'linked with a programme for the restructuring of the wine market' which was a legitimate goal of general interest of the European communities.[55] The whole reasoning of the Advocate General and the Court was developed based on a possible infringement of the right of property, while the effect of the regulations on freedom of trade was downplayed as a mere consequence: 'the restriction upon the free pursuit of the occupation of wine-growing, assuming that it

53. *Hauer*, para. 23.
54. Opinion of Advocate General Capotorti, Case C-44/79 (8/11/1979) 3755.
55. Opinion of Advocate General Capotorti, Case C-44/79 (8/11/1979) 3763, 3764.

exists, is justified by the same reasons which justify the restriction placed upon the use of property'.[56]

In a similar vein, still in the 1990s, the Court rejected the tendency of applicants to complain of violations of their basic freedoms measures which led to the loss of market shares and interests, and justified any limitations to these freedoms by the need to protect the internal market and to realize the objectives of international trade law. This appeared for example when, dealing with restrictions to the right to import third country bananas, the Court noted that any restriction 'imposed on the economic operators on the German market is inherent in the establishment of a common organization of the market designed to ensure that the objectives of Article 39 of the Treaty are safeguarded and that the Community's international obligations ... are complied with'.[57]

[C] Interim Conclusion

If private autonomy is interpreted in the traditional liberal meaning as freedom from State intervention, and if its constitutionalization were meant to protect that freedom from the State, then private autonomy as it has been developed at the European level does not seem to fit within the traditional meaning. In light of the various limitations in order to achieve the general objectives of the European communities and of the dichotomy of a legal order which on the one hand limits freedom of contract and on the other hand assumes free trade as a founding principle,[58] it is reasonable to affirm that fundamental freedoms are aimed at opening markets rather than guaranteeing freedom of contract per se.[59] In none of the cases did the Court accept that there had been a breach of the principle of autonomy, but found the regulatory interventions of the European communities to be justified. Over the years, the Court has heavily relied on the formula, giving the impression that, as long as the aims of the regulation restricting private autonomy are in line with the objectives of the Treaties and as long as the regulatory intervention is not disproportionate, it can be legitimated. The number of objectives that can justify restrictions to that freedom has progressively increased, in line with the increased number of the Union's 'objectives of general interests'.

§4.04 PRIVATE AUTONOMY VS. FUNDAMENTAL AND SOCIAL RIGHTS

In the constitutional case law of several Member States fundamental rights served as the counterpoise against one-sided private autonomy. The growing impact of fundamental rights in private law often resulted in a limitation of private parties' autonomy,

56. *Hauer*, para. 32.
57. *Federal Republic of Germany v. Council of the European Union*, para. 82.
58. H. Unberath, 'Freedom of contract', in *Max Planck Encyclopedia of European Private Law*, J. Basedow, K.J. Hopt, R. Zimmermann (eds) (Oxford, University Press, 2012) 755.
59. J.W. Rutgers, *The European Economic Constitution, Freedom of Contract and the DCFR*, 2 European Review of Contract Law 95, 104 (2009) referring to the Opinion of Advocate General Poiares Maduro, Case 158/04 and 159/04 (30/03/06).

in that it can require State intervention to set aside the effects of a contract which has been validly formed with the consent of the parties.[60] Scholars[61] have read this case-law as meant to protect the true and genuine will of the weaker parties to an agreement, so that fundamental rights would be employed in defence rather than against private autonomy. In so doing, national case law used the constitutionalization of private autonomy rather as a means to protect certain social parties. Such a development is clearly more advanced at the national level than at the European level, although this does not mean that fundamental rights cannot have an impact on the private law reasoning of the European Court as well.[62] However, there is no similar clear pattern to be discovered in the case-law brought before the ECJ. Even in the most prominent field of anti-discrimination law, preliminary references are not necessarily brought forward to increase the standard of protection but to 'complain' about unequal treatment of men and women, which might very well lead to a downgrading of protection in the name of equal treatment.

Two celebrated cases may be touched upon in order to demonstrate that before the CJEU it is much more the Member State and the margin left to the Member State which is at stake in balancing conflicting rights, economic freedoms against fundamental rights, or one fundamental right against the other. The first famous case in this context is *Schmidberger*,[63] in which freedom of expression was given precedence over the free movement of goods. The facts of the case were quite controversial, and the question was here whether a Member State could be liable for allowing a demonstration by a group of protesters who were blocking roads and hereby obstructed the free movement of goods. On the surface the circumstances look familiar: fundamental rights and economic freedoms. However, at a second glance we are not in a classical situation of private autonomy but in a social conflict where particular groups in the society disagree on the role and importance of environmental protection. EU law – the freedom of goods – is the trigger to engage the CJEU in the conflict. One of the most striking examples of the way in which fundamental rights can occasionally limit fundamental freedoms is said to be the *Omega*[64] case. The freedom to provide services beyond borders – as well as, at the domestic level, of parties to conclude service contracts which allow people to play a game in which they simulate the killing of human beings – was restricted because of the fact that the game infringed on human dignity. The Court held that the limitation of economic freedoms by national authorities could be justified by the need to protect human dignity, provided that the purpose of protecting that fundamental right could not be achieved by less restrictive measures. Again it is not really a conflict between private parties like in the German *Bürgschaft*

60. The clearest example of this is provided by the German Suretyship-case, BVerfG NJW 1994, 36.
61. A. Colombi Ciacchi, 'Concluding Remarks' in G. Brüggermeier, A. Colombi Ciacchi, G. Comandé (ed) *Fundamental Rights and Private Law in the European Union. Volume II: Comparative Analyses of Selected Case Patterns* (Cambridge, University Press, 2010) 429-430.
62. See V. Kosta, *Internal Market Legislation and the Private Law of the Member States – The Impact of Fundamental Rights*, 6(4) European Review of Contract Law 409 (2010).
63. *Eugen Schmidberger, Internationale Transporte und Planzüge v. Republik Österreich*, 2003 I-05659, Case C-112/00 (12/6/2003).
64. *Omega Spielhallen- und Automatenaufstellungs-GmbH v. Oberbürgermeisterin der Bundesstadt Bonn*, 2004 I-09609, Case C-36/02 (14/10/2004).

case. The preliminary reference was triggered by the service provider who challenged the administrative action taken against him by the German authorities. Whilst it is in essence a conflict about the reach of the private autonomy and the freedom to do business, the conflict is only indirectly one between private parties. It is not one of the customers who were requesting protection against this sort of cruel games but the public authorities fighting against a non-national provider.

From the possible array of cases to be discussed in more detail we have chosen three, one dealing with freedom of expression, one dealing with occupational health and safety and one dealing with consumer protection. Only the third fits into the categories established before national constitutional courts – the weaker party invoking protection against the suggested abuse or misuse of private autonomy – however again in a way which is hard to imagine in a purely national environment.

[A] *Mesopotamia/Roj TV* (Freedom of Expression vs Human Dignity)

In *Mesopotamia/Roj TV*,[65] the European Court held that a restriction to the freedom to provide services, based on the general principles of German constitutional law, could be justified. More specifically, the Court had to decide whether the broadcasting directive, which provided that 'Member States shall ensure freedom of reception and shall not restrict retransmissions on their territory of television broadcasts from other Member States for reasons which fall within the fields coordinated by this Directive', precluded the German authorities from blocking the activities of a TV broadcaster incorporated under Danish law which was accused of infringing the German constitutional principle of international understanding. Mesopotamia, a company established under Danish law, owned a TV channel, Roj TV, which broadcasted programmes in Kurdish to other countries including Turkey. The company was accused of promoting the activities of the Kurdish Party PKK, which was listed as a terrorist organization in the European Union. The directive provides that Member States should ensure that broadcasts do not contain any incitement to hatred on grounds of race, sex, religion or nationality and, on the basis of these provisions, the Turkish government complained with the Danish Radio and Television Board, which considered that the activities of Roj TV were covered by the right of freedom of expression and information and were, as a result, not in breach of the Danish legislation implementing the European directive. It must be recalled that the directive has the purpose of creating a free market of information by making it possible for all subjects to provide their services everywhere in Europe – which again means an extension of autonomy beyond national borders. However, it also responds to the more basic necessity to guarantee freedom of expression as recognized in Article 10(1) of the Charter, while Article 11(2) protects respect of freedom and pluralism of the media. The instrument through which this aim is pursued is the usual 'home country control' mechanism, according to which the country from which the television broadcasts emanate must monitor the compliance of

65. *Mesopotamia Broadcast A/S METV and Roj TV A/S v. Bundesrepublik Deutschland*, Joined cases C-244/10 and C-245/10 (22/9/2011).

the transmission with the directive, while the receiving Member States cannot exercise this control. In this case, this meant that since the Danish authorities had considered the broadcasting activities to be legal, German authorities could not impede the broadcasting of those programmes on the German territory. German authorities argued that, as an association, Roj TV also had to comply with the general rules of the German Association Law. The German Administrative Court suspected that the activities of Roj TV could be considered an infringement of its law of associations and the provision laid down in Article 9(2) of the Basic Law, which sets the limits to freedom of association for those entities 'whose purposes or activities infringe criminal laws, or which conflict with the constitutional order or the principles of international understanding are prohibited'. German authorities indeed considered that the activities of Roj TV could infringe the German public order by exacerbating the relations between Turkish and Kurdish communities on its territory.

The European Court considered most of the worries of the German authorities – while rejecting the argument based on the presence of Turkish and Kurdish minorities in Germany – and held that the provisions of the directive did not prevent a Member State from adopting on the basis of general laws such as those of Association Law and Basic Law measures against a broadcaster established in another Member States, as long as these measures did not impede retransmission on the territory of the receiving Member State. In so deciding, the Court referred to previous case law which had found that the directive did not prevent receiving Member States from applying different rules, like rules of consumer protection in the cases *Agostini/TV-Shop*.[66] With this judgment, the Court again accepted limitations to the freedom to provide services which could be justified by national constitutional law. It should be noted that the Court avoided any consideration of Mesopotamia's right to freedom of expression and did not balance it with any other rights, which is what the Danish authority had done. This was also possible since the Court defined the concept of 'incitement to hatred' included in the directive and considered that the activities of Roj TV represented a case of incitement to hatred which could not be considered to be covered by the freedom of information and expression. This complied with the argument of the Advocate General, who had based his position on the respect for human dignity: 'the freedom of expression guaranteed in Article 11 of the Charter ceases to operate when the message infringes other principles and fundamental rights recognised by the Charter, such as the protection of human dignity and the principle of non-discrimination'.[67] The directive, which prohibits broadcasts with discriminatory content, also aims to protect human dignity.[68] Following the advice of its Advocate General, the Court gave priority to human dignity over the principle of freedom of expression and information, allowing the German State to limit the economic freedom of Mesopotamia.

66. *Konsumentombudsmannen (KO) v. De Agostini (Svenska) Förlag AB and TV-Shop i Sverige AB*, 1997 I-03843, joined cases C-34/95, C-35/95 and C-36/95 (9/7/1997).
67. *Mesopotamia*, para. 68.
68. *Mesopotamia*, para. 77.

[B] *Spain and Finland versus the Parliament and the Council* (Health and Safety)

While in the cases discussed above the European Court accepted that fundamental rights can justify restrictions to market freedoms, in other cases the Court has also used fundamental rights contained in the Charter in order to justify even clearer limitations to private autonomy. The usual formula which has been employed since the 1970s to justify restrictions to private autonomy by the need to build a common market can be used to identify new grounds to justify restrictions. In *Spain and Finland v. the European Parliament and Council*[69] the Court had to decide over the claim for the annulment of Directive 2002/15 on the organization of the working time of persons performing mobile road transport activities The directive regulated the working time of self-employed drivers, setting limits to the number of hours they could devote to their activity of road transport, requiring the keeping of a record of the working time, and fixing the frequency and minimum length of breaks for self-employed drivers too. The imposition of these requirements meant that the directive was not only establishing common rules for the market of road transport in Europe, but was also pursuing other important objectives such as health and road safety. Recital 4 of the directive reads: 'it is therefore necessary to lay down a series of more specific provisions concerning the hours of work in road transport intended to ensure the safety of transport and the health and safety of the persons involved', while the first Article of the directive clarifies that it purports 'to establish minimum requirements in relation to the organization of working time in order to improve the health and safety protection of persons performing mobile road transport activities and to improve road safety and align conditions of competition'. It is indeed both intuitive and scientifically proved that hours spent driving have a direct negative effect on the tiredness and health of the transport worker and, as a consequence, on road safety. However, the Republic of Finland and the Kingdom of Spain were not convinced that this argument could justify the requirements imposed by the directive. Finland questioned firstly whether those measures were appropriate to achieve their goals and complained that the directive would limit the working time rather than the driving time. The Court stated that the regulation of the working time of self-employed drivers contributed 'to realizing the objectives of road safety and alignment of conditions of competition'. More substantively, the Kingdom of Spain and the Republic of Finland also claimed that the directive would entail an infringement of the autonomy of self-employed workers. According to Spain, the directive had the effect of preventing them 'from devoting all their time and effort to the prosperity of their undertaking and constitutes an impermissible infringement of their freedom to pursue an occupation and their freedom to conduct a business'.[70] In particular, Spain argued that while there may be the need for social legislation to protect employees, 'no such need for protection exists for self-employed

69. *Kingdom of Spain and Republic of Finland v. European Parliament and Council of the European Union*, 2004 I-07789, Joined cases C-184/02 and C-223/02 (9/9/2004).
70. *Spain and Finland v. European Parliament and Council*, para. 46.

workers, who must remain free to organize their activities as they wish'.[71] In this line of thought, intrusions on private autonomy may be justified to different degrees depending on the subject who is exercising autonomy: a need to protect socially weaker parties could justify stronger intrusions on the autonomy of employees, while the same level of intrusion would not be required in the case of other economic and social subjects. In the same vein, Finland claimed a violation of proportionality principle, since protection of road safety could be achieved through different regulatory instruments such as Regulation 3820/85 on the harmonization of certain social legislation relating to road transport, which would cause 'less interference with the freedom to pursue an occupation'[72] than the regulation of the working time of self-employed drivers. According to Finland, the 'freedom to pursue an occupation includes the organisation of the working time one intends to devote to one's business activities',[73]

The Court referred to its well-established formula:

> Those freedoms are not absolute rights, however, but must be considered in relation to their social function. Consequently, restrictions may be imposed on their exercise provided that the restrictions correspond to objectives of general interest and do not constitute in relation to the aim pursued a disproportionate and intolerable interference, impairing the very substance of the rights guaranteed.[74]

Since road safety was an objective of general interest, the Court considered the directive valid since it governed 'the time spent on activities directly linked to road transport, without encroaching on the freedom of a driver who has chosen to be self-employed to organize the general work inherent in that status as he wishes'.[75] The element that appears predominant in justifying a restriction of private autonomy is not purely the making of a well-functioning common market, which had been almost exclusively dominant in the case law started in the 1970s, but rather the protection of health and road safety. However, these objectives can certainly be seen as general objectives of the European Union. The protection of human health is found in the famous 'horizontal clause' of Article 9 TFEU, which, while it does not create any self-standing legal basis in those areas, provides that in defining and implementing its policies and activities the Union shall take into account requirements linked to the promotion of a high level of employment, the guarantee of adequate social protection, and the protection of human health. Article 168 adds that a 'high level of human health protection shall be ensured in the definition and implementation of all Union policies and activities'. The Charter of Fundamental Rights states in Article 31 that 'every worker has the right to working conditions which respect his or her health, safety and dignity. Every worker has the right to limitation of maximum working hours, to daily and weekly rest periods and to an annual period of paid leaves'. This provision was not explicitly referred to neither by the Court nor by the Advocate General, probably due to

71. *Spain and Finland v. European Parliament and Council*, para. 47.
72. *Spain and Finland v. European Parliament and Council*, para. 48.
73. *Spain and Finland v. European Parliament and Council*, para. 49.
74. *Spain and Finland v. European Parliament and Council*, para. 52.
75. *Spain and Finland v. European Parliament and Council*, para. 56.

the fact that at the time, the Charter was not yet legally binding. However, even without such a reference, it seems clear that the objective of protection of human health, or in light of the Charter of Fundamental Rights the right to 'working conditions which respect the worker's health and safety', can be characterized as a legitimate functionalization of private autonomy.

A similar reference to the objective of protecting human health was made to restrict economic freedoms in *Interseroh*,[76] a case about the protection of commercial secrets. Here, the Court considered that freedom to conduct a business could not cover the protection of commercial secrets to the extent of relieving shippers from the obligation to disclose information concerning the transported materials (waste), as this obligation was laid down in a directive which aimed at protecting and improving the quality of environment and human health. The Court did not explicitly undertake any balancing of rights and rather relied on the quite ambiguous argument that:

> even if the obligation to disclose the name of the waste producer to the consignee of a shipment of waste were to constitute a breach of the protection of the business secrets of intermediary dealers, that could not have the consequence of restricting the scope of a provision of secondary law that is clear and unconditional.[77]

[C] *Mohammed Aziz* (Consumer Protection)

The Court appears quite moderate in referring to fundamental rights and in applying them in private law relationships, especially when it comes to social rights which often require explicit action from the public power and as for which the Union does not even have autonomous legislative competences. Even if the Court avoids too explicit references to those rights, it still uses them at least in part in its legal reasoning. A clear example of this tendency can be found in the very recent *Aziz* case,[78] which dealt with a core area of European contract law: the unfairness of contract terms. The unfair term directive is the clearest example of a European intervention into contract law issues. Mr Aziz had concluded a loan agreement secured by a mortgage on his home, which was then seized as a result of him failing to pay the monthly instalments after he became unemployed. The seizure of his home occurred on the basis of a contract term which stipulated that the bank could immediately quantify the amount due by submitting a certificate indicating the amount. The Spanish judge sought guidance from the European Court to be able to examine the compatibility of the Spanish procedural system, which deferred the control of the fairness of the contract term to a later declaratory procedure without suspensory effect.

Thousands of Spanish consumers have been evicted from their home based on identical or similar contract terms. It is against this background that the judgment of the

---

76. *Interseroh Scrap and Metal Trading GmbH v. Sonderabfall-Management-Gesellschaft Rheinland-Pfalz mbH*, Case C-1/11 (29/3/2012).
77. *Interseroh*, para. 44.
78. *Mohamed Aziz v. Caixa d'Estalvis de Catalunya, Tarragona i Manresa (Catalunyacaixa)*, Case C-145/11 (14/3/2013).

Court should be read, when it affirms that the Spanish system does not offer adequate consumer protection stating that its reasoning:

> applies all the more strongly where, as in the main proceedings, the mortgaged property is the family home of the consumer whose rights have been infringed, since that means of consumer protection is limited to payment of damages and interest and does not make it possible to prevent the definitive and irreversible loss of that dwelling.[79]

A reference to Article 34(3) of the Charter of Fundamental Rights, to Article 31 of European Social Charter or the several international conventions which establish a right to housing is missing. Both the Court and the Advocate General avoided any reference to the Charter of Fundamental Rights, to the various social rights,[80] even to the Spanish constitution, which is quite outspoken in section 47 'All Spaniards have the right to enjoy decent and adequate housing', contrary to Article 34(3) of the Charter which vaguely proclaims that 'the Union recognizes and respects the right to social and housing assistance so as to ensure a decent existence for all those who lack sufficient resources'. What the CJEU is doing might be called 'hidden constitutionalization', in that it avoids explicitly referring to fundamental rights, whilst in practice using them to justify the restriction of private autonomy. This may suggest that the legal constitutional framework of the European Union is not yet ready to support a process of constitutionalization of private autonomy in light of the principle of the social State as it has occurred, for instance, in Germany.

[D] Interim Conclusion

If autonomy at the European level cannot be equated with the traditional idea of the freedom from the State as it has previously been shown, neither can it be said that it corresponds to the more innovative understanding of autonomy which has been developed at the national level through the application of fundamental rights in private law relations. Indeed, at the European level the judicial use of fundamental rights in issues relating to private law had different contours. These differences could certainly be explained by procedural reasons and in particular by the issue of competences of the Court of Justice, which are different and limited compared with those of national courts. The cases discussed above are still too few in number to be able to develop a comprehensive theory on the issue, but the present tendencies suggest certain hypotheses. While the Court is generally known for employing fundamental rights in its reasoning, and the most visible developments in that respect can be seen in the famous *Kadi*[81] case, in the realm of private law this development has been more nuanced. First of all, it can be noted that, as famous cases like *Omega* and also *Mesopotamia/Roj TV* reveal, the Court tends to respect fundamental rights as they are qualified at the

79. *Mohamed Aziz*, para. 61.
80. See the contributions in *Social and Labour Rights in a Global Context. International and Comparative Perspectives*, B. Hepple (ed.) (Cambridge, University Press, 2002).
81. *Yassin Abdullah Kadi and Al Barakaat International Foundation v. Council of the European Union and Commission of the European Communities*, 2008 I-06351, Case C-415/05 (3/9/2008).

national level, trying to avoid interference between European legislation and national constitutional interests. In this way, fundamental rights might serve as a side-constraint against potentially overarching economic freedoms.[82] References to fundamental rights in purely private law reasoning are on the contrary scarcer in the jurisprudence of the Court. This might also be due to the fact that only since the Treaty of Lisbon the European legal order has a clear list of explicitly formulated and legally binding fundamental rights at its disposition. More substantially, it seems that the extent to which autonomy can be instrumentalized and fundamental rights can be employed in private law reasoning depends on the different areas: the autonomy of the employee is not the same as that of the consumer. The application of (or the reference to) fundamental rights, even of what is usually understood as 'social fundamental rights', appears to be easier when the referred rights can also be based on other provisions of the Treaty: in those cases the reference to the Charter may merely serve as a supplementary reference, and it can even be wondered whether that constitutional jargon has a normative meaning of its own. The recent *Aziz* case gives occasion to suppose that the application is less explicit, but that it could still play an indirect normative role when constitutionalization concerns rights which do not fall directly within the competences of the Union. From this point of view, European regulated autonomy seems to differ from private autonomy as it has been qualified in national contexts, firstly in light of contractual justice theories and later in light of the principle of the social State. Shifting our focus to the areas which have been subject of such constitutionalization tendencies, it appears that these developments affect peripheral areas of private law rather than core areas of contract law, where the tendency to constitutionalization appears to be more covert, at least if we set aside anti-discrimination law. To confirm this observation, the next section will highlight that the strongest use of constitutional categories in private law takes place in quite different and 'innovative' areas of law, mostly those concerning the so-called information society.

§4.05 REGULATED AUTONOMY IN THE INFORMATION SOCIETY

Information and copyright law governs a large area of the modern economy and society whose importance is now becoming clear, and which also needs new instruments of regulation, because personal rights can more easily be infringed. In this context, fundamental rights acquire a new meaning and function. It does not come as a complete surprise then that this is exactly the area in which the Court of Justice has made the very outspoken use of constitutional provisions in private law relations. The express reference to the protection of intellectual property in the Charter of Fundamental Rights has facilitated a certain constitutionalization of the legal reasoning in that area, since it has made it necessary to expressly justify all the other rights and interests

82. On this aspect see A. Colombi Ciacchi, 'National and European Fundamental Rights in European Private Law: A Shield Against the Instrumentalisation of Private Law' in *European Constitutionalism without Private Law. Private Law without Democracy*, C. Joerges and T. Ralli (eds) (ARENA Report No 3/11, RECON Report No 14, Oslo, 2011).

which could infringe on the right to protection of intellectual property. But more substantially, an evolution of the internal market seems to be perceivable. While autonomy was regulated in the 1970s with the main aim of the 'common organization of the market', more recently new aspects of the internal market begun to be regulated. In an area in which technology often precedes legislation, private autonomy receives a particular importance, and it is exactly for this reason that it cannot be left alone and needs to be 'regulated' itself. Therefore, autonomy has to be adapted to facilitate the creation of a common society of information and technology. For a number of years the Commission has spoken about the emergence of an information society triggered by new technologies.[83] The Commission quickly identified the policy instruments to build and regulate that society to promote 'a competitive environment', which included the liberalization of the infrastructure in the telecommunications sector, standardization and interoperability, and also the availability of new intellectual property rights measures.[84] Copyright law was put at the centre of the discussion on the information society.[85] At the same time, this framework should provide for 'a fair balance of rights and interests between the different categories of rightholders, as well as between rightholders and rightusers'.[86] The information society does not just mean copyright protection to the extent to which this is necessary to protect economic investments; it also involves free circulation of knowledge. The Commission qualified the free movement of knowledge within the Union, qualifying this in quite suggestive terms as the 'fifth freedom' which, encouraging innovation and the spread of technologies across the Union, symbolizes the 'new frontiers' of the Internal Market.[87]

[A] Intellectual Property and Economic Freedoms

The first series of cases to be considered concern copyright law. The interaction between copyright law and fundamental rights is quite a complicated and controversial issue. While it can occasionally breach certain personal rights, intellectual property is still a particular form of private property, and as such is explicitly considered by the Charter in the same Article which provides for the right to property. At the same time, its protection is considered necessary to allow the economic compensation of intellectual professions and to protect the profitability of several industrial activities, which means that it is fundamental to the freedom to pursue a business. While private autonomy can be considered at least partially covered by the constitutional freedom of trade, its relation to the protection of copyright remains more multi-faceted. This has resulted in the case law of the Court pointing in quite different directions. In *Metronome*

83. Commission, *White paper on Growth, competitiveness, employment. The challenges and ways forwards into the 21st century*, COM(93)700, 5.12.1993.
84. Commission, *Europe's way to the information society: an action plan*, COM(94) 347 final, 19.7.1994.
85. Commission, *Green Paper on Copyright and related rights in the information society*, COM(95) 382 final, 19.7.1995.
86. Commission, *Follow-up to the green paper on copyright and related rights in the information society*, COM(96) 568 final, 1.3.
87. Commission, *A single market for 21st century Europe*, COM(2007) 724, 20.11.2007, 2.3.

the Court held that 'the general principle of freedom to pursue a trade or profession cannot be interpreted in isolation from the general principles relating to protection of intellectual property rights and international obligations entered into in that sphere by the Community and by the Member States'.[88] Directive 92/100 is said to require Member States to provide a right to authorize or prohibit the rental and lending of originals and copies of copyright works. This right, however, does not infringe the freedom to pursue a trade or profession, since the provisions of the Directive were necessary to protect industrial and commercial property. Rental rights contribute to 'guarantee that authors and performers can receive appropriate income and amortize the especially high and risky investments required particularly for the production of phonograms and films',[89] and, therefore, achieves the protection of literary and artistic property, which is one of the objectives of general interest pursued by the Community. The Advocate General was even more explicit in emphasizing that individuals can enjoy access to culture, which is qualified as a human right by several international conventions the European Union has subscribed to.[90] In later years, when the relationship between copyright law, autonomy and fundamental rights became increasingly more difficult, the Court adopted a new approach: linking autonomy and fundamental rights against excessive protection of intellectual property rights.

[B] *Promusicae*

The tendency to extend the number of fundamental rights referred to in copyright law cases – although not yet the right to conduct a business – became already clear in *Promusicae*[91]. Only a decade had passed since Metronome but already demonstrates an unbridgeable technological distance: while Metronome was about the rental of audio and video recordings, *Promusicae* was about the possibility for individuals to download music for free, thereby infringing copyright simply through using a personal computer and an internet connection. *Promusicae*, a non-profit-making organization of Spanish music producers, sought an order to require an internet access service provider to disclose the personal data of a group of users who could possibly have infringed *Promusicae*'s copyrights through the illegal downloading of music through P2P software. The internet access provider resisted the Court's order and claimed that under the Spanish legislation those data could only be disclosed for the purpose of safeguarding public security and national defence. The Spanish Court asked the European Court whether Member States are entitled under European law to limit the duty of providers of access to telecommunications services to retain and make available the data of the users of their services to criminal investigations or the safeguard of public security and national defence, especially in light of Articles 17 and 47 of the Charter of Fundamental

88. *Metronome Musik*, para. 26.
89. *Metronome Musik*, para. 22.
90. Opinion of Advocate General Tesauro, Case C-200/96 (22/1/1998) para. 12.
91. *Productores de Música de España (Promusicae) v. Telefónica de España SAU*, 2008 I-00271, Case C-275/06 (29/1/2008).

Rights, which provide protection to the right to intellectual property and establish the right to an effective remedy.

The European Directive 2002/58 protects the confidentiality of electronic communications and the related traffic data, and in general prohibits the storage of such data except for technical reasons. Article 15(1) of the Directive establishes a broad exception, allowing Member States to 'adopt legislative measures to restrict the scope of the rights and obligations' established in the Directive, among which the duty of confidentiality of traffic data:

> when such restriction constitutes a necessary, appropriate and proportionate measure within a democratic society to safeguard national security (i.e. State security), defence, public security, and the prevention, investigation, detection and prosecution of criminal offences or of unauthorized use of the electronic system, as referred to in Article 13(1) of Directive 95/46/EC.

That very Article, in turn, authorizes Member States to further restrict the obligation of confidentiality of personal data for 'the protection of the data subject or of the rights and freedoms of others', which certainly includes the economic rights of the copyright holder. The European Court concluded that European Directives allow but do not oblige Member States to impose an obligation to disclose personal data in the context of civil proceedings. At the same time, the case concerned another fundamental right too, 'namely the right that guarantees protection of personal data and hence of private life'.[92] This is clearly stated in Article 8 of the Charter. The Directive itself provides in Recital 2 that it 'seeks to respect the fundamental rights and observes the principles recognized in particular by the Charter of fundamental rights of the European Union. In particular, this Directive seeks to ensure full respect for the rights set out in Articles 7 and 8 of that Charter'.[93] Therefore the mechanism set up in the directive, which allows the Member States to restrict the obligation to confidentiality should be understood as to contribute to reconciling different fundamental rights. A fair balance of fundamental rights requires that:

> when implementing the measures transposing those directives, the authorities and courts of the Member States must not only interpret their national law in a manner consistent with those directives but also make sure that they do not rely on an interpretation of them which would be in conflict with those fundamental rights.[94]

What is needed is balancing different fundamental rights against each other, with all the problems a balancing test yields with regard to the weighing criteria.

[C] *Scarlet*

The troublesome relationship between intellectual property and personal data protection ended up in front of the European Court again in 2011, when the Court had to

92. *Promusicae*, para. 63.
93. *Promusicae*, para. 64.
94. *Promusicae*, para. 68.

decide the *Scarlet v. Sabam*[95] case. In this case, it used the freedom to conduct a business to strike a balance between the two conflicting principles. The facts are in substance identical to those of the Promusicae case. However, in *Scarlet* the copyright holder did not ask the access provider to disclose the personal data of the users, but rather to proactively prevent further infringements by making it impossible for its customers to send or receive files containing musical works covered by Sabam's copyright. This could be done by installing particular filtering systems. Scarlet claimed that such a filtering system would be ineffective and, even more importantly, would be a violation of the European rules on the storage and use of personal data. Therefore, the Court of Appeal in Brussels stayed the proceedings and asked the European Court whether the European directives, interpreted in the light of Articles 8 and 10 of the European Convention on the Protection of Human Rights and Fundamental Freedoms, which protect the right to respect for private life and the freedom of expression, permitted national Courts to order the installation of a filtering system for the prevention of copyright infringements. The Court held that an order requiring the installation of such a system would breach Article 3 Directive 2004/48, which prescribes that the measures set up by Member States to ensure the enforcement of intellectual property rights shall be 'fair and equitable and shall not be unnecessarily complicated or costly'. Moreover, they should be 'effective, proportionate and dissuasive and shall be applied in such a manner as to avoid the creation of barriers to legitimate trade'. The Court clarified that an injunction would breach European fundamental rights: even if intellectual property is a fundamental right recognized in Article 17(2) of the Charter, there is 'nothing whatsoever in the wording of that provision or in the Court's case law to suggest that that right is inviolable and must for that reason be absolutely protected'[96] and, citing *Promusicae*, that the right 'must be balanced against the protection of other fundamental rights'.[97] However, the Court added a new element going beyond *Promusicae* Whereas in that case the only other right to be balanced was the protection of personal data, in *Scarlet* the rights to be balanced are 'on the one hand, the protection of the intellectual property right enjoyed by copyright holders, and, on the other hand, that of the freedom to conduct business enjoyed by operators such as ISPs'.[98] An injunction compelling the ISP to install a costly and partially ineffective filtering system would infringe on its economic freedoms. However, this is not yet the end of the matter. The freedom of information is to be included in the balancing test. This is so because the filtering system could block lawful communications, since it could not distinguish between lawful and unlawful contents.[99] The Court put on the one side of the balance the right to intellectual property, and on the other side 'the freedom to conduct business, the right to protection of personal data and the freedom to receive or impart information'.[100] Three rights read

95. *Scarlet Extended SA v. Société belge des auteurs, compositeurs et éditeurs SCRL (SABAM)*, Case C-70/10 (24/11/2011).
96. *Scarlet*, para. 43.
97. *Scarlet*, para. 44.
98. *Scarlet*, para. 49.
99. *Scarlet*, para. 52.
100. *Scarlet*, para. 53.

together outweigh the protection of intellectual property. While the referring Court had made reference to the possible impact on the right to respect private life and freedom of expression (including the right 'to receive and impart information and ideas without interference by public authority'), the Court added a reference to the 'right to conduct a business' laid down in the Charter of Fundamental Rights as part of its judgment. The Court used the right to conduct a business to support personal fundamental rights, and in so doing decided in favour of personal data protection over intellectual property.

[D] *Netlog*

Imposing the installation of a filtering system on an ISP may turn out to be inefficiently discriminatory, costly and in breach of a number of fundamental rights. However, the situation could be different if such filters were installed more selectively, identifying those websites where copyright infringement took place. The opportunity appeared in *Netlog*[101]. Sabam also brought an action to protect the intellectual property rights of its associates against Netlog, which was the owner of an online social networking platform where registered users could, among other things, upload and listen to music. Netlog argued along the same lines as Scarlet, 'introducing such a filtering system would mean that personal data would have to be processed which would have to satisfy the provisions of EU law relating to the protection of personal data and the confidentiality of communications'.[102] The Court confirmed that while:

> the protection of the right to intellectual property is indeed enshrined in Article 17(2) of the Charter of Fundamental Rights of the European Union ('the Charter') [t]here is, however, nothing whatsoever in the wording of that provision or in the Court's case-law to suggest that that right is inviolable and must for that reason be absolutely protected.[103]

Again, an unusual alliance is established between the right to conduct a business, the right to data protection and freedom of information to prevent the imposition of a controversial filtering system which would signify a constant monitoring which 'has no limitation in time, is directed at all future infringements and is intended to protect not only existing works, but also works that have not yet been created at the time when the system is introduced'.[104]

These cases could be interpreted as an indication of a growing concern that an extensive use of copyright law could infringe the rights of users and more generally of citizens. This is in line with the strong political reaction against ACTA (Anti-Counterfeiting Trade Agreements).[105]

---

101. *Belgische Vereniging van Auteurs, Componisten en Uitgevers CVBA (SABAM) v. Netlog NV*, Case C-360/10 (16/2/2012).
102. *Netlog*, para. 24.
103. *Netlog*, para. 41.
104. *Netlog*, para. 45.
105. European Parliament legislative resolution of 4 July 2012 on the draft Council decision on the conclusion of the Anti-Counterfeiting Trade Agreement between the European Union and its Member States, Australia, Canada, Japan, the Republic of Korea, the United Mexican States, the

[E] *TV2 Danmark*

In another case in the area of the 'information society', *TV2 Danmark*,[106] the Court had the opportunity to elaborate on the relation between intellectual property and the freedom to conduct a business. Article 2 of Directive 2001/29 provides for an exclusive right for authors to authorize or prohibit direct or indirect reproduction of their work, but at the same time Article 5 allows Member States to provide exceptions or limitations to that right 'in respect of ephemeral recordings of works made by broadcasting organizations by means of their own facilities and for their own broadcasts'. The question was whether this exception covers recordings made by independent external television production companies which had been commissioned by a public radio and television broadcasting organization. The Court answered affirmatively and broadened the exception to intellectual property. It briefly mentioned fundamental rights, and stated that:

> in the assessment of the choices of interpretation available to the Court, that approach finds support in the fact that it ensures that broadcasting organisations have a greater enjoyment of the freedom to conduct a business, set out in Article 16 of the Charter of Fundamental Rights of the European Union, while at the same time not adversely affecting the substance of copyright.[107]

[F] *Sky Österreich*

In the area of TV broadcasting, the fundamental right to conduct a business was outweighed by the freedom of information. *Sky Österreich* deals with the compatibility of Article 15(6) of the Audiovisual Media Service Directive 2010/13 with Articles 16 and 17 of the Charter of Fundamental Rights. 'In order to safeguard the fundamental freedom to receive information and to ensure that the interests of viewers in the Union are fully and properly protected', as Recital 55 reads, Article 15 of the Audiovisual Media Service Directive provides that 'for the purpose of short news reports, any broadcaster established in the Union has access on a fair, reasonable and non-discriminatory basis to events of high interest to the public which are transmitted on an exclusive basis by a broadcaster under their jurisdiction'. To this end, holders of the broadcasting rights must grant broadcasters access to their signal, while Member States ensure the modalities, conditions and limits for the provision of those short extracts. Article 15(6) specifies that 'where compensation is provided for, it shall not exceed the additional costs directly incurred in providing access.' On the basis of the legislation implementing those rules, the Austrian authority for telecommunications decided that Sky, the holder of broadcasting rights for certain sport events, had to grant another broadcaster, ORF, the right to produce short news reports and that no remuneration

---

Kingdom of Morocco, New Zealand, the Republic of Singapore, the Swiss Confederation and the United States of America (12195/2011 – C7-0027/2012 – 2011/0167(NLE)).

106. *DR and TV2 Danmark A/S v. NCB - Nordisk Copyright Bureau*, Case C-510/10 (26/4/2012).

107. *TV2 Danmark*, para. 57.

was required for these reports. Sky considered this a disproportionate interference of its property rights. The European Court acknowledged that the Directive's provisions limit the freedom to exercise an economic or commercial activity, in that they restrict both the freedom to choose with whom to do business and the freedom to set the price, which are both core elements of the freedom of contract.[108] However, the usual formula applies: 'in accordance with the Court's case law, the freedom to conduct a business is not absolute, but must be viewed in relation to its social function'.[109] Freedom to conduct a business 'may be subject to a broad range of interventions on the part of public authorities which may limit the exercise of economic activity in the public interest'.[110] Any limitation to that right must comply 'with the principle of proportionality, must be necessary and actually meet objectives of general interest recognized by the European Union or the need to protect the rights and freedoms of others'.[111] In this case, the conflicting rights and interests at stake were, on the one hand, the freedom to conduct a business – covering freedom of contract – and, on the other hand, the freedom to receive information and freedom and pluralism of the media. The Court held that the limitations were proportionate, since they did not exhaust the possibilities of the right's holder to exploit the broadcasting rights, but simply provided that short reports shall be made available for free to other broadcasters to safeguard information and media pluralism. The Court confirmed its willingness to construe autonomy in the particular economic and political contexts. It appeared worried that the continuous marketization of general events on an exclusive basis could result in an increasing limitation of the fundamental right of information.[112] The Directive is said to only exclude remuneration for the preparation of reports for general news programmes, but not entertainment programmes, 'which have a much greater economic impact than general news programmes'.[113] Limitations could be justified by the need to build up an information society,in particular if the service at stake can be associated to a universal service.

Sky Österreich plainly confirms the relation between the constitutional law category of fundamental rights and the private law principle of autonomy:

> In the light, first, of the importance of safeguarding the fundamental freedom to receive information and the freedom and pluralism of the media guaranteed by Article 11 of the Charter and, second, of the protection of the freedom to conduct a business as guaranteed by Article 16 of the Charter, the European Union legislature was entitled to adopt rules such as those laid down in Article 15 of Directive 2010/13, which limit the freedom to conduct a business, and to give priority, in the necessary balancing of the rights and interests at issue, to public access to information over contractual freedom.[114]

108. *Sky Österreich*, para. 42.
109. *Sky Österreich*, para. 45.
110. *Sky Österreich*, para. 46.
111. *Sky Österreich*, para. 48.
112. *Sky Österreich*, para. 52.
113. *Sky Österreich*, para. 62.
114. *Sky Österreich*, para. 66.

[G] Interim Conclusion

The most innovative developments on the concept of private autonomy and its relation to fundamental rights and market freedoms are not found in the traditional areas of contract law, where the Court has adopted quite a humble approach towards the constitutionalization of private law, but rather in more peripheral areas of private law. These can only be considered 'peripheral' for traditional European private lawyers because in today's European economy and society those peripheral areas, the private law in regulated markets as well as IP law have come to take a central role. They regulate areas which are becoming more and more significant, not last from the perspective of the construction of the internal market. In that respect, the use of the freedom to conduct a business in copyright law, where that freedom has been used in quite unexpected ways to 'counterbalance' the constitutionalized protection of intellectual property stands for a much broader transformation process.

The a shift to constitutionalization in copyright law can be explained in different ways. First of all, the constitutionalization should be understood as a response to globalization and the role and function of the internet which in itself requires an adjustment of the changing European economic constitution.[115] Property rights are given a constitutional outlook, they have to be brought into line with the four freedoms and they have to be counterbalanced against conflicting fundamental rights. Secondly, the key actor in the process of constitutionalization is the European Court of Justice. Insofar constitutionalization enhances the role and function of the judiciary.[116] Thirdly the inclusion of freedom of trade in the Charter did not mean total protection of private autonomy. Rather, fundamental rights obligations meant to foster the creation of a European information society have been imposed on economic actors. Not much phantasy is needed to predict that further references will emerge where the freedom to conduct business via the use of property rights clashes with user rights, data protection or freedom of information. In copy right law the CJEU has begun to reconstrue private autonomy as a frame governed by conflicting fundamental rights, each with a constitutional status. This is regulated autonomy in its most explicit form.

§4.06 CONCLUSION

In contrast to what has been discussed in several national contexts, the possible constitutionalization of private autonomy has not signified the recognition of the inviolability of private autonomy by State powers, neither has it led (yet) to a reconstruction of autonomy in light of the principle of the social state, which has to a large extent driven the constitutionalization of private law. Rather, at the European level constitutionalization coincides with the functionalization of private autonomy in

115. See *Cahiers À Thème, La Constitution Économique Européenne Revisitée, Revue Internationale du Droit Economique*, (2011/4) 411-600, with contributions by J. Drexl, J. Stuyck, R.M. Hilty, M. Pallemaerts, L. Azoulai, K. Tuori
116. On 'juristrocacy', see R. Hirschl, *Towards Juristocracy. The Origin and Consequences of the New Constitutionalism* (Harvard University Press, 2004).

order to achieve the policy objectives of, first, the European Communities and, later, the Union. As a consequence, the content and the contours of the principle of autonomy in the jurisprudence of the European Court of Justice are not so easily compatible with the concepts of autonomy developed in national civil and constitutional laws. At the European level, the shift from autonomy to regulation, which can be observed also at the nation state level around the world has taken a particular and a unique form.

In order to produce/advance that functionalization, constitutionalization at the European level does not just mean protection of autonomy as such, be it to the benefit of the supplier or against the supplier to benefit of the customer, worker, citizen. European autonomy is regulated autonomy in that it serves to open up new opportunities, whilst at the same time setting boundaries to the newly gained opportunities. In order to show the interplay between opening and closing in the transnational European context, this contribution has looked into the orientations of the Court of Justice of the European Union, from its earlier judgments until the most recent cases, highlighting the different elements that have contributed to functionalization in its two forms of opening and closing. Regulated autonomy is used to steer the economic behaviour of private subjects in the direction of the policy aims of the Union. These aims have increased in number over the years, together with the extension of the competences of the EU and the legal bases for secondary legislation, as well as the entry into force of the Charter of Fundamental Rights. Therefore, reconstructing autonomy at the European level tells the story of European integration, from market integration to social regulation,[117] from the economic constitution to the many constitutions.[118]

While autonomy in the Member States was often rhetorically linked to basic fundamental freedoms, hallowed in general provisions of national constitutions or declarations of human rights, the European legal order initially embarked upon the process of marketization of autonomy. With this expression we mean not just the emphasis on the economic dimension of private autonomy, which would basically coincide with freedom of contract, but more importantly the definition of its role in the creation of a common market, which was the immediate goal of the European treaties. In the early jurisprudence of the Court of Justice in the 1970s autonomy encompassed general freedom of trade, qualified as a fundamental right drawn from the constitutional heritage of the Member States. The recognition of freedom of trade and the super-primary hierarchical position of the economic freedoms facilitated an extension of the borders of private autonomy, which became more than just a principle governing private law relationships, but a medium shaping the interaction between national citizens and their administrations. Put this way, constitutionalization processes should not be simply understood as to prevent national or European administration from regulating the economy through freedom restriction interventions. The market building

117. H.-W. Micklitz and St. Weatherill, *European Economic Law, Casebook* (London, Dartmouth, 1997).
118. K. Tuori and S. Sankari (eds), *The Many Constitutions of Europe* (Farnham, Ashgate, 2010).

process led to an extension of the boundaries of private autonomy in. The principle abandoned its purely national dimension and started to govern the relationships between subjects in different Member States, as a precondition for the establishment of a market without borders, a phenomenon which is widely recognized,[119] but has not lead to a rethinking of the concept of autonomy.

In contrast to an ideal purely liberal economic order which safeguarded the autonomy of the will of individuals, the EU system was meant to integrate markets rather than simply eliminate state intervention. Regulatory interventions of the EU could be considered to infringe the traditional interpretation of autonomy, or even on freedom of trade, as a negative freedom against Member State intrusions in the economic affairs of citizens. Reading the jurisprudence of the Court of Justice on autonomy and freedom of trade, we often find a particular dynamic: Member States adopt a wider and more liberal understanding of freedom of trade, and complain that the interventions of the EU infringed their citizens' autonomy. Despite opposition from Member States, the European Court justified the more interventionist approach of the European legislator which limited individual autonomy. The Court created a famous formula which remained unchanged, according to which limitations to a right are justifiable due to overarching public interests provided the substance of the right is left untouched. The Court has elaborated those constraints in constitutional jargon. The most evident consequences of this functionalization, at least at a conceptual level, became visible once the EU legal order pierced the veil of the Member State laws and extended the application of at least some of the free movement provisions to private subjects, on the basis of the de facto regulatory function of those subjects.[120] Individuals were directly affected, their private autonomy mutated into regulated autonomy.

The more the European Union embarked into new fields of law and policy, the more the CJEU became involved in areas where it could not restrict itself to weighing national freedoms against European freedoms, but to balance Europeanized freedoms with different policy objectives. From the perspective of private autonomy most of the research so far was dedicated to consumer law, labour law and in particular anti-discrimination law. Setting aside anti-discrimination, the analysis suffers from a national bias, in other words constitutionalization of private autonomy was very much discussed as a national phenomenon - e.g. in consumer law, or as a shield of national social policies against a European market driven ideology - labour and employment law. This contribution cannot carry out successfully an analysis of the case law of the

119. P.-C. Müller-Graff, 'Basic Freedoms - Extending Party Autonomy across Borders' in *Party Autonomy and the role of Information in the Internal Market*, S. Grundmann, W. Kerber, S. Weatherill (eds) (Berlin, Walter de Gruyter, 2001) 133-150.

120. *Union Royale Belge des Sociétés de Football Association ASBL v. Jean- Marc Bosman and others*, 1995 ECR I-4921, Case C-415/93 (15/12/1995) .The literature is vast, most recently, see among others, H. Schepel, 'Constitutionalising the Market, Marketising the Constitution, and to Tell the Difference: On the Horizontal Application of the Free Movement Provisions in EU Law' (2012) 10 *European Law Journal* 177-200; B. van Leeuwen, 'An Illusion of Protection and an Assumption of Responsibility: The Possibility of Swedish State Liability after Laval' (2012) 14 *Cambridge Yearbook of European Legal Studies* 453-473.

CJEU in all the different areas. In order to make our argument, but nevertheless demonstrating the implications of the ever growing fields of European policies for the shaping of regulated autonomy, we have chosen three areas condensed in three key policy fields – freedom of information, health and safety at work and consumer protection. This might sound rather arbitrary, but it has to be recalled that we have been looking in particular in cases, in which private autonomy in one way or the other came to the fore, directly or indirectly.

It appears that while Member States justified restrictions on autonomy on the basis of the public good clause, which can be found in several constitutions and has occasionally been interpreted in different ways by national courts,[121] the European Court usually directly referred to the policy objectives of the EU and the reasons for market and social regulation. This is self-explanatory and reflects the balancing process which was triggered by the wave of regulation in the aftermath of the Single European Act. The particular focus of our contribution gives the well-known debate a new twist. The freedom to do business as the starting point has to be confronted with conflicting fundamental rights, as enshrined in the different policy areas. The degree to which fundamental rights play a role differs according to policy field. Free speech has a clear fundamental rights dimension, health and safety at work to some extent, consumer protection only indirectly. The bottom-line of the case law is that that economic freedoms cannot always prevail and that, although a hierarchy between economic freedoms and fundamental rights is not possible, fundamental rights common to the Member States (but interpreted in the particular light of the legal tradition of those states) can occasionally limit those economic freedoms.

From diversification of policies to fragmentation is only a small step. Although it is certainly too early to say with certainty what the impact of the Treaty of Lisbon on private law relationships and autonomy could be, those legal bases have made a new functionalization of autonomy possible. After having used autonomy as an instrument to safeguard personal rights in several cases on the protection of intellectual property, the Court has come to strongly regulate even the freedom to set prices in cases on the information society. One of the reasons behind this evolution could be the recognition of the role of the 'information society' in the internal market. The realization of an integrated information society and market has become one of the new policy aims of the Union, combined of course with the realization of the internal market in the more traditional sense (so that the line of reasoning inaugurated in older cases which have been discussed in this contribution may still be found in more recent decisions). It should not go unnoticed that the CJEU allowed Italy in *Federutility* to define the energy prices for private customers, though without invoking fundamental rights or the like.[122] Both TV services and energy services bear a universal services dimension. Access to the services is key for the participation of the citizens in the economic and social life.

121. For Italy, see, with references to older cases, Corte Costituzionale 270/2010 (23/6/2010).
122. *Federutility and Others v. Autorità per l'energia elettrica e il gas*, 2010 I-03377, Case C-265/08 (20/4/2010).

In sum, private autonomy has received some kind of quasi-constitutional recognition at the EU level through the four freedoms and the recognition of a freedom to trade, which has eventually evolved into the freedom to conduct a business expressed in the Charter of Fundamental Rights. The marketization of autonomy meant to open up access to the Internal Market is outweighed by the increased instrumentalization of fundamental rights to set boundaries to an unrestricted opening. The result of the process is what we have termed regulated autonomy.

CHAPTER 5

European Law versus Private Law: Transformation or Deformation of the Paradigm?

Marek Safjan

§5.01 PRELIMINARY REMARKS

With a high degree of confidence we can say that today, due to the expansion of community instruments, private law in an integrated Europe has created an entirely different context from the one which existed several decades ago. The influence of European law is visible not only in specific solutions adopted in private law, but also in the methodology that imposes a certain style of legal interpretation which must ensure the co-existence of various systems. Pluralism of the systems which make up the body of modern private law does not entail parallel autonomous systems with clearly delineated boundaries of competence, but a much more complex structure. Contemporary pluralism, or systemic multi-centrism, requires that law should be applied in a way that allows for its simultaneous evaluation from the point of view of various ideologies, objectives and of a different hierarchy of principles.[1]

Evolution of private law, understood as a gradual change of a methodological perspective, ever more important differences in axiological premises, and changes of reference point in the process of reconstruction of an appropriate norm, is unquestionable. Are the changes which have already transformed considerable areas of private law like, for example, the sale of consumer goods, competition, intellectual property

1. Cf. in this question *inter alia* F. Cafaggi, H. Muir–Watt, Making European Private Law: Governance Design, (Edward Elgar Publishing 2008); S. Weatherill, European Private law between positive and negative integration: an assessment of the impact of the case law of the European Court of Justice on national private law, (Working paper, Florence 2009).

protection or liability for damages caused by a state institution so significant as to be called revolutionary? Has a new paradigm of private law, based on 'community' axiology, been accepted? It seems such a conclusion would still be premature. Nonetheless, definitely at the present stage of the development of European law, new challenges appear, which – should they reinforce current tendencies – may accelerate the evolution of private law. So perhaps we are on the verge of a revolution?

§5.02 A NEW PARADIGM OF EUROPEAN PRIVATE LAW

A new paradigm of European private law is often sought in the concept of social justice in private law. This new direction in thinking about private law has been most thoroughly expressed so far in 'Manifesto'.[2] The document entitled, 'Study Group on Social Justice in European Private Law' says *inter alia*, 'The modern statement of the principle of the private law of contract needs to recognize its increasingly pivotal role in establishing distributive fairness in society'.[3] It is not surprising that the starting point for this approach is 'the issue of fairness or social justice. [As a matter of fact,] the chosen market order has to embrace and protect a distributive pattern of outcomes, that ensures fair treatment for every European citizen and guarantees that the rules of the market system do not permit exploitation and social exclusion'.[4]

This tendency is accompanied by a trend which could be called a 'global law paradigm'. It focuses on a person holding universal and inalienable rights, both as an individual and as a member of a community, or – finally – as a member of global humanity. The individual is the subject of law in the broadest sense, overcoming the traditional division between public and private law. To quote Rafael Domingo: 'The Law is ever personal, relating to a specific person (the individual dimension), to a group of persons (the social dimension), or the entirety or totality of persons, that is to say, humanity as a whole (the universal dimension)',[5] and that is why 'The global human community leads to a new global legal paradigm for this reality, one that is pan-human in nature, and goes beyond the international statist paradigm'.[6] The leading idea underlying this concept as it exists in EU law assumes that the legal relationships between individuals are affected by the rules and values coming from other types of relationships, i.e., those which refer to social groups, and those which concern the human community as a whole. The interdependencies between these relationships are multilateral because:

> [t]he three dimensions are interrelated as they are all essentially personal (i.e. deal with human beings), but are quantitatively distinct. When the individual legal dimension does not take into consideration the social dimension of the laws, one

2. Cf. Study Group, Social Justice in European Contract Law: A Manifesto, vol. 10 No. 6 ELJ, 653–674 (November 2004).
3. M. Bianca, H. Collins, S. Grundman (President), E. Hondius, S. Stijns, Manifesto, Study Group on Social Justice in European Private Law [in] The Politics of a European Civil Code, 185 (ed. by M.W. Hesselink, Kluwer Law International, 2006).
4. *Ibid.*, 184.
5. R. Domingo, Gaius, Vattel, and the New Global Law Paradigm, vol. 22 no. 3 EJIL 211, 627-647.
6. *Ibid.*, 629.

> rapidly falls into legal (or judicial) individualism. There, law becomes gradually closed to the idea of solidarity with others in the human family. Alternatively, when the social dimension does not properly consider laws' universal dimension, it easily leads to imperialism, which aims to impose the rules and outlook of a specific political community on the global community, or part thereof. If the universal dimension of law fails to recognize the other dimensions (individual and social), personal rights are suffocated and suppressed, and self-government of institutions is paralysed. Subsidiarity is not respected, turning the world into a sort of centralized and standardized legal wilderness 'where one size fits all'. This is ultimately incompatible with the true role of law and the respect for the individual that it entails.[7]

This way not only the traditional paradigm based on a clear division between the spheres of public and private law is overcome, but also it seems that, in consequence, the regulatory function of the instruments of traditional private law is changed. The relationships between individuals can show individual needs and interests, provided that the value of people's cooperation is respected in the social and global sense. The proposals of Rafael Domingo try to conciliate two different approaches to the role played by private law instruments. An essential value of the concept is to indicate mutual interdependencies between 'two faces' of modern private law. None of them is more important than the other. It means that too strong an attachment either to individual rights' protection or to the social dimension can raise the risk of deformation of the function of private law. In fact, the problem is not as to whether two faces of private law are necessary (this question seems to be rhetorical), but where should the point of balance be sought, and how can a correct proportion between 'individualistic' and 'social' factor in private law be ensured. Does that point exist? I will here try to explore some elements of this issue and to formulate a few hypotheses related to the presence of social and public dimension in European private law. A short analysis seems to be necessary to diagnose whether the potential risk of infringement of the equilibrium between two faces of private law exists in European law. This gives rise to several questions:

(1) Can exactly the same motif which is present in classical debates on equity in private law be found in the contemporary discussion on 'social justice in private law'?
(2) Is the current introduction of contemporary 'social justice' into private law an element of a 'socialist' experiment – to wit, from relatively recent experience – which systematically tries to eliminate the division between private and public law?
(3) Is the tendency toward social justice in private law an intrinsic feature of European law or is it rooted in national legal systems, which are more and more oriented towards the constitutionalization of all branches of law? Is the constitutionalization of private law in line with expectations connected to the introduction of 'social dimension' into private law?

7. *Ibid.*, 644.

(4) Are the directions of the evolution of private law in national legal systems actually convergent with the trends within European law? Or, in the field of European private law, should one rather speak about vectors acting in many different directions?

Only when these questions are answered (sections §5.02[A] to §5.02[D] below) can a rational debate be started on the appropriate methodology to create European private law and to reconcile the present tendencies with the traditional functions of civil law.

[A] Traditional Justice versus Social Justice

The idea of equity in private law is as old as the oldest structures of private law rooted in Roman law. At least since the times of Ulpian the rule *lex est ars boni et aequi* has been considered an essential feature of legal relationships between individuals, while the Roman concept of *iniustum ius* was, in fact, a model for the contemporary doctrine of 'abuse of rights'. The idea of introducing into law of an equity corrective factor which limits the autonomy of the will and freedom of legal relationships for the sake of 'fairness' is firmly based on the oldest traditions of private law. The discussion on social justice in law did not start in the twentieth century when European law 'exploded'; as an example the trend represented by Leon Duguit[8] can be mentioned, or an opposite position, that of Marcel Planiol or Georges Ripert,[9] who defended the inviolable corpus of the principles of private law. If, today, it is required that private law more often absorbs the values of social solidarity such as justice and equality or protection of the weaker party to the contract, does it mean a fundamental, qualitative change, a 'Copernican revolution' in private law, or rather a natural phase in the development of the same idea which was already present a long time ago?

Apparently, arguments in favour of the first alternative prevail. Firstly, the postulated move towards social justice, publicisation, constitutionalization of private law is much more fundamental than the application of traditional instruments restoring equity in private law. 'Social justice', or 'constitutionalization', is, therefore, not a simple or even only a bit broader 'equity correction' applied to the relationships established within the framework of private law, but it is done with the help of different

8. Cf. Leon Duguit: 'The legal norm which governs people does not have at its basis respect or protection of non-existent individual rights or a manifestation of individual will, which in itself cannot have any social impact. Its basis is the fundament of a social structure, a necessity to maintain the community between different social factors by fulfilling a social function by each individual, by each social group' (Source: the Polish edition of Kierunki rozwoju prawa cywilnego od początku XIX wieku, 26-30 (Warsaw, 1938)). See also Leon Duguit, Préface à la deuxième édition du Traité de droit Constitutionnel (Paris 1920): 'La construction juridique individualiste, subjectiviste et métaphysique, qui par la révolution nous est venue de Rome et de la scolastique médiévale, a fait son temps, qu'il est impossible de plier aux vieux cadres les relations si complexes, si variées, naissant aujourd'hui entre les individus et les collectivités, et qu'il faut définitivement bannir de la jurisprudence les concepts métaphysiques de substance, du sujet de droit, de droit subjectif, sources de controverses sans fin, épuisantes et stériles'.
9. Cf. M. Planiol et G. Ripert, Traité Pratique de droit civil français t. VI, Obligations (Paris: LGDJ Pichon & Durand-Auzias 1952). See also G. Ripert, Le déclin du droit (Études sur la législation contemporaine (Paris: LGDJ 1949).

methods and has, in fact, a different objective. 'Equity correction' is, by nature, done *in casu and a posteriori* with regard to the existing individual legal relationships. Constitutionalization, on the other hand, is a process which pervades all the structures on which the legal system is built, including civil law. More and more frequently, it is an independent motif of the lawmaker's interference, meant to create protective instruments aimed at the protection of certain groups such as consumers, tenants, employees, the elderly or young people, etc. At the same time, constitutionalization presupposes a different method of establishing the sense and content of the binding legal norm, which should express an obligation to respect a certain axiology and an appropriate hierarchical structure of norms. In the traditional concept, 'equity correction' is in a sense an exception while, in the modern concept, the 'quest for justice' (in accordance with a well-established constitutional axiology) is a rule and a universal duty also addressed to the lawmaker.[10]

[B] Socialist Lesson

It can therefore be assumed that the postulate of social justice and constitutionalization is a call for a radical change in the paradigm of private law, which was supposed to ensure the freedom and autonomy of the parties, and not the achievement of goals and values external to the parties of a legal relationship. The tendencies to publicize private law, which seem to question its autonomous goals and values and to blur the division between private and public law, are nothing new in the history of the twentieth century. Being aware of all the differences, we must not forget an experiment carried out for decades in Eastern and Central Europe which systematically undermined the idea of private law and its status as a branch of law independent from public law, elevating to an axiological rank the superiority of public and community interest over the interest of individuals regulating their relations by means of private law relationships. Naturally, we must not forget that at that time public interest was very often identified with the interest of the state or of the communist party.[11] Therefore, simple comparison between a 'vulgar publicisation' experienced in communist countries and the request to introduce social justice into private law in modern Europe would be a considerable and totally unsubstantiated simplification. However, to some extent the lesson learnt from that 'experiment' may be useful and instructive in as much as it shows that there is an impassable border to the interference with private law, beyond which there is a risk of damaging the core of its structures. Breaking the 'correct' proportions between the protection of public and individual interests may lead to a deep deformation of private law mechanisms.

10. Cf. A. Clapham, Human Rights in the Private Sphere (Oxford-New York 1993); C.W. Canaris, Grundrechte und Privatrecht (Berlin-New York 1999); Human Rights in Private Law (ed. D. Friedmann, D. Barak-Erez, Oxford-Portland 2001); The Constitution in Private Relations: Expanding Constitutionalism (ed. A. Sajo, R. Uitz, The Hague 2005).
11. Cf. O.S. Ioffe and M.W. Janis, Soviet law and economy (Dordrecht: Nijhoff, 1987); O.S. Ioffe, Soviet civil law (Dordrecht: Nijhoff, 1988).

[C] 'National' Constitutionalization *versus* 'European' Constitutionalization

For a few decades, in a Europe which experienced war and totalitarianism, there has been constitutionalization of legal systems, including private law. This has been done by means of pro-constitutional interpretation, an application of the Constitution in the assessment of the horizontal relationship, including the technique of '*Drittwirkung*',[12] i.e., the introduction of constitutional axiology by means of new, adaptive private law regulations. The new approach based on constitutional values has been included gradually in the field of private law: from labour law and employees' protection through the protection of consumers, tenants and many other individuals being a weaker and non-professional party, to such basic civil law categories as property. Needless to say, the mechanisms of constitutional 'radiation' were much different from the classical instruments of restoring equity in private law in respect of the individual legal relationship, and they resembled a phenomenon which, nowadays, is most often called 'social justice in private law'. It is, therefore, clear that due to the impact exerted by these trends, private law in contemporary EU Member States looks quite different to that of the first half of the twentieth century.

It would not, therefore, be correct to assume that a particular 'social touch' – a phenomenon noted in contemporary European private law – is an exclusive manifestation and effect of the axiology promoted in the area of European law. It derives, at least partially, from the spirit of transformation taking place in national legal systems as a result of long, gradual evolution, while the pro-social tendencies oriented towards solidarity, justice and protection of the human dignity, visible in some segments of European law, are a certain sublimation of the phenomena rooted in national legal systems, even though, today, they are based on autonomous sources of European law.

[D] Specific Features of European Private Law: New Trends

This leads us to an essential question as to whether one could justify a thesis about the specific character of the development of European private law as opposed to the phenomena so clearly visible in national systems.

Undoubtedly, the phenomena and tendencies occurring now in European law and in national legal systems are, to some extent, convergent. This refers *inter alia* to the social justice (or constitutionalization) in private law, and is also reflected in the discussion about the horizontal effect of fundamental rights in European law, which is equally animated in national legal systems.[13]

12. Canaris, Grundrechte.
13. Cf. O.O. Cherednychenko, Fundamental Rights. Contract Law and the Protection of the Weaker Party. A Comparative Analysis of the Constitutionalisation of Contract Law, with Emphasis on Risky Financial Transaction (München 2007); Human Rights and the Private Sphere. A comparative Study (ed. D. Oliver, J. Fedtke, London-New York 2007); Ch. Mak, Fundamental Rights and European Contract Law. A comparison of the Impact of Fundamental Rights on Contractual Relationships in Germany, the Netherlands, Italy and England (The Hague 2008). See also M. Safjan, P. Mikłaszewicz, Horizontal effect of the general principles of EU law in the

[1] Fundamental Rights and the Horizontal Effect in European Private Law

In its famous *Defrenne* case, the European Court of Justice concluded that the prohibition on discrimination between men and women applies not only to the action of public authorities, but also extends to all agreements which are intended to regulate paid labour collectively, as well as contracts between individuals.[14] A tendency towards this approach can also be found in later judgments of the European Court of Justice.[15] A question arose as to whether certain contractual clauses, i.e., clauses adopted on the basis of freedom of contract and autonomy of the parties, may limit the influence of fundamental freedoms stipulated in the Treaty related to the free movement of persons. Following this path would mean enhancing the 'reversal of paradigm' of private law by adding 'heterogeneous implants', representing an approach different from that of classical civil law, which is based on individual evaluation of private interest. There are, however, important reasons for which this approach is considered fully justified. It is compliant with the concept of effective application of European law, which should operate in all types of legal relationships,[16] and, in consequence, in the sphere of horizontal relationships.

The entry into force of the Charter of Fundamental Rights undoubtedly strengthens the importance of the protection of fundamental rights in the sphere of European law. Although the protection of human rights has long been considered in the case law of the European Court of Justice as a necessary element of general principles,[17] the

sphere of private law, no. 3 ERPL, 475 ff. (2010); Cf. M. Safjan, Efekt horyzontalny praw podstawowych w prawie prywatnym: autonomia woli a zasada równego traktowania, no. 2 KPP, 297 ff. (2009); M. Szpunar, Odpowiedzialnoćć..., especially 104 ff.; Cf. also J. KrzemińskaVamvaka, Horizontal effect of fundamental rights and freedoms - much ado about nothing? German, Polish and EU theories compared after Viking Line, J. Monnet, Working Paper 11/09, http://centers.law.nyu.edu/jeanmonnet/.

14. Defrenne, Case 43/75, ECR (1976) 455, par. 39 (ECJ 8 April 1976). It is an example of direct application of a Treaty principle set out in Art. 157 TFEU (ex Art. 141 TEC). A characteristic example of application of the non-discrimination principle on grounds of age in connection with labor relations is the judgment in Mangold, Case C-144/04, ECR (2005) I-9981, (ECJ 22 November 2005). It illustrates a possibility of adopting a far fetched approach towards the 'horizontal application' of a directive provided it includes a precision of a principle of EU law or extension of a fundamental right in a certain sphere of relationships, despite a coherent jurisprudence delimiting the horizontal effect of directives, cf. e.g. Pfeiffer, C-397-403/01, (2004) ECR I-8835, (ECJ 5 October 2004); Carp, C-80/06, (2007) ECR I-4473, (ECJ 7June 2007).
15. Cf. e.g. Union royale belge des sociétés de football association *ASBL v. Bosman*, Case C-415/93, (1995) ECR I-4921, (ECJ 15 December 1995); Schmidberger, Case C-112/00, (2003) ECR I-5659, (ECJ 12 June 2003); Omega Spielhallen, Case C-36/02, (2004) ECR. I-9609, (ECJ 14 October 2004); International Transport Workers' Federation et Finnish Seamen's Union (Viking Line), Case C-438/05, (2007) ECR I-10779, (ECJ 11 December 2007); *Olympique Lyonnais SASP v. Olivier Bernard and Newcastle UFC*, Case C-325/08, (2010) I-2177, (ECJ 16 March 2010).
16. Such is among others the argument of N. Reich, Rights without duties? Reflections on the State of Liability Law in Multilevel Governance System of the Community: Is there a need for a more coherent approach in European Private Law, EUI Working Papers, LAW 2009/2010, cf. footnote 26.
17. Cf. e.g. Hauer, Case C-44/79, (1979) ECR. 3727, (ECJ 13 December 1979); ERT, Case C-260/89, (1991) ECR I-2925 (ECJ 18 June 1991); Schmidberger, Case C-112/00, (2003) ECR I-5659, (ECJ 12 June 2003); Familiapress, Case C-368/95,(1997) ECR I-3689, (ECJ 26 June 1997); *Connolly*

present catalogue of fundamental rights, which have the status of primary law, may change the perspective and add new quality to the axiology expressed in the Charter. It seems that in the process of enlarging the field of application of fundamental rights into the sphere of private law relationships, a special role will be played by the principles of non-discrimination and equality stipulated in the Charter of Fundamental Rights (Articles 20 and 21) in a general way, and, therefore, larger than in ex Article 12 TEC (Article 18 TFEU), which prohibits discrimination on the grounds of nationality.[18] Application of this principle gives the greatest opportunity to interfere with private law relationships, and carries the biggest risk of diminishing the importance of a decisive factor for such relationships. As was mentioned above, for many years this trend has been present in the case law of the European Court of Justice in the context of legal relationships traditionally marked by the idea of weak party protection i.e., labour law[19] or consumer.[20]

However, we must not forget that the effective protection of fundamental freedoms guaranteed by the Treaty requires strict application of the principle of non-discrimination, which has a direct impact on the sphere of economic activity i.e., also on private law relationships, and may increase the distance between these segments of EU law and the traditional model of private law, ensuring a much greater freedom for the individual market participants. The problem of relationship between fundamental rights and fundamental freedoms granted by the Treaty has not yet been clearly addressed in the case law but some issues related to it appeared in *Schmidberger*[21] and *Viking Line*[22] cases. The question of hierarchy of protected values and the respective position of the autonomy of the parties and freedom of contract which are enshrined in fundamental rights is of primary importance. Paradoxically, the entry into force of the Charter of Fundamental Rights, may question the thesis of absolute superiority of fundamental freedoms granted by the Treaty over the autonomy of individuals in private law relationships, especially if we take into consideration the fact

v. Commission, Case C-274/99 (2001) ECR I-1611 (ECJ 6 March 2001); Omega Spielhallen, Case C-36/02, (2004) ECR I-9609, (ECJ 14 October 2004).

18. Although ECJ's case law approached Art. 12 TEC (new Art. 18 TFEU) broadly and flexibly, cf. e.g. Sotgiu, Case 152/73, (1974) ECR 153, (ECJ 12 February 1974); Gravier, Case 293/83, (1985) ECR 593, (ECJ 13 February 1985); Grzelczyk, Case C-184/99, (2001) ECR I-6193, (ECJ 20 September 2001); Baumbast et R, Case C-413/99, (2002) ECR I-7091, (ECJ 17 September 2002); Bressol and Chaverot, Case C-73/08, (2010) ECR I-2735, (ECJ 13 April 2010). Cf. Also F. Sudre, Droit communautaire des droits fondamentaux, (Bruylant 2007). See also A. Hartkamp, European Law and National Private Law, secs. 53-54 (Wolters Kluwer 2012).
19. Cf. ECJ judgments referring to the principle of non-discrmination in labour relations, see e.g. ECJ judgments: Defrenne, Case 43/75, (1976) ECR 455, (ECJ 8 April 1976); Mangold, Case C-144/04, (2005) ECR I-9981, (ECJ 22 November 2005); Maruko, Case C-267/06, (2008) ECR I-1757, (ECJ 1 April 2008); Seda Kücükdeveci, Case C-555/07, (2010) ECR I-365, (ECJ 19 January 2010).
20. The concept of consumer protection is based on the assumption of restoring balance between parties to a contract, cf. H. Schulte-Nölke, The EC consumer law compendium: a pan-European knowledge base for politicans, business and consumer organizations 20 Eur. bus. law rev. 383, (2009); H-W. Micklitz, Understanding EU consumer law (Antwerp: Intersentia, C2009); F. Cafaggi, New frontiers of consumer protection: the interplay between private and public enforcement (Antwerp: Intersentia, C2009).
21. Cf. Schmidberger, Case C-112/00, (2003) ECR I-5659, (ECJ 12 June 2003).
22. Cf. International Transport Workers' Federation and Finnish Seamen's Union (Viking Line), Case C-438/05, (2007) ECR I-10779, (ECJ 11 December 2007).

that, as mentioned above, the freedom of contract is undoubtedly also protected by the Charter, especially as inalienable part of the general guarantees provided by the Article 6 (right to liberty).[23]

Axiology expressed in the general principles of EU law and in the Charter creates the framework for implementation of the idea of social justice in European law through lawmaking in the areas which lie within the scope of Union competence.[24] The most characteristic manifestation of the 'protectionist' tendency is, without a doubt, and as we have already mentioned, the position presented in the famous 'Manifesto', which directly proposes the application of the model of distributive fairness in private law as a model which reflects EU constitutional principles.[25]

Of particular interest are the instruments of consumer law, including those which regulate unfair terms. The concept of unfair terms adopted in European consumer law,[26] and reinforced in the case law of the European Court of Justice, led not only to the transformation of the traditional understanding of equity clauses (clauses of good faith and good practice) in national systems, but to a special petrification of behavioural patterns.[27] At the same time, in the context of open and often insufficiently precise concepts of European legislation, therefore the development of the correct practice in this area is currently in the sphere of the responsibility of the European Court of Justice.[28] The concept of *unfair terms* adopted in this field seems to have an influence on the evolution of these notions in other domains of private law, including those outside the field of consumer transactions.[29]

23. Cf. M. Safjan, P. Mikłaszewicz, Horizontal effect of the general principles of EU law in the sphere of private law, no. 3 Eur Rev Priv L, 475 ff. (2010).
24. Against this background there is a debate on the scope of application in private law of the concept of distributive fairness - characteristic for social law - which often occurs to the detriment of classical solutions of contract equity. In my opinion, those who would like to maintain clear difference between the distributive function and contract equity are right. Cf. e.g. M. Meli, Social Justice, Constitutional Principles and Protection of the Weaker Contractual Party, conference proceedings, no. 2 ERCL, 164 ff. (2006); cf. also R. Sefton-Green, Social Justice and European Identity in European Contract Law, no. 2 ERCL, 274 ff. (2006). Cf. also H. Schepel, The Enforcement of EC Law in Contractual Relations: Case Studies in How Not to 'Constitutionalize' Private Law, no. 5 Eur Rev Priv L, 661 ff. (2004).
25. Cf. Study Group on Social European Private Law, Social Justice in European Contract Law: A Manifesto, no. 10 ELJ, 653 ff. (2004).
26. Cf. here Directive 2005/29/EC of the European Parliament and of the Council concerning unfair business-to-consumer commercial practices in the internal market (11 May 2005), OJ 2005 L 149/22–39.
27. Cf. here the question of Hans-W. Micklitz (Jack is out of the box – the Efficient Consumer -Shopper, no. 3–4 JFT, 435 [2009]) if such concepts as good faith, good practices and equity can be still used to protect the consumer in a way which is different from the one adopted in the EU. The concept of full harmonisation of protection in the field of unfair market practices seems to exclude such a possibility.
28. Cf. to illustrate this thesis, how complicated consequences may arise here with respect of the division of competences between the ECJ and national justice systems see Oceano Groupo Editorial and Salvat Editores, Cases C–240/98 to C–244/98, (2000) ECR I-4941, (ECJ 27 June 2000); and Freiburger Kommunalbauten, C-237/02, (2004) ECR I–3403, (ECJ 1 April 2004).
29. Cf. G. Teubner, Legal Irritations: Good Faith in British Law or How Unifying Law Ends Up in New Divergences, vol. 61 MLR, 11 ff. (1998); cf. also Association Henri Capitant des Amis de la Culture Juridique Francaise, Terminologie Contractuelle Commune, 223 ff.(ed. B. Fauvarque-Cosson, Denis Mazeaud, Paris 2008). See also V. Trstenjak, E. Beysen, European Consumer Protection Law: Curia simper dabit remedium, 48/2011 CMLRev 95, 95-124 (2011).

[2] *Objectives of the European Union versus the Principles of Private Law*

A separate phenomenon, which has to be seen as a specific feature of European private law, is related to the fact that the mechanisms of European private law are dominated by the goals to which the European Union aspires as a separate, autonomous legal and political body. The classical instruments of private law on national levels are supposed to regulate the behaviour of individual market participants. First of all they allow for the expression of various individual interests, however, they also protect freedom and autonomy, at the same time, respecting the value of public order, equity and common good. It has become clear that the goals of these two orders are not the same. The starting point for the regulatory instruments of classical private law is an individual and its autonomy; while the starting point for the European regulatory instruments including the sphere of private law are specific aims related in particular to the Treaty freedoms and to the principles on which the European legal order is based, that is eg. the priority, effectiveness and unity of European law. In the latter case, 'private law' mechanisms seem to be deprived of their own autonomous objectives and they are becoming a necessary instrument to achieve the superior aims of the common market.[30]

I fully realized this whilst working as a reporting judge on a recently-settled case *Volvo Car*,[31] in which ECJ had to deal with a question about the interpretation of a dealership agreement in German law from the perspective of a European directive relating to self-employed commercial agents. A preliminary reference from the German Supreme Court was apparently simple. It concerned a refusal to grant compensation due to the agent after expiry of the agreement which was terminated according to contractual notice, after which it appeared that the dealer had failed to comply with his contractual obligations. The directive envisages a refusal to grant compensation if the principal has terminated the agency contract because of default attributable to the commercial agent. This hypothesis, however, was not met since the principal learnt about the wrongful behaviour of the agent only after the agreement had ended. Is it acceptable to refuse compensation using an analogy justified by equity, which is one of the methods commonly accepted in classical private law, and which was supported by the case law of the German Federal Tribunal? The European Court of Justice chose defending the freedom of 'undistorted' competition, hence limiting flexible application of the principles which could lead to an unequal competitive position of entities operating in the market in similar situations. The clash of the concepts of classical law (analogy and equity) with European law appears here with all its strength. In high probability, we can assume that this situation would be assessed differently on the basis of national law alone.[32]

30. Regardless of the fact that the concept of the common market assumes freedom and autonomy of entities operating on the market.
31. *Cf. Volvo Car Germany v. Autohof Weidensdorf GmbH*, Case C-203/09, (2010) ECR I-10721, (ECJ 28 October 2010).
32. However, see also A. Hartkamp, European Law and National Private Law (Wolters Kluwer 2012). The author stressed that the case law of the ECJ is very careful with regard to the

Another example of such an approach are the rulings in *Bosman*[33] or *Olympique Lyonnais*[34] cases, in which the restrictions imposed by the contract are not analysed from the perspective of the protection of freedom of contract but from the point of view of the protection of the principle of free movement of persons. Likewise, interference with the institution of 'golden share' is based not only on an abstract postulate of freedom of economic entities, but rather on the desire to ensure the free movement of capital.[35]

In my opinion, the phenomenon described here shapes the perspective of European private law quite differently from traditional private law: it places it closer to public law by adopting a different scale and hierarchy of values.

On the one hand, autonomy of the parties, freedom of contract and formal equality of entities give priority to the tendencies leading de facto to the levelling of the position of market participants, and ensure that all barriers to the common market are eliminated.

On the other hand, we observe a special 'protectionist leaning' of European law with respect to certain categories of entity in accordance with the systems of values which allude to the idea of a social market economy.

The demarcation line that divides public from private law in the European sphere often becomes invisible, while the mutual blending of mechanisms and methods typical for each of these domains is considered as inevitable, and closely related to the nature of the concepts of European law.

These two factors strongly characterize the present condition of European private law. At the same time, we must not forget the fact that these special features concern only certain segments of private law: those which lie within the scope of the application of the European law. We can formulate a hypothesis that this selective impact on EU private law makes the trajectories of the development of private law on the national level and on the EU level different.

[3] At Which Point Are We?

It seems that a thesis may be put forward that the evolution of European private law is not a simple reflection of the tendencies occurring on a national level, nor is it a special 'compilation' of the activity focused on social justice in private law or constitutionalization of private law in individual Member States. European law, let me stress – has its own goals and functions – defined up to now, equally, by the protectionist and pro-social tendencies, as well as by attempts to eliminate barriers blocking fundamental freedoms, on which the efficient operation of the common market depends. We often see that these goals not always bring forth identical results.

---

freedoms that are only intended to ban discrimination, but have developed into general prohibitions on restrictions (sec. 34).

33. Bosman, Case C-415/93, (1995) ECR I-4921, (ECJ 15 December 1995).
34. Olympique Lyonnais, Case C-325/08, (2010) ECR I-2177, (ECJ 16 March 2010).
35. *Commission v. Republic of Portugal*, Case C-543/08, (2010) ECR I-11241, (ECJ 11 November 2010).

Therefore, European law is affected by vectors acting in many different directions, which result from the nature of legal instruments applied in this area by the EU institutions which pursue their independent, autonomous goals regardless of the functions typical for the usual path of private law development and, therefore, oriented towards equilibrating individuals' interest by means of autonomy of the parties and contractual freedom. Therefore, is it not reasonable to think that orienting private law in the EU towards the goals which lie outside the field of private law leads to an infringement of the correct proportions between the social-public factor and the element originating in the autonomy of individuals and, in consequence, to a deformation of the private law paradigm?

The reason for this situation is that - as mentioned above - the interventions of the European lawmaker and ECJ's case law in this field are selective and occurring, somehow, 'by the way' and, therefore, partial. They are not in line with the postulate of coherent, cohesive, and 'subordinated to common goals' assumptions and clear the axiological construction of legal mechanisms making up this area of law. The reasons for this are well known and widely described in legal literature. To a great extent, they are linked to an unresolved dispute about the range of EU competences in the area of private law.[36] However, the problem remains.

In consequence, the construction process of the mechanisms of private law is subject to a dichotomy which is somehow enhanced by the praetorian development of private law.[37] In fact, the case law of the ECJ is not being developed according to common and homogenous criteria and, what is more, the ECJ deals only with matters that fall within its remit.

The unilateral character of the action oriented towards publicisation, social justice in European law with a regulatory loophole in the field of classical institutions of private law results in the difference between this phenomenon on the European level and the influence mechanisms of social justice and constitutionalization have on private law in national legal systems. In national legal systems, constitutionalization,

36. It is also believed that the provisions of the Treaty do not imply that the EU has wider competences in the sphere of private law, cf. Jürgen Basedow, Freedom of Contract in the European Union, 6/2008 Eur Rev Priv L, 901-923 (Kluwer International BV 2008).

37. Praetorian law created by case law of the European Court of Justice is based on the autonomous concepts, adapted to the requirements and goals of European law, which are not a simple transposition of well-known and well-established principles of the classical private law. A good example is application in case law of the concept of unjust enrichment when assessing the exercise of the substantive rights guaranteed in the EU order together with the principle excluding interest from unlawful behavior and with the principles of equivalency and effectiveness. Cf. Courage and Crehan, Case C-453/99, (2001) ECR I-6297, par. 30 (ECJ 20 September 2001); cf. also here Walter van Gerven, About Rules and Principles, Codification and Legislation and Convergence and Education in the Area of Contract Law, in: Continuity and Change in EU Law: essays in honor of Sir Francis Jacobs, 403 (ed. A. Arnull, P. Eeckhout, T. Tridimas, Oxford University Press 2008). Another example is transformation of the private law concept of an abuse of substantive right for the evaluation of a given behavior in the sphere of public law. A specific presentation of liability conditions within the concept of responsibility of a public authority, especially the causal link and unlawfulness, as well as an transformation of equity clauses to consumer trade, etc. can also be mentioned.

based on the gradual blending of traditional instruments of private law with social-, equality- and solidarity-oriented axiology, is less likely to breach the proportions between the social dimension and traditional dimension of private law. In European private law, that process of introducing social justice into certain segments of private law is not balanced by the existence of regulatory mechanisms which would express the classical axiology of private law, and guarantee its fundamental mission.[38]

Introduction of the Charter of Fundamental Rights, which strengthens the trend towards constitutionalization of European law, may paradoxically deepen the discrepancy between the axiology, the structure and the objectives of EU private law and private law in national legal systems, also due to the fact that the Charter acts within the field strictly delineated by the scope of application of European law, and therefore, does not create the basis for interference in areas outwith EU law. The Charter will act predominantly in these areas which are currently intensively explored by the European legislator. This does not mean that it may not play an important role in the future as a co-factor creating new European private law, subordinated to a coherent axiology being in line with the fundamental ideas of social market economy which we want to build in the European Union. However, for this, a decisive move towards creating a thorough integrated instrument of European private law would be needed. The European Civil Code could play this part.

[4] Looking for Development Possibilities

Today we face dilemmas related to an attempt to define the goals of European private law, as well as the methods of its creation and expansion in the future. Both these questions are closely related.

The present constellation of the European sphere is based on pluralism of national systems connected by common principles and common axiology. The interaction between fields of competence of the European Union and national bodies is a rather complex relationship, and all attempts to clearly and rigidly delineate the areas of competence are bound to fail. Is it, therefore, correct to maintain the individual, separate character of the legal systems? The idea of creating a coherent system of European private law must be seen in this perspective.

It would be difficult to deny that the creation of a homogenous European private law will be marked by the idea to attain the goals related to the construction of the

38. For these reasons I can agree that the crucial issue which concerns the relation between European law and private law is expressed in the question raised by Carla Sieburgh: 'which approaches should be chosen in case of confrontation of a field of law, private law, containing refined rules with a field of law, European Union law, containing less detailed rules and more concrete policies that do not specifically aim at private law relationships? In other words, which approaches should be taken when confronting a system that has developed into utmost refinement with a system that has started to be built up only a few decades ago? (See C. Sieburgh, Principles in Private Law: From Luxury to Necessity – Mutli-layered Legal Systems and the Generative Force of Principles, 2/2012 Eur Rev Priv L, 311-312 [2012]).

common legal area and common legal sphere.[39] It will, therefore, take the form of further 'publicisation' of private law, which will include horizontal application not only of the freedoms guaranteed by the Treaty, but also of fundamental rights related in principle to the sphere of private law. The traditional flexibility and freedom to shape private law relationships and variety of implementation methods of legal instruments resulting from the pluralism of national systems will most probably have to give way to other, stronger protected legal values of the European Union. Such a concept is clearly expressed in the statement made by Ruth Sefton-Green, who says that social justice is not only a simple manifestation of distributive concepts but something much more important as it symbolically expresses European cultural identity, which should pervade private contract law.[40] We can say that, should this assumption be followed, the sphere of application of the 'community method' – used so far in consumer law or applied to employment relationships and, therefore based, on levelling inequalities and guaranteeing stronger protection of one party of a given legal relationship – will probably expand. Shall this be so, the imperative to eliminate all cases of discrimination in the name of a common market could then become a crucial determinant of legal relationships – also, in the relations between undertakings and in consequence limit the sphere of freedom of contract. That is why in my opinion only a coherent system of contract law could diminish the disparity between the area of 'protectionist' impact, and the one in which such instruments are not applicable.[41]

Nevertheless, even if the change of the private law paradigm should be inevitable, I strongly believe that it should consist in a transformation and not deformation of its fundamental mission of expressing individual interests, in order to satisfy the goals related to the construction of the common legal area. The evolution of European private law, taking place over recent decades, should not lead to a questioning of the goals and the fundamental mission of private law. If subordinated, in all areas, to the primary role of the common interest private law will lose its function as the most

39. However, it has to be noted there is no unanimity about necessity to create the European civil code at the present stage, regardless of the vision of private law. It is so not only because in the sphere of private law uncodified methods allowing merging the systems gradually may be more effective, but also because it is not believed that uniformisation of private law would be good in itself. Additionally, EU Member States are not yet ready to adopt such a far-reaching instrument as a unified code in the matters concerning sensitive areas of the state, strongly connected with legal tradition and national identity. (cf. W. van Gerven, About Rules and Principles, Codification and Legislation and Convergence and Education in the Area of Contract Law, in: Continuity and Change in EU Law, 409; M. Meli, Social Justice, Constitutional Principles and Protection of the Weaker Contractual Party, 160).

40. Cf. R. Sefton-Green, Social Justice and European Identity in European Contract Law, no. 2 ERCL, 275 ff. (2006).

41. Cf. the remarks of van Gerven (About Rules and Principles, Codification and Legislation and Convergence and Education in the Area of Contract Law, in: Continuity and Change in EU Law, 406), who notices that the distance between the two blocks of contract law is today a source of many problems on the national and European level, and the best solution would be the systematization and integration of the protective contract law with the general law of contracts. This tendency could be important for the strengthening of social face of civil law. The author also notices (page 407), that [...] codification of civil law, if undertaken, should not be based exclusively on the principle of autonomy of the will but also on that of fairness and due regard and that accordingly, general and protective contract law should be integrated in one legal enactment.

sensitive and subtle instrument expressing a multitude of aspirations, motives, interests and economic goals. In consequence, it could not play its role anymore which, at the same time, is a condition for the existence of the free market and undistorted competition.

Can the construction of a harmonious space of European private law be reconciled with this postulate? I do not think that we can find a definitive answer to this question today.

CHAPTER 6

Horizontal Effect of Fundamental Rights: In Search of Social Justice or Private Autonomy in EU Law?

Dorota Leczykiewicz

§6.01 INTRODUCTION

What is the role of EU fundamental rights in cases involving two private parties? Does the category of 'fundamental rights' as concepts of EU law infuse that legal system primarily or exclusively with social values or is perhaps a vehicle of another transformation, towards greater liberalization and deregulation? Much depends on the content of 'fundamental rights' and the frequency with which parties to disputes reach for particular kinds of arguments. This article will argue that until recently 'fundamental rights' were used *horizontally* primarily in order to achieve greater social justice rather than to enhance private autonomy.[1] I will substantiate this thesis by looking at the application of Treaty provisions, directives and general principles protecting fundamental rights. I will pay special attention to the Charter of Fundamental Rights,[2] which has already featured prominently in horizontal cases referred to the Court of Justice of the EU. Despite employing fundamental rights to alter the content of private law relationships in the light of progressive goals,[3] EU law has not managed to ensure true

1. Hugh Collins, 'The constitutionalization of European private law as a path to social justice?' in Hans-W. Micklitz, *The Many of Social Justice in European Private Law* (Edward Elgar Publishing Cheltenham 2011) 133; Aurelia Colombi Ciacchi, 'The Constitutionalization of European Contract Law: Judicial Convergence and Social Justice' (2006) 2 European Review of Contract Law 167.
2. Charter of Fundamental Rights of the European Union [2010] OJ C 83, p. 389; [2012] OJ C 262, p. 391.
3. For more on the role of EU law in shaping private law relationships see contributions in Dorota Leczykiewicz and Stephen Weatherill (eds), *The Involvement of EU Law in Private Law Relationships* (Hart Publishing Oxford 2013).

'social justice' in the horizontal context. Following Mickltiz, I will distinguish between 'social justice' understood in redistributive terms, and 'access justice', which only ensures participation in the market and non-discrimination, without guaranteeing just results of market transactions.[4] This thinner version of 'social justice' is largely reconcilable with a version of private autonomy which insists on substantive freedom and removal of informational asymmetries and negative externalities. However, neither the full blown concept of social justice, nor its 'access justice' version, are directed towards promoting private autonomy in a liberal sense, understood as freedom from regulation and coercion. The article will look at how this latter freedom has so far been protected by EU law.[5] While it has been implicitly recognized as part of the Internal Market freedoms, and, in particular, of the principle of proportionality, the verbal layer of EU law did not include a principle of private autonomy. As such, private autonomy could not be expressly weighed against the pursuance of legitimate aims by the Member States in conflict with the Internal Market. Neither could it be invoked against expansive interpretation of secondary law, whose 'full effectiveness' often promoted the measure's objective at the expense of private autonomy of those who were subjected to regulation. This explains why the recent cases in which applicants are relying on the Charter of Fundamental Rights often engage its Article 16, which guarantees 'freedom to conduct a business'.[6] The case *Scarlet Extended*[7] is a very good example of the change in the role of fundamental rights reasoning in horizontal cases in EU law. The fact that the case was horizontal did not constitute any obstacle to application of Article 16 of the Charter because freedom to conduct a business was used there in the interpretation of a Directive in order to delineate the scope of discretion left to the Member States in its implementation and application. Equally, as the article will explain, we can conceive of the application of 'freedom to conduct a business' in 'pure' horizontal cases, such as those in which a private party is bound by free movement provisions.[8] While legal certainty, both as a principle and a relevant consideration, has been providing the first bulwark against the encroachment of horizontal private transactions by publicly-focused EU goals, fundamental rights offer private parties a more concrete and entrenched mechanism of resisting regulatory effects of national and EU law.

---

4. Hans-W. Micklitz, 'Social Justice and Access Justice in Private Law', EUI Working Paper LAW No. 2011/02.
5. See also the contribution in this book by Guido Comparato and Hans-W. Micklitz, Chapter 4.
6. For an in-depth analysis of the role of freedom to conduct a business in EU law, see the contribution of Peter Oliver in this volume, Chapter 12.
7. Case C-70/10 *Scarlet Extended SA v. Société belge des auteurs, compositeurs et éditeurs SCRL (SABAM)*, Judgment of 24 November 2011.
8. See Case C-171/11 *Fra.bo SpA v. Deutsche Vereinigung des Gas- und Wasserfaches eV (DVGW) - Technisch-Wissenschaftlicher Verein*, Judgment of 12 July 2012.

§6.02 WHEN MAY PRIVATE PARTIES RELY ON EU FUNDAMENTAL RIGHTS IN HORIZONTAL SITUATIONS?

Reliance on EU fundamental rights in horizontal situations is not unlimited. The first restriction on horizontal application of EU fundamental rights stems from the requirement of the case falling within the scope of EU law. If the claimant can point to a substantive Treaty provision protecting a fundamental right, such as the right to receive equal pay for equal work regardless of gender (Article 157 TFEU), the situation is straightforward. This provision, however, while horizontally directly effective, has a very limited scope of application. Another substantive Treaty provision protecting a fundamental right is Article 18 TFEU prohibiting discrimination on the ground of nationality. Despite its apparent breadth, the prohibition operates only '[w]ithin the scope of application of the Treaties, and without prejudice to any special provisions contained therein'. Thus, it can only be invoked alongside one of the Internal Market freedoms or the Treaty provisions on citizenship. Equally, general principles of fundamental rights apply only 'within the scope of Union law', and so thus the Charter of Fundamental Rights (Article 51(1)).[9] The situation with Directives is slightly more complex. While the fundamental rights they protect apply within the scope of application of the relevant Directives, the complex case law of the Court of Justice specifies exactly how and since when a Directive may generate effects in horizontal situations.[10] This is a problem in particular where a Directive which implements a fundamental right has not been correctly transposed by a Member State. Since the Court of Justice rejects horizontal application of Directives,[11] commentators often point

9. In Case C-617/10 *Åklagaren v. Hans Åkerberg Fransson*, Judgment of 26 February 2013, paras 19-20, the Grand Chamber of the Court of Justice held: 'The Court's settled case-law indeed states, in essence, that the fundamental rights guaranteed in the legal order of the European Union are applicable in all situations governed by European Union law, but not outside such situations... That definition of the field of application of the fundamental rights of the European Union is borne out by the explanations relating to Article 51 of the Charter, which, in accordance with the third subparagraph of Article 6(1) TEU and Article 52(7) of the Charter, have to be taken into consideration for the purpose of interpreting it (see, to this effect, Case C-279/09 *DEB* [2010] ECR I-13849, para. 32). According to those explanations, 'the requirement to respect fundamental rights defined in the context of the Union is only binding on the Member States when they act in the scope of Union law'.'

10. Case 14/83 *Sabine von Colson and Elisabeth Kamann v. Land Nordrhein-Westfalen* [1984] ECR 1891; Case C-427/06 *Birgit Bartsch v. Bosch und Siemens Hausgeräte (BSH) Altersfürsorge GmbH* [2008] ECR I-7245.

11. Case 152/84 *M. H. Marshall v. Southampton and South-West Hampshire Area Health Authority (Teaching)* [1986] ECR 723, Case C-91/92 *Paola Faccini Dori v. Recreb Srl* [1994] ECR I-3325, Case C-201/02 *The Queen on the application of Delena Wells v. Secretary of State for Transport, Local Government and the Regions* [2004] ECR I-723.

out that EU law suffers from 'implementation imbalance' or 'social deficit'.[12] Ordoliberal Internal Market law to a large extent does apply horizontally,[13] while more socially focused regulatory law enacted in the form of Directives finds full horizontal application only if the Member States correctly performed their obligation of implementation. The Court has tried to rectify the situation of imbalance between the market and social values by narrowing down the definition of a private party in EU law,[14] by inventing other channels of effectiveness, such as the obligation of consistent interpretation, and by making general principles of fundamental rights horizontally applicable.[15] However, all these methods have limits, arising either from the status of the defendant or the wording of national provisions, or are dependent upon the existence of a piece of secondary EU law which implements a general principle and in this way brings the case within the scope of EU law.[16]

§6.03 HORIZONTAL APPLICATION OF FUNDAMENTAL RIGHTS IN EU LAW: THE SOCIAL JUSTICE PARADIGM

In this light it is not surprising that 'fundamental rights' have been used horizontally by the Court of Justice predominantly to promote social justice. In the first case in which the Court recognized horizontal effect of a Treaty provision protecting a fundamental right[17] it stressed the fact that the provision in question (now Article 157 TFEU) 'form[ed] part of the social objectives of the Community, which is not merely an economic union, but is at the same time intended, by common action, to ensure social

12. Stephen Weatherill, 'Addressing Problems of Imbalanced Implementation in EC Law: Remedies in an Institutional Perspective' in Claire Kilpatrick, Tonia Novitz and Paul Skidmore (eds), *The Future of Remedies in Europe* (Hart Publishing Oxford 2000) 87; Christian Joerges and Florian Rödl, 'Informal Politics, Formalised Law and the 'Social Deficit' of European Integration: Reflections after the Judgments of the ECJ in *Viking* and *Laval*' (2009) 15 European Law Journal 1.
13. Articles 101 and 102 TFEU regulate directly the conduct of private parties and are therefore directly horizontally applicable. The Court has recognised that free movement provisions have horizontal application in the following cases: Case 36/74 *B.N.O. Walrave and L.J.N. Koch v. Association Union cycliste internationale, Koninklijke Nederlandsche Wielren Unie and Federación Española Ciclismo* [1974] ECR 1405; Case C-415/93 *Union royale belge des sociétés de football association ASBL v. Jean-Marc Bosman* [1995] ECR I-4921; Case C-281/98 *Roman Angonese v. Cassa di Risparmio di Bolzano SpA* [2000] I-4139; Case C-438/05 *International Transport Workers' Federation and Finnish Seamen's Union v. Viking Line ABP and OÜ Viking Line Eesti* [2007] ECR I-10779; Case C-341/05 *Laval un Partneri Ltd v. Svenska Byggnadsarbetareförbundet* [2007] ECR I-11767; Case C-171/11 *Fra.bo SpA v. Deutsche Vereinigung des Gas- und Wasserfaches eV (DVGW) - Technisch-Wissenschaftlicher Verein*, Judgment of the Court of 12 July 2012. On the questions arising in the context of horizontal application of free movement law, see Harm Schepel, 'Constitutionalising the Market, Marketising the Constitution, and to Tell the Difference: On the Horizontal Application of the Free Movement Provisions in EU Law' (2012) 18 European Law Journal 187; Julio Baquero Cruz, 'Free movement and private autonomy' (1999) 24 European Law Review 603.
14. See Case C-188/89 *A. Foster and others v. British Gas plc* [1990] ECR I-3313.
15. Case C-144/04 *Werner Mangold v. Rüdiger Helm* [2005] ECR I-9981.
16. In Case C-427/06 *Birgit Bartsch v. Bosch und Siemens Hausgeräte (BSH) Altersfürsorge GmbH* [2008] ECR I-7245.
17. Case 43/75 *Gabrielle Defrenne v. Société anonyme belge de navigation aérienne Sabena* [1974] ECR 455.

progress and seek the constant improvement of the living and working conditions of their peoples, as is emphasized by the Preamble to the Treaty'.[18] In *Angonese*, a case involving a question of horizontal application of the Treaty prohibition of discrimination on the ground of nationality, the Court's reasoning also referred to the need of ensuring that there was no discrimination on the labour market.[19] The Court allowed arguments based on fundamental rights also to create a more socially focused framework to economic freedoms.[20] In the case of fundamental rights protected by Directives the *Pfeiffer* judgment[21] shows that the doctrine of indirect effect of Directives enables an employee to rely on EU social rights against another private party by imposing on national courts a particularly strong obligation of ensuring the achievement of the Directives' objectives through interpretation of national law.[22] *Mangold* can obviously also be seen as a case where the Court of Justice wished to promote social justice by allowing a private party to rely directly on a general principle of non-discrimination on the ground of age against his employer. In *Kücükdeveci*,[23] the Court asked the national court to disapply any provision contrary to the principle of non-discrimination 'as given expression in Directive 2000/78',[24] once again signifying that there is a strong link between equal treatment Directives and 'fundamental rights', protected now both as 'general principles' and as Charter rights.[25]

---

18. *Ibid.*, para. 10.
19. Case C-281/98 *Roman Angonese v. Cassa di Risparmio di Bolzano SpA* [2000] ECR I-4139, para. 35.
20. Case C-36/02 *Omega Spielhallen- und Automatenaufstellungs-GmbH* [2004] ECR I-9609; Case C-341/05 *Laval un Partneri Ltd v. Svenska Byggnadsarbetareförbundet* [2007] ECR I-11767; Case C-438/05 *International Transport Workers' Federation and Finnish Seamen's Union v. Viking Line ABP and OÜ Viking Line Eesti* [2007] ECR I-10779; Case C-244/06 *Dynamic Medien Vertriebs v. Avides Media* [2008] ECR I-505; Joined Case C-570/07 and C-571/07 *José Manuel Blanco Pérez and María del Pilar Chao Gómez v. Consejería de Salud y Servicios Sanitarios* [2010] ECR I-4629. See Phil Syrpis and Tonia Novitz, 'Economic and social rights in conflict: political and judicial approaches to the reconciliation' (2008) 33 European Law Review 411.
21. Joined cases C-397/01 to C-403/01 *Bernhard Pfeiffer v. Deutsches Rotes Kreuz, Kreisverband Waldshut eV* [2004] ECR I-8835.
22. The case concerned two Directives: Council Directive 89/391/EEC of 12 June 1989 on the introduction of measures to encourage improvements in the safety and health of workers at work, OJ 1989 L 183, p. 1, and Council Directive 93/104/EC of 23 November 1993 concerning certain aspects of the organisation of working time, OJ 1993 L 307, p. 18.
23. Case C-555/07 *Seda Kücükdeveci v. Swedex GmbH & Co. KG* [2010] ECR I-365, para. 51.
24. Council Directive 2000/78/EC of 27 November 2000 establishing a general framework for equal treatment in employment and occupation, OJ 2000 L 303, p. 16.
25. See also Case C-447/09 *Reinhard Prigge and Others v. Deutsche Lufthansa AG*, Judgment of 13 September 2011, para. 38, where the Court held that a clause in a collective agreement that fixed at 60 the age limit from which pilots were considered as no longer possessing the physical capabilities to carry out their professional activity while national and international legislation fixed that age at 65 was precluded by the Directive, and stressed that the Directive gave specific expression in domain of employment and occupation to *a principle of non-discrimination on grounds of age*, whose existence the Court had acknowledged in *Kücükdeveci*, and which was 'incorporated in Article 21 of the Charter of Fundamental Rights of the European Union, which, from 1 December 2009, has the same legal status as the Treaties'; and Joined cases C-297/10 and C-298/10 *Sabine Hennigs v. Eisenbahn-Bundesamt and Land Berlin v. Alexander Mai*, Judgment of 8 September 2011, where the Court relied on the Charter of Fundamental Rights even more directly. It held that a collective agreement which provides that, within each salary group, the basic pay step of a public sector contractual employee is determined on appointment by reference to the employee's age is precluded by the principle of non-discrimination on grounds

Yet, not in all horizontal cases has the Court been receptive to fundamental rights arguments.[26] In *Dominguez*[27] the Court of Justice sitting in Grand Chamber held that 'Article 7(1) of Directive 2003/88/EC of the European Parliament and of the Council of 4 November 2003 concerning certain aspects of the organisation of working time must be interpreted as precluding national provisions or practices which make entitlement to paid annual leave conditional on a minimum period of ten days' or one month's actual work during the reference period' but decided *not* to apply the Charter or the general principles of fundamental rights horizontally to make its interpretation of the Directive binding regardless of the status of the defendant. Instead, the Court of Justice left it to the national court to determine 'taking the whole body of domestic law into consideration' and 'applying the interpretative methods recognised by domestic law' whether it could find an interpretation of that law that allowed the absence of the worker due to an accident on the journey to or from work to ensure that the entitlement to paid annual leave was not subjected to a condition that the worker has actually worked during the reference period laid down by that State. The Court held that if the objective of the Directive could not be achieved through interpretation, the national court should assess whether the claimant could rely on 'direct effect' of Article 7(1) of the Directive, this being conditional on whether the defendant could be treated as an emanation of the State. If this option was also not possible, the Court suggested that the injured party should rely on *Francovich* to obtain 'compensation for the loss sustained'.[28] The case constitutes clear confirmation of the absence of horizontal direct effect of Directives in EU law, but also an indication of the Court's caution in using fundamental rights to review individual contracts as opposed to collective agreements.[29] This is particularly visible when the judgment in *Dominguez* is contrasted with the opinion of Advocate General Trstenjak in the case,[30] where horizontal application of the Charter of Fundamental Rights and of general principles of fundamental rights is discussed extensively.

§6.04 'SOCIAL JUSTICE' OR 'ACCESS JUSTICE'?

The discussion so far has pointed to many instances of horizontal use of fundamental rights in EU law for the purpose of better realization of values which could be regarded as falling under the umbrella concept of 'social justice' (equal treatment, better working conditions). At this stage it is necessary to ask about the relationship

of age '*proclaimed in Article 21 of the Charter of Fundamental Rights* of the European Union and given specific expression in Council Directive 2000/78/EC of 27 November 2000 establishing a general framework for equal treatment in employment and occupation, and more particularly Articles 2 and 6(1) of that directive' (emphasis added).

26. See also the applicants' unsuccessful attempts to rely on the Charter in Case C-149/10 *Chatzi*, judgment of 15 September 2010.
27. Case C-282/10 *Maribel Dominguez v. Centre informatique du Centre Ouest Atlantique and Préfet de la région Centre*, Judgment of the Court (Grand Chamber) of 24 January 2012.
28. *Ibid.*, para. 43.
29. See Dorota Leczykiewicz, 'Horizontal Application of the Charter of Fundamental Rights' (2013) 38 European Law Review 479.
30. Opinion of AG Trstenjak of 8 September 2011 in *Dominguez*, above.

between horizontal invocability of fundamental rights and the advancement of social justice in EU law, on the one hand, and the protection of private autonomy, on the other. Does horizontal application of 'fundamental rights' lead to restricting private autonomy? In what sense does horizontal application of fundamental rights contribute to social justice? These two questions are in fact closely linked. If we accept that private autonomy should be protected in a substantive sense, as an actual ability for example to enter into market transactions and to make informed decisions, a layer of regulation is necessary to address economic imbalances, informational asymmetries and negative externalities. In the context of consumer law, freedom of contract and regulation are reconciled through the notion of 'consumer confidence'. The notion of 'consumer confidence' offers a justification for Internal Market regulatory law in the form of improving confidence of consumers to shop cross-border, which substantially extends their choice and contractual opportunities of EU traders. In the context of employment law, Deakin and Browne eloquently defended the view that social rights are necessary for market order, using in their argument the so-called capability approach.[31] In the same time, however, there are aspects of EU regulatory law (Directives) which exemplify a decisively paternalistic outlook. They promote social justice at the expense of restricting autonomy of the parties who receive protection, and potentially restricting their access to goods and services due to the increased price. Despite often paternalistic motives, redistributive effects of EU law are very limited. This has led Micklitz to maintain that EU law is not at all based on the idea of social justice. Instead it promotes what he describes as 'access justice'.[32] Weatherill, on the other hand, questions the whole constitutional competence of the EU to deliver social justice.[33]

However, not all EU social law may be reconciled with private autonomy. Inevitably there are situations where social regulation conflicts with contractual freedom. The two cases which show the aforementioned clash most vividly are *Viking* and *Laval*.[34] There, trade unions were attempting to rely on employees' fundamental right of collective action as a defence against companies that invoked free movement provisions. The Court directly relied in those cases on the fact that the conduct of trade unions had regulatory effects.[35] This is significant because it presupposes, at least in the horizontal context, a deregulatory or 'economic due process' interpretation of

31. Simon Deakin and Jude Browne 'Social Rights and Market Order: Adapting the Capability Approach' in Tamara K. Hervey and Jeff Kenner (eds), *Economic and Social Rights under the EU Charter of Fundamental Rights. A Legal Perspective* (Hart Publishing Oxford 2003) 27.
32. Hans-W. Micklitz, 'Social Justice and Access Justice in Private Law' EUI Working Papers Law 2011/02.
33. Stephen Weatherill, 'The Constitutional Competence of the EU to Deliver Social Justice' (2006) 2 European Review of Contract Law 136
34. Case C-341/05 *Laval un Partneri Ltd v. Svenska Byggnadsarbetareförbundet* [2007] ECR I-11767; Case C-438/05 *International Transport Workers' Federation and Finnish Seamen's Union v. Viking Line ABP and OÜ Viking Line Eesti* [2007] ECR I-10779.
35. Case C-438/05 *International Transport Workers' Federation and Finnish Seamen's Union v. Viking Line ABP and OÜ Viking Line Eesti* [2007] ECR I-10779, para. 60; Case C-341/05 *Laval un Partneri Ltd v. Svenska Byggnadsarbetareförbundet* [2007] ECR I-11767, paras 98-99. It would then seem that what justifies application of much of EU law against actors other than Member States is their regulatory capacity.

Internal Market freedoms.[36] Internal Market freedoms engaged horizontally seem to entail a freedom from (unjustified) private regulation. This is confirmed by an examination carried out by Davies of the relationship between free movement law and freedom of contract.[37] He argues that the Court of Justice should allow horizontal application of the principle prohibiting nationality discrimination only in cases in which one of the parties to the dispute acts as a 'third party' regulator. In such a situation the third party is intervening into the freedom of contract of others. This proves that according to Davies, at least in horizontal situations, there is a link between Treaty free movement provisions and protection of private autonomy, understood as freedom from third party's (regulator's) intervention. Where regulatory effects created by private parties are justified by social goals they will be allowed to continue. The two stages of the trade barrier test applied in horizontal situations each then perform a specialized task. Applicability of free movement provisions against private parties will ensure protection of private autonomy by enabling claimants to challenge private regulation creating obstacles to free movement, while at the justification stage the party subjected to the operation of free movement provisions will invoke social values to show necessity and proportionality of the regulatory effects. It is only when regulatory effects of private conduct go beyond what is necessary to promote social values that EU free movement law will restrict such conduct. It is important to note that this restriction will in itself be imposed in order to protect the private autonomy of others.

§6.05 FUNDAMENTAL RIGHTS AND PRIVATE AUTONOMY

I have explained above that free movement law may be used to protect private autonomy and in the same time ensure a proper place for non-economic values. Could the concept of 'fundamental rights' be employed to strengthen the protection in EU law of private autonomy, understood in the legal context most frequently as economic freedom? The formally binding Charter of Fundamental Rights may be the catalyst of such change. It includes two provisions which protect economic freedom. Article 15 guarantees freedom to choose an occupation and right to engage in work, while Article 16 recognizes freedom to conduct a business. The interesting question is in what horizontal configurations these two provisions could be used to protect private

36. For the discussion of different approaches to the interpretation of free movement provisions see Miguel Poiares Maduro, *We, the court. The European Court of Justice and the European Economic Constitution* (Hart Publishing Oxford 1998) 58 ff. Under the 'economic due process' approach the Court of Justice examines the reasonableness of public intervention in the market. See Case C-171/11 *Fra.bo SpA v. Deutsche Vereinigung des Gas- und Wasserfaches eV (DVGW) - Technisch-Wissenschaftlicher Verein*, Judgment of the Court of 12 July 2012, para. 30, where the fact that the lack of certification from the defendant, a private-law body, lead to a 'considerable restriction' on the marketing of the products concerned was provided by the Court as one of the justifications why the defendant was bound by Article 34 TFEU.
37. See Gareth Davies, 'Freedom of Movement, Horizontal Effect, and Freedom of Contract' [2012] European Review of Private Law 805 and Gareth Davies, 'Freedom of Contract and the Horizontal Effect of Free Movement Law' in Dorota Leczykiewicz and Stephen Weatherill (eds), *The Involvement of EU Law in Private Law Relationships* (Oxford Hart Publishing 2013) 53.

autonomy. The more obvious context are cases involving interpretation of EU secondary (regulatory) law, which has bearing on a horizontal dispute pending before a national court. In *Promusicae*, a case concerning three Directives, on electronic commerce, on copyright and on the enforcement of intellectual property rights,[38] the Court of Justice held that:

> when transposing those directives, the Member States [were required to] take care to rely on an interpretation of them which allows a fair balance to be struck between the various fundamental rights protected by the Community legal order. Further, when implementing the measures transposing those directives, the authorities and courts of the Member States must not only interpret their national law in a manner consistent with those directives but also make sure that they do not rely on an interpretation of them which would be in conflict with those fundamental rights or with the other general principles of Community law, such as the principle of proportionality.[39]

The judgment in *Promusicae* is important for my discussion in two respects. Not only does it explicitly state that the Member States should use their discretion under a Directive in a manner compatible with fundamental rights, it also maintains that the principle of proportionality requires the Member States to strike a fair balance between two fundamental rights when they stand in conflict. In *Promusicae* this conflict concerned the protection of intellectual property and the right to protection of personal data. It was the latter right, to protection of personal data, that was challenging the interpretation of the Directives that would ensure most fully their effectiveness.

Private autonomy, now expressly, albeit only partially, recognized as a fundamental right (in the form of freedom to conduct a business), has been used recently in a manner similar to that in which the right to protection of personal data was used in *Promusicae*, namely to challenge the regulatory reach of EU secondary law. *Scarlet Extended*[40] concerned an internet service provider ('ISP'), which provided its customers with access to the internet without offering other services such as downloading or file sharing. Despite that SABAM, a management company which represented authors, composers and editors of musical works in authorizing the use of their copyright-protected works by third parties, formed a view that Scarlet had an obligation under EU law[41] to prevent its customers from downloading works in the SABAM's catalogue

38. Directive 2000/31/EC of the European Parliament and of the Council of 8 June 2000 on certain legal aspects of information society services, in particular electronic commerce, in the Internal Market, OJ 2000 L 178, p. 1; Directive 2001/29/EC of the European Parliament and of the Council of 22 May 2001 on the harmonisation of certain aspects of copyright and related rights in the information society, OJ 2001 L 167, p. 10; Directive 2004/48/EC of the European Parliament and of the Council of 29 April 2004 on the enforcement of intellectual property rights, OJ 2004 L 157, p. 45, and corrigendum, OJ 2004 L 195, p. 16.
39. Case C-275/06 *Productores de Música de España (Promusicae) v. Telefónica de España SAU* [2008] ECR I-271.
40. Case C-70/10 *Scarlet Extended SA v. Société belge des auteurs, compositeurs et éditeurs SCRL (SABAM)*, Judgment of 24 November 2011.
41. Directive 2000/31/EC of the European Parliament and of the Council of 8 June 2000 on certain legal aspects of information society services, in particular electronic commerce, in the Internal Market, OJ 2000 L 178, p. 1; Directive 2001/29/EC of the European Parliament and of the Council of 22 May 2001 on the harmonisation of certain aspects of copyright and related rights in the

from the internet. The appeal court in Brussels asked the Court of Justice whether national courts could impose an injunction on an ISP, which would require it to install, for all its customers, in abstracto and as a preventive measure, exclusively at the cost of that ISP and for an unlimited period, a system for filtering all electronic communications, both incoming and outgoing, passing via its services, in particular those involving the use of peer-to-peer software, in order to identify on its network the movement of electronic files containing a musical, cinematographic or audio-visual protected by intellectual property rights, and subsequently to block the transfer of such files. In its reply, the Court of Justice used the framework it had developed in *Promusicae*. Just as it had used the right to protect personal data against various Directives in *Promusicae*, in *Scarlet Extended* it pointed to the freedom to conduct a business enjoyed by operators such as service providers as a consideration which should be balanced against the fundamental right to protection of intellectual property promoted by the relevant Directive.[42] It then observed that:

> the injunction requiring the installation of the contested filtering system involves monitoring all the electronic communications made through the network of the ISP concerned in the interests of those rightholders. Moreover, that monitoring has no limitation in time, is directed at all future infringements and is intended to protect not only existing works, but also future works that have not yet been created at the time when the system is introduced.[43]

The Court held that 'such an injunction would result in a serious infringement of the freedom of the ISP concerned to conduct its business'.[44]

The Court of Justice used almost identical reasoning in *SABAM v. Netlog*.[45] This case concerned the extent of obligations imposed on companies running online social networking platforms to prevent at their own cost violations of intellectual property rights. In particular, the national court inquired whether it had a duty to impose an injunction on Netlog to introduce, for all its customers, for an unlimited period, a system for filtering most of the information which was stored on its servers in order to identify electronic files containing musical, cinematographic or audio-visual work in respect of which SABAM claimed to hold rights, and subsequently to block the exchange of such files. Once again, the Court held that the injunction requested by SABAM would constitute a serious infringement of the freedom of the hosting service

information society, OJ 2001 L 167, p. 10; Directive 2004/48/EC of the European Parliament and of the Council of 29 April 2004 on the enforcement of intellectual property rights, OJ 2004 L 157, p. 45, and corrigendum OJ 2004 L 195, p. 16; Directive 95/46/EC of the European Parliament and of the Council of 24 October 1995 on the protection of individuals with regard to the processing of personal data and on the free movement of such data, OJ 1995 L 281, p. 31; and Directive 2002/58/EC of the European Parliament and of the Council of 12 July 2002 concerning the processing of personal data and the protection of privacy in the electronic communications sector, OJ 2002 L 201, p. 37.

42. Case C-70/10 *Scarlet Extended*, para. 46.
43. *Ibid.*, para. 47.
44. *Ibid.*, para. 48.
45. Case C-360/10 *Belgische Vereniging van Auteurs, Componisten en Uitgevers CVBA (SABAM) v. Netlog NV*, Judgment of 16 February 2012.

provider to conduct a business.[46] Also in *DR, TV2 Danmark*[47] the Court of Justice, while interpreting the Copyright Directive,[48] used Article 16 of the Charter to determine the scope of rights of a broadcasting organization to make ephemeral recordings of their own broadcasts. The Directive allowed the Member States to permit such recordings when the broadcasting organizations were making them 'by their own facilities'. The dispute concerned the question of whether the exception for ephemeral recordings also covered recordings made by legally independent television production companies. That depended on whether the broadcasting organization's 'own facilities' included facilities of a person acting 'on behalf of or under the responsibility of the broadcasting organisation', although legally independent. The Court compared different language versions of the relevant provision of the Directive and came to the conclusion that the external production company has to be acting *either* on behalf of the broadcasting organization *or* under its responsibility. The two requirements did not have to be met jointly. The Court justified such interpretative choice by the fact that the approach it adopted 'ensure[d] that broadcasting organisations ha[d] a greater enjoyment of the freedom to conduct a business, set out in Article 16 of the Charter of Fundamental Rights of the European Union, while at the same time not adversely affecting the substance of copyright'.[49]

In *Scarlet Extended, SABAM v. Netlog* and *DR, TV2 Danmark* reliance on freedom to conduct a business led to an interpretation of the Directive which was less protective of the Directive's objective. In its earlier case law the Court of Justice often argued from the consideration of ensuring 'full effectiveness' of the Directive, regardless of how much it thereby intruded into national regulatory autonomy and individual freedom. Here, 'full effectiveness' was not employed because it would conflict too starkly with the duty to take account of the operators' commercial freedom. In another horizontal case, *McDonagh*,[50] concerning interpretation of Air Passenger Rights Regulation,[51] the Court relied on another Charter provision, Article 38 stating that 'Union policies shall ensure a high level of consumer protection,' to reject Ryanair's submission for more restrictive interpretation of air carriers' obligations to passengers in the event of flight cancellation, as prescribed by Article 16 of the Charter. Article 52(1) of the Charter allows limitations on the exercise of rights enshrined by it as long as the limitations are 'provided for by law and respect the essence of those rights and freedoms', and, '[s]ubject to the principle of proportionality, are necessary and genuinely meet objectives of general interest recognised by the European Union or the need to protect

46. *Ibid.*, para. 48.
47. Case C-510/10 *DR and TV2 Danmark A/S v. NCB - Nordisk Copyright Bureau*, Judgment of 26 April 2012.
48. Directive 2001/29/EC of the European Parliament and of the Council of 22 May 2001 on the harmonisation of certain aspects of copyright and related rights in the information society, OJ 2001 L 167, p. 10.
49. Case C-510/10 *DR, TV2 Danmark A/S*, para. 57.
50. Case C-12/11 *Denise McDonagh v. Ryanair Ltd*, Judgment of 31 January 2013.
51. Regulation (EC) No 261/2004 of the European Parliament and of the Council of 11 February 2004 establishing common rules on compensation and assistance to passengers in the event of denied boarding and of cancellation or long delay of flights, and repealing Regulation (EEC) No 295/91, OJ 2004 L 46, p. 1.

the rights and freedoms of others'. It seems that in the light of the demanding wording of Articles 16 and 52(1) straightforward reliance by the Court on the 'full effectiveness' of a Directive to extend the scope of private parties' obligations under EU law is no longer a viable option. The Court understandably prefers to rely on another Charter provision to counterbalance arguments based on the Charter-protected freedom to conduct a business. If that is the case, the expansive reading of EU regulatory law is now more directly mitigated by relying on a fundamental right. It also follows that after the Lisbon Treaty, and largely thanks to Article 16 of the Charter of Fundamental Rights, private actors can enjoy a more explicit recognition of their autonomy in EU law.

Yet, applying fundamental rights in interpretation of Directives, even if it affects obligations of a private party, is arguably a less controversial instance of their horizontal application. Much more challenging in doctrinal terms is horizontal application of fundamental rights alongside or against horizontally applicable Internal Market freedoms. Private parties, such as professional bodies, sports associations, trade unions and standardization organizations are bound by Articles 34, 49 and 56 TFEU for their capacity to generate regulatory effects creating obstacles to free movement.[52] Reliance on the fundamental freedom to conduct a business in the interpretation of free movement provisions could alter the trade barrier test, leading to an easier burden of proof for parties challenging private regulation. Because private regulators also enjoy 'private autonomy', the Court will have to balance their freedom of action against the right to cross-border trade. Non-regulatory activities of private parties should, on the other hand, be protected from challenge by the Internal Market law as an element of the protection of private autonomy in EU law.

The practical effect of horizontal application of free move movement provisions is either disapplication of national law or its reinterpretation so as to restrict the power or freedom guaranteed to the private defendant by national law. Much less frequent and scarcely discussed is another scenario, where a party wishes to rely on EU primary law in order to claim invalidity of a secondary act affecting their dispute with another private party. In fact, the Court of Justice has decided only two such cases involving a reference to fundamental rights in the context of free movement law. *Association Kokopelli* concerned a dispute between two competitors.[53] The claimant sought compensation for loss it had suffered due to the defendant's marketing of vegetable seeds, excluded from circulation by a Directive.[54] In its defence the defendant argued that the relevant provision of the Directive was invalid because it violated Article 34 TFEU and the principle of proportionality, and also its freedom to conduct a business. The opinion of Advocate General Kokott concludes that the provision from the Vegetable Seed Directive should be held invalid because, in the first instance, it violates Article 16 of the Charter by being 'manifestly disproportionate'.[55] 'In addition' the Advocate General also establishes violation of the free movement of goods provision

52. See above.
53. Case C-59/11 *Association Kokopelli v. Graines Baumaux SAS*, opinion of 19 January 2012.
54. Council Directive 2002/55/EC of 13 June 2002 on the marketing of vegetable seed, OJ 2002 L 193, p. 33 ('Vegetable Seed Directive').
55. Case C-59/11 *Association Kokopelli*, opinion, para. 110.

exactly on the same grounds as in the case of violation of Article 16 of the Charter.[56] The Court of Justice did not agree with the conclusion of the Advocate General. In the judgment it held that while 'it [was] true that the acceptance regime for vegetable seed laid down by Directives 2002/55 and 2009/145 [was] capable of restricting the freedom of traders in old seed, such as Kokopelli, to pursue their professional activity', the Directive was 'intended to secure improved productivity in vegetable cultivation in the European Union, the establishment of the internal market for vegetable seed by ensuring its free movement within the European Union, and the conservation of plant genetic resources, which are objectives of general interest'.[57] The Court then held that the measures laid down by the Directive were not inappropriate to the attainment of those objectives, and therefore the obstacle to the freedom to pursue an economic activity which such measures represented could not, in the light of the aims pursued, be regarded as disproportionately impairing the right to exercise that freedom.[58] While the Court did not follow the opinion of the Advocate General, in order to arrive at a different conclusion, it had openly to admit that the purpose of the Directive was not liberalization of the market in vegetable seeds of conservation varieties.[59] The result of the judgment is that the defendant before the national court will be liable to pay the claimant compensation for loss arising from its 'uncompetitive' behaviour and refrain from marketing and advertising of the old vegetable and flower varieties originating from organic agriculture. The link between (in)validity of the EU Directive and the horizontal situation is provided here by national competition law and its remedial provisions.

Sky Österreich[60] was another case where the Court's validity review of a Directive had direct consequences for a private dispute. Sky had acquired exclusive rights to broadcast Europa League matches. Under the Broadcasting Directive,[61] as amended in 2007, Sky was required to allow broadcasters, for the purpose of short news reports, to use short extracts from the matches to which it had exclusive rights at a compensation not exceeding the additional costs in providing access. Yet, according to a contract between Sky and ORF, ORF was to pay Sky EUR 700 per minute for such reports. ORF made a request to the Austrian communications regulator to set aside this obligation because the additional costs directly incurred by Sky in providing access to the satellite signal were none. The private contract, which envisaged substantial compensation,

56. *Ibid.*, paras 112-114.
57. Case C-59/11 *Association Kokopelli v. Graines Baumaux SAS*, Judgment of 12 July 2012, paras 78-79.
58. *Ibid.*
59. *Ibid.*, para. 65: '[T]he EU legislature was not pursuing the liberalisation of the market for seed of conservation varieties and of varieties developed for growing under particular conditions, but was seeking to ease the rules of acceptance while preventing the emergence of a parallel market for such seed, which was likely to constitute an impediment to the internal market for seed of vegetable varieties'.
60. Case C-283/11 *Sky Österreich GmbH v. Österreichischer Rundfunk*, Judgment of the Court (Grand Chamber) of 22 January 2013.
61. Council Directive 89/552/EEC of 3 October 1989 on the coordination of certain provisions laid down by law, regulation or administrative action in Member States concerning the pursuit of television broadcasting activities, OJ 1989 L 298, p. 23, amended by Directive 2007/65/EC of the European Parliament and of the Council of 11 December 2007, OJ 2007 L 332, p. 27.

was in conflict with a Directive, which allowed only very limited, almost nominal, compensation. The Austrian regulator agreed with ORF but, at the same time, determined the conditions under which ORF could exercise the right to use short extracts of Sky matches. Both parties appealed against that decision and the institution considering the appeal, the Bundeskommunikationssenat, referred to the Court of Justice a question of validity of a Directive's provision restricting the value of compensation to be paid to the holder of exclusive broadcasting rights. The case raises a question of protection of private autonomy in EU law because the level of remuneration for the use of short extracts from matches had been set in a contractual agreement and the Directive would require the setting aside of this freely negotiated contractual term, which moreover predated the Directive. However, if a party could challenge successfully validity of the Directive on freedom-related grounds, the contractual term would remain enforceable.

The Court's judgment directly engages with the argument based on Sky's freedom to conduct a business. Freedom to conduct a business is extended by the Court to include the freedom of contract[62]. The Court accepts that the consequence of the Directive is that the holder of exclusive broadcasting rights cannot decide freely with which broadcasters it will enter into an agreement regarding the granting of the right to make short news reports and at what price. For these reasons, the Directive interferes with the freedom to conduct a business of holders of exclusive broadcasting rights.[63] However, freedom to conduct a business is not absolute and may be subject to a broad range of interventions on the part of public authorities, which may limit the exercise of economic activity in the public interest.[64] To define the public interest at stake the Court invokes the right of access of the general public to information, which is part of the fundamental freedom to receive information, now guaranteed also by Article 11(1) of the Charter of Fundamental Rights. The safeguarding of the freedom protected under Article 11(1) of the Charter constitutes a legitimate aim in the general interest capable of justifying the interference.[65]

Because the Court was asked only the specific question concerning validity of one of the Directive's provisions it did not have to address the difficult issue of its application to the facts of the case. As part of the proportionality review the Court held that 'the Member States are required to define the modalities and conditions regarding the provision of extracts from the signal used by taking due account of exclusive broadcasting rights.'[66] Nevertheless, the Court tacitly accepted, as it did in *Association*

62. In Case C-283/11 *Sky Österreich GmbH v. Österreichischer Rundfunk*, Judgment of 22 January 2013, paras 42-43, the Court explained that '[t]he protection afforded by Article 16 of the Charter covers the freedom to exercise an economic or commercial activity, the freedom of contract and free competition, as is apparent from the explanations relating to that article, which, in accordance with the third subparagraph of Article 6(1) TEU and Article 52(7) of the Charter, have to be taken into consideration for the interpretation of the Charter... In addition, the freedom of contract includes, in particular, the freedom to choose with whom to do business' (references omitted).
63. Case C-283/11 *Sky Österreich*, para. 44.
64. *Ibid.*, paras 45-46.
65. *Ibid.*, para. 66.
66. *Ibid.*, para. 63.

Kokopelli, that fundamental rights could be used to invalidate EU acts also in horizontal cases pending before national courts. The *Sky Österreich* case is particularly indicative because in that case, as explained above, upholding validity of the Directive in the light of the fundamental right to freedom to conduct a business had a direct bearing, given the national procedural context, on enforceability of a contractual term.

§6.06 CONCLUSION

The case law of the Court of Justice is showing a constantly growing tendency of accepting reliance on fundamental rights in horizontal cases. However, it is a recent phenomenon that the Court invokes freedom to conduct a business in cases involving disputes between two private parties. Cases in which this freedom is used to assess validity of an EU measure are not new and there the horizontal context, as in *Association Kokopelli* or *Sky Österreich*, seems largely irrelevant to the Court. In free movement cases where a private party challenges applicability of a national regulatory measure, the horizontal context is again hardly significant, despite the fact that it could raise issues of legal certainty and legitimate expectations. Here, the *Mangold* doctrine could be employed to justify why national regulatory measures incompatible with free movement law, interpreted in the light of the fundamental right to carry out an economic activity, should be disapplied in horizontal cases, even if national law separates the outcome of a horizontal dispute from (in)compatibility of national rules with EU law. Because private autonomy is protected under the rubric of freedom to conduct a business it is an inherent feature of these 'horizontal' cases that there be a public or private regulatory measure which constitutes an allegedly unlawful restriction. Thus, these cases are similar to triangular cases where it is not the other private party but a public actor which is the source of restriction.[67] The situation is more interesting in cases involving questions about interpretation of EU acts affecting interpretation of national law and the judicial obligations of ensuring full effectiveness of rights guaranteed by the EU acts. Cases that have reached the Court of Justice so far concerned primarily the protection of intellectual property rights, which tend to have an obvious restrictive effect on economic freedom. It remains to be seen whether social protection Directives, such as those guaranteeing equal treatment, consumer protection and various employees' rights, will also in the future be interpreted by the Court in the light of not only social fundamental rights but also freedom to conduct a business.[68] Finally, fundamental rights will understandably be invoked by private parties bound by EU free movement law. The Internal Market is a public good with, arguably, beneficial consequences for both private autonomy (commercial opportunities and contractual freedom) and social goals (consumers' choice and lower prices, availability of employment, access to healthcare services). Free movement law often applies horizontally in order to protect the liberal goals of the Internal Market. When so invoked against private parties it protects the economic freedom of cross-border traders

67. See Angela Ward's contribution in this volume, Chapter 14.
68. See the reference in Case C-426/11 *Alemo-Herron and Others*, Opinion of AG Cruz Villalón of 19 February 2013.

by restricting autonomy of other private parties. Therefore, the latter should be allowed to rely on fundamental rights to counterbalance these expansive tendencies of free movement rights. In these cases fundamental rights would be invoked directly against non-state actors to achieve greater private autonomy of private regulators which, according to their chosen purpose, could serve economic as well as social goals.

Part III: Horizontal Direct Effect

CHAPTER 7

The Concept of (Direct and Indirect) Horizontal Effect of EU Law: The Terminology of European Law Scholars and of Private Law Scholars Compared

Arthur Hartkamp

§7.01 INTRODUCTION

The Treaty on the Functioning of the European Union (as its predecessor, the EC Treaty) nearly exclusively contains rules of a public law character. However, some of its central provisions (prohibitions of discrimination, fundamental freedoms) have acquired significance for private law too, because the Court of Justice has interpreted them in such a way that they – at least to some extent – have become directly applicable to relationships between individuals, in the sense that they create subjective rights and obligations between them. Put in another way: those provisions now produce a direct horizontal effect in – at least some – private law relationships. See for examples in the Court's jurisprudence cases such as *Defrenne II* (43/75), *Walrave* (36/74), *Bosman* (C-415/93), *Angonese* (C-281/98), *Viking* (C-438/05) and *Fra.bo* (C-171/11).

The same is of course true for the provisions of Articles 101 and 102 TFEU, whose direct horizontal effect is enshrined in the Treaty itself (Article 101 paragraph 2) and elaborated by the Court of Justice (*Courage/Crehan,* C-453/99).

Moreover, Treaty provisions may have other kinds of horizontal effects ('indirect' or 'incidental' horizontal effect), in particular through the review (in disputes between individuals) of the compatibility of national legislation (both of a public law and a private law nature) with EU law and through the interpretation of open-textured standards of national law such as good faith or reasonableness and fairness, accepted principles of morality ('*boni mores*'), public order/public policy and general criteria for unlawful acts (negligence, conduct acceptable in society).

The concepts of direct and indirect effect and of vertical and horizontal effect have been coined in the doctrine of European law. To those studying the effects of European law on private law the definitions used by scholars of European law are not always clear. For a private lawyer to be able to describe the different effects of European law on private law it is necessary to analyse the differences more in detail than, apparently, is customary in the professional literature on European law.

It is not the intention of this paper to embark upon a discussion of the nature of the difference(s) between public law and private law or on exact definitions of the two. Speaking about private law I refer to general private law which comprises *i.a.* contract law, tort law, the law of restitution (unjust enrichment) and property law. For clarity's sake and in order to avoid misunderstandings I only consider relationships between private individuals, although of course in a number of jurisdictions private law extends to (some) relationships between private individuals and public authorities, e.g., unlawful acts or undue payments.

For an orderly discussion of private law effects of European law at least the following distinctions must be made:

- Primary/secondary EU law and its effect on national legislation of a private law character.
- Primary/secondary EU Law and its effect on national legislation of a public law character, as far as the application of EU law indirectly affects relationships between individuals.
- Primary/secondary EU Law and its direct impact on (legal) acts of private parties, in the sense that a rule or principle of EU law itself creates, extinguishes or modifies rights and obligations between them.

This paper will pay attention to the terminology used by European law scholars and confront that terminology with the one focused on private law.

§7.02 DIRECT EFFECT IN EUROPEAN LAW PARLANCE

In European law terminology 'direct effect' means that a norm of European law can be invoked by a party in a national court. The following references relate to vertical relationships, meaning the situation, normal in European law, that individuals invoke EU law against a Member State or public authority (or a legal person according to private law which exercises public power[1]).

According to Paul Craig and Gráinne de Búrca:

> (t)he meaning of direct effect remains contested. In a broad sense it means that provisions of binding EU law which are sufficiently clear, precise, and unconditional to be considered justiciable can be invoked and relied on by individuals before national courts. There is also a 'narrower' or classical concept of direct

1. The latter case is labeled 'administrative direct effect' by Paul Craig and Gráinne de Búrca, *EU Law* (Oxford: OUP 2011) 198.

> effect, which is defined in terms of the capacity of a provision of Union law to confer rights on individuals.[2]

The first definition is referred to as 'objective' direct effect, the second as 'subjective' direct effect.

It would seem that the broader definition is the more common one. 'Direct effect can be provisionally defined as the capacity of a norm of Union law to be applied in domestic court proceedings.' And:

> Originally, direct effect was often defined, not least by the Court of Justice itself, as the creation of rights for individuals which the national courts must protect. That expression was gradually superseded by what the French call *invocabilité*, namely the capacity of the norm to be invoked by individuals in national courts which are bound to apply them. The reason for this shift was the gradual realization that many norms of Community law, particularly norms contained in directives, though not having as their object the attribution of a benefit to individuals, may very well serve as a standard for reviewing the legality of Member State action when individuals can show a sufficient interest in the outcome of such a review.[3]

De Witte goes on (p. 331) to state the following:

> EU norms can therefore be used by parties in a national court case both as a sword (that is, as a source of new rights) and as a shield (that is, as a protection against conflicting national norms). In the former case, EU law has a 'substitution effect', taking the place of a national norm that would otherwise be applicable; in the latter case, EU law has an 'exclusionary effect': it merely excludes the application of a conflicting national norm, but is not itself a source of new rights.

And a final quotation (p. 331): 'Therefore, direct effect really boils down, as far as courts are concerned, to a test of justiciability: is the norm 'sufficiently operational in itself to be applied by a court' in a given case.'[4] In a similar vein, Prechal offers the following definition: 'Direct effect is the obligation of a court or another authority to apply the relevant provision of Community law, either as a norm which governs the case or as a standard for legal review'.[5]

§7.03 HORIZONTAL EFFECT IN EUROPEAN LAW PARLANCE

According to Peter Oliver and Wulf-Henning Roth:[6]

> (A) further question is whether private parties are or should be considered addressees of, and therefore directly bound by, the four freedoms. The issue is

2. Paul Craig and Gráinne de Búrca, *EU Law* (Oxford: OUP 2011) 180 ff.
3. Bruno de Witte, 'Direct effect, primacy and the nature of the legal order', in Paul Craig and Gráinne de Búrca (eds), *The evolution of EU law* (Oxford: OUP 2011) 323 ff., at 323 and 330. See in the same vein the leading Dutch expert Barents, in Barents and Brinkhorst, *Grondlijnen van Europees recht*, 13e ed. (Deventer: Kluwer 2012), no. 102.
4. In this sense AG Van Gerven in the Banks case (C-128/92), para. 27.
5. Prechal, *Directives in EC law* (Oxford: OUP 2005) 241.
6. Peter Oliver and Wulf-Henning Roth, 'The internal market and the four freedoms', CMLR 2004, 407 ff., 421.

> sometimes referred to as one of 'horizontal' application. However, such terminology is not precise enough. It is, indeed, beyond dispute that the four freedoms are not only vertically, but also horizontally applicable insofar as in proceedings among private parties the four freedoms come into play when national regulations, either from the realm of private or public law, have to be interpreted in the light of the four freedoms. The Court's case law concerning national intellectual property law or the law of unfair competition has long proceeded on this basis. This question has, however, to be distinguished from the other, much discussed issue as to whether, to what extent and in what manner private persons (individuals) are bound by the four freedoms when exercising their private autonomy (footnotes omitted).

So it seems that these authors use the term 'horizontal application' (or 'the direct application of the freedoms to private persons'[7]) to denote both the review of legality of national regulations in proceedings between private parties and the situation where private persons (individuals) are directly bound by the freedoms.

Bruno de Witte at first seems to restrict the concept of 'horizontal direct effect (in relationships between private parties)' to the situation where private persons are directly bound by an EU norm. He also calls that 'horizontal application' or 'the (EU norm) may be relied upon against private parties' (p. 334). However, speaking of directives (p. 335), he refers to the settled case law since *Marshall* on the absence of horizontal effect of directives[8] which he describes as 'absence of horizontal direct effect', meaning that he includes in this term the absence of legal review of national regulations in proceedings between individuals. Discussing the words 'of itself' he mentions several exceptions[9] which he brings under the heading of 'indirect' or 'triangular' horizontal effect, to conclude (referring to Dashwood) with the denomination 'indirect horizontal effect cases'.[10]

For Craig and the Búrca 'horizontal direct effect' means imposing obligations on individuals.[11] Treaty articles may have such effect, as well as regulations, but not directives since they cannot of themselves impose obligations on individuals. Where exceptionally a directive may be invoked by an individual for the purpose of legal review of a national legislative measure they speak of 'incidental horizontal effect'.[12]

---

7. *Ibid.*, p. 426.
8. 'According to settled case-law, a directive cannot of itself impose obligations on an individual and cannot therefore be relied upon as such against an individual.' This formulation includes (1) that a directive cannot create rights and obligations in a relationship between individuals vis-à-vis each other and (2) that it cannot be relied upon by an individual in proceedings with another individual in order to have a national measure reviewed for its compatibility with a directive.
9. ECJ 30 April 1996 *CIA Security/Signalson and Securitel* C-194/94 [1996] I-2201; ECJ 7 January 2004 *Wells/Secretary of State* C-201/02 [2004] I-723.
10. Bruno de Witte, 'Direct effect, primacy and the nature of the legal order', in Paul Craig and Gráinne de Búrca (eds), *The evolution of EU law* (Oxford: OUP 2011), 335 with footnote 45.
11. Paul Craig and Gráinne de Búrca, *EU Law* (Oxford: OUP 2011), 180. As an example of horizontal direct effect they mention (189) the *Viking* case (ECJ 11 December 2007 *ITWF/Viking* C-438/05 [2007] I-10779). Regulations, too, have direct effect (191).
12. '(A) directive can in certain cases be legally invoked in proceedings between private parties (incidental effect) so long as the directive does not in itself impose a legal obligation on one of the parties' (p. 180), and p. 182/3 sub 6: 'incidental horizontal effects', whereby a directive can preclude reliance on a provision of national law that is inconsistent with the provisions of the

For harmonious interpretation they use the term 'indirect effect'.[13] Sometimes it seems that these authors comprise both situations in *Marshall* under the absence of horizontal direct effect, sometimes it seems that they call the second situation absence of incidental effect.[14]

Instead of 'horizontal effect' we also find expressions such as third party effect, *Drittwirkung*, effects between private persons, direct application of EU law to acts of private persons, etc.

§7.04 THE EUROPEAN LAWYER'S AND THE PRIVATE LAWYER'S OUTLOOK COMPARED

It is clear that for European law scholars the concept of 'direct effect' is of primordial importance. In fact, the tandem 'primacy' and 'direct effect' belong to the core of European law. Direct effect is one of the most important vehicles for the realization of primacy, because it enables national courts at the request of interested individuals to resolve the conflict between EU law and national law in favour of the former.

However, primacy and direct effect are not inextricably linked. Primacy also operates through ways other than by means of individuals invoking (direct effect of) norms before the courts in proceedings against a state authority. For instance, it also operates through the intermediary of an obligation imposed on administrative bodies and through the intermediary of an obligation of harmonious interpretation imposed on the courts. Direct effect originated in vertical relationships with conflicting EU and national norms (and as such was linked to the notion of primacy), but gradually also came to play a role in horizontal relationships without conflicting EU and national norms.

Primacy does not play a large role in a private lawyer's conceptual thinking. Of course, a private lawyer acknowledges that a contract may be at variance with mandatory provisions of law, but he would not call that 'primacy of mandatory law over a private contract'. The concept of primacy is concerned with several layers of public regulations and as such is a constitutional principle.

For the same reason, a private lawyer would not normally use the term 'review' or the expressions 'substitution effect' and 'exclusion effect' (which in European Law parlance are used in relation to legality review of national regulation) in relation to the

---

directive even in an action between private parties.' See also p. 208, where the same situation is called 'indirect horizontal reliance'. It is an exclusionary, rather than substitutionary effect (p. 210).

13. *Ibid.*, pp. 180, 200.
14. This corresponds with an inherent ambiguity in the Court's formulation, since the second situation according to its literal meaning covers both the case where one party invokes an obligation against the other party (the first situation) and the case where the provision of a directive is invoked for the purposes of legal review of a national provision.

assessment of the consequences of EU law in private law relationships (e.g., assessing the validity of a contract or the legality of factual conduct in the light of a free movement provision).[15]

For a scholar of public law the difference between the two situations repeatedly alluded to under 2 and 3 – that is, on the one hand, relying on a EU norm which serves to review the compatibility of a national regulation with EU law and, on the other hand, relying on a norm of EU law which creates a right for the party concerned – seems to be not very large. Often they are captured under the same heading. The first situation (legality review) seems to be the most important one to him; the concept of conferring rights and obligations is a corollary. As was mentioned in above (section §7.02), legality review was originally phrased in terms of the conferment of rights and obligations on private persons, even if it was unclear what kind of rights were involved (certainly not always subjective rights; perhaps not more than the right to invoke the EU norm).

A private law scholar looks at matters from the opposite side. Reviewing national measures against higher ranking European legislation is not a normal part of his activity. He will associate direct effect in the first place with the contents of a legal relationship, not with the review of legality of a national measure. He will be interested to know whether norms of European law directly influence the validity, substance or interpretation of legal relationships between individuals; in other words, where they create, modify or extinguish rights and obligations between the parties.

Only occasionally the answer to this question will be influenced by legal review of national norms against norms of EU law. National norms of private law are only rarely reviewed against EU law.[16] National norms of public law are often reviewed against EU law, but not normally in a private law context.[17] And even if the context is a private law relationship, the outcome will not normally be that the national norm that is 'excluded' due to its incompatibility with a European norm will be 'substituted' by the latter norm in the sense that it creates rights or obligations between the parties. More often, the exclusion of the conflicting national regulation will lead to the re-applicability of the contractual norm or the national norm that was applicable between the parties in the first place.

Finally, as a matter of terminology, I note that European law scholars normally use the expression 'horizontal direct effect', whereas private lawyers seem to prefer 'direct horizontal effect'. This bears witness to the fact that in European law the focus is on the concept of direct effect (can the EU norm be directly applied by a national court?), which subsequently is qualified by horizontal (as opposed to vertical);

15. See in that sense, however, Mirjam de Mol, 'The Novel Approach of the CJEU on the horizontal direct effect of the EU Principle of non-discrimination: (unbridled expansionism of EU law?', MJ 2011, 109 ff, at 110/111.
16. Examples are ECJ 24 Jan. 1991 *Alsthom Atlantique/Sulzer* C-339/89 [1991] I-107 and ECJ 13 October 1993 *CMC Motorradcenter GmbH/Baskiciogullari* C-93/92 [1993] I-5009.
17. Examples of the latter are ECJ 9 June 1992 *Delhaize/Promalvin and AGE* C-47/90 [1992] p. I-3669 and ECJ 26 Sep. 2000 *Unilever/ Central Food* C-443/98 [2000] I-7535.

whereas in private law the focus is on the contents of a (horizontal) relationship, which is either directly or indirectly influenced by public (EU) law.[18]

§7.05 A PRIVATE LAWYER'S APPROACH

Based on the considerations developed above (section §7.04) I have classified the several horizontal effects as follows.[19]

'Direct horizontal effect' is the situation where European law – e.g., a Treaty rule or a rule in a regulation – directly influences the validity, substance or interpretation of legal relationships between individuals; in other words, where it creates, modifies or extinguishes rights and obligations between the parties. This may have the result, for example, that a contract concluded between parties is null and void or that one citizen's act constitutes an unlawful act vis-à-vis another citizen because the contract or act is at variance with a Treaty provision.

All other cases where European law influences private law in more indirect or incidental ways may be called 'indirect horizontal effects'.[20] I mention the following cases:

(a) Interpretation of national law, either obligatory (with respect to non-implemented or incorrectly implemented directives) or based on the discretion of national courts (influence exerted by EU law through open-ended principles of national private law, such as good faith, reasonableness and fairness, conduct acceptable in society, public order/public policy, public morals etc.).
(b) Positive obligations: the TFEU can be construed to imply an obligation for the Member States to protect the rights deriving from the free movement provisions as well as the prohibitions on discrimination and to safeguard these rights vis-à-vis their citizens, also in horizontal relationships.[21]
(c) Review of compatibility of provisions of national law (either of public law or of private law) with EU law in proceedings between individuals. It is particularly on this point that the private law inspired terminology conflicts with the terminology of European law, where this case is subsumed under (and is the prime expression of) the concept of 'direct effect'; see section §7.02 et seq above. However, from the point of view of the relationship between the parties the influence often is indirect, because what will happen

18. I thank Mirjam de Mol for this observation.
19. A.S. Hartkamp, *European Law and National Private Law. Effect of EU Law and European Human Rights Law on Legal Relationships between Individuals* (Kluwer: Deventer 2012), nos. 12 ff and passim.
20. In European law parlance 'indirect horizontal effect' seems to be the expression most often used (in particular in connection with harmonious interpretation), but there are a number of variations, such as incidental effect, triangular effect and diagonal effect. They do not seem particularly useful to me.
21. ECJ 9 December 1997 *Commission/France* C-265/95 [1997] I-6959; ECJ 12 June 2003 *Schmidberger/Austria* C-112/00 [2003] I-5659.

to that relationship after the 'exclusion' of the national regulation will depend on the nature of the EU law provision against which it was reviewed. If the EU norm does create rights and obligations between the parties, it is a case of direct horizontal effect in the sense mentioned in section §7.05. If it does not, the relationship between the parties will be determined by another rule: in some cases another EU law rule which does have direct horizontal effect, but more often a rule of national law or a valid agreement between the parties.[22]

(d) Yet another type of indirect effect via private law is produced by means of the *Francovich* principle (state liability for incorrect application of EU law by national public authorities).[23]

(e) An individual's successful reliance on a directive against the authorities (i.e., in a 'vertical' relationship) may have negative consequences for another individual (*Wells,* C-201/02).

(f) In *Viamex*[24] the ECJ ruled that while it is true that directives cannot impose obligations on individuals, it cannot be precluded that its provisions may be binding on individuals by means of a regulation that refers expressly to the directive.

(g) The ECJ's reasoning in *Mangold* and *Kücükdeveci*[25] has been considered a 'disguised' exception to the prohibition on horizontal effect of directives.

Not to be discussed here but to be distinguished from the 'indirect horizontal effects' mentioned in section §7.05 above, which relate to the effects of EU rules on specific legal relationships between individuals, are situations where EU law may have broader 'spill over effects' on the national laws (including private law) of Member States. Examples are:

22. The *Delhaize* judgment (ECJ 9 June 1992 *Delhaize/Promalvin and AGE* C-47/90 [1992] p. I-3669 is a good example. A Spanish seller of wine invoked force majeure against his Belgian buyer, because national (Spanish) legislation prohibited exporting the wine. The buyer sued the seller, claiming performance of the agreement and arguing that the Spanish legislation contravened Article 29 EC (currently Article 35 TFEU). This position turned out to be correct, so that the legislation could not be applied. As a result the seller was bound to deliver the wine pursuant to the agreement. It is true that in this case the non-applicability of the national law on account of contravention of the treaty provision did have consequences for the legal relationship between the parties, but I would not call this direct horizontal effect, because I use this term only where a Treaty provision or other rule or principle of European law *itself* creates rights and obligations in legal relationships between individuals. - *Delhaize* was about reviewing the compatibility of a rule of (economic) administrative law with a Treaty provision. The same is true in the case of review against EU law rules of a different nature, subject to the proviso that in principle individuals cannot rely on incompatibility of national legislation with a directive. But where this is different – the *CIA Security* case law, for example – the same is true again (ECJ 26 Sep. 2000 *Unilever/ Central Food* C-443/98 [2000] I-7535).

23. This systematization presupposes of course that the relationship between the Member State and the individual is considered a relationship in private law. See above section §7.01[A] in fine.

24. ECJ 17 January 2008 *Viamex/Hauptzollamt Hamburg-Jonas* C-37 and 58/06 [2008] I-69.

25. ECJ 22 November 2005 *Mangold/Helm* C-144/04 [2005] I-9981; ECJ 19 January 2010, *Seda Kücükdeveci/Swedex*, C-555/07 [2010] I-365.

(1) broader harmonization than is envisaged by a directive;
(2) effective sanction: e.g., the introduction of full reimbursement of legal costs on a specific area of law, may ultimately spill over to other areas of law;
(3) the principle of equality may demand an equal treatment of internal and external (EU) situations.

§7.06 CONCLUSION

To conclude: the concepts of (in)direct effect and horizontal effect are complex and may be defined differently by scholars of European law and scholars of private law. The main reason is that scholars of European law are principally concerned with the constitutional aspects of the relationship between EU law and national law (primacy, direct effect), whereas private lawyers focus on the contents of relationships between individuals. European law cannot be properly explained to private lawyers without taking into account the distinctions made in this paper; and a debate between European lawyers and private lawyers cannot be intelligible to both without an understanding of their differing approaches.

CHAPTER 8

The Expectation of Legal Certainty and Horizontal Effect of EU Law

Juha Raitio

§8.01 THE EXPECTATION OF LEGAL CERTAINTY AND SOME CONTEMPORARY DEFINITIONS OF LEGAL CERTAINTY IN NORDIC LEGAL THEORY

The subtopic leads us back to the Nordic legal theory of the 1980s. According to Finnish legal theorist *Aulis Aarnio*, the expectation of legal certainty *sensu stricto*[1] means that every citizen has the right to expect legal protection.[2] Furthermore, the courts' obligation to give legal protection is such that the citizen's legal problem is dealt with in accordance with the law. The courts must also make a justified legal decision in the case at hand.[3] In the same tone Aarnio's Swedish colleague *Aleksander Peczenik* hold that legal decisions must be supported by a source of law and in hard cases they must even be supported by moral value statements. Thirdly he maintained that one must be able to reconstruct legal decision-making as a logically correct process of reasoning.[4]

According to both Aarnio and Peczenik, the expectation of legal certainty *sensu largo* contains two substantial elements: the demands that arbitrariness must be avoided (formal legal certainty) and that the decision must be proper and thus

1. On the terms *sensu stricto, sensu largo* and *sensu largissimo*, see MacCormick, D. Neil – Summers, Robert S. (eds.), Interpreting Statutes, A Comparative Study, Aldershot, pp. 12-13, (MacCormick-Summers 1991).
2. See Aarnio, Aulis, *The Rational as Reasonable, A Treatise on Legal Justification*, Dordrecht, 1987, p. 3, (Aarnio 1987).
3. See Aarnio, Aulis, *Reason and Authority, A Treatise on the Dynamic Paradigm of Legal Dogmatics*, Aldershot, 1997, pp. 189-190, (Aarnio 1997) and Peczenik, Aleksander, *On Law and Reason*, Dordrecht, 1989, pp. 29-31, (Peczenik 1989).
4. See Peczenik 1989, pp. 29-31.

acceptable (substantive legal certainty).[5] Formal legal certainty can be defended by stating that courts have to behave so that the citizens are able to plan their activities on a rational basis, which in turn is a necessary condition for the continuity of the society.[6] The need to eliminate randomness from the judicial decision-making requires in turn rational legal reasoning.[7] The minimum precondition for such reasoning is that the courts support their decisions with legal norms. This precondition is connected with the principle of legality, which has significance especially in criminal and penal law. On the other hand, the courts must use proper interpretation methods to adapt legal norms to moral or teleological arguments and to the facts of the case.[8] The expectation of legal certainty requires also that the decision as an outcome of the rational legal reasoning is reasonable. Thus the substantive aspect of legal certainty means that the judicial interpretation must be in accordance with the law and it has to meet certain minimum distinctive criteria of equity and justice.[9] Thus the formal and substantive legal certainty intertwine in judicial decision-making.

In the more recent Nordic jurisprudence even more elaborated conceptions of legal certainty have been presented.[10] For example, *Gustafsson* has presented an idea of social acceptability and moral acceptability in the context of substantive legal certainty. My contribution in turn has been the threefold conception of legal certainty, namely the formal, factual and substantive legal certainty. The three elements of the conception of legal certainty may illustrate the Legal Positivism, Legal Realism and Natural Law theories, respectively. Factual legal certainty is a logical derivation of *Wróblewskian* conception of factual validity.[11] Actually, the factual legal certainty is part of the broader conception of substantive legal certainty, which in turn resembles the idea of social and moral acceptability by Gustafsson. However, the idea of stability in the (factual) legal certainty is actually not a novelty at all.[12]

In Denmark, Norway and Sweden, there has been a tendency to advocate for substantive legal certainty, not only the formal one. For example, Gustafsson has presented an idea of social acceptability and moral acceptability (*etisk godtagbarhet*) in the context of substantive legal certainty.[13] In Finland, perhaps the most far-reaching attempt to emphasize the substantive legal certainty is presented by *Paunio*, although

5. See Aarnio 1987, p. 3 and Aarnio 1997, p. 191 and Peczenik 1989, p. 32.
6. See Aarnio 1987, p. 4 and Peczenik, Alexander, *Vad är rätt? Om demokrati, rättssäkerhet, etik och juridisk argumentation*, Stockholm, 1995, p. 90, (Peczenik 1995).
7. See Aarnio 1997, p. 191.
8. See Peczenik 1989, p. 34.
9. See Aarnio 1997, pp. 191-192.
10. See Raitio, Juha, *The Principle of Legal Certainty in EC Law*, Dordrecht, Kluwer Academic Publishers, 2003, pp. 347-387, (Raitio 2003) and Gustafsson, Håkan, *Rättens polyvalens; En rättsvetenskaplig studie av sociala rättigheter och rättssäkerhet*, Lund, 2002, 1 ff, (Gustafsson 2002).
11. See Wróblewski, *The Judicial Application of Law*, ed. By Zenon Bankowski and Neil MacCormick, Dordrecht, Kluwer Academic Publishers, 1992, pp. 75-83, (Wróblewski 1992). According to him, the validity of norms is based on systemic, factual and axiological validity.
12. See Bydlinski, Franz, *Juristische Methodenlehre und Rechtsbegriff*, Wien: Springer Verlag, 1982, pp. 325-329. *Bydlinski* has already in the 1980s listed the following elements for the legal certainty: '*Rechtsklarheit, Sicherung der Rechtsdurchsetzung, Stabilität des Rechts, Zugänglichkeit des Rechts*'.
13. See Gustafsson, 2002, 1 ff.

in the context of analysing the decisions of the multilingual European Court of Justice. She seems to think that legal certainty consists of a more substantive element that that of predictability. According to her views substantive legal certainty is related to substantive acceptability of legislation adjudication.[14] In many cases legal certainty can be understood as a means for justifying a certain outcome or interpretative choice. Paunio claims that coherence in legal reasoning promotes legal certainty in its substantive form.[15] However, the problematic feature of substantive legal certainty is the obscure scope of application. Additionally, the criteria of acceptability of judicial decision-making are not to be thoroughly described either.

At least some elements of the contemporary academic discussion concerning the teleological interpretation and the expectation of legal certainty can be linked to the rights-based and morality-oriented approach to law, which is popular especially in the Anglo-American legal culture. There people tend to openly discuss moral issues in the context of legal problems and the teleological argumentation is relatively often employed by the courts.[16] In common law countries there are no law codifications in the same sense as in many Continental (European) countries, the case law might be sporadic and known only by legal professionals, so the considerations based on moral issues –or notions of 'fairness' or 'acceptability'– are likely to dominate the public discourse in such circumstances. This resembles the situation within the European union as regards the EU law, which is difficult to systematize and interpret. What is acceptable and what is not appears to be a populist argument, which qualified lawyers or scholars of EU law would probably hesitate to use, since the questions of legality as arguments in judicial decision-making are on grounds of their special skills more important to them than questions of fairness. The public discourse concerning EU law does not necessarily deal with issues of morality or acceptability, but invariably touches on various policy considerations as well. All this can be formulated in words by Finnish legal theorist *Siltala's* terminology by stating that the professionals of EU law prefer to employ the arguments with the high or mixed level of legal formality, whereas the public discourse tends to employ arguments with a low level of legal formality or not at all.[17]

One might wonder are there any universal criteria of acceptability in judicial decision-making. I have intentionally left this question unanswered and studied the argumentation patterns, levels of justification and rational interpretation instead.[18] One might note the universal nature of human and fundamental rights, though. The concept of 'acceptability' is connected with the material content of the interpretation

14. See Paunio, E, *Beyond Words, The European Court of Justice and Legal Certainty in Multilinqual EU Law*, Helsinki, Unigrafia, 2011, p. 7, (Paunio 2011).
15. *Ibid.*, 113. One might note that the underlying theoretical framework of Paunio's research is based on hermeneutical philosophy as well as on Habermas' work on discourse theory of law.
16. See MacCormick-Summers 1991, pp. 359-459.
17. See Siltala, Raimo, *A Theory of Precedent, From Analytical Positivism to a Post-Analytical Philosophy of Law*, Oxford, Hart Publishing, 2000, pp. 54-63, (Siltala 2000).
18. On the various argumentation models from the comparative perspective see MacCormick-Summers 1991, pp. 9-27 and 461-551.

and not with the form of reasoning itself. The reasonable result of the interpretation must correspond to the knowledge and values of the legal community in question.[19]

Inevitably, the substantive aspect of legal certainty is at least partially a subjective notion, since there is scant evidence of a uniform value-basis in modern societies. Still, if the requirement of legal certainty is exhausted merely by referring to the predictability and legality of the judicial decision-making, this would make any legal decision acceptable irrespective of its content or consequences. In general then, predictability can be related to the inner logic of judicial decision-making, to the subsumption of the fact and norm premises, whereas acceptability relates to the content of the decision.

§8.02 HOW THE EUROPEAN COURT OF JUSTICE HAS DEFINED LEGAL CERTAINTY AND HORIZONTAL EFFECTS OF EU LAW IN ITS EARLY CASE LAW?

The threefold conception of legal certainty (formal, factual, substantive) or Gustafsson's in effect similar definition (formal legal certainty and two-dimensional substantive legal certainty) can be illustrated by the famous case *Defrenne v. Sabena*[20] concerning the equal pay for men and women and the exceptional temporal effects of the judgment. Rasmussen has emphasized the significance of the *Defrenne v. Sabena* case by stating that it continued the development of the law of integration where the *van Gend en Loos* case[21] ended.[22] As is well known, in this case a Belgian air hostess had initiated proceedings in Belgium on the basis of the equal pay Article 119 EEC (Article 157 TFEU), because she did not earn as much as the male flight attendants, who had in fact the same tasks than air hostesses. The Court confirmed the direct effect of Article 119 EEC, but it applied the principle of legal certainty in order to limit the retroactive effect.

Firstly, the ECJ held that Article 119 EEC (Article 157 TFEU) was directly effective against a private party, the employer Sabena.[23] The *Van Gend en Loos* case introduced the vertical direct effect between the individuals and a Member State, whereas the scope of direct effect was broader in the *Defrenne v. Sabena* case, namely even the horizontal direct effect between individuals was held to be acceptable by the ECJ. One might also note that in the *Defrenne v. Sabena* case the direct effect was upheld despite the broad and underdeveloped terms of Article 119 EEC. Thus the ruling increased the efficiency of the EU law and access to justice within the national judiciaries. Therefore it was to be expected that the Court applied the horizontal direct effect between

19. On the concept of 'rational acceptability' as well as the terms 'L-rationality and D-rationality' see Aarnio 1987, pp. 158-229, esp. pp. 188-193.
20. Case 43/75 *Defrenne v. Sabena* (1976) ECR 455.
21. Case 26/62 *Van Gend en Loos* (1963) ECR 1.
22. See Rasmussen, Hjalte, *The European Court of Justice*, Copenhagen 1998, pp. 324-325, (Rasmussen 1998).
23. *Ibid.*, p. 476, para. 39.

individuals or private entities in its subsequent cases such as *Angonese,*[24] *Raccanelli*[25] or even in a politically a bit controversial case *Viking Line.*[26]

Secondly, the ECJ restricted the implications of its ruling and the direct effect of Article 119 EEC on the basis of legal certainty. Without temporal restrictions it would have been impossible to enforce the judgment in practice within the Member States on grounds of considerable financial consequences and difficulties involved in calculating the loss women had suffered in the past. One of the most important tasks of the ECJ is to safeguard the full functioning of the internal market and it would not have been in keeping with this task to give a judgment which would have placed both private and public undertakings in huge financial difficulties and driven some of them inevitably to bankruptcy.[27]

This stance based on the principle of legal certainty led to the conclusion that the direct effect of Article 119 EEC cannot be relied on in order to support claims concerning pay periods prior to the date of this judgment, except as regards those workers who have already brought legal proceedings or made an equivalent claim. I find that this ruling takes into consideration in a well-balanced way the demands of the factual legal certainty, or social acceptability in Gustafsson's terms, since both the practical reasoning in the background of the judgment and even the practical consequences of the judgment have been taken into account. However, it is important to emphasize that such an exceptional restriction of judgments' temporal effects has occurred relatively rarely, and typically in the 1990s in the context of case law concerning various social benefits.[28] In recent case law it has been stated that such temporal restrictions are possible under two essential criteria, namely that those concerned acted in good faith and there is a risk of serious difficulties.[29] In various circumstances legal relations established in good faith seems to be protected by the Court.[30] In any case normally the more predictable formal legal certainty seem to prevail in the argumentation of the temporal effects of the judgments.[31]

The *Defrenne v. Sabena* case is also illustrative in a sense that it shows that the principle of legal certainty is one of the widest generality as 'an underlying principle' of law. In comparison to the principle of equal pay this becomes easily understandable. The principle of equal treatment between men and women, i.e., equality in general, might be understood as forming the background to Article 157 TFEU, according to

24. Case C-281/98 *Angonese* (2000) ECR I-4139, paras 30, 34 and 36. The Court made it clear that the prohibition of discrimination on grounds of nationality laid down in Article 48 of the Treaty (Article 45 TFEU, free movement of workers) must be regarded as applying to private persons as well.
25. Case C-94/07 *Raccanelli* (2008) ECR I-5939, paras 41-46.
26. Case C-438/05 *Viking Line* (2009) ECR I-10779.
27. Case 43/75 *Defrenne v. Sabena* (1976) ECR 455, para. 74.
28. Cases 43/75 *Defrenne v. Sabena* (1976) ECR 455, 24/86 *Blaizot* (1988) ECR 379, C-262/88 *Barber* (1990) ECR I-1889, C-163/90 *Legros* (1992) ECR I-4625, C-485 & C-486/93 *Simitzi* (1995) ECR I-2655, C-415/93 *Bosman* (1995) ECR I-4921, C-308/93 *Cabanis-Issarte* (1996) ECR I-2097, C-262/96 *Sema Sürül* (1999) ECR I-2685 and C-437/97 *Evangelischer Krankenhausverein Wien* (2000) ECR I-1157.
29. Case C-73/08 *Bressol* (2010) ECR I-2735, para. 91
30. Case C- 161/06 *Skoma-Lux* (2007) ECR I-10841, para. 67.
31. Cases C-137/94 *Richardson* (1995) ECR I-3407 and C-423/04 *Richards* (2006) ECR I-3585.

which the principle of equal pay for male and female workers for equal work of equal value must be ensured. The principle of equal pay and its scope of application can be defined relatively accurately by reference to the case law[32] and to the secondary legislation. There is for example case law concerning the meaning of 'pay', which the ECJ has interpreted in a very broad fashion to include any benefit paid in respect of the employment.[33] Legal certainty in turn can be related to various circumstances, not only to the relationship between an employer and employee. The sporadic case law in which the principle of legal certainty has been mentioned as an argument is more difficult to systematize than the case law of the principles which have a relatively narrow scope of application.

The extensive scope of application of the legal certainty can be illustrated by referring to the recent case law of the European Court of Justice. The principle of legal certainty has been mentioned in the relatively recent *Intertanko*-case[34] in the context of ship-source pollution and on the introduction of penalties for infringements. In this context the predictability aspect of legal certainty seems to be more relevant than more casualistic acceptability aspect. The European Court of Justice (ECJ) clarified the content of legal certainty as follows:

> The general principle of legal certainty, which is a fundamental principle of Community law, requires, in particular, that rules should be clear and precise, so that individuals may ascertain unequivocally what their rights and obligations are and may take steps accordingly.[35]

However, this citation does not really suffice as a definition of legal certainty and it has not even supposed to be interpreted like that. Both of these examples illustrate that in the context of EU law the principle of legal certainty has come to the fore in various contexts and legal principles.[36] The specific fields where legal certainty is at stake are, for example, the principles of legitimate expectations,[37] acquired rights,[38] the non-retroactivity of EU legislation,[39] lack of procedural time-limits[40] or the demand of understandable language.[41]

32. See Klami Hannu Tapani, *Methodological Problems in European and Comparative Law*, Helsinki 1997, p. 12.
33. See e.g. cases 80/70 *Defrenne v. Belgian State* (1971) ECR 445, esp. pp. 450-452 (retirement pensions), 12/81 *Garland* (1982) ECR 359, esp. pp. 367-371 (concessionary travel facilities provided for employees after the termination of the employment) or 262/88 *Barber* (1990) ECR I-1889, esp. pp. I-1948 - I-1952 (redundancy pay and pension payments).
34. Case C-308/06 *Intertanko* (2008) ECR I-4057.
35. *Ibid.*, para. 69 and also C-110/03 *Belgium v. Commission* [2005] ECR I-2801, para. 30 .
36. See more thorougly e.g. Raitio 2003, pp. 187-263.
37. See 112/77 *Töpfer* (1978) ECR 1019, esp. pp. 1032-1033, paras 18,19 and 212-217/80 *Salumi* (1981) ECR 2735, esp. p. 2751, para. 10.
38. See 23/68 *Klomp* (1969) ECR 43, esp. p. 50 and 10/78 *Belbouab* (1978) ECR 1915, esp. p. 1924-1925.
39. See 98/78 *Racke* (1979) ECR 69, esp. p. 84, paras 15 and 212-217/80 *Salumi* (1981) ECR 2735, esp. p. 2751, paras 9-10.
40. See the Steel Subsidies case 59/70 *Netherlands v. Commission* (1971) ECR 639, esp. p. 653, paras 15-19.
41. See 66/74 *Farrauto* (1975) ECR 157, esp. p. 162, para. 6 and C-161/06 *Skoma-Lux* (2007) ECR I-10841, para. 67.

§8.03 NON-DISCRIMINATION ON GROUNDS OF AGE AND THE HORIZONTAL EFFECT OF GENERAL PRINCIPLES

Nowadays one can argue that the principle of non-discrimination on grounds of age can be regarded as a general principle of EU law, because it has been designated as such in the *Mangold* case.[42] On the other hand, one can find a description of the principle of non-discrimination in Article 19 TFEU (Article 13 EC) as well as in Article 2 of Directive 2000/78/EC[43] and a more specific scope of application as regards the principle of non-discrimination on grounds of age in Article 6(1) of the Directive 2000/78/EC.[44] It is important to note, however, that the ECJ holds that the actual source of the forms of equal treatment in employment and occupation can be found in various international instruments and in the constitutional traditions of the Member States.[45] The Court stated that national courts must guarantee the full effectiveness of the general principle of non-discrimination in respect of age, setting aside any provision of national law which may conflict with EU law, even when the period prescribed for transposition of that Directive has not yet expired.[46] The Court's argumentation as regards the horizontal effects of discrimination on grounds of age was controversial in such a way that many requests for a preliminary ruling originated especially from German or Austrian courts after *Mangold*.[47] This leads one to conclude that legal certainty comes to the fore in the argumentation when Member States enjoy broad discretion in their choice of the measures capable of attaining their objectives in the field of social and employment policy.

The *Mangold*-judgment has been criticized by A-G *Mazák* in *Palacios de la Villa* case.[48] In his view neither Article 19 TFEU (Article 13 EC) nor Directive 2000/78/EC necessarily reflect an already existing prohibition of all the forms of discrimination to which they refer.[49] Therefore one may pose a question, whether not only prohibition to discriminate on grounds of age, but all specific prohibitions of the types of discrimination referred in Article 19 TFEU or Directive 2000/78/EC would have to be regarded as general principles of EU law.[50] A-G *Mazák* does not regard as particularly compelling the conclusion drawn on *Mangold* case as to the existence of a general principle of non-discrimination on grounds of age. It is relevant to point out that various international instruments and constitutional traditions common to the Member States to

42. See C-144/04 *Mangold* (2005) ECR I-9981, para. 75.
43. See OJ, No. L 303, 2.12.2000, p. 16, at p. 18.
44. *Ibid.*, at p. 19.
45. See C-144/04 *Mangold* (2005) ECR I-9981, para. 74.
46. *Ibid.*, para. 78.
47. See e.g. C-45/09 *Rosenbladt* (2010) ECR I-9391, C-341/08 *Petersen* (2010) ECR I-47, C-229/08 *Wolf* (2010) ECR 1, C-88/08 *Hütter* (2009) ECR I-5325 (Austria), C-555/07 *Kücükdeveci* (2010) ECR I-365 and C-427/06 *Bartsch* (2008) ECR I-7245
48. See C-411/05 *Palacios de la Villa* (2007) ECR I-8531 and the Opinion of A-G Mazák, delivered on 15 February 2007.
49. Discrimination is prohibited on grounds of religion, disability, age or sexual orientation in Article 1 of the Directive 2000/78/EC.
50. See e.g. C-13/05 *Chacón Navas*, the Opinion of A-G Geelhoed, delivered on 16 March 2006, para. 53. A-G Geelhoed found no room for widening the scope of Article 13 EC by relying on the general policy of equality.

which the ECJ refers in the *Mangold* case enshrine the general principle of equal treatment, but not - except a few cases, such as the Finnish constitution - the specific principle of non-discrimination on grounds of age as such.[51]

In the subsequent *Kücükdeveci* case the Court referred to the non-discrimination on grounds of age not merely as a general principle of EU law but as a Charter right.[52] In *Kücükdeveci* the non-discrimination on grounds of age was applied in legal proceedings between two individuals eventually so that a conflicting norm of national legislation was left unapplied. The Court confirmed on the basis of the *Mangold* case that the principle of non-discrimination on grounds of age is a general principle of European Union law in that it constitutes a specific application of the general principle of equal treatment, which in turn can be derived from various international instruments and from constitutional traditions common to the Member States.[53] In this context the Court has applied systemic argumentation by referring to analogy as regards the *Defrenne* case.[54] On the other hand, the Court stated that Article 6(1) TEU provides that the Charter of Fundamental Rights of the European Union is to have the same legal value as the Treaties and that under Article 21(1) of the Charter any discrimination based on age shall be prohibited.[55] This shows in concrete way that the coming into force of the Lisbon Treaty has been noted by the Court. The Court also relied on its traditional means to enforce the impact of EU law in the national sphere, namely it referred to the significance of the indirect effect of EU law[56] and even to the primacy of EU law.[57]

It is to be noted, though, that the Court confirmed the horizontal effect of the non-discrimination on grounds of age in spite of the fact that Article 51 of the Charter does not seem to allow for horizontal application of its provisions. Based on the wording of Article 51(1) it seems to be clear that the Charter provisions are applicable only in relation to EU institutions and to Member States when they are applying and implementing EU law. The Court has actually interpreted Article 51(1) literally according to it's wording,[58] which I think is in coherence with the expectation of legal certainty. Article 51(1) is central to the relation between EU fundamental rights and the Member States' legal systems and it has its background in the case law of the Court.

---

51. See C-411/05 *Palacios de la Villa*, the Opinion of A-G Mazák, delivered on 15 February 2007, para. 88.
52. See C-555/07 *Kücükdeveci* (2010) ECR I-365.
53. *Ibid.*, paras 20 and 50.
54. *Ibid.*, para. 21 and by analogy Case 43/75 *Defrenne* (1976) ECR 455, para. 54.
55. *Ibid.*, para. 22.
56. *Ibid.*, para. 47 and 48.
57. *Ibid.*, para. 54.
58. See e.g., C-27/11 *Vinkov*, Judgment of 7 June 2012, not yet reported, paras 57-60, C-411/10 and C-493/10 *N.S.*, Judgment of 21 December 2011, not yet reported, paras 64,65,68 and 69, C-483/09 and C-1/10 *Gueye*, Judgment of 15 September 2011, not yet reported, para. 69 and C-400/10 PPU, *McB* (2010) ECR I-8965, paras 44, 45 and 50-52.

Especially the cases *Wachauf*[59] and *ERT*[60] are relevant in this context, but also the more subsequent cases *Annibaldi*[61] and *Karlsson*.[62]

Therefore it has been relatively often noted in the legal literature that the *Kücükdeveci* decision signifies a considerable step in development of the scope of application of the EU fundamental rights.[63] However, based on the clear wording of the case, the horizontal direct effect of Directives was not established by the Court.[64] The problematic interpretation relates to the question, how far-reaching is the requirement of consistent interpretation, i.e., the indirect effect of the Articles of a Directive.[65] The Court has analysed the Article 6(1) of the Directive 2000/78 and aspects of non-discrimination on grounds of age in its subsequent case law even further.[66]

However, in this context it is relevant to mention the *Römer* case,[67] in which the Court adopted a much more restrictive interpretation as regards the discrimination based on sexual orientation than it has done as regards discrimination on grounds of age in the *Mangold* line of cases. This seems to be a bit controversial issue in the sense that the Court did not follow Advocate General *Jääskinen's* opinion on this matter. However, I find that the Court respected the expectation of legal certainty for not following the line of argumentation adopted in *Mangold*. In this respect it is relevant to note that in the circumstances of the *Römer* case the applicant could rely on his rights as regards non-discrimination based on sexual orientation only after the expiry of the period for transposing the Directive 2000/78/EC.[68]

§8.04 HOW THE EMPHASIS ON FUNDAMENTAL RIGHTS AND THE CHARTER HAS AFFECTED TO THE CASE LAW OF THE COURT?

It has become clear that EU fundamental rights are not only binding on EU Institutions, but Member States are also bound by them when implementing EU law.[69] For example, as regards the Charter of Fundamental Rights the Court has consistently held that it must be taken into consideration only when some other EU norm is to be applied in a national sphere.[70] This obligation applies to Member State legislators when transposing Directives into national legal order and to national courts when interpreting EU

59. 5/88 *Wachauf* (1989) ECR 2609.
60. C-260/89 *ERT* (1991) ECR I-2925.
61. Case C-309/96 *Annibaldi* (1997) ECR I-7493, paras 21-23. In this case the Court denied the applicability of fundamental rights on the basis of an analysis showing that the national law at issue did not present sufficient links to EU law.
62. Case C-292/97 *Karlsson* (2000) ECR I-2737, para. 37.
63. See e.g. Pech, Laurent: Union Founded on the Rule of Law: Meaning and Reality of the Rule of Law as a Constitutional Principle of EU Law, 6 European Constitutional Law Review (2010) 359, 384-385.
64. See C-555/07 *Kücükdeveci* (2010) ECR I-365, para. 46.
65. *Ibid.*, para. 47.
66. See C-447/09 *Prigge et al.*, Judgment of 13 September 2011, not yet reported.
67. See C-147/08 *Römer* (2011) ECR I-3591.
68. *Ibid.*, paras 58-64.
69. See e.g. 5/88 *Wachauf* (1989) ECR I-2609 and C-260/89 *ERT* (1991) ECR I-2925.
70. See e.g. C.400/10 PPU, *McB* (2010) ECR I-8965, paras 44,45 and 50-52, C-411/10 and C-493/10 *N.S.*, Judgment of 21 December 2011, not yet reported, paras 64,65, 68 and 69 or C-27/11

secondary law.[71] Directives must not be interpreted in a manner, which collides with EU fundamental rights or other general principles of EU law. It is also noteworthy that when a certain fundamental right is to be found both in Charter and in the European Convention of Human Rights, is suffices to rely on the Charter Article only.[72] However, the emphasis on fundamental rights and the importance of the Charter should not be overestimated. One has to take into consideration the systemic interpretation of EU law. This can be shown in the recent case law.

For example, the *Dominguez* case,[73] is interesting in this respect. It concerned the interpretation of Directive 2003/88/EC, the right to paid annual leave and thus social policy. It is to be noted that the Court first stated the entitlement of every worker to paid annual leave must be regarded as a particularly important principle of European Union social law, but it did not explicitly designate it as a general principle of EU law like it did in the context of non-discrimination on grounds of age.[74] Then the Court emphasized the importance of consistent interpretation of EU law, or indirect effect of EU law, as well as the full effectiveness of EU law, which in turn pinpoints the importance of systemic interpretation.[75] In this context it is important to note, though, that like in *Kücükdeveci* the Court did not accept the horizontal direct effect of Directives, which is in line with the settled case law.[76] It is interesting that although Advocate General *Trstenjak* had analysed the facts of the case also in the context of Charter rights, this was not done by the Court in the grounds of the judgment. However, one might pose a question, would it have been necessary in *Dominguez* case to elaborate the Charter rights. I don't think it was necessary, but on the other hand, I intentionally advocate for a systemic interpretation of EU law. Those, who emphasize more teleological approach, would probably have wished for a rights-based approach.

Additionally, I find that the recent case law on EU citizenship and the principle of non-discrimination on grounds of nationality is illustrative.[77] These cases can typically be related to social policy as well. In *Zambrano*,[78] protecting citizens against the deprivation of their genuine enjoyment of the substance of their rights is rooted

Vinkov, Judgment of 7 June 2012, not yet reported, paras 57-60, C-23/12 *Zakaria*, Judgment of 17 January 2013, not yet reported, para. 39 and C-87/12 *Ymeraga*, Judgment of 8 May 2013, not yet reported, para. 43

71. See e.g. C-275/06 *Promusicae* (2008) ECR I-271, para. 68.
72. See e.g. C-386/10 P, *Chalcor v. Commission*, Judgment of 8 December 2011, not yet reported, para. 51 and C-199/11 *Otis*, Judgment of 6 November 2012, not yet reported, para. 47. The Court seems to have taken this stance already in case C-400/10 PPU, *McB* (2010) ECR I-8965, para. 53.
73. See C-282/10 *Dominguez*, Judgment of 24 January 2012, not yet reported.
74. *Ibid.*, para. 16.
75. *Ibid.*, paras 24 ad 25.
76. *Ibid.*, para. 42 and for example, C-397/01 and C-403/01 *Pfeiffer* (2004) ECR I-8835, para. 109.
77. See e.g. C-135/08 *Rottmann* (2010) ECR I-1449, C-34/09 *Zambrano* (2011) ECR I-1177, C-434/09 *McCarthy*, (2011) ECR I-3375 and C-256/11 *Dereci*, Judgment of 15 November 2011, not yet reported and C-356/11 and C-357/11 *O and S*, Judgment of 6 December 2012, not yet reported.
78. See C-34/09 *Zambrano* (2011) ECR I-1177.

exclusively in EU citizenship without any recourse to the Charter.[79] In *Dereci*[80] the Court mentioned the right to family life under Article 7 of the Charter, but in the end left it to the national court to decide whether the situation of the applicants comes within the scope of Union law, i.e., whether the Article 7 of the Charter is applicable.[81]

To my mind, *Dereci* is a case in which emphasis is in the interpretation of Article 20 TFEU, not in a relevant way to the Charter rights such as the respect for private and family life.[82] The difficult point in this case was that the EU citizens concerned have never exercised their right to free movement and have always resided in a Member State of which they are nationals. EU citizenship is a fundamental status of nationals of a Member State. *Zambrano* and *Dereci* can be linked together so that they both relate to the question of 'genuine enjoyment of the substance of the rights' conferred by virtue of the EU citizenship.[83] This in turn refers to situations in which the EU citizen has to leave not only the territory of the Member State of which he is a national but also the territory of the Union as a whole. In those circumstances, EU citizens would, in fact, be unable to exercise the substance of the rights conferred on them by virtue of their status as citizens of the Union, as the Court aptly put it.[84]

§8.05 HOW THE RECENT CASE LAW ON THE APPLICATION OF FUNDAMENTAL RIGHTS CAN BE LINKED TO THE EXPECTATION OF LEGAL CERTAINTY: A QUESTION OF INTERPRETATION MODELS

Then one might pose a question how this analysis concerning Article 51(1) of the Charter and the emphasis on fundamental rights can be linked to legal certainty. This is a relevant question in a sense that in *Mangold, Kücükdeveci, Zambrano, Dereci* and *Dominguez* the expectation of legal certainty did not come to the fore in the argumentation of the Court. However, this does not mean that an underlying principle such as legal certainty would have been left unnoticed. I find that the way to effectively bring legal certainty to the spotlight of this discussion is to analyse the various interpretation models the Court seems to apply, namely literal, teleological and contextual (systemic) ones.[85] My hypothesis is that the more the Court would be inclined to apply various fundamental rights and rely on Charter rights the more teleological the Court rulings become. On the other hand, it seems to me that the Court has not been willing to 'run wild', but instead of ultra-teleological rights-based interpretations it has applied its

79. See Ladenburger, Clemens: European Union Institutional Report, in Laffranque Julia (ed.), The Protection of Fundamental Rights Post-Lisbon, Reports of The FIDE Congress, Tallinn Tartu University Press, 2012, pp. 141-215, at p. 162.
80. See C-256/11 *Dereci*, Judgment of 15 November 2011, not yet reported.
81. Walkila, Sonya, The Use of the Charter of Fundamental Rights of the European Union in Court Adjudication – Stronger Rights for the Union Citizens, Europarättsligt Tidskrift, 4/2012, p. 616.
82. See C-256/11 *Dereci*, Judgment of 15 November 2011, not yet reported, paras 70 and 71.
83. See C-256/11 *Dereci*, Judgment of 15 November 2011, not yet reported, paras 62-69 and C-34/09 *Zambrano*, (2011) ECR I-1177, paras 41-44.
84. C-256/11 *Dereci*, Judgment of 15 November 2011, not yet reported, para. 65.
85. *Ibid.*, para. 54, in which the Court expressly mentioned the literal, telological and contextual interpretation models.

traditional systemic interpretation model in which it has relied on its previous case law and to the concepts of EU law often connected to the terms of internal market such as 'the citizenship of the Union'. However, it seems to be clear that the Court will have to develop its case law on fundamental rights even further. For example, a step ahead are the *Åkerberg Fransson* and *Melloni* cases, which clarify the question concerning the application of EU law in the context of Article 51(1) of the Charter.[86]

This hypothesis concerning the connection between the fundamental rights and teleology leads me to a more theoretical issue of coherence in legal decision-making. I am a bit hesitant as regards Paunio's emphasis on the originally *Soriano's* modest notion of coherence,[87] which focuses on analysing the legal reasoning of the European Court of Justice instead of formulating the whole legal system as a coherent unit based on a limited number of principles. It ensures that value choices are expressed in the justification. Her ideas lead me to pose some questions, which are in fact connected to expectation of legal certainty as well. Will the emphasis on substantive legal certainty lead to increasing casuism, to context-bound discussions of fairness or to emphasizing legal certainty too much from an individual's point of view instead of a more communitarian way emphasizing stability and predictability? Will the emphasis on substantive legal certainty advocate for more Anglo-American way to justify legal decisions than has been the Court's practise so far?

I oppose this kind of ultra-teleological interpretation of EU law. The Court decisions should be context-bound, but this does not mean that the coherence of the legal system as a whole can be hampered. It is not enough to make sure that a decision contains coherent arguments from the beginning to the end of it. I call such a casuism as 'the Casanova-method' named after the famous playboy.[88] Casanova was successful, because he told to the partner whatever she wanted to hear. He could trust that no one really knew how the stories differed from one another. Courts don't have this possibility, because the judgments are published and known. If the courts settle for casuism and tend to neglect the systemic interpretation, the coherence of the legal system will be hampered, which in turn is a threat to the legal certainty.

Then again, one could argue that my criticism against the modest notion of coherence is too far-reaching. It is indeed true that Soriano has emphasized the coherence of legal argumentation instead of coherence of legal rulings. A modest notion of coherence is meant an indeterminate criterion of rightness which is not able to provide an ultimate answer for every case. It provides 'a criterialess criterion of legal reasoning'.[89] He asks, whether the argumentation which supports a certain ruling cohere and how one can find coherence in connecting, or 'netting' reasons, which

86. See C-617/10 *Åkerberg Fransson*, Judgment of 26 February 2013, not yet reported, para. 29 and C-399/11 *Melloni*, Judgment of 26 February 2013, not yet reported, para. 60.
87. About modest notion of coherence see Soriano Leonor Moral, 'A Modest Notion of Coherence in Legal Reasoning. A Model for the European Court of Justice', 16 *Ratio Juris*, 2003, pp. 296-323, (Soriano 2003).
88. See a more thorough presentation on Casanova-method in Raitio, Juha: 'Legal Certainty as an Element of Objectivity in Law', in Husa, Jaakko and van Hoecke Mark (eds.), *Objectivity in Law and Legal Reasoning*, Oxford, Hart Publishing, 2013, pp. 85-108.
89. See Soriano 2003, p. 307.

support the ruling. In his article he has first taken as an example of the traditional approach to interpret EU law the following words originally written by Judge Edward:

> The judge's role cannot be confined to that of providing a technocratic literal interpretation of texts produced by others. () As a system based on case law the judge must proceed from one case to another seeking, as points come up for decision, to make the legal system consistent, coherent, workable, and effective.[90]

This citation naturally underlines the significance that the rulings cohere, i.e., systemic interpretation, which is exactly my point as well. One way to interpret Soriano's modest notion of coherence is that it would merely mean that he underlines the 'netting of arguments' and advocates for a better quality in the reasoning of the Court of Justice. Then in the end one may once more state in a relieved tone that the European Court of Justice is not 'running wild'.[91]

---

90. See Edward David, 'Judicial Activism: Myth or Reality?' in Angus, Campbell and Meropi Voyatzi (eds.), *Legal Reasoning and Judicial Interpretation of European Law*, London, Trenton, 1996, 29-67, esp. pp. 66-67 and Soriano 2003, p. 298.
91. See Cappelletti, Mauro, The Judicial Process in Comparative Perspective, Oxford, Clarendon Press, 1989, pp. 384-401 and Rasmussen, Hjalte, On Law and Policy in the European Court of Justice, A Comparative Study in Judicial Policymaking, Dordrecht, 1986, pp. 13-14. Rasmussen has described and commented the criticism of Professor Hamson, whose paper 'Methods of Interpretation - a Critical Assessment of the Results' was submitted to a Judicial and Academic Conference held at the ECJ in 27-28, September 1976. One might point out, though, that Hamson eventually held the ECJ's ruling in Van Gend en Loos case to be justifiable, although he warned that the Court should not become 'more royalist than the King'.

CHAPTER 9

Horizontal Effect of General Principles: Bold Rulings and Fine Distinctions

Takis Tridimas

§9.01 INTRODUCTION

Although traditionally the case law was reluctant to accept that general principles of law bind individuals,[1] recent cases suggest otherwise. This chapter seeks to examine the direct and indirect horizontality of general principles.[2] It is structured as follows. After some short introductory remarks, it revisits *Mangold*.[3] Although the judgment has been the subject of extensive commentary, many of its aspects remain unexplored. This contribution seeks to discuss in detail the Court's reasoning and its implications. It then assesses the response of the Bundesverfassungsgericht and, in the light of *Dominguez*,[4] whether the *Mangold – Kücükdeveci*[5] approach can be extended to other general principles. Finally, it looks at the indirect horizontality of general principles. The analysis does not seek to discuss in detail the possible horizontal effect of the EU Charter of Fundamental Rights nor does it examine the horizontal effect of fundamental freedoms.

By way of introduction, the following points may be made. First, a distinction may be drawn between direct and indirect horizontality.[6] Direct horizontality occurs where a private party seeks to rely directly on a constitutional norm, e.g., the founding

1. See e.g. Case C-2/92 *Bostock* [1994] ECR I-955.
2. The chapter borrows heavily from my analysis in the second chapter of the third edition of *the General Principles of EU Law*.
3. Case C-144/04 *Mangold v. Helm* [2005] ECR I-9981.
4. Case C-282/10 *Dominguez v. CICOA*, judgment 24 January 2012.
5. Case C-555/07 *Seda Kücükdeveci v. Swedex GmbH & Co. KG*, judgment of 19 January 2010.
6. For the horizontal effect of fundamental rights, see in general D. Oliver and J. Fedtke (Eds), Human Rights and the Private Sphere (Routlege, 2007); A. Clapham, *Human Rights Obligations of Non-State Actors* (Oxford: OUP, 2006); A. Clapham, *Human Rights in the Private Sphere*

Treaties, the Charter, or a general principle of law, against another private party. Direct horizontality was accepted in *Mangold* and *Kücükdeveci* in relation to the general principle of non-discrimination on grounds of age. Indirect horizontality may take several forms but, essentially, occurs where private relations are affected through the imposition of duties on state authorities, mostly the courts. Depending on how extensively indirect horizontality is understood, the distinction between direct and indirect horizontality may lie more in the formal reasoning that underpins them and less in their effects. The two forms of horizontality can best be viewed as different sides of the same coin.

Secondly, although the case law has accepted that some Treaty provisions may produce horizontal effect, the extent of such effect remains unclear and its rationale inarticulate. The ECJ has not sought to elaborate a theory of horizontality and seems more preoccupied with the facts of each case. Thus, horizontal effect has been grounded on the objectives of the Treaty provision in issue,[7] its importance and its effectiveness,[8] the 'private governance'[9] model, the market power of private associations[10] or the market access foreclosure model.[11] As we shall see a similar lack of clarity also characterizes the horizontality of general principles.

Thirdly, although cases of direct horizontality are rare, there is nothing to preclude *a priori* the horizontal effect of general principles. They are rules of primary law which, according to the principle of primacy, can in appropriate circumstances be invoked by an individual against another.[12] It may be argued that the historical origins and purpose of general principles, which is to protect the individual against public authorities, suggests a negative reply. That reasoning focuses on the role of fundamental rights as part of the liberal bargain. They are the quid pro quo for the citizen conceding powers to the state and can therefore be invoked only against state authorities. But that argument is not conclusive. In the modern pluralist State, the traditional public–private dichotomy is not categorical. In certain cases, fundamental

(Oxford University Press, 1993); D. Spielmann, *L'effet potentiel de la Convention européenne des droits de l'homme entre personnes privées* (Brussels: Bruylant, 1995).

7. This applies, for example, in relation to Articles 101 and 102 TFEU.
8. See e.g. Case 43/75 *Defrenne v. Sabena* [1976] ECR 455; Case C-281/98 *Angonese v. Cassa di Risparmio di Bolzano SpA*, [2000] ECR I–4139.
9. C. Barnard, The Substantive Law of the EU, 3rd Ed., OUP, Oxford, 2010 at 234. According to this rationale, Treaty freedoms bind private bodies where they exercise a regulatory task or quasi-legislative power: see e.g. Case 36/74 *Walrave v. Association Union Cycliste Internationale* [1974] ECR 1405; Case C-415/93 *Bosman* [1995] ECR I-4921; and more recently, in relation to the free movement of goods, Case C-171/11 *Fra.bo SpA v. Deutsche Vereinigung des Gas- und Wasserfaches eV (DVGW)*, judgment of 12 July 2012.
10. See e.g. Case C-438/05 *International Transport Workers' Federation and Finnish Seamen's Union v. Viking Line ABP* [2007] ECR I-10779
11. According to this rationale, Treaty freedoms produce horizontal effect where it is necessary to overcome a restriction on market access which could not be remedied by the application of the ordinary rules of free market and liberal competition. See e.g. *Angonese, supra*. This economic rationale of horizontality was articulated by Maduro AG in his Opinion in Case C-438/05 *International Transport Workers' Federation and Finnish Seamen's Union v. Viking Line ABP* [2007] ECR I-10779, paras 41 et seq. of the Opinion.
12. See K. Lenaerts and J. Gutiérrez-Fons, The Constitutional Allocation of Powers and General Principles of EU Law, at 1641-2, and see also K. Lenaerts and Corthaut, Of Birds and Hedges: The Role of Primacy in Invoking Norms of EU Law, 31 (2006) ELRev 287 at 290-291.

rights deserve to be protected as much against private entities as against public ones. The horizontal effect of a general principle may be justified for many reasons. It may be necessitated on functional grounds where a private entity exercises de facto public power or a power traditionally reserved to the state. It may be justified because of the value that the principle incorporates. It may be said, for example, that the prohibition of discrimination on grounds of race or gender are of such constitutional value that they should trump the principle of private autonomy and bind both public and private actors. Finally, horizontality may be dictated by the objectives and the effectiveness of a principle. Thus, the prohibition of discrimination on grounds of gender may be said to be intended to cover relations between individuals since, otherwise, its effectiveness would be much diminished. Whether a general principle is capable of binding individuals will be a matter of interpretation and depend on the purpose for which the general principle is invoked in the circumstances of the case. It will thus be necessary to establish that (a) a general principle with a sufficiently ascertainable normative content exists and (b) it is appropriate to apply it in a horizontal situation. *Mangold* suggests that the ECJ is prepared to be bold. Similar developments have occurred in national laws. In a case decided in 2001, the French *Cour de Cassation* held that an employer had breached the employee's right to private life by gaining unauthorized access to his personal emails stored in a computer provided to him by the employer.[13] Similarly, in 1996, the *Cour de Cassation* held that a housing association which prohibited tenants from living with relatives had breached Article 8 ECHR.[14] Thus, the courts of at least some Member States are prepared to grant horizontal effect to the European Convention in certain circumstances.[15]

§9.02 *MANGOLD* AND ITS AFTERMATH: THE INTERACTION BETWEEN GENERAL PRINCIPLES AND EU LEGISLATION

In *Mangold*[16] the Court held that the prohibition of discrimination on grounds of age is a general principle of law which can be relied upon against private parties. *Mangold* set an important precedent in relation to the horizontality of general principles but the reasoning of the judgment is problematic and its ramifications remain unclear.

The case concerned the compatibility of German law with the Framework Directive on Equal Treatment[17] which prohibits, *inter alia*, discrimination on grounds of age. A German labour law (TzBfG) permitted the conclusion of fixed-term employment contracts only if there were objective grounds for doing so. The law had been introduced to implement Directive 1999/70, which seeks to prevent the use of

13. *Cour de Cassation* (Chambre sociale), Judgment No 4164 of 2 October 2001.
14. *Cour de Cassation*, Judgment of 6 March 1996, Cass.3rd civ. J.C.P., ed. G (1996) IV, 973).
15. For further discussion, see Clapham, *supra*, Ch. 9 and for various examples of indirect horizontality in the laws of various Member States, see Maduro AG in Case C-438/05 *International Transport Workers' Federation and Finnish Seamen's Union v. Viking Line ABP* [2007] ECR I-10779 at n 38 of the Opinion.
16. Case C-144/04 *Mangold v. Helm* [2005] ECR I-9981.
17. Council Directive 2000/78 establishing a general framework for equal treatment in employment and occupation, OJ 2000 L 303/16.

successive fixed-term employment contracts with a view to protecting the workforce.[18] By way of exception, Article 14(3) of the TzBfG provided that the conclusion of a fixed-term contract did not require justification if the worker had reached the age of 58 by the time when the employment relationship began. The purpose of that exception was to facilitate the reintegration of older persons in the workforce. Subsequently, by a Law which took effect after the Framework Directive came into force but before the time-limit for its implementation had expired, Article 14(3) was amended and the permissible age limit was lowered to 52. Mr Mangold, who was 56 years of age, concluded a fixed-term contract to work for Mr Helm. Since Mr Mangold was more than 52 years old, the contract was valid under the amended version of Article 14(3) TzBfG but he argued that that provision was contrary to the Framework Directive.

The Court held that Article 14(3) differentiated against older employees and such difference in treatment was not objectively justified.[19] It was therefore incompatible with the Framework Directive. Following this finding, it became necessary to ascertain the consequences of incompatibility. Conventional wisdom would suggest that, in the circumstances of the case, the incompatibility between Article 14(3) and the Framework Directive could not assist Mr Mangold. First, when the contract was concluded, the period for the implementation of the Framework Directive had not yet expired. Secondly, in any event, directives are not by themselves capable of imposing obligations on individuals. The Court however followed an alternative approach. In relation to the first point, it held that during the period prescribed for the transposition of a directive, Member States must refrain from taking any measures liable seriously to compromise the attainment of the result prescribed by it.[20] On that basis, and taking into account the specific context of the case, it held that the fact that, when the contract was concluded, the period prescribed for the implementation of the Framework Directive had not yet expired could not call into question the finding of incompatibility.

On the issue of horizontality, the Court reasoned as follows. It held that the principle of equal treatment is not established by the Framework Directive itself. The Directive merely expresses that principle, its actual source being, as stated in the preamble, various international instruments and the constitutional traditions common to the Member States. It followed that the principle of non-discrimination on grounds of age must be regarded as a general principle of EU law.[21]

This reasoning is remarkable. The judgment posits that there is a general principle of EU law which prohibits discrimination on grounds of age in the field of employment. The sources of that principle are to be found in the international instruments listed in the preamble to the Directive and the constitutional traditions

18. Council Directive 1999/70, OJ 1999 L 175/43.
19. Article 6(1) of the Directive permits Member States to provide for differences in treatment on grounds of age if they are objectively and reasonable justified by a legitimate aim, including legitimate employment policy, labour market and vocational training objectives. The ECJ however took the view that the exception of Article 14(3) was too inflexible and too broad and therefore breached the principle of proportionality.
20. See Case C-129/96 *Inter-Environnement Wallonie* [1997] ECR I-7411.
21. Paras 74-75.

common to the Member States. This reasoning however is 'far from compelling'.[22] The preamble refers to a number of fundamental international conventions which pertain to the principle of equality before the law and the principle of equal treatment.[23] Only one of them makes express reference to age and this is only in a specific context.[24] The reference to the common constitutional traditions of the Member States appears unsubstantiated since it is not backed by any comparative analysis of national laws or case law. In fact, the constitutions of only two Member States recognized the principle at the time of the judgment.[25] The truth is that, until the very recent past, national laws were ripe with provisions creating differential treatment on grounds of age.[26] Neither the international conventions referred to in the preamble nor the constitutional traditions of the Member States point unequivocally to the derivation of a right against age discrimination in employment with a sufficiently specific ascertainable content. Whilst *Mangold* can be viewed as a bold and forward-looking judgment, its reasoning is axiomatic. The Court derives a right against age discrimination on the basis of the overarching principle of non-discrimination. It also posits that this general principle can be invoked against private parties. The horizontal effect was assumed without any discussion. This is, in fact, the first case where the ECJ accepts that a general, unwritten, principle of EU law has horizontal effect.[27]

The establishment of a general principle of non-discrimination on grounds of age is by no means objectionable. It would be hard to argue that an employer must be free to differentiate among employees on arbitrary grounds. The law cannot sanction arbitrary or capricious conduct. The judgment however is problematic in a number of respects. First, it raises problems in the way the Court applied the principle of proportionality to find that the German legislation was not objectively justifiable.[28] In practical terms, this is the most important aspect of the case. Critics would argue that the Court lays down social policy on the strength of the barest statutory background. In that respect, *Mangold* is, undoubtedly, a highly activist judgment although it could be counter-argued that, if the equality is to be taken seriously as a general principle, courts

22. See Opinion of Mazák AG in Case *Palacios de Villa*, para. 94 and see the criticism by M. Herdegen, General Principles of EU Law – The Methodological Challenge in U. Bernitz, J. Nergelius and C. Cardner (Eds), General Principles of EC Law in the Process of Development, Kluwer 2008, 343-355.
23. Recital 4 refers to the Universal Declaration of Human Rights, the United Nations Convention on the Elimination of All Forms of Discrimination against Women, the United Nations Covenants on Civil and Political Rights and on Economic, Social and Cultural Rights, the European Convention for the Protection of Human Rights and Fundamental Freedoms, and ILO Convention No 111 which prohibits discrimination in the field of employment and occupation.
24. See ILO Convention No 111, *supra*, Article 5(2).
25. These were the Finnish and the Portuguese constitutions, see Lenaerts and Gutiérrez-Fons, at 1654, n. 142.
26. Age restrictions applied under many jurisdictions, for example, to employment in the civil service or admission to the Bar.
27. Tizzano AG referred in support of horizontality to Case C-27/95 *Woodspring District Council v. Bakers of Nailsea* [1997] ECR I-1847, para. 21. This case however provides scant support as it referred to a trader who relied on the principle of equal treatment in proceedings against a local authority to challenge the validity of a Community agricultural regulation.
28. See paras 62-65.

are entitled to interpret and apply it even if they reach results that the political branch finds unpalatable.

Irrespective of the above, the reasoning of the Court raises a number of issues especially as regards the linkage between the general principle and the Framework Directive. Prima facie, there is an oxymoron: If the prohibition of discrimination on grounds of age is a general principle of EU law, Mr Mangold could have relied on it even in the absence of the Framework Directive. In fact, Tizzano AG was not averse to that argumentation. Why then did the Court go at lengths to discuss the Directive and delved into its effects before the period for its implementation had expired? The role of the Framework Directive in activating the dormant general principle of non-discrimination on grounds of age is normatively unclear and methodologically unsound.

One possible interpretation of the judgment is that the reference to the Directive was by way of secondary argument. According to the judgment, the fact that the period for the implementation of the Directive had not yet expired could not rescue the German law for two reasons: first, because directives produce effects even before the expiry of their time-limit and, secondly, and in any event, because the prohibition of discrimination on grounds of age is a general principle of EU transcending the provisions of the Framework Directive. The principal argument is clearly the second. In the absence of a general principle of law, the applicant could not have relied on the Framework Directive even if it produced some effect before the expiry of the time-limit for its implementation since directives may not produce horizontal effect. The invocation of a general principle as a rule of primary law was therefore essential. Arguably, Mr Mangold would have succeeded even in the absence of the Framework Directive. His situation would still be within the scope of EU law as a result of Directive 1999/70.[29] This interpretation is tenable[30] and perhaps logically more persuasive. It overlooks, however, that the role of the Directive in the reasoning of the Court was crucial. This is evident from the ruling where the ECJ refers to the effect of and the obligations deriving from Article 6(1) of the Framework Directive.[31] This linkage between directives and general principles is normatively unpersuasive and, as we shall see below, gives rise to problems.

A further difficulty with the judgment is that the Court treated the content of the general principle as coterminous with the provisions of the Framework Directive. Presumably, only those provisions of the Directive which can be said to reflect the pre-existing general principle can have horizontal effect. But the distinction is extremely difficult, if not impossible, to draw. There will be a temptation by litigants to

29. The Court expressly held that the situation fell within the scope of EU law by virtue of the fact that the German legislation in issue was intended to implement Directive 1999/70: see para. 75.
30. It receives support from para. 74 where the Court outlines the argument based on the general principle of non discrimination as a separate ground from the effects of the Framework Directive.
31. See para. 78 of the judgment and the second paragraph of the ruling. This also appears to be the way Trstenjak AG understood the judgment in her Opinion in *Dominguez*. The Advocate General distinguished between the recognition of a general principle of law *simpliciter* and the *Mangold – Kücükdeveci* approach. See below §9.04.

elevate a rule contained in a directive to a general principle of law and attribute to it a specific content with the benefit of hindsight, i.e., in the light of the provisions of the directive. There is a thus risk that provisions of directives would be interpreted as illustrations of pre-existing general principles and attributed the status of primary law leading to their horizontal effect and benefiting from enhanced remedies. This fusion between primary and secondary sources of law was rightly criticized by the Advocate General in *Dominguez.*[32]

The judgment may also be criticized on procedural grounds. Arguably, since the ECJ intended to rely on the general principle of non-discrimination on grounds of age, and given that the questions posed by the national court did not raise such a possibility, it should have reopened the oral procedure offering to the parties and the Member States the possibility to submit argument. In that respect, the case contrasts sharply with *Pfeiffer*[33] where the oral procedure was reopened on the ground that the case raised fundamental issues pertaining to the effect of directives, in particular, the consequences of incompatibility of national law with directly effective provisions in horizontal situations.

Mangold was reiterated in *Kücükdeveci.*[34] German law provided for an incremental increase in the period of notice that an employer must give to an employee to terminate his employment depending on the length of the employee's service. By way of exception, however, an employee's periods of employment before the age of 25 were to be disregarded. The Court found that such differential treatment was not justified and, confirming *Mangold*, it held that it was contrary to the general principle of non-discrimination on grounds of age as given expression by the Framework Directive.[35]

The theoretical model of the *Mangold – Kücükdeveci* approach appears to be the following. General principles of law are rules of primary law and, in contrast to directives, they are not precluded from producing horizontal effect. Whether a general principle exists and, if so, whether it may produce horizontal effect is a matter of judicial interpretation and therefore, ultimately, for the ECJ to determine. The content of a general principle, however, is to be determined by close reference to EU legislation which covers the same field. This appears to be justified on policy rather than normative grounds. It ensures that the discovery of general principles does not threaten the vertical allocation of powers between the EU and the Member States by bypassing the legislative process. Secondly, it satisfies the requirements of legal certainty since, otherwise, the co-existence of overlapping general principles and concrete statutory rules at variance with each other would lead to uncertainty and over-fine distinctions. On this analysis, the value of the general principle lies not in its normative content,

32. See below §9.04.
33. Joined Cases C-397/01 to C-403/01 *Pfeiffer and Others* [2004] ECR I-8835.
34. Case C-555/07 *Seda Kücükdeveci v. Swedex GmbH & Co. KG*, judgment of 19 January 2010.
35. See paras 21 et seq.

which is determined by the provisions of the directive which concretizes it, but in its remedial force.[36]

Still, this analysis is not without problems. The truth is that the Court failed to provide an intellectually robust explanation of the linkage between the Framework Directive and the general principle and how the former influences the normative recognition and/or judicial application of the latter. To appreciate the interaction between the general principles of non-discrimination and the Framework Directive one might ask the following question: what would be the possible outcomes in the hypothetical case where facts similar to those in *Mangold* took place in the complete absence of the Framework Directive? Although this exercise is speculative and somewhat counter-intuitive, it helps us to cast light on the interaction between general principles and statutory law. In such a hypothetical case, the situation would continue to fall within the scope of EU law as a result of Directive 1999/70[37] but it is not at all clear that the Court would have reached the same conclusion. One could distinguish the following scenarios. According to a first scenario, in the absence of the Framework Directive, the prohibition of discrimination on grounds of age would not be recognized as a general principle of law. This scenario treats the Framework Directive as part of the recognition process of the general principle. It is however incorrect since in its judgment the Court did not base, not even in part, its finding that there is a general principle on the existence of the Directive. Such a supposition would indeed be incorrect since it would put the cart before the horses, i.e., derive a rule of primary law on the basis of a rule of secondary law. Although in normative terms, the absence of the Framework Directive would not have affected the existence of the general principle, it is quite possible that the Court would not have relied on the latter. It was the Framework Directive that spurred the Court to recognize the general principle and, at the very least, in terms of judicial psychology the value of the Directive is difficult to discount.

According to a second scenario, the prohibition of age discrimination would be recognized as a general principle of EU law but the applicant could not rely on it since, in the absence of the Framework Directive, it would not be sufficiently ascertainable. The principle therefore would exist in a statutory vacuum. This approach has the benefit of giving effect to the legislative solution chosen by the Member States by adopting the Framework Directive but remains normatively lacking. It determines the content of a general principle *ex posto facto* by reference to specific rules which concretise it. The role of the general principle is therefore solely to give the status of primary law to specific provisions of directives.

According to a third scenario, the prohibition of age discrimination would be recognized as a general principle of EU law and the applicant could still invoke it because it would be considered that the principle had a minimum normative content

36. This is also the view taken by Bot AG in *Kücükdeveci*, para. 34; in accord: See Lenaerts and Gutiérrez 1647; Prechal, Competence Creep and General Principles of Law 3 (2010) Rev.Eur. Adm. L. 8 at 18-19
37. The Court expressly held that the situation fell within the scope of EU law by virtue of the fact that the German legislation in issue was intended to implement Directive 1999/70: see para. 75.

and the German law in question went beyond the discretion permitted to the Member States. In this case, the same result would have been reached as that reached in *Mangold* on the basis of the Framework Directive. This is the most theoretically cogent approach although it is doubtful whether the Court would have followed it. If a general principle of constitutional status is said to exist then neither its recognition nor its minimum content can be conditional on the adoption of legislation. To the extent that a general principle is insufficiently concrete and therefore cannot give rise to specific rights, it can inform the interpretation of legislation but cannot accord to that legislation the status of primary law.

True horizontality occurs only under the third scenario. The truth is that it is impossible to know how the case would have been decided in the absence of the Framework Directive. It is clear that the right not to be discriminated on grounds of age recognized to the applicant in *Mangold* was the result of the combined effect of the general principle prohibiting age discrimination and the Framework Directive. The *Mangold – Kücükdeveci* approach grants normative effect to the combined application of a general principle of law and the Framework Directive in a way which remains intellectually unpersuasive.

[A] The Effects of Reliance on a General Principle

What are the practical effects of elevating the prohibition of discrimination on grounds of age to a general principle of law? How does that better the position of the applicant?

If an individual based her claim solely on a directive, she would not be able to rely on it against another individual. Directives do not produce horizontal effect. The directive would still be relevant in that it would trigger the duty of consistent interpretation. That duty is extensive[38] but nonetheless subject to limitations, since it cannot justify a *contra legem* interpretation of national law,[39] and remains dependent on the discretion of the national court. By contrast, reliance on a general principle of EU law has a stronger effect. The national court has the responsibility to provide the legal protection which individuals derive from EU law and to ensure its full effectiveness, setting aside any provision of national law which may conflict with EU law.[40] A general principle can be relied upon against a private party directly and has a *Simmenthal*[41] foreclosing effect. The national court must set aside any offending provision and there is no need for the judicial acrobatics of the *Marleasing* variety.[42]

38. It requires the national court to procure a directive compliant construction 'taking the whole body of domestic law into consideration': See *Dominguez*, para. 27; Case C-212/04 *Adeneler and Others* [2006] ECR I-6057, para. 111; and *Angelidaki and Others*, para. 200.
39. *Dominguez*, para. 25; Case C-268/06 *Impact* [2008] ECR I-2483, para. 100, and *Angelidaki and Others*, Joined Cases C-378/07 to C-380/07 *Angelidaki and Others* [2009] ECR I-3071, para. 199.
40. *Mangold*, para. 77; *Kücükdeveci*, para. 51.
41. Case 106/77 *Simmenthal* [1978] ECR 629.
42. This added value of the foreclosing effect is made clear especially by comparing the analysis of the Court in *Kücükdeveci* paras 49 et seq. and the different language employed by the ECJ in *Dominguez*, paras 31 et seq.

The foreclosing effect of general principles, however, still remains unclear. It appears that the national court is under an obligation to set aside the offending norm of domestic law but in some cases it may not be clear what it should apply in its stead. It appears that in *Mangold* the national court would need to set aside the fourth sentence of Article 14(3) of the TzBfG which lowered the age in relation to which there was no need to provide objective justification from 58 to 52.[43] One assumes that in *Kücükdeveci* the national court must disregard the rule of German law which provided that periods of employment completed by an employee before reaching the age of 25 are not to be taken into account in calculating the notice period and therefore take into account such periods completed in the case in issue.

Finally, it will be noted that the fact that the general principle of non-discrimination on grounds of age may have horizontal effect does not in itself mean that it may be relied upon. It is a necessary condition of invokability that the situation of the applicant must fall within the scope of EU law. This occurs in the following cases:

(1) Where the national law in issue intends to implement a directive or other specific EU norm.
(2) Where the situation of the applicant is covered by the Framework Directive and the time-limit for its implementation has expired.
(3) Where there is another connecting factor that brings it within the scope of EU law.

Mangold fell in the first category. Article 14(3) of the TzBfG came within the ambit of EU law because it was a measure implementing Directive 1999/70. *Kücükdeveci* fell within the second category because the conduct complained of took place after the expiry of the period for the implementation of the Framework Directive.[44] By contrast, in *Bartsch*,[45] where the applicant sought to challenge rules of a corporate provident fund on the ground that they gave rise to age discrimination, the Court declined to apply the underlying general principle on the ground that the rules in question were not measures implementing the Framework Directive and the facts occurred before the expiry of the time-limit for its implementation. A similar finding was made in *Römer*[46] which concerned sexual orientation. The Court held that Article 13 EC (now Article 19 TFEU) could not, as such, bring within the scope of application of EU law situations which did not fall within the framework of the measures adopted on the basis of that article, before the expiry of the time-limit prescribed for their transposition.

43. This is how the judgment was understood by the German Federal Labour Court in subsequent proceedings leading to the judgment of the Federal Constitutional Court 2 BvR 2661/06, 6 July 2010, on which see below §9.03.
44. *Kücükdeveci*, *supra*, para. 24.
45. Case C-427/06 *Bartsch* [2008] ECR I-7245.
46. Case C-147/08 *Römer v. Freie und Hansestadt Hamburg*, judgment of 10 May 2011, para. 62.

§9.03 THE RESPONSE OF THE BUNDESVERFASSUNGSGERICHT

Following the *Mangold* judgment, the German Constitutional Court (FCC) rejected a complaint that the ECJ had acted *ultra vires*.[47] The complaint was raised by a private employer against a judgment of the Federal Labour Court which had applied the findings in *Mangold* to a fixed-term contract. The FCC confirmed that it retains residual power to review whether an act adopted by the EU institutions is beyond the power conferred to the European Union but subjected its review to very strict criteria. It held that it would intervene only if a breach of competence by the EU institutions was 'sufficiently qualified'. This will occur only if the act in question is 'manifestly' in breach of EU competence and leads to a structurally significant shift in the allocation of competences between the EU and the Member States.[48]

Although the precise tipping point at which such a structural shift occurs is difficult to determine, it is clear that the threshold is very high, consistently with the FCC's approach that its *ultra vires* review must be exercised in a way which is 'open towards European law'.[49] However, as the FCC stated, a structural shift may exist even though the breach of competence by the EU act does not reach the level of impinging on the constitutional identity of the state.[50] It would occur where case law 'changes clearly recognisable statutory decisions' or 'creates new provisions without sufficient connection to legislative statements' or 'makes fundamental policy decisions over and above individual cases'.[51] The truth is that the FCC enjoys here enormous discretion which it appears committed to exercise in favour of the ECJ.

The FCC found that the *Mangold* judgment did not reach that threshold. Whilst it acknowledged that the reasoning of the ECJ was not clear, it interpreted the judgment as reviewing the German fixed-term employment law by applying the provisions of the Framework Directive and not merely the standard of the unwritten general principle of law.[52] With regard to the applicability of the directive, despite the fact that the time-limit for its transposition had not yet expired, the FCC held that such interpretation did not restrict the discretion of Germany to such a degree as to bring about 'a structurally effective shift of competences'.[53] Similarly, the attribution of horizontal effect to the directive could be seen as developing from the ECJ's case law which allows directives to impose negative effects on individuals. It served to require Member States to carry out existing obligations and did not create any new obligations.[54]

Seen in that context, whether a general principle of non-discrimination on grounds of age could be derived from the constitutional traditions common to the

---

47. BVERFG, 2 BvR 2661/06, 6 July 2010. For the English version, see http://www.bverfg.de/entscheidungen/rs20100706_2bvr266106en.html
48. *Supra*, para. 61.
49. Para. 58.
50. *Supra*, para. 65 and see commentary by M. Mahlmann, The Politics of Constitutional Identity and its Legal Frame—the *Ultra Vires* Decision of the German Federal Constitutional Court, 11 (2010) German Law Journal 1407 at 1410.
51. Para. 64.
52. Para. 71.
53. Para. 76.
54. Para. 77.

Member States and their international agreements was in fact immaterial.[55] The FCC continued as follows:[56]

> A putative further development of the law on the part of the Court of Justice of the European Union, which would no longer be justifiable in terms of legal method, would only constitute an evident breach of the principle of conferral if it also had the effect of establishing competences in practice. With the disputed general principle of the prohibition of discrimination based on age derived from the constitutional traditions common to the Member States, however, neither a new field of competences was created for the Union to the detriment of the Member States, nor was an existing competence expanded with the weight of a new establishment. This would only be the case if without the issuance of a secondary legal act – seen here as having an advance effect – not only rights, but also obligations of citizens were introduced by virtue of further development of the law which would prove to constitute both encroachments on fundamental rights and a shift of competence to the detriment of Member States. Even if they guarantee the protection of fundamental rights at Union level, general principles may not expand the field of influence of Union law over and above the existing competences of the Union or indeed establish new tasks and competences (see Article 51.2 of the Charter of Fundamental Rights).

This suggests that the interpretational technique of the ECJ paid off. Whatever the soundness of its methodology, the linking of the general principle with the Framework Directive was sufficient to provide interpretational legitimacy. The FCC was prepared to allow the ECJ wide margin for judicial activism and gave it the benefit of the doubt. But the approach of the FCC also suggests that the development of the law merely on the basis of unwritten general principles and the creation of concomitant obligations on private parties might cross the threshold of a sufficiently qualified breach.[57] All in all, the reaction of the FCC provides testament to the imperfect but workable system of constitutional symbiosis on which the primacy of EU law is founded and the mutual deference which characterizes the relationship between the ECJ and the national constitutional courts.

§9.04 CAN THE MANGOLD - KÜCÜKDEVECI APPROACH BE EXTENDED TO OTHER PRINCIPLES?

The question arises whether the status of general principle of law may be granted not only to the prohibition of discrimination on grounds of age but also to the other forms of discrimination prohibited by Article 19 TFEU (formerly Article 13 EC) and the Framework Directive. The compact reasoning of *Mangold* inserted a considerable

55. Para. 78.
56. Para. 78.
57. Notably, Justice Landau delivered a dissenting opinion. He considered that the majority departed from the test established in the *Lisbon judgment* by requiring that a breach of EU competence must not only be manifest but also lead to a structurally significant shift in the division of competences between the EU and the Member States. In his view, this additional condition was not justified by the basis of the *ultra vires* review exercised by the FCC which was to ensure the democratic legitimation of EU powers. He also took the view that in its judgment, the ECJ has manifestly transgressed the limits of justifiable interpretation.

degree of unpredictability as to how the case law might develop. It could be argued that equality of treatment irrespective of religion or belief, disability, and sexual orientation are also elevated to general principles of law. *Mangold* suggested that all these grounds are specific expressions of the underlying idea of substantive equality.[58] The Court appeared to endorse that view in *Römer*,[59] which concerned discrimination on grounds of sexual orientation. It reiterated that the principle of equal treatment in the field of employment and occupation, and not solely non-discrimination on grounds of age, derives from various international instruments and the constitutional traditions common to the Member States. The Framework Directive merely lays down a framework for combatting discrimination on various grounds.[60]

In any event, the issue is perhaps of less importance given that Article 21(1) of the Charter expressly endorses a general substantive principle of non-discrimination referring to a long but indicative list of grounds.[61] It may therefore be possible to rely on the Charter. More generally, *Mangold* and *Kücükdeveci* open the possibility that statutory provisions of EU law might be considered to be express illustrations of general principles other than the principle of non-discrimination. It is submitted that this approach should be avoided and construed narrowly. As has been pointed out both by Advocates General and academic commentators, it is liable to create confusion between primary and secondary sources of law and leave individuals and national courts uncertain as to the origin, scope and effect of rights.[62]

So far, the *Mangold - Kücükdeveci* approach has not been extended beyond discrimination. *Dominguez*[63] provides an interesting juxtaposition between the Court and the Advocate General. The case concerned an employee's right to annual leave which is provided by Article 7 of the Working Time Directive.[64] French law fell short of the requirements of Article 7 and one of the questions referred by the Cour de Cassation was whether a national court must disregard a conflicting national provision in proceedings before private parties. The Court provided a conventional answer reiterating that directives may not produce horizontal effect but that courts are under a strong *Marleasing* duty of consistent interpretation. It referred to the right to annual leave as a particularly important principle of EU social law[65] but did not characterize it as a general principle.

58. See *Mangold, supra*, para. 74, and Mazák AG in *Palacios de Villa*, para. 96 of the Opinion.
59. Case C-147/08 *Römer v. Freie und Hansestadt Hamburg*, judgment of 10 May 2011.
60. *Supra*, para. 59.
61. Article 21(1) states that any discrimination based on any ground such as sex, race, colour, ethnic or social origin, genetic features, language, religion or belief, political or any other opinion, membership of a national minority, property, birth, disability, age or sexual orientation shall be prohibited.
62. This critique was persuasively articulated by the Trstenjak AG in *Dominguez* (see below in this section) and also by Mazák AG in *Palacios de Villa, supra*, and Geelhoed AG in Case C-13/05 *Chacón Navas* [2006] ECR I-6476. For academic commentary, see among others, Herdegen, *supra*; for a defence of *Mangold*, see Lenaerts and Gutiérrez-Fons, *supra*, 1654 et seq.
63. Case C-282/10 *Dominguez v. CICOA*, judgment 24 January 2012.
64. Directive 2003/88 concerning certain aspects of the organisation of working time, OJ 2003 L 299/9.
65. Para. 16.

Trstenjak AG was more adventurous and examined three alternative approaches, namely, Article 31(2) of the Charter, the possible direct application of a general principle of EU law, and the *Mangold – Kücükdeveci* approach. It is worth examining her view in more detail.

Article 31(2) of the Charter provides for the right to annual leave.[66] The AG opined that that article lays down a right and not merely a principle but came to the conclusion that it could not be relied upon against an individual because, under Article 51(1) of the Charter, its provisions lack horizontal effect. The Advocate General then took the view that the right to annual leave could be considered to be a general principle of EU law. It pre-existed the Working Time Directive having long been recognized as a fundamental social right in many international instruments. In relation to national constitutional laws, the AG drew a distinction between new and old Member States. Whilst in the majority of old Member States the right to a minimum period of paid annual leave was based on ordinary legislation, the constitutions of the States which acceded in 2003, with the exception of Cyprus, expressly refer to that right. She concluded that the right to annual leave permeates the national legal systems which recognize it as a core element of labour law, it is granted constitutional status by the Charter, and exhibits a minimum substantive degree of normative certainty. It could thus be viewed as a general principle of EU law. The Advocate General opined that, although as a general principle it could produce horizontal effect, such effect could not be recognized because it would lead to inconsistency with the Charter. An individual would then be able to rely on the right to annual leave as a general principle of EU law to circumvent the lack of horizontality of the Charter.[67]

Finally the AG considered whether it might be possible to follow the *Mangold -Kücükdeveci* approach i.e., whether it might be possible to apply the general principle of annual leave as exemplified in the Working Time Directive. She came against that approach. It risked mixing separate sources of law and was problematic from the point of view of legal certainty. Individuals could not be certain if the source of a right provided in a directive could be an unwritten general principle with enhanced status and effects which would trump the specific provisions of the directive. National law might also be eroded since courts might decline to apply a much greater range of provisions of domestic law on the ground that they would run counter to a general principle. Finally, that approach would also be inconsistent with the lack of horizontality of the Charter. All on all, Trstenjak AG came to the view that none of the alternative avenues that she examined would be able to give the applicant any additional rights than those granted by the Working Time Directive.

The most prominent aspects of the Opinion are that the Advocate General expressed doubts as to the suitability of the *Mangold -Kücükdeveci* approach and also that she was prepared to grant priority to the Charter over general principles of law. In

66. It states that 'Every worker has the right to limitation of maximum working hours, to daily and weekly rest periods and to an annual period of paid leave'.
67. In any event, the AG took the view that, even if the invocation of the right to annual leave in horizontal situations as a general principle of EU was not inconsistent with the Charter, the general principle lacked the requisite degree of specificity. It was not a right but a principle that required legislative configuration and was not substantively unconditional.

her view, since the Charter may not produce horizontal effect, it would be incorrect to allow individuals to rely on a general principle of law to undermine the Charter's lack of horizontality. This view is questionable. First, in *Kücükdeveci* the Court did not follow this approach. It referred to Article 21(1) of the Charter which prohibits discrimination on grounds of age but focused its analysis on the *Mangold* rationale and applied the general principle of non-discrimination. It would appear therefore that, where a general principle of law can be said to exist, it may produce horizontal effect even if an equivalent provision of the Charter may not do so. This would accord with Article 6 TEU which appears to view both the Charter and the general principles of EU law as sources of primary law of equivalent status. Secondly, it is questionable whether the Charter may not produce at least indirect horizontal effect. There is nothing to exclude *a priori* the possibility of the Charter imposing, in appropriate circumstances, a duty of national courts to provide effective legal protection for individuals.

There is a further aspect of the Opinion which is problematic. The Advocate General took the view that, even if the invocation of the right to annual leave in horizontal situations as a general principle of EU was not inconsistent with the Charter, the general principle lacked the requisite degree of specificity. It was not a right but a principle that required legislative configuration and was not substantively unconditional. It is however difficult to see why the general principle of entitlement to annual leave is more abstract than Article 31(2) of the Charter which the AG recognized to include a right and not merely a non-binding principle. The issue is whether, as the AG put it, it 'exhibits a minimum substantive degree of normative certainty',[68] in other words, whether in has a minimum ascertainable substantive content which circumscribes the discretion of the decision-maker.

§9.05 INDIRECT HORIZONTALITY

The above sections examined instances where a private party may rely directly on a general principle against another private entity. More often the horizontal effect of general principles will be indirect. Indirect horizontality may take several forms. First, it arises from the duty of constitutional interpretation. EU and national measures which fall within the scope of EU law must be interpreted so as to comply with the general principles of law and the Charter. This derives from the general rule of constitutional construction under which rules belonging to a lower tier must be interpreted, as far as possible, so as to comply higher ranking norms of the constitutional order.[69] It is an obligation deriving from the principle of hierarchy of norms and similar to the *Marleasing* duty of consistent interpretation. It applies to all measures, including those which regulate relations between individuals, and can therefore affect private rights and obligations. Horizontality is here limited in that it is conditioned by the process of interpretation: it assumes that a construction of the law which is compatible with the general principles is possible.

68. *Supra*, at para. 113 of the Opinion.
69. See e.g. Case 218/82 *Commission v. Council* [1983] ECR 4063, para. 15; Case C-314/89 *Rauh* [1991] ECR I-1647, para. 17.

Indirect horizontality may however go further and arise as a result of sharper obligations imposed on state actors. Where they act within the scope of EU law, public agencies may not exercise their powers in a way which is contrary to the general principles of law and the Charter. This obligation attaches to all state authorities including the courts. It could therefore be argued that, even though general principles and Charter rights may not bind individuals directly, national courts have an obligation to enforce them in the exercise of their state powers. Under this approach, even though the right to family life or the freedom of expression may not bind directly a private employer, in adjudicating in a dispute between an employer and its employee, a court may not exercise its judicial functions in a way that leads to those rights being infringed. A classic example of such indirect horizontality is provided by the seminal judgment of the US Supreme Court in *Shelley v. Kraemer*.[70] A white couple who owned property in a district covered by a restrictive covenant sought to prevent a black couple from moving in the district. The covenant prohibited the occupancy of property by 'any person not of the Caucasian race'. The Supreme Court accepted that the equal protection clause inhibits only state conduct and that private agreements standing alone could not be regarded as a violation. It held however that the action of state courts was State action. It noted that 'but for the active intervention of the state courts, supported by the full panoply of state power, petitioners would have been free to occupy the properties in question without restraint'.[71] It then concluded that the Fourteenth Amendment inhibited judicial enforcement by state courts of restrictive covenants based on race.

The limits of indirect horizontality differ in various constitutional orders depending, *inter alia*, on the wording of constitutional laws and the willingness of courts to infuse constitutional standards in civil litigation. If the obligation on courts to respect fundamental rights is understood broadly, it could lead to full horizontality by the back door. It could conceivably lead a court to be under an obligation to take account of fundamental rights in all civil disputes and refuse to enforce a private contract or exercise a power which would violate them.[72] Take for example the situation where a private creditor seeks enforcement of a debt by requesting a judicial order to auction the debtor's assets including his private home in way that would leave the debtor and his family destitute and homeless. Could the debtor raise the argument that, although the creditor is not directly bound by the right to private life, the court may not exercise its powers in a way that would be in breach of that right? So far, the ECJ has not ruled in relation to such a situation. It may be said, however, that in the hypothetical case where the ECJ was called upon to rule on facts similar to those in *Shelley v. Kraemer*, and assuming that they fell within the scope of EU law, it is likely that it would apply not only indirect but also direct horizontality. Indirect horizontality should also be recognized as a feature of EU law. In a different context, the Court has held that a private agreement may under no circumstances derogate from mandatory provisions of

70. 334 U.S. 1 (1948).
71. 334 U.S. 1 (1948) at 19.
72. This does not necessarily mean that the court would be under an obligation to raise an issue of fundamental rights on its own motion.

the Treaty on the free movement of goods.[73] If that is the case in relation to free movement, it is also *a fortiori* in relation to fundamental rights as enshrined in the Charter or the general principles of EU law. This view is also supported by the *Mangold* line of case law.

More broadly, however, it appears that the case law does not place national courts under a general duty not to enforce private law obligations which run counter to general principles, beyond the duty of consistent interpretation. In *Luksan*[74] a dispute arose between the director and the producer of a documentary film as to who had the right to exploit the film in digital networks. The Commercial Court of Vienna asked whether various copyright directives should be interpreted as meaning that rights to exploit a film vest to the principal director in his capacity as author of the work and, consequently, precluded national legislation which allocated those rights by operation of law exclusively to the producer. The Court answered in the affirmative. It relied on the provisions of several directives, the objectives of Directive 2001/29, and Article 17(2) of the Charter which provides for the protection of intellectual property. Having established that, under the directives, the principal director must be regarded as having lawfully acquired the right to own the intellectual property, it held that national legislation which denied him the exploitation rights would be tantamount to depriving him of his right contrary to Article 17(2) of the Charter.

Luksan is an example of indirect horizontality. The Charter was relied upon to determine the correct interpretation of EU copyright directives which, in turn, determined whether Austrian law was compatible with them. The meaning of the judgment is that an interpretation of Austrian law which allocates exploitation rights by operation of law exclusively to the producer of the work is precluded by EU law. The question whether such preclusive effect could be raised in proceedings between individuals was not touched by the judgment. In other words, the judgment pertains to the interpretation of law and not to judicial powers. It did not require the national court in the main proceedings to set aside the offending provisions of the Austrian law in all circumstances. The ruling presupposes that it is possible to interpret Austrian law in a way which is compatible with EU law and it is thus consistent with the prohibition of horizontal effect of directives.

One might wonder why it would not be possible to transplant the *Mangold-Kükükdeveci* model to *Luksan*. To the extent that the Austrian legislation contravened Article 17(2) of the Charter, it ran counter to a rule of primary law and the national court might therefore be considered to be under an obligation to set it aside even if it was not possible to force a consistent interpretation of national law. Still, as stated above, there are good reasons against the extension of the *Mangold- Kükükdeveci* approach and the fusion between primary and secondary sources of law.

In *Scarlet Extended SA,*[75] SABAM, a management company representing composers of musical works, brought proceedings against Scarlet, an internet service provider (ISP), arguing that internet users using Scarlet's services were downloading illegally

73. Case 58/80 *Dansk Supermarked v. Imerco* [1981] ECR 181, para. 17.
74. Case C-277/10 *Luksan v. van der Let*, judgment of 9 February 2012.
75. Case C-70/10 *Scarlet Extended SA v. SABAM*, judgment of 24 November 2011.

works in SABAM's catalogue. It sought an injunction requiring Scarlet to make it impossible for its customers to have access to musical files without permission. Although the order was granted at first instance, Scarlet claimed on appeal that that injunction was contrary to EU law because it would de facto impose upon it a general obligation to monitor communications on its network.

The Court stated that, under Directive 2001/29 on information society[76] and Directive 2004/48 on the enforcement of intellectual property rights,[77] holders of intellectual property rights may apply for an injunction against ISPs. It also pointed out, however, that the national laws introduced to implement those directives and their application by national courts must observe the limitations arising from Directive 2000/31 on electronic commerce,[78] Article 15(1) of which prohibits national authorities from adopting measures which would require an ISP to carry out general monitoring of the information that it transmits. Furthermore, under Article 3 of Directive 2004/48, remedies must be fair and equitable and not too costly.

On that basis, the Court found that an injunction which would require the ISP to install the contested filtering system would be incompatible with EU law, essentially, for three reasons.[79] First, it would require the ISP to monitor actively the individual data of all customers and such a general monitoring obligation would be incompatible with Article 15(1) of Directive 2000/31. Secondly, it would result in a serious infringement of the ISP's freedom to conduct its business which is guaranteed by Article 16 of the Charter. The Court held that, although the right to intellectual property is protected by Article 17(2) of the Charter, it is not inviolable and must be balanced against the protection of other rights.[80] In the circumstances, the granting of the injunction would not strike a fair balance between the protection of copyright and the SPI's protection of the right to trade. Finally, the injunction would infringe the fundamental rights of the ISP's customers, namely their right to protection of their personal data and their freedom to receive and impart information which are guaranteed by Articles 8 and 11 of the Charter.

In *Scarlet* the Court invoked Directive 2003/31 and the Charter as supplementary grounds to hold that the granting of an injunction by a national court was incompatible with EU law. The judgment could be understood in different ways. It could be understood as a case where the Court specifies what EU law requires and leaves it up to the referring court to decide whether national law can be interpreted so as to comply with it. But it could be understood as going further, i.e., as excluding the power of a national court to issue an injunction where that would conflict with the Charter, even if national law cannot be interpreted consistently under the *Marleasing* doctrine. As stated above, it is possible to suggest that national courts, where they act within the scope of EU law, may not exercise their powers in a way which is incompatible with

76. Directive 2001/29 on the harmonization of certain aspects of copyright and related rights in the information society, [2001] OJ L 167/10.
77. Directive 2004/48 on the enforcement of intellectual property rights, [2004] OJ L157/45.
78. Directive 2000/31 on certain legal aspects of information society services, in particular electronic commerce, in the Internal Market, [2000] L 178/1.
79. *Scarlet Extended*, *supra*, paras 40-52.
80. See further on this, Case C-275/06 *Promusicae* [2008] ECR I-271.

human rights. Such an approach would be beneficial to the party concerned where it would not be possible to interpret national law in conformity with the EU directives applicable. *Scarlet* comes close to recognizing the indirect horizontality of the Charter but it should be borne in mind that in the circumstances of the case the Charter was invoked in the context of a specific EU statutory framework established by Directives 2000/31, 2001/29, 2004/48 and also Directive 95/46[81] and Directive 2002/58[82] on the processing of personal data. It is notable that the operative part of the ruling provides an interpretation of those directives in the light of the requirements of fundamental rights and does not refer expressly to the Charter.[83]

In conclusion, the indirect horizontality of the general principles of law and the Charter is wide. So far, however, the case law has not gone as far as to rely solely on the indirect horizontality of a general principle or the Charter in the absence of EU legislation. It is thus not evident that in *Luksan* the plaintiff could have achieved the same result if he had relied solely on Article 17(2) of the Charter in the absence of EU secondary legislation. For one thing, such legislation brought the matter within the scope of EU law. For another, it provided a statutory determination of rights and obligations within which Article 17 of the Charter could operate. Whether in some cases Charter rights or general principles might have sufficient concretized content to exclude specific national legislation even in the absence of any concrete legislation will depend on the circumstances. In this respect, a paradox may arise. The concretization of a general principle by legislation may have a constraining effect on it to the extent that its substantive content is determined exclusively by reference to the legislation. Conceivably, in its absence, the minimum normative content of the general principle could be said to be wider.

Before leaving this section, it is pertinent to refer to another form of indirect horizontality, which is borne in particular by the European Convention, and arises through the imposition of positive obligations on States. The case law of the ECtHR imposes upon States the duty 'take reasonable measures to protect individuals from infringement of their Convention rights by other private persons'.[84] The case law on positive obligations is well-established and multi-faceted.[85] Thus, to give but few examples, the Strasbourg Court has accepted that the right to private life establishes obligations for the States which involve 'the adoption of measures designed to secure respect for private life even in the sphere of the relations of individuals between themselves'.[86] Also the right to life includes an obligation on state authorities to

81. Directive 95/46 on the protection of individuals with regard to the processing of personal data and the free movement of such data, [1995] OJ L281/31.
82. Directive 2002/58 concerning the processing of personal data and the protection of privacy in the electronic communications sector, [2002] OJ L 201/37.
83. *Scarlet Extended* was confirmed in Case C-360/10 *SABAM v. Netlog*, judgment of 16 February 2012.
84. See A. Mowbray, The Development of Positive Obligations under the European Convention of Human Rights by the European Court of Human Rights (Oxford, Hart Publishing, 2004) at 225.
85. For a discussion, see Mowbray, *supra* and Clapham, Human Rights Obligations of Non-State Actors (Oxford, 2006), pp. 349 et seq.
86. *X and Y v. the Netherlands*, Judgment of 26 March 1985, para. 23; see also, in relation to Articles 8 and 11 ECHR, *Plattform Ärzte für das Leben*, Judgment of 21 June 1988, para. 32.

investigate properly and punish killings by non-state actors.[87] This positive obligations model also applies to EU law. The provisions of the Treaties and the Charter, as well the general principles of law, impose obligations on states to take measures to protect human rights from being breached by non-state actors.[88]

§9.06 CONCLUSION

The case law lacks a coherent theoretical framework on horizontality. *Mangold* is a bold, brave judgment predicated on the imperative of equality as a constitutional value but its reasoning is perplexing. The Court failed to provide an intellectually robust explanation of the inter-relationship between EU legislation and general principles and explain how the former influence the normative recognition and the judicial application of the latter. The judgment fuses primary and secondary sources of law in a way which is doctrinally unsound and makes it difficult to replicate results. In that respect, it does not aid legal certainty.

Although in some cases general principles of law may produce directly horizontal effects, it is more likely that, in most cases, the Court will opt for indirect horizontality. This approach has advantages. It respects the public – private divide and avoids thorny theoretical issues pertaining to the horizontal effects of constitutional norms. It should be recognized that, at least in some cases, the general principles and the Charter may produce indirect horizontal effects via the imposition of duties on national courts. Although in *Scarlet Extended* the Court came close to doing so, even in that case the presence of EU legislation was crucial to its ruling. All in all, the horizontal effect of general principles remains a work in progress.

87. See e.g. *Ergi v. Turkey*, Judgment of 28 July 1998, *Paul and Audrey Edwards v. United Kingdom*, Judgment of 14 March 2002.
88. See e.g. in the context of the free movement of goods, Case C-265/95 *Commission v. France* [1997] ECR I-6959; Case C-112/00 *Schmidberger* [2003] ECR I-5659.

CHAPTER 10

General Principles and the Charter in Private Law Relationships: Constructive and Critical Input from Private Law

Carla Sieburgh

§10.01 THE GENERATIVE FORCE OF EU LAW ARGUMENTS IN PRIVATE LAW: A CASE FROM DAILY LIFE

Imagine, you are a private party, a so-called individual, for example a Bank. You are looking for new employees. Your bank is situated in the north of the Netherlands, in Friesland, a province known by many for organizing the eleven cities tour for skaters. Friesland is known for its eleven cities and for its own language, which is legally protected under the European Charter for Regional or minority Languages. Many Frisians speak this language and many of them do not speak any other language. So whenever your Bank needs new employees, they need to be fluent in Frisian. And to lessen all kinds of administrative work, years ago you entered into a cooperation with a language centre that twice a year organizes a language exam. Like the headquarters of your Bank the language centre is located in Leeuwarden.

The notice for the recruitment of new employees has been published. It imposes the requirement of the possession of a Certificate obtained by passing the exam organized by the language centre in Leeuwarden. You receive many reactions to the advert. One of those is from Mr Angonese, living in and originating from Austria. He is not only fluent in Italian, German, English and Slovene, but also in Frisian. However, he does not have a Certificate obtained by passing the exam organized by the language centre in Leeuwarden.

You answer Mr Angonese that he does not meet the conditions to enter the selection procedure. Subsequently he confronts you with a new element in your daily life. You are infringing EU law.

Being an experienced player, Mr Angonese can explain why. The requirement of having obtained a Certificate by passing an exam organized by the language centre in Leeuwarden restricts the free movement of workers (Article 45 TFEU) and is discriminating against people who do not live in Friesland or the Netherlands but who are fluent in Frisian anyway. The fact that Mr Angonese is not in the possession of the proper Certificate is not a valid ground to deprive him from entering the selection procedure.[1]

The sequence just described is a part of daily life. Most legal subjects do not have any normative opinion about the fact that EU law enters their daily life and legal relationships with other individuals. But what they keep in mind for ever is, that if EU law confers rights to other individuals (like Angonese) and obligations to them, it might also confer rights to them and obligations to other individuals.

For each creative legal mind the confrontation with EU law in real life will be a powerful reason to study with care the chances given by this source of law. If the director of the Bank in Leeuwarden ever wants to move his company to the city of London and gets confronted with a collective action of Bank employees, he knows that the Dutch national judge will test this collective action against the European Social Charter. Normally the collective action will be regarded lawful. Nothing in national law as it stands can help him out of this situation. But in the TFEU he will find an interesting rule, Article 49, prohibiting the restriction of the freedom of establishment. He starts an investigation on the internet, looking for EU law and its relevance in private law matters and finds interesting case law and materials.[2]

§10.02 POINTS OF DEPARTURE

[A] Bottom-Up Approach: EU Law as a Fact in Private Law

Why do I confront the reader with a story about a specific person, the director of a Bank in Leeuwarden, Friesland, The Netherlands? Isn't it of more importance to discuss legality issues, constitutional aspects of multiple layers of law, the relation between supranational law and national law and supremacy and direct effect?[3] In other words: shouldn't a chain be analysed – a chain of reactions provoked by the law in force – EU

1. Compare CJEU 6 June 2000, C-281/98, Jurispr. 2000, p. I-4139 (Angonese/Cassa di Risparmio di Bolzano).
2. Compare CJEU 11 December 2007, C-438/05, Jurispr. 2007, p. I-10779 (ITWF/Viking), CJEU 18 December 2007, C-341/05, Jurispr. 2007, p. I-11767 (Laval/Svenska Byggnadsarbetareförbundet). See for analysis and exhaustive materials A.S. Hartkamp, European Law and National Private Law. Effect of EU Law and European Human Rights Law on Legal Relationships between Individuals, Deventer 2012. See for a comparable approach E. Steindorff, EG-Vertrag und Privatrecht, Baden-Baden: Nomos 1996.
3. See for sources relating to constitutional law: A. von Bogdandy, Grundprinzipien des Unionsrechts – eine verfassungstheoretische und – dogmatische Skizze, EuR 2009, 749; M. Poiares Maduro, Interpreting European Law: Judicial Adjucation in a Context of Constitutional Pluralism, European Journal of Legal Studies 2007; H.C.F.J.A. de Waele, Rechterlijk activisme en het Europese Hof van Justitie, Den Haag 2009; N. Reich, Procedural Autonomy of Member States vs. Effective Legal Protection in Recent Court Practice – On the Way to "Procedural plurality", in: Private Law: past, present and future, Liber Amicorum Valentinas Mikelenas, Vilnius 2008,

law in force? At the end of this chain-reaction a legal relationship may be found, either vertical or horizontal. But should the analysis of a concrete relationship not be left to practitioners?

However, legal reality is that EU law touches upon private law rules and horizontal relationships. In other words: EU law is a fact in private law. Therefore carrying out research in the field of EU law and private law also involves the consideration of concrete horizontal relationships. These horizontal relationships need not necessarily have been brought to court. One of the starting points for the analysis of the impact of EU law in private law is the horizontal relationship.[4] Taking the relationship as a given, an attempt can be made to get a picture of the law that governs the relationship and that moulds it into its final shape. The law in force applicable to that relationship is the entire set of rules and arguments that determine the concrete juridical situation.[5]

[B] Individuals Use EU Law as Creative Source

Another aspect that I want the reader to imagine is that parties that are for some reason wondering about the concrete features of their relationship and use whatever argument

---

p. 271-286; J. Priban, Multiple Sovereignty: On Europe's Self-Constitutionalization and Legal Self-Reference, Ratio Juris 2010, pp. 41-64.

See for sources relating to the development of a method for EU law: S. Grundmann, Die Auslegung des Gemeinschaftsrechts durch den Europäischen Gerichtshof, Konstanz 1997; S. Grundmann, K. Riesenhuber, Die Auslegung des Europäischen Privat- und Schuldvertragsrechts, JuS 2001, pp. 529-536; M. Potacs, Effet utile als Auslegungsgrundsatz, EuR 2009, pp. 465-486; E. Paunio, Beyond Predictability - Reflections on Legal Certainty and the Discourse Theory of Law in the EU Legal Order, German Law Journal 2009, p. 1469, C. Höpfener en B. Rüthers, Grundlagen einer europäischen Methodenlehre, Archiv für die civilistische Praxis, 2009, p. 1-36; A. Fritzsche, Discretion, Scope of Judicial Review and Institutional Balance in European Law, CMLR 2010, pp. 361-403; T. von Danwitz, Die Aufgaben des Gerichtshofes bei der Entfaltung des europäischen Zivil- und Zivilverfahrensrechts, ZEuP 2010, pp. 463-476.

See for sources regarding the comparison of methods in national law: S. Vogenauer, Die Auslegung von Gesetzen in England und auf dem Kontinent Band I und II, Tübingen, 2001; K. Riesenhuber, System und Prinzipien des Europäischen Vertragsrechts, Berlin 2003.

See for sources regarding inconsistencies between the EU law methods and methods in national law: C. Busch, C. Kopp, M.R. Mc Guire, M. Zimmermann, Konvergenz und Diskrepanz nationaler und europäischer Methodik: Der Einfluss des Gemeinschaftsrechts auf dat äussere System des deutschen Privatrechts, GPR 2009, pp. 150-159; J. Basedow, Der Europäische Gerichtshof und das Privatrecht, Archiv für die civilistische Praxis 2010, pp. 157-195.

The legitimacy of the confrontation of European Union law and national private law was subject of a discussion paper by to the Dutch Jurist Association 2011: C.H. Sieburgh, Legitimiteit van de confrontatie van Europees recht en burgerlijk recht van nationale origine, in: Controverses rondom legaliteit en legitimiteit, Handelingen Nederlandse Juristen-Vereniging 2011-1, Deventer 2011, pp. 187-242.

4. See for a method to substantively guide the involvement of EU law in private law matters that combines the top-down approach with a bottom-up approach: C.H. Sieburgh, A Method to Substantively Guide the involvement of EU Law in Private Law Matters, ERPL 2013, section 3. The conventional top-down analysis of the effectuation of EU law in private law matters starting from the supremacy and direct effect of EU public law over national private law is combined with a bottom-up approach taking into account the concrete horizontal relationship.
5. See for such a bottom-up approach H.-W. Micklitz, The Politics of Judicial Co-operation in the EU, Cambridge 2005.

they can find. As soon as they get sense of the possibility to rely on primary EU law – the Treaty provisions, the general principles of EU law, the Charter, the judgments of the CJEU and the General Court – they will try as much as possible to use that type of sources. Besides this they use their private law systems and apply that to facts coming from EU law.

I give an example: the fact that Article 101 paragraph 2 TFEU renders automatically void an agreement infringing the prohibition of paragraph 1 to prevent, restrict or distort competition within the internal market, implies in private law that an act infringing Article 101 TFEU constitutes and unlawful act. So, the giant leap for EU law mankind made in the CJEU's judgment *Courage/Crehan*[6] was a small step for private law men: an organic development of the private law anti-trust doctrine.

In the same vein as inferring from prohibition and nullity unlawfulness and damages, one can assume that Article 101 TFEU also is a basis for claims on ground of unjust enrichment and undue payment and for injunctions. The nullity as laid down in Article 101 TFEU unfolds as it were the whole net of other remedies in private law.

The same applies to a private law mind if the CJEU grants an injunction, like in *Muñoz, Viking* or *Laval*.[7] The injunction is granted for a situation that can be regarded as an unlawful act. Consequently, comparable unlawful acts can be the basis for a claim in damages.[8]

[C] Direct Horizontal Effect

As explained above, individuals make use of each argument they find. And, moreover, as a consequence of several rules of EU law producing direct horizontal effect, individuals become forced to use arguments that are anchored in EU law.

The dynamic envisioned is as follows. In the first place a provision of EU law produces direct horizontal effect according to its explicit wording (like Article 101 TFEU) or is declared to do so by the CJEU (like Article 18, Article 157, Article 45, Article 49, Article 56 TFEU). By direct horizontal effect I mean: 'the invocation of [that provision of] EU law between individuals, with the result that one individual can enforce a right or be released from an obligation vis-à-vis another individual'.[9] When EU law creates, modifies or extinguishes rights and obligations between parties, 'this

6. CJEU 20 September 2001, C-453/99, Jurispr. 2001, p. I-6297 (Courage/Crehan).
7. CJEU 17 September 2002, C-253/00, Jurispr. 2002, p. I-7289 (Muñoz/Frumar), CJEU 11 December 2007, C-438/05, Jurispr. 2007, p. I-10779 (ITWF/Viking), CJEU 18 December 2007, C-341/05, Jurispr. 2007, p. I-11767 (Laval/Svenska Byggnadsarbetareförbundet).
8. See for this approach applied to EU law in general Hartkamp, European Law and National Private Law, 2012 (note 2). See for the follow up judgment in the Laval case (granting damages), Swedish Labour Court, Judgment no 89/09, Case No 268/04, translation in English by L. Carlson, in: M. Rönnmar, Labour Law, Fundamental Rights and Social Europe, Oxford 2011, pp. 227-276 and U. Bernitz & N. Reich, Case note, CMLR 2011, pp. 603-623.
9. Hartkamp, European Law and National Private Law, 2012 (note 2), nr. 12. See for a broader understanding of the concept of direct horizontal effect by EU law scholars (in contrast to both private law scholars and constitutional law scholars): B. De Witte, Direct effect, supremacy, and the nature of the legal order, in: P. Graig & G. De Búrca, The Evolution of EC Law, Oxford 2011, pp. 329-333; M. de Mol, The novel approach of the ECJ towards the horizontal direct effect of the EU principle of non-discrimination: (Unbridled) expansionism of EU law?, MJ 2011, pp. 110-111.

may have the result, for example, that a contract concluded between parties is null and void or that one citizen's act constitutes an unlawful act vis-à-vis another citizen because the contract or act conflicts with a treaty provision.'[10] Regarding the market freedoms the production of direct horizontal effect implies that individuals are not allowed to restrict these market freedoms in their horizontal relationships.

Consequently the autonomy of parties is limited. To be able to take justifiable private law interests into consideration and to balance them in the context of a horizontal relationship it is to be assumed that parties must be able to rely on arguments that relate to their horizontal relationship by way of justification for an infringement of EU law.[11] That type of arguments come from private law and will be brought into connection with EU law. For example, it might be allowed for (potential) buyers or organizations of (potential) buyers of laser targeting devices and sensory tags, to conclude a contract holding that devices and tags to be used to play at killing people will not be bought. The reason is that the contracting parties are convinced that the simulated killing of human beings infringes a fundamental value, namely human dignity, which to the conviction of these parties is an important value within their undertakings.[12] If the importer invokes his right to freely provide services (and/or his right to the free movement of goods that are related to the provision of the service), the argument of the (potential) buyers or organizations of (potential) buyers to restrict these rights can be based on their conviction (party autonomy) and be related to Article 10 Charter.

The CJEU case law accepts this kind of justifications if they are related to the public order.[13] Recently the CJEU elaborated upon justifications based on fundamental rights that refer to the right to property (Article 17 Charter),[14] the freedom to choose an occupation (Article 15 Charter)[15] and to the freedom to conduct a business (Article 16 Charter). Within the freedom to conduct a business it recognizes aspects of the doctrine of private autonomy. The protection afforded by Article 16 Charter covers the freedom to exercise an economic or commercial activity and the freedom of contract and free competition. The freedom of contract includes in particular the freedom to choose with

10. Hartkamp, European Law and National Private Law, 2012 (note 2), nr. 12.
11. See hereinafter para. 10.04.A and 10.04.B. From CJEU 15 December 1995, C-415/93 Jurispr. 1995, p. I-4921 (ASBL/Bosman) and CJEU 7 May 1997, C-350/96, Jurispr. 1998, p. I-2521 (Clean Car/Landeshauptmann Wien) it follows that individuals may rely on the grounds of justification as provided for by the TFEU. Given the fact of direct horizontal effect the system of exceptions cannot remain unchanged. See C.H. Sieburgh, Western Law of Contract, Chapter 6 in M. Bussani & F. Werro (eds.), European Private Law. A Handbook, Volume I, Berne 2009, pp. 161-202; Hartkamp, European Law and National Private Law, 2012 (note 2), nr. 64-66; M. Kumm, Who is Afraid of the Total Constitution? Constitutional Rights as Principles and the Constitutionalization of Private Law, German Law Journal 2006, pp. 362-268.
12. Compare CJEU 14 October 2004, C-36/02, Jurispr. 2004, p. I-9606 (Omega Spielhallen).
13. CJEU 12 June 2003, C-112/00, Jurispr. 2003, p. I-5659 (Schmidberger/Austria), para 74; CJEU 14 October 2004, C-36/02, Jurispr. 2004, p. I-9606 (Omega Spielhallen), para. 35.
14. CJEU 22 January 2013, C-283/11, n.y.r. (Sky Österreich GmbH/Österreichischer Rundfunk), paras 31-40.
15. CJEU 6 September 2012, C-544/10, n.y.r. (Deutsches Weintor eG/Land Rheinland-Pfalz), paras 54.

whom to do business and the freedom to determine the price of a service.[16] From this reasoning it can be deduced that the CJEU may in the future accept a private party relying in a horizontal relationship on fundamental rights if they are presented in relation to interests of individuals.[17]

[D] Two Strands

It is for this reasons that I am convinced that research in the field of EU Private law should involve both elements. First, the analysis of the way EU law technically works out in private law rules and/or horizontal relationships. Against the background of legitimacy required, part of this research may well be the development of critical comments. The influence of EU law in private law matters can be seen as an effect prescribed by supranational law. Coming from above, it is the effectuation of a top-down mechanism. This top-down approach should be combined with a second strand of research. In this bottom-up approach, the question is: Given the impact of EU law on private law matters, what reactions can be expected from private law actors; how are they going to use the given facts in EU law?

Certainly, they will not restrict themselves to simply reflecting. The very fact of the existing influence of EU law in the realm of private law and horizontal relationships creates a strong incentive to rely on that influence, both to invoke a right granted by EU law and to construe arguments against individuals that rely on such rights. Individuals will bring the existing possibilities into practice and will elaborate creatively on those possibilities.

Much scholarly work is devoted to the first strand of research. For that reason this contribution focuses on the approach of research to be done in relation to the second strand. As rules of EU law producing direct horizontal effect penetrate private law rules and relationships in the most pertinent way, they drastically appeal to the invention of pertinent arguments. Either to invoke a right provided for by EU law, or to make clear that there are convincing arguments to limit such a right. Moreover horizontal cases, in which EU law produces direct horizontal effect, are most urgently in need of a substantive recognition of the aims, requirements, possibilities and limitations of private law. Therefore this contribution deals with cases which touch upon rules that produce direct horizontal effect. They are used to demonstrate the questions, reasonings, arguments and reactions that will come up from individuals who get confronted with EU law and who seek solace in EU law.

16. CJEU 6 September 2012, C-544/10, n.y.r. (Deutsches Weintor eG/Land Rheinland-Pfalz), para. 54; CJEU 22 January 2013, C-283/11, n.y.r. (Sky Österreich GmbH/Österreichischer Rundfunk), paras 41-46.

17. For the elaboration upon the Charter provisions as an instrument that can translate the private law principles in a given case into arguments that are suitable to substantively interact with other EU law principles at stake: Sieburgh, ERPL 2013 (note 4), sections 3 and 5.

§10.03 PRIVATE LAW REASONING BASED ON CASE LAW OF CJEU

[A] Interaction Individuals and Courts

Individuals do not in the first place develop sophisticated theories and insights about the ability or inability of EU law to produce horizontal effects and the legitimacy of this technique. Neither do they care about the coherence of their own national law.

So the theory that EU primary law, apart from competition law, should not produce direct horizontal effects does not work anymore, since individuals have been confronted with advantages and disadvantages of direct (horizontal) effects of EU law. For the same reason the argument coming from private law scholars that private law becomes incoherent and gets destroyed due to influences of EU primary law, has lost its (practical) relevance.

Besides that, I am not convinced that, once the CJEU considers a rule of primary EU law to be able to produce effects in a horizontal relationship, either by conferring rights and obligations or by being a basis for a legality review of the applicable rule, EU law scholars and private law scholars really can achieve a turning back of the Court. Not these scholars but individuals bring, via national judges, the next case to the court. And these individuals will gratefully employ the new opportunity to develop arguments.

Not only individuals, also EU judges and national judges who decide on horizontal relationships, will creatively build on the facts they find in the law in force: the national legislation, the Human Rights provisions, the Treaty on the Functioning of the EU, the general principles of EU law and the Charter, the case law of the Human Rights Court, the Court of Justice and the General Court.[18]

[B] Reactions from Legal Doctrine: Analysis and Proactivity

That however does not imply that EU law scholars and private law scholars have to sit and wait until the CJEU invents another new trick or tool. Or to put it neutrally: another instrument, for example another provision producing direct horizontal effect (as with regard to free movement of goods (Articles 34 and 35 TFEU) may follow from its decision in *Fra.bo*),[19] or another general principle of EU law, to bypass the restrictive aspects of directives in horizontal cases.[20]

Scholars originating from both fields of law, EU law and private law, can study the few facts in detail and try to calculate the precise features of the interactions between these fields. With this knowledge they can use the matter appropriately, both constructively, thinking proactively about new analogies and possible applications,

18. Compare S. Iglesias Sánchez, The Court and the Charter: The Impact of the Entry into Force of the Lisbon Treaty on the ECJ's Approach to Fundamental Rights, CMLR 2012, p. 1609.
19. CJEU 12 July 2012, C-171/11, n.y.r. (Fra.bo/DVGW).
20. See for a bottom-up analysis of this mechanism: Sieburgh, ERPL 2013 (note 4), section 4.

and critically, identifying proactively disadvantages of possible developments and systematic inconsistencies.[21]

To a certain level the interaction of EU law and national private law can be compared with graphene. Long before the physical substance was isolated, graphene existed as an idea. Scientists were aware of its properties: its magnetic behaviour, its superconductivity and its strength. With those characteristics in mind they where able to anticipate possible applications in practice. In the same vein the few facts that are available in the field of EU private law can be used to predict and anticipate possible applications in the future.

[C] Guidance on Two-Way Traffic

This building process needs some guidance. Legislators, judges, lawyers, individuals and scholars need to be informed and need to inform each other about how to proceed in a sensible way in a situation of not knowing exactly how the substance looks like and in the same time having the ability to predict all kinds of disasters and splendid possibilities and chances.

In the inevitable process of convergence of EU law and private law, both fields of law must take into consideration their respective aims, requirements, possibilities and limitations. For that purpose, a two-way traffic, a substantive exchange between EU law and private law must be established.[22]

The aims (EU law aims and private law aims) and interests (general interests/ public interests/EU law interests, private law interests) at stake in a concrete case or in a concrete category of cases can be linked with different levels of importance for the respective field of law.

Subsequently, weighing and balancing of the relevant aims and interests can take place, taking into account the degree of importance of the interest at stake for EU law and/or private law. The standard for distinction between competing principles is the degree in which an aim or interest typical for EU law is addressed (like supremacy and direct effect) and the degree in which an aim or interest is addressed that is typical for private law (like unjust enrichment).[23]

§10.04 APPLICATION TO GENERAL PRINCIPLES AND CHARTER PROVISIONS

Against the background of a mutual exchange between EU law and private law, I will elaborate upon analysing, calculating, proactively drawing analogies and possible

21. See more extensively on this C.H. Sieburgh, Principles in Private Law: From Luxury to Necessity – Multi-layered Legal Systems and the Generative Force of Principles, ERPL 2012, pp. 300-301, 308-311; J. Nergelius, General Principles of Community Law in the Future, in: U. Bernitz & J. Nergelius (eds.), General Principles of European Community Law, 1999, p. 232.
22. See Sieburgh, ERPL 2012 (note 21), pp. 301, 304 and Sieburgh, ERPL 2013 (note 4), section 3.
23. See for a more detailed description of this categorization Sieburgh, ERPL 2012 (note 21), pp. 309-310.

applications and developing criticisms referring to disadvantages of possible developments and systematic inconsistencies.

The law as it stands recognizes general principles of EU law. A well known general principle of EU law is the prohibition to discriminate on the ground of age. For horizontal relationships this became clear in the decisions of the CJEU in the cases *Mangold* and *Kücükdeveci*. The CJEU used the general principle of EU law to review a rule of national law, applicable to the horizontal relationship. Since the provision of national law was not in conformity with the principle and could not be interpreted harmoniously, it had to be disapplied. The consequence in the *Mangold* case was that the provision of national law had to be disapplied, and subsequently that the clause in the employment contract between the parties Mangold and Helm that provided for the fixed time ran counter to the remaining rules of national origin, and was null and void. The implication of the invalidity of the fixed time clause of the employment contract was not that the entire employment contract was void, but that it was held to be concluded for unlimited time. In the *Kücükdeveci* case the consequence was that the calculation of the period of notice for dismissal changed, that the severance pay had to be recalculated and that the employer had to pay more.[24]

[A] General Principles and Charter as Standard for Legality Review or as Justifying Argument

It can be expected that the Court of Justice will develop other general principles of EU law, to recognize them as standard for a legality review of applicable provisions of national law. I am aware of the critical attitude vis-à-vis that aspect of the Court's case law from a constitutional point of view.[25] Nevertheless I am convinced that for each court it is inevitable to use legal sources like general principles.[26] First, to create a more consistent body of law than the piecemeal provisions of EU law provide for. Second, to create room for necessary flexibility.[27] In this legal reasoning I distinguish, next to the

24. See for a detailed analysis of the consequences in the specific cases C. Sieburgh, The Union Law Principle of Equality and its Effect on Private Law, in: A. Hartkamp, C. Sieburgh, L. Keus, J. Kortmann & M. Wissink, The Influence of EU Law on National Private Law, forthcoming (2014); M. de Mol, Kücükdeveci: Mangold Revisited – Horizontal Direct Effect of a General Principle of EU Law, European Constitutional Law Review 2010, 293 and the contribution in this book by N. Reich, Chapter 13.
25. (Critical) E. Spaventa, The Horizontal Application of Fundamental Rights as General Principles of Union Law, in A. Arnull e.o. (eds.), A Constitutional Order of States? Essays in EU Law in Honour of Alan Dashwood, Oxford 2011,199; M. Dougan, In Defence of Mangold, in A. Arnull e.o. (eds.), A Constitutional Order of States? Essays in EU Law in Honour of Alan Dashwood, Oxford 2011, 219; O. Mörsdorf, Unmittelbare Anwendung von EG-Richtlinien zwischen Privaten in der Rechtsprechung des EuG, EuR 2009, 219.
26. Compare amongst others Kumm, German Law Journal 2006 (note 11), pp. 345-346, 362-268.
27. T. Tridimas, The General Principles of EU Law, Oxford 2006, 17-18: 'Lacunae are more likely to arise in Community law, especially in the early stages in its development, since it is a new legal order. Community law simply lacks the accumulated judicial experience, buttressed in case law, that national legal systems possess. The need to feel gaps is exacerbated by the distinct characteristics of the Community legal order. Community law is not only a new legal order but also a novel one in the sense that it has no historical precedent or indeed contemporary equivalent. It represents a new development in the law of international organizations. Also the

interpretive, derogating and supplementing function attributed to general principles,[28] a generative function.[29]

It is also clear that the CJEU will gratefully rely on the Charter, as a source to creatively develop new general principles.[30] It uses these general principles as grounds for justification in case of restrictions of market freedoms (like in *Laval* and *Viking*) and as grounds for legality review of national measures (like in *Mangold* and *Kücükdeveci*).

From these separate considerations the conclusion can be drawn that the Charter is a source of inspiration for the development of new general principles of EU law, for justification of prima facie infringements of EU law and for developing standards for legality reviews. It is now possible to start drawing the contours of the influences of the Charter on EU law and consequently of the influences of the whole body of EU law on private law and horizontal relationships.

[B] Application in Private Law Matters

[1] Case 1: Justifications for Restriction of Market Freedoms Derived from General Principles and Adjusted to Horizontal Relationships and the Interest of Individuals

What proactive thinking can be based on these assumptions? I give one example. In the *Laval* case, the CJEU held that a party in a horizontal relationship may rely on the freedom to provide services (Article 56 TFEU). An individual who restricts this freedom in a cross-border situation infringes the prohibition enshrined in Article 56 TFEU. Of course, within the framework of the provision, the party restricting the market freedom can rely on certain grounds for justification (Article 52 TFEU): public policy, public security or public health.[31] As the Court explicitly held, justification may also be found in the right to collective action.[32] This right is laid down in Article 12 of the Charter.

EC Treaty is a traité cadre. It provides no more than a framework. It is ramplant with provisions overpowering in their generality and uses vague terms and expressions which are not defined.' Regarding the gap filling function see Tridimas, The General Principles of EU Law, 18; K. Lenaerts and J.A. Gutiërrez-Fons, The constitutional allocation of powers and general principles of EU law, CMLR 2010, 1629, at 1631.

28. Tridimas, The General Principles of EU Law (note 27).
29. Sieburgh, ERPL 2012 (note 21), pp. 301, 306-308.
30. Lenaerts and Gutiërrez-Fons, CMLR 2010 (note 27), 1654-1660; Iglesias Sánchez, CMLR 2012 (note 18), pp. 1598, 1610. See for the general principle of non-discrimination and the Charter: N. Reich, The Impact of the Non-Discrimination Principle on Private Autonomy, in: D. Leczykiewicz & S. Weatherill (eds.), The Involvement of EU Law un Private Law Relationships, Oxford 2013, Chapter 11.
31. CJEU 15 December 1995, C-415/93 Jurispr. 1995, p. I-4921 (ASBL/Bosman) and CJEU 7 May 1997, C-350/96, Jurispr. 1998, p. I-2521 (Clean Car/Landeshauptmann Wien).
32. CJEU 11 December 2007, C-438/05, Jurispr. 2007, p. I-10779 (ITWF/Viking), CJEU 18 December 2007, C-341/05, Jurispr. 2007, p. I-11767 (Laval/Svenska Byggnadsarbetareförbundet). Other justifications related to fundamental rights are known from CJEU 12 June 2003, C-112/00, Jurispr. 2003, p. I-5659 (Schmidberger/Austria) and CJEU 14 October 2004, C-36/02, Jurispr. 2004, p. I-9606 (Omega Spielhallen).

Whereas the right to collective action protects an interest of a general nature, for a restriction to be justified in a horizontal relationship there must also be a possibility to take into consideration party interests of a more typically private law nature.[33] The very general notion of private autonomy is unfit for that purpose, since it is clear that almost the whole body of EU law as applicable in horizontal relationships can easily be counterbalanced and in the end undermined if a mere reference to private autonomy would suffice. However, this does not mean that arguments relating to private law and interests of individuals are never fit to justify an infringement of EU law. The point is that an argument of this nature has to be more specific than merely referring to private autonomy.

To work out general principles of EU law, the CJEU gratefully relies on Charter provisions. For that reason, in the context of the interaction of EU law and private law, the Charter can be a first source of inspiration.[34] One may think of tailoring to a horizontal relationship the freedom of thought, conscience and religion (Article 10 Charter), the freedom of expression and to receive information (Article 11 Charter) and the freedom to choose an occupation (Article 15 Charter). Suppose that individual A relies on the freedom to supply services or to transport goods from UK to Germany, which are intended for use in laser games. The players of these games simulate the act of killing each other. Party B may argue that the restriction of the freedom to provide services or of the free movement of goods he caused by agreeing with his colleagues C and D to not sell these devices is justified by their conviction (Article 10 Charter) that such play infringes human dignity.

Other Charter provisions that can play a role in the exchange between EU law and private law are the freedom to conduct a business (Article 16 Charter), and the right to property (Article 17 Charter).[35]

While drawing these contours there is room to proactively calculate what can happen. What is the outreach of the principle of the freedom to conduct a business? Of course the provision in the Charter limits this principle to the boundaries set by Union law, national law and practices. But since the principle is a part of the very EU law, it will shape the future law in force.

33. Hartkamp, European Law and National Private Law, 2012 (note 2), nr. 66, AG Trstenjak, Opinion in CJEU 12 July 2012, C-171/11, n.y.r. (Fra.bo/DVGW), paras 55 ff, N. Reich, The Impact of the Non-Discrimination Principle on Private Autonomy, 2013 (note 30), under 1, A. Colombi Ciacchi, European Fundamental Rights, Private Law and Judicial Governance, in: H. Micklitz (ed.), The Constitutionalisation of European Private Law, Oxford University Press (2014 forthcoming).
34. Compare H. Collins, On the (In)compatibility of Human Rights Discourse and Private Law, LSE Law, Society and Economics Working Papers 7/2012.
35. See for the consideration of these provisions as a means to justify the infringement of a provision of EU law CJEU 22 January 2013, C-283/11, n.y.r. (Sky Österreich GmbH/Österreichischer Rundfunk).

[2] *Case 2: Justifications for Restriction of the Prohibition of Anti-competitive Agreements Derived from General Principles and Adjusted to Horizontal Relationships and the Interest of Individuals*

The dynamic explained under §10.04[B][1] is as follows. An argument related to the private interest of a party is interlinked with the Charter. Subsequently it is used to shape and adjust the obligations under EU law applicable in horizontal relationships in a way that respects the particularities of a horizontal relationship. From that dynamic, another question comes up, which is relevant for competition law, especially for the prohibition of Article 101 TFEU.

This part of EU law is directed towards individuals. Article 101 TFEU prohibits agreements between undertakings, decisions by associations of undertakings and concerted practices which may affect trade between Member States and which have as their object or effect the prevention, restriction or distortion of competition within the internal market. Agreements (e.g., contracts) that infringe this prohibition are declared automatically void. However, if certain conditions are met, such agreements may be allowed. These conditions are laid down in Article 101 paragraph 3 TFEU. It is generally assumed that permitted exceptions are limited to those provided for by Article 101 paragraph 3.

The Charter has the same legally binding force as the TFEU and therefore the same binding force as Article 101 TFEU. Consequently (arguments anchored in) the Charter may be able to change the situation that each exception to the prohibition and nullity has to meet the requirements of Article 101 paragraph 3 TFEU.[36]

By taking into consideration the possibility of Charter provisions providing for arguments to justify a derogation from the prohibition of Article 101 TFEU, an analogy can be drawn with the Charter-based justifications of the restriction of a market freedom. That type of justification can, through the intermediary of the rights and principles enshrined in the Charter, be connected with arguments commonly used in private law. For example, if the contract between B, C and D that restricts the freedom of A to freely deliver services (see under §10.04[B][1]) would be justified with arguments laid down in the Charter, like the right to have one's own convictions, it would be inconsistent to assume that nevertheless such contract would be void under Article 101 TFEU.[37]

The CJEU has not yet decided on this subject. If it would indeed consider the Charter to be a (second) source providing for exceptions to the prohibition, that would be interesting for two reasons. A lively debate on the possibility in competition law to justify restrictive agreements and practices for non-economic reasons has taken place in the past.[38] The CJEU has cautiously accepted the possibility to acknowledge more

36. G. Monti, Article 81 EC and Pubic Policy, CMLR 2001, 1057-1099; C. Townley, Article 81 EC and Public Policy, Oxford 2009, Chapter 2.
37. Townley, Article 81 EC and Public Policy (note 36), Conclusion.
38. See with references to more literature Townley, Article 81 EC and Public Policy (note 36) and C. Townley, Which goals count in Article 101 TFEU?: Public policy and its discontents, European

'soft', value related considerations as a ground for justification. This cautious approach would be supported if grounds of justification following from the Charter were to be acknowledged. The Charter-values are almost all of a non-economic nature. Development in this manner would be a solid and fertile ground for the integration of non-economic values in economic law. It would allow for a broader range of arguments relating to the interests of individuals, such as the preference to conduct a business consistently with one's convictions.

[3] Case 3: Moulding an EU Law Remedy of a Private Law Origin by Balancing Mutual Aims

To elaborate upon the creative and grounding force of the Charter provisions in horizontal relationships, I give a third example. In this case the approach of a creative and critical exchange, taking into consideration requirements of both EU law and private law and the respective systems, in my opinion has worked out well. I have in mind the so-called passing on defence in competition law cases. The defence of passing on means that the party who infringes competition law (e.g. a brewery that sets prices) and who has to pay damages to the party who was the victim of the infringement (e.g. a pub), argues that the damage for which the other party claims compensation has been passed on – for instance to consumers. This defence is a normal argument in private law: damage that not has been suffered (e.g., because it was passed on), should not be compensated. Compensation would enrich the claimant and therefore would run counter the principle that prohibits unjustified enrichment.

From the initial point of view of EU law, the defence endangers the effectiveness of competition law: a successful defence prevents the infringer (defendant) from feeling that he did something wrong.

We know however that EU law has its hours of glory through the assistance of national law. To ensure a long-lasting effectiveness it is wise not to ruin unnecessarily the private law systems of the Member States. That is why the private law related argument of enrichment changed the position of the Commission.[39] It dropped its initial idea to prohibit the passing on defence.

In my view, this is a convincing example of an interaction between EU law and private law that leads to convergence of both fields of law.

It may be argued however that, to withstand an argument coming from a source of law, declared by itself as supreme and capable of being directly effective, one needs solid ground. Is there a more solid ground for the enrichment argument?

Competition Law Review 2011, 441; S. Lavrijssen, The Protection of Non-Competition Interests; What Role for National Competition Authorities after Lisbon, European Law Review 2010, 634-659.

39. COM (2008) 165 def.

The principle of prohibition of enrichment is applied *inter alia*[40] by the CJEU in the sphere of Article 340 TFEU, the liability of the Union for damages (*Masdar*)[41] and in the sphere of (vertical) undue payment and unduly levied charges.[42] Until now, the defence derived from enrichment in horizontal relationships has only been accepted by the Court in competition law cases (the passing on defence, discussed above).[43] In the *FIAMM* case the possibility to claim damages (in a restricted number of cases) in case of lawful acts of the Union, was technically linked with the fundamental right to property as enshrined in Article 1 Protocol No. 1 ECHR and the freedom to pursue a trade or profession.[44]

Now I make this combination of ingredients (the acknowledgment of the prohibition of unjustified enrichment in EU law as a ground for compensation in case of lawful acts, and the connection between the possibility to claim compensation with the fundamental right to property) instrumental in the next step of development: if the enrichment argument can be linked to Article 1, First Protocol, ECHR, it also can be linked to the right to property as laid down in Article 17 Charter. Let us turn back to the passing on defence and apply the reasoning. It can be argued that the idea of enrichment as it emanates from the possibility to rely on the passing on defence, being a derogation from EU competition law effectiveness, has a solid ground, namely in the Charter, holding that no one may be deprived of his or her possessions without valid reason.

[C] What Could Be the Next Step?

We can wait for the next step: the development of the concept of 'the right to property'. From the case law of the ECHR on Article 1, First Protocol it is clear that this concept can fly very high - almost covering the entire private law[45] – both the law of obligations (contracts and tort) and property law. So this Charter provision can, taken into consideration Article 52 Charter, become a link through which a considerable part of private law reasoning can be introduced in EU law.[46]

40. The prohibition of enrichment is developed by the CJEU in public law cases. See A.S. Hartkamp, Unjustified enrichment and condictio indebiti in European community law, in K. Boele-Woelki & W. Grosheide (eds.), The Future of European Contract Law, Essays in Honour of Ewoud Hondius, 2007, pp. 291-306.
41. CJEU 16 December 2008, C-47/07P, Jurispr. 2008, p. I-9761 (Masdar/Commission).
42. CJEU 27 February 1980, 68/79, Jurispr. 1980, p. 501 (Just/Skatteministeriet); CJEU 9 November 1983, 199/82, Jursipr. 1983, p. 3595 (Amministrazione delle Finanze dello Stato/SpA San Giorgio), CJEU 14 January 1997, C-192-218/95, Jurispr. 1997, I-165 (Comateb/Directeur général des douanes). See moreover CJEU 20 October 2011, C-94/10 n.y.r., (Danfoss A/S/ Skatteministeriet). See on these cases Hartkamp, European Law and National Private Law, 2012 (note 2), nr. 87-88.
43. CJEU 20 September 2001, C-453/99, Jurispr. 2001, p. I-6297 (Courage/Crehan).
44. CJEU 9 September 2008, C-121/06, Jurispr. 2008, p. I-6513 (FIAMM/Council and Commission), paras 182 et seq.
45. Hartkamp, European Law and National Private Law, 2012 (note 2), nr. 211-219.
46. See in more detail Sieburgh, ERPL 2013, sections 3, 5 and 6.

§10.05 GENERAL PRINCIPLES AND CHARTER AS A SOURCE FOR ARGUMENTS IN EU LAW AND PRIVATE LAW

In the work to be done as envisioned in this paper: the bottom-up analysis of horizontal relationships, the construction of the mutual influence of EU law and private law and the development of criticism towards results of mutual influences (and mostly a combination of the two) – the influx of the Charter (and general principles of EU law backed up by the Charter) into EU law and from EU law into private law and horizontal relationships, can be a source of substantive inspiration and new arguments within techniques known for a long time in EU law. Even though the Charter not necessarily changes the techniques (legality review, generative, supplementing, derogating function of general principles of EU law), it will add to the arguments used by individuals: for example in case of justifying a restriction of EU law that is necessary to meet reasonable needs in private law relationships or to have an applicable rule of national law reviewed where the Charter provision turns out to be a basis for a general principle of EU law.

Moreover, the Charter will be used by private law scholars to connect private law arguments and EU law reasoning – both to co-develop and co-shape EU law applicable in horizontal relationships and to develop arguments on and criticism against the way EU law tries to come to effect in specific fields of private law or concrete horizontal relationships. It is for this reason that the Charter has a promising future in private law.

CHAPTER 11

The Horizontal Direct Effect of the Four Freedoms: From a Hodgepodge of Cases to a Seamless Web of Judicial Protection in the EU Single Market?

Sybe de Vries & Robert van Mastrigt[*]

§11.01 INTRODUCTION

Ever since the outbreak of the financial, economic and monetary crisis in Europe, the attention for the EU Single Market seems to have relented. Yet, the crisis in Europe calls for a renewed commitment to the internal market, once the cornerstone of European integration and still a key task for the European Union in the attainment of the objectives of the Treaties.[1] Although the internal market appears to be the 'least disputed' area of European cooperation at first sight, the spread of the Treaty rules on free movement, which form the backbone of the internal market, causes anxiety among the Member States in sensitive non-economic fields as well. This is due, first of all, to the broadly defined substantive scope of application of the four freedoms. Whereas the main principles regarding the substantive scope of application have now – more or less – crystallized in the Court's case law, this is much less so in respect of the *personal* scope of application, which concerns the question as to whom the Treaty freedoms are addressed. But also here, we see that the outer limits of internal market law have

* We would like to thank Peter Morris for the editing of this paper.

1. From the much-debated speech by D. Cameron of 23 January 2013 on the relationship between the UK and Europe, it appears that Cameron sees the EU mainly as a single market with a high level of competitiveness: http://www.bbc.co.uk/news/uk-politics-21013771 (last consulted 29 March 2013).

gradually been stretched, the Court having been induced to apply EU free movement law to practices of private individuals in horizontal situations.

In our contribution we will investigate this development and we will focus on the question whether traces of a coherent approach can be discerned from the case law, or rather whether we are still faced with a hodgepodge of cases with a variable impact of the four freedoms on relationships between private individuals.

The starting point for our analysis is that the EU provisions on free movement, although their wording may suggest otherwise, were primarily drafted for the Member States, 'the authorities', and are not directed at private individuals. For such private individuals, the drafters of the Treaty envisaged the provisions on competition.[2] This dividing line has been marked by the terms '*imperium*' and '*dominium*', or public and private interests.[3] But the question is how strict is this dividing line? Could we picture EU free movement law and the EU competition rules as the Roman god *Janus*, with two faces looking in opposite directions? Or could and should we force *Janus* to look in the same direction, whereby for the sake of market integration the four freedoms must be applied in horizontal situations without (any) reservation?

In the following we seek to address these questions by first briefly discussing the broad *substantive* scope of application of the four freedoms, which is also relevant for understanding the *personal* scope of application. We will then analyse the case law of the Court on horizontal direct effect. After this analysis we can discuss the rationale of the Court's case law and the implications for private parties being obliged to respect the four freedoms as well. Lastly, before we present our summary we will briefly discuss whether there are no alternatives to horizontal direct effect.

§11.02 THE SUBSTANTIVE SCOPE OF THE FOUR FREEDOMS AND COMPETITION RULES

[A] The Four Freedoms

The Treaty prohibitions on the restrictions to free movement are in two ways broadly interpreted by the ECJ. Firstly, it appears that what is prohibited on the basis of the rules on free movement does not only include discriminatory measures but also all measures restricting free movement; the Court moved towards a market access test as a leading criterion. Secondly, not only legislation but also private actions may fall under the definition of a measure, or a restriction.

2. S. Prechal & S. De Vries, *Seamless Web of Judicial Protection in the Internal Market?*, 34 ELRev. 5, 13 (2009).
3. See K. Mortelmans, *Towards Convergence in the Application of the Rules on Free Movement and on Competition?*, 38 CMLRev. 613, 623 (2001), who refers to the words used by Röpke, 'Economic order and international law', (1954) RCADI, 224; this concerns 'the genuinely liberal principle of government and economy, of sovereignty and economic exploitation, of Imperium and Dominium, or of political power and economic power'.

[1] Market Access as a Leading Criterion

The threshold for applying EU free movement law is generally low.[4] And, although the principle of non-discrimination on grounds of nationality remains the cornerstone of the four freedoms,[5] the development of the Court's case law shows that the prohibitive rules on free movement are more broadly applicable. Market access has now become the main criterion for adjudicating national measures under the prohibitive rules on free movement, which entails that national rules preventing or hindering market access are unlawful, irrespective of whether they discriminate against other persons, services or capital. The *Dassonville* case[6] and subsequent cases, in particular *Cassis de Dijon*,[7] serve as a powerful illustration of this trend that even non-discriminatory or indistinctly applicable product requirements are caught by the prohibition on restricting trade in goods as contained in Article 34 TFEU.[8] The legal commitment to free trade and free movement entails a regime, which is directed at prohibiting any unjustified obstacle to trade rather than at merely eliminating discrimination and protectionism.[9] In a similar vein, in the context of the provisions on services and persons, the Court has clarified that these provisions also apply to indistinctly applicable measures.[10] Irrespective of *Keck*, where the ECJ retreated and overruled parts of its case law on the free movement of goods in respect of certain selling arrangements, the Court has generally preferred to adopt a 'market access-based test' and has never been willing to apply *Keck* beyond the field of the free movement of goods.[11] But *Keck* itself also appears to be limited in scope as the Court decided in two more recent cases that rules restricting or prohibiting the *use* of certain goods – like personal watercraft on waters other than general navigable waterways in Sweden[12] and trailers for motorcycles or mopeds in

4. S. Weatherill, 'From Economic Rights to Fundamental Rights', in *The Protection of Fundamental Rights in the EU After Lisbon*, 14 (S. de Vries, U. Bernitz & S. Weatherill (eds), Oxford: Hart Publishing 2013).
5. C. Barnard, *The Substantive Law of the EU: The Four Freedoms*, 18 (3rd ed., Oxford: Oxford University Press 2010).
6. Case 8/74, *Dassonville* [1974] ECR 837.
7. Case 120/78, *Cassis de Dijon* [1979] ECR 649.
8. S. Weatherill, 'From Economic Rights to Fundamental Rights', in *The Protection of Fundamental Rights in the EU After Lisbon*, 14 (S. de Vries, U. Bernitz & S. Weatherill (eds), Oxford: Hart Publishing 2013); C. Barnard, *The Substantive Law of the EU: The Four Freedoms*, 79-80 (3rd ed., Oxford: Oxford University Press 2010); P. Oliver (assisted by Malcolm Jarvis), Free Movement of Goods in the European Community: Under Article 28 to 30 of the EC Treaty, 115-118 (London: Sweet and Maxwell 2003).
9. See on the dispute which cut to the heart of the international trade regime: J.H.H. Weiler, 'The Constitution of the Common Market Place', in *The Evolution of EU Law*, 352 (P. Craig & G. de Búrca (eds), 1st ed., Oxford: Oxford University Press 1999).
10. Case C-415/93, *Bosman* [1995] ECR I-4921 (workers); Case C-55/94, *Gebhard* [1995] ECR I-4165 (establishment); Case C-76/90, *Säger* [1991] ECR I-4221 (services); Case C-384/93 *Alpine Investments*, [1995] ECR I-1141 (services).
11. C. Barnard, *The Substantive Law of the EU: The Four Freedoms*, 242-246 (3rd ed., Oxford: Oxford University Press 2010). In Case C-405/98, *Gourmet International* [2001] ECR I-1795, the Court had the possibility to extend its *Keck* approach to the free movement of services, but did not do so.
12. Case C-142/05, *Mickelsson and Roos* [2009] ECR I-04273; Case C-110/05, *Commission v. Italy* [2009] ECR I-519.

Italy – did impede market access. According to the Court, such a prohibition has a considerable influence on the behaviour of consumers, which in turn affects the access of that product to the market.[13]

[2] *A Broad Conception of What Constitutes an Obstacle or Restriction*

Not only has the Court provided for a broad interpretation of the *prohibitions* through the introduction of a market access test, but it has also provided a broad conception of *what* actually constitutes an obstacle or restriction.[14] There is a line emerging in the case law according to which the question whether there is an obstacle to free movement or a discriminatory act contrary to the Treaty is separated from the question whether the actor at the origin of the restriction is a person bound by the relevant Treaty prohibitions.[15] In other words, there seems to be *a self-standing test* in which it is first of all of importance to determine what exactly the restriction consists of – does it consist of legislation, binding decisions or also of actual practice? – and secondly who causes the restriction? Is it the legislature, the central or local government, a civil servant, a public organization, is it a sporting federation or a trade union or even individuals holding demonstrations?

The origins of this line of reasoning are already relatively old and can be found in the above-mentioned *Dassonville* case. The term 'measures having equivalent effect' contained in Article 34 TFEU is not further defined in the Treaty and has been interpreted very widely by the Court. According to the *Dassonville* definition, many arrangements, such as licences, inspections, safety regulations, advertising and labelling rules and price measures can be covered by the term 'measure'. Another illustration of this very broad approach is *Commission v. France,* a case on franking machines, where the Court held that the fact that a law or regulation conforms, in formal terms, to Article 34 TFEU is not sufficient to discharge a Member State of its obligations under that provision.[16] Later case law also determined that judicial decisions, decisions of professional organizations[17] and even conduct that is not legally

13. Case C-110/05, *Commission v. Italy* [2009] ECR I-519, para. 56.
14. S. Prechal & S. De Vries, *Seamless Web of Judicial Protection in the Internal Market?*, 34 ELRev. 5-24 (2009).
15. The term 'obstacle' is used here for both discriminatory measures and indistinctly applicable measures restricting market access. See with regard to the terms obstacle, restriction, and hindrance: C. Barnard, *The Substantive Law of the EU: The Four Freedoms*, 257-261 (3rd ed., Oxford: Oxford University Press 2010).
16. Case C-21/84, *Postal franking machine* [1985] ECR 1355, para. 11: 'Under the cloak of a general provision permitting the approval of machines imported from other Member States, the administration might very well adopt a systematically unfavourable attitude towards imported machines.'
17. P.J.G. Kapteyn, & P. VerLoren van Themaat, *Het recht van de Europese Unie en van de Europese Gemeenschappen*, 534 (Deventer: Kluwer 2003); C. Barnard, *The Substantive Law of the EU: The Four Freedoms*, 73-75 (3rd ed., Oxford: Oxford University Press 2010). With regard to judicial decisions, see e.g. Opinion of AG Van Gerven in Case C-93/92, *Motorradcenter* [1993] ECR I-5009; Regarding decisions of professional organizations, see e.g. Joined Cases 266/87 and 267/87, *Royal Pharmaceutical Society* [1989] ECR 1295; Case C-292/92, *Hünermund* [1993] I-6787.

binding can be considered as 'measures'. The *Buy Irish* case concerned a campaign to promote the sale and purchase of domestic products – the 'Buy Irish' campaign – that, according to the Court, was contrary to the prohibition of Article 34 TFEU. In fact, this campaign was financed by the Irish government.[18]

Many years later in the *A.G.M.-COS.MET* case the Court even considered that comments expressed in public by a Finnish state official regarding the alleged non-safety of Italian car lifts were a measure having equivalent effect, in view of the fact that as a consequence of these comments the sales in Finland of the car lifts produced by the Italian company AGM, dropped.[19]

Also in the context of the other freedoms, various types of measures and practices can be or are considered to be a restriction and are thus, in principle, subject to the prohibitions. Article 45 TFEU on workers, for instance, pertains not only to qualification requirements, language requirements or conditions of residence, but also to transfer rules drafted by sports federations.[20] From the *Köbler* case it appears that judicial decisions may lead to conflicts with the free movement of workers, for which the Member State may be held liable.[21]

We can see a similar development regarding the free movement of services. According to the Court, not only can certain licence requirements, authorization requirements for medical treatment abroad or other mandatory provisions come within the scope of Article 56 TFEU, but also the selection rules determining that Christine Deliège was not allowed to compete in the Paris International Judo Tournament in the under-52 kg category – even though these rules were in the end not considered to be in breach of Article 56 TFEU.[22] In the *Viking* and *Laval* cases the Court considered trade union action and the right of unions to take collective action, as a result of which undertakings established in other Member States may be forced to join a collective employment agreement, to be restrictions within the meaning of Articles 49 and 56 TFEU, the freedom of establishment and the free movement of services respectively. According to the Court the abolition, as between Member States, of obstacles would be compromised, 'if the abolition of State barriers could be neutralised by obstacles resulting from the exercise of their legal autonomy by associations or organisations not governed by public law'.[23]

18. Case C-249/81, *Commission v. Ireland* [1982] ECR 4005.
19. Case C-470/03, *A.G.M.-COS.MET* [2007] ECR I-2749. See also the annotation by S. de Vries, CMLRev. 569-585 (2008).
20. Case C-415/93, *Bosman* [1995] ECR I-4921.
21. Case C-224/01, *Köbler* [2003] ECR I-10239.
22. Joined Cases C-51/96 and C-191/96, *Deliège* [2000] ECR I-2549. In the *Deliège* case the Court applied the so-called inherent restriction approach (see also S. de Vries, *Tensions within the Internal Market*, 44-45). In the *Grogan* case a prohibition issued by an Irish court on providing information on the availability of legal abortions in the United Kingdom was, however, not considered to be a restriction within the meaning of Article 56 TFEU, since, according to the Court, the link between the activity of the students' associations of which Mr Grogan and the other defendants were officials and the medical termination of pregnancies carried out in clinics in another Member State is too tenuous for the prohibition on the distribution of information to be capable of being regarded as a restriction within the meaning of Article 56 TFEU: Case C-159/90, *SPUC v. Grogan*, [1991] ECR I-4685, para. 24.
23. Case C-341/05, *Laval* [2007] ECR I-11767, para. 98; See also section §11.03 below.

And, lastly, the *Premier League* case, on the compatibility of territorial restrictions on broadcasting rights for English Premier League matches, illustrates that even contractual provisions between the broadcasters and their customers can be considered as a restriction within the meaning of Article 56 TFEU. In applying the free movement of services provision the Court held that the 'actual origin of the obstacle to the reception of such services is to be found in the contracts concluded between the broadcasters and their customers, which in turn reflect the territorial restriction clauses included in contracts concluded between those broadcasters and the holders of intellectual property rights'.[24]

[3] Who Causes the Restriction Is Irrelevant

This trend of interpreting the concept of measures and restrictions so broadly that actual actions also fall under their definition also shows that it is apparently irrelevant *who* causes the restriction for the determination of whether there *is* a restriction of free movement. At issue in *A.G.M-COS.MET* were the statements of a civil servant, in the sports cases rules introduced by sports federations were a bone of contention, and in *Viking* and *Laval* the actions of trade unions were at issue, in particular collective actions. In the *Spanish Strawberries*[25] and *Schmidberger*[26] cases it in fact concerned private action by angry farmers and an environmental organization respectively, which constituted an obstacle to free movement. And, although in *Premier League*[27] the fact that national law conferred legal protection on the territorial restrictions might have sufficed to trigger the application of Article 56 TFEU, the Court, by admitting that the actual origin of the restriction derives from contractual provisions, took the autonomous behaviour of private parties, i.e., the broadcasters and the holders of intellectual property rights, as a starting point for its analysis of Article 56 TFEU.[28]

The *Premier League* case confirms the Court's approach in applying this self-standing test. By separating the question whether contractual provisions could in principle qualify as a restriction from the addressee issue, contractual provisions, which are traditionally considered as a matter of competition law and not regarded as an obstacle to free movement,[29] could easily be brought within the ambit of the free

24. Joined Cases C-403/08 and C-429/08, *Premier League* [2011] n.y.r., para. 88.
25. Case C-265/95, *Spanish Strawberries* [1997] ECR I-6959. But certain conditions must be met. In the light of a number of specific factors and given the frequency and seriousness of the incidents cited by the Commission, the Court concluded that the measures adopted by the French government were manifestly inadequate to ensure the freedom of intra-Community trade in agricultural products.
26. Case C-112/00, Schmidberger [2003] ECR I-5659.
27. Joined Cases C-403/08 and C-429/08, *Premier League* [2011] n.y.r.
28. S. De Vries, *Case Note on Premier League and Karen Murphy Joined Cases C-403 & 429/08 Football Association Premier League Ltd, NetMed Hellas SA, Multichoice Hellas SA (C-403/08) v. QC Leisure et al., and Karen Murphy v. Media Protection Services Ltd (C-429/08), Judgment of the Court (Grand Chamber) of 4 October 2011, nyr.*, 50 CMLRev. 591-622 (2013).
29. Case C-159/00, *Sapod Audic* [2002] ECR I-5031. But there were exceptions, for example, in the fields of sports (e.g. the transfer rules set up by UEFA that were at issue in Case C-415/93, *Bosman* [1995] ECR I-4921) or in the field of certain professional services (e.g. the decision by the Dutch bar association (association of undertakings) to prohibit integrated partnerships

movement rules. Only upon a second analysis could they be removed from the scope of free movement, namely when it would transpire that the obstacle can in no way be attributed to an authority which is bound by the free movement provisions (see hereafter §11.03).[30]

[B] EU Competition Rules

[1] Own Modes of Application

Where competition rules are applied, it must be assessed whether the rules emanate from an *undertaking* in the first place and restrict competition in a particular market to an appreciable extent, or whether the rules are the result of unilateral action by one or more dominant firms. Article 101 TFEU distinguishes between agreements having as their object the restriction of competition and agreements having as their effect the restriction of competition. The first category of agreements is presumed to restrict competition to an appreciable extent and includes so-called hardcore restrictions.[31] With respect to the second category, account should be taken of *inter alia* the economic context in which the undertakings operate.[32]

The free movement rules and the competition rules therefore continue to have their own 'modes of application'. Several situations may exemplify this. Certain types of national measures, for example, that are likely to infringe the free movement rules may not be at all problematic in the light of the competition rules. Quality standards and product requirements, for example, are generally not considered to restrict competition within the meaning of Article 101 TFEU (the cartel prohibition). As long as certain transparency requirements are met, market access will not be affected and competition between competitors will not be excluded. However, as stated above, national rules on product standards are considered to restrict the free movement of goods within the meaning of Article 34 TFEU.

Price restrictions, on the other hand, may not be problematic in the light of the free movement rules, but will almost certainly be prohibited by Article 101 TFEU. The same holds true for market sharing or the control of outlets, which are considered as obvious restrictions on competition and which will normally fall within the scope of Article 101(1) TFEU. Hence, the specific requirements of Articles 101 and 102 TFEU,

---

between lawyers and accountants, which was at issue in Case C 309/99, *Wouters* [2002] ECR I-1577 and which were also found to restrict Article 56 TFEU.

30. As we will briefly discuss below, in section §11.03, there are already exceptions for organizations which regulate, by virtue of their own autonomous powers, employment or self-employment.
31. This clear distinction between object and effect has been reinforced by the Court in cases like Case C-8/08P, *T-Mobile* [2009] ECR I-4529; Joined Cases C-501/06, C-513/06, 515/06 & 519/06 P, *GlaxoSmithKline* [2009] ECR I-9291; Joined Cases C-403/08 and C-429/08, *Premier League* [2011] n.y.r.; See also A. Gerbrandy, *Case Note on Case 8/08 P, T-Mobile Netherlands BV, KPN Mobile NV, Orange Nederland NV, Vodafone Libertel NV v. Raad van bestuur van de Nederlandse Mededingingsautoriteit, [2009] ECR I-4529*, 47 CMLRev. 1206-1207 (2010).
32. Joined Cases T-374/94, T-375/94, T-384/95 and 388/95, *European Night Services* [1998] ECR II-3141.

which differ from the requirements set by the four freedoms, must be met. In this respect the Court in the *Meca-Medina* case on anti-doping rules issued by the International Olympic Committee clearly held that:

> if those rules do not constitute restrictions on freedom of movement because they concern questions of purely sporting interest and, as such, have nothing to do with economic activity [see *Walrave and Koch* and *Donà* – SdV & RvM][33] that fact means neither that the sporting activity in question necessarily falls outside the scope of Articles 101 and 102 TFEU, nor that the rules do not satisfy the specific requirements of those articles.[34]

Furthermore, it must also be stressed that the competition rules apply in the goods and services markets, but not – at least not in full – in the labour market. This is also clear from the Court's case law regarding collective labour agreements (the *Albany* and *Brentjens* jurisprudence), where collective labour agreements enjoy, to a certain extent, anti-trust immunity.[35] Hence, obstacles to the labour market in another Member State could only be successfully challenged on the basis of the free movement rules, which would justify a broad interpretation of the concept 'obstacle'.[36]

The competition rules will not apply where contracts between private parties or unilateral behaviour are clearly prescribed by law. Here the Court has developed the so-called state action defence doctrine, also referred to as the *Ladbroke* doctrine.[37] In this situation, companies infringing the cartel prohibition by concluding restrictive agreements are excused and are not liable for their actions, since the state prescribes their behaviour.[38]

§11.03 THE PERSONAL SCOPE OF THE TREATY FREEDOMS

In competition law, matters seem to be relatively straightforward. Articles 101 and 102 TFEU contain prohibitions addressed to private parties and also to public authorities when the latter engage in an economic activity. According to well-established case law, the concept of undertaking includes any entity – potentially this can also be a single individual – engaged in an economic activity, irrespective of its legal status and the way it is financed.[39] The situation is somewhat more complicated in the area of the Treaty freedoms. It is tempting to see horizontal direct effect as a logical consequence of the

33. Case 36/74, *Walrave and Koch* [1974] ECR 1405; Case 13/76, *Donà* [1976] ECR 1333.
34. See Case C-519/04 P, *Meca-Medina* [2006] ECR I-6991, paras 30-32.
35. Joined Cases C-115/97, C-116/97 and C-117/97, *Brentjens* [1999] ECR I-6025; Case C-67/96, *Albany* [1999] ECR I-5751.
36. One may wonder, however, whether the Court, at the time, arrived too easily at the conclusion that collective agreements should be kept outside the scope of Article 101 TFEU. In fact AG Jacobs in the *Albany* case suggested a more subtle approach, and indicated that it is not necessarily obvious that collective employment agreements on work and employment conditions cannot have negative effects on the goods and services markets and have negative consequences for third parties.
37. Case C-359/95 P and C-379/95 P, *Commission v. Ladbroke Racing Ltd* [1997] ECR I-6265.
38. The state may be liable, however, under Article 4(3) TEU in conjunction with Articles 101 or 102 TFEU for the resulting restrictions on competition (see Case C-198/01, *CIF* [2003] ECR I-8055).
39. Case C-41/90, *Höfner* [1991] ECR I-1979, para. 21.

applicability of the free movement provisions to 'non-government action' (see above §11.02 A[2]). The Court also seems to point in that direction in some of its case law.[40] That this is not necessarily so follows from other cases such as *Spanish Strawberries* and *Schmidberger*, which will be discussed hereafter. In other words, as was already observed above, the question 'what actions can restrict free movement and who is at the origin of those actions?', and the question 'for whom do the free movement provisions create obligations?', must apparently be kept separate. In turn, from the latter obligations one may deduce against whom these provisions may be relied upon.

Before we discuss the development in the case law on considering individuals bound by the free movement provisions in certain situations and consequently to grant these provisions (limited) horizontal direct effect, the concept of direct effect needs to be briefly introduced.

[A] The Concept of Direct Effect in General

The recognition of the principles of direct effect and supremacy in the *Van Gend & Loos* and *Costa v. Enel* cases have been crucial for the European integration process.[41] *Van Gend & Loos* is probably the most important case in the history of European legal integration. The Court, by deducing from the spirit, the general scheme and the wording of the EEC Treaty a new autonomous and independent legal order, which is intended to confer rights upon individuals, formulated a number of requirements which a provision must meet in order for it to have direct effect: there must be a clear and precise obligation for the Member States; the obligation must be unconditional; compliance with the obligation must not require any further legal act and the Member States have no discretion regarding the implementation of the obligation.[42]

In subsequent case law the Court gradually extended the doctrine of direct effect, at first in the following two ways. Firstly, the conditions of direct effect have been relaxed in the Court's case law, which now entail that provisions of EU law are directly effective whenever they are sufficiently precise and unconditional.[43] As a matter of fact, the Court has gradually turned the concept of direct effect into a test of justiciability: is the norm sufficiently operational to be applied by a court?[44]

And secondly, the Court, by offering a pragmatic and functional approach to the question of 'against whom can a provision of EU law be relied upon?', has interpreted the concept of a state broadly and thereby widened the scope of *vertical* direct effect, i.e., extending the possibilities to rely on a provision of EU law in a national court vis-à-vis the Member State. The case *Foster v. British Gas* serves as an illustration of this approach by the Court. This approach prevents the search 'for exhaustive and

40. Cf. the already mentioned points in Case C-341/05, *Laval*, [2007] ECR I-11767, paras 98 and 99. See also the somewhat peculiar reference in Case C-438/05, *Viking* [2007] ECR I-10779, para 62.
41. Case 26/62, *Van Gend & Loos* [1963] ECR 1; Case 6/64, *Costa v. ENEL* [1964] ECR 585.
42. J.H. Jans, R. De Lange, S. Prechal & R.J.G.M. Widdershoven, *Europeanisation of Public Law*, 65 (Groningen: Europa Law Publishing 2007).
43. *Ibid.*
44. Cf. B. De Witte, 'Direct Effect, Primacy and the Nature of the Legal Order', in *The Evolution of EU Law*, 331 (P. Craig & G. De Burca (eds), Oxford: Oxford University Press 2011).

polarized definitions of "the state" and "private individual"' and the drawing of a strict dividing line between *imperium* and *dominium*.[45] Public bodies that are established pursuant to a measure adopted by the state in order to provide a public service under the control of the state will, just like the government, have to comply with provisions of EU law, including Directives.[46]

[B] Towards the Horizontal Direct Effect of Treaty Rules on the Free Movement of Persons and Services

Although the Court in *Foster v. British Gas* offered an expansive understanding of the notion of a state, thereby opening the door to the application of the notion of direct effect in 'grey zones' between the state and private parties, it was for a long time unclear whether the fundamental freedoms impose direct obligations on non-public, private law bodies. In *Walrave* the Court finally clarified the issue and held that 'the rule on non-discrimination applies in judging *all legal relationships* [emphasis added]'.[47] According to the Court non-discrimination applied, in addition to public authorities, also to rules of 'any other nature aimed at collectively regulating gainful employment and services'.[48] Later case law indicated that the Court did not intend - at least thus far - to move towards full horizontal direct effect but merely meant an extension of vertical direct effect.

[1] Case Law on Collective Regulations

The Court has included actions aimed at regulating gainful employment in a collective manner or regulating the activities of the self-employed collectively, and actions by trade unions designed as a threat in order to compel the signing or application of a collective agreement. Regarding the first type of actions, the case *Walrave* concerned a rule of the Union Cycliste Internationale, which prescribed that in races the pacemaker must be of the same nationality as the stayer. The question was whether this alleged discrimination on grounds of nationality by a private sporting organization was compatible with the free movement of workers and the free provision of services. The Court ruled for the first time that those fundamental freedoms not only apply to rules imposed by public authorities, but likewise extend to rules adopted by organizations which are governed by private law and aimed at regulating, in a collective manner, gainful employment and the provision of services.[49]

In *Bosman*[50] rules set up by national sporting associations, restricting the extent to which foreign footballers could be recruited or fielded in a match, and the transfer

45. Case C-188/89, *Foster v. British Gas* [1990] ECR I-3313; E. Szyszczak, Case Law: Case C-188/89, *Foster and Others v. British Gas plc*, Preliminary Reference under Article 177 EEC by the House of Lords, Decision of the European Court of Justice of 12 July 1990, 27 CMLRev. 859, 867(1990).
46. *Ibid.*, 859-871.
47. Case 36/74, *Walrave and Koch* [1974] ECR 1405, para. 28.
48. *Ibid.*, para. 17.
49. Case 36/74, *Walrave and Koch* [1974] ECR 1405, para. 17.
50. Case C 415/93, *Bosman* [1995] ECR I-4921.

rules laid down by UEFA were at issue. The Court held that these rules were contrary to Article 45 TFEU as the first rule discriminated against foreign players and restricted the opportunities for employment, and the second rule prevented and deterred players from leaving the clubs to which they belong after the expiry of their contract. Important is that, different from *Walrave,* the second rule did not directly discriminate against others, but constituted a restriction. *Bosman* is thus very significant in that the Court broadened the scope of horizontal direct effect to truly non-discriminatory measures. But it was still unclear whether Article 45 TFEU applied to all kinds of 'private' measures or only to collective regulations.[51]

Non-governmental regulatory bodies that impose collective rules can also be found outside the area of sports. In *Wouters,* for example, it was affirmed that the Dutch Bar Association needs to comply with the freedom of establishment and cannot prohibit multi-disciplinary partnerships between lawyers and accountants.[52]

Under the second type of actions, horizontal direct effect can be found in situations where collective actions are organized by trade unions. The Court held in the *Viking*[53] and *Laval*[54] judgments that a trade union established by private law can be subject to the provisions of the free movement of services and establishment. In *Viking* a group of trade unions initiated a collective action when a Finnish undertaking was planning to reflag its ship to Estonia where lower wages could be paid. According to the Court a private undertaking may rely on Article 49 TFEU against a trade union or an association of trade unions as they regulated, in a collective manner, gainful employment, self-employment and the provision of services. The Court came to a similar conclusion with regard to Article 56 TFEU in *Laval,* which concerned a blockade on a construction site in Sweden, because the Latvian construction company, which posted its own Latvian workers, refused to sign the applicable collective labour agreement. Interestingly *Viking* and *Laval* concerned a phase before the introduction of collective rules in the form of collective labour agreements. After all, in both cases the aim of the collective action by the trade unions was to get foreign employers to sign or apply a certain collective agreement.[55]

All of the above-mentioned cases, dealing with either the free movement of workers, the freedom of establishment, or the free provision of services, have in common that the powers of the bodies and organizations resemble, in practice, state-made rules. But it is thereby not necessary, different from *Foster v. British Gas,* that the state exercises direct or indirect control over the organizations.[56] These rules, either discriminatory or non-discriminatory and merely restrictive, are thus treated similarly. Sporting associations have by their very nature de facto the exclusive power

51. S. Van den Bogaert, 'Horizontality; The Court Attacks?', in *The Law of the Single European Market – Unpacking the Premises,* 127-128 (C. Barnard and J. Scott (eds), Oxford and Portland: Hart Publishing 2002).
52. Case C 309/99, *Wouters* [2002] ECR I-1577.
53. Case C-438/05, *Viking* [2007] ECR I-10779.
54. Case C-341/05, *Laval* [2007] ECR I-11767.
55. S. Prechal & S. de Vries, *Seamless Web of Judicial Protection in the Internal Market?,* 34 ELRev. 5, 14 (2009).
56. Case C-188-89, *Foster v. British Gas* [1990] ECR I-3313, paras 18-20.

to adopt rules in the area of sport for which they are responsible; intervention by other parties would render such a system nugatory. Intervention by the State is in this area only marginal or even non-existent.[57] Trade unions have, in a similar vein, a substantial power to force undertakings by way of collective action to comply with a collective agreement. Fact remains that horizontal direct effect is still limited in its impact due to the fact that the rules only apply to private parties if well-defined rule-making powers are present.

[2] Extending the Scope of Horizontal Direct Effect in the Field of Workers

In the area of the free movement of workers the Court seems to have gone further by extending the personal scope of EU law to private individuals, regardless of the existence of regulatory powers. The case *Angonese*[58] concerned an Italian bank in the bilingual region of Balzano which required their prospective employees to have a certificate of bilingualism (in German and Italian). This certificate could only be obtained through the local authority. The Court held that Article 45 TFEU could be relied upon in a dispute between private individuals, emphasizing that Article 45 TFEU 'constitutes a specific application of the general prohibition of discrimination contained in [Article 18 TFEU]'.[59] The Court added that like Article 157 TFEU, 'it is designed to ensure that there is no discrimination on the labour market' and thereby referred to the *Defrenne II* judgment.[60]

Although the central considerations of the Angonese case point in the direction of 'full horizontal direct effect', this must be put into perspective for the following three reasons. Firstly, it must be reiterated that the contested action by the bank was indirectly based on a collective employment agreement for savings banks.[61] This would suggest that there was some 'collectiveness' present in this case.

Furthermore, the regional practice in relation to access to employment was one of the reasons that the bank was dominant when it came to hiring employees. In the *Ferlini* case the Court explicitly referred to the existence of dominance as a relevant factor in this respect:

> the first paragraph of Article 6 of the Treaty [now Article 18 TFEU] also applies in cases where a group or organisation such as the EHL [Entente des Hôpitaux Luxembourgeois] exercises a certain power over individuals and is in a position to impose on them conditions which adversely affect the exercise of the fundamental freedoms guaranteed under the Treaty.[62]

57. P. Oliver, *Oliver on Free Movement of Goods in the European Union*, 71 (Oxford and Portland: Hart Publishing 2010).
58. Case C-281/98, *Angonese* [2000] ECR I-4139.
59. *Ibid.*, para. 35.
60. Case 43/75, *Defrenne II* [1976] ECR 455, para. 34.
61. S. Prechal & S. de Vries, *Seamless Web of Judicial Protection in the Internal Market?*, ELRev. 5, 15 (2009).
62. Case C-411/98, *Ferlini* [2000] ECR I-8081, para. 50.

And lastly, the Court in *Angonese* emphasized the significance of the prohibition of discrimination as contained in Article 45 TFEU, which constitutes a specific application of the general principle of non-discrimination contained in Article 18 TFEU. This suggests that it is first and foremost the principle of discrimination that triggered the horizontal direct effect of Article 45 TFEU in the *Angonese* case.[63]

Recapitulating the above-discussed judgments in *Walrave, Bosman* and *Angonese,* we can discern the following development in the doctrine of horizontal direct effect. In *Walrave* the Court indicated that Article 45 TFEU applies to private parties that have a regulatory function, but only in the case of discriminatory measures. From *Bosman* the conclusion can be drawn that Article 45 TFEU is applicable to private parties having a regulatory function, but also in the case of non-discriminatory or indistinctly applicable restrictions on free movement. In *Angonese,* however, Article 45 TFEU also applies to private parties *not* having a regulatory function, but only in the case of discrimination.

The *Angonese* judgment and the argument of non-discrimination was confirmed by the Court's judgment in *Raccanelli,*[64] which involved a dispute between the Max Planck Institute (MPI), which offered research places, and a foreign doctoral student. Although the case concerned a dispute between two private individuals as the MPI is governed by private law, it should be observed that like in *Angonese* an element of dominance was present. The MPI, which is a unique and prestigious research institute, has substantial powers over the offering of research places to junior researchers. In addition, the institutions pursued a public interest, namely education and research. However, since the Court did not really pronounce on the issue of dominance, it is unclear how much weight should be given to these considerations. What is important, though, is that *Raccanelli* is the first confirmation of *Angonese,* decided by a chamber of the Court of only three judges, which might suggest that the 'Angonese approach' to horizontal direct effect was considered as settled case law by the Court'.[65]

[C] The Horizontal Direct Effect of the Treaty Rules on Goods?

The famous *Dassonville* formula of 'all trading rules *enacted by Member States* which are capable of hindering, directly or indirectly, actually or potentially, intra-Community trade' seems to indicate that only measures enacted by the *state* are subject to Article 34 TFEU on goods, thereby excluding private parties as addressees. It was more or less generally accepted that the provisions on the free movement of goods have no horizontal direct effect. One of the main arguments used here is that it is the competition rules that are drafted for the behaviour of private parties that affect the free

63. S. Prechal & S. De Vries, *Seamless Web of Judicial Protection in the Internal Market?*, 34 ELRev. 5, 16 (2009).
64. Case C-94/07, *Raccanelli* [2008] ECR I-5939.
65. See C. Krenn, *A Missing Piece in the Horizontal Effect 'Jigsaw': Horizontal Direct Effect and the Free Movement of Goods*, 49 CMLRev. 177, 194 (2012) (footnote 110); S. Prechal & S. De Vries, *Seamless Web of Judicial Protection in the Internal Market?*, 34 ELRev. 5, 15 and 18 (2009).

movement of goods.[66] This view seemed to be confirmed by the Court's judgment in *Sapod Audic,* wherein it ruled that 'a contractual provision cannot be regarded as a barrier to trade for the purposes of [Article 34 TFEU] since it was not imposed by a Member State but agreed between individuals'.[67] Likewise, in *Van de Haar* the Court emphasized that Article 101 TFEU is addressed to undertakings, whereas Article 34 TFEU is directed at measures taken by Member States that hinder imports.[68]

However, the Court has not always been fully consistent on the matter and in the earlier case *Dansk Supermarked,* dating from 1980, it ruled that 'it is impossible in any circumstances for agreements between individuals to derogate from the mandatory provisions of the Treaty on the free movement of goods.'[69] And, most recently, the Court in the *Fra.bo* case indicated that in *some* circumstances Article 34 TFEU can be relied upon vis-à-vis a private law association; however, without explicitly mentioning horizontal direct effect.[70]

[1] The Fra.bo Case

The *Fra.bo* case concerned a dispute between the German association of gas providers (Deutsche Vereinigung des Gas- und Wasserfaches eV), established by private law, and a manufacturer of copper fittings. The association required a certificate, which could only be issued by that association, and the manufacturer argued that this constituted an obstacle to the free movement of goods. The Court held that:

> Article 28 EC [now Article 34 TFEU] must be interpreted as meaning that it applies to standardisation and certification activities of a private-law body, where the national legislation considers the products certified by that body to be compliant with national law and that has the effect of restricting the marketing of products which are not certified by that body.

In arriving at this conclusion the Court heavily relied on the factual circumstances of the case and stated that '[i]n such circumstances, it is clear that a body such as the DVGW, by virtue of its authority to certify products, in reality holds the power to regulate the entry into the German market ...'.[71] Additional reasons for the Court to apply Article 34 TFEU here are that (1) the national law states that products certified by the association are compliant with national law,[72] (2) the association is de facto the only possibility for obtaining the certificate,[73] and (3) the referring court decided that it placed a considerable restriction on market access.[74]

Contrary to Advocate General Trstenjak the Court refrained from explicitly mentioning horizontal direct effect, although its reasoning by emphasizing the power

66. P. Oliver & W-H. Roth, *The Internal Market and the Four Freedoms*, 41 CMLRev. 407, 421 (2004).
67. Case C-159/00, *Sapod Audic* [2002] ECR I-5031, para. 74.
68. Joined Cases 177/82 & 178/82, *Van de Haar* [1984] ECR 1797, paras 11-12.
69. Case 58/80, *Dansk Supermarked* [1981] ECR 181, para. 17.
70. Case C-171/11, *Fra.bo* [2012] n.y.r.
71. *Ibid.*, para. 31.
72. *Ibid.*, para. 27.
73. *Ibid.*, para. 28.
74. *Ibid.*, para. 30.

of the DVGW to regulate market access fits within the case law that is referred to by the Advocate General.[75] AG Trstenjak had proposed to apply the case law on Articles 45, 49 and 56 TFEU for collective agreements by analogy on the basis of the *effet utile* rationale:[76]

> There are no fundamental objections to the application of the argument developed in case-law on the limited horizontal effect of the freedom of movement for workers, the freedom of establishment and the freedom to provide services to a case such as the present one, in which the applicability of the principle of the free movement of goods to a private-law association with de facto rule-making competence is at issue.[77]

Considering the careful approach of the Court the exact scope of the judgment remains unclear.[78] It appears that the Court regards the fact that the national law refers to the certification scheme as a determining factor, which could indicate that the 'legislative and regulatory context' of the Member State is relevant rather than the fact that it concerns a private or public law body. Hence, *Fra.bo* may not entail the full recognition of the horizontal direct effect of Article 34 TFEU, but certainly constitutes a – albeit careful – step towards this.

§11.04 THE RATIONALE OF THE COURT'S CASE LAW AND THE IMPLICATIONS THEREOF

The foregoing has shown that in the area of freedom of establishment and the free movement of services, a limited form of horizontal direct effect has been accepted,[79] whereas in the area of workers the Court has recognized a broader form of horizontal direct effect, meaning that private persons can directly rely on the Treaty provision vis-à-vis another private person, but only in so far as it concerns the principle of non-discrimination.[80] And, with respect to the free movement of goods the situation remains unclear.

---

75. Cf. H. van Harten en T. Nauta, *Nog geen horizontale rechtstreekse werking van het vrije verkeer van goederen?*, 10 NTER 329, 333 (2012).
76. Opinion of AG Trstenjak in Case C-171/11, *Fra.bo* [2012] n.y.r., para. 43.
77. *Ibid.*, para. 45.
78. N. Shuibhne, *The Treaty is Coming to Get You*, 4 ELRev. 367, 367 (2012).
79. In one way this seems close to a mere extension of vertical direct effect to non-governmental regulatory bodies. See for the resemblance with the broad interpretation of a 'measure' within the meaning of Article 34 TFEU: J. Snell, 'And then there were two: Products and citizens in Community Law', in *EU Law for the Twenty-First Century: Rethinking the New Legal Order* vol. II, 57 (T. Tridimas and P. Nebbia (eds), Oxford: Hart Publishing 2004). Noteworthy, is the similar reluctance of the Court to acknowledge horizontal direct effect explicitly in the Court's case law on directives: e.g. Case C-188/89, *Foster* [1990] ECR I-3313; Case C-106/89, *Marleasing* [1990] ECR I-4135; Case C-555/07, *Kücükdeveci* [2010] ECR I-365.
80. A. Dashwood, *Viking and Laval: Issues of 'Horizontal Direct Effect'*, 10 Cambridge Yearbook of European Legal Studies 525, 525 (2008); Cf. S. Prechal & S. De Vries, *Seamless Web of Judicial Protection in the Internal Market?*, 34 ELRev. 5, 16 (2009).

[A] The Rationale: Three Strands of Argumentation

If we look at the cases that have been decided so far, we see that the Court uses different arguments in different types of cases to accept some form of (limited) horizontal direct effect of the Treaty freedoms. We can essentially discern the following three strands of argumentation in the Court's case law. The first argument is based on the *effet utile* principle, which implies that neither the State nor private law bodies may detract from the useful effectiveness of EU law. The free movement provisions would be prevented from functioning effectively if private organizations were allowed to create or maintain obstacles that governments are not allowed to create or maintain. This *effet utile* line of argumentation can be found in the *Warave and Koch, Bosman* and *Viking & Laval* cases. In *Bosman* the Court formulated this as follows:

> The Court has held that the abolition as between Member States of obstacles to freedom of movement for persons and to freedom to provide services would be compromised if the abolition of State barriers could be neutralized by obstacles resulting from the exercise of their legal autonomy by associations or organizations not governed by public law (see *Walrave*, cited above, paragraph 18).
>
> It has further observed that working conditions in the different Member States are sometimes governed by provisions laid down by law or regulation and sometimes by agreements and other acts concluded or adopted by private persons. Accordingly, if the scope of Article 48 of the Treaty were confined to acts of a public authority there would be a risk of creating inequality in its application (see *Walrave*, cited above, paragraph 19). That risk is all the more obvious in a case such as that in the main proceedings in this case in that, as has been stressed in paragraph 24 above, the transfer rules have been laid down by different bodies or in different ways in each Member State.[81]

A second and related argument for the Court to accept a (limited) form of horizontal direct effect is the aspect of dominance, or, in other words, the fact that certain private organizations exercise a certain power over (other) individuals. This argument was clearly and explicitly referred to in the *Ferlini* judgment, but more implicitly present in the Court's judgments in *Angonese* and *Raccanelli*. In *Angonese* it was the dominance of the bank in respect of hiring personnel, whereas in *Raccanelli* it was the prestigious research institute, Max-Planck-Gesellschaft, which undoubtedly exercises some powers over especially young researchers. This dominance or power aspect of the regulatory body may have played a similar role in *Fra.bo SpA*, as the German private law body held the power to regulate the entry into the German market of certain products.[82]

The third and last argument relates to the fundamental (mandatory) nature of the freedoms and the key role of the principle of non-discrimination therein. Regarding the fundamental character of the four freedoms we find various references in the case law

81. Case C-415/93, *Bosman* [1995] ECR. I-4921, paras 83-84.
82. S. De Vries, *Case Note on Premier League and Karen Murphy Joined Cases C-403 & 429/08 Football Association Premier League Ltd, NetMed Hellas SA, Multichoice Hellas SA (C-403/08) v. QC Leisure et al., and Karen Murphy v. Media Protection Services Ltd (C-429/08), Judgment of the Court (Grand Chamber) of 4 October 2011, nyr.*, 50 CMLRev. 591, 612 (2013).

of the ECJ indicating that there is a close nexus between the fundamental freedoms and fundamental rights.[83] The Court itself uses words like 'fundamental freedom',[84] 'one of the fundamental principles of the Treaty',[85] or 'fundamental Community provision'.[86] The 'fundamental nature' of the freedoms can be deduced from the substantive scope of the Treaty freedoms, whose dogmatic foundation is provided for in *Dassonville*.[87] In a similar vein, Article 34 TFEU has been described as a 'fundamental political right', or as 'subjective public rights'.[88]

Other arguments to support the fundamental character of the freedoms are that, firstly, the freedoms have played a vital role in building Europe's economic constitution. According to the Ordo-liberal school, which originates from the German town of Freiburg in the 1930s, the constitution should protect the economic freedoms, 'which are as integral to the protection of human dignity, and as indicative of a free society, as political freedoms, which are themselves liberal in nature and which therefore underscore individual economic freedoms'.[89] And, secondly, the economic freedoms can often be defined in terms of the freedom to pursue a trade or profession, which is a fundamental right laid down in Article 16 of the Charter of Fundamental Rights.[90]

Lastly and very importantly, rights that are implicit in the economic freedoms, such as the right to equal treatment (non-discrimination), the right to move and reside in another Member State, transcend beyond the economic dimension of the free movement rules. The principle of non-discrimination is in fact transformed into a fundamental right to protect individual personality and human dignity.[91] The fact that the principle of non-discrimination may have triggered horizontal direct effect could be deduced from *Angonese*, wherein the Court emphasized the fact that Article 45 TFEU constitutes a specific application of the general principle of non-discrimination as contained in Article 18 TFEU. It could therefore be argued that the fundamental rights

83. P. Oliver & W-H. Roth, *The Internal Market and the Four Freedoms*, 41 CMLRev. 407, 407-411 (2004).
84. For instance, Case C-112/00, *Schmidberger* [2003] ECR I-5659 (goods); Case C-281/98, *Angonese* [2000] ECR I-4139 (workers); Case C-341/05, *Laval*, [2007] ECR I-11767 (services); Case C-36/02, *Omega* [2004] ECR I-9609 (services).
85. Case C-265/95, *Spanish Strawberries* [1997] ECR I-6959.
86. See Case C-49/89, *Corsica Ferries France* [1989] ECR I-4441, para. 8: 'As the Court has decided on various occasions, the articles of the EEC Treaty concerning the free movement of goods, persons, services and capital are fundamental Community provisions and any restriction, even minor, of that freedom is prohibited'. See recently the cases which the Commission has started against a couple of Member States regarding the profession of notaries, such as Case C-50/08 *Commission v. France* [2011] nyr., para. 67.
87. C. Barnard, *The Substantive Law of the EU: The Four Freedoms*, 73-74 (3rd ed., Oxford: Oxford University Press 2010).
88. M.P. Maduro, *We the Court. The European Court of Justice and the European Economic Constitution*, 81 (Oxford, Hart Publishing, 1998); T. Kingreen, *Struktur der Grundfreiheiten des Europäischen Gemeinschaftsrechts*, 15 (Berlin: Duncker & Humblot 1999). Cf. P. Oliver & W-H. Roth, *The Internal Market and the Four Freedoms*, 41 CMLRev. 407, 410 (2004).
89. D. Chalmers, 'The Single Market: From Prima Donna to Journeyman', in *New Legal Dynamics of European Union*, 57 (J. Shaw & G. More (eds), Oxford: Clarendon Press 1995).
90. S. Prechal & S. De Vries, *Viking/Laval en de grondslagen van het internemarktrecht*, 11 SEW 425, 434 (2008). See on a discussion of the freedom to conduct a business under Article 16 of the Charter also the contribution in this book by P. Oliver, chapter 12.
91. *Ibid.*, at 435.

character of the non-discrimination principle is crucial in creating obligations for private individuals. A similar approach can be found in the cases *Defrenne* and *Viking & Laval*.

[B] Implications of Accepting Horizontal Direct Effect

So what are the consequences of accepting horizontal direct effect for private individuals? And, does the recognition of horizontal direct effect of provisions of primary EU law, the Treaty, have ramifications for the adoption of EU legislation, secondary law, as well?

[1] Primary EU Law

The acceptance of a (limited) form of horizontal direct effect of provisions of primary EU law has several important consequences.

[a] Horizontal Direct Effect and Private Autonomy

Firstly, the prohibitive rules on free movement do not only impose binding obligations on the State, within the broadest sense of its meaning, but also on private parties, which directly encroaches upon their (contractual) autonomy. It has been argued 'that applying the four freedoms to the acts of private persons may constitute an inappropriate interference in their autonomy'.[92] Private persons cannot be compared to the state and their autonomy constitutes the very basis of the internal market.[93] The consequences of horizontal direct effect for private autonomy and thus for private law as such have been described by some as 'dramatic'.[94] In addition, as the application of the four freedoms in horizontal situations leads to direct intrusion in the domestic private law systems, it may undermine the coherence of the system.[95]

However, private or contractual autonomy should not in our opinion be a reason to deny horizontal direct effect at the outset, as autonomy in general has to be exercised within the limits of the law that is sufficiently clear for these purposes.[96] Furthermore, if there are good reasons for private parties to breach EU obligations, this can be weighed in the context of a possible justification (see hereafter).

92. P. Oliver & W-H. Roth, *The Internal Market and the Four Freedoms*, 41 CMLRev. 407, 427 (2004).
93. *Ibid.*, p. 427.
94. Cf. O. Cherednychenko, *EU Fundamental Rights, EC Fundamental Freedoms and Private Law*, 14 ERPL 23, 43 (2006). For a more nuanced approach see, e.g., A. Hartkamp, 'Fundamental Rights, Fundamental Freedoms and Contract Law', in *Constitutional Values in European Contract Law*, 103-106 (S. Grundmann (ed.), Alphen a/d Rijn: Kluwer Law International 2008).
95. T. Kingreen, '14 – Fundamental Freedoms', in *Principles of European Constitutional Law*, 548 (A. von Bogdandy & J. Bast (eds), Oxford: Hart Publishing 2010).
96. S. Prechal & S. De Vries, *Seamless Web of Judicial Protection in the Internal Market?*, 34 ELRev. 5, 18 (2009).

[b] *Horizontal Direct Effect and Liability*

Secondly, and as a consequence of the above-mentioned, a private law body may be held liable for an infringement of the Treaty freedoms and possibly be ordered to pay damages. Although the Court will undeniably be confronted with balancing conflicting rights, the right of individuals would be impaired if individuals were unable to obtain redress when their rights are infringed by EU law.[97] However, the ECJ has so far only provided for remedies for private parties within the sphere of competition law and not within EU free movement law.[98] And the *Francovich* and *Brasserie* case law applies to infringements of EU free movement law by the State only, not by private parties.[99]

We will have to wait and see whether the ECJ is willing to further expand its case law on damages into EU free movement law, covering horizontal relations between private parties as well. In *Raccanelli* the ECJ clearly hinted at the possibility to claim damages in a situation where a foreign doctoral student did not have the opportunity to conclude an employment contract with Max-Planck-Gesellschaft and would as a result be discriminated against:

> [I]n the event that the applicant in the main proceedings is justified in relying on damage caused by the discrimination to which he has been subject, it is for the referring court to assess, in the light of the national legislation applicable in relation to non-contractual liability, the nature of the compensation which he would be entitled to claim.[100]

But the ECJ has never explicitly pronounced itself on a claim for damages. And, horizontal liability in the context of free movement raises issues concerning retroactivity, legitimate expectations and legal certainty for the future.[101] In the follow-up case of *Laval* the Swedish labour court may have predicted the future case law of the ECJ by ordering the Swedish trade union to pay compensation to Laval. In a rather innovative and also well-founded judgment the Swedish court argued along the lines of *inter alia Francovich, Manfredi* and the above-mentioned *Raccanelli* case to establish that the Swedish labour unions are liable for the damages incurred by Laval as a result of the boycott.[102]

97. U. Bernitz, 'Horizontal Effects of Private Rights Vested by Union Law on Damages to be Paid by another Private Party: The Laval Case a Model', in *The Protection of Fundamental Rights in the EU After Lisbon*, 141 (S. de Vries, U. Bernitz & S. Weatherill (eds), Oxford: Hart Publishing 2013).
98. Case C-453/99, *Courage* [2001] ECR I-6297; Joined Cases 295-298/04, *Manfredi* [2006] ECR I-6619.
99. Joined Cases C-6/90 and 9/90, *Francovich* [1991] ECR I-5357; Joined Cases C-46/93 and 48/93, *Brasserie du Pêcheur* [1996] ECR I-1029.
100. Case C-94/07, *Raccanelli* [2008] ECR I-5939, para. 52.
101. M. Mörk, 'An End to the Possibilities – on Horizontal Liability in *Laval* and the Limits of Judicial Rights Protection', in *The Protection of Fundamental Rights in the EU After Lisbon*, 132 (S. de Vries, U. Bernitz & S. Weatherill (eds), Oxford: Hart Publishing 2013).
102. U. Bernitz, 'Horizontal Effects of Private Rights Vested by Union Law on Damages to be Paid by Another Private Party: The *Laval* Case as a Model', in *The Protection of Fundamental Rights in the EU After Lisbon*, 139-150 (S. de Vries, U. Bernitz & S. Weatherill (eds), Oxford: Hart Publishing 2013); U. Bernitz & N. Reich, *Case No. A 268/04, The Labour Court, Sweden*

[c] *Horizontal Direct Effect and the Growing Convergence between EU Free Movement Law and Competition Rules*

It has also been submitted that by accepting horizontal direct effect the EU competition rules and free movement rules may become too much intertwined. As stated above, the free movement rules and the competition rules continue to have their own 'modes of application'. The specific requirements of Articles 101 and 102 TFEU, which differ from the requirements set by the free movement rules, must be met.[103] But at the same time it must be observed that there is also a certain degree of convergence between the free movement and competition rules in respect of the prohibitive rules and the exceptions.[104] Ever since the landmark judgment in *Consten & Grundig* agreements that are capable of constituting a threat, either direct or indirect, actual or potential, to the freedom of trade between Member States harm the attainment of the objectives of a single market between Member States. The Court's judgment in *Dassonville* on measures having equivalent effect to quantitative restrictions (Article 34 TFEU) was strongly inspired by the judgment in *Consten & Grundig*.[105] Furthermore, the Court in *Consten & Grundig* held that agreements containing a clause that provides absolute territorial protection must be regarded as having the object to restrict competition within the meaning of Article 101 TFEU. Absolute territorial protection is in fact a 'mortal sin' under EU competition law.

And, although *Consten & Grundig* dates from 1966 and *Dassonville* from 1974, the way in which restrictive agreements are adjudicated in the light of the cartel prohibition and measures in the light of Article 34 TFEU has, in principle, not changed.[106] The message that the Court sends out in *Grundig & Consten* is that EU competition law is also – and very much so – concerned with market integration, next to the growing importance of consumer welfare. The EU competition rules play an important role in the creation of the EU Single Market in addition to the free movement provisions.[107]

Although this conventional approach of the Court in competition cases has been under attack for some years,[108] the more recent judgment in the *Premier League* case reveals that market integration, as an aim of EU competition law, is very much alive and kicking.[109] In this case the Court applied EU free movement law, i.e., the free

(Arbetsdomstolen) Judgment No. 89/09 of 2 December 2009, Laval un Partneri Ltd. V. Svenska Byggnadsarbetareförbundet et al., 48 CMLRev. 603, 603 (2011).

103. Case C-519/04 P, *Meca-Medina* [2006] ECR I-6991.

104. See in general the 'ground-breaking' article on convergence by K. Mortelmans, *Towards Convergence in the Application of the Rules on Free Movement and on Competition?*, 38 CMLRev. 613-649 (2001).

105. *Ibid.*, 623.

106. A. Gerbrandy, 'Consten en Grundig', in *Het recht van de Europese Unie in 50 klassieke arresten*, 29 (T.W.B. Beukers, H.J. van Harten & S. Prechal (eds), The Hague: Boom 2010).

107. More recently Protocol No. 27, which is attached to the Lisbon Treaty, emphasizes this important role of EU competition law by stating that the internal market comprises a system ensuring that competition is not distorted.

108. E.g. B.E. Hawk, *System Failure: Vertical Restraints and EC Competition Law*, 32 *CMLRev.* 973-989 (1995).

109. Joined Cases C-403/08 and C-429/08, *Premier League* [2011] n.y.r. This judgment is in line with other recent cases on Article 101 TFEU wherein the Court clearly made a distinction between

movement of services provision contained in Article 56 TFEU, and EU competition law, i.e., the cartel prohibition of Article 101 TFEU, simultaneously. By tackling both the free movement rules and competition rules the Court emphasized their joint aim in realizing and safeguarding the functioning of the internal market. And the breeding ground for such a convergence approach is undoubtedly the territorial restrictions imposed by agreements between undertakings.

Furthermore, convergence between the rules on free movement and on competition is also motivated by the, albeit sometimes hesitant, readiness of the Commission and the EU Courts to take account of non-competition or public interests within the context of Article 101(3) TFEU. Particularly in the field of the environment this development has been remarkable.[110] However, convergence has its limits here as well. According to the Commission in its Guidelines on the application of Article 81(3) of the Treaty (now Article 101(3) TFEU) a strict approach is desirable as public interest goals can be taken into account only to the extent that they can be subsumed under the four conditions of Article 101(3) TFEU.[111] But in the *Premier League* case it appeared that the more 'rigid conceptual framework' of Article 101(3) as compared to the exceptions to the Treaty freedoms did not prevent the Court from applying the *same* reasoning as with regard to the rule of reason exceptions in the context of free movement. It is striking to see that the Court focused on the public interests of the protection of intellectual property rights and the objective of encouraging the public to attend football stadiums, apparently built in Article 101(3) TFEU, and then on the application of the proportionality test whether these justification grounds allow a hardcore competition restriction to be exempted from the cartel prohibition. Efficiency issues, which are normally investigated under Article 101(3) TFEU, appeared to be irrelevant in this scenario as well as the requirement for competition restrictions to pass a cumulative series of four separate tests.[112]

Hence, irrespective of the degree of convergence between EU free movement law and the EU competition rules, it must be prevented that these rules become too much

the object and effect of an agreement, such as *T-Mobile* and *GlaxoSmithKline*: Case C-8/08, *T-Mobile* [2009] ECR I-4529; Joined Cases C-501/06, C-513/06, 515/06 & 519/06 P, *GlaxoSmithKline* [2009] ECR I-9291.

110. See e.g. Commission Decision 2000/475, *CECED* O.J. 2000, L187/47, which involved an agreement for domestic washing machines set up by members of CECED, an association comprising manufacturers of domestic appliances, and national trade associations, not to manufacture and import washing machines that do not meet a certain standard of energy efficiency. See S. de Vries, *Tensions within the Internal Market: The Functioning of the Internal Market and the Development of Horizontal and Flanking Policies*, 220-221 (Groningen: Europa Law Publishing 2006). Cf. H. Vedder, *Competition Law and Environmental Protection in Europe: Towards Sustainability?* (Europa Law Publishing 2003); Cf. S. Lavrijssen, *The Protection of Non-Competition Interests: What Role for Competition Authorities after Lisbon?*, 35 ELRev. 634–659 (2010). The new Guidelines on Horizontal Co-operation Agreements no longer contain a separate chapter on environmental agreements (O.J. 2001, C 3/2); however, there are various references to *inter alia* safety and environmental concerns which the Commission takes into account in assessing restrictive agreements under Article 101(3) TFEU: Guidelines on the Application of Article 101 of the Treaty on the Functioning of the European Union to Horizontal Co-operation Agreements, O.J. 2011, C 11/1.
111. O.J. 2004, C101/97, para. 42.
112. J. Goyder, *EC Competition Law*, 127 (Oxford: Oxford University Press 2003)

intertwined so that the specific requirements that apply to the two sets of rules will not be met.

[d] Horizontal Direct Effect and Justification

The foregoing observations lead us to another important consequence of granting horizontal direct effect, i.e., the (im)possibility to invoke *exceptions*. The sting is often in the tail, because if private law bodies would be directly subject to EU free movement law, they should have recourse to a justification ground as well. AG Trstenjak in her Opinion in the *Fra.bo* case mentions three possibilities for private parties to rely on justification grounds:

> The [German Gas and Water Association (DVGW)] could attempt to claim justification on a special ground of private interest, emphasising its own private-law nature. Referring to the judgment in *Angonese*, DVGW might also cite 'objective considerations' to justify the restriction at issue. DVGW might, furthermore, refer to its private-law nature and rely on the protection of the fundamental rights guaranteed in the Charter of Fundamental Rights, such as the freedom to conduct a business guaranteed in Article 16 of the Charter of Fundamental Rights, and endeavour to demonstrate a collision between the free movement of goods and one or more fundamental rights, between which a fair balance would have to be struck in application of the principle of proportionality.[113]

The first option the Advocate General refers to is to rely upon interests of a private law nature in case there is an infringement of one of the fundamental freedoms. The Advocate General refers to the Court's judgments in *Olympique Lyonnais* and *Bosman*.[114] In both judgments the Court considered that rules set up by a football association, which restrict the freedom of movement for workers, could be justified in principle by their objective of guaranteeing a balance among the clubs, while preserving a certain equality of opportunity and the uncertainty of results, and of promoting the recruitment and training of young players, provided that the principle of proportionality was observed.[115]

The second option for private law bodies would be to invoke *public or general* interest exception grounds. In *Bosman* the Court, in response to the argument raised by UEFA that only Member States are able to rely on the exception contained in Article 45(3) TFEU, had no problem at all in accepting that '[t]here is nothing to preclude individuals from relying on justifications on grounds of public policy, public security or public health. Neither the scope nor the content of those grounds of justification is in any way affected by the public or private nature of the rules in question.'[116] The Court's judgment, however, has been rightfully criticized for its lack of subtlety, particularly since public policy and public security are typical general interests that cannot be left

113. Opinion of AG Trstenjak in Case C-171/11, *Fra.bo* [2012] n.y.r., para. 56.
114. Case C-325/08, *Olympique Lyonnais* [2010] ECR I-2177, paras 38 et seq.; Case C-415/93, *Bosman* [1995] ECR. I-4921, paras 106 et seq.
115. Opinion of AG Trstenjak in Case C-171/11, *Fra.bo* [2012] n.y.r., para. 38.
116. Case C-415/93, *Bosman* [1995] ECR. I-4921, para. 86.

to private organizations.[117] Hence, there must be limits to the possibilities of private parties to rely on public interest grounds, which relate to the above-mentioned *imperium* and *dominium* divide.[118]

But *Bosman* was confirmed by *Angonese* in that the Court accepted that requirements imposed by the bank relating to the acquired linguistic knowledge could in principle be justifiable, provided that the requirements are based on objective factors unrelated to the nationality of the persons concerned and that it is in proportion to the aim legitimately pursued.[119] This entails that indeed not only Member States but also private law bodies may, within the limits that EU free movement law sets, pursue a linguistic policy. *Viking* and *Laval* in a way build upon this case law by accepting the possibility for trade unions to justify their collective or industrial action by invoking the fundamental right to strike, as now recognized in Article 28 of the EU Charter.[120]

The fact that private law bodies may rely on specific public interest grounds is supported by developments in the sphere of competition law. As stated above, although the conditions contained in the exception to the cartel prohibition, Article 101(3) TFEU, primarily relate to the economic interests of the private parties (undertakings) and to the market in general,[121] a development in the Commission's decision practice and the Court's case law has taken place to consider also non-economic public interests under Article 101(3) TFEU.[122]

The third and last option is to rely on the EU Charter and one of the fundamental rights contained therein. Private autonomy as a 'principle' is linked to Article 16 of the EU Charter, which lays down the right to conduct a business. According to the Explanation on Article 16 of the Charter, this Article is based on the case law of the ECJ, which has recognized the freedom to exercise an economic or commercial activity, the freedom of contract and free competition.[123] In a horizontal dispute between private law bodies various economic rights can conflict with each other. In *Scarlet Extended*, for instance, the Court was confronted with a clash between the intellectual property rights of music producers and the economic rights of Internet providers. The Court for the first time applied Article 16 of the EU Charter. In this case the ECJ considered that the requirement for an ISP, ordered by the Belgian civil court, to install a filter system

117. K. Mortelmans, *Towards Convergence in the Application of the Rules on Free Movement and on Competition?*, 38 CMLRev. 613, 642 (2001); Cf. case note of K. Mortelmans, *Annotatie van Zaak C-415/93, KBVB, Royal Club Liégeois, Uefa t. Bosman*, SEW 141, 144 (1996).
118. K. Mortelmans, *Towards Convergence in the Application of the Rules on Free Movement and on Competition?*, 38 CMLRev. 613, 623 (2001).
119. Case C-281/98, *Angonese* [2000] ECR I-4139, para. 42.
120. Case C-341/05, *Laval* [2007] ECR I-11767, para. 103; Case C-438/05, *Viking* [2007] ECR I-10779, para. 77.
121. See K. Mortelmans, *Towards Convergence in the Application of the Rules on Free Movement and on Competition?*, 38 CMLRev. 613, 635 (2001).
122. See e.g. C. Townley, *Article 81 EC and Public Policy* (Oxford: Hart Publishing 2009); O. Odudu, *The Boundaries of EC Competition Law, the Scope of Article 81 EC* (Oxford: Oxford University Press 2005); G. Monti, *Article 81 EC and Public Policy*, 39 CMLRev. 1057-1099 (2002); S. Lavrijssen, What Role for National Competition Authorities in Protecting Non-Competition Interests after Lisbon?, 35 ELRev. 636-659 (2010); S.A. de Vries, *Tensions within the Internal Market – the Functioning of the Internal Market and the Development of Horizontal and Flanking Policies* (Groningen: Europa Law Publishing 2006).
123. OJ 2007, C 303/23.

with a view to preventing and combating infringements of intellectual property rights is contrary to the freedom to conduct a business. According to the Court in *Sky Österreich* the freedom to conduct a business is - of course - not absolute, but must be viewed in relation to its social function.[124] And this should be ensured by respecting the principle of proportionality as enshrined in Article 52(1) of the EU Charter.[125]

But it is clear that the Court's case law needs to be developed further here, as was also admitted by Advocate General Trstenjak in her Opinion in the *Fra.bo* case. She stated that:

> [i]f, in the main proceedings, DVGW were convincingly to present special grounds of private interest, "objective considerations" or a position protected by the Charter of Fundamental Rights to justify the restriction of the free movement of goods ..., the referring court should address a new request for a preliminary ruling to the Court and submit a substantiated request for information on whether and, if so, under what conditions those arguments advanced by DVGW might be brought to bear in a case such as the main proceedings. For, in the light of the current state of case-law on the horizontal effect of the fundamental freedoms and on the relationship between the fundamental freedoms and the fundamental rights, it is my view that the answer to those questions cannot yet be unequivocally deduced from the Court's case-law.[126]

[C] Secondary EU Law: Trigger and Creep?

Broadening the personal scope of application of the four freedoms through horizontal direct effect may also trigger a legal basis for EU secondary legislation. The argument is that, by recognizing the horizontal direct effect of the Treaty freedoms, the EU legislature becomes competent to regulate acts of private individuals.

According to Advocate General Maduro in his intriguing Opinion in the *Vodafone* case the regulation of roaming prices by the EU legislator under Article 114 TFEU, which concern actions of private parties in the telecommunications sector, can *inter alia* be justified by applying 'the logical consequences of its case law on the horizontal application of free movement rules to its analysis of Article 95 [now Article 114 TFEU]'.[127] The Advocate General referred to the case law of the ECJ on horizontal direct effect, including cases such as *Viking & Laval, Bosman* and *Schmidberger*. And, as, according to him, private parties disfavour cross-border economic activity by charging high roaming prices for calls outside the Member State, their acts, which directly disfavour a cross-border economic activity, could be regulated by the EU.

However, the Advocate General's Opinion has been heavily criticized in the legal literature on this point as the text of Article 114 TFEU unequivocally requires that the provisions are laid down by law, regulation or administrative action in Member

124. Case C-283/11, *Sky Österreich* [2013] nyr., para. 45.
125. *Ibid.*, para. 47.
126. Opinion of AG Trstenjak in Case C-171/11, *Fra.bo* [2012] n.y.r., para 57.
127. Opinion of AG Maduro in Case C-58/08, *Vodafone* [2010] ECR I-4999, para. 21. Cf. S. Weatherill, *The Limits of Legislative Harmonization Ten Years after Tobacco Advertising: How the Court's Case Law Has Become a 'Drafting Guide'*, 12 German Law Journal 828, 841 (2011).

States.[128] And parallelism between the free movement rules and Article 114 TFEU would undermine the principle of conferral, or the legality principle.[129] Nevertheless, the 'significant stretch' of Article 114 TFEU as proposed by AG Maduro is not wholly unprecedented, and his ideas are certainly thought-provoking.[130] Furthermore, they fit within a tendency to interpret Article 114 TFEU ever more broadly.[131]

Other examples of this process of 'trigger and creep' are the Monti I regulation and the former proposal for a Monti II regulation. The Monti I regulation on the functioning of the internal market in relation to goods was adopted as a direct consequence of the Court's judgment in *Spanish Strawberries*.[132] Through *inter alia* the inclusion of an intervention mechanism that provides the European Commission with the power to intervene in cases where the free movement of goods is seriously disturbed, the EU legislature obliges the Member States to implement the Court's case law further.[133]

In a similar vein the Monti II proposal for a Council Regulation on the exercise of the right to take collective action,[134] which has now been withdrawn,[135] shows how an extensive interpretation of primary law, in this case the application of Articles 49 and 56 TFEU to strike action in horizontal relationships, has induced the EU legislature to take action. Monti II was designed 'to clarify the general principles and applicable rules at EU level with respect to the exercise of the fundamental right to take collective action within the context of the freedom to provide services and the freedom of establishment, including the need to reconcile them in practice in cross-border situations'.[136] If Monti II had been adopted, it would have been a perfect example of how free movement rules

128. M. Brenncke, *Case C-58/08, Vodafone Ltd and Others v. Secretary of State for Business, Enterprise and Regulatory Reform, Judgment of the Court of Justice (Grand Chamber) of 8 June 2010*, 47 CMLRev. 1793, 1808 (2010).
129. K. Riesenhuber & S. Wichary, *Drittwirkung der Grundfreiheiten als Kompetenzbegründung?: Anmerkung zu den Schlussanträgen des Generalanwaltes Maduro vom 1. Oktober 2009 - Rs. C-58/08 Vodafone u.a. / Secretary of State for Business, Enterprise and Regulatory Reform'*, Zeitschrift für Gemeinschaftsprivatrecht 8, 10 (2010).
130. Weatherill refers to the Regulation on cross-border payments in euros, which is based on Article 114 TFEU and requires the bank charges for cross-border payments in euros to be the same as charges for payments made in euros within a Member State (Regulation 2560, OJ 2001, L 344/13, which has been replaced by Regulation 924/2009, OJ 2009, L 266/11): S. Weatherill, *The Limits of Legislative Harmonization Ten Years after Tobacco Advertising: How the Court's Case Law has become a 'Drafting Guide'*, 12 German Law Journal 828, 841 (2011).
131. S. de Vries, *Tensions within the Internal Market: The Functioning of the Internal Market and the Development of Horizontal and Flanking Policies*, Chapter 4 (Groningen: Europa Law Publishing 2006).
132. Case C-265/95, *Spanish Strawberries* [1997] ECR I-6959.
133. S. Prechal, S. de Vries & H. van Eijken, 'The Principle of Attributed Powers and the "Scope of EU Law"' in *The Eclipse of the Legality Principle*, 235-236 (L. Besselink, F. Pennings & S. Prechal (eds), Alphen a/d Rijn: Kluwer Law International 2011).
134. Proposal for a Council Regulation on the exercise of the right to take collective action within the context of the freedom of establishment and the freedom to provide services, COM(2012) 130 final.
135. The proposal has been withdrawn after nineteen national parliaments held that the proposal did not comply with the subsidiarity principle as laid down in Article 5 TEU ('yellow card procedure' referred to in Article 352 TFEU, which was the legal basis of the Commission's proposal).
136. COM(2012) 130 final, p. 10.

interact with a Treaty provision constituting the legal basis for a measure addressing private practices.

§11.05 ALTERNATIVES TO HORIZONTAL DIRECT EFFECT?

The question is: do we actually need horizontal direct effect? Are there no alternatives which are less intrusive for private autonomy? In *Viking* and *Laval* the Court almost completely ignored an option of *indirect* horizontal effect that was mentioned by AG Maduro.[137] Such indirect horizontal effect can be realized in EU law in roughly three ways. Firstly, by refraining from applying provisions of national law that are incompatible with the relevant Treaty provisions in the particular situation. Secondly, by interpreting national law in such a way that the result is in compliance with EU law. As is known, both cases concern a 'technique' that is also used to circumvent the prohibition of the horizontal direct effect of directives.[138] In essence such an approach has long been inherent in the free movement of goods, where intellectual property legislation must be applied in such a way that it is in compliance with Articles 34 and 36 TFEU in disputes that are usually between private individuals (see also above §11.03 [C]).[139]

These two techniques relating to indirect horizontal effect – the interpretation of national law or the setting aside of relevant provisions – first of all concern the national courts and are applied in the context of a dispute between two private parties.

A different – third – version of indirect horizontal effect is the obligation of the state/government to protect the rights granted to private individuals by the Treaty freedoms, by application of *inter alia* Article 4(3) TEU (and thus to guarantee the effectiveness of free movement). Although the obligation of the courts described above can also be traced back to the '*Schutzpflicht*' of the state,[140] the most important difference between the two types of approaches is that in the first and second case, actions against private individuals are at stake, while in the third case the proceedings are started against the state. This opens 'the way to approach the impact of the four

137. AG Maduro relies primarily on the American doctrine of State action. In continental Europe a well-elaborated equivalent is the 'mittelbare Drittwirkung'. See on this O. Cherdnychenko, *EU Fundamental Rights, EC Fundamental Freedoms and Private Law,* 14 ERPL 23 (2006).

138. That is the interpretation of national law in conformity with the directive and, in some cases, the setting aside of national rules which are incompatible with the directive. It would seem that ever since Joined Cases C-397-403/01, *Pfeiffer* [2004] ECR I-8835, the latter option is not a viable one.

139. See Case 58/80, *Dansk Supermarked* [1981] ECR 181; the reasoning in Case C-61/97, *Laserdisken* [1998] ECR I-5171; and in relation to Article 12 EC Joined Cases C-92/92 and C-326/92, *Phil Collins* [1993] ECR I-5145.

140. It is in particular in German literature that for several decades a discussion has taken place about the various modalities of protecting fundamental rights in private law relationships. This debate has spilled over to the effects of the Treaty freedoms. One of the issues in this debate concerns the question in how far indirect effect (the 'mittelbare Drittwirkung') is a species of the State's duty to protect the constitutional rights of individuals (the 'Schutzpflicht'). For a dicussion of both the German theories of the protection of fundamental rights and the situation in EC law, see O. Cherdnychenko, *EU Fundamental Rights, EC Fundamental Freedoms and Private Law,* 14 ERPL 23 (2006); Cf. also R. Alexy, *Theorie der Grundrechte,* 484-493 (Baden-Baden: Nomos 1994).

freedoms on private persons not primarily as a matter of direct applicability of the freedoms, but as matters resolved by law of the Member States'.[141]

As briefly outlined above, the Court applied Article 4(3) TEU in conjunction with Article 34 TFEU for the first time in *Spanish Strawberries*,[142] where it was held that Article 34 TFEU requires Member States, on the basis of the principle of sincere cooperation in Article 4(3) TEU, to take all necessary and appropriate action to ensure that the free movement of goods is respected. This meant that France should have taken all necessary steps to prevent angry French farmers from *inter alia* violently attacking trucks importing Spanish strawberries. According to the Court, Member States do enjoy a margin of appreciation in order to determine what measures are appropriate in a given situation.[143] But considering the seriousness and the number of incidents in France, it was not difficult to establish a breach of Articles 4(3) TEU and 34 TFEU.

The judgment in *Spanish Strawberries* was confirmed in *Schmidberger*,[144] which involved a demonstration by environmentalists on the Brenner motorway in Austria, thereby closing the motorway to traffic for nearly thirty hours. The question was whether the Austrian authorities could be held liable for an infringement of Article 34 TFEU in conjunction with Article 4(3) TEU, as the Austrian authorities had granted permission for this demonstration on such an important motorway. According to the Court, the free movement of goods was indeed restricted but these restrictions were justifiable by the protection of fundamental rights, which form an integral part of the general principles of EU law. Since the blockade was only on one single route, at one single location, and lasted only thirty hours, Austria did not, contrary to France in *Spanish Strawberries*, misuse its margin of discretion by authorizing the demonstration.

But there are some deficiencies inherent in indirect horizontal effect.[145] Firstly, horizontal indirect effect on the basis of Article 4(3) TFEU is only applicable in case of a persistent and manifest failure by a Member State.[146] After all, in *Spanish Strawberries* the Court made clear that the Member States enjoy a wide margin of discretion. Furthermore, certain sensitivities could come into play regarding, for instance, the question to what extent the state is allowed or obliged to interfere with the autonomy of private law bodies. This issue was raised in the context of the autonomy of social partners as a consequence of the *Viking* and *Laval* judgments.[147]

141. P. Oliver & W-H. Roth, *The Internal Market and the Four Freedoms*, 41 CMLRev. 407, 427 (2004).
142. Case C-265/95, *Spanish Strawberries* [1997] ECR I-6959.
143. *Ibid.*, para. 33.
144. Case C-112/00, *Schmidberger* [2003] ECR I-5659.
145. C. Krenn, *A Missing Piece in the Horizontal Effect 'Jigsaw': Horizontal Direct Effect and the Free Movement of Goods*, 49 CMLRev. 177, 208 (2012).
146. Cf. Case C-265/95, *Spanish Strawberries* [1997] ECR I-6959, para. 65.
147. S. Prechal & S. De Vries, *Seamless Web of Judicial Protection in the Internal Market?*, 34 ELRev. 5, 22 (2009); Cf. Case C-184/89, *Helga Nimz v. Freie und Hansestadt Hamburg* [1991] ECR I-297; Cf. Case C-15/96, *Kalliope Schöning-Kougebetopoulou v. Freie und Hansestadt Hamburg* [1998] ECR I-47.

Secondly, because of the absence of the possibility for private individuals to initiate proceedings, they are dependent on the discretion of the Commission or Member States to commence enforcement proceedings.[148] And starting proceedings against the state is probably not the quickest route – provided that there is an appropriate legal remedy – and the result is far from certain.

Finally, it has been observed that horizontal indirect effect grants a margin of discretion to Member States in balancing the appropriateness of infringing fundamental freedoms (such as the freedom of assembly)[149] which leads to legal uncertainty.[150] It can therefore be argued that, despite the usefulness in certain cases, it should be possible for private individuals to invoke the Treaty freedoms directly.

§11.06 SUMMARY: FROM A HODGEPODGE TO A SEAMLESS WEB?

Although the Court has advanced *different* arguments in a variety of cases to support the horizontal direct effect of the four freedoms, there appears to be some *logic* in the reasoning of the Court. Rather than what at first sight might appear to be a hodgepodge of cases, considering the sometimes shaky and incomplete argumentation of the Court,[151] we can discern a returning pattern in the evolution of the concept of horizontal direct effect, whereby the Court on each occasion seeks to fill in the remaining 'gaps' in the EU system of judicial protection.

Considering the role that private law bodies play in our mixed economies, since they may, due to their quasi rule-making or similar powers, often be in a position of relative dominance, the other side of the coin is their enhanced responsibility under the Treaty provisions on free movement. Private autonomy cannot be used as a mere justification to avoid obligations arising out of EU law.[152]

Especially in situations where private behaviour is not necessarily caught by the competition rules, due to the different requirements of Articles 101 and 102 TFEU, it is important that the 'device' of horizontal direct effect can be used to develop a more seamless web of judicial protection in the internal market. Hence, horizontal direct effect first and foremost relates to the *effet utile* of the internal market and must thus not be rejected *a priori*.

As has been described above, there is already a degree of convergence between the scope of application of the EU free movement rules, which even includes actions by

148. See Articles 258–260 TFEU. The second deficiency was raised in J. Snell, 'Private Parties and the Free Movement of Goods and Services', in *Services and Free Movement in EU Law*, 239 (M. Andenas & W-H. Roth (eds), Oxford: Oxford University Press 2002).
149. Cf. Case C-112/00, *Schmidberger* [2003] ECR I-5659.
150. J. Snell, 'Private Parties and the Free Movement of Goods and Services', in *Services and Free Movement in EU Law*, 239 (M. Andenas & W-H. Roth (eds), Oxford: Oxford University Press 2002).
151. Cf. C. Krenn, *A Missing Piece in the Horizontal Effect 'Jigsaw': Horizontal Direct Effect and the Free Movement of Goods*, 49 CMLRev. 177, 177 (2012); Cf. S. Van den Bogaert, 'Horizontality: The Court Attacks?', in *The Law of the Single European Market – Unpacking the Premises*, 143 (C. Barnard & J. Scott (Eds), Oxford: Hart Publishing 2002).
152. C. Krenn, *A Missing Piece in the Horizontal Effect 'Jigsaw': Horizontal Direct Effect and the Free Movement of Goods*, 49 CMLRev. 177, 214 (2012).

private individuals and contractual provisions, and the competition rules. And because the substantive scope of application and the issues of judicial protection are closely related, the recognition of horizontal direct effect is the logical consequence of this.

But the question is, of course: how far should horizontal direct effect reach and where are its limits? We do realize that, through the explicit recognition of horizontal direct effect, the Court has extended EU competence 'deeply into the sphere of private law'.[153] The four freedoms intrude into the private autonomy of private law bodies. And although private autonomy is not absolute, a careful approach is desirable. For that matter, exceptions are available, also for private parties. We therefore come up with the following proposal.

Our starting point is that a limited form of horizontal direct effect should be accepted for all four freedoms, meaning that in the words of the Court, whenever there is a degree of dominance on the part of the private law body or a form of collectiveness in the regulations adopted by a private party, the four freedoms could be invoked before the national court to challenge the actions of private law bodies that impede market access. And we see no compelling reason to exclude the free movement of goods provision from this approach. It is therefore really unfortunate that the Court did not, contrary to the Advocate General, embroider on the possible horizontal direct effect of Article 34 TFEU in the *Fra.bo* case. If we take the *effet utile* argument as a starting point, as Krenn did in his seminal article on the horizontal direct effect of the free movement of goods provision, also Article 34 TFEU could impose direct obligations on private parties, whenever there is a need to use this provision as an instrument of market integration.

However, Article 34 TFEU should not be stretched so far that the scope of application of the EU competition rules is undermined. As argued above, the provisions continue to have their own modes of application, whereby the (potential) sphere of application of EU free movement law, e.g., Article 34 TFEU – or of Article 56 TFEU on services – is much broader.[154] The horizontal direct effect of the Treaty provisions on free movement should therefore not mean that the provisions on EU competition law, in particular Articles 101 and 102 TFEU, become redundant.[155] Where, on the other hand, the scope of application of EU free movement law and the EU competition rules coincide, there is no such danger and both sets of provisions could be applied simultaneously, as the *Premier League* case shows.

In his article Krenn proposes to introduce a *de minimis* requirement to determine the limits of horizontal direct effect in respect of the free movement of goods. He refers to the *Commission v. Italy* case (see also, section §11.02[A] above), wherein the Court in respect of an Italian law prohibiting the towing of trailers by motorcycles held that 'a prohibition on the use of a product in the territory of a Member State has a considerable influence on the behaviour of consumers, which, in its turn, affects the

153. S. Van den Bogaert, 'Horizontality: The Court Attacks?', in *The Law of the Single European Market – Unpacking the Premises*, 141 (C. Barnard & J. Scott (Eds), Oxford: Hart Publishing 2002).
154. *Ibid.*, 140.
155. *Ibid.*, 140.

access of that product to the market of that Member State'.[156] Consumer behaviour is then used to measure the impact on market access, which suggests a more economic approach to Article 34 TFEU. The inclusion of the word 'considerable' would entail that the market access test is subject to the requirement that the restriction impedes market access to a sufficient degree.[157] The problem is, however, that in the field of EU free movement law an in-depth economic test is generally absent.[158] And the Court has continuously rejected attempts to plead *de minimis*.[159] Furthermore, it is eventually the national courts that have to apply this rule in individual cases and they will be confronted with an economic test, for which they might need further guidance, like in the field of competition law.[160]

In order to prevent EU free movement law from becoming too much conflated with economic thinking – economic analysis is an infamously uncertain science – another perhaps rather formal and legalistic approach but more in line with the Court's case law can be used here. Factors that can be taken into account are the collectiveness of the rules, the dominant position of the regulating private law body, the de facto regulating power of the private party and the legislative framework in which it operates. Advocate General Trstenjak refers to the de facto rule-making competence of a private law association as a determining factor for a limited form of horizontal direct effect of Article 34 TFEU. In a similar vein, promotional campaigns that are carried out *without* governmental support or state intervention, such as 'buy national' campaigns like Buy Irish, could be caught by the free movement rules and in particular by Article 34 TFEU. Such promotional campaigns draw on nationalism and ethnicity as strong motives for influencing consumer behaviour with a considerable impact on trade and may therefore be covered by Article 34 TFEU.[161] But purchasing choices by (individual) undertakings favouring domestic products would then fall outside the scope of Article 34 TFEU.

---

156. Case C-110/05, *Commission v. Italy* [2009] ECR I-519, para. 56.
157. T. Hornsley, *'Anyone for Keck': Case Note on Case C-110/05, Commission v. Italy, Judgment of the Court (Grand Chamber) of 10 February 2009, not yet reported; Case C-142/05, Åklagaren v. Percy Mickelsson and Joakim Roos, Judgment of the Court (Second Chamber) of 4 June 2009, not yet reported; Case C-265/06, Commission v. Portugal, Judgment of the Court (Third Chamber) of 10 April 2008, [2008] ECR I-2245*, 46 CMLRev. 2001, 2015 (2009).
158. S.A. de Vries, *'Goods Revisited' – Nieuwe inzichten in de rechtspraak over het vrije verkeer van goederen*, 4 NTER,127 (2009).
159. L.W. Gormley, *Free Movement of Goods and Their Use – What Is the Use of It?*, 33 Fordham International Law Journal 1589, 1625 (2011); Cf., for instance, Joined Cases 177 & 178/82, *Van der Haar* [1984] ECR 1979 or Case C-67/97, *Bluhme* [1998] ECR I-8033. In his Opinion in the *Leclerc* case Advocate General Jacobs advocated a *de minimis* approach to Article 34 TFEU: Opinion of AG Jacobs in Case C-412/93, *Leclerc-Siplec* [1994] ECR I-182, paras 42-49.
160. Cf. K. Lenaerts and D. Gerard, *Decentralisation of EC Competition Law Enforceent: Judges in the Frontline*, 27 World Competition 313-349 (2004).
161. See C. Krenn, *A Missing Piece in the Horizontal Effect 'Jigsaw': Horizontal Direct Effect and the Free Movement of Goods*, 49 CMLRev. 177-216(2012); Cf. S. de Vries, *Consumer Protection and the EU Single Market Rules – The Search for the 'Paradigm Consumer*, 4 Journal of European Consumer and Market Law 228, 240 (2012); Case C-249/81, *Commission v. Ireland ('Buy Irish')* [1982] ECR 4005; J. Hojnik, *Free Movement of Goods in a Labyrinth: Can Buy Irish Survive the Crises*, 49 CMLRev. 291, 304-305 (2012), who does not exclude the possibility of applying Article 34 TFEU to ethnocentric, promotional campaigns.

Full horizontal direct effect of the free movement rules must not be excluded, but applies only in specific circumstances. Whereas limited horizontal direct effect may extend to indistinctly applicable measures restricting market access, full horizontal direct effect should, in the spirit of the *Angonese* case, only cover discriminatory practices. This can be justified by the principle of non-discrimination or the right to equal treatment, which is the cornerstone of the four freedoms and which can be transformed into a fundamental right to protect individual personality and human dignity. Party autonomy here has its limits in the rights of others in respect of human dignity & fundamental rights. Hence, it is the fundamental rights character of the prohibition of discrimination on grounds of nationality that creates the obligation for private individuals, with as the ultimate consequence, full horizontal direct effect.[162] Examples may include contractual provisions containing an exclusivity right for the broadcasting of football matches (*Premier League* case), having the effect of dividing the internal market into separate markets. But also situations similar to *Buy Irish*, such as 'buy domestic campaigns', might be contrary to the equality principle.[163] Considering this fundamental rights twist, we would want to exclude that even a broader 'restriction reading' of the Treaty freedoms binds purely private situations.[164]

This is, however, not the end of the story. Both restrictions and discriminatory practices are justifiable, for example, by the private party's desire to preserve its autonomy or to protect general interests. And in sensitive cases, the Court should adopt a rather lenient proportionality test.[165]

§11.07 CONCLUSION

Although the original idea was to draft the four freedoms solely for the Member States,[166] the wording of the fundamental freedoms does not necessarily indicate that private individuals can only rely on these provisions vis-à-vis Member States.[167] Faced with private law bodies having regulatory powers, the Court after a while accepted a limited form of horizontal direct effect. But ever since one of its first judgments, in particular *Walrave and Koch*, the Court has struggled to define the boundaries of horizontal direct effect. Most problematic in this respect, given the existence of competition rules, has been the free movement of goods provision. It is therefore not surprising that the Court at first excluded the free movement of goods provision from

162. See also section §11.04[A] above and N. de Boer, *Fundamental Rights and the EU Internal Market: Just How Fundamental are the EU Treaty Freedoms? – A Normative Enquiry Based on John Rawls' Political Philosophy*, Utrecht Law Review 148-168 (2013).
163. Hojnik, *Free Movement of Goods in a Labyrinth: Can Buy Irish Survive the Crises*, 49 CMLRev. 291, 304-305 (2012).
164. S. Prechal & S. De Vries, *Seamless Web of Judicial Protection in the Internal Market?*, 34 ELRev. 5, 17 (2009).
165. See in respect of the *Viking* and *Laval* case law: C. Barnard, *A Proportionate Response to Proportionality in the Field of Collective Action*, ELRev. 117-135 (2012).
166. S. Prechal & S. De Vries, *Seamless Web of Judicial Protection in the Internal Market?*, 34 ELRev. 5, 13 (2009).
167. Case C-281/98, *Angonese* [2000] ECR I-4139, para. 30.

having horizontal direct effect, and relied merely on horizontal *indirect* effect.[168] It was much easier for the Court to recognize full horizontal direct effect for the free movement of workers provision in the *Angonese* case. In this field, the EU competition rules will hardly be undermined by the application of the Treaty rules on free movement, considering the limited scope of application of the competition rules to the labour market.

We welcome the Court's approach to the horizontal direct effect of the four freedoms, particularly from the perspective of the judicial protection of individuals, whenever there is a gap in the system of judicial protection. But we would also like to stress that the Court's reasoning in the different cases could be improved. And, the implications of accepting horizontal direct effect should be further clarified in case law, particularly where it concerns liability of private parties under EU free movement law and the possibilities to rely on justification grounds.

168. However, it must be noted that this seems equally true for the free movement of services, which is also subject to competition rules. See: J. Snell, 'And Then There Were Two: Products and Citizens in Community Law', in *EU Law for the Twenty-First Century: Rethinking the New Legal Order* vol. II, 58 (T. Tridimas and P. Nebbia (eds), Oxford: Hart Publishing 2004).

CHAPTER 12

What Purpose Does Article 16 of the Charter Serve?

Peter Oliver[*]

§12.01 INTRODUCTION

Since its inception, the whole of what is now Union law has been suffused with economic rights: the 'common market', now the 'internal market', consisting of the four economic freedoms and competition has always been its cornerstone. At the core of fundamental economic rights lie the freedom to choose an occupation and the right to engage in work (now enshrined in Article 15 of the Charter), the freedom of enterprise (Article 16 of the Charter) and the right to property (Article 17 of the Charter). Yet paradoxically the freedom to conduct a business appears to have had little resonance with the Court of Justice: time and again, it has given short shrift to arguments based on this right. Why is this? Now that the Court has delivered such recent landmark judgments in *Scarlet Extended v. SABAM*[1] and *Sky Österreich v. Österreicher Rundfunk*,[2] the time is ripe for an examination of this important question.

§12.02 A CHRONOLOGICAL OVERVIEW

Unlike the right to property, which is enshrined in Article 1 of Protocol 1 to the European Convention on Fundamental Rights (ECHR), the freedom to conduct a business is not recognized in that Convention or its Protocols.[3] Indeed, the right to

* The author wishes to thank Thomas Bombois and Wouter Wils for their very helpful comments on an earlier draft of this article. However, the views expressed here are personal to the author and any errors are attributable to him alone.

1. Case C-70/10 (judgment of 24 November 2011).
2. Case C-283/11 (judgment of 22 January 2013) (Grand Chamber).
3. However, the European Court of Human Rights has held that an existing professional practice or business constitutes 'possessions' within the meaning of Article 1 of Protocol 1 to the ECHR: *van*

property as provided for in Protocol 1 only covers the right to retain property and transfer it,[4] not to acquire it.[5] Rather, the freedom to conduct a business is rooted in the Constitutions of a number of Member States,[6] including Germany,[7] Ireland[8] and Italy.[9]

Marle v. Netherlands (judgment of 26 June 1986) *Wendenburg v. Germany* (decision of 6 February 2003); this includes goodwill (*Wendenburg*). But this principle does not extend to future earnings (*Ian Edgar (Liverpool) Ltd v. United Kingdom* (judgment of 25 January 2000), as Article 1 does not confer the right to acquire property; see note 5 below. On the other hand, since a 'legitimate expectation' of obtaining an asset will itself be protected under Article 1 of Protocol 1 in certain circumstances: it was held in *Centro Europa 7 v. Italy* (judgment of 7 June 2012, Grand Chamber) that, by granting the applicant company a television broadcasting licence without granting it any broadcasting frequency, Italy was in breach of that provision.

Furthermore, the same court has ruled, albeit only in extreme cases, that restrictions on the individual's access to employment may be a breach of Article 8 ECHR: *Sidabras v. Lithuania* (judgment of 27 October 2004), *Bigaeva v. Greece* (judgment of 28 August 2009); see O'Connell 'The Right to Work in the European Convention on Human Rights' 2012 EHRLR 176, Oliver 'The Protection of Privacy in the Economic Sphere before the European Court of Justice' 46 CMLRev. (2009) 1443, 1452.

4. Thus the unlawful and unjustified withdrawal of a licence to operate a business is in breach of Article 1 of Protocol 1: *Capital Bank v. Bulgaria* (judgment of 24 November 2005) and *Centro Europa 7* (note 3 above), para. 177.
5. *van der Mussele v. Belgium* (judgment of 23 November 1983), para. 48; *Stec v. United Kingdom* (judgment of 12 April 2006 GC), para. 53. See generally Allen 'Property and the Human Rights Act 1998' (Hart Publishing, 2005), Burgorgue-Larsen 'La Convention européenne des droits de l'homme' (2012, LGDJ), 173ff., Harris, O'Boyle and Warbrick (Oxford University Press, 2nd ed., 2009), ch. 18, Meyer-Ladewig 'Europäische Menschenrechtskonvention' (Nomos, 3rd ed., 2011), 413ff., Sudre 'Droit européen et international des droits de l'homme' (Presses Universitaires de France, 10th ed., 2011), 633ff., van Dirk *et al.* (eds.) 'Theory and Practice of the European Convention on Human Rights' (Intersentia, 4th. ed., 2006), ch 17.

   Other articles of the Convention may however be in point in certain cases. Thus in *Centro Europa 7* (note 3 above), the measure in issue was also held to be in breach of Article 10 of the Convention on freedom of speech.
6. For a detailed overview, see Frederik Schmidt 'Die unternehmerische Freiheit im Unionsrecht' (Duncker & Humblot, 2010) 70ff.; see also Bernsdorff's commentary on Article 16 of the Charter in Meyer (ed) 'Charta der Grundrechte der Europäischen Union' (3rd ed., Nomos 2011) 293, 294 and the materials referred to in footnote 27 to the AG's Opinion in Case C-426/11 *Alemo-Herron* (judgment of 18 July 2013). The French Constitution does not contain any express provision on the freedom to conduct a business, but the Conseil Constitutionnel has deduced it from Article IV of the Declaration of the Rights of Man of 1789, which provides for a general right to freedom; see *inter alia* its decisions 2013-317 QPC of 24 May 2013 together with the commentary thereto, and 2013-672 DC of 13 June 2013.
7. Article 12(1) of Germany's Basic Law is drafted in the following terms: 'All Germans shall have the right freely to choose their occupation or profession, their place of work and their place of training. The practice of an occupation or profession may be regulated by or pursuant to a law.' This provision must be read with Article 19(3), which states: 'The basic rights shall also apply to domestic legal persons to the extent that the nature of such rights permits.' See Schmidt (note 6 above), 74ff. and sources cited there, including numerous quotations from the judgments of the Federal Constitutional Court.
8. Article 45(3) of Ireland's Constitution reads: '1. The State shall favour and, where necessary, supplement private initiative in industry and commerce. 2. The State shall endeavour to secure that private enterprise shall be so conducted as to ensure reasonable efficiency in the production and distribution of goods and as to protect the public against unjust exploitation.'
9. The first two sentences of Article 41 of Italy's Constitution are worded as follows: 'Private economic enterprise shall be free. It may not be carried out against the common good or in such a manner as to harm safety, liberty and human dignity.'

This right was first recognized by the Court of Justice in its seminal judgment in *Nold v. Commission*[10] in 1974, and this ruling was subsequently confirmed on numerous occasions. In the year 2000, this right was enshrined in Article 16 of the Charter of the Fundamental Rights of the Union,[11] which reads:

> The right to conduct a business in accordance with Union law and national laws and practices is recognized.

Initially, the Court of Justice merely took the Charter into account;[12] but, on the entry into force on the Treaty of Lisbon on 1 December 2009, the Charter in a somewhat amended form became binding with the 'same legal value as the Treaties'.[13] At that moment, it is submitted, Article 16 seamlessly replaced the pre-existing fundamental right to conduct a business which had existed as a general principle of Union law.

Manifestly, it would serve no purpose for the general principle to subsist alongside Article 16 if the two were identical. Yet what would be the point in maintaining in existence two overlapping but slightly different fundamental rights?[14] The open-ended wording of Article 16 is sufficiently flexible to accommodate the pre-existing general principle. Even if that were not the case, the co-existence of two similar but discrete fundamental rights would undoubtedly give rise to considerable legal uncertainty. As the Vice-President of the Court has put it, 'a dual regime should be avoided, since it would give rise to arbitrary divergences as to the actual quality and potency of those rights'.[15] Similarly, Ladenburger has pointed out that it would 'undermine the overall coherence of the Union's legal system if one attempted to develop ... a separate set of horizontal rules differing from those of the Charter.'[16]

Admittedly, Article 6(3) TEU provides: 'Fundamental rights, as guaranteed by the European Convention for the Protection of Human Rights and Fundamental Freedoms and as they result from the constitutional traditions common to the Member States,

10. Case 4/73 [1974] ECR 491.
11. The original version of the Charter as 'solemnly proclaimed' in that year is to be found in 2000 OJ C364/1.
12. The first case in which the Court acknowledged that it took the Charter into account was Case C-540/03 *European Parliament v. Council* (Directive on family reunification) [2006] ECR I-5769, para. 38.
13. Article 6(1) TEU. The revised version of the Charter is contained in 2007 OJ C303/1 and 2010 OJ C83/389. The European Court of Human Rights appears to attach some importance to the fact that the Charter has become binding: *Michaud v. France* (judgment of 6 December 2012), para. 106.
14. Hofmann and Mihaescu argue in favour of the continued development of general principles alongside virtually identical rights enshrined in the Charter. They see this as a source of dynamism in the Union's legal system which would then continue to act as 'an incubator of innovative legal solutions to new problems of European integration': 'The Relation between the Charter's Fundamental Rights and the Unwritten General Principles of EU Law: Good Administration as a Test Case' 9 (2013) European Constitutional Law Review 73.
15. Judge Lenaerts 'Exploring the Limits of the EU Charter of Fundamental Rights' (2012) 8 European Constitutional Law Review 375, 402.
16. EU Report on 'Protection of Fundamental Rights Post-Lisbon' at the FIDE Conference of 2012 http://www.fide2012.eu/index.php?doc_id=88 page 5.

shall constitute general principles of the Union's law'. However, as Ladenburger has pointed out, this provision is no obstacle to the view propounded here, since 'Article 6(3) TEU is now the basis of a *residual* category of fundamental rights, to which the Court is likely to resort only in case of a gap in the fifty articles of the Charter that cannot be closed even by creative interpretation.'[17]

In addition, it is true that, on the issue of whether fundamental rights subsist as general principles alongside the Charter, the case law gives us a mixed picture. In *Dominguez* Advocate General Trstenjak suggested that a positive answer be given to this question,[18] while Advocate General Cruz Villalón appeared to take the opposite view in *Prigge*[19] and *Scarlet Extended*.[20] What is more, although the Court frequently decides cases on the basis of the Charter, several judgments relating to rights enshrined in that instrument have inexplicably omitted any reference to it. Examples include the rulings of the Grand Chamber in *Dominguez*[21] and *Toshiba*.[22] On the other hand, in answering a preliminary question which referred merely to general principles, the Court has been known to frame its judgment exclusively in terms of the Charter.[23] Furthermore, in *Chalkor*, the Court appeared to assert that, in relation to the principle of effective judicial protection, it would now look exclusively to Article 47 of the Charter.[24] Finally, one might conceivably have regard here to the Court's statement in *Åkerberg Fransson* that: 'The applicability of European Union law entails applicability of the fundamental rights guaranteed by the Charter'.[25] However, to take this very general assertion, which was made in another context, as confirmation of the view that the Charter ousts pre-existing general principles in so far as they cover the same subject-matter may seem far-fetched.

At all events, in its recent judgments on Article 16, the Court continues to refer to its pre-Lisbon case law,[26] which also suggests that this provision has taken over the mantle of the general principle.

17. *Ibid.*; emphasis in the original.
18. Case C-282/10 (judgment of 24 January 2012), paras 89 ff., especially para. 131. This case concerned the right to annual leave (Article 31(2) of the Charter).
19. Case C-447/09, not yet reported, para. 26. *Prigge* concerned age discrimination (Article 21 of the Charter).
20. Paras 29 to 34 of his Opinion.
21. See note 18 above.
22. Case C-17/10 (judgment of 14 February 2012). This case primarily concerned the principle of *ne bis in idem*. Although that principle is now enshrined in Article 50 of the Charter, the judgment contains no mention of that provision at all. This is all the more anomalous in that the referring Czech court mentioned Article 50 in one of its preliminary questions and AG Kokott repeatedly mentioned it in her Opinion. Even more baffling is the fact that the Court did refer to Article 49 of the Charter in its judgment, even though it was less important to the case! See Oliver and Bombois '*'Ne bis in idem'* en droit européen: un principe à plusieurs variants' 2012 Journal de droit européen 266, 270.
23. Case C-279/09 *DEB* [2010] ER I-13849, para. 32, see the case note by Oliver 2011 (48) CMLRev. 2023.
24. Case C-386/10P (judgment of 8 December 2011), paras 51 and 52.
25. Case C-617/10 (judgment of 26 February 2013, Grand Chamber), para. 21.
26. E.g. Case C-544/10 *Deutsches Weintor* (judgment of 6 September 2012), para. 54, Case C-1/11 *Interseroh Scrap* (judgment of 29 March 2012), para. 43.

For all these reasons, in the absence of a clear ruling from the Court on this point, we shall proceed on the basis that, with the entry into force of the Treaty of Lisbon, the general principle first recognized by the Court in *Nold* has been purely and simply replaced by Article 16 of the Charter.

§12.03 THE WORDING OF ARTICLE 16

The striking feature of Article 16 is the almost diffident terms in which it is formulated, in two respects. First, the phrase 'the freedom to conduct a business ... is recognised' contrasts with the much stronger language to be found in several other provisions of the Charter.[27] Numerous articles, including Article 15 and Article 17, begin with the words 'Everyone has the right ...', which is manifestly more forceful. Second, the phrase 'in accordance with Union law and national laws and practices' further lessens the intensity of Article 16.[28]

As we shall see, the relatively weak language of Article 16 reflects the pre-existing case law on the right to conduct a business. In addition, this language reflects the drafting history of Article 16 which was introduced as a counterweight to the social rights in Title IV:[29] the intention of the drafting Convention was to give Article 16 the same weight as those social rights.[30]

At the same time, there appears to be a degree of consensus about the fact that Article 16 was not intended to be more limited than the pre-existing general principle on the freedom to conduct a business.[31]

§12.04 THE 'EXPLANATIONS'

Article 6(1) TEU requires the Charter to be interpreted with 'due regard' to the official Explanations on that instrument.[32] For good measure, this requirement is repeated in

27. Other rights which are merely 'recognised' in the Charter include Article 10(2) on the right to conscientious objection (see note 28 below), Article 25 on the rights of the elderly and Article 26 on the rights of persons with disabilities.

    It is true that Article 52(1) and (2) uses the word 'recognised by this Charter' in relation to all the rights spelt out there. That does not alter the fact that the use of 'recognised' in Article 16 weakens it in comparison with such provisions as Articles 15 and 17.
28. In both respects, Article 16 is comparable to Article 10(2) of the Charter which reads: 'The right to conscientious objection is recognised, in accordance with the national laws governing the exercise of this right.' Naturally, the latter provision does not mention Union laws, since the Union has no competence with regard to military service. On the other hand, perhaps some significance should be attached to the fact that Article 10(2) refers only to national laws, whereas Article 16 mentions national laws and practices.
29. It is customary to refer to these rights in Title IV as 'social and economic rights'. However, in this paper, the term 'social rights' will be used to avoid any confusion with the economic rights enshrined in Articles 15, 16 and 17 of the Charter.
30. Bernsdorff (note 6 above), 295; Blanke in 'Europäische Grundrechte-Charta' (eds. Tettinger and Stern) (2006, Beck); 427; Schwarze, commentary on Article 16 in 'EU-Kommentar' (ed. Schwarze) (3rd ed., 2012, Nomos) 2649.
31. Schwarze (note 30 above), 2649 and sources cited there.
32. The Explanations, which had originally been drafted in 2000, were also amended. For the current version, see 2007 OJ C303/17. See Ziller 'Le fabuleux destin des Explications relatives à

Article 52(7) of the Charter itself. The Court has duly applied the principles on several occasions.[33] Indeed Vice-President Lenaerts has stated:

> it would be very difficult for the ECJ to interpret the provisions of the Charter in a way conflicting with those Explanations. Otherwise, the ECJ would be engaging in judicial activism. In my view, only where the Explanations relating to the Charter provide no (complete) answer to the questions of interpretation with which the ECJ is confronted may the latter have recourse to other methods of interpretation.[34]

At all events, the 'Explanation' on Article 16 is of particular assistance for those who share the view of Advocate General Cruz Villalòn that the case law has not provided 'a full and useful definition' of the freedom enshrined in this article.[35] In view of its great importance in the present context, this 'Explanation' must be quoted here *in extenso*. It reads as follows:

> This Article is based on Court of Justice case-law which has recognised freedom to exercise an economic or commercial activity (see judgments of 14 May 1974, Case 4/73 *Nold* [1974] ECR 491, paragraph 14 of the grounds, and of 27 September 1979, Case 230/78 *SpA Eridiana and others* [1979] ECR 2749, paragraphs 20 and 31 of the grounds) and freedom of contract (see *inter alia Sukkerfabriken Nykøbing* judgment, Case 151/78 [1979] ECR 1, paragraph 19 of the grounds, and judgment of 5 October 1999, C-240/97 *Spain v. Commission* [1999] ECR I-6571, paragraph 99 of the grounds) and Article 119(1) and (3) of the Treaty on the Functioning of the European Union, which recognises free competition. Of course, this right is to be exercised with respect for Union law and national legislation. It may be subject to the limitations provided for in Article 52(1) of the Charter.

Thus, according to the Explanations, Article 16 constitutes a bundle of three discrete rights, namely: the freedom to exercise an economic or commercial activity; freedom of contract; and the right to free competition. As is plain from the Explanations, the first two rights are recognized in the case law; and we shall discuss this shortly. In contrast, the third right is based on the wording of the Treaties; and it is therefore appropriate to consider it at this juncture.

As to the third right, Article 119 TFEU falls within Title VIII of that Treaty, which relates to economic and monetary policy. Paragraphs (1) and (3) are of a rather general nature. The only relevant language appears to be the statement in Article 119(1) that 'the activities of the Member States and the Union shall include ... the adoption of an economic policy which is ... conducted in accordance with the principle of an open market economy with free competition'. This language is not new, since precisely the same wording was to be found in the 'predecessor' to Article 119(1), namely Article 4(1) EC.

---

la Charte des droits fondamentaux de l'Union européenne' in 'Chemins d'Europe – Mélanges en l'honneur de Jean-Paul Jacqué' (Dalloz, 2010).

33. The first occasion was *DEB* (note 23 above), para. 32. See also *Sky Österreich*, para. 42, *Åkerberg Fransson* (note 26 above), para. 20.
34. Note 15 above, 402.
35. *Alemo-Herron* (note 6 above), para. 49.

In short, Article 16 of the Charter read with the revised Explanations recognizes a right to free competition. This is all the more important in that – as is well known – the Treaty of Lisbon removed the reference to competition policy which had been in Article 3(1)(g) EC and relegated it to Protocol 27 on the Internal Market and Competition. To be more precise, Article 3(3) TEU simply provides that 'The Union shall establish an internal market'; and this is supplemented by the statement in the preamble to Protocol 27 that Article 3 TEU 'includes a system that competition is not distorted'.

Having said that, it is a moot point whether the 'right' to free competition is enforceable. Schwarze is among the authors who have questioned whether it is.[36] Yet, even if it is not, the mere fact that this 'right' is mentioned in Article 16 read with the Explanations is not without legal significance. We shall return to this point in §12.06 below.

At all events, after referring to Protocol 27, the Court in *TeliaSonera Sverige* spoke of the importance of competition in ensuring the well-being of the Union in terms which has given us the welcome assurance that, in the Court's eyes, the Treaty of Lisbon has not downgraded competition policy in any way.[37] The Charter was not even mentioned by the Court or the Advocate General. Having said that, as Weatherill has pointed out, this was a straightforward competition law case on abusive pricing, and the real test will come when the Court is faced with the need to balance the freedom of competition against other values or rights.[38]

The subsequent ruling in *Commission v. Italy*, a State aids case, repeated the essence of the Court's statement in *TeliaSonera*, albeit in bolder terms: it went so far as to speak of 'the vital nature of the Treaty rules on competition'.[39] Once again, the Charter was not mentioned but no other fundamental right was at stake.[40]

§12.05 THE MAIN CASES

In this section, we shall consider the salient judgments chronologically, beginning with *Nold* and ending with *Sky Österreich*, the most recent case.

[A] *Nold*

The proceedings in *Nold* concerned a complex decision taken by the Commission under the ECSC Treaty involving the conditions of operation of Ruhrkohle AG. Nold objected primarily to the fact that the Commission made the right to purchase coal directly from that company dependent on the conclusion of a two-year contract whereby the purchaser undertook to buy at least 6,000 metric tons a year of Ruhr coal for the

36. Schwarze (note 30 above), 2649 and sources cited there.
37. Case C-52/09 [2011] ECR I-527, paras 20-22.
38. 'From Economic Rights to Fundamental Rights' in De Vries, Bernitz and Weatherill (eds) 'The Protection of Fundamental Rights in the EU after Lisbon' (Hart Publishing, 2013), 11 at 33.
39. Case C-496/09 (judgment of 17 November 2011), para. 60.
40. Similarly, see Case T-48/09 *Slovak Telekom* (judgment of 22 March 2012), paras 36 and 37.

domestic and small consumer sector. As a result of the Commission's decision, Nold lost its right to act as a direct wholesaler of Ruhr coal, as did some sixty other dealers. Nold relied on a 'right akin to a property right' and on its freedom to pursue a business activity. The Court dismissed this argument in the following terms:

> If rights of ownership are protected by the constitutional laws of all the Member States and if similar guarantees are given in respect of their right freely to choose and practise their trade or profession, the rights thereby guaranteed, far from constituting unfettered prerogatives, must be viewed in the light of the social function of the property and activities protected thereunder. For this reason, rights of this nature are protected by law subject always to limitations laid down in accordance with the public interest. Within the Community legal order it likewise seems legitimate that these rights should, if necessary, be subject to certain limits justified by the overall objectives pursued by the Community, on condition that the substance of these rights is left untouched. As regards the guarantees accorded to a particular undertaking, they can in no respect be extended to protect mere commercial interests or opportunities, the uncertainties of which are part of the very essence of economic activity.
>
> The disadvantages claimed by the applicant are in fact the result of economic change and not of the contested decision ...[41]

In its subsequent case law, the Court has reiterated the principles spelt out in the first of these two paragraphs. On the basis of the assertion in the second of these paragraphs, the action was dismissed. As we shall see, in virtually all the later cases, pleas based on the freedom to conduct a business have been equally unsuccessful.

[B] *Hauer*

In *Hauer*,[42] the applicant claimed that a ban on all new planting of vines imposed by a Council Regulation was in breach of her right to property and the freedom to pursue her occupation as a wine producer. Both Advocate General Capotorti and the Court treated the latter right as a mere adjunct to the former. Their detailed examination of the laws of the Member States and of the ECHR was confined to the right to property.

Concentrating on the right to property, the Court stressed that regard must be had to its social function[43] and that it must consider whether the restriction in issue constituted a 'disproportionate and intolerable interference with the rights of the owner impinging on the very substance of the right to property'.[44] The purpose of the contested measure was found to be two-fold, namely: on the one hand, to establish a lasting balance on the wine market at a price level which was profitable for producers and fair to consumers and, on the other, to obtain an improvement in the quality of

41. Paras 14 and 15 of the judgment.
42. Case 44/79 [1979] ECR 3727.
43. Para. 20.
44. Para. 23.

wines marketed.[45] Seen in this light, the measure did not entail any undue limitation on the right to property.[46]

As to the applicant's freedom to pursue her trade, the Court first recalled its ruling in *Nold* and then found that 'the restriction upon the free pursuit of the occupation of wine-growing, assuming that it exists, is justified by the same reasons which justify the restriction placed upon the use of property'.[47]

[C] *Milk Quotas and More*

Following *Nold* and *Hauer*, the Court delivered a large number of judgments in which it reiterated the principles laid down in those two judgments, namely: the freedom to pursue a business activity is not an absolute right, but must be considered in relation to its social function, provided that the restrictions are in the public interest and do not constitute a disproportionate and intolerable interference, impairing the very substance of the rights guaranteed.[48] In all of these cases, the plea based on the freedom to conduct a business failed.

However, two cases deserve a special mention.

In *Neu*,[49] which concerned the milk quota regime, the Court held that the freedom to pursue a trade or profession included the freedom to 'choose whom to do business with'.[50] That right would not be guaranteed if a producer's decision to switch to a different dairy were to result in a reduction of its reference quantity, the Court held. Since such a reduction would not be justified by the need to ensure that the quantities of milk marketed respected the overall guaranteed quantity for the Union, the contested legislation must be construed as not providing for such a reduction in these circumstances. Accordingly, while the application of the general principle now enshrined in Article 16 of the Charter did not lead to the provision in question being declared invalid, it did result in it being interpreted in a particular way.

The other case is *ABNA*,[51] which related to a provision that required manufacturers of feedingstuffs to provide customers with the exact ingredients of their

45. Para. 25.
46. Para. 29.
47. Para. 32.
48. E.g. Cases 265/87 *Schräder v. Hauptzollamt Gronau* [1989] ECR 2237, para. 15, C-177/92 *Kühn* [1992] ECR I-35, para. 16, Case C-280/93 *Germany v. Council* (bananas) [1994] ECR I-4973 (see Tridimas 'The General Principles of EU Law' (2nd ed., 2006, Oxford University Press), 315), C-306/93 *SMW Winzersekt* [1994] ECR I-5555, para. 22, C-248/95 *SAM Schiffahrt* [1997] ECR I-4475, para. 72, C-210/03 *Swedish Match* [2004] ECR I-11893, para. 72, C-154/04 *Alliance for Natural Health* [2005] ECR I-6451, para. 126 and C-184/02 and C-223/02 *Spain and Finland v. European Parliament and Council* [2004] ECR I-7789, para. 52.
    A high proportion of these cases concerned measures adopted under the Common Agricultural Policy.
49. Case C-90/90 *Neu* [1991] ECR I-3617.
50. The freedom to 'choose whom to do business with' is of course subject to the 'right' to free competition which is also enshrined in Article 16: under Articles 101 and 102 TFEU, undertakings are not always free to decline to conclude contracts, or to supply goods or services, to particular parties.
51. Case C-453/03 [2005] ECR I-10423, para. 87.

products, at the risk that those customers or third parties would be in a position to manufacture those feedingstuffs themselves. This requirement was held to be contrary to the principle of proportionality, given that it was not justified on health grounds or indeed any other grounds. It was therefore held to be invalid.[52] This was more or less tantamount to a finding that the contested provision constituted a breach to the freedom to conduct a business. Consequently, it is somewhat anomalous that the Court then went on to consider whether the right to property and the freedom to conduct a business were infringed. In view of its finding on the principle of proportionality, the Court found it unnecessary to decide the point.[53]

[D] *Scarlet Extended*

Scarlet Extended[54] was a very rare – perhaps unique – case in which the Court expressly held a measure to be in breach of Article 16, albeit not in isolation, but read with Union legislation.

SABAM is a Belgian copyright society which represents authors, composers and editors of musical works. Scarlet Extended is an 'ISP'. SABAM brought legal proceedings against the ISP, claiming that copyright had been infringed by unauthorized file-sharing by users of the latter's services. The President of the Tribunal de première instance of Brussels found that that was indeed the case. On this basis, he granted an injunction against the ISP requiring it in effect to monitor all electronic communications made on its services and, if necessary, to block them at its own expense and for an unlimited period. Scarlet Extended appealed to a higher Belgian court which asked the Court of Justice in effect whether such an injunction was compatible with a complex web of Directives[55] read in the light of the applicable fundamental rights. The most significant provision in this legislation was Article 15(1) of Directive 2000/31 of the European Parliament and the Council[56] on electronic commerce which read:

> Member States may not impose a general obligation on providers … to monitor the information which they transmit or store, nor a general obligation actively to seek facts or circumstances indicating unlawful activity.

As the Court recognized, in this case the right to intellectual property under Article 17(2) of the Charter was pitted against the right to conduct a business under Article 16;

52. Paras 82-85. See also AG Tizzano in the same case.
53. Paras 87 and 88.
54. Note 1 above.
55. Directive 95/46 of the European Parliament and the Council on data protection (1995 OJ L281/31), Directive 2000/31 of the European Parliament and the Council on electronic commerce (2000 OJ L178/1), Directive 2001/29 of the European Parliament and the Council on certain aspects of copyright and related rights on the information society (2001 OJ L167/10), Directive 2002/58 of the European Parliament and the Council on privacy and electronic communications (2002 OJ L201/37) and Directive 2004/48 of the European Parliament and the Council on the enforcement of intellectual property rights (2004 OJ L157/45 and corrigendum 2004 OJ L195/16).
56. Note 54 above.

and it stressed the need to strike a fair balance between the two rights.[57] In the key passage of the ruling, the Court stated:

> In the present case, the injunction requiring the installation of the contested filtering system involves monitoring all the electronic communications made through the network of the ISP concerned in the interests of those right-holders. Moreover, that monitoring has no limitation in time, is directed at all future infringements and is intended to protect not only existing works, but also future works that have not yet been created at the time when the system is introduced.
>
> Accordingly, such an injunction would result in a serious infringement of the freedom of the ISP concerned to conduct its business since it would require that ISP to install a complicated, costly, permanent computer system at its own expense ...[58]

Consequently, the Court found that the injunction failed to strike a fair balance.[59] In effect, it was disproportionate. Moreover, the Court added:

> the effects of that injunction would not be limited to the ISP concerned, as the contested filtering system may also infringe the fundamental rights of that ISP's customers, namely their right to protection of their personal data and their freedom to receive or impart information, which are rights safeguarded by Articles 8 and 11 of the Charter respectively.[60]

The Court therefore concluded that such an injunction was incompatible with the Directives concerned, read in the light of 'the requirements stemming from the applicable fundamental rights'.[61] Plainly, then, although the right to conduct a business under Article 16 was the fundamental right primarily in issue, Articles 8 and 11 of the Charter played supporting roles.[62] Subsequently, this judgment was confirmed in *Netlog*.[63]

57. Paras 43 ff.
58. Paras 47 and 48. At the end of para. 48, the Court also referred to Article 3(1) of Directive 2004/48 (note 54 above) according to which measures intended to ensure the respect of intellectual property rights must not be unnecessarily complicated or costly.
59. Para. 49.
60. Para. 50.
61. Compare Case C-275/05 *Promusicae* [2008] ECR I-271 (Grand Chamber) which also concerned the illegal file-sharing of music and which also arose out of an action brought by a copyright society. In that case, the right of intellectual property was at odds with the right to data protection under Article 8 of the Charter. As to the difference between the two cases, see para. 4 of the Opinion of AG Cruz Villalón in *Scarlet Extended*; but these differences do not fully explain the Court's significantly less indulgent approach to the protection of intellectual property in the latter case.
62. The AG in *Scarlet Extended* also found that such an injunction was contrary to the Directives concerned read with the Charter; but he referred to Articles 7, 8 and 11 of the Charter and did not mention Article 16 at all.
63. Case C-360/10 (judgment of 16 February 2012). A related case is Case C-314/12 *Constantin Film* (pending).

[E] *Sky Österreich*

The judgment of the Grand Chamber in *Sky Österreich*[64] is particularly significant. This case concerned the validity of Article 15(6) of the Audiovisual Media Services Directive.[65] Article 15(1) to (5) required a broadcaster to allow competitors to reproduce coverage of 'events of high interest to the public' to other broadcasters for the purpose of short news reports. By virtue of Article 15(6), where Member States chose to provide for compensation, that compensation could not exceed the 'additional costs in providing access'. At issue was a series of excerpts from broadcasts of football matches, which Sky Österreich did not wish to make available to another Austrian broadcaster in accordance with these provisions. In the instant case, the costs directly incurred in providing access to the satellite signal were non-existent. The Austrian court hearing the dispute referred a question for a preliminary ruling asking whether Article 15(6) was compatible *inter alia* with Article 16 of the Charter.

After endorsing the Explanation on the latter provision,[66] the Court asserted:

> In addition, the freedom of contract includes, in particular, the freedom to choose with whom to do business (see, to that effect, Joined Cases C-90/90 and C-91/90 *Neu* [1991] ECR I-3617, paragraph 13), and the freedom to determine the price of a service (see, to that effect, Case C-437/04 *Commission v. Belgium* [2007] ECR I-2513, paragraph 51, and Case C-213/10 *F-TEX* [2012] ECR I-0000, paragraph 45).[67]

Next, it found that, since it prevented the holder of exclusive broadcasting rights from deciding freely on the price to be charged for access to the signal for the purpose of making short news reports, Article 15(6) of the Directive amounted to an interference with the freedom to conduct a business.[68]

However, the Court went on to hold that the restriction was justified. In a crucial passage, after referring to various cases in which it had held once again that the freedom to conduct a business is not absolute but must be viewed in the light of its social function, the Court stated:

> On the basis of that case-law and in the light of the wording of Article 16 of the Charter, which differs from the wording of the other fundamental freedoms laid down in Title II thereof, yet is similar to that of certain provisions of Title IV of the Charter, the freedom to conduct a business may be subject to a broad range of interventions on the part of public authorities which may limit the exercise of economic activity in the public interest.[69]

Thus the Court took the view that the words 'in accordance with Union law and national laws and practices' in Article 16 gave public authorities greater leeway to restrict the freedom to conduct a business in the public interest than they would

64. Note 2 above.
65. Directive 2010/13 of the European Parliament and the Council (2010 OJ L95/1 and corrigendum 2010 OJ L263/15).
66. Para. 42.
67. Para. 43.
68. Para. 44.
69. Para. 47.

have otherwise. It also emerges from this passage that the Court considers this language to have been inserted into Article 16 so as to reflect its own case law which has always been ambiguous towards the freedom to conduct a business.[70] This is a statement of very considerable importance for the understanding of this provision.[71] What is more, the parallel which the Court has made with the social rights in Title IV can come as no surprise since, as mentioned in §12.03, the intention of the Convention in drafting Article 16 had been to seek to ensure that the freedom to conduct a business would be treated on a equal footing with those rights.

The contested provision did not 'affect the core content of the freedom to conduct a business' since it did not 'prevent a business activity from being carried out as such by the holder of exclusive broadcasting rights'.[72] Moreover, the purpose of Article 15 of the Directive was to 'safeguard the fundamental freedom to receive information, guaranteed under Article 11(1) of the Charter, and to promote pluralism of the media in the production and programming of information in the European Union, protected under Article 11(2) of the Charter'.[73] This undoubtedly constituted 'a legitimate aim in the general interest'.[74] On a detailed analysis of the Directive, the Court went on to find that Article 15(6) was both appropriate and necessary to achieve that end.[75] Accordingly, although this provision restricted the freedom to conduct a business under Article 16 of the Charter, it was justified under Article 52(1). This ruling closely matches the Opinion of Advocate General Bot.

[F] *McDonagh*

McDonagh v. Ryanair[76] concerned Regulation 261/2004 of the European Parliament and the Council on air passengers' rights.[77] The plaintiff in the main case had booked a flight from Faro in Portugal to Dublin for 17 April 2010. However, two days before that date Irish airspace was closed following the eruption of the Eyjafjallajökull volcano in Iceland, and she was unable to return to Ireland until 24 April. The Court construed the Regulation to mean that in such circumstances air carriers are required to pay passengers' board and lodging and local transport expenses without any temporal or

70. By the same token, the right to property is not only subject to the general exception contained in Article 52(1) of the Charter, but is also qualified by the exception contained in the second and third sentences of Article 17(1) itself. As explained below, there is a close link between Articles 16 and 17.
71. Moreover, as is clear from the passage cited, this statement also has major repercussions for the interpretation of Title IV of the Charter ('Solidarity'). A number of the provisions in this Title also contain the words 'in accordance with Union law and national laws and practices' or similar language: e.g. Articles 27 (workers' rights to information and consultation within the undertaking), 28 (right to collective bargaining and to strike) and 30 (protection against unjustified dismissal). See further note 85 below.
72. Para. 49.
73. Para. 51.
74. Para. 52.
75. Paras 53 ff.
76. Case C-12/11 (judgment of 31 January 2013).
77. 2004 OJ L46/1.

monetary limitation, so long as such expenses are necessary, proportionate and reasonable.

Next, the Court considered the Ryanair's claim that the Regulation as so understood ran counter to Articles 16 and 17 of the Charter, since it had the effect of depriving air carriers of part of the fruits of their labour and of their investments. On this point, the Court referred to Article 38 of the Charter which seeks to ensure a high level of protection for consumers. In the light of this provision, it found no breach of Articles 16 and 17. This part of the judgment is notable for its brevity, as the Court scarcely attempted a serious balancing exercise.

[G] *Alemo-Herron*

Finally, an important ruling has been delivered in *Alemo-Herron*,[78] which related to Council Directive 2001/23 on safeguarding employees' rights in the event of transfers of undertakings.[79] The Supreme Court of the United Kingdom posed a series of questions asking whether the Directive permitted Member States to allow "dynamic clauses referring to collective agreements". These are clauses which have been agreed between the employees and the transferor employer to abide by the conditions agreed in future collective agreements, even where the employer cannot be a party to the negotiations leading to that agreement. In addition, the Supreme Court asked in effect whether such clauses were compatible with fundamental rights.

Advocate General Cruz Villalón found that generally speaking such clauses were compatible with the Directive. As to fundamental rights, a key passage of his Opinion reads as follows:

> Of course, the right to acquire a particular undertaking does not form part of the freedom recognised under Article 16 of the Charter. Nevertheless, to make acquisitions subject to such draconian requirements that, in practice, they are a strong disincentive to the acquisition or take-over of undertakings, may result in an infringement of this article. The fact that the employer may be indefinitely bound, in the event of the transfer of an undertaking, by terms and conditions of employment to which it did not agree, starts to resemble a restriction on the freedom of contract, which is one of the component parts of the freedom to conduct a business, according to the explanations of Article 16 of the Charter.[80]

He went on to conclude that such legislation is compatible with Article 16, provided that the requirement is not unconditional or irreversible.[81]

Similarly the Court stated that, by virtue of Aricle 16, the transferee of the business must be able to assert its interests in a contractual process and to negotiate the aspects determining changes in the working conditions of its employees.[81a] Where the transferee could not do so, the very essence of its freedom to conduct a business

78. Note 6 above.
79. 2001 OJ L82/16.
80. Para. 54.
81. Para. 58.
81a. Para. 33.

was liable to be adversely affected.[81b] Accordingly, the Direction must be interpreted as precluding Memeber States from providing for dynamic clauses in such a situation.

§12.06 SOME GENERAL ISSUES

[A] Does Article 16 Lay Down a Right or a Principle?

One question which has given rise to some discussion is whether Article 16 lays down a directly enforceable right or merely a 'principle'. According to Article 52(5) of the Charter, principles have no legal force by themselves but must be 'implemented by legislative and executive acts taken by institutions, bodies, offices and agencies of the Union, and by acts of Member States when they are implementing Union law, in the exercise of their respective powers.'[82] The Explanations on this provision do not give any clear indication as to whether the freedom enshrined in Article 16 constitutes a right or a principle. Picod took the view that, because Article 16 Charter refers to 'Union law and national laws and practices', it only lays down a principle,[83] while others have espoused the view that it provides for a right .[84]

As regards freedom of contract, this controversy has now been laid to rest by the ruling in *Sky Österreich*. In that case, as we noticed, the Court appeared to treat that freedom as a right rather than a mere principle, even though, in view of the reference to 'Union law and national laws and practices', the grounds of justification were broader than they otherwise would be, since the public authorities were entitled to proceed to a 'broad range of interventions' in the public interest.[85]

81b. Para. 35.

82. Article 52(5) was inserted into the Charter in 2007. However, the distinction between rights and principles was present in the Charter from its inception in Article 51(1). This provision requires the rights enshrined in it to be 'respected', while the principles are merely to be 'observed'. On this distinction, see Craig 'EU Administrative Law' (2nd ed., Oxford University Press 2012) 467ff., Ladenburger, commentary on Article 52(5) in Tettinger and Stern (note 30 above), 803ff. and the same author's FIDE report (note 16 above), 31 ff.

83. 'Pour un développement durable des droits fondamentaux de l'Union européenne' in 'Chemins d'Europe' (note 32 above), 528, 533.

84. E.g. Jarass 'Die Gewährleistung der unternehmerischen Freiheit in der Grundrechtecharta' 2011 EuGRZ 360.

85. As we noticed earlier (note 71 above and the accompanying text), the same applies to a number of provisions in Title IV of the Charter. The very purpose of incorporating the concept of 'principles' into Article 52(5) appears to have been to ensure that some social rights enshrined in the Charter would not be directly enforceable: Judge Lenaerts (note 15 above), at 399-400 and sources cited there. However, although they were delivered prior to the entry into force of the Treaty of Lisbon which gave binding force to the Charter, the judgments in Cases C-438/05 *Viking Line* [2007] ECR I-10779 and C-341/05 *Laval* [2007] ECR I-11767 strongly suggest that Article 28 of the Charter lays down a directly enforceable right, not a mere principle. Indeed, the judge describes these judgments as clear authority on the point. In contrast, according to the Explanations on Article 52(5), one provision in Title IV, Article 37 on environmental protection, lays down a mere principle, while two others (Article 33 on family and professional life, and Article 34 on social security and social assistance) 'may contain both elements of a right and of a principle'.

It is hard to imagine how the first of the three rights mentioned in the Explanations on Article 16, namely the freedom to exercise an economic or commercial activity, could be treated differently from freedom of contract. On the other hand, as we noticed earlier, the 'right' to free competition may not be enforceable as such, in which case it is a mere principle. The Explanations on Article 52(5) specifically state that one and the same article may contain both a right and a principle.[86]

[B] How Does Article 16 Relate to Articles 15 and 17?

As we mentioned at the outset, Article 16 is closely related to its immediate neighbours in the Charter, namely Articles 15 and 17. Article 15 provides for the right to work and the freedom to choose an occupation. The Court has held that the latter freedom coincides with the freedom which is now enshrined in Article 16.[87] To what extent Articles 16 and 17 overlap will depend on how broadly the words 'possessions' and 'property' in the latter provision are interpreted. In *Interseroh Scrap*, the Court appeared to suggest that the protection of commercial secrets falls under Articles 15, 16 and/or 17 – without indicating which.[88]

In *Alemo-Herron*, Advocate General Cruz Villalón asserted that the right to property applies to tangible and intangible assets, whereas the freedom to conduct a business 'protects economic initiative and the ability to participate in a market rather than the actual profit, seen in financial terms, that is earned in that market'.[89] Whether this is a workable distinction is an open question.

[C] Which Categories of Person May Rely on Article 16?

The wording of Article 16 does not indicate which persons may rely on it. Beyond any doubt, it applies in favour of natural persons who hold the nationality of a Member State. The question is: what other categories of person can benefit from this provision?

Plainly, legal persons can also do so, although they are not mentioned.[90] In most of the cases concerning the freedom to conduct a business – including *Nold, Scarlet*

86. The Explanations give three examples of measures which contain both a right and a principle, namely Articles 23 (equality between men and women), 33 (family and professional life) and 34 (social security and social assistance). Since these are merely examples, nothing turns on the fact that Article 16 has been omitted from this list.
87. Cases C-184/02 and C-223/02 *Spain and Finland v. European Parliament and Council* [2004] ECR I-7789, para. 51. See also para. 83 of the Opinion of AG Trjstenjak in Case C-316/09 *Sharp & Dohme* [2011] ECR I-3259 and para. 26 of AG Wahl's Opinion in Case C-101/12 *Schaible* (pending); and Bernsdorff (note 6 above), 296-297 and Jarass (note 77 above), 360-361.
88. Note 26 above, para. 43. The facts of this case – but not the outcome – are somewhat similar to those of *ABNA* (note 51 above). For the purposes of the TRIPS Agreement ([1994] OJ L336/214), certain business secrets are treated as intellectual property (see Articles 1(2) and 39 of that Agreement); on that basis, they fall within Article 17(2) of the Charter.
89. Para. 51 of the judgment (note 6 above).
90. E.g. Bernsdorff (note 6 above), 299, Ruffert, commentary on Article 16 of the Charter in Callies/Ruffert 'EUV/ AEUV Kommentar' (4th ed. Beck, 2011) 286, Sasse 'Die Grundrechtsberechtigung juristischer Personen durch die unternehmerische Freiheit gemäß Article 16 der Europäischen Grundrechtecharta' 2012 EuR 628, Schwarze (note 30 above), 2650 and the

Extended and Sky Österreich – the party invoking this right was a company. Indeed, if Article 16 were confined to natural persons, it would be largely ineffective. Furthermore, there appears to be no reason to exclude entities which lack legal personality, provided of course that they are able to bring legal proceedings.[91]

Having said that, Article 16 only applies to entities which carry out a 'business'. As to what constitutes a 'business', the French version of Article 16 uses the word '*entreprise*', the word which also corresponds to the term 'undertaking' in Articles 101 and 102 TFEU. It therefore seems logical to have regard to the meaning of the latter term.[92]

By the same token, there is no reason to exclude third country nationals and companies,[93] although of course Article 16 does not give them the right to establish themselves in the Union. The same applies to stateless persons.[94]

On these issues, the recent ruling in *Bank Mellat v. Council*[95] appears to be of assistance. In that case, the Applicant was an Iranian bank which contested a Council Regulation imposing sanctions on it. The Council and the Commission claimed that the bank was an emanation of the Iranian State. They also maintained that legal persons who are emanations of third countries could not rely on fundamental rights protection and guarantees. The General Court dismissed this argument, saying:

> neither in the Charter of Fundamental Rights of the European Union (OJ 2010, C 83, p. 389) nor in European Union primary law are there any provisions which state that legal persons who are emanations of States are not entitled to the protection of fundamental rights. On the contrary, the provisions of the Charter which are relevant to the pleas raised by the applicant, and in particular Articles 17, 41 and 47, guarantee the rights of 'everyone', a wording which includes legal persons such as the applicant.[96]

Accordingly, the General Court held that the applicant could rely on various fundamental rights such as its right of defence and its right to effective judicial protection. Although the freedom to conduct a business was not in issue in that case, there is every reason to suppose that this ruling extends to that right.

literature cited there. In *DEB* (note 23 above), paras 39ff. the Court set out two criteria for assessing whether a provision of the Charter applies to legal persons; but they are surely not needed in the present context. See generally Oliver 'The Fundamental Rights of Corporations' (Hart Publishing, forthcoming).

Some authors have expressed regret that the Charter does not contain a provision modelled on Article 19(3) of Germany's Basic Law (cited in note 7 above): Bernsdorff (note 6 above), 299, Schwarze 'Der Grundrechtsschutz für Unternehmen in der Europäischen Grundrechtscharta' 2001EuZW 517, 518.

91. Sasse (note 90 above).
92. Bernsdorff (note 6 above), 297.
93. Bernsdorff (note 6 above), 299, Sasse (note 90 above), Schwarze (note 30 above), 2650.
94. Bernsdorff (note 6 above), 299.
95. Case T-496/10 (judgment of 29 January 2013).
96. Paras 36 and 37.

§12.07 WHY ARE ARGUMENTS BASED ON ARTICLE 16 SO RARELY SUCCESSFUL?

As the above survey has shown, the success rate of arguments based on the freedom to conduct a business is low, *Scarlet Extended* and *Alemo-Herron* being the only clear exceptions, although it is submitted that *ABNA* should also be regarded as such a case.

In considering the low success rate of such arguments, it must be borne in mind that this fundamental right is closely akin to the right to property. Pleas founded on the right to property itself have nearly always been roundly rejected by the Court.[97] No doubt, this is due in part to the broad justifications which the European Court of Human Rights accepts on restrictions on the right to property under Article 1 of Protocol 1 to the ECHR.[98] Consequently, it is scarcely surprising that parties who invoke Article 16 so rarely meet with any success.

However, that is not the end of the matter. The reality is that, as Tridimas has pointed out,[99] where a measure seriously threatens the freedom to carry out a business, the Court frequently prefers to accept the claim on other grounds such as the principle of equality[100] or the protection of legitimate expectations.[101]

In addition, of course, the four economic freedoms can be called in aid in many cases, provided that an interstate element is present. Ironically there is some risk of their becoming a surrogate for Article 16. Advocate General Tesauro pointed out in *Hünermund* that Article 34 TFEU does not provide for a general freedom to trade or the right to the unhindered pursuit of one's commercial activities, but is aimed at restrictions on imports.[102] An assertion to the same effect was made by Advocate General Poiares Maduro in *Alfa Vita*.[103] These statements are incontrovertible. None of the four freedoms applies in the absence of an interstate element, but in practice the Court has eroded this requirement in cases such as *Pistre*[104] and *Karner*.[105] Similarly, in cases involving facts confined to a single Member State, the Court has considered questions on the four freedoms to be admissible, thus leaving the possibility to the national

97. See e.g. *Nold*, *Hauer* and Cases C-22/94 *Irish Farmers's Association* [1997] ECR I-1809, paras 26-29, and C-20/00 *Booker Aquaculture* [2003] ECR I-7411, paras 64 ff., *Sky Österreich* (paras 34 ff.). A spectacular exception is Case C-402/05 *Kadi* [2008] ECR I-6381, paras 345 ff. Also, in Case C-277/10 *Luksan* (judgment of 9 February 2012), paras 69-70, Austrian legislation granting exploitation rights to a cinematographic work to the producer rather than to the director was held to infringe the latter's right to property, but this was ancillary to its incompatibility with various EU Directives on copyright. For criticism of the latter ruling from the viewpoint of an intellectual property lawyer, see Griffiths 'Constitutionalising or Harmonising? The Court of Justice, the Right to Property and European Copyright Law' (2012) 38 ELRev. 65, 74.
98. See the literature referred to in note 5 above.
99. Note 48 above, 315.
100. e.g. Case C-309/89 *Cordoniu v. Council* [1994] ECR I-1853.
101. e.g. Cases 120/86 *Mulder I* [1988] ECR 2321 and C-189/89 *Spagl* [1990] ECR I-4539.
102. Case C-292/92 *Hünermund* [1993] ECR I-6787, 6813.
103. Case C-158/04 [2006] ECR I-8135, paras 37 and 41.
104. Case C-321/94 [1997] ECR I-2343. See also Case C-72/03 *Carbonati Apuani* [2004] ECR I-8027.
105. Case C-71/02 [2004] ECR I-3025, paras 19-20.

court to apply the relevant Treaty provisions even to purely internal situations.[106] In so doing, where commercial transactions are involved, the Court has come close to treating the four freedoms as a general freedom to trade.[107,108]

Quite apart from all those considerations, Article 16 has an important role to play away from the courtroom. It is axiomatic that public authorities are expected to apply the law without waiting for the courts to strike down their acts.[109] Consequently, the mere fact that Article 16 features in the Charter means that all public authorities acting within the scope of EU law – and in particular the Union legislator – are required to take full account of the freedom to conduct a business and balance it against other fundamental rights. For example, as has been pointed out, 'ultimately all the Union's social policy legislation can be analysed as operating some sort of balancing between social rights and principles, as now reflected in Title IV of the Charter, and countervailing rights including the freedom to conduct a business'.[110] In other circumstances, the Union legislator will have to weigh that freedom against other rights provided for in the Charter. That in itself shows that Article 16 is far from an empty letter.

§12.08 CONCLUSION

With the entry into force of the Treaty of Lisbon, the general principle of the freedom to conduct a business appears to have been replaced seamlessly by Article 16 of the Charter. As before, the success rate of pleas founded on this right is very low. The only clear exceptions are its judgments in *Scarlet Extended* and *Alemo-Herron*, although even those rulings were based in large part on various Union Directives; and it is submitted that *ABNA* should be classed together with this judgment, even though that judgment is formally based on the principle of proportionality. In any event the Court's consistent reluctance to find breaches of this fundamental right is tempered by its considerably more stringent attitude when adjudicating on alleged infringements of other more specific rules benefiting enterprise such as the four freedoms and the principles of equality and legitimate expectation.

Accordingly, it seems clear that Article 16 is reserved for extreme cases, its primary function being to act as a counterweight to other fundamental rights.[111] This

106. E.g. Cases C-6/01 *Anomar v. Portugal* [2003] ECR I-8621, C-515/99 *Reisch v. Salzburg* [2002] ECR I-2157, C-300/01 *Salzmann* [2003] ECR I-4899 and C-384/08 *Attanasio* [2010] ECR I-2055.
107. See generally Oliver on Free Movement of Goods (5th ed., 2010, Hart Publishing); 131-132 and 142ff.
108. Article 16 of the Charter cannot be read as broadening the scope of the four freedoms, in view of Article 52(2). That provision reads: 'Rights recognised by this Charter for which provision is made in the Treaties shall be exercised under the conditions and within the limits defined by those Treaties.'
109. See generally Case 103/88 *Fratelli Costanzo* [1989] ECR 1839, paras 28 ff.
110. Ladenburger FIDE report (note 16 above), 38. At pages 8ff. of the same report, he describes the mechanisms which the Commission, the European Parliament and the Council have set in place to ensure that Union legislation is compatible with the Charter.
111. AG Cruz Villalón in *Alemo-Herron* (note 6 above), para. 52.

author is certainly not alone in believing that that is its proper place. Equally, the Convention was undoubtedly right to include this provision in the Charter: its mere presence should generally act as reminder to the institutions and bodies of the Union as well as to the Member States acting within the scope of EU law that they must have regard to this fundamental right in all their actions, as well as to the other rights enshrined in the Charter, including the social rights set out in Title IV.

CHAPTER 13

The Principle of Effectiveness and EU Private Law

*Norbert Reich**

§13.01 ARTICLE 47 CHARTER/19 TEU: ANYTHING NEW?

This chapter will be concerned with a specific aspect of the 'Constitutionalisation of private law', namely the principle of effectiveness now written into Article 47(1) of the Charter of Fundamental Rights in the EU (in the following: Charter) which reads:

> Everyone whose rights and freedoms guaranteed by the law of the Union are violated has the right to an effective remedy before a tribunal in compliance with the conditions laid down in this Article.

Article 19(1) sentence 2 TEU puts the responsibility for 'providing remedies sufficient to ensure effective legal protection in the fields covered by Union law' on Member States resp. their courts of law as 'Union courts'. A similar provision was contained in

* The paper continues prior reflections which will not be cited individually, namely: Individueller und kollektiver Rechtsschutz im EU-Verbraucherrecht – Von der 'Nationalisierung' zur 'Konstitutionalisierung' von Rechtsbehelfen, Schriftenreihe der Juristischen Studiengesellschaft Hannover Bd. 51, 2012; (with Hans Micklitz Peter Rott and Klaus Tonner) Understanding EU Consumer Law, 2009, 2nd edition in preparation for 2013, § 8 (Legal Protection of Individual and Collective Consumer Interests); Effective Private Law Remedies in Discrimination cases, in: R. Schulze (eds.), Non-discrimination in European Private Law, 2011, 57-80; The Social, Political and Cultural Dimension of EU Private Law, in: R. Schulze, European Private Law - Current Status and Perspectives 2011, pp. 57-88; The interrelation between rights and duties in EU Law: Reflections on the state of liability law in the multilevel governance system of the Union – Is there a need for a more coherent approach in European private law?, in: Oxford Yearbook of European Law (YEL), 2010, 112-163. References to other authors are kept at a minimum.

Article I-29(1) of the Draft EU Constitution which was rejected in the Dutch and French referenda, but which later formed the basis of the TEU.[1]

In a traditional reading, the constitutional 'tandem' of Article 47 Charter and Article 19 TEU does not seem to contain anything new. It simply restates the existing EU-*acquis* based on the so-called 'procedural autonomy' of Member States for enforcing Union rights, with some specific limitations developed under the so-called *REWE/Comet* case law to be discussed later. Its importance for private law still remains to be discovered – or even more radical cannot be discovered at all because it simply doesn't seem to exist.

This chapter will develop a different approach. The argument takes three steps in order to find out the different functions and approaches of the effectiveness principle in the case law of the CJEU:

- The first and rather traditional reading understands 'effectiveness' as an *'elimination rule.'*
- The second uses it as a *'hermeneutical'* i.e., interpretative principle.
- The third is concerned with its *'remedial'* function.

The argument will be limited to CJEU case law which has a reference to private law and illustrated by case studies – a relatively new area of EU law which will explain some hesitations and inconsistencies of it. But it seems that a new, more functional and more aggressive approach of the Article 47/19 tandem can be discovered and will be discussed in the last section.

§13.02 THE ELIMINATORY FUNCTION OF THE EFFECTIVENESS PRINCIPLE

The effectiveness principle was, as is well known, first developed in the *Comet/Rewe* cases dating from 1976 and basically requires that national remedies and procedural rules must not render the exercise of Union rights *practically impossible*[2] or – as was later added[3] – *excessively difficult*. In parallel to this, the CJEU developed the principle of *'equivalence'* based on non-discrimination considerations: rights under EU law should not be treated less favourably than those similar to domestic actions.[4] However, these principles only allow a 'minimum', not an 'adequate' protection, as AG van Gerven had observed;[5] they have a mostly 'negative' content, as the intense case law

1. Tridimas, *The General Principles of EU Law*, 2nd ed. 2006, p. 419; the more recent study by D. Poelzig, *Normsetzung durch Privatrecht*, 2013, p. 270 analyses the principle of effectiveness as starting point for individual enforcement of Union law, but does not even mention Art. 47 of the Charter.
2. Case 33/76 *Rewe Central Finanz* [1976] ECR 1989 para. 5; 45/76 *Comet* [1976] ECR 2043 paras 13-16.
3. Case 199/82 *San Georgio* [1983] ECR 3595 at para. 14.
4. Case law on defining equivalence in practice has been quite complex and cannot be adequately discussed here; the Court prefers a broad teleological, not a narrow formal approach, see Tridimas, note 1 above, p. 418.
5. V. Gerven, *Of Rights, Remedies, and Procedures*, CMLRev 2000, 501 p. 504/529.

shows; I therefore call it the *'eliminatory function'* of the effectiveness principle (in parallel with the equivalence principle): They eliminate restrictions *to* protection, but do not create remedies *for* protection. As a consequence it can be said: Once the CJEU (or a national court) has established that a national rule makes the implementation of EU rights excessively difficult, or that it does not put national and EU law rights on an equal footing, the competent national court must either disapply the incriminated national provisions, or interpret it in conformity with EU law under the principles of (limited) horizontal direct effect.

The explanation for this limited effect of the effectiveness principle – in contrast to what the wording seems to suggest – is the so-called 'procedural autonomy' of Member States. Its standard formula reads:

> (I)n the absence of Community rules on this subject, it is for the domestic legal system of each Member State to designate the courts having jurisdiction and to determine the procedural conditions governing actions at law intended to ensure the protection of the rights which citizens have from the direct effect of Community law...[6]

Later litigation tried to clarify the scope and limits of the principle of procedural autonomy, which has remained a controversial principle in doctrine in its balancing with the seemingly opposing principles of 'effectiveness' and 'equivalence'. Therefore, some authors criticize or even deny the existence of such a principle of 'procedural autonomy' or find a more or less contradictory, sometimes only symbolic application by the Court.[7] In my opinion, it seems that this controversy is to some extent rendered superfluous by a closer look at the more recent case law of the CJEU to which I will be turn at a later stage of this chapter.

The main area of application of the effectiveness principle – together with equivalence – has indeed been administrative law and procedure, for instance in scrutinizing time limits for recovery of overcharged duties, tariffs or taxes, or limitation periods for compensation in state liability cases.[8] I have found only a limited number of genuine private law cases where the Court referred to them:

Levez[9] concerned prescription periods for claims of compensation in discrimination cases. The referring English court stated that Ms. Levez was caught by a two-year prescription period – which as such did not violate the effectiveness principle – because of a wrong information on her case by her employer. The Court found:

6. See the above mentioned *Rewe/Comet* cases.
7. A. Adinolphi, 'The "Procedural Autonomy" of Member States and the Constraints Stemming from the CJEU's Case Law: Is Judicial Activism Still Necessary', in Micklitz/de Witte (eds), *The CJEU and the Autonomy of Member States*, Intersentia 2012, p. 281; Bobek, Why there is No Principle of 'Procedural Autonomy of the Member States, in: Micklitz/de Witte (eds.), at p. 305; D.-U. Galetta, 'Procedural Autonomy of EU Member States: Paradise Lost?', Springer 2011, p. 34 referring to the principle of consistent interpretation as a limitation of procedural autonomy, in particular in sex discrimination cases, p. 41.
8. For a recent restatement see cases C-445/06 *Danske-Slagterier* [2009] ECR I-2119 para. 32; C-533/10 *CIVS v. Receveur des Douanes de Roubaix* [2012] ECR I-(14.6.2012) para. 22; for an overall discussion see Tridimas, note 1 above p. 427.
9. Case C-326/96 *Levez v. Harlow Pools* [1998] I-7835; for a somewhat different analysis of the effectiveness principle see case C-249/09 *S. Bulicke v. DBS* [2010] ECR I-7003 at para. 41.

> In short, to allow an employer to rely on a national rule such as the rule at issue would, in the circumstances of the case before the national court, be manifestly incompatible with the principle of effectiveness referred to above. Application of the rule at issue is likely, in the circumstances of the present case, to make it virtually impossible or excessively difficult to obtain arrears of remuneration in respect of sex discrimination. It is plain that the ultimate effect of this rule would be to facilitate the breach of Community law by an employer whose deceit caused the employee's delay in bringing proceedings for enforcement of the principle of equal pay (para 32).

In *Manfredi*[10] as a follow-up of *Courage*[11] concerning compensation for breaches of competition rules the Court wrote:

> the full effectiveness of Article 81 EC (now Article101 EU) and, in particular, the practical effect of the prohibition laid down in Article 81(1) EC would be put at risk if it were not open to any individual to claim damages for loss caused to him by a contract or by conduct liable to restrict or distort competition...As to the award of damages and the possibility of an award of punitive damages ... it is for the domestic legal system of each Member State to set the criteria for determining the extent of the damages, provided that the principles of equivalence and effectiveness are observed.. it follows from the principle of effectiveness and the right of any individual to seek compensation for loss caused by a contract or by conduct liable to restrict or distort competition that injured persons must be able to seek compensation not only for actual loss (*damnum emergens*) but also for loss of profit (*lucrum cessans*) plus interest (paragraphs 90–95).

Vale[12] concerns the conversion of a company from one state (Italy) to another (Hungary) where the Court, in restating the applicability of the principles of equivalence and effectiveness within the directly applicable fundamental freedom of establishment guaranteed to companies which however must be compromised with national company law as source of the creation of companies as such, wrote:

> Consequently, the authorities of the host Member State are required, pursuant to the principle of effectiveness, to take due account, when examining a company's application for registration, of documents obtained from the authorities of the Member State of origin certifying that that company has indeed complied with the conditions laid down in that Member State, provided that those conditions are compatible with European Union law (paragraph 61).

A fourth case, *Alassini*,[13] concerned an Italian requirement for consumer complaints against telecommunication operators to first undertake an ADR/ODR proceeding as foreseen in Directive 2002/22[14] before going to court. The Court discusses this requirement both under equivalence and effectiveness principles, but did not find a violation. It wrote:

10. Joint cases C-295-298/04 *Vicenzo Manfredi et at v. Lloyd Adriatico Asssicurazioni SpA et al.* [2006] ECR I-6619
11. C-453/99 *Courage Ltd v. Crehan* [2001] ECR I-6297
12. Case C-378/10 *Vale Építési* [2012] ECR I-(12.7.2012)
13. Case C-317/08 *Rosalba Alassini et al. v. Telecom Italia*. [2010] ECR I-2213.
14. Directive 2002/22/EC of 7 March 2002 of the EP and of the Council on Universal Services in Electronic Communications, [2002] OJ L 108/ 51

> In those circumstances, it must be held that the national legislation at issue in the present case complies with the principle of effectiveness in so far as electronic means is not the only means by which the settlement procedure may be accessed and in so far as interim measures are possible in exceptional cases where the urgency of the situation so requires' (paragraph 60).

In *Aziz*[15] the Court was confronted with the protection of defaulting debtors of an outstanding mortgage loan who under existing Spanish law cannot oppose the claim of the creditor against execution even if clauses in the contract on acceleration, default interests and unilateral determination of the amount of unpaid debt may be found to be unfair under Article 3 of Directive 93/13. In her opinion of 8 November 2012, AG Kokott refers to the principle of effective legal protection of the debtor which must give the judge the possibility to stay execution proceeding in order to find out whether the incriminated clause is abusive or not (paragraph 57). The Court in its judgment of 14 March 2013 followed suit, referring that the principle of effectiveness must be assessed 'by reference to the role of that provision in the procedure, its progress and its features, viewed as a whole, before the various national bodies' (paragraph 53).

The cases are somewhat specific insofar as *Levez, Vale, Alassini* and recently *Aziz* are closely linked to a procedural enforcement of Union rights, namely non-discrimination, freedom of establishment in a cross-border situation of conversion, and consumer rights of effective complaint handling resp. defences against unfair terms. In *Alassini*, the Court also refers to the importance of Article 47 Charter even though it does not extract any 'extra legal value' out of it; its use as an argument looks rather superficial and not well-elaborated legally. *Manfredi* seems to be somewhat broader as it defines minimum substantive requirements of effectiveness concerning the head of damage which cannot be limited to actual economic loss as such but must also include loss of (future) profit – an important general principle of the law of compensation, which can be generalized to other claims arising under EU law, as the Court did with regard to state liability.[16] More specific questions had been treated in *Manfredi* under the traditional reading of effectiveness with regard to limitation periods (paragraph 78) and equivalence with regard to the award of punitive damages (paragraph 93). On the other hand, there is also a strong procedural element in *Manfredi* which stems from its origin in *Courage:* a damage claim is seen as a corollary to effective enforcement of competition law. This link between substantive and procedural remedies seems to be particular important and will be taken up later.[17]

§13.03 EFFECTIVENESS AS A HERMENEUTICAL PRINCIPLE

There are many cases where the Court went beyond the merely 'eliminatory' approach of the classical *Rewe/Comet* formula and developed a positive *effet utile* or 'full

15. Case C-415/11, *M. Aziz v. Catalunyacaixa*, [2013] ECR I-(14.3.2013).
16. Joined cases C-46 and C-48/93 *Brasserie du Pêcheur v. Germany and the R v. Secretary of State for Transport ex parte Factortame Ltd.* [1996] ECR I-1029 para. 87
17. Ch. Mak, Rights and Remedies – Article 47 EUGR and Effective Judicial Protection in European Private Law Matters, unpubl. Paper at file with the author.

effectiveness' test[18] as mentioned in *Manfredi*. This requires a two step approach of the Court concerning EU law:

It must first find out the Union right which must be protected by an adequate remedy (*ubi ius-ibi remedium*).[19] This is basically a matter of interpretation of Union law which is the prime (but not exclusive) responsibility of the Court itself. With regard to primary EU law, it has been active in the field of competition law. A similar case law does not yet exist in free movement law, but has been to some extent announced in *Raccanelli:*[20]

> In the event that the applicant ... is justified in relying on damage caused by the discrimination to which he has been subject, it is for the referring court to assess, in the light of the national legislation applicable in relation to non-contractual liability, the nature of the compensation which he would be entitled to claim (paragraph 57).

What is somewhat surprising is the rather short and not well-elaborated mentioning of the possibility of compensation, without any reference to the principles of effectiveness or equivalence as in *Manfredi*. Or is the Court suggesting a different treatment of claims arising out of breaches of the (horizontally applicable) free movement rules than of the competition provisions? It should be mentioned that the Swedish Arbetsdomstolen, in its follow-up judgment to the *Laval*-saga, used the reference to *Raccanelli* as a justification for awarding compensation to Laval against the illegal boycott of the Swedish labour unions.[21]

With regard to secondary law, the Court will first find out the remedies provided by regulations or directives. As an example one could refer to the case law concerning compensation under the Air-Passenger Regulation 261/2004[22] not only for cancellation but also for 'long delays' exceeding three hours. In its controversial *Sturgeon* case[23] the Court, despite a legislative decision to the contrary, allowed such an extension of compensation for reasons of equality: the passenger suffering from a long delay was said to be in a comparable situation as the one suffering from a cancellation; there was no justification for treating these two similar situations differently. The principle of 'equal treatment' justified an analogy despite, as was in particular criticized in German doctrine,[24] of an absence of a legislative 'gap'.

Many national courts criticized the CJEU's approach to extend liability against the intention of the EU legislator and therefore referred the question again. In its recent

18. For a critique see J. Lindholm, *State Procedure and Unions Rights*, (J. Foerlag Umaea, 2007) at p. 126; for a differing view Reich, Federalism and Effective Legal Protection, *FS Brüggemeier*, 2009, 381
19. Tridimas, note 1 above at p. 422; V. Gerven, note 5 above at p. 511.
20. C-94/07 *Raccanelli v. MPG* [2008] ECR I-5939.
21. For details see the comment by Bernitz/Reich, CMLRev 2011, 603 at p. 608.
22. [2004] OJ L 46/1.
23. C-402 + 432/07 [2009] ECR I-10923 para. 54
24. Riesenhuber, Interpretation and Judicial Development of EU Private Law – The Example of the Sturgeon Case, 2010 ERCL 2010, 384; a more nuanced appraisal has been put forward by Garben, Sky-high controversy and high-flying claims? The *Sturgeon* case in the light of judicial activism, euroscepticism, and eurolegalism, CMLRev 2013, 15.

Nelson judgment[25] the Grand Chamber of the CJEU implicitly rejected any criticism against the *Sturgeon* judgment of its Forth Chamber without adding anything new. It simply referred to the comparable situation of passengers with long delays and those with cancellations:

> In addition, passengers in either group are in practice denied the opportunity to reorganise their travel arrangements freely, since they are faced either with a serious incident in the operation of their flight which is about to depart or already underway, or with the cancellation of their flight giving rise, as the case may be, to an offer to re-route. Consequently, if, for one reason or another, they are absolutely required to reach their final destination at a particular time, they cannot avoid the loss of time inherent in the new situation, having no leeway in that regard (paragraph 35).

The Court however does not address the more fundamental question of its competence to simply extend the scope of an EU act beyond its clear wording and without finding a 'legislative gap' which in legal methodology[26] seems to be the prerequisite of an analogy; instead the Court apparently sticks to its jurisdiction under Article 267 TFEU concerned only with the '*interpretation*' of acts of the Union! As far as the question of 'effective application' of Reg. 261/2004 according to recital 7 is concerned, the Court does not refer to it, but implicitly seems to take the view that without extending liability of air carriers also to long delays, the protection of passengers remains insufficient and therefore must be regarded as ineffective.

As far as interpreting remedies provided in directives, the CJEU has not hesitated to extend them under an implicit recognition of the effectiveness principle as will be shown in the following case studies, e.g., with regard to non-discrimination and consumer protection law. Under Article 19(1) 2nd TEU sentence it is the task of Member State courts to provide for remedies 'sufficient' to ensure the protection of EU granted rights.

Much more difficult and controversial are the steps to be taken in the interpretation of national law concerning implementation of EU law rights. Under the principle of division of competences, it not up to the CJEU to interpret national law; this must be left to the competent courts of Member States.[27] On the other hand, in reference proceedings, the Court has frequently given guidelines on how to understand national

25. Joined cases C-582 + 629/10 *Nelson et al. v. Deutsche Lufthansa et al.* [2012] ECR I-(23.10.2012).
26. For a general methodological discussion see the contributions in K. Riesenhuber (ed.), Europäische Methodenlehre, (Springer 2nd ed. 2010), particularly by Chr. Baldus, Auslegung und Analogie im 19. Jh., p. 6; R. Stotz, Die Rechtsprechung des EuGH, p. 653; concerning 'Rechtsfortbildung' (continuous development of EU law) see M. Pechstein/C. Drechsler, Die Ausbildung und Fortbildung ders Primärrechts, p. 224; concerning a rather restrictive use of the argument of analogy in secondary law, see J. Köndgen, Die Rechtsquellen des Europäischen Privatrechts at p. 189. For a broader discussion based on 'general principles of EU law' see M. Herdegen, General Principles of EU Law – the Methodological Challenge in: U. Bernitz et al. (eds.), General Principles of Community Law as a process of development, (Kluwer Int. 2008) at p. 343; Tridimas, note 1 above at p. 17 (gap-filling function of general principles) and p. 51 (rules of Treaty interpretation); see also Bernitz/Reich, note 21 above at p. 612.
27. V. Gerven note 5 above at p. 502, suggesting that the concept of 'procedural autonomy' should be seen as a question of 'procedural competence'; see also R. Stotz, in Riesenhuber note 26 above at p. 663 referring to Art. 267 TFEU.

law in the light of Union law. There is an indirect spill-over of EU law to national law, at least insofar as an inconsistent application can be stated, and the Court will rule that a certain application or interpretation of national law is 'precluded' by EU law – a formula used in many highly controversial cases. The mechanism of 'preclusion' in the end is nothing more than the imposition on national law of an interpretation given to EU law by the CJEU with consequences on available remedies to be discussed in the next section.

§13.04 EFFECTIVENESS AS A REMEDIAL PRINCIPLE: 'UPGRADING' NATIONAL REMEDIES

The remedial function of the effectiveness principle requires Member State courts to create or improve remedies of their own '*sufficient*' for the effective protection of Union rights, of which I will give some examples later. Article 19(1) sentence 2 TEU posits a clear link between 'effective protection' and 'sufficient remedies'. Both concepts are those of Union, not of Member State law, and are therefore subject to autonomous interpretation by the CJEU. They are not limited to administrative and procedural effectiveness,[28] but include as *prerequisite also remedies under substantive private law*, e.g., compensation, restitution, avoidance of contracts to be implemented before courts of law,[29] as could already be shown under the 'eliminatory function' of the effectiveness test (section §13.02 above). It will of course not be easy to measure in a concrete case whether this relationship between 'rights' and 'remedies' – whether substantive or procedural – in the spirit of '*ubi res – ibi remedium*' paradigm are fulfilled in a positive or rather a negative sense. In the latter case, the Commission may bring infringement proceedings against non-complying Member States under Article 260 TFEU which it does rather seldom.[30] In the end it will be the task of Member State courts as 'EU courts' themselves to guarantee this equilibrium between rights and remedies.

This EU law process of linking rights to remedies (and in the end procedures before courts of law) should be done by what I have called a *hybridisation approach.*[31] It combines Member State autonomy – whether remedial or procedural – with the imperatives of enforcement of EU granted rights. In short it requires a three-step test:

28. In this sense A. Eser, 'Comment Art. 47 para. 19', in J. Meyer (ed.), Charta der Menschenrechte in der EU Kommentar (3d. ed. Nomos 2011): '... ernsthafte und unparteiliche Prüfung durch ein Gericht'; H.J. Blanke, comment to Art. 47 Charta para. 2 in: Calliess/Ruffert, Kommentar zum EUV/AEUV (4th. ed. Beck 2011).
29. V. Gerven, note 5 above at pp. 509, 516; Trstenjak & Beysen, 'European Consumer Protection Law: *Curia semper dabit remedium?*, CMLRev 2011, 95, 109; A. Hartkamp, 'The Impact of EU Law on National Private Laws', 2012, para. 111; D. Poelzig, note 1 above at p. 306.
30. See case C-144/99 *Commission v. Netherlands* [2001] I-3541 at para. 21 insisting that a directive conforming interpretation (Dir. 93/13 on unfair terms ion consumer contracts) of national (Dutch) law 'cannot achieve the clarity and precision needed to meet the requirement of legal certainty. That, moreover, is particularly true in the field of consumer protection'.
31. Horizontal liability' in EC Law – 'Hybridization' of remedies for compensation in case of breaches of EC rights, CMLRev 2007, 705 at p. 708, Bernitz & bReich, note 21 above at p. 615.

- The first step is concerned with finding appropriate national remedies in case of violations of EU granted rights (whether primary or secondary law); therefore, the applicable Member State law has to be clarified, in the end by the competent national court of law.
- Second, this 'national remedy' has to be measured:

  - against the yardstick of the 'negative, eliminatory' EU principles of effectiveness and equivalence; and
  - if the result is unsatisfactory from an EU law point of view as interpreted as providing 'insufficient remedies', it has to be 'upgraded' to meet EU standards.

- This remedy thus found is a '*hybrid*' insofar as it takes up elements of national law in the limits of the principle of procedural autonomy, as well as effectiveness in its different functions. It should be '*sufficient*' to ensure effective protection in the words of Article 19(1) paragraph 2 TEU, that is to meet the 'adequacy' standard by AG van Gerven.[32]

The circular relationship between:

- remedies under national law ('procedural autonomy');
- the effectiveness principle (Article 47 Charter) in a broad, remedy oriented reading;
- their 'upgrading' via the principle of consistent interpretation to 'hybrids' (Article 19(1) TEU can be demonstrated in a graph:

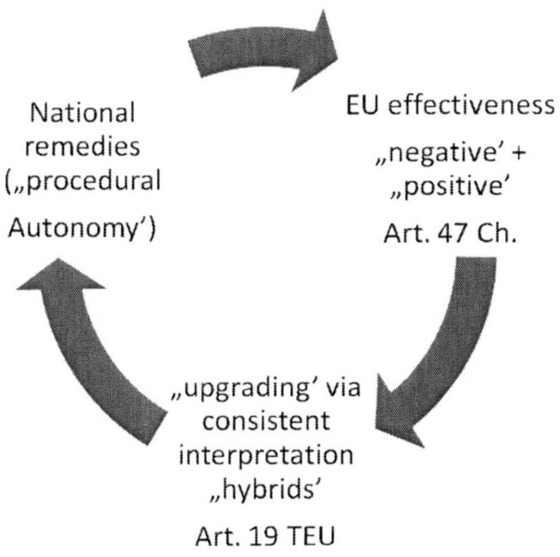

32. At p. 529.

§13.05 SOME EXAMPLES APPLYING THE EFFECTIVENESS TEST IN EU PRIVATE LAW

[A] The Classical Case: *Von Colson and Kaman* – from a Conditional to a Direct Remedy

Von Colson[33] concerned the refusal to employ a women as a warden in a male prison. This was clearly regarded as a discrimination based on the sex of the candidate which could not be justified under the restrictive regime of justifications under the then applicable Directive 76/206/EEC, now Directive 2006/54.[34] Whether this refusal could be qualified as a contract or a tort case depends on the national law which is not a matter of the CJEU to decide. Under German law, this case came under the principle of *culpa in contrahendo* as a matter of (pre-) contractual liability[35] which allows only compensation of the so-called 'negative interest', that is the damage which would not have occurred had the defendant acted legally. In the specific situation this would have to be limited to the costs of making the (unsuccessful) application, e.g., costs for mailing, transportation for an interview and the like, but not to the 'positive interest' under a contract.

This rather trifle amount of compensation did not suffice in the eyes of the Court which insisted on the principle of effectiveness in a *positive, remedial sense* regarding the provision of a remedy:[36]

> [Compensation must] be such as to guarantee real and effective judicial protection, ... have a real deterrent effect on the employer [and] must in any event be adequate in relation to the damages sustained ... purely nominal [compensation] eg the reimbursement of expenses incurred by them [the candidates] in submitting their application, would not satisfy the requirement of an effective transposition of the directive.

In this still very important and often cited judgment, the Court rejected a merely symbolic compensation as incompatible with the principle of effectiveness in a positive sense, including also the scope of the remedy under contract law (or pre-contractual obligations as under German *culpa* principles). It is not quite clear on what legal principle the Court based its principle of full compensation since the Directive was silent on this point, especially as the Court held at the same time that Mrs von Colson did not have the right to a contract. In this light it would be difficult to explain the claimant's right to full compensation on the basis of a traditional contract theory. In my opinion, the damage which the Court strove to remedy by its ruling was primarily 'moral'. This raises the question whether EU law should require non-material damages to be awarded more generally for breaches of EU sex-discrimination prohibitions which

33. Case 14/83 *Von Colson and Kamann v. Land Nordrhein-Westfalen* [1984] ECR 1891.
34. Recast Directive 2006/54/EC of the EP and the Council of 5 July 2006 'on the implementation of the principle of equal opportunities and equal treatment of men and women in matters of employment, [2006] OJ L 204/23.
35. This is different now under the EU conflict law regimes of Art. 1 (2) (i) of Reg. 593/5008 (Rome I) and Art. 12 of Reg. 864/2007 (Rome II), even though the applicable law will be that of the contract had it been entered into.
36. Paras 23–24.

I think would be justified, provided a certain threshold of injury is met.[37] The overall context of this case law on compensation as inaugurated by *Von Colson*, even though not phrased in these terms, certainly has a constitutional dimension which is now well settled under Article 47 Charter as mentioned, in connection with the prohibition on sex-discrimination in Article 23 Charter.

The follow-up case law tries to develop the effectiveness principle further; there is no need to go into details.[38] Just to mention some leading cases:

- Liability does not depend on the fault of the offender.[39]
- The head of damage to be compensated includes interest as 'adequate compensation'.[40]
- Upper limits to compensation in cases of multiple victims are subject to a strict proportionality test.[41]
- Discrimination may occur not only before getting or within the job, but also after its ending.[42]

[B] An Open Constitutional Dimension: *Kücükdevici*

The question of an effective remedy in discrimination matters clearly popped up in the case *Kücükdevici*[43] but not so much regarding compensation or restitution, but as precluding the application of a provision in national contract law shortening the periods of notice for young employees which violated the Framework Directive 2000/78[44] forbidding age discrimination. The problem of this remedy consisted that it stood in contrast to well-established principles not allowing a horizontal direct effect of directives. In the prior *Mangold* case[45] the CJEU had seemingly allowed such an effect

37. The Court recognises this with regard to compensation for 'lost holiday' in package tours, see case C-168/00 *Simone Leitner v. TUI Deutschland* [2002] ECR I-2631; there is no reason to treat discrimination cases less stringently.
38. For details under German law before 1996 see Steindorff, *EG-Vertrag und Privatrecht*, 1996, p. 375; Reich, 'Effective Private Law Remedies in Discrimination Cases', in Schulze (ed.), *Non-Discrimination in European Private Law*, 2011, 57; Poelzig, note 1 above at p. 272 insisting on a 'functional creation of subjective right (funktionale Subjektivierung)' as a structural principle of Union law to enforce EU market legislation.
39. Case 177/88 *Dekker v. Stichting Vormingscentrum voor Jong Volwassenen (VJV-Centrum) Plus* [1990] ECR I-3941 para. 23
40. Case C-271/91 *Marshall v. Southhampton Health Authority* [1993] ECR I-4367 paras 26/31.
41. Case C-180/95 *Draempaehl v. Urania* [1997] ECR I-2195 para. 37; for a discussion see U. Magnus and W. Wurmnest, *Casebook Europäisches Haftungs- und Schadensrecht*, 2002 at p. 101.
42. Case C-185/97 *Coote v. Granada Hospitality* [1998] ECR I-5199; for a discussion of the issues see H.-W. Micklitz, *The Politics of Judicial Co-operation*, 2005, at pp. 210–13, 269–70.
43. Case C-555/07 *Seda Kücükdevici Swedex GmbH* [2010] ECR I-365, recently confirmed by case C-447/09, *R. Prigge et al. v. Lufthansa,* [2011] ECR I-(13.9.2011) para. 38;; the broad approach of the Court has been criticised M. Dougan, In Defence of *Mangold*?, in: Arnull et al., A Constitutional Order of States – Essays in Honour of A. Dashwood, 2011, p. 219 f.
44. Council Directive 2000/78/EC of 27 November 2000 establishing a general framework for equal treatment in employment and occupation [2000] OJ L 303/16.
45. Case C-144/04 *Werner Mangold v. Rüdiger Helm,* [2005] ECR I-9981; confirmed for German law by the German Constitutional Court in the *Honeywell*-case, BVerfGE 126, 286 with dissenting opinion by Judge Landau referring to the Lisbon judgment and criticising the *Mangold*-judgment

based on an alleged 'general principle of age discrimination', but the reasoning remained shaky and controversial.

The question concerned the dismissal periods in a contract for employment which would increase with age, but beginning only after having reached the age of 25 years. The CJEU in its judgment of 19 January 2010, referring to Article 21 (but not Article 47) of the Charter,[46] under the principle of '*full effectiveness*' required the national court to disapply the discriminatory provision without the necessity to first refer the case to the Court.[47] The Bundesarbeitsgericht (the Federal Labour Court) followed suit and in the judgment of 9 September 2010 simply set aside the contested German provision (§ 622(2) paragraph 2 BGB) which discriminated against young employees with regard to the notice period for termination of employment by excluding from calculation the employment period accrued before the age of 25.[48] In its stead the court used the general rule contained in § 622(2) paragraph 1 BGB on the calculation of the length of employment.

[C] Effective Protection against Unfair Terms in Consumer Contracts: *Invitel/Camino/ Aziz*

The Unfair terms Directive 93/13/EEC[49] has led to a number of spectacular judgments of the CJEU insisting on the principle of effective protection justified by the unequal bargaining power of the parties, lately highlighted by the recent *Invitel*- and *Aziz*-judgments.[50] This concerns the requirement imposed on national courts to apply ex officio certain protective provisions, in particular its Article 6. The case law started with *Océano* concerning jurisdiction clauses,[51] was continued in *Claro*[52] and *Asturcom*[53] with arbitration clauses in consumer contracts, confirmed and refined in *Pannon*:[54]

of the CJEU, pp. 318, 324. For an assessment of the cooperation between the CJEU and the BVerfG see the paper by Sauer, Europas Richter Hand in Hand?, EuZW 2011, 94.

46. At para. 22.
47. At para. 54.
48. BAG, 2 AZR 714/08, Zeitschrift für Wirtschaftsrecht (ZIP) 2011, 444.
49. Council Directive 93/13/EEC of 5 April 1993 on unfair terms in consumer contracts [1993] OJ L 95/29. For an overview (in German) see now Micklitz/Reich, Von der Klausel- zur Marktkontrolle, EuZW 2013, 457.
50. Case C-472/10 *Nemzeti Fogyaszróvédelni Hatóság v. Invitel* [2012] ECR I-(26.4.2012); comment Micklitz/Reich, AGB-Recht und UWG – (endlich) ein Ende des Kästchendenkesn nach Pernivoca und Invitel, EWS (Europäisches Wirtschafts- und Steuerrecht) 2012, 257; the prior opinion AG Trstenjak of 6.12.2011 has been commented by Micklitz/Reich, EuZW 2012, 126.
51. Joined case C-240-244/98 *Océano Grupo ed. V. Quintero et al.* [2000] ECR I-4941
52. Case C-168/05 *E.M.M. Claro v.Centro Movil Milenium* [2006] ECR I-10421.
53. Case C-40/08 *Asturcom v. Christina Rodrigues Nogueria* [2009] ECR I-9579; comment H. Schebasta, Does the National Court Know European Law, in: Micklitz/Reich (eds,), The Impact of the Internal Market on the Private Law of Member countries, EUI Working Papers 2009/22 at pp. 47 = ERPrL 2010, 847, insisting that in *Asturcom* which concerned a consumer who 'in total inertia' did not raise any defences against an arbitration proceedings, including the *res iudicata* of the final award against her (para. 34), the CJEU did not apply the effectiveness, but the less stringent equivalence test.
54. Case C-243/08 *Pannon v. Erzsébet Sustikné Győrfi [*2009] ECR I-4713; see also case C-137/08 *VB Penzügyi Lizing v. Ferenc Schneider* [2010] ECR I-10847 para. 56 concerning investigation on its own motion whether the court has jurisdiction or not according to the incriminated clause.

> The court seised of the action is therefore required to ensure the effectiveness of the protection intended to be given by the provisions of the Directive. Consequently, the role thus attributed to the national court by Community law in this area is not limited to a mere power to rule on the possible unfairness of a contractual term, but also consists of the obligation to examine that issue of its own motion, where it has available to it the legal and factual elements necessary for that task, including when it is assessing whether it has territorial jurisdiction (paragraph 32).

The problem of this approach is the seeming conflict with the principle of procedural autonomy of Member States, but already the *van Schinjdel* case[55] which is cited as the clearest recognition of this principle in civil proceedings which depend on the initiative of the parties, expressed a reservation. It is often overlooked that the Court made an exception for a court intervention on its own motion based on a *public interest* test. A joint paper by AG V. Trstenjak/Boysen[56] have justified this case law with the following remarks:

> a less stringent application of the concept of procedural autonomy of the Member States can be observed in the case law of the CJEU with regard to the enforcement of consumer rights under the different consumer protection directives.

The case to be discussed here concerns the effects of an action for an injunction by the Hungarian consumer protection office against the fixed-line telephone network *Invitel* whose general business conditions (GBC) introduced clauses on fees for money order (and additional postal fees) without specifying the calculation of these fees, and were thus charged as being unfair under Article 3 and the (indicative) Annex of the Unfair Terms Directive. Two questions were submitted to the Court, one concerning the fairness of these clauses which will not be discussed in this context, the other more interesting here on the effects of a successful injunction on individual consumer contracts.

Under German law, this problem is seemingly 'solved' by the so-called 'Einredelösung' of § 11 Unterlassungsklagengesetz: once the judgment prohibiting the use of such a clause has attained force of res judicata, the consumer can object to its further use, but only with effects to the future and only with regard to the specific defendant, not with regard to other businesses even if using the same incriminated clause.[57] In practice this solution has played no role and has not been an effective remedy of the individual consumer having been the object of an incriminated clause.

Invitel offers a much more far-reaching solution under an implicit principle of 'remedial effectiveness' of this problem which means that German law will have to be changed: The Court first insists on 'the deterrent nature and dissuasive purpose of the

55. Case C-430-432/93 *Van Schijndel and Van Veen v. Stichting Pensioenfonds* [1995] ECR I-4705 para. 21; do a detailed discussion of the later case-law narrowing the *Van Schijndel* formula see Hartkamp, note 29 above at paras 124-130.
56. Trstenjak/Beysen, note 29 above at p. 119.
57. Critique Micklitz/Reich, note 50 above at p. 261 with further references.

measures to be adopted' under Article 7(2) of the Unfair Terms Directive (paragraph 37). It then goes on to say:

> (W)here the unfair nature of the term included in the GBC of consumer contracts has been recognised in an action for an injunction ... the national courts are required, of their own motion, and also as regards to the future, to draw all the consequences provided for by national law in order to ensure that consumer who have concluded a contract to which those GBC apply will not be bound by that term (paragraph 43).

It is clear that these consequences must be attached to national law, as suggested in the *hybridisation approach*, but they must take two directions:

- One concerning the individual contract in which the incriminated clause is 'not binding on the consumer' according to Article 6, which as a consequence means that money paid under the unfair clause must be returned to the consumer under the national doctrines of unjust enrichment or restitution.
- The second is concerned with future effects of the unfair terms whose continued used must be prohibited under Article 7(1).

National – in my understanding German – law has to be upgraded accordingly. The so-called 'Einredelösung' will have to be substituted to a 'Unwirksamkeitslösung' to be applied ex officio by the competent national court and not depending on a motion of the consumer.

The recent *Aziz* case as mentioned above[58] was concerned with remedies of the consumer against the execution of a mortgage containing unfair terms to the detriment of a defaulting consumer:

> It follows from the above that, under Spanish rules of procedure, the final vesting of mortgaged property in a third party is always irreversible, even if the unfairness of the term challenged by the consumer before the court hearing the declaratory proceedings results in the annulment of the mortgage enforcement proceedings, except where that consumer made a preliminary registration of the application for annulment of the mortgage before that marginal note. In that regard, taking into account the progress and the special features of the mortgage enforcement proceedings at issue in the main proceedings, such an eventuality must however be regarded as remote because there is a significant risk that the consumer in question will not make that preliminary registration within the period prescribed for that purpose, either because of the rapidity of the enforcement proceedings in question or because he is unaware of or does not appreciate the extent of his rights ...It must therefore be held that such procedural rules impair the protection sought by the directive, in so far as they render it impossible for the court hearing thedeclaratory proceedings – before which the consumer has brought proceedings claiming that the contractual term on which the right to seek enforcement is based

58. Note 15 above.

> is unfair – to grant interim relief capable of staying or terminating the mortgage enforcement proceedings, where such relief is necessary to ensure the full effectiveness of its final decision (paragraphs 57–59)

This rigid mechanism of the Spanish enforcement proceedings violated the effectiveness principle because the consumer did not have a remedy like interim relief to escape the consequences of an unfair clause. The court could not on its own motion – as required by the case law of the CJEU – stop in time the execution proceedings even if the contract contained unfair clauses concerning acceleration, unilateral determination of the amount of unpaid debt, and default interests to be determined by the court (paragraphs 73–75). The Court also referred to the risk that the consumer in execution proceedings will lose his home without a possibility to recover it even if the term was unfair; the mere possibility to obtain reparation would violate the principle of effectiveness:

> That applies all the more strongly where, as in the main proceedings, the mortgaged property is the family home of the consumer whose rights have been infringed, since that means of consumer protection is limited to payment of damages and interest and does not make it possible to prevent the definitive and irreversible loss of that dwelling (paragraph 61).

On the other hand, the remedy provided must be commensurate to the purpose the directive, as the Court insisted in *Camino* and may therefore exclude the remedy of adaptation of the incriminated clause:[59]

> if it were open to the national court to revise the content of unfair terms included in such contracts, such a power would be liable to compromise attainment of the long-term objective of Article 7 of Directive 93/13. That power would contribute to eliminating the dissuasive effect on sellers or suppliers of the straightforward nonapplication with regard to the consumer of those unfair terms ... in so far as those sellers or suppliers would remain tempted to use those terms in the knowledge that, even if they were declared invalid, the contract could nevertheless be modified, to the extent necessary, by the national court in such a way as to safeguard the interest of those sellers or suppliers... (paragraph 69).

In the same judgment, the CJEU insisted that the principle of effectiveness is not excluded by a simplified procedure for the recovery of debts:

> In that context, it must be stated that such a procedural arrangement, which completely prevents the court before which an application for order for payment has been brought to assess of its own motion, *in limine litis* or at any other stage

59. Case C-618/10 *Banco espagnol de Credito/Camino* [2012] ECR I- (of 14.6.12); comment Rott, ERCL 2012, 470 (475). The case law of the German Bundesgerichtshof (Federal Court – BGH), VIII ZR 80/12 NJW 2013, 991 allows a an adaption of the incriminated clause by what is called 'ergänzende Vertragsauslegung' (supplementary interpretation of the contract based on the hypothetical, legally justified will of the parties), arguing this should not be identified with a 'revision of the content' (geltungserhaltende Reduktion) in the sense of *Camino* – a very problematic judgment which will be discussed in a different context. Unfortunately, the BGH did not refer this question to the CJEU!

> during the proceedings, even though it already has all the legal and factual elements necessary for that task available to it, whether terms contained in a contract concluded between a seller or supplier and a consumer are unfair where that consumer has not lodged an objection, is liable to undermine the effectiveness of the protection intended by Directive 93/13. In the light of the order for payment procedure..., its progress and its special features, viewed as a whole, there is a significant risk that the consumers concerned will not lodge the objection required either because of the particularly short period provided for that purpose, or because they might be dissuaded from defending themselves in view of the costs which legal proceedings would entail in relation to the amount of the disputed debt, or because they are unaware of or do not appreciate the extent of their rights, or indeed because of the limited content of the application for the order for payment submitted by the sellers or suppliers, and thus the incomplete nature of the information available to them (paragraphs 53–54).

The judgment does not seem to require the court to always examine ex officio the unfairness of a term in an expedited proceeding. The CJEU is not criticizing the existence of such proceedings for the rapid recovery of debts, but the strict prohibition for the judge not to examine the merits of the claim even if there is evidence before him of the use of unfair terms.

[D] The Extent of Strict Liability in Sales Law: *Weber-Putz*

The facts of the litigation in cases *Weber* and *Putz*[60] decided by the CJEU on 16 June 2011 against the critical opinion of AG Mazak of 18 May 2010 are probably well known to the readers and need not be discussed in detail here; they are a good and at the same time controversial example of the impact of EU law on traditional concepts on remedies in sales law beyond the wording of Directive 99/44.[61] They concern reimbursement of additional costs by the consumer for replacing a defective product and installing a conforming one, e.g., by tearing off and replacing the defective tiles which had been used for floor panelling, or by dis-and reconnecting the dishwasher which did not function. The AG rejects this claim under EU law, but the CJEU upheld it as a causal consequence of the seller's obligation to deliver a conforming good. The reasoning of the Court is surprisingly short and based on the rather unspecific provisions in the directive that repair and replacement should be done within 'a reasonable time', 'free of charge' and 'without significant inconvenience to the consumer', even if the contract did not include installation. This creates a *strict liability regime* of the seller not only for the act of replacing the non-conforming good as such, but also for the emerging follow-up costs even after the transfer of the risk. In order to avoid an overcharging of the seller, the Court referred to its possibility to an action on recourse against the previous seller/producer according to Article 4 of Directive 99/44 (paragraph 48). The Court was also asked whether Article 3(3) of Directive 99/44 wasto be read as an 'absolute' or a 'relative' defence of the impossibility of the seller to repair or replace the non-conforming good. The 'dominant opinion' (*herrschendeMeinung*) of German law

60. Joined cases C-65/09 and C-87/09 *I. Gebr. Weber et al v. J. Wittmer et al.* [2011] ECR I-5257.
61. [1999] OJ L 171/12.

of the time understood the implementing provision of § 439 BGB as an 'absolute proportionality test': if one of the remedies was impossible and the other disproportionate regarding costs, this had the consequence of a total loss of first stage remedies under sales law. The Court however opted for a 'relative proportionality defence' as corroborated by recital 11: even if one remedy (repair) would be impossible and the other (replacement) provokes disproportionate costs on the seller, the consumer would not be at a complete loss of his first stage remedies; disproportionate costs of replacement (including cost for dis- and reconnecting) would only allow the seller to reduce them 'to an amount proportionate to the value the goods would have if there were no lack of conformity and the significance of the lack of conformity' (paragraph 74). The reference point therefore are not the – possibly much higher – cost for removal of the non-conforming or/and installation of a conforming good, but its lower net value. This seems to be a fair balancing of the different interests of the parties.

The German Federal Court (BGH), in its judgment of 21 December 2011[62] followed suit under the principle of consistent interpretation extending the scope of replacement beyond a mere disconnection also to a reconnection which thus far was rejected by its earlier case law. It also followed suit concerning the 'relative proportionality test' under Article 3(3) Directive 44/99, and interpreted § 439 BGB restrictively using the method 'teleological reduction' of German law which it had already applied in its follow-up judgment to *Quelle*.[63] It discussed in detail the different proposals in legal writing on how to implement the proportionality criteria; it found an amount of EUR 600 to be reimbursed to the consumer to be adequate for the value of conforming tiles (EUR 1200) and the importance of their non-conformity.

I will not discuss the *efficiency* problems of the judgment, particularly concerning its possible negative effects on distance selling. In my context, I'm concerned with the *effectiveness* argument with reference to the consumer protection objective of the Directive which is given a broad reach by the Court, but at the same time reduced by a balancing element taking into account the economic situation of the seller, or rather of the specific transaction. Under the 'relative proportionality test', the Court avoids a complete loss of the consumer's first stage remedies which would have been the consequence of the 'absolute test', hereby seriously undermining the principle of effective consumer protection under Article 47 Charter read together with Directive 99/44. Under these criteria, the judgment certainly has a certain deterrent effect concerning the sale of non-conforming goods, especially when they need to be installed like a dishwasher or put into place like the tiles which is well aware to the seller. At the same time, the Court used a proportionality argument based on a 'fair balancing' (paragraph 75) principle, which means that the consumer has to bear some of the risks of this transaction. Such a balancing is also possible under a strict liability regime for

62. BGH, VIII ZR 70/08 NJW 2012, 1073; the BGH however did not extend this principle to B2B transactions, VIII ZR 226/11 of 17.10.2012, EuZW 2013, 157.
63. BGH NJW 2009, 427.

compensation of costs caused as result of the delivery of a non-conforming good. Thus, the effectiveness argument leads to a *specific risk-sharing and risk-distribution* between the seller and the consumer, protecting at the same time the consumer's rights under Directive 99/44 without excessively increasing the risks of the seller. Effectiveness of consumer protection does not mean that the consumer's transaction is completely risk free – but he should at least not carry all its risks.

[E] A Missed Opportunity: The Heininger-Saga

This chapter may seem to exaggerate the importance of the effectiveness principle in the CJEU case law in EU private law. There are however also judgments where the Court did not seem to be ready to take a more forward-looking approach to providing remedies in protecting EU law rights. The best and often criticized example concerns the so-called *Heininger*-saga[64] where the effects of a withdrawal from a mortgage credit of a bank entered into by the consumer at the doorstep on the financed real estate transaction by a project developer were before the Court. The BGH was very quick at giving its answer based on the doctrine that the real estate and the credit transactions are legally separated from each other.[65] The withdrawal of one (the mortgage credit) does not affect the other (purchase of real estate). The only consequence of withdrawal from the credit contract is to avoid it. What are the consequences of avoidance? Does the consumer have to pay back the credit in full and without the privilege of instalments, as the case law of the BGH seemed to suggest? Does he have to pay the contracted interests, including those which will accrue over time? Does it make any difference that he has not been informed about an eventual right of withdrawal? Could he raise a claim of compensation against the bank for not having been adequately informed under the German theory of '*culpa in contrahendo*'?[66] Or could one even argue, as the Commission did, that the credit and the purchase contract form an economic unity which must be judged together, even if formally separated?

These were the questions which came to the CJEU via references of lower courts which were quite opposed to the restrictive case law of the BGH in the follow-up cases of *Schulte*[67] and *Crailsheimer Volksbank*.[68] In its reasoning, the Court put forward the following legal doctrines:

64. C-481/99 *Heininger v. Bayr. Hypo und Vereinsbank* [2001] ECR I-9945.
65. BGH NJW 2002, 1884.
66. For a discussion see N. Reich, Balancing in Private Law and the Imperatives of the Public Interest: National Experiences and (Missed?) European Opportunities, in: R. Brownsword et al. (eds), Modern Tendencies in Private Law, 2011,221; H. Unberath and A. Johnston, 'The Double Headed Approach of the CJEU Concerning Consumer Protection, CMLRev 2007, 1237, 1261; T. Möllers and P. Grassi, Die Europarechtswidrigkeit der Schrottimmobilienrechtsprechung zur Haustürwiderrufs-RiLi 85/577/EWG durch deutsche Gerichte (2010) Verbraucher und Recht 2010, 3.
67. Case C-350/03 [2005] ECR I-9215.
68. Case C-229/04 [2005] ECR I-9293.

- Starting from a formal approach in following the opinion of Advocate General Léger,[69] it held that the withdrawal by the consumer avoided the credit transaction and that therefore the parties had to re-install the original state of affairs, namely, that the consumer had received the credit without justification and therefore had to pay back the money immediately and in full (*Schulte* paragraph 87).
- It was of no relevance for which purpose the credit was used; the CJEU indirectly rejected the idea of 'linked contracts' as a principle of EU law, which would however not be precluded under national law (paragraph 80).
- The consumer had to pay market interest for the credit money used without justification, thus restoring the *status quo ante* (paragraph 92).
- However, States have to 'ensure that their legislation protects consumers who have been unable to avoid exposure to such risks (loss of rental income and property value incurred because of not knowing of their right of cancellation under the Directive), by adopting suitable measures to allow them to avoid bearing the consequences of the materialization of those risks' (paragraph 101).

In the end this meant that the consumer's economic situation is not improved after withdrawal; a claim for compensation will be difficult to prove in practice. The Court did not attach any importance to the effectiveness principle it had used in other cases.[70] Instead, it relied on the theory of a formal separation of transactions, as confirmed in the Opinion of Advocate General Léger of 29 October 2004 in *Schulte*:

> I think a purposive interpretation of the Directive, just like its practical effect, do not permit a requirement that the cancellation of the secured credit agreement should produce an effect, in one way or another, on the validity of the property purchase contract (paragraph 95).

Whether the effectiveness paradigm used here would allow different answers remains an open question; it will not give easy answers. It is to some extent caught in between the 'full autonomy' of Member States to protect citizens as they wish under their national rules of remedies and procedures unless there has been express EU legislation (the *Heininger*-saga being an example in this direction because the 'Doorstep' Directive 85/577 left the provision of remedies to national law) – and the seemingly opposite 'full effectiveness' approach relevant whenever there is a deficiency in the available remedies under national or EU law as in the cases studied here. But even under the 'full effectiveness' approach compromise solutions must and will be sought by the CJEU

69. Opinion of AG Léger in *Crailsheimer Volksbank* (2 June 2005) paras 54,72
70. See Micklitz, The CJEU between the Individual Citizen and the Member States –A Plea for a Judge Made European Law on Remedies, in: Micklitz/de Witte (eds.), The CJEU and the Autonomy of Member States, Intersentia 2012, p. 349 at p. 386; more positive Hartkamp, note 29 above at para. 174: 'unexpected outcome'.

which will often result in a *balancing of different interests.*[71] This balancing should not be done so much under formal competence aspects, but under substantive proportionality criteria, as has been recently demonstrated in *Weber/Putz.*

[F] Overview of the Case Studies

CJEU case	*EU-rights*	*nat. Remedies*	*nat. Procedures*	*EU 'upgrade'*
Von Colston	No sex-discrimination – Directive 76/2007	Culpa in contrahendo – token compensation		Adequate compensation, deterrent effect
Kücükdevici	No age discrimination – Directive 2000/78	No special dismissal protection for young employees		Preclusionary effect of Directive 2000/78 read together with Article 21 Charter
Invitel/ Camino/Aziz	No unfair terms – Directive 93/13/ Ex officio control of unfair terms	No 'geltungs-erhaltende' Reduktion/ only compensation	'Abstract' injunction / no defence against execution	Spill-over effect on individual contract / Effective defence of consumer
Weber-Putz	Conformity of product and installation – Directive 1999/44	replacement only; earlier BGH case law: only disconnection - § 439 BGB: absolute proportionality: if one remedy is disproportionate the other also fails		Strict liability for dis- and re-connecting – 'relative proportionality test' – limited to either repair or replacement - Proportionate reduction of recoverable costs

71. See my paper, note 66 above; critique also by H. Rösler, Europäische Gerichtsbarkeit auf dem Gebiet des Zivilrechts, 2012, p. 156: '... der EuGH (hat) die wirkliche Dimension und dogmatische Komplexität des Problems wohl nicht recht erfasst'. The new Consumer Rights Directive 2011/83/EU of 25 October ([2011] OJ L 304/6) which repealed Dir. 85/577 excludes financial services form its cope of application (Art. 3 (3) (d) and therefore excludes a continuation of the '*Heininger*-saga'!

CJEU case	*EU-rights*	*nat. Remedies*	*nat. Procedures*	*EU 'upgrade'*
Heininger-saga as an anti-dote	Directive 85/577 (repealed by Dir. 2011/83): Withdrawal from doorstep mortgage credit; no time-limit in case of non-information; consequences of withdrawal left to national law, Article 7	Rejection of remedies: No 'Einwendungs-durchgriff'	Necessity to pay back the amount credited in full with market interest	No EU remedies, Article 4(4) 'appropriate measures of consumer protection' – CJEU: limited to compensation because of non-information of right of withdrawal

§13.06 THE IMPORTANCE OF ARTICLE 47 CHARTER/19 (1) TEU FOR EU PRIVATE LAW REVISITED

[A] A Substantive Understanding of the Article 47 Charter/19 TEU Tandem

The case studies should have given an impression of the complex interpretation and balancing problems behind the effectiveness requirement on EU private law. However, Article 47 Charter seems to be a 'sleeping' beauty which has not really been 'kissed awake' in *Alassini*. The other cases where the CJEU refers to Article 47 Charter[72] seem to be too far away from private law as to allow an impact of remedies like compensation or restitution. Should one therefore follow the sceptical view of D. Leczykiewicz?[73]

> However, the right of access to a court and the right to an effective remedy (under Article 47) are on their own incapable of overriding all limitations to the enforceability of Union rights and of empowering to the EU to introduce a harmonised general regime of remedies.

72. Case C-432/05 *Unibet v. Justiekanslern* [2007] ECR I-2271 on standing in administrative proceedings, C-279/09 *DEB Deutsche Energiehandels- und Beratungsgesellschaft mbH v. Bundesrepublik Deutschland*, [2010] ECR I-13849 on legal aid for legal persons, C-402 + 415/05P *Kadi et al. v. Council of the EU* [2008] ECR I-6351 on protection of persons charged with terror activities, and C-12/08, *Mono Car Styling* [2009] ECR I-6653 para. 47 with regard to workers' right of action to enforce information owed to them in case of collective redundancy; C-249/09 *Fuß v. Stadt Halle* [2010] ECR I-9849 para. 66 concerning protection against reprisal measures of the employer against an employee insisting on his EU rights.
73. '"Where Angels Fear to Tread": The EU Law of Remedies and Codification of European Private Law', ERCL 2012, 58.

Or is the more optimistic approach of H. Micklitz justified?[74]

> I'm arguing for an active court, a court which takes the imbalance between the three legal orders (economic, social, citizen) seriously and which is ready to develop RRP's (rights, remedies, procedures) in the social legal order...Article 47 will have to play a key role in that respect.

In my opinion it must be remembered that, even though the Court refers to Article 47 Charter in a private law setting only in the *Alassini* case, the principles on which it is based form the 'hidden agenda' of the Court ever since *Von Colson*. An express reference to Article 47 Charter/19 (1) TEU does not attach substantial new elements to the principle of effectiveness, rather makes it conform to the more recent Constitutionalization of EU private law.[75] Effectiveness has, as could be seen, a 'negative', that is an 'eliminatory' and a 'positive', that is a 'hermeneutical' and 'remedial' side, both now enshrined in Article 47 Charter: 'Negative' insofar, as it allows a first test of national law on whether it makes the implementation of private law rights under EU primary and secondary law 'impossible or excessively difficult'. It still is a forceful and to some extent straightforward argument which the Court has used lately in *Alassini*. It is supplemented by the equivalence test preventing Member State law to prescribe lower standards for EU based claims than for those under national law; *Asturcom* is a good case in this direction concerning the ex- officio protection of the consumer against an unfair term.

But effectiveness also has a *positive* side in interpreting existing remedies and even imposing newly shaped remedies, and the case studies should exactly have demonstrated this. It results in what I have called an 'upgrading' of remedies, both in a substantive and in a procedural context. The so-called 'remedial' and 'procedural' autonomy of Member States is put on trial, but not completely abandoned.

Such a result conforms to the wording and the purpose of Article 47 Charter/19 (1) TEU. A somewhat closer look at the structure and contents of Article 47 (in relation with Article 19 (1) sentence 2 of the TEU) may be useful for our purposes. It requires first that a '*right*' exists under Union law. Article 47 Charter shares the concept of protecting *individual rights as subjective rights in a liberal spirit*. In private law this is limited to those EU law provisions which intend to create *mandatory standards* in favour of a specific individuals; if EU law leaves contractual autonomy more or less untouched, Article 47(1) cannot be invoked.[76]

This mandatory nature is usually the case in contract law matters concerning non-discrimination and consumer protection discussed here. It is however not limited to EU contract law, as has been shown by referring to *Manfredi*[77] on compensation for breaches of the competition rules, and to the *Valé*[78] -case on making cross-border

74. Note 70 above at p. 392
75. In the same sense Mak note 17 above.
76. An example would be Dir. 2011/7/EU of 16.2.2011 combating late payments, [2011] OJ L 47/1, referring to freedom of contract in setting payment dates in Art. 3 (5) in the limits of the 'grossly unfairness principle' of Art. 7
77. Note 10 above.
78. Note 12 above.

conversion of companies possible. It will depend on the applicable EU law or secondary legislation as interpreted by the CJEU. In addition to their mandatory nature, these provisions should take direct effect under general principles of EU law, that is must be sufficiently precise and unconditional.

This individual subjective right must be provided by Member States with '*remedies sufficient to ensure effective legal protection*'. In my understanding, the English term is somewhat broader that the German translation '*wirksamer Rechtsbehelf*' and the French term '*recours effectif*'; while the German and French terminology seem to be restricted to access to and management of court proceedings, the English term includes also remedies based on substantive provisions of contract, tort and company law. This is corroborated by the case studies in the beginning part of this essay. In a purpose oriented interpretation of EU law as required by Article 52 Charter, I therefore prefer the broad English concept of remedy instead of the narrow German and French understanding. Indeed, there could and would be no effective 'judicial protection' without the prior grant of remedies also in the area of private law rights.

These remedies may relate both to substance and/or to procedures: *Substantive remedies* include compensation, restitution, avoidance of a contract term, and preclusion of the application of a non-conforming national rule.[79] *Procedural remedies* relate to issues of standing, injunctions, time-limits, evidence rules.[80] However it should be kept in mind that it will not always be easy to differentiate exactly between substantive and procedural remedies, and this depends very much on applicable national law which uses different criteria in distinguishing between substantive and procedural remedies, eg in the area of prescription periods. Obviously they must find their legal basis in EU law. These remedies must in the end be able to be enforced before a tribunal; but this does not exclude alternative dispute resolution mechanisms (ADR) if they do not preclude access to courts, as the CJEU stated in *Alassini*.

The approach advocated in this chapter results, as has been mentioned before, in a '*hybridisation' of remedies* which have to be introduced into national law by using the classical method of 'directive conforming interpretation', supplemented lately by a 'negative horizontal effect' of directives if they can be based on the Charter of Fundamental Rights, in particular the non-discrimination provisions of Articles 21 and 23. It seems arguable that the principle of consumer protection in Article 38 Charter read together with Article 12/169 TFEU allows a similar 'preclusionary direct effect' of horizontal EU directives.[81]

To avoid possible fears of an 'overextension' of the effectiveness principle it should be remembered that it is only relevant in areas where EU law creates or intends to create rights, for example in favour of individuals coming under the umbrella of the competition or free movement rules, or those protecting discriminated persons or

79. Hartkamp, note 29 above at paras 113-114.
80. See the seminal paper by V. Gerven, note 5 above with examples on p. 522; Hartkamp paras 115-116.
81. This is the interesting argument by O. Mörsdorf, Die Auswirkungen des neuen 'Grundrechts auf Verbraucherschutz' gem. Art. 38 GrCh auf den nationalen Verbraucherschutz, Juristenzeitung 2010, 759.

consumers. This is always a matter of interpretation and requires in my understanding that the provisions on which these are based are *mandatory* in nature.

[B] 'Full' Effectiveness: Too 'Full', Too 'Empty', or 'Just Right'? – The Need for a Balancing Approach

My next point is concerned with a legal-political question: Isn't the Court sidestepping its mandate limited to interpretation of EU law when it goes about to reshape remedies based on national law? This critique does not so much rely on the effectiveness and equivalence principles in the negative sense – they have been recognized as general constitutional principles of EU law ever since, and are of course not limited to administrative and procedural issues but have also been extended to private law matters, including (mandatory) contract law. The critique is directed against the *positive 'full effectiveness'* principle with its hermeneutical and remedial aspects – which the Court had developed in the cases analysed here and which sit square to traditional Member State remedial and procedural 'autonomy' and competence. The 'use' (some say: 'abuse') of compensation for deterrence purposes, the abrogation of the fault principle for compensation in contract law substituted by strict liability rules, the limitation of party autonomy in proceedings concerning unfair terms, the extension of seller's liability in consumer sales beyond the transfer of risk, the recognition of ADR-instruments as a prerequisite for later proceedings before courts of law under certain qualifying conditions – not much 'autonomy' of Member States seems to be left. Isn't the CJEU acting '*ultra vires*', as was argued by the plaintiffs in the *Honeywell* litigation before the German Constitutional Court criticizing *Mangold*, but finally rejected by the same BVerfG which confirmed the wide scope and competence the CJEU enjoys in interpreting and in the end developing EU law, even at the 'detriment' of cherished principles of Member States' law?[82]

It must also be remembered that even in cases where the CJEU required an 'upgrading' of national remedies and procedures to protect rights granted under EU law, it left a wide margin of discretion to national courts to accomplish the right balancing between conflicting interests. The best example it the *Putz/Weber* case itself. Even if the extension of the strict seller's liability beyond the mere 'bodily' quality of the sold goods at the time of transfer of risk itself may seem 'revolutionary', the ensuing remedies of the consumer nonetheless are still limited by a proportionality argument taking into account the legitimate interests of the seller and the character of the transaction itself. It is of no surprise that the BGH[83] in its follow-up judgment quite straight-forwardly divided the risk between seller and consumer to one half for each!

A similar approach can also be seen in discrimination cases. As a prerequisite in all cases granting compensation to victims of discrimination, there must be at the outset a national rule in this regard; the original EU Directive 76/207 did not provide for such a remedy and left it as an option to Member States. Once the States had made use

82. Note 45 above.
83. Note 62 above.

of this option, it was 'upgraded' in the case law of the CJEU to meet the standards of effectiveness. Only later legislation, in particular Directive 2002/73/EC[84] expressly provided for the remedy of compensation also as mandatory under EU law.[85] Its Article 6(2), now replaced by Article 13 of the Recast Directive 2006/54,[86] to some extent codified as mandatory what had been developed as an effective remedy by the CJEU alongside, thus completing the originally only optional regime of compensation.

[C] Relevance of the Effectiveness Principle for Collective Remedies?

The effectiveness of collective remedies like injunctions by consumer organizations or labour unions has been recognized in the opinions of several AGs. In her opinion of 6 December 2011 in the *Invitel* case AG Trstenjak wrote:[87]

> The collective action as a means of enforcing collective rights not only provides access to this legal remedy but also has characteristics that make it an effective deterrent. As can be seen from the abovementioned judgment, this assessment is shared by the Court. Collective actions offer many advantages over individual actions. By bundling consumers' common interests together, they make it possible to enforce them judicially. By means of collective actions, consumer protection associations give consumers a voice and a weight that they would often not have in this form in isolated proceedings because of their generally weaker position. Lastly, a collective action helps to enhance the status of the consumer at the procedural level and relieves him of the risk of costs in civil proceedings if he is unsuccessful, which may deter a consumer from individually asserting his rights just as much as a low value in an individual case, for which it would not be worthwhile for an individual to incur the expense. The successful enforcement of rights by way of a collective action creates a just balancing of the interests of consumers and undertakings, ensures fair competition and shows that collective actions are just as necessary as individual actions in order to protect the consumer (paragraph 41).

However, the effectiveness principle in this context is not linked to protecting individual rights as under Article 47 Charter, but rather as an 'abstract remedy' intended to 'clear the market' from unfair contract terms or unfair commercial practices, but also to sanction discriminatory practices.[88] But what are the effects on the individual consumer who has been object to them? Is there an obligation on

84. Directive 2002/73/EC of the European Parliament and of the Council of 23 September 2002 amending Council Directive 76/207/EEC on the implementation of the principle of equal treatment for men and women as regards access to employment, vocational training and promotion, and working conditions [2002] OJ L 269/15
85. Reich note 38 above at p. 60.
86. Note 34 above.
87. Case C-472/10 *Nemzeti FH/ Invitel nnv* [2012] ECR I-(26.4.2012); similar AG Jacobs, opinion 27.1.2000, para. 47 in case C-195/98 *Öst. Gewerkschaftsbund, Gewerkschaft öffentlicher Dienst/ Republik Österreich*, [2000] ECR I-10497 para. 47.
88. For an example in this direction, see case C-54/07 *Centrum voor gelijkheid van kansen en voor racismebestrijding (CGKR) v. Firma Feryn NV*, [2008] ECR I-5187 para. 39 where the Court left the choice of an 'effective, proportionate and dissuasive' measure under Art. 15 of the Race Directive 2000/43 to the Member States, including 'an award of damages to the body bringing the proceedings.'

Member States law to rectify the consequences of unfair terms or practices (Folgenbeseitigungsanspruch)? Wouldn't this be the consequence of a correct understanding of Article 47 Charter in its remedial function? Shouldn't there be a right of the injured to reclaim sums unduly paid as a general principle?[89] *Invitel* could be understood as a first step in this direction.[90] There the Court wrote:

> It follows that, where the unfair nature of a term included in the GBC of consumer contracts has been recognised in an action for an injunction, such as that here at issue in the main proceedings, the national courts are required, of their own motion, and also as regards the future, to draw all the consequences provided for by national law in order to ensure that consumers who have concluded a contract to which those GBC apply will not be bound by that term (paragraph 43).

A similar consequence for the injunction under Directive 2005/29 seems to be excluded by its Article 3(2), but in its recent *Perenicova*[91] judgment the Court insisted:

> a finding that a commercial practice is unfair is one element among others on which the competent court may base its assessment of the unfairness of contractual terms under Article 4(1) of Directive 93/13 (paragraph 42)

The Court seems to suggest a link between collective and individual remedies which must be followed on in the future.

On the other hand, Article 47 Charter cannot be 'upgraded' to a mechanism of providing collective remedies of its own. Such an interpretation would clearly be contrary to the limited scope of the EU Charter under its Article 51(1) and to the understanding of 'general principles' as excluding any direct effect. Article 47 must be seen together with existing EU law and implementing Member State law on collective remedies. It allows, as was said before, an 'upgrading' of existing but not a 'creating' of new remedies. The difference between the two concepts may be difficult to draw, but this is again a matter of interpretation under Article 267 TFEU. Therefore, an extension of the existing collective remedy of injunction to individual compensation in consumer protection and anti-discrimination cases is certainly within the jurisdiction of the CJEU, but not the creation of a free-standing group action for compensation in competition or discrimination cases. Of course, Article 47 Charter may serve as a legal-political argument in adopting EU legislation on collective redress. But this discussion will not be followed up here.

89. Hartkamp, note 29 above at para. 134.
90. Micklitz/Reich, note 50 above at 263.
91. Case C-453/10 *Perenicova and Perenic* [2012] ECR I-(15.3.2012).

CHAPTER 14

Remedies under the EU Charter in the Context of Disputes Arising in Private Law

Angela Ward[*]

§14.01 INTRODUCTION

Remedies under the EU Charter of Fundamental rights ('the Charter') present somewhat of a paradox. There are no provisions of the Charter that laying down detailed substantive rules on the legal sanctions to be available in the event of its breach. Yet, the principles that have been included in the Charter, and which are pertinent to the question of remedies, provide support, in almost equal measure, to both victims of Charter violations seeking adequate redress, and alleged perpetrators in whose interests such efforts would be scuppered.

This paper will commence by providing an overview of Charter rules on effective judicial remedies, and place them within the context of EU rules of general application in this field. It will then provide a brief outline of the circumstances in which the Charter can be enforced horizontally in private legal actions, before turning to the specific questions of remedies, with emphasis on private enforcement of the Charter. It will be here shown that, although the Charter provides the impression that it is a classical human rights instrument binding agencies of government only, there are significant opportunities for its horizontal enforcement between private sector actors. This may include an obligation on national courts to see to the provision of adequate sanctions when EU laws vests individuals with rights in a private law context.[1]

* All views expressed are solely of the author and do not reflect those of any institution or organization.

1. With respect to horizontal enforcement of general principles see M. Safjan and P.Miklaszewicz 'Horizontal Effect of the General Principles of EU Law in the Sphere of Private Law' (2010) 18 *European Review of Private Law* 475; Editorial Comment 'Horizontal Direct Effect – A Law of Diminishing Coherence' (2006) 43 *Common Market Law Review*; X.Groussot, L. Pech and G.T.

§14.02 OVERVIEW OF CHARTER RULES CONCERNING EFFECTIVE JUDICIAL PROTECTION IN THE CONTEXT OF THE COURT'S ESTABLISHED CASE LAW

From one perspective, the Charter speaks strongly in favour of robust judicial enforcement. It proclaims, in Article 47, that everyone 'whose rights and freedoms guaranteed by the law of the Union are violated has the right to an effective remedy before a tribunal in compliance with the conditions laid down in this Article'. This provision might be viewed as a re-expression of Article 19(1), second paragraph, TEU, which binds Member States to 'provide remedies sufficient to ensure effective legal protection in the fields covered by Union law'.[2] A commitment to remedial protection might also be inferred from the preamble to the Charter, which states that it is necessary 'to strengthen the protection of fundamental rights in the light of changes in society, social progress and scientific and technological developments'.

Tangential support for a remedial regime that is sympathetic to victims can also be gleaned from parts of Title VII entitled 'General Provisions Governing the Interpretation and Application of the Charter'. Article 52 restricts 'any limitation on the exercise of rights and freedoms recognised by this Charter' (which I would argue includes remedial protection) to limitations that respect the essence of the right, which comply with the principle of proportionality and which meet objectives of general interest recognized by the Union, along with the rights and freedoms of others.[3] Article 52(3) can be read as supportive in that the remedial case law of the Strasbourg Court under Article 13 of the European Convention of Human Rights (the 'Convention') has been set as the minimum standard for available sanctions. This is so because Article 52(3) states that, when Charter rights correspond with those of the Convention, as is the case with Article 47 vis-à-vis Article 13 of the Convention,[4] 'the meaning and scope of those rights shall be the same as those laid down by the said Convention'. Article 52(3) goes on to add that this 'provision shall not prevent Union law providing more extensive

Petursson 'The Scope of Application of Fundamental Rights on Member States' Action: In Search of Certainty in EU Adjudcation' Eric Stein Working Paper No 1/2011.

2. See the Opinion of Advocate General Kokott in of 17 January 2013 in Case C-583/11P *Inuit Tapiriit Kanatami*, para. 121 where she hints that Article 19 (1) second paragraph may have strengthened EU rules on remedies. The Advocate General observed that, in general, 'Member States must provide remedies sufficient to ensure effective legal protection in the fields covered by Union law. Since the entry into force of the Treaty of Lisbon, this duty has been expressly laid down in the second subparagraph of Article 19(1) TEU. This means not least that conditions for admissibility of actions before national courts, including possible preventive actions for declarations or injunctions, may not be excessively restrictive.' See also on the principle of effectiveness and EU private law the contribution of Norbert Reich in this book, Chapter 13.
3. See generally S. Peers 'Taking Rights Away? Limitations and Derogations' in S. Peers and A. Ward (eds) *The EU Charter of Fundamental Rights:Politics, Law and Policy* (Hart Publishing 2004) p. 141.
4. See explanations to Article 47. Pursuant to the preamble to the Charter it will be 'interpreted by the Courts of the Union and the Member States with due regard to the explanations prepared under the authority of the Praesidium of the European Convention' while Article 52 (7) states that the 'explanations drawn up as a way of providing guidance in the interpretation of this Charter shall be given due regard by the courts of the Union and of the Member States.' See also Article 6(1) third paragraph TEU.

protection.' And finally, the remedial standards for breach of human rights available at Member State level might be viewed as supplying a minimum benchmark. Article 52(4) states that in so far as the Charter 'recognises fundamental rights as they result from the constitutional traditions common to the Member States, those rights shall be interpreted in harmony with those provisions.'[5]

Finally, Article 6(1) TEU states that the Charter is to have the 'same legal value as the Treaties'. This means that it 'stands on an equal footing' with both the TEU and the TFEU,[6] while some of the Advocates General of the Court of Justice have declared that the Charter 'forms part of the primary law of the Union'.[7] Thus, all of the Court's case law on effective proportionate and dissuasive remedies,[8] and which is addressed to Member State courts and tribunals, equally extend to cases in which enforcement of the Charter is sought, whether that be vertically against government authorities or horizontally between private sector actors in civil disputes, provided that the relevant Charter provisions meets the requirements set by that case law.

However, an equally visible feature of the Charter is the manner in which its enforcement is restrained. In contrast with Article 1 ECHR, which secures human rights protection to 'everyone' within the jurisdiction of the contracting parties to the Convention,[9] the impact of the Charter is significantly limited with respect to Member State action. Pursuant to Article 51(1), Member States are only bound by the Charter when they are 'implementing' EU, a restriction that has already been subject to lively debate in academic literature,[10] and deeper elaboration by the Court of Justice.[11] It

5. This is subject, however, to the restrictive interpretation of Article 53, and the role of Member State human rights law, afforded in the judgment of the Court of Justice of 26 February 2013 in Case C-399/11 *Criminal Proceedings Against Stefano Melloni*. See also L.S. Rossi 'How Fundamental are Fundamental Rights? Primacy and Fundamental Rights After Lisbon' 27 YEL (2008) p. 77.
6. See Lenaerts, K 'Exploring the Limits of the EU Charter of Fundamental Rights ' 8 (2012) *European Constitutional Law Review* 375 at 375.
7. See e.g., Advocate General Sharpston of 18 October 2012 in Case C-396/11 *Radu*, para. 52.
8. For a recent analyses see S. Prechal and R. Widdershoven 'Redefining the Relationship between 'Rewe-effectiveness' and Effective Judicial Protection' 4 *Review of European Administrative Law* (2011) 31; A. Arnull 'The Principle of Effective Judicial Protection in EU Law: An Unruly Horse?' 36 (2011) *ELRev* 51.
9. A provision which, nonetheless, has been the subject of vigorous litigation before the Strasbourg court, byt mostly with respect to extra-territorial effects, see eg Application No 31821/96 *Issa and Others v. Turkey*, judgment of 16 November 2004, Eur. Ct. H.R.
10. See e.g. Lenaerts, note 6 above and the following excellent commentaries on the meaning of Article 51(1); R. Rosas 'When Is the EU Charter of Fundamental Rights Applicable at National Level' (forthcoming) *Lithuanian Journal of European Law*; H. Kalia 'The Scope of Application of the Charter of Fundamental Rights of the European Union in the Member States' in P. Cardonnel et al. (eds) *Constitutionalising the EU Judicial System: Essays in Honour of Pernilla Linh* (2012, Hart Publishing); T. von Danwitz and K. Paraschas 'A Fresh Start for the Charter: Fundamental Questions on the Application of the European Charter of Fundamental Rights' (2012) 35 *Fordham International Law Journal* 1400; M. Sajan 'Areas of Application of the Charter of Fundamental Rights of the European Union: Fields of Conflict?' *EUI Working Paper* 2012/22.; X. Groussot, L. Pech and G. Thor Petursson 'The Scope of Application of Fundamental Rights non Member States' Action: in Search of Certainty in EU Adjudication' *Eric Stein Working Paper* No 1/2011; D. Anderson and C.Murphy 'The Charter of Fundamental Rights: History and Prospects on Post-Lisbon Europe' *EUI Working Paper* Law 2011/08.
11. See most recently Case C-617/10 *Aklagaren v. Fransson*, judgment of 26 February 2013.

means, however, that absent the requisite link with EU law, the Charter will be of no help to those faced with potential human rights violations at the hands of a Member State. They will remain outside the scope of the Charter *ratione materiae*. Their remedy will remain within the realm of ECHR law and domestic human rights protection. Further, one Advocate General has concluded that Article 51(1) has a particularly restraining effect in private litigation. Advocate General Trstenjak has said that Article 51(1) shows an 'intentional restricting of the parties to whom fundamental rights are addressed',[12] so that the Charter cannot support disapplication of national laws in horizontal actions concerning private parties.[13]

Article 51 does not impose an analogous restriction on actions brought against EU institutions. Here the text is clear, the Charter is addressed to 'the institutions, bodies, offices and agencies of the Union'. However, the remedial standards for the enforcement of the Charter remain problematic for different reasons. None of the case law that I have mentioned above concerning the obligation to provide effective proportionate and dissuasive remedies is opposable to EU institutions. All of it is directed to actions which *Member State* courts are bound to take to enforce EU law, whether that be Charter rights or otherwise, and none of it, with the exception of the rules on liability for damages,[14] is relevant when determining the remedies which the General Court are bound to issue to correct violation of the Charter. Unlike the Member State Courts, the General Court is limited to the range of sanctions provided in the Treaties, and can take no unilateral action to ensure the provision of a remedy that is effective, proportionate, and dissuasive of breach.

Given that the Treaty of Lisbon preserved the restriction on the orders which the General Court is able to issue to (i) a declaration that the measure is void, leaving it to the institution concerned to take the appropriate action (Articles 264 and 266 TFEU) (ii) interim relief and suspensory measures (Articles 278 and 279 TFEU) and (iii) damages (Articles 268 and 340), the Charter, and in particular Article 47, cannot be expected to alleviate concerns on the difficulty of securing an effective judicial remedy before the General Court. Indeed, early indications are that the relaxation of the applicability of the *locus standi* rule on 'individual concern' that appeared in Article 263, so that it does not prevent nullity actions before the General Court with respect to 'a regulatory act which is of direct concern to [the applicant] and does not entail implementing measures' will not be susceptible to an applicant 'friendly' interpretation due to the legal obligations imposed by Article 47 of the Charter and the right to an effective remedy.[15] This means that, when failure to comply with the Charter is alleged against an EU institution, the primary avenue for securing its enforcement will remain Member State courts and Article 267 validity review.[16]

---

12. See para. 80 of her opinion in Case C-282/10 *Dominguez* judgment of 24 January 2012.
13. *Ibid.*, para. 83.
14. The liability of EU institutions to pay compensation was aligned with Member State liability in Case C-352/98 P *Bergaderm and Goupel v. Commission* [2000] ECR I-5291.
15. See Opinion of Advocate General Kokott in of 17 January 2013 in Case C-583/11P *Inuit Tapiriit Kanatami*, and the ruling before the General Court, T-18/10 of 6 September 2011.
16. D. Leczykiewicz 'Effective Judicial Protection' of Human Rights After Lisbon: Should National Courts be Empowered to Review EU Secondary Law?' 35 (2010) *ELRev* 326.

Moreover, the prospects for legislative intervention to correct enforcement problems arising from the limitations imposed by Article 51(1) on the enforceability of the Charter *ratione materiae* against Member States, or the remedial regime for challenging compliance of EU institutions with the Charter would appear to be slim. This is so because under Article 6(1) TEU it has been written into primary EU law that the 'provisions of the Charter shall not extend in any way the competences of the Union as defined in the Treaties.' Article 51(2) of the Charter repeats this, and adds that nor does the Charter 'establish any new power or task for the Union, or modify powers and tasks as defined in the Treaties.' Further, the last sentence of Article 51 provides that both the Member States and the EU institutions 'shall...respect the rights, observe the principles and promote the application thereof in accordance with their respective powers and respecting the limits of the powers of the Union as conferred on it in the Treaties;' Thus, if either of the difficulties here described are to be addressed by the EU legislature, this could only be done if legal bases otherwise available under the Lisbon Treaty could be identified. Depending on the precise legislative intervention taken, it is by no means a foregone conclusion that such a foundation exists.[17]

Finally, mention needs to be made of a provision of the Charter that has a limiting role that is of particular pertinence to its horizontal enforcement. Pursuant to Article 52(3), rights 'recognised by this Charter for which provision is made in the Treaties shall be exercised under the conditions and within the limits defined by those Treaties.' Classically, free movement of workers, the free movement of services, the freedom of establishment, and rights have been held to be directly effective horizontally.[18] These rights are also now reflected in the Charter, respectively, through combination of Articles 15(2) and 45.[19] While these rights remain enforceable horizontally, it does not appear to be open to the Court to interpret Articles 15(2) and 45 beyond the parameters of established principles of free movement law.

§14.03 HORIZONTAL EFFECTS OF THE CHARTER

Rosas and Armati identify three scenarios that are relevant to the discourse on horizontal direct effect of the Charter.[20] First, they note that in the case of litigation between private party (A) and a state authority (S) concerning a public measure which

17. During the drafting of the Charter, some Member States feared it would have a federalising device. In order to avoid this, Title VII was crafted. For a discussion see Lenaerts note 6 above at p. 376.
18. Case 36/74 *Walrave and Koch* [1974] ECR I-1405, para. 17; Case 13/76 *Donà* [1976] ECR I-1333, para. 17; C-415/93 *Bosman* [1995] ECR I-4921, para. 82; Joined cases C-51/96 and C- 197/97 *Deliège* [2000] ECR I-2549, para. 47; Case C-281/98 *Angonese* [2000] ECR I-4139, para. 31; Case C-309/99 *Wouters and Others* [2002] ECR I-1577, para. 120.
19. Article 15 (2) states that'Every citizen of the Union has the freedom to seek employment, to work, to exercise the right of establishment and to provide services in any Member State' while Article 45 provides that 'Every citizen of the Union has the right to move and freely reside within the territory of the Member States'. See C. Landenburger 'European Union Institutional Report' in J. Laffranque (ed) '*The Protection of Fundamental Rights Post-Lisbon: the interaction between the Charter of Fundamental Rights of the European Union, the Europan Convention on Human Rights and National Constitutions*', 142 at section 3.1.9.
20. See A. Rosas and L. Armati *EU Constitutional Law* (Hart Publishing, 2012) pp. 179 - 180.

is addressed to another private party, a triangular situation arises, which they point out is not a question of horizontal direct effect in the proper sense, but it contains horizontal elements.[21] It is interesting to note, however, that if a public measure of this kind were promulgated by an EU institution, the remedial consequences for the party seeking to challenge it for breach of fundamental rights would be significant. I will address this question in Part IV below.

Rosas and Armati also refer to the situation where, in a civil dispute between two private parties, one of them argues that a Member State measure does not comply with EU law.[22] Under this scenario, national judges are bound to disapply national measures that are inconsistent with general principles of EU law, such as the prohibition on discrimination on the basis of age (now reflected in Article 21 of the Charter) when the inconsistency arises within the field of application of relevant EU legislation. Thus, the case law supporting this principle suggest that, to the extent to which an established general principle of law has been re-stated in the Charter, it will have full horizontal direct effect in civil litigation of this kind, by 'trumping' any inconsistent national measures, the private nature of the dispute notwithstanding, and provided that the general principle is supported by EU legislation.[23] This situation too creates interesting remedial issues that will be explored in Part IV.

Finally, Rosas and Armati refer to the scenario in which a civil dispute between two private parties does not concern any state or public measure. This they describe as a 'bilateral' rather than a 'triangular' situation. This situation entails a clash of rights, in which one party is seeking to rely on fundamental right A, with the other seeking to rely on fundamental right B, and both A and B have the status of horizontally directly effective rights.[24] As will be explained in Part IV below, this type of problem is governed, by the Court's limited by important case law on the right to an effective remedy in fully horizontal situations.[25]

21. They cite Case C-112/00 *Schmidberger* [2003] ECR I-5659 and note that in that case the state invoked freedom of assembly (see Charter Article 12) and freedom of expression (see Charter Article 11) enjoyed by another private party as against A's rights under the law on the free movement of goods. in pending Case C-536/11 *Donau Chemie* the Court will again be asked to consider thus type of triangular problem. Here a private sector actors is invoking the Article 47 right to effective judicial protection against an organ of the state, which is in turn relying on the privilege against self-incrimination and the rights of the defence of a third (private) party to resist the action. The rights of the defence are now protected by Article 48 (2) of the Charter.
22. They cite Case C-144/04 *Mangold* [2005] ECR I-9981 and Case C-555/07 *Kücükdeveci* [2010] ECR I-365; Case C-71/02 *Karner* [2004] ECR I-3025; Case C-244/06 *Dynamic Medien* [2008] ECR I-505. To these examples I would add Case C-282/10 *Dominguez*, judgment of 24 January 2012, which concerned whether national legislation was inconsistent with the right to paid annual leave. The Court held at para. 16 that the right to paid annual leave is a particularly important principle of EU social law, without acknowledging that it is now protected by Article 31 (2) of the Charter. The triangular situation, in which a piece of national legislation was argued to be inconsistent with fundamental rights, in a dispute of a purely private nature, was also considered by the Court in Case C-400/10 PPU *Mc B* [2010] ECR I-8 965.
23. For a detailed discussion of horizontal direct effect of general principles see Safjan and Miklaszewicz note 1 above.
24. They cite C-438/05 *International Transport Workers Federation (Viking Line)* [2007] ECR I-10779 and C-341/05 *Laval* [2007] ECR I-11 767.
25. See notably Case C-295/04 and C-298/04 *Manfredi* [2006] ECR I-6619 and Case C-453/99 *Courage Crehan* [2001] ECR I-6297.

To these examples I would add two more. Given that the Charter has the 'same legal value' as the Treaties, as prescribed by Article 6(1) TEU, and forms part of the 'primary' law of the EU,[26] it can always be used as an aid to interpretation in the event of any ambiguity in either treaty, regulations, directives, and decisions, or in Member State laws that implement EU measures. The doctrine of sympathetic interpretation, as it is known, has been applied to both Treaty articles[27] and Directives,[28] while the pertinence of Regulations to support civil actions has long been established.[29] This suggests that it is incontrovertible that the Charter can be used for the same purpose, at least when there is argument over the meaning of any of the legal measures here mentioned in civil actions.[30]

The doctrine of sympathetic interpretation will perhaps be of most use in the enforcement of provisions of the Charter that amount to legal principles as opposed to rights Pursuant to Article 52(5) of the Charter, principles are only 'judicially cognizable' with respect to the interpretation of EU and Member State legislative and executive acts that implement them. According to the explanations, Charter Articles 25 and 26 on the rights of the elderly and integration of persons with disabilities, and Article 37 on environmental protection are examples of principles, while other Charter articles may contain elements of both a right and a principle. The provisions mentioned within this rubric are Article 23 on equality between men and women, Article 33 on family and professional life, and Article 34 on social security and social assistance. It has also been suggested that Article 22 on cultural and linguistic diversity, Article 35(2) which guarantees a high level of human health protection, and Article 36, access to services of a general economic interest and promotion of social and territorial cohesion are all principles.[31]

Here too complex questions arise with respect to the sanctions that might be imposable by Member State Courts in civil litigation. Occasionally, the Court of Justice has applied the right to an effective remedy in a context in which the doctrine of sympathetic interpretation was the EU constitutional norm pertinent to the resolution of a dispute,[32] but the reasoning accompanying these decisions has not always been full. This question too will be address in Part IV below.[33]

Finally, no discussion of the horizontal effects of the Charter would be complete without special reference to the special nature of Article 47. This provision, I would argue, is horizontal by virtue of its content because it guarantees to '[e]veryone whose

26. See note 7 above.
27. E ;G C-165/91 *Simon J Munster* [1994] ECR I-4661 at paragpraph 34.
28. Established in Case C-106/89 *Marleasing* [1990] ECR I - 4135
29. Case C-253/00 *Muñoz v. Frumar* [2002] ECR I-7 289.
30. For a notable example see Case C-282/10 *Dominguez*, judgment of 24 January 2012.
31. J. Laffranque 'General Report' in of J. Laffranque (ed) '*The Protection of Fundamental Rights Post-Lisbon: the interaction between the Charter of Fundamental Rights of the European Union, the European Convention on Human Rights and National Constitutions*' p. 63 at p. 110.
32. See notably Case C-185/97 *Coote v. Granada Hospitalty* 1998] ECR I-5199, which concerned enforcement of a Directive by one private party against another. See also Case C-268/06 *Impact* [2008] ECR I-2483 and Case C-444/09 *Gavierro* [2010] ECR I-14031
33. For further reflections see D. Leczykiewicz 'Horizontal Application of the Charter of Fundamental Rights' un-published manuscript on file with the author.

rights and freedoms guaranteed by law of the Union are violated has the right to an effective remedy before a tribunal'. In other words, if the substantive right or freedom that has been breached is horizontal in nature such as, for example, rights protected under Regulations,[34] or treaty provisions that have horizontal direct effect, then an effective remedy must necessarily follow. This means, therefore, that the substantive guarantees reflected in the Article 47 right to an effective remedy[35] are opposable to civil litigation as soon as it is shown that one private party has failed to respect an EU principle *vis à vis* another private party, when that norm has horizontal direct effect.[36]

§14.04 MEMBER STATE REMEDIES IN A PRIVATE LAW CONTEXT

The most striking consequence of attempting to connect the Court's case law on effective remedies, with its rulings to date on the legal effect of the Charter, is the extent to which the two bodies of principle do not easily match. Originally, the Court's case law on provision of effective, non-discriminatory remedies literally 'piggy-backed' on its case law on direct effect and indeed, it was not until that ruling in Joined Cases C – 6/90 and C-9/90 *Francovich*[37] that it became clear that Member States courts would be bound to supply such sanctions, and more specifically damages, in a context in which an EU measure lacked direct effect but nonetheless vested individuals with rights.

However, the Court of Justice is yet to vest any provision of the Charter with 'direct effect', or indeed declare that an Article of the Charter vests individuals with rights. So far, the Charter has most commonly invoked as an aid to interpretation of relevant EU legislation and/or the corresponding implementing measure,[38] with the high water-mark, perhaps, of the Court's case law tying Member States to exercise discretion available to them under EU legislation in conformity with the Charter.[39] As I have mentioned above, additional influence of the Charter on national law has been secured through the construction of a delicate bridge between the Charter and general principles of law,[40] so that, as discussed in section §14.03 above, Charter articles that are equally reflected in general principles require disapplication of inconsistent national measures, when a Charter article is relied on in an EU legislative context in private litigation.[41]

34. See Case C-253/00 *Muñoz v. Frumar* [2002] ECR I-7 289
35. See notably Case C-69/10 *Diouf* of 28 July 2011.
36. One commentator has put the field of application of Article 47 even higher, and has argued as follows: 'For Article 47 to apply, it suffices that a litigant can convincingly claim, in a national court, to have a subjective right under Union law (other than the Charter) that might be violated by a national act. Then that court is required to perform its role as Union court under Article 19 TEU by granting judicial protection, and its action is covered by Article 47, regardless of any connection between the national act challenged and Union law and whether the subjective right eventually proves to exist'. See Ladenburger, cited note 19 above, para. 3.1.9.
37. Joined Cases C-6/90 and C-9/90 *Francovich* [1991] ECR I-5357.
38. See e.g. Case C-282/10 *Dominguez*, judgment of 24 January 2012 and Case C-400/10 PPU *Mc B* [2010] ECR I-8 965.
39. Joined Cases C-411/10 and C-493/10 *NS*, judgment of 21 December 2011.
40. See most notably Case C-282/10 *Dominguez*, judgment of 24 January 2012 and Case C-400/10 PPU *Mc B* [2010] ECR I-8 965.
41. See note above 23.

Of the three scenarios isolated by Rosas and Armati, the remedial aspects of only two of them have been directly addressed in the case law. With respect to case example 1, in which one private party challenges a public measure directed at another party, two sub-divisions can be discerned. The first appertains to challenge to Member State conduct taken in the context of implementation of an EU measure. Here it is established that, even if the EU measure underpinning Member State action is a Directive, the full gamut of EU rules on Member State remedies and procedures will continue to apply, even though consequence follow for the legal position of another private party who might otherwise have been able to rely on the horizontal direct effect of a directive.[42] In Case C-201/02 *Delena Wells*,[43] in the context of a case concerning enforcement of the Environmental Assessment Directive[44] by a private individual against a Member State government agency, the Court of Justice put to one side the ramifications of the action for the developer. It was held that 'mere adverse repercussions on the rights of third parties, even if the repercussions are certain, do not justify preventing an individual from invoking the provisions of a directive against the Member State concerned'.[45] The Court went on to apply its classical formula, and held that the detailed procedural rules to allow this to occur were within the province of the Member States, subject to the principles of effectiveness and non-discrimination.[46] Significantly, the Court made no reference to whether or not the relevant provisions of the Environmental Assessment Directive was directly effective, but rather alluded to relevant parts of that Directive as measures which individuals were entitled to invoke in the event of Member State conduct that was inconsistent with them.[47]

This means, therefore, that the same principle should apply when a Charter provision is pertinent to the interpretation of a Directive vesting individuals with rights, or indeed a Regulation, in cases in which non-compliance thereof is alleged against Member State agencies. Any national rules that impedes the full effectiveness of the Charter provision, as rendered pertinent by the need to interpret EU legislation in conformity with it, will need to be set aside. Under the Court's classical case law, such measures include onerous rules of evidence,[48] unreasonable time limits,[49] and disproportionate barriers to the availability of interim relief.[50] In defined circumstances, and provided the measure concerned vests individuals with rights, it can also entitle those affected to damages.[51]

The legal architecture, however for instituting legal challenge when an EU measure underpins this type of triangular situation is somewhat different. When an EU measure is addressed to a person other than the person who wishes to challenge it, as

42. See classically Case C-91/92 *Faccini Dori* [1994] ECR I-325.
43. [2004] ECR I-723.
44. Directive 85/337 OJ 1985 L 175, p. 40.
45. Note 43 above at para. 57.
46. Note 43 above para. 67.
47. Case C-201/02 *Delena Wells* [2004] ECR I-723 paras 55 to 58
48. Eg Case C-199/82 *San Giorgio* [1983] ECR 3595
49. Eg Case C-188/95 *Fantask* [1997] ECR I-6783.
50. Considered, for example, in Case C-432/05 *Unibet* [2007] ECR I-2271.
51. See classically Joined Cases C-46/93 and 48/93 *Brasserie d Pëcheur and Factortame III* [1996] ECR I-1029.

I have pointed out above, direct access to the General Court is normally precluded.[52] As mentioned above, the remedial obligations of the General Court are different from those of the Member State Courts. Thus, if a private party wishes to challenge an EU measure for non-compliance with the Charter, or to seek an interpretation of the relevant EU measure in conformity with it, they will need to do so via the national courts, and seek an Article 267 reference to the Court of Justice. Criticism of this procedure has been well documented elsewhere.[53] They include delay, difficulties in persuading a national judge to make the reference,[54] and the need to isolate a national implementing measure so that a Member State court can take jurisdiction. To this I would add, in the context of validity review, the need to establish that a provision of the Charter reflects a general principle of law, given that there has been no indication to date in the case law of the Court of Justice that mere infringement of the Charter is a basis for validity challenge.

Of the three scenarios for horizontal effect of the Charter described by Rosas and Armati, example 3 fits most easily into the Court's established case law. It will be recalled that case study 2 entailed a situation in which a civil dispute between two private parties did not concern any state or public measure, but rather involved competition between, or clash of rights. Here the case law of the Court of Justice has been clear. In the leading Case of C – 453/99 *Courage Crehan*[55] the Court considered the obligations on national courts when one private party sought enforcement of Article 101 of the TFEU against another, a measure having horizontal direct effect, in circumstances in which a rule of national law precluded the institution of proceedings. There the Court of Justice reverted to its classical jurisprudence, citing authority such as *van Gend en Loos* and *Costa*, both of which were elaborated in vertical situations against the state. The salient passages of the *Courage Crehan* judgment merit reproduction. They are as follows:

> 19. It should be borne in mind, first of all, that the Treaty has created its own legal order, which is integrated into the legal systems of the Member States and which their courts are bound to apply. The subjects of that legal order are not only the Member States but also their nationals. Just as it imposes burdens on individuals, Community law is also intended to give rise to rights which become part of their legal assets. Those rights arise not only where they are expressly granted by the Treaty but also by virtue of obligations which the Treaty imposes in a clearly defined manner both on individuals and on the Member States and the Community institutions (see the judgments in Case 26/62 *Van Gend en Loos* [1963] ECR 1, Case 6/64 *Costa* [1964] ECR 585 and Joined Cases C-6/90 and C-9/90 *Francovich and Others* [1991] ECR I-5357, paragraph 31).
> 20. Secondly, according to Article 3(g) of the EC Treaty (now, after amendment, Article 3(1)(g) EC), Article 85 of the Treaty constitutes a fundamental provision which is essential for the accomplishment of the tasks entrusted to the

52. For a recent assessment see Opinion of Advocate General Kokott in of 17 January 2013 in Case C-583/11P *Inuit Tapiriit Kanatami*.
53. See the Opinion of Advocate General Jacobs in Case C-50/00 P *UPA* [2002] ECR I-6677; D. Leczykiewicz 'Effective Judicial Protection' of Human Rights After Lisbon: Should National Courts be Empowered to Review EU Secondary Law?' 35 (2010) *ELRev* 326.
54. Case C-314/85 *Foto-Frost* [1987] ECR 4199.
55. C-453/99 *Crehan* [2001] ECR I-6279.

> Community and, in particular, for the functioning of the internal market (judgment in Case C-126/97 *Eco Swiss* [1999] ECR I-3055, paragraph 36)....
> 23. Thirdly, it should be borne in mind that the Court has held that Article 85(1) of the Treaty and Article 86 of the EC Treaty (now Article 82 EC) produce direct effects in relations between individuals and create rights for the individuals concerned which the national courts must safeguard (judgments in Case 127/73 *BRT and SABAM* [1974] ECR 51, paragraph 16, ('*BRT I*') and Case C-282/95 P *Guérin Automobiles* v *Commission* [1997] ECR I-1503, paragraph 39).
> 24. It follows from the foregoing considerations that any individual can rely on a breach of Article 85(1) of the Treaty before a national court even where he is a party to a contract that is liable to restrict or distort competition within the meaning of that provision.
> 25. As regards the possibility of seeking compensation for loss caused by a contract or by conduct liable to restrict or distort competition, it should be remembered from the outset that, in accordance with settled case-law, the national courts whose task it is to apply the provisions of Community law in areas within their jurisdiction must ensure that those rules take full effect and must protect the rights which they confer on individuals (see *inter alia* the judgments in Case 106/77 *Simmenthal* [1978] ECR 629, paragraph 16, and in Case C-213/89 *Factortame* [1990] ECR I-2433, paragraph 19).
> 26. The full effectiveness of Article 85 of the Treaty and, in particular, the practical effect of the prohibition laid down in Article 85(1) would be put at risk if it were not open to any individual to claim damages for loss caused to him by a contract or by conduct liable to restrict or distort competition...
> 28. There should not therefore be any absolute bar to such an action being brought by a party to a contract which would be held to violate the competition rules.

These principles bode well for litigants who might wish to challenge deficient Member State remedial regimes in a context in which a Charter right is fully horizontally enforceable, and the case concerns a clash of rights between private parties rather than Member State laws that are alleged to be incompatible with EU measures. Just as the obstructive rule in issue in *Courage Crehan* had to be set aside, so too would any national measure that impeded the enforcement of Charter rights having horizontal direct effect. Further, all of the principles elaborated by the Court in *Courage Crehan* concenring effective remedies are equally opposable to a Charter context; Charter rights must take full effect, and they would, in practical terms, be equally compromised if it were not open to individuals to claim damages.

Of the three scenarios described by Rosas and Armati, the second is most problematic from the point of view of remedies. What remedial rules of EU law apply when one of the parties in horizontal litigation is able to show incompatibility of national law with a general principle of EU law, and which is also reflected in the Charter, when the case falls within the field of application of EU law by virtue, for example, of the pertinence of a Regulation or a Directive to the dispute? This situation is problematic because of the dearth of Court of Justice authority on the duty of national courts, with respect to remedies, when the case does not concern directly effective EU measures, or rules vesting individuals with rights, but enforcement of general principles. There has simply been no flow of case law under the Article 267 reference mechanism in which private parties have sought to argue that a national sanction or procedural rules obstructs the enforcement of general principles. How then, might the Court of Justice deal with this problem if it arises in the context of general principles which are supported by the Charter in horizontal cases?

I would suggest that the answer to this lies in the combined force of Article 47 of the Charter and Article 19(1) TEU. As noted above Article 47 obliges tribunals to supply an effective remedy whenever 'rights and freedoms guaranteed by law of the Union are violated'. Article 19(1) TEU states that Member States (and thus the Courts) shall provide remedies sufficient to ensure effective legal protection in the 'fields covered by Union law.' These two provisions combined point firmly toward application of the Court's remedial case law in our example 2 scenario in which national law obstructs the application of general principles in horizontal situations, even though this consequence has not been a prominent feature of the Court's remedial case law to date.

Mention should also be made of the position, with respect to remedies when an EU measure does not vest individuals with rights, but is not the less relevant to a dispute as an aid to interpretation. This so-called doctrine of sympathetic interpretation arises when a directive is being invoked by one private party against another, and requires relevant national laws to be interpreted in conformity with the directive, provided that this does not result in *contra legum* interpretation.[56] If a Charter article is pertinent in the context of such disputes, the relevant directive must undoubtedly be interpreted, in turn, in conformity with that Charter provision. But does this mean that the Court's case law on effective, proportionate and dissuasive remedies is also applicable to this type of dispute?

The ruling of the Court of Justice in Case C-185/97 *Coote v. Granada Hospitality*[57] suggests that they would. That case concerned interpretation of Directive 76/207 on the implementation of the principle of equal treatment for men and women as regards access to employment, vocational training, promotion and working conditions,[58] and which an individual alleged that national remedies provide an insufficient deterrent against breach of the principle of equal treatment between men and women, which is now enshrined in Charter Article 21(1). Given that the former employer was a private sector actor, the doctrine of sympathetic interpretation, rather than direct effect or individual rights, was the only argument available to Mrs Coote for bringing the directive into the national proceedings. Nonetheless, the Court held:

> that all persons have the right to obtain an effective remedy in a competent court against measures which they consider to interfere with the equal treatment for men and women laid down in the Directive. It is for the Member States to ensure effective judicial control of compliance with the applicable provisions of Community law and of national legislation intended to give effect tothe rights for which the Directive provides.[59]

56. Se classically Case C-106/89 *Marleasing* [1990] ECR I-4135. See more recently Case C-282/10 *Dominguez*, judgment of 24 January 2012
57. [1998] ECR I-5199.
58. OJ 1976 L 39 p. 40.
59. Note 57 above at para. 22.

However, there is tension between the findings of the Court of Justice in *Coote* and some of its more recent authority. For example, it was held in Case C – 268/06 *Impact*,[60] that, if a national Court were to find that the system of remedies and procedural rules set by national law to safeguard rights protected by EU law infringed the principle of effectiveness, then it would be for the national court to '*interpret* the domestic jurisdictional rules in such a way that, wherever possible, they contribute to the attainment of the objective of ensuring effective judicial protection of an individual's rights under Community law' (my emphasis).[61] This would appear to be a more modest obligation on the national court than that imposed by the Court of Justice in *Coote*. Thus the route to be taken by the Court in any future cases on effective remedies and interpretation of the Charter is by no means clear.

Finally, it should be apparent from the above discussion that, to some degree, the question of whether specific Charter articles are directly effective, or vest individuals with rights, is to some degree academic in any debate concerning their enforability. As explained in section §14.03 above the remit of the Charter is limited, due to Article 51(2) and Article 6(1) TEU competence *ratione mataerie* of the Union, and the Charter cannot be called in aid to extend it. Thus, the Charter can only ever be of relevance when either (i) interpretation of the Treaty provisions is in issue (ii) the EU has exercised its competence to pass measures in a field in which power has been attributed to it, or (iii) arguably, the Union has such competence but is yet to exercise it. Therefore, in the vast majority of cases, the Charter will enter the fray as a secondary norm to buttress either existing Treaty rights or rights protected in an EU legislative measure of some kind. The exception to this may be the determination of whether breach of a particular Charter article vests individuals with rights for the purposes of state liability (provided of course that the breach has occurred within EU competence)[62] given that State liability has evolved as a discrete area of legal principle.

§14.05 CONCLUSION

It is to be hoped, therefore that, despite the initial impression of 'orthodoxy' presented by the Charter, in the sense of securing enforcement of its terms against governmental agencies only (whether they be EU or Member State) the established case law of the Court on effective judicial protection, and the obligation on Member States to respect general principles of EU law in the legislative process, has provided potential, which is not insignificant, for certain Charter articles to be enforceable horizontally, including an obligation of some kind on national courts to secure adequate remedial protection. This may be particularly so with respect to Charter rights that are fleshed out by EU legislative measures. As one Advocate General observed:

---

60. [2008] ECR I-2483.
61. *Ibid.*, at para. 54. See similarly Case C-240/09 *Lesoochranárske zoskupenie* [2011] ECR I-1255, para. 51.
62. For a detailed discussion see A. Ward 'Damages under the EU Charter' *ERA Forum* 12 (2012) p. 589.

> [G]iven the ever increasing intervention of Community law in relations between private persons, the Court will, in my view, be inevitably confronted with other situations which raise the question of the right to rely, in proceedings between private persons, on directives which contribute to ensuring observance of fundamental rights. Those situations will probably increase in number if the Charter of Fundamental Rights of the European Union becomes legally binding in the future, since among the fundamental rights contained in that charter are a number which are already part of the existing body of Community law in the form of directives.[63]

Yet the case law is the most highly evolved, I would argue, in the context in which individuals seek to enforce competing horizontal rights against one another, given that the detailed principles on effective remedies elaborated by the Court of Justice in *Courage and Crehan*[64] is directly opposable to this situation. Perhaps ironically, the remedial landscape remains the most pessimistic in the context of calling EU institutions to account for compliance with an 'EU' Charter, given the subsisting complexities in the judicial architecture for instituting and completing such actions.

63. See the Opinion of AG Bot in *Kücükdeveci* note above 22.
64. Note above 55.

Part IV: Competition Law and General Principles

CHAPTER 15

From Regulation 17/62 to Article 52 of the Charter of Fundamental Rights

Ian S.Forrester[*]

§15.01 INTRODUCTION

This article will review some features of the procedural history of European competition law to consider whether the current regime is acceptable in the light of the Charter of Fundamental Rights[1] which now forms an integral part of the EU legal framework.

In the early days, the Commission was the policy-maker, and it was obviously an administration with cautious habits. It was the Commission which drafted the block exemptions, which set its enforcement priorities, which chose which law to make via its rare flagship decisions, which imposed penalties, and which spoke up for the principle of competition within the deliberations of the European institutions. Its quite rare decisions were often selected to advance the law rather than to resolve a particular conflict.

The Commission's decision-making processes were adopted in 1962 and have not fundamentally changed since then. Although they have been improved, they

* Queen's Counsel at the Scots Bar; Honorary Professor, University of Glasgow; White & Case, Brussels. I thank Marika Harjula, Solicitor of the Bar of England and Wales, and Emilie Eriksson, *jur.kand.* (Sweden), for ideas and insights. I have written more fully about the themes covered in this paper in a number of articles, including: *A Bush in Need of Pruning: the Luxuriant Growth of 'Light Judicial Review'*, European Competition Law Annual 2009: The Evaluation of Evidence and its Judicial Review in Competition Cases, Oxford and Portland Oregon (2011); *Due Process in EC competition cases: a distinguished institution with flawed procedures* (2009) 34 E.L. Rev. 817; *A Challenge for Europe's Judges: The Review of Fines in Competition Cases* (2011) 36 E.L.Rev. 185.

1. The Charter of Fundamental Rights of the European Union, 2010 OJ C 83/389, which has the same legal value as the Treaties, according to Article 6(1) of the Treaty of the European Union. The Charter is binding on the EU institutions, according to Article 51(1) of the Charter.

remain administrative, not prosecutorial. I respectfully suggest that in light of the Commission's current role, and its policies and fining practices, these procedures are now inadequate. It would be foolish to say that they always condemn innocent companies. Indeed, the system yields 'acquittals' in the sense that allegations in the statement of objections may be abandoned or narrowed in the final decision. Officials are careful to respect the interests of the defence within the framework ascribed to them. Nor do I assert that those who engage in cartel activity should be generously treated. I simply add my voice to the groundswell of opinion in favour of procedures that are worthy of the distinguished institution and appropriate for the important role it discharges.

§15.02 THE EARLY DAYS

Since *BRT SABAM*,[2] it has been known that the competition rules[3] had direct effect and could be invoked in national courts. However, there was an unreality which muddled the process of the analysis of whether a problem existed. The prohibition of Article 85(1)[4] was deemed to have a broad, extensive scope. It caught (according to the Commission's conservative choice of enforcement priorities in the early 1960s) both basically good agreements which had restrictive features but achieved and pursued a pro-competitive goal, and basically bad agreements which could not be redeemed. The reach was therefore vast: tens of thousands of agreements signed each year containing exclusivity provisions were in theory caught by Article 85(1), rendered null by Article 85(2)[5] and were theoretically liable to fines. If they did not fit the narrow confines of the available block exemptions, the theoretically indispensable remedy against unenforceability and fines was the filing of a notification seeking an exemption. In theory, exemptions would be granted on their merits. In reality, exemptions were almost never granted in specific cases. Specific exemption decisions were reserved for interesting and important cases where the Commission wished to make new law (or soft targets, like trade fairs, which could be good for the statistics).[6]

The Commission was the only entity which could grant exemptions. Courts could not do so. As a result, much legal and procedural creativity was deployed: national courts preferred to find that Article 85(1) was inapplicable, to avoid ceding jurisdiction to the Commission.

This history is still relevant today. There is a link between procedural and substantive law. National courts will seek to escape the constitutional consequences of

---

2. Case 127/73, *BRT v. SABAM* [1974] ECR 313. See e.g. Ian Forrester, *Jurisdiction of National and Community bodies in competition matters after SABAM*, Common Market Law Review (1974).
3. Former Articles 85 and 86 of the Treaty of Rome.
4. Now Article 101(1).
5. Now Article 101(2).
6. Among the trade fair and bourse cases were decisions on office equipment (*VIFKA*, 1986 OJ L 291/46); freight futures (*Baltic Freight Futures Exchange Limited (BIFFEX)*, 1987 OJ L 222/24); dentistry equipment (*International Dentalschau*, 1987 OJ L 293/48 and *British Dental Trade Association*, 1988 OJ L 233/15); and machine tools (*CECIO/EMO*, 1989 OJ L 37/11).

European competition law if the consequences of strictly applying it seem unpalatable. If courts feel that the procedures strictly applicable can lead to unjust results, the substantive law will be adapted. It is not a coincidence that in the United States, while dire procedural entanglements await those credibly accused in the civil courts of anti-trust infringements, the courts are conservative, indeed reluctant, in recognizing new categories of anti-trust infringement. Intellectual creativity by plaintiffs and enforcers is more welcome in Brussels.

Because of the primary role of the Commission, great (maybe excessive) weight was in the past attached to any indication of its opinion on the merits, and the Commission was correspondingly exceedingly cautious in expressing any view to assist the courts in applying EC law in national litigation. It developed the 'comfort letter', which was less than an exemption but more than a silence in response to a notification. The comfort letter was a source of some reassurance in the sense that it confirmed the Commission had no fundamental concerns; but it was a source of discomfort in that it gave no exemption even where Article 85(1) applied (and therefore nullity was a theoretical consequence).

There arose cases of tension between the determinations of national judges and European proceedings. The handling of national litigations unfolds according to quite well-established procedures, according to a predictable timetable. Commission proceedings were far from predictable. Decisions were few and rare, sometimes as few as ten per year, reserved for flagship cases where the Commission wanted to advance the law. Indeed, this unpredictability made judges reluctant to cede responsibility to a public authority which was notably slow. Although the issues at stake were not as serious as today, and although there was more acceptance of the Commission's role as defender of the faith, it was evident that a Commission decision was more of an accusatory than a judicial document. And since in many cases there was likely not to be a decision, an excessive amount of energy was devoted to arguing propositions such as 'If the Commission were to decide, it would find in my client's favour'. And when they did emerge, decisions would often lack the judicious review of both sides of the argument which a court would normally deploy. The law developed, a rather small number of decisions was taken, and a number of judgments handed down, the shadow of which, especially in dominance cases, still influences today's law and practice.

§15.03 THE FIRST ROUND OF REFORM

The next phase of competition law history can be marked from the adoption of the EU's first Merger Regulation 4064/89 on 21 December 1989. It came into force on 21 September 1990.[7] Now, a merger control regime had been proposed by the Commission as early as 1973. Member States had differing opinions on whether and how mergers should be controlled at Community level. There were doubts as to whether the Commission, which in its antitrust function was slow, perfectionist and reluctant to say

7. Regulation 4064/1989 was amended by Regulation 1310/97 and repealed and replaced in 2004 by the current Merger Regulation, Regulation 139/2004.

'no' (and even more reluctant to say 'yes'), would be capable of taking decisions in a prompt and timely fashion. However, to the surprise of many, including myself, the Commission was able to produce high quality business-like decisions addressing the key points of a contemplated merger.

During 1991, the first full year of operation for the Merger Regulation,[8] the Merger Task Force received sixty-three notifications and disposed of sixty. It found in five cases that the transaction did not fall within the Regulation (either too small or not a concentration). It blessed fifty transactions under Article 6(1)(b) as raising no serious doubts. In six cases, serious doubts were raised and the procedure of thorough investigation began. In four cases, the transaction was declared compatible with the Common Market, subject (in three of the four cases) to the giving of certain undertakings. A fifth case had not been disposed of at the end of 1991. In the most celebrated case, *Aerospatiale-Alenia/de Havilland,*[9] there was a declaration of incompatibility. The Commission's first condemnation of a notified merger aroused fierce political debate, aligned largely along national lines. The responsible Commissioner, Sir Leon Brittan, was subject to extravagant criticisms in a debate before the European Parliament, and there was extensive governmental lobbying. However, the decision was made and was procedurally respected. No political crisis was created, a confirmation of the maturity of EC competition policy.

Since the adoption of the Merger Regulation the Commission has cleared more than 4,600 transactions and blocked twenty-two.[10] Experience did not confirm early fears of slow, bureaucratic or overly burdensome application of the Regulation. The demands for information have been less extravagant than is routine in the US. Small teams of officials have been able to make a thorough and realistic assessment of each pending transaction, and to do so conclusively, in most cases, within a fixed (though frequently elastic in the sense of being liable to postponement) period. Thus the legal certainty of a specific transaction was delivered routinely by the Merger Task Force. Its decisions were clear, untheoretical, and straightforward. Of course, they were often controversial. Thus the Commission had shown its capacity to reach practical, workmanlike decisions inside a quite short time. The process of getting a merger blessed is intensely confrontational and involves the balancing of contrasting predictions of future events. While its decisions on mergers were occasionally challenged, its rare judicial reverses have enhanced the Commission's credibility.

The story is different with respect to antitrust, notably the repression of cartels, which was transformed by the adoption of the European leniency programme. The earlier adoption by the US authorities of a successful regime offered important advantages in exchange for being the first to confess and to implicate. Despite initial reluctance, the Commission adopted a regime which offered powerful incentives to the first participant in cartels to confess with full details incriminating other participants.

---

8. Regulation 4064/89, 1989 OJ L 395/1.
9. Commission Decision 91/619/EEC, Case IV/M05, *Aerospatiale-Alenia/de Havilland*, 1991 OJ L 334/42.
10. Commissioner Almunia speech: http://europa.eu/rapid/press-release_SPEECH-12-917_en.htm.

One procedural consequence of the success of the leniency programme has been that delations of supposed co-conspirators have increased. The classic chain of events is that a business with a guilty conscience approaches the Commission to report that it has discovered its sales managers have been participating in secret, imprudent and illegal meetings with competitors, and that each of several named people (nearly always men) had participated in these meetings for years. As a condition of not being fined, the confessing company implicates its fellow competitors. There is an interest in accusing them widely of grave economic wrong-doing or plain criminality, and an evident risk of error, embellishment or exaggeration. Such circumstances call for rigorous checking of facts and identities.

Article 16 of Regulation 1/2003 provides that a national court ruling on anti-competitive practices which are already the subject of a Commission decision 'cannot take decisions running counter to the decision adopted by the Commission'. The green shoots (or black ones, depending on one's viewpoint) of follow-on damages actions by aggrieved competitors and customers are appearing in national courts in several Member States (especially England), encouraged by the Commission and the promise of riches on an American litigation scale.

Criminal liability can flow in some Member States for individuals inculpated by Commission findings. I believe that as of the writing of this article, no citizen is in prison in Europe for cartel offences (though several have been tried), but the day will soon come when that will no longer be the case. Dozens of Europeans are in American prisons for cartel offences. These potential consequences in national law are a further reason to demand rigour in Brussels.

§15.04 DECENTRALIZATION AND WIDER ENFORCEMENT

On 1 May 2004, Regulation 17 of 1962 was replaced by Regulation 1/2003 which brought major changes to the Commission's enforcement powers.[11] The Commission surrendered its Article 85(3) monopoly powers, both the abolition of the notification system ('do nothing without seeking Commission blessing'), and the abolition of its monopoly over exemptions ('only the Commission can be trusted to interpret Article 85(3)'). It shared enforcement, thus bringing into being a decentralization of power towards national authorities. This was matched by a surge in cooperation between national competition agencies and a rise in private enforcement.

Competition law is increasingly important around the world, and the European Commission is probably its most influential public enforcer, because it is usually more radical than its US counterparts and is subject to lighter judicial review. This brings us to how Commission decisions are taken, a topic which is familiar, but which is also troubling.

11. Ian Forrester, *Sector-Specific Price Regulation or Antitrust Regulation – A Plague on Both Your Houses?*, European Competition Law Annual 2007: A Reformed Approach to Article 82 EC, Hart Publishing (2008).

§15.05 HOW COMMISSION DECISIONS ARE TAKEN

If we work backwards from the decision itself, we may note the circumstances in which the decision is taken. A College of twenty-seven Commissioners (soon to be twenty-eight when Croatia arrives) sits round a table (usually on a Wednesday) with the Secretary General of the Commission, and adopts a number of decisions on important matters falling within its remit. The Commission is an international organization, so its role and functioning is different to that of a national cabinet of ministers, but there are similarities in that each Member of the Commission is (like a minister in a national government) responsible for a different portfolio, that there is collective responsibility, and that deals between Commissioners are hammered out politically with give-and-take reflecting the portfolios, nationalities and political persuasions of the Commissioners.

It is therefore possible that the disposition of a particular competition case may be the subject of political lobbying to any Commissioner, or to the Commissioner specifically responsible for competition matters. Most competition law practitioners in Brussels can cite several examples. In the modern convention, the Competition Commissioner endeavours to limit the number of communications of a lobbying nature which are made to him or her directly; and if one side is received by the Commissioner, all sides will likely be received. Other Commissioners are certainly in the habit of receiving representations from governments, companies and trade associations relevant to pending competition cases. I know of at least one celebrated case (in the 1990s) where the decision was adopted as part of the unblocking of a number of stalled dossiers. Thus the imposition of anti-dumping duty on bicycle parts, the protection of the herring population, and the taking of a controversial competition decision could be traded-off the one against the other. It is of, course, welcome that in modern practice the Competition Commissioner and his cabinet try to limit the opportunity for political lobbying by governments, compatriots, interested parties or others. However, it cannot be justified that a political body staffed by political figures takes decisions on guilt or innocence or imposes penalties of criminal severity.

Administrations can regulate, legislate, investigate and reach conclusions with perfect propriety. They can, in certain cases, impose penalties, as do tax authorities, refuse collectors, and parking administrators. A cabinet of ministers cannot vote on the guilt or innocence of a company accused of an economic crime. It is unimaginable that a new Member State would be allowed to adopt a competition law regime under which the Prime Minister and cabinet of the country decided on guilt, innocence and penalty in a competition matter. The Commissioner is neither in person nor in function a judge. And the College of Commissioners is assuredly not a court. It is a political body, and political bodies in a democracy cannot well decide matters of guilt or innocence.

Additional thoughts in the same direction are that the Commissioner, although briefed by expert staff, has not attended the hearing of the accused company and will not have heard in a comprehensive way from the accused company about the case. The Commissioner may have been given copies of key documents and will certainly have discussed matters with his staff; and in very large cases, he will often have received delegations from interested parties. These commendable steps are not enough to make the process lawful.

[A] The Hearing

Article 6(1) of the ECHR contemplates a public hearing for a criminal proceeding, unless there are exceptional circumstances which justify dispensing with such a hearing.[12] The purpose of this right[13] is to protect litigants from 'the administration of justice in secret with no public scrutiny',[14] to maintain public confidence in the courts and the administration of justice.[15] According to the ECtHR case law the right to be present and to participate effectively is fundamental to the fairness of the proceedings, and it includes not only physical presence, but also the ability to hear and follow the proceedings,[16] to understand the evidence and arguments, to instruct the lawyers, and to give evidence.[17] According to the ECtHR this is particularly important where the proceedings are adversarial in nature.[18]

The oral hearing provided for in Article 27(1) of Regulation 1/2003, which takes place at a very advanced stage of a competition law case, is not a trial. Indeed, it barely corresponds to a hearing as the term is understood by most lawyers accustomed to civil or criminal advocacy. (An adequate hearing would be presided over by a decision-maker charged with deciding a factual or legal controversy.) Its purpose is to give the parties the opportunity to supplement their written defence by making oral presentations to the Commission. They will typically bring along lawyers and other experts, such as economists or scientists, and give a presentation to elaborate on specific points considered. There is no obligation on the Commission to respond to points or questions. The hearing is held in a large conference room, with the opposing parties facing one another across long rows of tables, the Member States round the edge of the room, with the Hearing Officer and members of the Commission Legal Service looking on from another long table. The curious physical layout is a metaphor for the obscure role of the hearing. The hearing is not a trial. There is only a limited opportunity for the accused company to challenge the evidence against it, including the witnesses upon whose testimony the Commission relies. Functionally, it is an opportunity for the case team to conclude that despite four years of effort it may have been mistaken all along. It should be an opportunity for a trier of fact to decide whether Mr Smith or Ms. Dupont is more believable in describing who attended the meeting on 13 January 2007.

The danger of a lack of rigour in handling the evidence is particularly relevant with respect to the evidence provided by companies with interests hostile to those of the company under attack. Take, for example, leniency applicants. There is no denying that leniency is a valuable tool in uncovering secret cartels. Cartels can be broken by

12. *Jacobsson v. Sweden* (No. 2) (1998) R.J.D. 1998-I, para. 46.
13. See, *Schuler-Zgraggen v. Switzerland* (1993) 16 E.H.R.R. 405, para. 58.
14. *Pretto v. Italy* (1983) 6 E.H.R.R. 182, para. 21.
15. *Diennet v. France* (1995) 21 E.H.R.R. 554, para. 33.
16. *Stanford v. United Kingdom* (1994) Series A, No. 282-A
17. *T and V v. United Kingdom* (2000) 30 E.H.R.R. 121.
18. *Hulki Gunes v. Turkey*, App. No. 28489/95, Judgment of 19 June 2003.

the risk of confessions implicating others in exchange for immunity from fines. Leniency applicants have a clear interest in showing serious wrong-doing by their competitors. The juicier the information they provide, the more chance they have of being deemed to have provided 'significant added value' and obtaining a reduction in their fine, or total immunity; and, in the process, they will have created big trouble for their competitors. The same concern arises, *mutatis mutandis*, in the case of complainants, who assert that the factual realities of the marketplace reveal the existence of an infringement and a need for Commission intervention. It is very common for the facts to be the subject of diametrically opposite views. So while it is certain that disputed points of evidence will be considered, that evidence will not be sifted, balanced and analysed at a hearing by a neutral decision-maker who has heard both parties.

The hearing takes place in the absence of the final decision-makers. The Commission's case team and other officials (such as representatives of the Commission's Legal Service) will be present, and will listen with courteous care to the arguments made by the accused company (in most cases those arguments will have been heard before).

The Member States, in the form of the Advisory Committee, look on and put questions and, in due course, may vote on the wisdom of the proposed decision. The Advisory Committee is naturally deferential to the authority which has spent years preparing the case. So far as I am aware, the Advisory Committee has not in thirty years voted against the adoption of a Commission Decision. To the extent there are imperfections of procedure within the Commission, they are not remedied by the Advisory Committee.

We have come a long way since the early days of EU competition law, when cases were carefully picked, decisions were few and penalties were modest. In 1962, fines were not confiscatory though they could, in theory, be painful. At a time when the institution was young and the real and theoretical extent of its powers remained uncertain, the shaping of the procedures for the enforcement of EC competition law was affected by the enormous contributions of a number of individual officials. Their personal scholarship and their dedication to the shaping of sound law meant that they were reluctant to endorse decisions where there was factual or legal doubt and a risk of defeat in Court. In those days, the criticisms concerned more the choice of cases than the fairness of the process. I recollect that in the 1970s, hearings were conducted by the Director in charge of the case team. The Director, in a sense, was there to hear his staff and the accused company battle out their differences. He was evidently not neutral, but he was presiding over one stage in a continuing administrative process. The file was not very thick, and the contested facts might not be very many. Procedural reforms occurred to respond to particular problems in specific cases, such as the Commission's decision in 1981 to appoint an independent Hearing Officer to preside over the hearing.[19] When the hearing was chaired by the Director of the Directorate leading the investigation, this heightened a perception that the Commission, when reaching its decision, might be minded institutionally not to have an openness to alternative ideas.

19. Commission of the European Communities, *11th Report on Competition Policy* (1981), point 26.

This development followed a celebrated controversy. In the *IBM* Article 102 EC case,[20] relations between the company and the Commission's staff were tense; press comments suggested the Commission had made up its mind, and the hearing promised undignified fireworks. The decision was made to bring in an outsider, a retired DG IV Director, to preside over the hearing. That official was charming, and firm, and the hearing was a dignified event at which neither side convinced the other but where arguments were rigorously exchanged. Subsequently, the post of Hearing Officer was institutionalized. Each Hearing Officer (I recollect eight) has had long experience and enjoys a high reputation.

The Commission recognized the problem in its 11th Report on Competition Policy:

> Although the Commission has no reason to believe that they [the oral hearings] are not conducted fairly at present, it intends to emphasize the objectivity of the hearing. With this in mind it envisages appointing hearing officers, duly authorized to chair hearings, vested with genuine autonomy and the right of direct access to the responsible Member of the Commission. This would provide an even better guarantee that the Commission, when stating its views on an individual case as a decision-making authority, would be fully informed of all features of the case whether favourable or unfavourable to the undertakings.[21]

The Commission also referred to the possibility of introducing administrative law judges to investigate and decide competition cases, similar to the Administrative Law Judges who work within the US Federal Trade Commission. The Commission dismissed this suggestion, because it had not proved fully satisfactory in the competition field in the United States because such an authority 'does not seem compatible with the institutional scheme of the Treaty'. Indeed, a hearing by accusers is structurally not likely to be thought to show 'objectivity', regardless of the scrupulousness of the accusers.

Thus the original reason for the naming of a Hearing Officer was that of seemliness—the notion that no one should decide his own case, *nemo iudex in causa sua*, that it was undesirable to imply that the prosecuting service was in charge of concluding the case and organizing the hearing of the company's defence. At that stage, it could have been decided to alter the decision-making process itself, creating a hearing before the decision-maker, or before a person charged with clarifying factual issues. But the reform was, in reality, very modest. If successive Hearing Officers played a role in convincing the Commission that the case was on the wrong track, this was not by rendering a formal favourable ruling but by a quiet word with colleagues.

The Hearing Officer's role was initially limited to chairmanship, the organization and conduct of the hearing. It has, over time, widened to cover other procedural

20. The Commission's decision of 19 December 1980 to open an investigation and to issue a statement of objections regarding infringements of Article 86 (now 102) EC was unsuccessfully challenged before the ECJ (Case 60/81, *IBM v. Commission* [1981] ECR 2639). The case was eventually settled (European Commission's *14th Report on Competition Policy* (1984), point 94); see also, Ian Forrester and Christopher Norall, Yearbook of European Law, Clarendon Press, Oxford (1985), 395.
21. Commission of the European Communities, *11th Report on Competition Policy* (1981), point 26.

questions, in particular safeguarding the confidentiality of documents and business secrets, and access to the Commission's file. The Hearing Officer must report to the Commission on the procedure, and may report on the substance (those reports are not available to the parties). The Commissioner will also receive advice from the Legal Service, and commonly from other services, and will have ready access to all shades of opinion with the Competition Directorate-General.

This matches the pattern that emerged in the 1980s and 1990s of a growing awareness by the Commission of the need to be more procedurally scrupulous in taking competition decisions, while not fundamentally changing how decisions were taken. Access to the file was not addressed in the original Regulation 17[22] or any implementing legislation. In a line of judgments, the Courts restricted the Commission's ability to use documents which have not been disclosed to the defendant company, and confirmed the right of defendant companies and their advisors to examine documents which may be useful for their defence.[23] Following *Soda Ash,*[24] the Commission in 1997 issued a Notice setting out how the obligation to give parties access to the file would be discharged in practice. The rules were fine-tuned in light of experience by a 2005 Notice.[25]

The person who presides over the hearing, although a very distinguished civil servant of long experience, has no function to decide on the substance. The Hearing Officer's function is to ensure that the hearing proceeds correctly and that the established procedural rights of the accused company are respected. Those rights amount essentially to being able to make representations in knowledge of the case against it. The Hearing Officer determines such matters as confidentiality of documents, access to the file, the date and duration of the hearing, and the extent to which rights of defence have been respected. These are significant matters and it is good that they are competently and neutrally decided, but the officer's powers are manifestly not sufficient to satisfy modern standards for determining guilt or innocence. The hearing does not constitute what is called for by Article 6 of the ECHR. A hearing at which the decision-maker is absent and the decision-drafters, although present and politely attentive are deeply sceptical (although their minds may not formally already be made up), is not a 'public hearing by an independent and impartial tribunal'.

[B] Fusion of the Investigation and Decision-Making Functions

In a prosecutorial context, the same officials should not both investigate and decide. Police can gather evidence and accuse a suspect, but we do not allow them to decide

22. Regulation No.17: First Regulation implementing Articles 85 and 86 of the Treaty, 1962 OJ 13, pp. 204–211.
23. For instance, Cases 100-103/80, *Musique Diffusion Française v. Commission* [1983] ECR 1825; Case C-62/86, *AKZO Chemie BV v. Commission* [1991] ECR I-3359; and Case T-30/91, *Solvay et Cie v. Commission* ('Soda Ash') [1995] ECR II-1775.
24. Case T-30/91, *Solvay et Cie v. Commission* [1995] ECR II-1775.
25. Notice on the rules for access to the Commission file in cases pursuant to Articles 81 and 82 of the EC Treaty, Articles 53, 54 and 57 of the EEA Agreement and Regulation 139/2004, 2005 OJ C 325/7.

on guilt. A certain 'prosecutorial bias' can flow from the entrusting to a single set of persons the functions of investigation, prosecution and adjudication.[26] The existence of such bias is not in itself a criticism of individual officials, but is a reflection of the investigative structure itself once proceedings have been commenced and investigative resources have been deployed. These general psychological factors can affect the most talented and ethical professionals. Wouter Wils, a considerable scholar and well-experienced Commission official, distinguishes between confirmation bias, hindsight bias and policy bias.

Confirmation bias arises from the natural tendency for a case investigator to favour evidence that supports his belief that a competition infringement has been committed.[27] Police look for their suspect's fingerprints or footprints: that is perfectly normal. *Hindsight bias* flows from the natural desire to justify one's past efforts, in particular to hierarchical supervisors and outsiders. It has been argued that it:

> is understandable in human terms that Commission officials sometimes want to push through what they perceive to be 'their' case. And it explains why arguments put forward by the parties often appear to fall on deaf ears.[28]

As a result, case teams may be reluctant to adjust previously held views (honestly and legitimately held) in light of information coming to light later in the investigation.[29] In such circumstances, the official can be minded to continue to work towards an infringement decision, ignoring or diminishing the information adverse to the case, so as to justify and confirm the earlier decision to continue the investigation.

The third category of bias, *policy bias*, arises from the desire of officials and authorities to show a high level of enforcement activity. On this theory, promotions flow from taking decisions, and not from not taking decisions. The importance attached to the fines is exemplified by the statistics published by DG Competition on its website[30] and by the speeches of successive Competition Commissioners justifying decisions imposing fines and the high level of these fines. As Mr Wils notes, this entails:

> a potential risk of abuse, in that dubious cases might be pursued or fines might be inflated in order to keep up the statistics.[31]

I repeat yet again that these difficulties or weaknesses do not in any way impugn the skill or honour of the concerned officials. There is, however, a real danger of the kinds of institutional bias mentioned.

---

26. Wouter Wils, *The Combination of the Investigative and Prosecutorial Function and the Adjudicative Function*, 27 World Competition: Law and Economic Review (2004), 202.
27. Wils, *ibid.*, at 215.
28. Frank Montag, *The Case for a Radical Reform of the Infringement Procedure under Regulation 17*, (1996) 8 E.C.L.R 428, 430.
29. Wouter Wils, *The Combination of the Investigative and Prosecutorial Function and the Adjudicative Function*, (2004) 27 World Competition: Law and Economic Review 202, 216.
30. See: http://ec.europa.eu/comm/competition/cartels/statistics/statistics.pdf (accessed 13 March 2013).
31. Wouter Wils, *The Combination of the Investigative and Prosecutorial Function and the Adjudicative Function*, (2004) 27 World Competition: Law and Economic Review 202, 217.

The fusion of investigative and decision-making functions is not easy to reconcile with the notion of 'an independent and impartial tribunal established by law' enshrined in Article 6 of the ECHR. In *Dubus v. France*,[32] the lack of an 'organic separation' within the French *Commission Bancaire* between those sections which prosecuted and sanctioned Mr Dubus entitled the company to have reasonable doubts as to the independence and impartiality of the *Commission Bancaire*, such that there had been a breach of Article 6(1) of the ECHR. The features of the *Commission Bancaire's* procedures which caused concern to the ECtHR will sound very familiar to readers in Brussels: there was no clear distinction between the functions of prosecution, investigation and adjudication in the exercise of the *Commission Bancaire's* judicial power.[33] While the combination of investigative and judicial functions was not, in itself, incompatible with the need for impartiality, there should be no 'prejudgment' or the appearance thereof on the part of the *Commission Bancaire*.[34] The Strasbourg Court noted that the applicant company might reasonably have had the impression that it had been prosecuted and tried by the same people. The *Commission Bancaire*, in its various capacities, had brought disciplinary proceedings, notified the offences and pronounced the penalty.

Consistent rigour in verifying what happened, why it happened and who suffered as a result, is necessary from the first consideration of the problem, to the formal opening of the case, to the Commission decision, and on to the later stage of the European Courts' review. Factual rigour is especially desirable in light of the unique – and imperfect – procedures by which competition decisions are taken by the European Commission. These procedural imperfections mean that factual determinations by the Commission services are never publicly tested rigorously, certainly not with the rigour of a criminal trial.

An administration in such circumstances may well reach the right answer, and no doubt it does reach the right result in most cases. But an administrative body cannot readily conduct a trial. It can prosecute, and vigorously. It can regulate and administer, and shape policy goals. It may sometimes impose penalties. But there are risks in doing that, unless the penalties are modest reactions to modest errors or infringements. Administrative penalties can be imposed for parking too long, insanitary restaurant kitchens, environmental nuisances and similar infringements. Grave economic crimes require different treatment.

§15.06 JUDICIAL REVIEW: NEED FOR RIGOUR

Rigorous judicial oversight in turn encourages rigour within the decision-making authority. Under the Convention, a tribunal must have full jurisdiction, to examine all questions of fact and law relevant to the dispute before it.[35] Furthermore it must determine matters within its competence on the basis of rules of law, and its decisions

32. *Dubus S.A. v. France*, No. 5242/04, 11 June 2009.
33. *Ibid.*, para. 56.
34. *Ibid.*, paras 57-58.
35. See *Terra Woningen v. Netherlands* (1996) 24 E.H.R.R. 456 (para. 52).

must be legally binding.[36] It also has to be impartial and independent of the executive, and of the legislature.[37] It is not the case that enhanced procedures weaken the prosecutor. To the contrary: previous negative rulings of the European Courts have given the Commission the impetus to sharpen its own internal decision-making processes. It was the annulment of Commission merger control decisions such as *Tetra Laval*[38] and *Airtours*[39] that led to the establishment of peer review within the Commission, a process which surely enhances the quality of today's Commission decisions. There is no inconsistency between being opposed to wrong-doing while favouring effective protections for those accused. We learn from the 'war on terror' in my own and others' countries that errors and injustices can occur due to weak forensic procedures, over-enthusiastic prosecutors and over-tolerant juries.

§15.07 DEFERENCE

Whether a contested element in a Commission decision is deemed to be a question of 'fact' or a 'complex ... appraisal', will affect how the Court exercises its power of review,[40] making only a limited check of 'legality', often called 'light review' or 'marginal review'. It is not a review of the correctness or well-foundedness of the act in question. In the case of merger control, the Court of First Instance has indicated that the EC Merger Regulation confers discretion on the Commission to carry out an economic assessment of the likely effects of a merger. But at the same time the Court has been very interventionist in examining the Commission's decisions.[41] By contrast, in antitrust cases as to breaches of Articles 101 or 102, the Courts have sometimes been quite deferential to the Commission and at other times quite interventionist.[42] It is not always easy to see a clear dividing line to separate cases of rigorous factual review (as in *Woodpulp*[43]) from cases of deference to Commission discretion (as in *Wieland-Werke*[44] or *Microsoft*[45]). I suggest that it cannot be the case that all economic appraisals are 'complex'. Just because an economic assessment is difficult, for example, should not mean it is deemed to be 'complex'.

36. See *Belilos v. Switzerland* (1998) 10 E.H.R.R. 466 (para 64).
37. *Beamartin v. France* (1994) E.H.R.R. 485 at 503 (para. 38), *Campbell and Fell v. United Kingdom* (1984) 7 E.H.R.R. 165 (para. 78).
38. Case C-12/03 P, *Commission v. Tetra Laval* [2005] ECR-I 987.
39. Case T-342/99, *Airtours plc v. Commission* [2002] ECR II-2585.
40. Judge Vesterdorf has recently written that the exercise of unlimited jurisdiction is in practice the very rare exception: *The Court of Justice and Unlimited Jurisdiction: What Does it Mean in Practice?*, Global Competition Policy, Release 2 (2009).
41. See Case T-342/99, *Airtours* [2002] ECR II-2585, para. 64.
42. There is a remarkable contrast between *Woodpulp* and *Microsoft*. See Ian Forrester, *A Bush in Need of Pruning: the Luxuriant Growth of 'Light Judicial Review'*, European Competition Law Annual 2009: The Evaluation of Evidence and its Judicial Review in Competition Cases, Oxford and Portland Oregon (2011).
43. Joined Cases C-89/85, C-104/85, C-114/85, C-116/85, C-117/85 and C-125/85 to C-129/85, *A Ahlström Osakeyhtiö and Others v. Commission* [1993] ECR I-1307.
44. Case T-116/04, *Wielandwerke v. Commission* [2009] ECR II-1087.
45. Case T-201/04, *Microsoft Corp v. Commission*, [2007] ECR II-3601.

The language of deference has been cited so frequently that it may have become a sort of judicial mantra. The words have appeared in at least fifty competition cases since 1984. There have been many more cases where the Courts have favoured deference than cases where they have exercised their unlimited jurisdiction. I am doubtful if the appraisals of evidence by the Commission deserved judicial deference in every case where the familiar words have been pronounced.

The boundaries of '*complex economic assessments*' have expanded over the years. The Courts' exercise of unlimited jurisdiction may, in parallel, have been shrinking. Curiously, as the consequences of being found to be in the wrong have become more dire, the judicial control of such findings has, at least in appearance, become more deferential.

The doctrine of judicial deference to the Commission's assessments was first enunciated in a famous judgment, *Consten and Grundig*,[46] in which the ECJ in effect conceded that the Commission could choose its enforcement priorities. The doctrine was further elaborated in *Remia/Nutricia*.[47] In those days, the Commission defined the prohibition on 'restricting' competition contained in Article 85(1) very broadly, referring parties whose conduct was caught in this wide net to the possibility of obtaining an exemption under Article 85(3). Even if the end result – the conclusion that a given agreement or conduct was acceptable and even desirable from the point of view of competition policy – was clear, the Commission consistently considered it was to be reached, as a theoretical matter, by first condemning it under Article 85(1) and then redeeming it under Article 85(3). Agreements which were caught by Article 85(1) and unexempted were void and unenforceable. Voidness could be cured only by an exemption, only the Commission could issue exemptions, and it did so very rarely. Thus the question in *Remia/Nutricia* was whether a clause to regulate competition could be blessed under Article 85(1).

[A] *Remia/Nutricia*: Deference as a Lightening of Article 101(1)

Nutricia notified agreements under which it successively sold two subsidiaries, Remia specializing in the manufacture of sauces (to an individual in the Netherlands), and Luycks, a manufacturer of pickles and condiments as well as a few sauces (to a subsidiary in the Netherlands of the Campbell group). The 'Sauce Agreement', required Nutricia not to engage in the production or sale of sauces in the Netherlands for ten years; Nutricia was required to ensure that Luycks also complied with this clause. Remia received a two-year non-exclusive licence for the 'Luycks' trademark for sale of sauces to the hotel and catering trade. The 'Pickles Agreement' prohibited Nutricia from engaging in the sale or production of pickles in 'European countries' for five years, with an exception for certain bulk sales. The buyer also accepted the restriction on making and selling sauces imposed on Luycks, by virtue of the Sauce Agreement.

---

46. Joined Cases 56 and 58/64, *Etablissements Consten SARL and Grundig-Verkaufs-GmbH v. Commission* [1966] ECR 299.
47. Case 42/84, *Remia BV v. Commission* [1985] ECR 2545.

According to the Commission's theory, post-sale non-compete clauses, which in a narrow sense constitute clear and explicit restrictions of competition, were held not to be caught by Article 85(1) at all. This solution was achieved by an exercise in definitions.

The restriction was 'inherent' in the sale of business and thus was not a restriction. The question then became how much such restriction was 'inherent': for how many years could the seller be obliged not to compete? Now, was the restrictive period pro-competitive, or irretrievably bad, or was it overlong but curable by shortening? The Commission found the periods of non-competition were excessively long. But it did concede that where the sale of a business covered goodwill and clientele as well as material assets, a non-competition obligation imposed on the seller may be necessary to ensure transfer of '*the full commercial value of the business*'. Applying these criteria, the Commission found that four years rather than ten would have been appropriate for the Sauce Agreement; for the Pickles Agreement, it found that two years would be appropriate, and that the geographical scope of the clause should be appropriately limited.[48]

The Commission's approach made good sense to the business community but was legally controversial. Sales of businesses would be impossible without non-compete clauses. Thus they reinforce competition by increasing the number of enterprises on the market. But by arguing that a particular 'restriction' is pro-competitive and therefore not caught by Article 85(1), arguments normally reserved for Article 85(3) crept into the analysis under Article 81(1).

Advocate General Lenz spelled out the problem:

> There can be no doubt that a total ban on competition, that is to say an undertaking not to act directly or indirectly on a certain market for a specified period, must be seen as an agreement which has as its object or effect a restriction of competition...[49]
>
> I now turn to the question whether it is possible for the prohibition in Article 85(1) not to be applied to agreements in restraint of competition which in theory fall within its scope without adopting the exemption procedure under Article 85(3). If the answer to that question is positive it will then remain to be examined what rules of law must apply in the case of such a 'non-application' of Article 85(1) of the EEC Treaty...[50]
>
> Although the non-application of Article 85(1) finds no immediate support in the Treaty its permissibility is accepted in academic writings, in particular in the case of agreements for the transfer of undertakings...[51]
>
> In academic writings on Community law it is argued that, taken in the abstract, restrictions on competition agreed in the context of agreements for the transfer of undertakings may in principle be regarded as satisfying the factual criteria contained in Article 85(1) of the EEC Treaty...[52]

48. See Commission Decision 83/670, Case Nos IV 130.389 and IV/30.408, *Nutricia/de Rooij and Nutricia/Zuid-Hollandse Conservenfabriek* [1983] OJ L 376/22.
49. Case 42/84 *Remia v. Commission* [1985] ECR 2545, at 2556.
50. *Ibid.*, at 2558.
51. *Ibid.*, at 2558.
52. *Ibid.*, at 2558.

> I, too, agree that an exception, to the extent described above, to the prohibition of restrictive agreements laid down in Article 85(1) of the EEC Treaty is both conceivable and practicable...[53]

So the Advocate General was endorsing the Commission's approach as sound in principle, even though he noted that academic writing was not unanimous: one of the dissenters was the formidable Norbert Koch of the Commission Legal Service. The Advocate General then produced another reason to support the Commission:

> If this is right..., a further consequence will follow regarding the scope for judicial review of the Commission's decision. Since the conditions for an exemption are outlined only in a general manner, the Commission enjoys a wide discretion even in the case of a straightforward application of Article 85(3). The Court of Justice has recognized that Article 85(3) necessarily implies complex assessments of economic matters. Similarly, where such assessments are made in the case of prohibitions of competition agreed in connection with transfers of undertakings, the judicial review must take that fact into account and therefore confine itself to determining the correctness of the facts on which the assessments are based and the applicability to those facts of the relevant legal principles. As the Court of Justice has stated, judicial review must in the first place be carried out in respect of the reasons given for the Commission's decision, which must set out the facts and considerations on which the said assessments are based.

This was a big legal step in terms of the substantive law (which was recognized with relief by commentators, including myself), and it was a deeply important constitutional initiative (less noticed at the time by commentators).

The Court followed the Advocate General. The Commission was in a sense intelligently finding a middle way to reconcile opposing concerns; navigating between the Scylla and Charybdis of stubborn prohibition and lax toleration. At this moment, the notion of ancillary restraints had not been adopted in EC law. The approach of the Commission was commendably practical (even if the precise number of years could be debated: indeed, whether the correct period should be three, four or five years was a matter of appraisal where reasonable men could reasonably differ). As regards the duration of the non-compete clause, the Court endorsed the Commission's findings that the ten years agreed by the parties was too much, and that four years was sufficient.

In upholding the Commission's decision, the Court of Justice noted, echoing Advocate General Lenz, that:

> although as a general rule the Court undertakes a comprehensive review of the question whether or not the conditions for the application of article 85(1) are met, it is clear that in determining the permissible duration of a non-competition clause incorporated in an agreement for the transfer of an undertaking, the Commission has to appraise complex economic matters.

Consequently:

53. Case 42/84, *Remia v. Commission* [1985] ECR 2545, at 2559.

> the Court must therefore limit its review of such an appraisal to verifying whether the relevant procedural rules have been complied with, whether the statement of the reasons for the decision is adequate, whether the facts have been accurately stated and whether there has been any manifest error of appraisal or misuse of powers.[54]

Nutricia fertilized the small plant of judicial deference in competition matters. The bush subsequently burgeoned, being cited in dozens of subsequent competition judgments.[55] But the original seed was intended to commend the Commission's creativity in pragmatically solving a problem of principle. It was not meant, I submit, to be a shifting of primacy in the balance between the administration/prosecution and the judiciary.

[B] The *Microsoft* Case: Deference to Technical and Economic Assessments

The *Microsoft* case involved numerous hotly-debated factual matters concerning the design of computer operating systems, how software functions, the role of directories in networks of servers, and other topics. While these matters were assuredly technical and complex, the issues at stake were set forth with limpid clarity in the admirably accurate Report for the Hearing. The judges of the Court of First Instance were evidently able to decide on the merits of the case, as they had accurately identified the issues in dispute. However, in the judgment in 2007,[56] the formulation of light judicial review was extended to technical matters, not merely complex economic assessments:

> The Court observes that it follows from consistent case-law that, although as a general rule the Community Courts undertake a comprehensive review of the question as to whether or not the conditions for the application of the competition rules are met, their review of complex economic appraisals made by the Commission is necessarily limited to checking whether the relevant rules on procedure and on stating reasons have been complied with, whether the facts have been accurately stated and whether there has been any manifest error of assessment or a misuse of powers ... [citations omitted][57]
>
> Likewise, in so far as the Commission's decision is the result of complex technical appraisals, those appraisals are in principle subject to only limited review by the Court, which means that the Community Courts cannot substitute their own assessment of matters of fact for the Commission's (see, as regards a

54. Case 42/84, *Remia v. Commission* [1985] ECR 2545, at 2575.
55. See e.g., Joined Cases 142 and 156/84, *BAT and Reynolds v. Commission* [1987] ECR 4487, para. 62; Case T-44/90, *La Cinq SA v. Commission* [1992] ECR II-1, para. 85; Joined Cases T-39/92 and T-40/92, *Groupement des Cartes Bancaires 'CB' and Europay International SA v. Commission* [1994] ECR II-49, para. 109; Case T-17/93, *Matra Hachette SA v. Commission* [1994] ECR II-595, para. 104; Case T-471/93, *Tiercé Ladbroke SA v. Commission* [1995] ECR II-2537, para. 55.
56. Case T-201/04 *Microsoft Corp. v. Commission* [2007] ECR II-3601. For a rich review by a number of the participants in the case (as well as others), see Luca Rubini (Editor) *Microsoft on Trial: Legal and Economic Analysis of a Transatlantic Antitrust Case*, New Horizons in Competition Law and Economics (Edward Elgar 2010).
57. *Ibid.*, para. 87.

> decision adopted following complex appraisals in the medico-pharmacological sphere, order of the President of the Court of Justice in Case C-459/00 P(R) Commission v. Trenker [2001] ECR I-2823, paragraphs 82 and 83 ... [citations omitted][58]

These paragraphs expanded the Courts' deference to complex technical appraisals as well as to complex economic ones. The familiar standard was set forth accurately in paragraph 87 referring to 'complex economic appraisals' where the Court's task is 'necessarily limited to checking whether the relevant rules ... have been complied with, whether the facts have been accurately stated and whether there has been a manifest error of appraisal.' The Court's enunciation of a different standard of review in paragraph 88 is striking. The Court's reference to cases 'in the medico-pharmacological sphere' to present this new standard applicable to 'complex technical appraisals' seems unfortunate. In any competition case, the Commission is not assisted by a special agency entrusted with elucidating scientific controversies and making recommendations for action.

I suggest that while the EU Courts recognize that the Commission has a margin of appreciation in economic or technical matters, that does not mean that they must decline to review the Commission's interpretation of economic or technical data. The EU Courts must not only establish whether the evidence put forward is factually accurate, reliable and consistent but must also determine whether that evidence contains all the relevant data that must be taken into consideration in appraising a complex situation and whether it is capable of substantiating the conclusions drawn from it (see, to that effect, concerning merger control, *Tetra Laval*).[59]

Thus the doctrine of deference has expanded considerably from where it stood in 1965 at the time of *Consten and Grundig*. It has moved from the refusing of an exemption in light of overriding concerns relating to Community policy to reach very specific cases on very specific findings relevant to whether Article 101 or 102 were infringed. The deference shown to 'complex economic assessments' has spread, and has been referred to in scores of judgments, including some which I submit did not involve a complex regulatory exercise. If the *Microsoft* ruling is followed in future, deference (by which I mean either reciting the language of deference or genuinely according actual deference) now encompasses 'complex technical appraisals' as well as economic ones, and does not distinguish between where the Commission is advised by technical regulatory experts and where the Commission decides a competition case itself with no such expert guidance. Among the 'technical matters' could be a range of factual disputes, the determination of which connotes guilt or innocence of a competition law offence.

58. *Microsoft, ibid.*, para. 88.
59. Case C-12/03 P, *Commission v. Tetra Laval* [2005] ECR I-987, para. 39.

[C] Judicial Deference Spreads to Fines

The phenomenon of deference spread to appeals about the level of fines, in that the Courts sometimes reviewed in a 'deferential' manner how the Commission exercised its fining discretion:

> It is therefore for the Court to verify, when reviewing the legality of the fines imposed by the contested decision, whether the Commission exercised its discretion in accordance with the method set out in the Guidelines and, should it be found to have departed from that method, to verify whether that departure is justified and supported by sufficient legal reasoning. In that regard, it should be noted that the Court of Justice has confirmed the validity, first, of the very principle of the Guidelines, and, secondly, the method which is there indicated (Joined Cases C-189/02 P, C-202/02 P, C-205/02 P to C-208/02 P and C-213/02 P Dansk Rørindustri and Others v Commission [2005] ECR I-5425, paragraphs 252 to 255, 266, 267, 312 and 313).[60]

If any part of a Commission decision should not be subject to deference, it is the setting of the fine, which is explicitly subject to the unlimited jurisdiction of the European Courts. I question whether such an approach is consistent with a proper exercise of the Courts' unlimited jurisdiction.

[D] *Chalkor* and *KME*: Criticism of Deference in Fining Cases

On 8 December 2011, in its judgments in *Chalkor*[61] and *KME*,[62] the European Court of Justice pronounced on the level of judicial review which the General Court must carry out when reviewing Commission decisions in competition cases. The appellants did prevail as to their arguments of principle, but lost as to their appellate challenge to the judgment below. Although the ECJ rejected the appeals, it implicitly criticized previous cases where the EU Courts had exercised a deferential standard of review, and in contrast prescribed a rigorous standard of judicial review.

The ECJ held that in competition cases the EU Courts must make a full review of the law and the facts. This implies the power of the reviewing court to assess the evidence, annul the contested decision and alter the amount of the fine. The ECJ rejected the notion of limited judicial review. It stated that, although the Commission has a margin of discretion, the CFI (by then the General Court) cannot use that margin of discretion as a basis for dispensing with an in-depth review of the law and the facts or for refraining from reviewing the Commission's interpretation of information of an economic nature. The General Court should examine whether the evidence relied on is factually accurate, reliable and consistent, whether the evidence contains all the information which must be taken into account in order to assess a complex situation, and whether the evidence is capable of substantiating the conclusions drawn from it.

60. Case T-116/04, *Wieland-Werke v. Commission* [2009] ECR II-1087, para.30.
61. Case C-386/10P, *Chalkor v. Commission* [2011] ECR I-0000.
62. Case C-272/09P, *KME v. Commission* [2011] ECR I-0000.

The General Court has repeatedly recited that its competence was merely to verify that the Commission had acted within the scope of its own Guidelines, not to consider whether the fines were fair and proportionate. However, the ECJ's formulation indicates that such an approach would no longer be appropriate in light of the Charter of Fundamental Rights:

> The review provided for by the Treaties thus involves review by the Courts of the European Union of both the law and the facts, and means that they have the power to assess the evidence, to annul the contested decision and to alter the amount of a fine. The review of legality provided for under Article 263 TFEU, supplemented by the unlimited jurisdiction in respect of the amount of the fine, provided for under Article 31 of Regulation No 1/2003, is not therefore contrary to the requirements of the principle of effective judicial protection in Article 47 of the Charter.[63]

The *Chalkor* case thus offers good news and bad news. On the one hand, for the general interest, the ECJ criticizes the practice of deferentially reviewing fines; on the other hand, for Chalkor's interest, it found that although the Court of First Instance had used the offending language, the CFI had in fact actually performed a non-deferential review. Thus Chalkor lost its appeal.

§15.08 INTERNATIONAL STANDARDS

The Lisbon Treaty in 2009 gave to the EU Charter of Fundamental Rights status equivalent to the EU Treaties and made the Charter binding on all EU institutions (including the EU Courts).[64] The Charter requires that EU law affords at least the same protection for fundamental rights as that prescribed in the ECHR. Article 6(1) ECHR, or the corresponding Article 47 of the Charter, have been much studied by scholars and practitioners.[65]

Sadly, the tepid enthusiasm of the EU institutions for external interference may be inferred from the fact that *years* after the conclusion and entry into force of the Lisbon Treaty, which itself was no overnight development, there is no early prospect that the Union will expose itself to the scrutiny of the Strasbourg Court.

Article 6 of the ECHR and Article 47 of the Charter set out the requirement of a fair and public hearing and due process:

> 1. In the determination of his civil rights and obligations or of any criminal charge against him, everyone is entitled to a fair and public hearing within a reasonable time by an independent and impartial tribunal established by law...
> 2. Everyone charged with a criminal offence shall be presumed innocent until proved guilty according to law.
> 3. Everyone charged with a criminal offence has the following minimum rights:

63. Case C-386/10P, *Chalkor v. Commission* [2011] ECR I-0000.
64. Articles 6(1) of the Treaty of the European Union and Article 51(1) of the Charter.
65. Article 52(3) of the Charter stipulates that insofar as the Charter contains rights which correspond to the rights guaranteed by the ECHR, the meaning and scope of those rights shall be the same as those laid down in the ECHR, which does not prevent the Union law from providing more extensive protection.

(b) to have adequate time and the facilities for the preparation of his defence;
(d) to examine or have examined witnesses against him and to obtain the attendance and examination of witnesses on his behalf under the same conditions as witnesses against him.

These principles reflect the fundamental principle of favouring the rule of law,[66] which underpins the whole Convention system.[67,68]

Conduct subject to criminal sanctions deserves procedures which satisfy criminal standards of rigour, thoroughness and due process. The determination of a 'criminal charge' (as opposed to the determination of 'civil rights and obligations') requires additional safeguards. A defendant in such a case has the right to be informed promptly and in detail of the nature and cause of the accusation; to adequate time and the facilities to prepare a defence; to defend himself in person or through legal assistance of his own choosing (with free legal assistance if necessary); and to examine or have examined witnesses against him and to obtain the attendance and examination of witnesses on his behalf under the same conditions as witnesses against him.

[A] The Nature of the EU Competition Rules

Articles 101 and 102 TFEU are general rules applying to all undertakings and are, therefore, general norms of a binding character. A primary purpose of the competition rules and the Commission's power to enforce them is the protection of society against damage caused by anti-competitive conduct. The fines imposed on those who breach the rules have a punitive and deterrent character. They are, in relative and absolute terms, very heavy. They threaten a very serious financial sanction both in theoretical maximum and in actual practice. The punitive nature of competition fines is confirmed by the way in which they are announced by the Commissioner. There is plenty of stigma in the announcements of the punishment of the guilty. It is striking that a prosecution for a grave economic crime, susceptible to a penalty of tens or hundreds of millions of Euro, should be 'administrative' such that there is no need to grant a 'fair and public hearing ... by an independent and impartial tribunal' and that, likewise, the accused need not have the opportunity 'to examine or have examined witnesses against him'. I repeat that there is no hearing on facts (which may be hotly-contested) by a decision-maker, the decision-makers are high political functionaries, and the same officials investigate, charge, convict and punish. And the judicial review is of legality, not correctness (except as to fines since *Chalkor*). The appellate process is sometimes rigorous and sometimes not. The consistency of such a regime with the ECHR is not manifest: some would put it more forcefully.

66. See e.g. *Salabiaku v. France* (1998) 13 E.H.R.R. 379 (para. 28).
67. See e.g. *Sunday Times v. United Kingdom* (1979) 2 E.H.R.R. 245 (para. 55) referring to *Golder v. UK* (1975) 1 E.H.R.R. 524 (para. 34).
68. The rule of law is also expressely referred to in the Preamble to the Convention (see *Klass v. Federal Republic of Germany* (1978) 2 E.H.R.R. 214, para. 55) and in Article 3 of the Statute of the Council of Europe. See *Stran Greek Refineries and Stratis Andreadis v. Greece* (1994) 19 E.H.R.R. 293, para. 46.

It should be a cause for embarrassment that even though accession to the ECHR has been imminent for years, no relevant adaptation of processes has been effected. The relationship between EC/EU law and ECHR law has not been especially edifying. The Luxembourg Courts have consistently noted the terms of the Strasbourg Convention and jurisprudence but have rarely doubted the adequacy of the procedures applied by the institutions in Brussels. Although the advent of the Charter and the Convention can hardly have been a surprise for anyone, the implementation has been embarrassingly slow.

[B] Categorization of Criminal Matters by the ECtHR

This brings us to the scope and the meaning of the case law of the ECtHR, difficult topics. In *Engel v. Netherlands*,[69] the ECtHR established three criteria for determining whether proceedings are 'criminal' from the point of view of the ECHR, namely (i) the domestic classification, (ii) the nature of the offence, and (iii) the severity of the potential penalty. Subsequent judgments have also established that the criteria are to be assessed independently and that the third criterion is the most important.[70] So if the legal sanction imposed for breaching a rule has the principal objective of deterring future violations, where the violation of that norm is generally perceived as inherently 'bad' or contrary to the common values shared in a democratic society, and where the norm is generally addressed to an undefined group of persons, a truly 'criminal' charge under Article 6 would exist. ECtHR case law on Article 6 can be read as making a distinction between 'soft' quasi-criminal matters (withdrawal of an advantage, tax penalties, and administrative penalties) and 'hard' criminal matters (stigma, punishment, deterrence). However, the ECtHR has given inconsistent guidance on whether the particular (and procedurally controversial) features of an administrative process make the process incurably inadequate or whether rigorous judicial review can solve the problem.

One case helpful to those who are sceptical about an administrative penal process was *Dubus v. France*,[71] which concerned the disciplinary proceedings of the French *Commission Bancaire*. The ECtHR took the view that in condemning Mr Dubus, the *Commission Bancaire* should be regarded as a 'tribunal' for the purpose of Article 6 of the ECHR. After citing the *Engel* criteria,[72] the Court noted that, while the penalty

69. *Engel v. The Netherlands* (1976) 1 E.H.R.R. 647.
70. *Brown v. United Kingdom* (1998) 28 E.H.R.R. CD 233.
71. *Dubus S.A. v. France*, No. 5242/04, June 11, 2009.
72. That is, the nature of the offence and the nature and severity of the penalty: 'it is first necessary to know whether the provision(s) defining the offence charged belong, according to the legal system of the respondent State, to criminal law, disciplinary law or both concurrently. This however provides no more than a starting point. The indications so afforded have only a formal and relative value and must be examined in the light of the common denominator of the respective legislation of the various Contracting States. The *very nature of the offence* is a factor of greater import. ... However, supervision by the Court does not stop there. Such supervision would generally prove to be illusory if it did not also take into consideration the *degree of severity of the penalty* that the person concerned risks incurring. In a society subscribing to the rule of law, there belong to the 'criminal' sphere deprivations of liberty liable to be imposed as a

which had been imposed was categorized in domestic law as an administrative sanction, the penalty was removal from the register or a fine up to the level of its minimum capital, or both. It considered that such significant financial consequences can be regarded as penal sanctions. The penal nature of a sanction depends on the gravity of the potential sanction, and not on the gravity of the sanction in fact imposed. The sanction in this case was such as to affect the credit of the company, entailing undeniable consequences on the company's capital. The ECtHR not only took the view that the *Commission Bancaire*, when it imposed the fine, should be considered to be a 'tribunal' for the purpose of Article 6(1) of the ECHR, but also that, in the circumstances, the sanction had a '*coloration pénale*' and was a criminal charge for the purpose of that Article. There had been a breach of Article 6.

At first, *Dubus* seemed to imply that if a procedure had a *coloration pénale*, then an administrative forum in which the accusers were the deciders was unsatisfactory under Article 6 ECHR. The implications for the EU's competition law regime seemed obvious. Other decisions, however, have clouded the matter.

In *Jussila*,[73] the ECtHR was asked to assess whether imposing a tax surcharge was to be seen as a criminal matter under Article 6, even though it was deemed to be administrative under the Finnish system. The Court first discussed at length whether the *Engel* criteria should be used:[74]

> [it] is enough that the offence in question is by its nature to be regarded as criminal or that the offence renders the person liable to a penalty which by its nature and degree of severity belongs in the general criminal sphere. The relative lack of seriousness of the penalty cannot divest an offence of its inherently criminal character.

To justify the application of the *Engel* criteria, the Court referred to the assessment in *Janosevic*[75] saying that:

> No established or authoritative basis has ... emerged in the case-law for holding that the minor nature of the penalty, in taxation proceedings or otherwise, may be decisive in removing an offence, otherwise criminal by nature, from the scope of Article 6.[76]

The Court was not persuaded that the nature of tax surcharge proceedings was such that they should fall outside the protection of Article 6. Arguments to that effect had also failed in the context of prison disciplinary and minor traffic offences:[77]

> While there is no doubt as to the importance of tax to the effective functioning of the State, the Court is not convinced that removing procedural safeguards in the

punishment, except those which by their nature, duration or manner of execution cannot be appreciably detrimental. The seriousness of what is at stake, the traditions of the Contracting States and the importance attached by the Convention to respect for the physical liberty of the person all require that this should be so'.

73. *Jussila v. Finland* (2007) 45 E.H.R.R. 39.
74. *Ibid.*, para. 30.
75. *Janosevic v. Sweden* (2004) 38 E.H.R.R. 473.
76. *Jussila v. Finland* (2007) 45 E.H.R.R. 39, para. 35.
77. *Ibid.*, para. 36.

> imposition of punitive penalties in that sphere is necessary to maintain the efficacy of the fiscal system or indeed can be regarded as consonant with the spirit and purpose of the Convention.[78]

In its assessment, the Court then noted that 'that the surcharges were imposed by a rule whose purpose was deterrent and punitive'.[79] It considered that this established the criminal nature of the offence and that the minor nature of the penalty rendered the case different from previous case law but that this did not remove the matter from the scope of Article 6 and that Article 6 applied 'notwithstanding the minor nature of the tax surcharge:[80]

> Notwithstanding the consideration that a certain gravity attaches to criminal proceedings, which are concerned with the allocation of criminal responsibility and the imposition of a punitive and deterrent sanction, it is self-evident that there are criminal caes which do not carry any significant degree of stigma.
>
> ...
>
> Tax surcharges differ from the hard core of criminal law; consequently, the criminal-head guarantees will not necessarily apply with their full stringency...[81]

The ECtHR's assessment of Finland's compliance with Article 6 and the right to a hearing is relevant to competition cases and how to categorize them. After having established that 'the obligation to hold a hearing is not absolute',[82] and that 'national authorities may have regard to the demands of efficiency and economy'[83] and dispense with one, the Court distinguished 'criminal cases which do not carry any significant degree of stigma.'[84] It thus confirmed that there were clearly 'criminal charges' of differing weight and that the autonomous interpretation adopted by the ECHR institutions of the notion of a 'criminal charge' by applying the *Engel* criteria had labelled as criminal cases not strictly belonging to the traditional categories of the criminal law, such as administrative penalties, prison disciplinary proceedings, customs law, competition law, and penalties imposed by a tax court.

[C] The *Menarini* Judgment: Turning Point or Cross-Road?

In *Menarini*,[85] the ECtHR examined a fine imposed by the Italian competition authority.[86] As usual, the Court noted that it was not determinative that the infringement had been labelled 'administrative'. It held that the imposed fine was based on legislation with a penal and deterrent aim, and noted that the application of competition rules by a competition authority affecting the general interests of society had already been held to be criminal for the purpose Article 6 and that the imposed fine sought first and

78. *Ibid.*, para. 36.
79. *Ibid.*, para. 38.
80. *Ibid.*, para. 38.
81. *Ibid.*, para. 43.
82. *Ibid.*, para. 41.
83. *Ibid.*, para. 42.
84. *Ibid.*, para. 43.
85. *Menarini Diagnostics S.R.L. v. Italy*, No. 43509/08, September 27, 2011.
86. See also for a discussion of this judgment and its effects on EU competition law procedures the contribution by Helene Andersson in this book, Chapter 16.

foremost to have a punitive effect.[87] As regards the severity of the penalty, the Court held that the large fine, as well as the resulting deterrent effect, meant that the penalty indeed had a criminal nature.[88]

However, the Court then held that Menarini had been able to challenge the fine before the administrative court and to appeal against that court's decision to the *Consiglio di Stato*. The Italian courts had examined Menarini's various arguments in fact and in law and had in doing so examined the evidence produced by the Italian competition authority. Although the competition authority had discretionary powers, the administrative court's role was not limited to verifying the lawfulness of the competition authority's decision: the court was further able to verify whether the administration had made proper use of its powers.[89] The courts had been able to examine whether the authority's decisions had been substantiated and proportionate, and even to check its technical findings.[90] Moreover, both the administrative court and the *Consiglio di Stato* had been able to verify that the penalty was appropriate for the offence and could have changed it where necessary.[91] The *Consiglio di Stato* had gone beyond a 'formal' review (*'un contrôle "externe"'*) of the logical coherency of the authority's decision and had made a detailed analysis of the appropriateness, including the proportionality, of the penalty.[92] The competition authority's decision had thus been reviewed by judicial bodies having full jurisdiction. In this respect, there had been no breach of the Convention. The Court found (with one dissent) that there had been no breach of Article 6 by Italy. There seems an evident tension between *Jussila* and *Menarini*.

§15.09 POSSIBLE REMEDIES

Following *Jussila*, it appeared that matters which fell within the 'hard core of the criminal law' demanded at first instance the procedural protections of Article 6 of the ECHR. This conclusion was strengthened by such cases as *Dubus* and *Primagaz*. There appeared to be an evident inconsistency between the reality of how a European competition case was prosecuted and punished and the requirements of the Convention. That inconsistency was not incurable, however. We can distinguish between what is offensive in a formalistic sense (reflecting a mixing of the political and the judicial at the stage of the formal act of the institution) and what is unacceptable in a practical and common-sense way (reflecting unfairness or potential error in how the facts have been considered). A body of politicians, no matter how eminent, should not decide guilt or innocence and impose penalties in criminal cases or cases analogous to criminal cases. The situation of the European Commission is, I believe, unique on earth. The Commissioner cannot effectively be both chief decision-maker and chief of

87. *Menarini Diagnostics S.R.L. v. Italy*, No. 43509/08, September 27, 2011, para. 40.
88. *Ibid.*, paras 41–42.
89. *Ibid.*, para. 63.
90. *Ibid.*, para. 64.
91. *Ibid.*, para. 65.
92. *Ibid.*, para. 66.

the prosecution service. Both positions are honourable, but they should not be combined. The combination of the two roles is dangerous, though the substantive vice of politicization is, in reality, less acute than it might appear. In actual practice, in the great majority of cases, members of the College of Commissioners do not have a hand in drafting the decision, although they are consulted about it in the final stages.

Thus as a formal matter, the decision is criminal in nature, yet it is taken not by an independent and impartial tribunal but by twenty-seven political figures. And if the matter were ever to arrive competently before the ECtHR, this element would perhaps be the strongest and most obvious imperfection. By contrast, the level of resentment or sense of injustice felt by those who have been through the process arises not so much from the formalities of the final vote as from the perceived unfairness of the intellectual process of reaching a conclusion. When diligent and honest officials investigate a case over a period of time, say four years, and then issue the Statement of Objections once the case is, say, 80% concluded, they are understandably committed to the line chosen. So the hearing, regrettably, serves as a tardy opportunity for the case team and the hierarchy of the case team to be persuaded that, after years of investigation, they are indeed mistaken. It is not the function of the hearing to allow the Hearing Officer, who presides, to reach a decision on guilt or innocence or contested facts. There is no equiparation of the 'case for the prosecution' and the 'case for the defence'.

Matters would improve if there were a hearing by an independent person of the factual and legal merits of the accusations levelled by case teams in DG Competition against the accused company, a true '*contradictoire*' debate between opposing parties in the presence of a person who is neutral and impartial. If the decision-maker is functionally separate to the case team, then the problem of combined inconsistent roles is resolved. The case team would be the investigator-prosecutor, and would have to convince the decision-maker that there was a solid case. The substantive outcomes in particular cases would often not be much different, but their credibility would be greatly enhanced.

If the decision-shaping function were removed from the case team, the investigation could still be carried out, as today, by officials within DG Competition. One step further would be to establish an independent competition agency along the lines of OLAF.[93] This would isolate the fact-gathering function under one roof. The staff within such an agency could, for instance, deal with cases up to the statement of objections, and then submit the case to the Hearing Officer or the hearing tribunal.

Thus the system could be greatly improved and made more acceptable if the drafting of the decision were entrusted to an individual or group of individuals who had not been involved in the preparation of the prosecution case. Candidates for the discharge of such a function would be members of the judiciary, independent teachers or practitioners of law, and very senior Commission officials with the rank of deputy

93. For a fuller discussion of a possible independent European competition authority, see the working paper by Andreangeli et al., *Enforcement by the Commission – the decisional and enforcement structure in antitrust cases and the Commission's fining system*, in Merola & Waelbroeck (Editors), *Towards an optimal enforcement of competition rules in Europe*, Chapter 3, Bruylant, Brussels (2010).

director general or director general. The current Hearing Officers would be ideally suited to such a role. Indeed they already carry out an assessment of the substance of the cases in their interim report, but this report is not made public and has no formal influence on the final decision. If the persons were to sit in a tribunal as a trio, there could be a Commission representative alongside two others. If the 'Hearing Officer' were to be a sole individual, ideally the role should not be filled by a member of DG Competition, but by another person with experience of competition cases, who could be attached to, say, the Commission President or the Secretary General. The problem of independence would not be eliminated, but the problem would be less flagrant. If the person or persons taking the decision were obliged to act in independence, and were truly independent of DG Competition, the problem would be materially eased. The problem of bad procedure would have been palliated. It would not be a perfect solution, but it would be an improvement.

Endowing the Hearing Officers with more important functions would be a step in the right direction. The Hearing Officer could organize a proper hearing to get to the bottom of the facts, and could report in writing. If that report were made available to the parties its conclusions could not readily be ignored. This would call for time, staff, facilities and support far more extensive than is currently the case.

The hearing should take place in front of the person who will determine the facts. Otherwise, it is not really a hearing. Subject to confidentiality concerns, there is no reason why Commission hearings should not be public. The ECtHR has held that '[a]n oral and public hearing constitutes a fundamental principle enshrined in Article 6(1)'.[94] The presence of outsiders would engender an improvement in quality. It would require more solid standards of evidence, and of precision and moderation, than currently prevail. The hearing should provide for a more formal method of scrutiny, by allowing the defendant company to challenge the evidence against it, including the witnesses upon whose testimony the Commission relies. This would require modification to Regulation 1/2003: the hearing would no longer be optional for the parties. It would be an obligatory part of the procedure. (In a number of cases, accused companies have waived a hearing believing that it would change no minds.) The parties, as well as other natural and legal persons, would be obliged to appear before the decision-maker, to reply to the questions posed, and to tell the truth. A prosecution for dangerous driving should not have manifestly superior processes to determine facts than an important competition law prosecution on whose outcome thousands of jobs or millions of Euros or criminal liability may directly or indirectly depend. Thus reform is not at all inimical to efficient prosecution of important cases.

§15.10 CONCLUSION

In the process of finalizing the text of this chapter, I have tried to make sense of the apparent contradiction between *Jussila* and *Menarini*, and the uncertain augury of

94. *Jussila v. Finland* (2007) 45 E.H.R.R. 39 at [40].

Halcor/Chalkor and KME.[95] I have been helped by the brave attempt of the EFTA Court in 2011 in *Norge Post*[96] to reconcile the authorities. Let us recollect where things stood.

The citizen in dispute with the public authority has more procedural rights if the matter is 'criminal' than if it is not. The *Engel* criteria mean that if a matter is labelled criminal in domestic parlance, that will guarantee the applicability of Article 6 ECHR; but the domestic categorization of the infringement is no more than a starting point, implying that the authority cannot be sure of avoiding the inconvenience of Article 6 by calling the offence 'administrative'. Putting it differently, almost no deference or credit is given to how the state defines its regime. After *Engel*, the scope of what was eligible for the protections of Article 6 ECHR was expanded steadily to cover a range of controversies with the state.

It has to be recorded that the discussion about the application of the case law of the ECtHR to 'administrative' penalties is confused and confusing. In *Jussila*, the Court considered the imposition of a EUR 300 surcharge by an administrative authority. It made a distinction between what the literature calls hardcore criminal offences and others:

> it is self-evident that there are criminal cases which do not carry any significant degree of stigma. There are clearly 'criminal charges' of differing weight. Tax surcharges differ from the hard core of criminal law; consequently, the criminal-head guarantees will not necessarily apply with their full stringency (see *Bendenoun* and *Janosevic*, §46 and §81 respectively, where it was found compatible with Article 6§1 for criminal penalties to be imposed, in the first instance by an administrative or non-judicial body: *a contrario, Findlay v. the United Kingdom* ...[97]

Jussila was a decision of a Grand Chamber, therefore highly authoritative, but dissents by Judges Zupančič and Spielmann (now President) made it less authoritative. The Court also said 'there must be at first instance a tribunal which fully meets the requirements of Article 6'. Following *Jussila*, it seemed to me that the Court had declared unacceptable regimes under which an administrative agency imposed penalties in matters which did involve a 'significant degree of stigma'.[98]

Now, the public stigma of being condemned for competition infringement is much greater than losing an argument with the tax authorities. Citizens who have to pay tax penalties, or civil penalties for putting out rubbish on the wrong day or for customs irregularities, are not exposed to public disgrace. In tax cases, the facts in dispute are usually narrowly limited and the dispute turns on how to characterize them. The frequency and circumstances under which tax investigations are conducted substantially differ from the way the Commission conducts its competition investigations. Nor does the tax authority encourage private lawsuits against the infringer.

95. See also Helene Andersson's contribution in this book, Chapter 16, for a discussion of these cases and their effects for EU competition law.
96. Case E-15/10, *Posten Norge AS v. EFTA Surveillance Authority*, Judgment of the Court, 18 April 2012, [0000] EFTA Ct. Rep. 000.
97. *Jussila v. Finland* (2007) E.H.R.R. 39, para. 43.
98. See Ian Forrester, *A Challenge for Europe's Judges: The Review of Fines in Competition Cases*, 36 E.L. Rev. 185 (2011)

The ECtHR seems to have partially reversed *Jussila* by its judgment in *Menarini*. Perhaps 'reversed' is too strong. Maybe 'departed from' or 'elected not to follow' would be more accurate. In *Menarini*, the Court found that the imposition of a fine by the administrative agency in a competition case was acceptable under Article 6 in that the civil courts had jurisdiction over questions of fact and law on appeal, could review the evidence and could review how the authority had exercised its discretion in imposing the fine. If *Menarini* (not a Grand Chamber decision, and weakened by the dissent of Judge Pinto de Albuquerque) is reliable, then punishment by an administrative agency may be made acceptable by the intensity of the available judicial review.[99]

One way of approaching the matter is to conclude that there is no single test by which the requirements of Article 6 can be assessed. On this reasoning, the totality of what happens at first instance may be relevant to the adequacy of the treatment accorded to the citizen. This involves discarding *Jussila*'s convincing distinction between categories of controversy, with a special status for the 'hard core' of offences. This line was taken, not without some head-scratching, by the EFTA Court in *Norge Post*.

In any event, I respectfully suggest that the level of intensity of judicial review in EU competition cases is of uncertain adequacy. Judicial review of 'legality' is evidently lesser than judicial review of 'correctness'. As set forth above, the Courts in Luxembourg have saddled themselves with language which, in some cases, excuses a light check on formal adequacy and rationality, while in other cases they rigorously and sceptically challenge what the administration has done and how it has justified itself. While the judgments in *Chalkor* and *KME* confirm the Courts' duty to be non-deferential in assessing fines, the Courts' competence in appeals not involving fines is merely a check of legality. Sometimes the Courts robustly review the facts, and sometimes they do not.

I therefore submit that the case law of the ECtHR in Strasbourg is not clear; that the case law of the European Courts in Luxembourg is inadequate to satisfy the requirements of Article 6 of the Convention in all cases; and that the Commission's regime for deciding competition cases is deeply inadequate. It is profoundly troubling that scrutiny of these procedures by the ECtHR is being prolonged by the very regrettable slowness to accomplish the accession of the EU to the ECHR. I hope that when next this distinguished gathering occurs in Stockholm, the EU institutions will have either adapted their practices or exposed them to scrutiny in Strasbourg.

99. See further Renato Nazzini, *Administrative Enforcement, Judicial Review and Fundamental rights in EU Competition Law: a Comparative Contextual-Functionalist Perspective*, CMLR 49, 971 (2012).

CHAPTER 16

Judicial Review after *Menarini*: Any Need for Reform of the EU System?

Helene Andersson

§16.01 INTRODUCTION

Google 'due process and antitrust' and you will get nearly 2,000,000 results. Obviously, only a fraction of these have anything to do with due process in EU antitrust cases. Nonetheless, the number of articles dealing with this issue is significant, and there is an ongoing and much heated debate as to whether the system in place does actually meet the standards of the European Convention on Human Rights, standards which shall lay the floor for EU fundamental rights protection.

Those critical of the EU antitrust enforcement system[1] argue that an order where the European Commission acts as investigator, prosecutor and judge is incapable of safeguarding fundamental rights, and that those targeted by the Commission's investigations are denied access to rights such as the right to a fair trial. The subsequent judicial review of the Commission's decisions has also been criticized for being too deferential.

In September 2011, the European Court of Human Rights (the Strasbourg Court or the ECtHR) delivered its ruling in the *Menarini* case, giving its view on the standard of review to be performed in antitrust cases. According to some, the ruling should put an end to the debate, whereas others anticipate the debate to continue for many years. Given the subsequent rulings by the European Court of Justice (the ECJ or the Court) and the EFTA Court in the *KME* and *Norway Post* cases, as well as the recent and successful attempt by the Commission to wear yet another hat, this time as a plaintiff in an antitrust damages action, there is no indication that the debate will end at this stage.

1. See e.g., contribution by Ian Forrester in this book, Chapter 15.

§16.02 BACKGROUND TO THE DEBATE ON THE DUAL ROLES OF ANTITRUST AUTHORITIES

Contrary to what is the case in certain national legal systems, such as the Swedish for example, the European Commission has the powers both to investigate suspected infringements of the competition rules and to impose sanctions on competition law offenders.[2] During the last fifteen years, we have witnessed a more aggressive, or diligent if you so prefer, application of these powers by the Commission. This new approach has given rise to an intense debate on whether the EU antitrust enforcement system respects fundamental rights.

Although the debate is very heated at the moment, it is far from new. Already in the 1970s, complaints were made about the lack of separation of powers violating the European Convention for the Protection of Human Rights and Fundamental Freedoms (the ECHR), principally Article 6 and the right to a fair trial enshrined therein.[3]

Surely, those critical of the system already back then could not have imagined what would come. In the 1990s, the EU started to glance overseas at the US antitrust enforcement system, and decided to borrow two of its more successful features; sentencing guidelines and leniency programmes. This was followed by the implementation of the Modernization package in 2004. Today, the substantive competition rules may be more or less identical to those in force in the 1960s, but the administrative enforcement show few similarities, if any, with that of the early days of European integration.

The European Commission's Directorate General for Competition (DG COMP) is now perceived as an aggressive and diligent enforcer of the EU competition rules. At the same time, the EU Courts are perceived by their critics as anything but aggressive. Instead they are criticized for failing to perform the in-depth review of the Commission's decisions required of them in antitrust cases, thereby giving the Commission too much leeway, and failing to respect the principle of equality of arms.

It is not the approach of the EU Institutions alone that is the root of the heated debate. It has also been fuelled by recent changes in the legal landscape of the EU. Through the entry into force of the Lisbon Treaty in December 2009, EU fundamental rights protection has been strengthened in a number of ways, giving more weight and legitimacy to the criticism.

The on-going debate has not gone unnoticed by either the Commission or the EU Courts. In 2011, the Commission adopted a package of measures aimed at increasing interaction with parties in antitrust proceedings and strengthening the mechanisms for safeguarding parties' procedural rights.[4] However, it still appears unlikely that the

2. The EFTA Surveillance Authority (ESA) and the Italian Competition Authority do also have these powers, and it is their decisions that were challenged in the cases brought to the EFTA Court and the Strasbourg Court respectively.
3. A. Riley, *The Modernisation of EU Anti-Cartel Enforcement: Will the Commission Grasp the Opportunity?*, CEPS Special Report/January 2010, p. 11.
4. Commission notice on best practices for the conduct of proceedings concerning Articles 101 and 102 TFEU, OJ 2011/C 308/06.

debate will result in a more profound revision of the system, relieving the Commission of some of its powers.

On the contrary, at the same time as the Commission presents its best practices in antitrust cases, the lack of an effective legal framework for antitrust damages actions has urged it to take on yet another role. This time as plaintiff in an antitrust damages case.[5] It was in the wake of the elevator cartel proceedings,[6] that the Commission, not only an enforcer this time but also a customer of the elevator companies, chose to bring damages actions before a Belgian court against the members of the cartel.

This caused the defendants to argue that the Commission's actions were contrary to Article 47 of the Charter of Fundamental Rights of the European Union (and its right to an effective remedy and to a fair trial), as the Commission was (allegedly) acting as judge in its own cause and was disrespecting the principle of equality of arms. In a preliminary ruling, the Grand Chamber of the ECJ has now declared that the actions by the Commission are well in line with the Charter. The recent ruling has once again sparked the discussion on the Commission's practices.

Below is a brief and general background to the fundamental rights protection in the EU followed by a more specific discussion on fundamental rights issues relating to antitrust cases and the issue of the standard of review. This discussion will be conducted against the background of three recent rulings by three different European courts, all dealing with the issue of the intensity of the judicial review required in antitrust cases.[7]

§16.03 FUNDAMENTAL RIGHTS PROTECTION IN THE EU

In the early days of European integration, it all seemed so simple. Integration was then standing on two – clearly separate but equally important – limbs, one being market integration, the other human rights protection. At the time, the EEC dealt almost exclusively with economic matters, and was striving to achieve a common market where goods could flow freely between the Member States. The Council of Europe and the Strasbourg Court on the other hand were busy establishing a human rights agenda for Europe.

However, it soon became evident that the two regimes could not be kept apart, and over the years the ECJ has had to develop its own human rights jurisprudence. The initial reason for this development was arguably the adoption of the doctrine of supremacy in the 1960s,[8] a doctrine allowing all EU rules to take precedence over national rules of any type.

5. Case C-199/11, *Europese Gemeenschap v. Otis N.V. et al.* [2012] ECR I-000.
6. Cases C-494/11P, C-501/11P, C-503/11P to 506/11P, C-510/11P, C-516/11P and C-519/11P.
7. The ruling of the European Court on Human Rights in the case *A. Menarini Diagnostics S.R.L. v. Italy*, application no. 43509/08; the ruling(s) of the Court of Justice of the European Union in Cases C-272/09 P and C-389/10 P, *KME v. Commission* and C-386/10 P, *Chalkor v. Commission*, [2011] ECR I-000; and, finally, the ruling of the EFTA Court in Case E-15/10, *Posten Norge AS v. EFTA Surveillance Authority*.
8. The case *Costa v. ENEL* being considered as the landmark ruling; Case 6/64, *Flaminio Costa v. E.N.E.L*, [1964] ECR 585.

By adopting the doctrine of supremacy, the ECJ soon faced opposition from especially the German and Italian constitutional courts. These courts did not accept such supremacy as it implied that the fundamental rights protected by their constitutions would be at stake. Facing an ever growing criticism, the Court was more or less forced to find a solution to the problem created by the dichotomy between EU law and national constitutions.

The solution opted for by the ECJ was to let fundamental rights become general principles of Community law, and not only regard them as part of the Member State regimes. The first judgment where the Court applied a general principle that can be regarded as a fundamental right, was the *Max Gutmann* case concerning the application of the rule *ne bis in idem*.[9] Four years later, following the Court's judgment in *Stauder v. City of Ulm*,[10] no doubts remained as to whether fundamental rights formed part of the EU legal system, as the Court declared that:

> The provision at issue contains nothing capable of prejudicing the fundamental human rights enshrined in the general principles of Community law and protected by the Court.[11]

From thereon, we know that the Court has continued to develop its human rights jurisprudence. However, this jurisprudence has not gone hand in hand with legislative measures, and for the first forty years of European integration, the ECJ carried the burden of establishing and maintaining a platform for human rights protection more or less on its own.

In recent years, a number of legislative measures have been taken in order to achieve also a statutory framework. At the time when there was still an on-going debate as to whether the EU should have its own constitution, it was decided that the EU should at least have its own bill of rights. This bill of rights, or charter, was not intended to create new rights, but rather to assemble rights that were previously scattered over a range of sources including the ECHR and other international agreements.

However, the drafting of the charter proved to be a hard task, as opinions differed on both its purpose and its value. Whereas the Member States tended towards a declaratory text that would, at most, be politically binding, the Commission and the European Parliament were set on drafting a more significant document.[12] In the end, it was the Member States that got their way. When the EU Charter of Fundamental Rights (the Charter) was adopted in December 2000, it was not legally binding.

For a number of years, the Charter played a rather insignificant role, being undermined by its lack of binding legal effect. However, with the entry into force of the Lisbon Treaty in December 2009 it all changed. The legal landscape of human rights protection was redesigned, and the most significant changes lie in the amendments to Article 6 of the TEU.

9. Joined Cases 18 and 35/65, *Max Gutmann v. Commission of the European Communities*, [1966] ECR 103 and [1967] ECR 1961.
10. Case 26/69, *Erich Stauder v. Stadt Ulm, Sozialamt*, [1969] ECR 419.
11. *Ibid.*, at para. 7.
12. Anderson & Murphy, *The Charter of Fundamental Rights: History and Prospects in Post-Lisbon Europe*, EUI Working Paper Law, 2011/08, at p. 2.

According to Article 6 of the TEU, fundamental rights are now protected under three diverse and complementary perspectives: as general principles of the EU, as defined by the Charter and as protected by the ECHR.

Article 6(1) of the TEU gives the Charter the same legal value as the treaties, and Article 6(2) commits the EU to accede to the ECHR. Upon accession, the ECHR jurisprudence will become directly applicable before the European Courts and challenges may be brought before the Strasbourg Court for infringements committed by the EU. Article 6(3) confirms general principles as a source for fundamental rights.

As accession to the ECHR is still a question for the future, the most important change at this stage is the altered legal status of the Charter. In the four years following the entry into force of the Lisbon Treaty, the Charter has been referred to on many occasions by the ECJ.

The Charter contains all the rights encompassed in the ECHR, together with a number of additional rights, such as e.g., the right to good administration. An important feature of the Charter is its Article 52(3). Article 52(3) stipulates that, to the extent that the Charter affords rights that correspond to ECHR rights, the meaning and scope of those rights shall be the same as those laid down by the ECHR. EU law may only derogate from the ECHR if such derogation means more extensive protection. As a result, the ECHR and the case law of the Strasbourg Court now lays a floor in the protection of fundamental rights by the EU.[13] We have thus come a long way since the delivery of the ECJ's ruling in the *Max Gutmann case* in 1966. The question is, exactly how long?

§16.04 THE ECHR AS A MINIMUM STANDARD: WHAT ARE THE IMPLICATIONS FOR ANTITRUST PROCEEDINGS?

Today, companies challenging Commission decisions in antitrust cases appear to invoke violations of fundamental rights more or less on a regular basis. The debate is intense also outside the court rooms, and one of the more common objections against the EU system is that it fails to respect Article 6(1) of the ECHR and the right to a fair trial.

The critics argue that the protection provided by the EU Courts falls far short of the protection afforded under the ECHR.[14] Some even argue that the ECHR requires the Commission to be deprived of its adjudicating powers, and that fines in antitrust cases should instead be imposed by a court.

13. See e.g. the explanations to the Charter stating that the scope of the rights are not only determined by the wording of the ECHR, but also of the case law of the Strasbourg Court, and Case C-400/10 *PPU J McB v. LE*, [2010] ECR I-000, where the ECJ held that where Charter rights correspond to those in the ECHR, the Court should follow the clear and consistent jurisprudence of the ECtHR.

14. See e.g. Aslam and Ramsden, *EC Dawn Raids: A Human Rights Violation?*, The Competition Law Review, Volume 5 Issue 1, December 2008, pp. 61-87. See also the appeal by Saint Gobain SA which raises the question whether the imposition of a fine by an administrative body which holds powers both on investigation and sanction is compatible with the right to an independent and impartial tribunal and of the right to respect for the presumption of innocence. Case T-56/09, *Saint Gobain v. European Commission*, pending.

However, at this point, most accept the fact that the Commission has both investigatory and adjudicative powers. Instead the critique is focused on the judicial review performed by the EU Courts in general, and the General Court in particular. According to the critics, the General Court is too deferential towards the Commission, and is granting the Commission too large a margin of appreciation, failing to respect the principle of equality of arms. Some even refer to this as the 'judicial deference doctrine'.[15]

More specifically, the criticism against the Courts' (limited) review is focused mainly on two issues: the EU Courts' assessment of the fines imposed by the Commission in antitrust proceedings, and their review of any complex economic or technical assessments undertaken by the Commission.[16]

In order to assess the validity of these arguments, it is of course necessary to take a closer look at Article 6(1) of the ECHR. In short, the article provides that anyone charged with a criminal offence is entitled to a fair and public hearing within a reasonable time by an independent and impartial tribunal established by law.[17] Over the years, the Strasbourg Court has interpreted this to mean that, as for criminal offences within the core of the term, they shall be decided by a tribunal already at first instance whereas it is possible for an administrative authority to impose sanctions at first instance if the criminal offence comes within the wider meaning of the term, provided however, that such decisions may be appealed to a tribunal with full jurisdiction. As for the term 'full jurisdiction', the Strasbourg Court has on several occasions declared that this shall include the powers to quash a decision in all aspects, legal as well as factual.[18] In the *Silvester's Horeca* case, for example, the Strasbourg Court declared:

> Parmi les caractéristiques d'un organe judiciaire de pleine juridiction figure le pouvoir de *réformer* (emphasis added) en tous points, en fait comme en droit, la décision entreprise, rendue par l'organe inférieur. Il doit notamment avoir compétence pour se pencher sur toutes les questions de fait et de droit pertinentes pour le litige dont il se trouve saisi (Chevrol c. France, arrêt du 13 février 2003, § 77).[19]

Given the historic definition of the term full jurisdiction, many of the critics were expecting to be able to rely on the Strasbourg Court's ruling in the *Menarini* case, a case dealing with the standard of review in antitrust proceedings. Much to their surprise, the ruling of the Strasbourg Court turned out not to be quite in their favour.

---

15. See e.g. Jaeger, *The Standard of Review in Competition Cases Involving Complex Economic Assessments: Towards the Marginalisation of the Marginal Review?*, Journal of European Competition Law and Practice, 2011 2(4):295-314.
16. See also the contribution by Ian Forrester in this book, Chapter 15.
17. The Article also deals with civil rights.
18. See e.g. *Janosevic v. Sweden*, application no. 34619/97 and *Silvester's Horeca Service v. Belgium*, application no. 47650/99.
19. *Silvester's Horeca Service v. Belgium*, application no. 47650/99. Para. 27.

§16.05 THE STRASBOURG COURT AND ANTITRUST PROCEEDINGS: MUCH ADO ABOUT NOTHING?

In September 2011, the Strasbourg Court handed down its much awaited ruling in the *Menarini* case. The case of *A. Menarini Diagnostics S.R.L. v. Italy*[20] concerned the imposition of fines by the Italian Competition Authority, and its compatibility with Article 6 of the ECHR and the right to a fair trial.

To give a background to the dispute, the Italian medical diagnostics company A. Menarini Diagnostics S.R.L. (AMD) had – along with four of its competitors – been subject to a cartel investigation by the Italian competition authority Autorità Garante della Concorrenza e del Mercato (the AGCM).

In a decision of 30 April 2003, the AGCM had fined the company EUR 6 million for participation in a price fixing and market sharing cartel in the Italian diabetes diagnosis test market, stating that the penalty should serve as a deterrent to all pharmaceutical companies.[21] AMD appealed the decision to the regional administrative court (the TAR), requesting the TAR to overturn the decision of the AGCM on the grounds that AMD had not participated in any cartel activity, criticizing both the AGCM's legal analysis and its presentation of facts.

The TAR dismissed the appeal, reminding AMD that its judicial review is limited to a legality review. When reviewing AGCM's decision, the judge cannot substitute its appraisal to that of the competition authority. In its ruling, the TAR stressed that, although empowered to evaluate the facts and the application of the sanction, when assessing the facts gathered by the AGCM, the review has to be limited to the legality of the administrative decision. The TAR explicitly recognized that the judge cannot substitute its appraisal to that of the competition authority, the judge can only apply the legal norms identified by the competition authority and cannot modify the elements of the investigation or the very decision. The judicial control is limited to the verification of legality, of the logic and coherence of the decision.

AMD then turned to the *Consiglio di Stato,* arguing that, by limiting the judicial review to issues of law, the TAR had not evaluated the actions on which the determination of the fine had been made. AMD argued that the fine imposed was illegal and complained about the lack of courts with 'full jurisdiction' in the Italian administrative legal system.

The appeal was dismissed also by the *Consiglio di Stato*. Although recognizing that the powers of the administrative judge are limited to a review of issues of law, the judge may evaluate the proof gathered by the AGCM. In addition, when an authority has a margin of appreciation, the administrative court may not substitute its appraisal with that of the authority. However, the court may verify whether the authority has used its powers appropriately, and as for the imposition of fines, the court stated that the TAR has full jurisdiction to review the fines imposed.[22]

20. Application no. 43509/08.
21. Para. 9.
22. Para. 18.

AMD unsuccessfully turned to the Court of Cassation. Having exhausted all domestic remedies, AMD turned to the Strasbourg Court.

Relying on Article 6(1) of the ECHR, AMD argued that it had had no access to a court with full jurisdiction to review the administrative decision of the AGCM.[23,24] In its application, AMD stressed that, when reviewing the AGCM's decision, the judge (i) cannot substitute its appraisal to that of the competition authority, (ii) can only apply the legal norms identified by the competition authority, and (iii) cannot modify the elements of the investigation or the very decision. The judicial control is limited to the verification of legality, of the logic and coherence of the decision.[25]

In its ruling, the ECtHR confirmed that competition law could be considered penal and subject to the protections afforded by Article 6(1) ECHR given the severity and repressive character of the fine imposed.

However, the Strasbourg Court rejected AMD's main contention that there had been a breach of Article 6(1) ECHR. Instead it declared that the Italian Courts do in fact have full jurisdiction in competition cases, since they can examine the elements of proof, verify whether the administration has used the powers in an appropriate manner,[26] verify the reasonableness and proportionality of the choices within a decision, verify the technical matters,[27] as well as amend the sanction.[28]

The standard set by the Strasbourg Court in this ruling differs from its previous case law, as the court opens for a differentiated standard not only when it comes to the question of whether a case must be decided by a tribunal already at first instance or not, but also when it comes to the definition of the term 'full jurisdiction'. The Strasbourg Court is still adamant that the courts should have full jurisdiction in order to be able to ensure a fair trial, but nevertheless sets a different standard stating that:

> Par ailleurs, la Cour rappelle que la nature d'une procédure administrative peut différer, sous plusieurs aspects, de la nature d'une procédure pénale au sens strict du terme. Si ces différences ne sauraient exonérer les Etats contractants de leur obligation de respecter toutes les garanties offertes par le volet pénal de l'article 6, elles peuvent néanmoins influencer les modalités de leur application.[29]

The court seems to have settled for a 'good enough scrutiny' this time, choosing not so much to look at what the Italian courts are empowered to do as what they actually did.

23. Para. 51.
24. http://cmiskp.echr.coe.int/tkp197/portal.asp?sessionId=80512717&skin=hudoc-pr-en&action=request.
25. Para. 52.
26. Para. 63.
27. Para. 64.
28. Para. 65.
29. Para. 62.

§16.06 THE ECJ AND ANTITRUST PROCEEDINGS

Only two months after the Strasbourg Court delivered the ruling in the *Menarini* case, it was the ECJ's turn to give its view on the standard of review in antitrust proceedings. This was done in the two *KME* rulings and the *Chalkor* ruling, all of the same day.[30]

Here, the Commission had imposed fines on several companies for their participation in cartels on the markets of copper industrial tubes and copper plumbing tubes. KME was fined under both decisions, whereas Chalkor was fined under the copper plumbing tubes decision. Both companies unsuccessfully appealed the decisions to the General Court.

Turning to the ECJ, KME and Chalkor criticized the General Court's willingness to grant the Commission a margin of appreciation when it came to the calculation and imposition of fines, an area where the Commission has traditionally enjoyed a wide margin of appreciation, both when it comes to the choice of factors to be taken into account when calculating fines and the assessment of such factors. The companies argued that the Commission should not enjoy *any* margin of appreciation in this area as the EU Courts have full jurisdiction when it comes to fines. According to the applicants, the General Court had infringed EU law and the applicants' fundamental right to a full and effective judicial review under Article 47 of the Charter by failing to examine their arguments closely and thoroughly and had deferred, to an excessive and unreasonable extent, to the Commission's discretion.

In its judgment(s), the ECJ reiterated the statement made in *Tetra Laval*[31] regarding the standard of review to be carried out in complex economic matters, declaring that although the Commission has a margin of discretion in such areas, this does not relieve the Courts of their duty to evaluate the evidence presented by the Commission and to assess whether the evidence does actually substantiate the findings of the Commission. Furthermore as regards the determination of fines, the ECJ noted that this process requires the Commission to consider a large number of factors and that the Commission must therefore carry out a thorough examination of the circumstances of the infringement.[32] This in turn means that:

> the Courts must carry out the review of legality incumbent upon them on the basis of the evidence adduced by the applicant in support of the pleas in law put forward. In carrying out such a review, the Courts cannot use the Commission's margin of discretion – either as regards the choice of factors taken into account in the application of the criteria mentioned in the Guidelines or as regards the assessment of those factors – as a basis for dispensing with the conduct of an in-depth review of the law and of the facts.[33]

When reviewing the fines imposed by the Commission, the Court may thus no longer rely on the margin of discretion of the Commission, but has to conduct an in-depth

30. Cases C-272/09 P and C-389/10 P, *KME v. Commission* and C-386/10 P, *Chalkor v. Commission*, [2011] ECR I-000.
31. Case C-12/03 P, *Commission v. Tetra Laval*, [2005] I-00987.
32. Case C-272/09P *KME v. Commission* [2011] ECRI-000, at para. 98.
33. *Ibid.*, para. 102.

review of both the law and of the facts. As for the threshold of this in-depth review, the ECJ did not give any specifications as to what is required. However, it is apparent from the judgment that the standard of review conducted by the General Court in the present case was considered sufficient as the ECJ stated:

> It must be noted in that regard that although the General Court repeatedly referred to the 'discretion', the 'substantial margin of discretion' or the 'wide discretion' of the Commission, including in paragraphs 35 to 37, 92, 103, 115, 118, 129 and 141 of the judgment under appeal, such references did not prevent the General Court from carrying out the full and unrestricted review, in law and in fact, required of it.[34]

As for the applicants' claim that they were denied effective judicial protection, the ECJ concluded:

> The review provided for by the Treaties thus involves review by the Courts of the European Union of both the law and the facts, and means that they have the power to assess the evidence, to annul the contested decision and to alter the amount of a fine. The review of legality provided for under Article 263 TFEU, supplemented by the unlimited jurisdiction in respect of the amount of the fine, provided for under Article 31 of Regulation No 1/2003, is not therefore contrary to the requirements of the principle of effective judicial protection in Article 47 of the Charter.[35]

Judging from the Court's rulings, the limited review does have limits and the General Court should no longer resort to a manifest error test. However, although the ECJ has now eliminated any doubts as to whether the standard of review established in *Tetra Laval* applies also to Article 101 cases, and explicitly requires the General Court to carry out an in-depth review – both of the law and of the facts – when it comes to the determination of fines, it is also true that the Court is satisfied with the level of review actually performed by the General Court in this case, and that there is thus no reason for the General Court to apply a stricter standard than it does today. Like the Strasbourg Court, the ECJ seems to focus more on the review actually performed than the statutes regulating such review.

The only reason the EU Courts should be *forced* to adhere to a stricter standard would be if the Strasbourg Court would come to a different conclusion with regard to the standard of review required in order for an antitrust enforcement system to be compatible with Article 6(1) ECHR. At this stage, with the *Menarini* judgment as a bench mark, it appears as if the judicial review carried out by the General Court is to the satisfaction also of the Strasbourg Court.[36] The question then is of course whether the EU Courts should settle for 'the good enough standard' applied by the Strasbourg Court or whether the ruling of the court in Strasbourg should merely be considered as a minimum standard.

---

34. Para. 109.
35. Para. 106.
36. For a more cautious conclusion as to the question whether the procedures under EU law are adequate in the light of Article 6 ECHR see Ian Forrester's contribution to this book, Chapter 15.

§16.07 THE EFTA COURT AND ANTITRUST PROCEEDINGS

Also the EFTA Court has recently been given the opportunity to give its say on the standard of review in antitrust cases. In April 2012, the EFTA Court delivered its ruling in the *Norway Post* case.[37]

In June 2002, the EFTA Surveillance Authority (ESA), received a complaint that the former monopolist Norway Post was abusing its dominant position through certain exclusivity arrangements. Following investigations into the matter, ESA issued a decision against Norway Post, imposing a EUR 13 million fine on Norway Post for breach of Article 54 of the EEA Agreement.[38] According to the decision, Norway Post had abused its dominant position in the business-to-consumer parcel market in Norway during the period 2000 through 2006.

Norway Post appealed the decision to the EFTA Court, challenging the finding that its behaviour constituted an abuse. In its application to the EFTA Court, Norway Post contended that ESA should bear the burden of proof. Since the fine imposed was tantamount to a criminal charge, this meant that the existence of the circumstances that constitute the infringement must be proven beyond any reasonable doubt. Furthermore, Norway Post submitted that, in order for the procedure to be compliant with Article 6 of the ECHR, the EFTA Court must have full jurisdiction, including the power to quash in every respect, on issues of fact as well as law, the contested decision. Referring to Article 2 of Protocol 7 to the ECHR, Norway Post contended that this must apply *a fortiori* in the absence of a possibility to appeal to a second instance. ESA challenged the applicant's claim, arguing that as its assessment of the competitive situation is by its nature a complex economic assessment, and that the EFTA Court should thus not carry out an in-depth review, but must instead resort to a manifest error test.

In its judgment, the EFTA Court started out by acknowledging that the provisions of the EEA agreement should be interpreted in the light of fundamental rights and that both the ECHR and the case law of the Strasbourg court are important sources in the determination of such rights.[39] Not only did the EFTA Court rely on the ECHR, it also made express reference to the Charter and its Article 47.[40]

As for the burden of proof, the Court recalled that this lies on ESA, and that ESA must submit precise and consistent evidence in order to establish the existence of the infringement. It then went on to discuss its own review and assessment of the evidence presented by ESA, reiterating what the ECJ has said about complex economic assessments, and stating that ECJ's case law must be seen against the background of the limitation of the powers of review inherent in the concept of legality review.[41]

According to the EFTA Court, the legality review prevents it from annulling a decision if there can be no legal objection to the assessment of ESA, even if such

37. Case E-15/10, *Posten Norge AS v. EFTA Surveillance Authority*.
38. Corresponding to Article 102 of the TFEU.
39. Para. 85.
40. Para. 86.
41. Para. 96.

assessment is not the one which the court would consider to be preferable. This said, the EFTA Court went on to declare that it must not refrain from reviewing ESA's interpretation of information of an economic nature, and that Article 6(1) ECHR requires that the subsequent control of a criminal sanction is undertaken by a tribunal with full jurisdiction to quash in all aspects, factual as well as legal, the challenged decision. Against this background, ESA should not be regarded to have any margin of discretion when imposing fines in antitrust proceedings other than the leeway that '... *necessarily flows from the limitations inherent in the system of legality review*'.[42]

Furthermore, the EFTA Court acknowledged that it must be convinced that the conclusions drawn by ESA are supported by the facts presented. The court then concluded that the submission by ESA that the EFTA Court may intervene only if it considers a complex economic assessment of ESA to be manifestly wrong must be rejected.

§16.08 THREE RULINGS AND JUST AS MANY STANDARDS OF REVIEW?

Had the judgments of the ECJ and the EFTA Court been delivered in August 2011 – the month *before* the Strasbourg handed down its ruling in *Menarini* – it is my firm belief that those critical of the EU (and EEA) systems would have given the two rulings a fail, and argued that the requirements set by the two courts do not meet the standards of the ECHR.

Although many still argue that the judicial review performed by the EU and EEA Courts do not afford the protection required under Article 6(1), it is nonetheless hard to find support for such arguments in the *Menarini* case itself, as the Strasbourg Court chose to give the term *full jurisdiction* a more narrow meaning in administrative proceedings than in 'hard core' criminal proceedings. Furthermore, as is often the case, the Strasbourg Court chose to focus more on the review actually performed by the Italian courts than the frameworks provided to them by the Italian legislator.

Also the ECJ seems to apply somewhat of an *in casu* approach, noting that the General Court, although referring to the Commission's margin of discretion on numerous occasions, did actually carry out the full and unrestricted review, in law as well as in fact, required of it. A more general guidance as to the intensity of review required would have been welcome.

Instead, both the judgments of the ECJ and the EFTA Court leave a number of question marks as to the intensity of review to be performed in antitrust proceedings. For example – it is hard to determine exactly what the EFTA court means when it states:

> ESA should not be regarded to have any margin of discretion when imposing fines in antitrust proceedings other than the leeway that necessarily flows from the limitations inherent in the system of legality review.[43]

42. Para. 100.
43. Para. 100 of the ruling.

Likewise, the ECJ causes some confusion when it declares that the Commission should have no margin of appreciation and the General Court should carry out an in-depth review of facts and law also when it performs its legality review, but at the same time is satisfied with the review actually performed by the General Court.

Although we do know that the General Court may no longer refrain to a strict manifest error test, and the Court has in that respect raised the bar somewhat, it may take many years and number of rulings before we know exactly what is required by the courts in order for the judicial review in antitrust proceedings to meet the standards set by Article 6(1) of the ECHR.

Another aspect to be considered is of course whether the EU system should settle for the 'good enough standard' applied by the Strasbourg Court in the *Menarini* case, or whether it is actually more appropriate to regard that ruling only to 'set a floor', and strive to achieve a system which meets an even higher standard. This question is especially pertinent, as there is an additional dimension to be considered in EU antitrust cases.

The Strasbourg Court's ruling deals with a national system where an infringement of the competition rules may result in the imposition of fines. Here, we can draw a parallel to the EU system and argue that the same standards should apply in the EU as the sanctions are more or less the same and of an administrative character. However, although the *Commission* is not empowered to send anyone to prison, the authorities in several *Member States* do have such powers. Surely, there have been and there will be cartel cases brought by the Commission with effects also in national antitrust proceedings.

In the *Marine hose cartel* for example, a number of individuals were sentenced to prison in the US, and were then 'shipped' to the UK to face prosecution for the crimes under UK law. At the same time, the cartel was investigated by the Commission which later imposed fines of EUR 131 million.[44] Clearly, in a situation like this, it is hard to keep the different systems apart, especially since a decision by the Commission will have a binding effect on any national authorities that rule on agreements or practices that have already been the subject of such decision.[45]

Unlike the decision taken by the AGCM in the *Menarini* case, decisions by the Commission and the review of such decisions by the EU Courts may have severe implications for individuals in subsequent national proceedings concerning the same set of facts. Leaving a discussion on possible *ne bis in idem* problems to professor Wouter Devroe in his contribution in this book,[46] clearly this additional dimension makes it hard to draw a straight parallel to the *Menarini* case.

However, this has not (yet) been a concern of the ECJ. On the contrary, the ECJ's rulings in the *KME* and *Chalkor* cases, as well as the subsequent *OTIS* ruling, allowing the Commission to take on yet another role in antitrust cases, suggests that at this

44. Case COMP/39406 *Marine Hoses*.
45. Article 16 of Regulation 1/2003.
46. See contribution by Devroe in this volume, Chapter 18.

point, the Court sees no reason to raise the bar and to consider the ECHR standard only to lay the floor for EU fundamental rights protection in antitrust cases.

Irrespective of the ECJs current view on the matter, there are so many aspects to consider and so many differing opinions voiced in this debate, that it is highly unlikely that it will end here.

CHAPTER 17

Data Mirroring during Dawn-Raids: Right to Judicial Review

Ingeborg Simonsson

§17.01 INTRODUCTION

This contribution addresses the right to judicial review in Member State courts when large amounts of data are copied electronically at the premises of companies suspected of competition law infringements.

When competition authorities carry out investigations and inspections, the practice has spread in recent years of making extensive copies of contents of computers or servers. This is sometimes referred to as mirroring. The competition authority brings back the mirror image to its own premises in order to analyse it extensively with the help of forensic software. This type of indexing and searching can take anything from a few days to several months. Companies subjected to mirroring will ask themselves whether they can challenge the practice before a court.

For judicial review, there must be access to court. In addition, the standard of legal review must be sufficient to allow for a real review. The thesis put forward is that there is a right to judicial review under EU law and, in Member States, pursuant to the European Convention of Human Rights and Fundamental Freedoms (ECHR) of decisions authorizing mirroring of data. Such judicial review must meet the standards set by the EUCJ and, at least in Member States, by the ECtHR in *Primagaz, Canal Plus* and *Robathin*.

§17.02 SOURCES OF LAW

There are several sources of EU law in operation at the same time when competition law inspections are made; the rules in Regulation 1/2003,[1] the jurisprudence where the EUCJ has developed fundamental rights and general principles, and the Charter of Fundamental Rights of the European Union[2] as well as the jurisprudence that is being developed to interpret it.

For Member States, yet another source of law applies, namely that of the ECHR.

§17.03 STANDARD OF REVIEW CAN DIFFER DEPENDING ON THE TYPE OF DECISION

Standard of judicial review in competition law cases brought before Member State courts will be set by national law.[3] However, it will be necessary to check whether national law meets the requirements under EU law and the ECHR. Standard of judicial review has been addressed at length in the respective judgments of the ECtHR and of the EUCJ in *Menarini*[4] and *KME*. The EUCJ held in *KME* that the principle of effective judicial protection is a general principle of European Union law to which expression is now given by Article 47 of the Charter of Fundamental Rights.[5] However, those judgments concerned appeals against final decisions imposing fines on undertakings.

Although of great interest, the judgments in *Menarini* and *KME* are inconclusive as regards the standard of review of decisions authorizing inspections. Decisions prohibiting anti-competitive practices and imposing fines on companies are adopted after years of extensive investigation and legal analysis. On the other hand, decisions authorizing dawn-raids or other investigative measures will be adopted at an early stage in the proceedings. Such decisions may be based on evidence that is yet insufficient to prove an infringement. There may in addition be severe time-constraints for the investigating authorities, since an investigation must be carried out without alerting the companies involved, before they have time to destroy or manipulate any evidence. It should come as no surprise that the ECtHR and the EUCJ have had to develop *separate* lines of case law on judicial review of decisions authorizing investigative measures.

1. Council Regulation (EC) No 1/2003, [2003] OJ L 1/1.
2. According to Article 6(1) of the Treaty on European Union, the Union recognises the rights, freedoms and principles set out in the Charter of Fundamental Rights of the European Union of 7 December 2000, as adapted at Strasbourg, on 12 December 2007, which shall have the same legal value as the Treaties. According to Article 6(3) of the TEU, fundamental rights, as guaranteed by the European Convention for the Protection of Human Rights and Fundamental Freedoms (ECHR) and as they result from the constitutional traditions common to the Member States, shall constitute general principles of the Union's law. The provisions of the Charter of Fundamental Rights are addressed not only to the institutions, bodies, offices and agencies of the Union but also to the Member States, when they are implementing Union law (see article 51(1) of the Charter).
3. Joined Cases C-430/93 and C-431/93 *Van Schijndel and van Veen* [1995] ECR I-4705, at paras 17-19.
4. Judgment on 27 September 2011 in *A. Menarini Diagnostics v. Italy*, Case No 43509/08.
5. Case C-389/10 P *KME Germany and others v. Commission* [2011] ECR I-0000, paras 118-133.

§17.04 JUDICIAL REVIEW THROUGH STAND-ALONE ACTIONS OR RETROSPECTIVE CONTROL?

Procedural law before the EUCJ allows to a certain extent for stand-alone actions against Commission decisions authorizing inspections. Otherwise, claims relating to procedural errors will be tried within an appeal of a final decision.

The EUCJ has established that although certain rights of the defence relate only to the contentious proceedings which follow the delivery of the statement of objections, other rights, such as the right to legal representation and the privileged nature of correspondence between lawyer and client, must be respected as from the preliminary-inquiry stage.[6] The General Court considers that the administrative procedure under Regulation 1/2003, which takes place before the Commission, is divided into two distinct and successive stages, each having its own internal logic, namely a preliminary investigation stage and an *inter partes* stage.[7] This explains why claims on insufficient access to documents will be tried within an appeal, since it has to do with the second stage in the proceedings before the Commission.[8] Similarly, claims that incriminating questions were asked have been tried within the appeal of a final decision.[9] An undertaking may find out during the second stage of the proceedings that the Commission has gone outside of the subject-matter of the investigation when searching the premises *another* undertaking which is also suspected of the same infringement, and this could be tried within an appeal.[10]

Part of the logic underlying differential procedural treatment seems to be that some procedural errors can be set right afterwards by excluding evidence on appeal,[11] and yet other errors have no impact on the rights of the defence.[12]

The primary grounds for challenging inspection decisions on a stand-alone basis would be deficiencies in the evidential basis underpinning the decisions,[13] or that the Commission had not fulfilled its duty to state reasons.[14] Those two aspects often interact. One of the purposes of the requirement to give reasons for a particular decision is to enable the EU judicature to exercise its power to review the legality of the

6. Joined Cases 46/87 and 227/88 *Hoechst v. Commission* [1989] ECR 2859, at para. 16.
7. T-410/09 *Almamet v. Commission* [2012] REU II-0000, at para. 24 with references.
8. Joined Cases C-204/00 etc. *Aalborg Portland and others v. Commission* [2004] ECR I-123, at paras 68-73.
9. Joined Cases T-236/01 etc. *Tokai Carbon and others v. Commission* [2004] ECR II-1181, at paras 407-409.
10. *Almamet*, note 7 above, at para. 34.
11. Case 85/87 *Dow Benelux v. Commission* [1989] ECR 3137, at para. 18, Joined Cases C-238/99 P, etc. *Limburgse Vinyl Maatschappij and others v. Commission* [2002] ECR I-8375, at paras 298-300.
12. Case C-194/99 P *Thyssen Stahl v. Commission* [2003] ECR I-10821, at para. 31.
13. Case 374/87 *Orkem v. Commission* [1989] ECR 3283, Joined Cases 97/87 to 99/87 *Dow Chemical Ibérica and others v. Commission* [1989] ECR 3165, at paras 50-53, see also as regards requests for information order of the President of the Court of First Instance of 21 November 1990, Case T-39/90 R *SEP v. Commission* [1990] ECR II-649.
14. *Dow Chemical*, note 13 above, at paras 43-49.

decision, while the scope of the duty depends on the nature of the measure in question and on the context in which it was adopted.[15]

Another viable cause of action at the investigation stage, tried on a stand-alone basis by the General Court and the EUCJ, is that the decision does not comply with the principle of proportionality. The obligation imposed on an undertaking to supply information should not be a burden on that undertaking which is disproportionate to the needs of the inquiry. The need for protection against arbitrary or disproportionate intervention by the public authorities in the sphere of private activities of any person, whether natural or legal, is recognized as a general principle of EU law.[16]

In addition, the procedure before the EU Courts allows for stand-alone actions to determine whether documents are legally privileged, that is correspondence between independent lawyers and clients.[17] National rules on legal privilege need not be identical to EU law.[18] However, as will be set out here, it can be expected that a high degree of similarity will be required when applying national law.

This leads to the question how mirroring will be assessed – will it be tried on a stand-alone basis or only within the scope of an action for the annulment of the final decision? And this particular question has been tried by the General Court in *Nexans* and *Prysmian*, as will be set out later.

§17.05 STANDARD OF JUDICIAL REVIEW UNDER EU LAW

Standard of judicial review of investigation decisions has undergone a significant development in EU law. Back in the 1980s, the Commission seemed to enjoy nearly total discretion in deciding whether a request for information or an inspection was necessary.[19] In *Dow Chemical*, the applicants claimed that the Commission decisions infringed the principle of legality because they were not based on evidence or indicia of such a nature as to justify the inspections.[20] This was rejected by the Court of Justice because the applicants had in no way substantiated that claim.[21] It can be questioned whether the Court made any assessment at all of the evidence on which the Commission based the decisions. Following the establishment of the Court of First Instance, reviews were made of the evidence underlying such decisions.[22] In *Roquette Frères*, it was held that the review carried out by the EU courts is limited to ensuring that an investigation decision has not been adopted *in the absence of facts* capable of justifying the investigation. There must exist reasonable grounds for suspecting an infringement

15. Case T-340/04 *France Télécom v. Commission* [2007] ECR II-573, at para. 48, see also Case T-135/09 *Nexans France and Nexans v. Commission* [2012] REU II-0000, at para. 45.
16. *Dow Chemical*, note 13 above, at para. 16, Joined Cases T-458/09 and T-171/10 *Slovak Telekom v. Commission* [2012] REU II-0000, at para. 81.
17. Case 155/79 *AM & S v. Commission* [1982] ECR 1575, at para. 21, Order of the President of the Court of First Instance in Joined Cases T-125/03 R and T-253/03 R *Akzo Nobel Chemicals and Akcros Chemicals v. Commission* [2003] ECR II-4771, at para. 100.
18. Case C-550/07 P *Akzo Nobel v. Commission* [2010] ECR I-8301, at para. 105.
19. *Orkem*, note 13 above, at para. 15.
20. *Dow Chemical*, note 13 above, at para. 50.
21. *Ibid.*, at para. 52.
22. *SEP*, note 13 above, at para. 21.

of the competition rules by the undertaking concerned.[23] Although this principle is still reiterated, the intensity of legal review has increased considerably. In *Nexans*, the General Court analysed in relative detail the delimitation of the Commission's decision.[24]

[A] Must Standard of Judicial Review in Member State Courts Equal that of the EUCJ?

It was established in *Upjohn* that, when there are complex assessments, EU law does not require the Member States to establish a procedure for judicial review of national decisions which involves a more extensive review than that carried out by the Court of Justice in similar cases.[25] Nevertheless, any national procedure for judicial review of decisions of national authorities must enable the court or tribunal effectively to apply the relevant principles and rules of EU law when reviewing their legality.[26]

§17.06 CASES ON MIRRORING

As will be seen, case law on judicial review of decisions authorizing mirroring demonstrates a certain tension between the judgments coming from Strasbourg and Luxembourg respectively. In an interesting development, the General Court seems ready to develop its own case law without explicit references to the ECHR, while, on the other hand, the EFTA Court is openly relying on the recent cases from the ECtHR. We are yet to see how the EUCJ will address this intriguing question.

I will however take the liberty of beginning with a national case which demonstrates the most problematic situation of all; where there is no access to court.

[A] The AstraZeneca Case

The Swedish Competition Authority routinely makes exact copies of storage media (like hard drives, USB-memories, discs or CD-discs) for investigation. The authority then searches for evidence in the copy/ mirror image rather than in the computers or other storage media of the undertaking. The search is carried out in the authority's premises and the undertaking is allowed to be present. There is no particular legal framework for this, only rules that to a large extent mirror the Commission's investigation powers under Regulation 1/2003.

On 24 November 2010, Stockholm City Court authorized the Competition Authority to carry out a dawn-raid at the premises of AstraZeneca to investigate whether the undertaking had abused a dominant position in violation of Article 102 of the Treaty on the Functioning of the European Union (TFEU). The decision was adopted

23. Case C-94/00 *Roquette Frères* [2002] ECR I-9011, at paras 54-55.
24. *Nexans*, note 15 above.
25. Case C-120/97 *Upjohn* [1999] ECR I-223, at para. 35.
26. *Ibid.*, at para. 36.

without hearing AstraZeneca. The Competition Authority had made its application on behalf of the Dutch Competition Authority Nederlandse Mededingingsautoriteit (NMa).

AstraZeneca appealed the City Court's decision and demanded that the Market Court should grant leave for appeal. AstraZeneca accepted that the inspection was made, but demanded that the Market Court should decide that it could only be carried out at AstraZeneca's premises. With reference to mirroring, AstraZeneca demanded that copies taken by the authority should only encompass business documents etc. covered by the purpose and subject-matter of the investigation. The Market Court found that the appeal, as was evident from the documents, rather concerned an enforcement measure. The Market Court denied leave for appeal. This meant that no statement was made on the lawfulness of mirroring.[27]

The Competition Authority subsequently filed a new application and claimed that the City Court should allow the authority, within the framework of the inspection that commenced on 30 November 2010 at AstraZeneca, to copy digitally stored data collections to external storage devices (such as hard drives) and carry out indexing and searching in that data collection at the authority's premises. AstraZeneca opposed the claim.[28]

According to submissions made by AstraZeneca, the mirroring would have included volumes of electronic documents equalling (if printed) thirteen full truck lorries. It would have included documents outside the subject-matter of the investigation as well as legally privileged material. It would also have included highly sensitive business secrets such as product development.

Stockholm City Court interpreted the statements made by the Market Court to the effect that there was an absence of procedural jurisdiction to hear the mirroring issue. That is because in the procedural context, enforcement measures are for the authorities and not for the courts. Implicitly, the Market Court seemed to have left mirroring to the Competition Authority's discretion. There are no provisions in the national procedural code which would enable the courts to dismiss unlawfully gathered evidence in a subsequent proceeding on fines. This procedural gap raised the question whether there was nevertheless a requirement for the national legal order to provide for a free-standing action in certain cases.

There is indeed a procedure under Swedish law in cases of conflicts about whether a document is legally privileged. The document shall then be sealed and urgently submitted to the Stockholm City Court for examination and assessment. However, the Competition Authority had not relied on that procedure. And this proves an important point about mirroring; how standard procedures are not adapted to modern technology. The courts do not have the indexing or search systems that would be necessary to pick out legally privileged material from a copy of a hard drive.

Being the judge in the said case, I drafted a request for a preliminary ruling under Article 267 TFEU, essentially asking the EUCJ to say that the City Court must have

27. Market Court Case no A 5/10 *AstraZeneca v. Konkurrensverket*.
28. Stockholm City Court Case Ä 20087-10 *Konkurrensverket v. AstraZeneca*.

competence under EU law to hear the mirroring issue.[29] I questioned whether the absence of a procedural rule conferring competence on the City Court to examine the claim was compatible with the requirement on the Member State to ensure that fundamental rights are observed and that the competition law of the Union is given full effect, as well as to guarantee the right to effective review by a court. I suggested that a need for a stand-alone action exists at least to ensure the right of protection of legally privileged documents.[30]

The draft reference for a preliminary ruling was sent to the parties for comments on 15 December 2010. The Competition Authority then immediately withdrew its mirroring request. What was left was only to decide on costs and close the case. Consequently the request for a preliminary ruling was never sent to the EUCJ and we do not yet know what the answer would have been.

[B] The Canal Plus and Primagaz Cases before the ECtHR

On 21 December 2010, just a few days after the Swedish Competition Authority withdrew its case in AstraZeneca, as set out in the previous section, the ECtHR in Strasbourg handed down two judgments on standard of legal review of decisions on inspections (dawn-raids).[31]

In 2005, the French authorities responsible for competition, consumer affairs and fraud prevention acted against Primagaz, Canal Plus and two other companies. The companies were suspected of anti-competitive practices, and their premises were searched on the orders of the liberties and detention judge. Various documents and data media were seized. Before the ECtHR, Primagaz and Canal Plus relied in particular on Article 6 § 1 (right to a fair trial), complaining that there had been no effective judicial review of the lawfulness and well-foundedness of the search and seizure orders. In both cases, the ECtHR found that Article 6 § 1 of the ECHR had been violated.[32]

The facts of the cases can briefly be summarized as follows. The French competition authority Conseil de la concurrence suspected that Canal Plus and several other companies had infringed Articles 81 and 82 of the Treaty of Rome (now Articles 101 and 102 TFEU). On 8 February 2005 and 12 May 2005 respectively, the authorities

29. This was done with reference to the *Factortame* and *Simmenthal* jurisprudence, Case 106/77 *Simmentahl* [1978] ECR 629, paras 21-24, Case C-213/89 *Factortame* [1990] ECR I-2433, paras 19-20, and with reference to the EUCJ's statement in *VEBIC* that, under Regulation 1/2003, Member States shall ensure that fundamental rights are observed and that EU competition law is fully effective (Case C-439/08 *VEBIC* [2010] ECR I-12471, para. 63).

30. Case C- 550/07 P *Akzo Nobel Chemicals and Akcros Chemicals v. Commission*, at para. 105, Case 155/79 *AM & S v. Commission* [1982] ECR 1575, Joined Cases T-125/03 and T 253/03 *Akzo Nobel Chemicals and Akcros Chemicals v. Commission* [2007] ECR II-3523, at para. 82.

31. Judgments of 21 December 2010 in Affaire *Compagnie des Gaz de Pétrole Primagaz c. France*, no. 29613/08 and Affaire *Société Canal Plus et autres c. France*, no. 29408-08.

32. Article 6 § 1, first sentence, of the ECHR reads as follows: 1. In the determination of his civil rights and obligations or of any criminal charge against him, everyone is entitled to a fair and public hearing within a reasonable time by an independent and impartial tribunal established by law.

responsible asked the relevant courts in Paris and Lille for permission to carry out investigations through searches at the premises of the companies. Such permissions were granted according to decisions adopted by the said courts. The decisions were adopted by judges, setting out the facts which underpinned the suspicions. The same judges were also responsible to ensure that the investigations were carried out in accordance with the law. Based on the decisions, the companies' premises were searched and various documents and data media were seized.

The companies complained that their right to a fair trial and effective legal review had been violated. In particular, they argued that the only way to challenge the decision was through the Cour de Cassation according to the procedure entitled *pourvoi en cassation*. The procedure, said the companies, did not constitute an independent and impartial control of the substance of the decision.

It is not entirely clear from the judgments what kind of review a *pourvoi en cassation* includes, but it can be concluded from the ECtHR's reasoning and its reference to its judgment in *Ravon et autres c. France* (no 18497/03) that the *pourvoi de cassation* did not include a review of both the law and the facts on which the decisions were based.

The ECtHR reminded that the parties concerned had a right to obtain judicial control, in law and in fact, on the lawfulness of the decision authorizing the search, as well as, as the case was, the measures taken based on the decision. The possibility to contest the decision before the Cour de Cassation did not allow for an examination of the facts on which the authorizations of the searches were based. This meant that effective legal control in the sense of Article 6 § 1 ECHR was not guaranteed.

This was not remedied by a law enacted in 2008 which retroactively gave the companies a right to challenge the decisions before the Cour d'Appel. There had consequently been violations of Article 6 § 1 ECHR.

[C] Robathin before the ECtHR

On 3 July 2012 arrived a judgment on mirroring from the ECtHR, in *Robathin v. Austria*.[33] One of the limbs of the case was on Article 8 of the ECHR; respect for private and family life, home and correspondence.

Robathin started out with a search warrant at the office of an Austrian practicing lawyer who was suspected of aggravated theft, aggravated fraud and embezzlement. All files of the lawyer's computer system were copied. Representatives of the Vienna Bar Association were present and opposed this as being disproportionate. It was technically possible to search for and copy only those files which corresponded to the criteria set out in the search warrant.[34]

The ECtHR held that domestic law and practice must afford adequate and effective safeguards against any abuse and arbitrariness.[35] The Court found that the search was based on a warrant issued by a judge and based on reasonable suspicion at

33. Judgment of 3 July 2012 in Case of *Robathin v. Austria*, no. 30457/06.
34. *Ibid.*, at para. 10.
35. *Ibid.*, at para. 44.

the time of issuing the search warrant.[36] Several aspects of the search decision, in particular its scope, was discussed, and this is of great interest by way of comparison in relation to the EU law duty to state reasons. The ECtHR critizised the search warrant for being couched in very broad terms and authorizing in general and unlimited manner the search and seizure of documents, personal computers and discs and other documents. Deficiencies in the search and seizure warrant could however be offset by sufficient procedural safeguards.[37]

Of paramount interest is the Court's reasoning on right to legal review. If the owner objected to the seizure of documents or data storage media, Austrian law provided that they be sealed and put before a judge. There was also a possibility to apply for legal review to the Review Chamber. In these circumstances, the manner in which the Review Chamber exercised its supervisory function was held to be of particular importance. The Court found that the Review Chamber gave only very brief and rather general reasons when authorizing the search of all electronic data from the law office. This did not enable the Court to establish that the search of all electronic data was proportionate in the circumstances.[38] There should be particular reasons to allow the search of all other data, having regard to the specific circumstances prevailing in a law office. There were no such reasons either in the search warrant itself or in any other document. The ECtHR found that the seizure and examination of all data went beyond what was necessary to achieve the legitimate aim. There was a violation of Article 8 of the ECHR.[39]

[D] Nexans and Prysmian before the General Court

On 14 November 2012, the General Court handed down two judgments on mirroring.

In *Nexans*, the Commission had carried out a dawn-raid pursuant to Article 20.4 of Regulation 1/2003 at the premises of Nexans and Nexans France, on suspicions of a cartel on electric cables. The Commission decided to remove four DVD-ROM discs and a copy of the hard drive of the laptop of an employee of Nexans France, for review at its premises in Brussels at a later date. The inspection decision, as well as the mirroring measures and other measures, were appealed to the General Court.[40]

Central aspects of the decision authorizing the inspection were tried in relative detail by the General Court, notably whether the scope of the inspection decision was overly broad and vague. The intensity of legal review indicates that the General Court had found some inspiration in the ECtHR's judgments in *Primagaz* and *Canal Plus*, which apparently were in the file.[41] Parts of the judgment are deleted for reasons of confidentiality, which shows that the intensity of legal review must have been higher than what is immediately visible. This branch of the appeal had two grounds. The first

36. *Ibid.*, at paras 45-46.
37. *Ibid.*, at para. 47.
38. *Ibid.*, at para. 51.
39. *Ibid.*, at para. 52.
40. Case T-135/09 *Nexans France and Nexans v. Commission* [2012] REU II-0000. The case has been appealed, Case C-37/13 P *Nexans and Nexans France v. Commission*, pending.
41. *Ibid.*, at para. 17.

was whether the inspection decision was imprecise in its delimitation of the products concerned, and the second whether there were reasonable grounds for suspecting an infringement. The General Court found that the Commission has not demonstrated that it had reasonable grounds for ordering an inspection covering all electric cables and the material associated with those cables. There were however reasonable suspicions for high voltage underwater and underground electric cables and the material associated with those other cables. The decision was consequently partly annulled and partly upheld.

When it came to the question of mirroring, Nexans had claimed that the General Court should declare unlawful the Commission's decision to remove copies of certain computer files and of the hard drive of Mr C's computer for review at its offices in Brussels later. Following a lengthy discussion, this claim was deemed inadmissible.[42] The General Court reminded that acts against which an action for annulment may be brought are those which produce binding legal effects capable of affecting the applicant's interests by bringing about a distinct change in his legal position.[43] Therefore, in principle, an intermediate measure intended to pave the way for the final decision is not a challengeable measure.[44] Copying of computer files was such an intermediate measure.[45] The copying of each document during an inspection was not to be regarded as an act separable from the decision under which the inspection was ordered, but as a measure implementing that decision.[46] As regards Nexans' argument about legal privilege, the General Court pointed out that there was no claim at the time of the copying that the documents copied by the Commission or the information obtained by it would be eligible, under EU law, for protection similar to that conferred on the confidentiality of communications between lawyers and their clients.[47] Although Nexans had kept the originals, in either paper or electronic form, it had not identified specific documents or parts of documents which were protected under EU law.[48]

After reminding that Nexans could bring their claims within an appeal against a final decision, the General Court pointed out that Nexans could also bring an action for damages against the Commission if it believed that copying of several computer files and of a hard drive for later examination in its offices was illegal and had caused harm.[49]

In *Prysmian*, the Commission had carried out a dawn-raid pursuant to Article 20.4 of Regulation 1/2003 at the premises of Prysmian and Prysmian Cavi e Sistemi Energia, apparently on suspicions of the same electric cable cartel as that in *Nexans*. The Commission decided to extract a copy of the entire contents of the hard disks of three of the employees of Prysmian and to analyse the content thereof in its own offices

42. *Ibid.*, at paras 115-134.
43. *Ibid.*, at para. 115.
44. *Ibid.*, at para. 116.
45. *Ibid.*, at para. 119.
46. *Ibid.*, at para. 125.
47. *Ibid.*, at para. 129.
48. *Ibid.*, at para. 130.
49. *Ibid.*, at paras 132-133.

in Brussels. The inspection decision, as well as the mirroring measures, were appealed to the General Court.[50]

Just as in *Nexans*, a relatively detailed analysis was made in *Prysmian* on whether the inspection decision was imprecise in its delimitation of the products and geographic market concerned, and whether there were reasonable grounds for suspecting an infringement. The outcome was, once again, the annulment of part of the decision.

The General Court found inadmissible the claims that it should declare unlawful or abusive the Commission's decision to extract a copy of the entire contents of the hard disks of some of the directors of Prysmian and to analyse the content thereof in its own offices in Brussels. The reasoning was equal to that in *Nexans*.

[E] Schenker North before the EFTA Court

The EFTA Court ruled in a judgment of 21 December 2012 on access to documents in a competition law case. The EFTA Court referred to the above-mentioned case law of the ECtHR (*Primagaz, Canal Plus* and *Robathin*). The protection of a company's business premises afforded by Article 8 of the ECHR meant that seizure of documents during an administrative investigation procedure may constitute an interference with a company's rights. Outside the scope of investigation, there should be particular reasons to allow for search of all other data, having regard to the specific circumstances prevailing in a particular undertaking. Seizure and examination of data should not go beyond what is necessary to achieve the legitimate aim.[51]

§17.07 WHAT CONCLUSIONS CAN BE DRAWN; ON THE INTERACTION BETWEEN NATIONAL LAW, EU LAW AND THE ECHR?

Investigations of suspected infringements of Articles 101 and 102 TFEU carried out by national authorities must comply with general and fundamental principles of EU law.[52] The Member States are in addition bound by the ECHR. The case law of the ECtHR is repeatedly referred to by the EUCJ as inspiration in its jurisprudence on procedural issues in competition cases.[53]

The *Robathin* case concerned classic or hard core criminality. Depending on the circumstances, a competition law fine can be considered a criminal penalty.[54] Competition law cases nevertheless lean more towards the administrative enforcement side. The *Robathin* case arose because of a search and seizure at a law office, where there is

50. Case T-140/09 *Prysmian and Prysmian Cavi e Sistemi Energia v. Commission* [2012] REU II-0000.
51. Judgment of the EFTA Court in Case E-14/11 *Schenker North and others v. EFTA Surveillance Authority*, at para. 166.
52. See esp Case C-94/00 *Roquette Frères* [2002] ECR I-9011, at para. 25, Case C-176/99 P *ARBED v. Commission* [2003] ECR I-2737, at para. 19.
53. See *inter alia* Joined Cases C-204/00 etc. *Aalborg Portland and others v. Commission* [2004] ECR I-123, at para. 64.
54. Judgment on 27 September 2011 in *A. Menarini Diagnostics v. Italy*, Case no 43509/08, at paras 38-45.

little but legally privileged material to look for. In the context of a competition law investigation, legally privileged documents will be around, but to a much lesser proportion. It is furthermore easy to envisage that a search at a law office will risk revealing legally privileged documents or business secrets pertaining to third parties who have nothing whatsoever to do with the suspected criminality. The interest of protecting innocent third parties applies to a lesser extent during a competition law investigation, but it still applies. This follows from the now codified rule that the investigation must be kept to the subject-matter,[55] and from the jurisprudence which excludes copying of documents of a strictly personal nature.[56] For these reasons, the *Robathin* judgment is relevant when assessing mirroring during competition law investigations.

Two different procedural approaches can be observed if we compare the judgments of the ECtHR in *Primagaz, Canal Plus* and *Robathin* with the judgments of the General Court in *Nexans* and *Prysmian*. The ECtHR seems to envisage that the courts should assess the necessity and proportionality of mirroring in each case. The General Court, on the other hand, envisages a retrospective control within the appeal against a final decision.

Recent case law demonstrate an increased awareness of the need for intense review of the justification of decisions on seizure and search of electronic data. The method of looking at separate categories of documents and affording them different procedural protection is well-established in EU law. There is still reason to consider whether, in addition to the established actions, it should be possible to appeal on a stand-alone basis against various overarching aspects of mirroring. Through mirroring, huge amounts of data, including correspondence between lawyer and client, can be copied and brought back to the competition authority. The judgments in *Nexans* and *Prysmian* illustrate how the court may, based on established procedures, have to wait until the indexing and search has been made by the competition authority, before any assessment of the legality of the seizure can be made. That is because different legal standards apply to different kinds of documents encompassed by the mirroring. Legally privileged documents enjoy particularly high protection, substantively and procedurally. Conversely, documents that can determine whether or not the suspected infringement took place can be copied and the copies can be kept by the investigating authority. Documents that are outside the subject-matter of investigation should not be copied or kept, and the same applies to documents of a non-business nature.

Since the claims relating to unlawfulness or abusiveness of mirroring were inadmissible in *Nexans* and *Prysmian*, we are yet to learn whether mirroring is in principle legal, and if so, under what conditions. First, it will be interesting to see if the EUCJ will come to the same conclusion on admissibility. Secondly, the judgments leave open the question what would have been the outcome had there been legally privileged documents in the copies. It is well-established that whether documents were lawyer-client confidential can be tried on a stand-alone basis. If we accept, as a working hypothesis, that the General Court's view will be upheld on appeal, this raises the

55. Articles 12(2) and 28(1) of Regulation 1/2003.
56. *Roquette Frères*, note 52 above, at para. 45.

question whether a retrospective review is in line with the necessity and proportionality test envisaged by the ECtHR in *Robathin*. According to the ECtHR, there must be particular reasons to allow the search of all other data than those relating to the alleged criminal activities, having regard to the specific circumstances prevailing in a law office. A seizure and examination of all data must not go beyond what is necessary to achieve the legitimate aim. The EFTA Court has interpreted this as a general principle, not only applicable when law offices are searched during criminal proceedings, but for competition law investigations as well.

Necessity and proportionality was at the core of the ECtHR's judgment in *Robathin*. Proportionality has repeatedly been tried on a stand-alone basis as a claim for annulment of Commission decisions. I believe a combined necessity and proportionality test could be helpful when national judiciary try, on a case-by-case basis, whether mirroring is lawful.

CHAPTER 18

How General Should General Principles Be? *Ne Bis in Idem* in EU Competition Law

*Wouter Devroe**

§18.01 GENERAL

[A] Context

'*How much is too much?*' wonders a leading US antitrust observer when referring to overlapping international sanctioning of cartels.[1] Authorities enforce competition law ever more vigorously with high fines or even with criminal sanctions. Their actions are now complemented by private enforcement, on a scale not witnessed before. Few, if any, unilateral, bilateral[2] or global mechanisms are in place to limit the extraterritorial

* The authors also provide an overview of ECtHR and ECJ case law which may support these 'particular justifications' in other areas (notably ECtHR 23 November 2006, Jussila v. Finland; ECJ 9 November 2010, Case C-92/09, Schecke and Eiffert [2010] ECR I-11063; ECJ 22 December 2010, Case C-279/09 DEB [2010] ECR I-13849).

1. '*Few issues engender as much debate in antitrust circles as the concern of overlapping punishment of cartel offenders in international cartel cases. The mass proliferation of antitrust enforcement, rising criminal and civil penalties, and the seemingly boundless extraterritorial reach of national antitrust laws challenge traditional notions of proportional punishment and adequate deterrence*': J. Terzaken and P. Huizing, 'How much is too much? A Call for Global Principles to Guide the Punishment of International Cartels', 27 ABA Antitrust Magazine 2, Spring 2013, 53. Mr Terzaken is the former Director of Criminal Enforcement for the Antitrust Division of the US Department of Justice. He refers by way of example to the global air cargo cartel which was sanctioned in at least 10 jurisdictions (including the EU), leading to record combined fines on individual companies.
2. Bilateral instruments are in place. See recently e.g. Council Decision 2013/203/EU of 22 April 2013 'on the signing, on behalf of the European Union, of an Agreement between the European Union and the Swiss Confederation concerning cooperation on the application of their competition laws' (*Official Journal of the European Union (OJ)*, L 117/6, 27 April 2013). However, the bilateral instruments do not preclude double sanctioning.

reach and overlap of sanctions. This combination of factors gives rise to a risk of over-enforcement, which may be as undesirable as under-enforcement.

Internationally, the European Union (hereinafter 'EU') has become one of the most vigorous enforcers of competition law against global cartel offenders. Yet this is only one dimension. Ever more often, overlapping punishment of cartel offenders occurs *within the EU*.

A few examples can illustrate this. A national competition authority (hereinafter 'NCA') may want to investigate and possibly sanction an alleged cartel law infringement on the basis of EU and/or national competition law (a) before the European Commission (herein after 'Commission') starts an investigation into the same behaviour under EU competition law, or (b) after the Commission has started, or perhaps even terminated, its investigation. While under investigation by an NCA, a company may be informed that this investigation is suspended because the Commission has launched an investigation. After the Commission has concluded its investigation and administered fines, the undertaking may learn, to its surprise, that the NCA now intends to pursue its original investigation into the effects of the alleged infringement on national territory, with a view to imposing further fines. Third example: after one NCA has investigated and fined behaviour occurring in three Member States, the NCA of another of those three Member States imposes an additional fine, reflecting the negative effects of the infringement on its territory. Is this legal, and if so, is it desirable from a perspective of effective enforcement and procedural economy? The examples are not hypothetical.[3]

Now that Member States have developed effective national enforcement mechanisms and that the modernization of competition law has granted them new powers, the *parallel* application of national and EU competition law and the largely *parallel* competences of NCAs, national judges and the Commission in practice often lead to *parallel* (double, threefold, ...) fining. This raises new issues, or highlights existing issues, from an EU and fundamental rights perspective.

Parallel application and extraterritorial reach of EU and national competition laws are only two of several factors contributing to the risk of overlapping sanctioning, in practice if not in law. In addition:

(a) national regulatory authorities, such as telecom supervisors, are now also enforcing (aspects of) competition law;
(b) Article 3(2) of Regulation 1/2003[4] permits '*stricter national laws which prohibit or sanction unilateral conduct engaged in by undertakings*' (e.g., laws applying to economic dependency from non-dominant market operators), also outside regulated sectors;

3. Comp. the categorization by G. Di Federico 'EU Competition Law and the Principle of *Ne Bis in Idem*', *European Public Law* 2011, (241), 252-258, distinguishing between the 'vertical' (Commission after NCA, NCA after Commission), 'horizontal' (several NCAs) and 'superimposed' (concurrent application of EU and national competition laws) dimension of potential violations of *ne bis in idem*.
4. Council Regulation (EC) No 1/2003 of 16 December 2002 on the implementation of the rules on competition laid down in Articles 81 en 82 of the Treaty, OJ L 1/1, 4 January 2003.

(c) Article 3(3) of Regulation 1/2003 permits '*provisions of national law that predominantly pursue an objective different from that pursued by Articles 101 TFEU and 102 TFEU*';
(d) criminalization of competition law is on the rise in national legal systems;[5] and
(e) as above-mentioned, the same is true for private enforcement of competition law.[6]

Under EU law, the debate is to a large extent framed in terms of general principles of EU law. The general principle of proportionality – sanctions should not only be effective and dissuasive but also proportionate – and the general principle of *ne bis in idem* (*non bis in idem*, the 'double jeopardy rule') are supposed to guide, and if necessary limit, overlapping punishment of cartel offenders. A third relevant general principle was recognized by the European Court of Justice (hereinafter 'ECJ') in *Walt Wilhelm* as '*a general requirement of natural justice*'[7] and re-formulated by Advocate General (hereinafter 'AG') Cruz Villalón in his Opinion in the recent *Fransson* case as '*the principle of the prohibition of arbitrariness, which is inseparable from the rule of law (Article 2 TEU), [which] requires national law to enable criminal courts to have the power to take into account, by whatever means, the prior existence of an administrative penalty for the purposes of mitigating the criminal penalty*'.[8] Other general principles may apply.[9]

As is well known, the *ne bis in idem* principle examined here is recognized by Article 4 of Protocol 7 to the European Convention on Human Rights (hereinafter 'ECHR') as 'the right not to be tried or punished twice', by the case law of the European Court of Human Rights (hereinafter 'ECtHR') and by EU law.[10] The Court of Justice of

5. In terms of *ne bis in idem*, there will often be no unity of offender between criminal sanctions (individuals) and sanctions of an administrative nature that are criminal under the so-called *Engel* criteria (section §18.02[A] below).
6. Judgments on private enforcement are of a civil nature but this does not exclude all relevance from a *ne bis in idem* perspective: note 11 below.
7. ECJ 13 February 1969, Case 14/68, *Walt Wilhelm* [1969] ECR 1, para. 11.
8. Opinion of 12 June 2012 in Case C-617/10, *Åklagaren v. Hans Åkerberg Fransson*, not yet published (the *Fransson* Opinion), para. 93. There is a difference between the *Fransson* Opinion and the *Walt Wilhelm* judgment, which required that '*any previous punitive decision must be taken into account in determining any sanction which is to be imposed*' and not merely that 'national law enables criminal courts to have the power to take into account'. Comp. P. Oliver and T. Bombois, '"Ne bis in idem" en droit européen: un principe à plusieurs variantes', *JTDE* 2012, 272, footnote 122. The principle discussed here is sometimes referred to as 'Anrechnungsprinzip' (versus the 'Erledigungsprinzip' requiring 'a bar on further prosecution or punishment'). See N. Neagu, 'The ne bis in idem principle in the interpretation of European courts: towards uniform interpretation', *LJIL* 2012, 956.
9. In the *Toshiba* case, discussed below, the principle of retroactive application of the more lenient penalty (*lex mitius*), recognised by the ECJ as a general principle of EU law was also discussed: section §18.04[C][1] below.
10. There is abundant legal literature on *ne bis in idem* in EU and competition law. At least one Ph.D was written on the topic (B. van Bockel, *The ne bis in idem Principle in EU Law*, Kluwer Law International, 2010, xi + 267 p.), while others deal extensively with the topic (e.g. S. Brammer, *Co-operation between national competition agencies in the enforcement of EC competition law*, Hart, 2009, 344-419). The Ph.D theses are complemented by dozens of articles, which will not be listed here. However, special mention should be made of W. Wils, 'The Principle of Ne Bis in Idem in EC Antitrust Enforcement: A Legal and Economic Analysis',

the European Union finds no difficulty in recognizing that this '*fundamental principle of EU law*' (section §18.02[B] below), originally devised for criminal sanctions, is fully applicable to sanctions imposed under EU competition law.

In words, European law has never safeguarded the *ne bis in idem* principle better than at present. In addition to the above, the principle is now also enshrined in the Convention Implementing the Schengen Agreement (hereinafter 'CISA') and in Article 50 of the Charter of Fundamental Rights of the European Union (hereinafter 'Charter'), which has become a binding legal instrument since the entry into force of the Lisbon Treaty on 1 December 2009. Furthermore, the Charter and the Lisbon Treaty have linked EU law more closely than ever before to the ECHR, as interpreted by the ECtHR.

However, the words contrast sharply with the simple observation that in practice no one has so far been able to successfully raise a *ne bis in idem* argument in a competition law case before the General Court (hereinafter 'GC') or the ECJ.[11] The argument is raised but the ECJ systematically rejects it.[12]

[B] 'Legal Idem' versus 'Factual Idem'

This gap between words and practice is all the more remarkable since individuals do win cases on the basis of *ne bis in idem* in other areas of EU law, or before the ECtHR.

Apparently then, there is a difference between the application of *ne bis in idem* in competition law cases and in other areas of the law, and in particular in cases concerning the area of police and judicial cooperation in criminal matters (hereinafter for ease of use referred to as 'Schengen cases'). The difference is, in essence, that whereas EU law has gradually moved away from a so-called 'legal idem' in favour of a 'factual idem'[13] in Schengen cases, the GC and ECJ continue to apply a 'legal idem' in competition matters.

Interpreting the 'idem' in *ne bis in idem* as a 'factual idem' (*idem factum*) prohibits prosecution, trial, or punishment for a second offence if that second offence

World Competition 2003, 131-148 (see also W. Wils, 'The Principle of Ne Bis In Idem', in *Principles of Eurropean Antitrust Enforcement*, Hart, 2005, 93-110) as this was the first article to overtly question the traditional interpretation of *ne bis in idem* in EU competition law in light of modernisation and the Charter, and to do this on the basis of arguments that remain fully valid today.

11. Apparently there are instances where the argument was successfully raised before *national* courts. For example, *ne bis in idem* motivated the High Court in *Devenish* to deny exemplary damages in a follow-on damages suit, brought by direct purchasers in the vitamin cartel case after the Commission had already imposed fines on the defendants. This is an interesting case, as it concerns the combination of public and private enforcement of competition law. High Court of England and Wales, *Devenish Nutrition Ltd v. Sanofi-Avensis SA (France) and others* [2008] EWCA Civ. 1086; [2008] WLR (D) 317 (2008). The judgment was upheld by the England and Wales Court of Appeal. See for another example note 50 below.
12. See for a discussion of case law e.g. R. Nazzini, *Concurrent proceedings in competition law. Procedure, Evidence and Remedies*, Oxford, OUP, 2004, 114-124 and, also in other sectors (e.g. agriculture), P. Oliver and T. Bombois, note 8 above, *JTDE* 2012, 268-270.
13. Some authors use different terminology to denote the difference. See e.g. '*the 'natural' or 'legal' unity of conduct*' in B. van Bockel, *The ne bis in idem Principle in EU Law*, Kluwer Law International, 2010, 43 or '*in abstracto*' versus '*idem factum, in concreto*' in N. Neagu, above, 2012, 955.

arises from '*identical facts or facts which are substantially the same*'. Facts are substantially the same in case of '*a set of concrete factual circumstances involving the same defendant and inextricably linked together in time and space*' (sections §18.03[C] and §18.03[E] below). In competition law terms, the defendant's conduct will be decisive.

On the contrary, interpreting 'idem' as a 'legal idem' allows for a finding that the same conduct of the defendant may constitute separate offences, may be tried in separate proceedings and may lead to separate punishment depending on the legal qualification of the behaviour and/or the object or objectives of the rules infringed. Not the conduct but the legal qualification of the conduct is decisive, and this legal qualification may differ in function of the rules applicable to the conduct.[14]

The choice between a 'factual idem' and a 'legal idem' is crucial. As former Judge and Vice-President of the ECtHR Prof. Tulkens writes:

> It is not simply a technical question but a question which touches upon the very substance of fundamental rights. When making the choice, one necessarily sides either with better protection of persons (factual idem) or with the interest of repression and administration of justice (legal idem).[15]

In competition matters the choice between a 'factual' or 'legal idem' is equally crucial. Under a 'factual idem', the establishment and administration of an EU-wide cartel may only be investigated and sanctioned once, to the extent that the same defendants are involved and the concrete factual circumstances are inextricably linked together in time and space. However, applying a 'legal idem' makes it in theory possible to have the same cartel behaviour investigated by both the Commission (under EU law) and 1 up to 28 individual Member States (under national law and/or EU law), as long as EU and national law can be said to have different objects or objectives.

[C] Structure of this Chapter

Expanding on the above, this chapter examines what recent ECJ case law has added to the debate on overlapping punishment of cartel offenders and to existing European case law on *ne bis in idem*. The structure is as follows.

---

14. Under this approach there is formally not '*an offence for which [the person concerned] has already been finally acquitted or convicted*' under Art. 4 of Protocol No. 7 but there are *several* offences.
15. '*L'enjeu est important. Tout d'abord, nous sommes dans le contexte d'un droit indérogeable qui ne relève pas, en principe, de la marge d'appréciation des Etats. Ensuite, il ne s'agit pas simplement d'une question technique mais d'une question qui touche à la substance même des droits fondamentaux. En optant pour l'une ou l'autre voie, on prend nécessairement parti soit pour la protection accrue des personnes (idem factuel), soit pour les intérêts de la répression et de l'administration de la justice (idem légal).*' F. Tulkens, 'Non bis in idem. Un voyage entre Strasbourg et Luxembourg', forthcoming in *Mélanges en l'honneur de Renée Koering-Joulin*, para. 26. Comp. B. van Bockel who pleaded in favour of a 'factual idem' in his doctoral thesis and who noted that '*the majority of national systems of law emphasize the actual, historical event as the decisive element for the determination of idem*'. B. van Bockel, *The ne bis in idem Principle in EU Law*, Kluwer Law International, 2010, 44-45.

First, the traditional case law of the European courts on *ne bis in idem* will be briefly recalled (section §18.02). Subsequently, five evolutions in EU and ECHR law which might have altered the traditional approach will be highlighted (section §18.03). More or less in chronological order, these five evolutions are:

(i) the modernization of competition law (1999–2004);
(ii) the adoption of the Charter (first in 2000, again in 2007, with binding force since 2009);
(iii) the option for a 'factual idem' by the ECJ when applying Article 54 CISA (2006–2007);
(iv) the entry into force of the Lisbon Treaty (2009); and
(v) the decision by the ECtHR to align its interpretation of *ne bis in idem* to the ECJ's interpretation of CISA (2010).

The ECJ's *Toshiba* judgment of 14 February 2012[16] will then be analysed (section §18.04). In this judgment, the ECJ had to decide on the impact of these five evolutions on its existing restrictive interpretation of *ne bis in idem* in competition matters. The ECJ ruled in essence that nothing should change, so that the *ne bis in idem* principle is now interpreted differently in (a) competition law and (b) certain other areas of EU law and ECHR law. It is also striking that the reference to the ECHR, present in the older case law, is no longer present in *Toshiba* and is not replaced by a reference to the Charter.

Tentative conclusions will be drawn in section §18.05.

§18.02 TRADITIONAL APPROACH TO *NE BIS IN IDEM* IN EU COMPETITION LAW: ECHR AS SOURCE OF INSPIRATION – ADOPTION OF A 'LEGAL IDEM'

[A] ECHR as Source of Inspiration

In matters concerning *ne bis in idem* in competition law, the ECJ has traditionally made reference to Article 4(1) of Protocol No. 7 to the ECHR.[17]

Protocol No. 7 ECHR is now ratified by forty-three of forty-seven Members States of the Council of Europe. It is not signed by the UK and not ratified by Germany, the Netherlands and Turkey. In addition, five of the ratifying Member States have lodged reservations or declarations limiting the scope of the *ne bis in idem* so that it only covers double punishment in respect of criminal offences within the meaning of national law.[18]

---

16. References to '*Toshiba*' in this chapter refer to the *Toshiba* case and judgment: Judgment of the ECJ of 14 February 2012, Case C-17/10, *Toshiba Corporation and others / Úřad pro ochranu hospodářské souteže*, not yet published in the ECR (the *Toshiba* judgment).
17. '*No one shall be liable to be tried or punished again in criminal proceedings under the jurisdiction of the same State for an offence for which he has already been finally acquitted or convicted in accordance with the law and penal procedure of that State.*' The principle cannot be made subject to derogation under Article 15 ECHR in time of war or other public emergency threatening the life of the nation (Article 4(3) ECHR).
18. See for an overview the *Fransson* Opinion, para. 72 (although Belgium had already ratified at the date of the Opinion).

The fact that Article 4 of Protocol No. 7 was not ratified by all Member States has not until now (section §18.04[E][2][b] below) prevented the ECJ from referring to the provision in its pre-Charter case law.

There has been relatively little controversy surrounding the 'bis' element in the ECtHR's *ne bis in idem* case law (section §18.02[A] below). However, the 'idem' element has been shrouded in controversy and will be discussed separately below (section §18.03[E]).

In order to define the 'bis' element, the ECtHR cogitates the *ratione materiae* (relating to the criminal nature of proceedings), the *ratione temporis* (relating to the final character of the first decision at the time a second proceeding is launched) and the *ratione loci* (relating to the jurisdiction where second proceedings are launched).[19]

With respect to the *ratione materiae,* the two proceedings should be '*criminal*' under the so-called *Engel* criteria: (a) legal classification of the offence under national law, (b) nature of the offence, (c) degree of severity of the penalty that the person concerned risks incurring.[20] Under these criteria, a proceeding formally classified as administrative can be determined as criminal for ECHR purposes.

The 'bis' element makes provision for a threefold guarantee: no one shall be (a) prosecuted (b) tried or (c) punished for the same offence.[21] In its milestone *Franz Fischer v. Austria* judgment of 29 May 2001,[22] the ECtHR (Grand Chamber) ruled that reducing the quantum of the second sanction is not sufficient to avoid the application of *ne bis in idem* as '*Article 4 of Protocol No. 7 is not confined to the right not to be punished twice but extends to the right not to be tried twice.*'[23] It further appears from this judgment that Article 4 of Protocol No. 7 can be applicable to a combination of administrative and criminal sanctions, regardless of which of these are first imposed.

With respect to the *ratione temporis,* the second proceedings should occur after the person concerned has been '*finally acquitted or convicted*':[24]

19. C. Karakosta, 'Ne bis in idem: Une jurisprudence peu visible pour un droit intangible', *Rev. trim. dr. h.*, 2008, 29-34. F. Tulkens, above, paras 6-25.
20. ECtHR 8 June 1976, *Engel and others v. Netherlands.* The criteria are confirmed in a.o. the ECtHR's judgment of 10 February 2009, *Sergey Zolotukhin v. Russia,* para. 53. Comp. ECJ 5 June 2012, Case C-489/10, *Łukasz Marcin Bonda,* not yet reported, paras 36 et seq., where the ECJ rules that penalties in an agricultural Regulation are not of a criminal nature under the *Engel* criteria.
21. ECtHR 20 July 2004, *Nikitine v. Russia.*
22. ECtHR 29 May 2001, *Franz Fischer v. Austria.*
23. *Ibid.*, para. 29. Comp. J. Vervaele, 'The transnational *ne bis in idem* principle in the EU: Mutual recognition and equivalent protection of human rights', *Utrecht Law Review,* 2005, 102-103 (also J. Vervaele, 'The transnational *ne bis in idem* principle in the EU: Towards an EU system of general principles and human rights?', in *The European Composite Administration,* Antwerp, Intersentia, 2011, (535), 539) and W. Wils, note 10 above, 96. See also the Opinion of AG Colomer of 11 February 2003 in Case C-213/00 P, *Italcementi v. Commission* [2004] ECR I-230, para. 96: '*That principle* [*ne bis in idem,* WD] *is not a procedural rule which operates as a palliative for proportionality when an individual is tried and punished twice for the same conduct, but a fundamental guarantee for citizens*'.
24. See for a discussion of problems concerning the recognition of the final character of a judicial decision at the international level B. van Bockel, *The ne bis in idem Principle in EU Law,* Kluwer Law International, 2010, 41-43 and C. Karakosta, above, 32-34.

> [A] decision is final if, according to the traditional expression, it has acquired the force of res judicata. This is the case when it is irrevocable, that is to say when no further ordinary remedies are available or when the parties have exhausted such remedies or have permitted the time-limit to expire without availing themselves of them.[25]

However, (a) the continuation of a second proceeding after the first one has acquired force of res judicata can violate the *ne bis in idem* principle and (b) cumulative sanctioning in procedures where there is no res judicata can lead to the imposition of a disproportionate sanction (and thus violate the principle of proportionality).[26]

With respect to the *ratione loci,* the second proceedings should occur within the same Member State. This is materially different from the EU Charter and the CISA, but other Council of Europe conventions may be invoked to give transnational application to Article 4 of Protocol No. 7.[27]

[B] EU Competition Law

The ECJ fully recognizes the *ne bis in idem* principle, also in competition law cases.[28]

By making that recognition through explicit reference to the ECHR, the ECJ leaves no doubt that competition cases, although not strictly of a criminal nature, nevertheless fulfil the *Engel* criteria listed above:

> The principle of ne bis in idem, ... a fundamental principle of [EU] law also enshrined in Article 4(1) of Protocol No. 7 to the ECHR, precludes, in competition matters, an undertaking from being found guilty or proceedings from being brought against it a second time on the grounds of anti-competitive conduct in respect of which it has already been penalised or declared not liable by a previous unappealable decision.[29]

However, having duly recognized the principle, the ECJ subsequently interprets the 'idem' element as a 'legal idem', so that a three-prong test emerges:

> As regards observance of the principle ne bis in idem, the application of that principle is subject to the threefold condition of identity of the facts, unity of

25. Explanatory Report on Protocol No 7, para. 29 *juncto* para. 22.
26. Under the EU Schengen acquis, a settlement in a criminal case can also be final. ECJ 11 February 2003, Joined Cases C-187/01 and C-385/01, *Criminal proceedings against Hüseyin Gözütok and Klaus Brügge* [2003] ECR I-1345. This decision is regularly criticized.
27. See para. 27 of the Explanatory Report on Protocol No 7, referring to '*[s]everal other Council of Europe conventions, including the European Convention on Extradition (1957), the European Convention on the International Validity of Criminal Judgments (1970) and the European Convention on the Transfer of Proceedings in Criminal Matters (1972)*'.
28. See *Toshiba* judgment, para. 94: '*The ne bis in idem principle must be complied with in proceedings for the imposition of fines under competition law.*' The ECJ refers to ECJ 15 October 2002, Joined Cases C-238/99 P, C-244/99 P, C-245/99 P, C-247/99 P, C-250/99 P to C-252/99 P and C-254/99 P *Limburgse Vinyl Maatschappij and Others v. Commission* [2002] ECR I-8375, para. 59; ECJ 7 January 2004, Joined Cases C-204/00 P, C-205/00 P, C-211/00 P, C-213/00 P, C-217/00 P and C-219/00 P *Aalborg Portland and Others v. Commission* [2004] ECR I-123, para. 338-340; ECJ 29 June 2006, Case C-289/04 P *Showa Denko v. Commission* [2006] ECR I-5859, para. 50.
29. *Ibid.*

> offender and unity of the legal interest protected. Under that principle, therefore, the same person cannot be sanctioned more than once for a single unlawful course of conduct designed to protect the same legal asset.[30]

It is the view of the ECJ that there is no unity of the legal interest protected by EU competition law and competition law of third countries. The question of whether there is unity of legal interest between EU and national competition law is not entirely resolved (section §18.03[A] below).

The ECJ ruled as early as 1969 in *Walt Wilhelm* that '*Community and national law on cartels consider cartels from different points of view.*'[31] When asked whether the risk of double sanctioning by the Commission and an NCA '*renders impossible the acceptance for one set of facts of two parallel procedures*'[32] the ECJ answered in the negative:

> [T]he acceptability of a dual procedure of this kind follows in fact from the special system of the sharing of jurisdiction between the Community and the Member States with regard to cartels. If, however, the possibility of two procedures being conducted separately were to lead to the imposition of consecutive sanctions, a general requirement of natural justice [...] demands that any previous punitive decision must be taken into account in determining any sanction which is to be imposed.[33]

This explains why *ne bis in idem* arguments against the combined application of EU and national competition laws were systematically rejected.

§18.03 FIVE EVOLUTIONS IN THE LAW WHICH MIGHT HAVE ALTERED THE TRADITIONAL APPROACH

[A] Modernization of Competition Law (1999–2004)

The modernization of competition law since 1 May 2004 engenders both 'decentralisation' of a kind and increased economic thinking. Assuming that Regulation 1/2003 and its implementation are well known by now we limit ourselves to three aspects of particular relevance here.

Firstly, modernization promoted parallel application of national and EU law in various ways. By demanding that NCAs be entitled under their national law to apply EU competition law to restrictive practices which may affect trade between Member States,[34] by granting NCAs and national judges the power to apply Articles 101 and 102 TFEU in their entirety,[35] by promoting cooperation and exchange of information (even

30. *Toshiba* judgment, para. 97, under reference to para. 338 of the above-cited judgment in *Aalborg Portland and others v. Commission*.
31. ECJ 13 February 1969, Case 14/68, *Walt Wilhelm* [1969] ECR 1, para. 3.
32. *Ibid.*, para. 10.
33. '*In any case, so long as no regulation has been issued under Article 87(2)(e), no means of avoiding such a possibility is to be found in the general principles of Community law*': *Ibid.*, para. 11.
34. Article 3(1) of Regulation 1/2003.
35. Articles 5-6 of Regulation 1/2003.

confidential) between EU and national enforcers,[36] through the European Competition Network and otherwise, modernization has increased the scope for parallel enforcement and for cases where *ne bis in idem* issues may arise. Modernization should be understood in its widest sense here, including e.g., the raising of *de minimis* thresholds and the reform of the block exemption system.

Modernization makes it harder to maintain that national and EU competition law protect different legal interests. In its *ThyssenKrupp Liften* judgment of 13 July 2011,[37] the GC ruled that when applying Articles 101 and 102 TFEU, the Commission and NCAs are '*protecting the same legal asset, namely the free competition within the common market.*' The Court concluded from this that:

> [I]t must be held that the principle non bis in idem precludes an undertaking from being penalised a second time or made the defendant to proceedings brought by the Commission a second time for an infringement of Article 81 EC or 82 EC for which it has already been penalised, or of which it has been exonerated, by a previous decision of a national competition authority adopted under Article 5 of Regulation No 1/2003 which has become final.

This is in line with the earlier Opinion in the *Italcementi* case.[38]

Secondly, certain elements in Regulation 1/2003 create the impression that its drafters wanted competition cases in the EU to be handled by one best placed ('*most appropriate*') authority, and not by potentially 28 different authorities. For example, Recital 18 of the Preamble refers to '*the objective ... that each case should be handled by a single authority*', Article 13 allows NCAs and the Commission to suspend or terminate proceedings if another authority is dealing with the case and Article 11(6) states that initiation of proceedings by the Commission relieves NCAs of their competence to apply Articles 101–102 TFEU. These provisions could again be interpreted as a clear sign of aversion by the drafters of Regulation 1/2003 to multiple proceedings and as supporting a broader interpretation of *ne bis in idem*.

Finally, Regulation 1/2003 is important because it links modernized competition law to the Charter and to the ECHR. Recital 37 of Regulation 1/2003 reads as follows:

> This Regulation ... observes the principles recognised ... by the Charter .... Accordingly, this Regulation should be interpreted and applied with respect to those rights and principles.

It can be argued that, to the extent that the interpretation of the Charter is linked to the interpretation of the ECHR (section §18.03[B] below), the interpretation of Regulation

36. Exchanged confidential information can normally only be used by NCAs to apply Articles 101-102 TFEU. However the information exchanged can also be used for the application of national competition law '*where national competition law is applied in the same case and in parallel to [EU] competition law and does not lead to a different outcome*'. See Art. 12(2) of Regulation 1/2003.
37. Case T-144/07, not yet reported, para. 162.
38. Opinion of AG Colomer of 11 February 2003 in Case C-213/00 P, *Italcementi v. Commission* [2004] ECR I-230, para. 94. One could add that from a practical point of view, NCAs which apply national and EU competition law in parallel in accordance with Article 3(2) of Regulation, and which find a breach of both sets of rules, nevertheless impose only one sanction and not e.g. two separate fines.

1/2003 is also linked not only to the Charter but also to the interpretation of the ECHR. A change in the interpretation of *ne bis in idem* in the ECHR (like the reversal in the ECtHR's case law in 2010, opting for a 'factual idem' instead of a 'legal idem': section §18.03[E] below), would then also have to guide the interpretation of Regulation 1/2003.

[B] Charter of Fundamental Rights of the European Union (2000–2009)

Article 50 of the Charter confirms that the *ne bis in idem* principle is part of the EU legal order, and applies *ratione loci* to the entire EU and not just to a single Member State:

> No one shall be liable to be tried or punished again in criminal proceedings for an offence for which he or she has already been finally acquitted or convicted within the Union in accordance with the law.

Article 51(1) adds that the provisions of the Charter '*are addressed … to Member States only when they are implementing Union law*'.[39]

Also, of utmost importance is Article 52(3) of the Charter, which links the Charter to the ECHR:

> In so far as this Charter contains rights which correspond to rights guaranteed by the [ECHR], the meaning and scope of those rights shall be the same as those laid down by the said Convention. The provision shall not prevent Union law providing more extensive protection.

This again raises the question whether the option for a 'factual idem' by the ECtHR binds the ECJ in its interpretation of the Charter. In its recent *Fransson* judgment,[40] the ECJ appears to have ruled that it does not (section §18.04[E][2][b] below).

[C] The ECJ Applies a 'Factual Idem' in Schengen Cases (2006–2007)

Article 54 CISA contains yet another *ne bis in idem* provision.[41] When asked to interpret this provision in the *Van Esbroeck* case in 2006, the ECJ did not copy its restrictive interpretation of *ne bis in idem* cases from competition law. To the surprise

39. As will be seen below, the Commission argued in the *Toshiba* case that the Charter should not apply to the Czech Republic because that state applied its national law and not EU law, note 166 below.
40. Judgment of 26 February 2013, Case C-617/10, *Åklagaren v. Hans Åkerberg Fransson*, not yet reported (*Fransson* judgment).
41. '*A person whose trial has been finally disposed of in one Contracting Party may not be prosecuted in another Contracting Party for the same acts provided that, if a penalty has been imposed, it has been enforced, is actually in the process of being enforced or can no longer be enforced under the laws of the sentencing Contracting Party.*' See for an analysis of the ECJ case law on (and only on) Article 54 CISA, involving the 'Green Paper on conflicts of jurisdiction and the principle of non bis in idem' of 23 December 2005 (doc. COM(2005) 696 final) T. Rafaraci, 'The principle of non bis in idem in the jurisprudence of the European Court of Justice', in *Le contrôle juridictionnel dans l'espace pénal européen*, Editions Université libre de Bruxelles, 2009, 93-110.

of many, the ECJ opted for a 'factual idem' instead of a 'legal idem', on the following grounds:

> 27. In the first place [...] the wording of Article 54 of the CISA, 'the same acts', shows that that provision refers only to the nature of the acts in dispute and not to their legal classification.[42] [...]
> 30. There is a necessary implication in the ne bis in idem principle, enshrined in that article, that the Contracting States have *mutual trust in their criminal justice systems and that each of them recognises the criminal law in force in the other Contracting States even when the outcome would be different if its own national law were applied.*[43]
> 31. It follows that the possibility of divergent legal classifications of the same acts in two different Contracting States is no obstacle to the application of Article 54 of the CISA.
> 32. For the same reasons, the criterion of the identity of the protected legal interest cannot be applicable since that criterion is likely to vary from one Contracting State to another.
> *33. The above findings are further reinforced by the objective of Article 54 of the CISA, which is to ensure that no one is prosecuted for the same acts in several Contracting States on account of his having exercised his right to freedom of movement.*[44] *[...]*
> 36. In those circumstances, the only relevant criterion for the application of Article 54 of the CISA is identity of the material acts [...]. [...]
> *38. ...the definitive assessment in that regard belongs ... to the competent national courts which are charged with the task of determining whether the material acts at issue constitute a set of facts which are inextricably linked together in time, in space and by their subject-matter.*[45] *(emphasis added)*

The ECJ confirmed and developed this approach in its *Norma Kraaijenbrink* judgment of 18 July 2007.[46] It added that '*the starting point for assessing the notion of "same acts" within the meaning of Article 54 of the CISA is to consider the specific unlawful conduct ... as a whole.*'[47] At the same time, the ECJ was quick to point out that a mere subjective link between acts (*in casu* the same criminal intention) does not suffice to qualify these acts as 'same acts' under Article 54 CISA.[48] The ECJ again left it to the national court to make the assessment and decide.[49]

---

42. The ECJ notes in para. 28 that other international treaties, including the ECHR, use different terms, referring to 'offence' instead of 'acts'.
43. *'[C-385/01] Gözütok and Brügge [[2003] ECR I-1345], paragraph 33'.*
44. *'Gözütok and Brügge, paragraph 38, and Case C-469/03 Miraglia [2005] ECR I-2009, paragraph 32'.*
45. ECJ 9 March 2006, Case C-436/04, *Criminal proceedings against Leopold Henri Van Esbroeck* [2006] ECR I-2333. See for an analysis e.g. T. Rafaraci, 'The principle of *non bis in idem* in the jurisprudence of the European Court of Justice', in S. Braum and A.Weyembergh, 'Le contrôle juridictionnel dans l'espace pénal européen', Editions de l'Université de Bruxelles, 2009, 93-110.
46. ECJ 18 July 2007, Case C-367/05, *Criminal proceedings against Norma Kraaijenbrink* [2007] ECR I-6619.
47. ECJ 18 July 2007, para. 27 continues: '*Thus, Article 54 of the CISA can become applicable only where the court dealing with the second criminal prosecution finds that the material acts, by being linked in time, in space and by their subject-matter, make up an inseparable whole.*'
48. ECJ 18 July 2007, para 29-30. Comp. T. Rafaraci, above, 102-103.
49. ECJ 18 July 2007, para. 32.

The consequences of the different application by the ECJ of the *ne bis in idem* principle in Schengen and competition matters become clear from the results of the judgments: whereas persons won Schengen cases on the basis of *ne bis in idem,* the *ne bis in idem* arguments of undertakings continued to be rejected in competition cases.

There are two aspects which may hinder comparability of *ne bis in idem* under Article 54 CISA and *ne bis in idem* in competition law cases. Firstly, Article 54 CISA normally applies to natural persons and not to companies. Secondly, it is unclear whether Article 54 applies to cases that are not purely criminal.[50]

[D] Lisbon Treaty (2009)

One of the stated aims of the Lisbon Treaty was to give greater weight to fundamental rights. In order to attain this objective, the Treaty on European Union (hereinafter 'TEU') granted binding force to the Charter[51] and codified the link, already present in ECJ case law, between the ECHR and general principles of EU law.[52]

After the entry into force of the Lisbon Treaty, the interpretation of fundamental rights in the EU legal order appeared very closely linked to the ECHR:

- Article 52(3) of the Charter links the '*meaning and scope*' of the rights protected in the Charter to corresponding rights in the ECHR.[53]
- Recital 37 of Regulation 1/2003 links the application and interpretation of Regulation 1/2003 to the Charter, which itself is linked to the ECHR.
- Article 6(3) TEU links the general principles of EU law to the ECHR.

[E] The ECtHR Opts for a 'Factual Idem' under Reference to the ECJ (2010)

After EU law had thus linked Regulation 1/2003, the Charter and the general principles of EU law to the ECHR... the interpretation of the ECHR changed. Indeed, in 2010, in

50. However, I do know of one decision by a *national* (Belgian) financial market supervisor where Article 54 CISA was successfully invoked by a company to avoid an administrative fine for market manipulation. This is most surprising, as Article 54 CISA is generally considered to apply to 'hard core criminal law' and to natural persons. See 'Commission bancaire, financière et des assurances. Rapport du Comité de direction 2007' (www.fsma.be/nl/Doormat/Publications/Annual%20reports/~/media/Files/publications/ver/fr/cbfa_dc_2007.ashx), at p. 66.
51. Article 6(1) TEU: '*The Union recognises the rights, freedoms and principles set out in the Charter ... which shall have the same legal value as the Treaties.*'
52. Article 6(3) TEU: '*Fundamental rights, as guaranteed by the [ECHR] and as they result from the constitutional traditions common to the Member States, shall constitute general principles of the Union's law.*' The wording appears stronger than in the old Art. 6(2) EU which obliged the EU to '*respect fundamental rights, as guaranteed by the [ECHR]*'.
53. However, comp. the *Fransson* Opinion, paras 70 and 81-87. In view of the fact that certain Member States have not ratified Protocol No 7 or have lodged reservations and declarations on its Article 4, the AG pleads for an 'autonomous' interpretation of the general principle of *ne bis in idem* in EU law rather than an interpretation in light of the ECHR. Although not explicit in its motivation, the ECJ's judgment of 26 February 2013 appears to follows this approach.

a rare explicit reversal of its case law, the ECtHR decided to no longer interpret the *idem* in Article 4 of Protocol No. 7 as a 'legal idem' (or rather as an utterly unclear mix of interpretations: section §18.03[E] below) but as a 'factual idem' (section §18.03[E] below). Ironically, the ECtHR based this reversal on the ECJ case law in Schengen matters (discussed in, section §18.03[C] above).

As had been criticized by many and as the ECtHR itself finally admitted, ECtHR case law went in several directions. For too long, judgments on *ne bis in idem* adopting a 'factual idem' co-existed with judgments adopting a 'legal idem'.

The ECtHR's Grand Chamber judgment of 29 May 2001 in *Franz Fischer v. Austria* proved to be a milestone on this point as well, but not the final one. In what is now generally recognized as a 'compromise' solution, the ECtHR adopted the 'essential elements' doctrine: *ne bis in idem* applies if the two offences involved have the 'same essential elements'. The qualification of an offence or its name were no longer deemed to be decisive for the ECtHR.

However, unsatisfactory '*hybrid case law*' resulted, holding that *ne bis in idem* does not apply if the two offences '*only slightly overlap*', are committed by different persons (natural-legal) or are a repetition of the same offence.[54] This may all have been understandable but the ECtHR also ruled that *ne bis in idem* does not apply when two offences differ in their criminal intent or purpose[55] or were distinguishable in terms of their gravity and consequences or the social value being protected. Especially in latter instances, the 'essential elements' approach may have amounted to a renewed 'legal idem' approach.

The 'essential elements' approach was criticized in legal literature and the 'Freiburg proposal on concurrent jurisdictions and the prohibition of multiple prosecutions in the European Union', initiated by experts at the Max Planck Institute for Foreign and Criminal Law,[56] proposed to replace it by an outright 'factual idem' approach: *'Act' has to be understood as substantially the same facts, irrespective of their legal character.*

The Grand Chamber judgment of 10 February 2009 in *Sergey Zolotukhin v. Russia* reversed existing case law on the definition of 'idem':

> The Court considers that the existence of a variety of approaches ... engenders legal uncertainty incompatible with a fundamental right, namely the right not to be prosecuted twice for the same offence.[57]

54. E.g. a request for information by tax authorities is refused twice.
55. E.g. when '*the special aggravating element of drunken driving*' or '*the applicant's reliance on the incorrect information contained in the books when submitting his tax returns*' were established in only one set of proceedings. Case references are cited in the *Sergey Zolotukhin* judgment, para. 74-76.
56. See www.mpicc.de/ww/de/pub/forschung/forschungsarbeit/strafrecht/archiv/freiburg_proposal.htm.
57. Judgment *Sergey Zolotukhin*, para. 78. See for an analysis e.g. G. Di Federico, above, 244-245 and M. Puéchavy, 'L'arrêt *Zolotoukhine c. Russie*' in *Le principe ne bis in idem*, Brussels, Nemesis, 2012, 19-32. H. Mock, 'Ne bis in idem: Strasbourg tranche en faveur de l'identité des faits', *Rev. trim. dr. h.*, 2009, 867-881 is positive about the choice for an *idem factum*, but not about certain other aspects of the judgment.

In *Zolotukhin*, the ECHR refers to several other human rights instruments.[58] When analysing the ECJ case law on the issue, it explicitly mentions the '*different interpretation of idem*' in, on the one hand, the Schengen cases and, on the other hand, competition cases.[59]

The ECtHR then, courageously, opts for an explicit reversal of its own case law:

> While it is in the interests of legal certainty, foreseeability and equality before the law that the Court should not depart, without good reason, from precedents laid down in previous cases, a failure by the Court to maintain a dynamic and evolutive approach would risk rendering it a bar to reform or improvement.

The ECtHR, contrary to the ECJ in *Van Esbroeck*, rules that the use of the word 'offence' in Article 4 of Protocol No. 7 cannot be decisive (it refers to the wide variety in terminology worldwide: same 'offence', 'acts', 'cause', 'conduct'). The Court rather opts for an *effet utile* approach: '*[T]he Convention must be interpreted and applied in a manner which renders its rights practical and effective, not theoretical and illusory.*'[60]

The ECtHR rejects a 'legal idem' because it is '*too restrictive on the rights of the individual*' and '*risks undermining the guarantee enshrined in Article 4 of Protocol No. 7.*' The ECtHR opts for a 'factual idem' instead, using terminology copied from ECJ case law in Schengen cases:

> Ne bis in idem 'must be understood as prohibiting the prosecution or trial of a second 'offence' in so far as it arises from identical facts or facts which are substantially the same'.[61] 'The Court's inquiry should therefore focus on those facts which constitute a set of concrete factual circumstances involving the same defendant and inextricably linked together in time and space, the existence of which must be demonstrated in order to secure a conviction or institute criminal proceedings.'[62]

§18.04 THE ECJ'S *TOSHIBA* JUDGMENT: A *STATUS QUO*, AT BEST

[A] Facts and Procedures

This case relates to a restrictive agreement allegedly concluded on an international level in 1988 and discovered by the Commission in 2004. On 3 March 2004, one of the cartelists filed a leniency application and on 11 May 2004, the Commission carried out dawn-raids.[63] The end date of the infringement could be associated with either one of these dates but is heavily debated (section §18.05[A] below).

---

58. Apart from those listed in the Annex, also the Statute of the International Criminal Court, the case law of the Inter-American Court of Human Rights, the Constitution of the United States, and the case law of the US Supreme Court.
59. Judgment *Sergey Zolotukhin*, para. 37.
60. Comp. F. Tulkens, above: (translated) 'protection of persons is more important than *ius puniendi*'.
61. Judgment *Sergey Zolotukhin*, para. 82.
62. *Ibid.*, para. 84.
63. Continued on 12 May 2004.

On 30 September 2004, the Commission wrote a letter to the Czech NCA. The precise content of that letter is also uncertain but according to the ECJ, the letter informed the Czech NCA of the Commission's intent to initiate proceedings (or to fine?) only in relation to the infringement prior to 1 May 2004 and relating to the territory of the old EU Member States.[64]

On 20 April 2006, after an investigation of almost two years, the Commission adopted a Statement of Objections. On 24 January 2007, the Commission adopted a final decision by which it imposed fines of ca. EUR 750 million on the parties.[65] The parties started an action for annulment against the Commission Decision before the GC. By judgments dated 12 July 2011, the GC partially annulled the Decision for some parties, but only in relation to the calculation of fines.[66] Most, but not all, parties brought appeals against the GC judgments before the ECJ and these are still pending.[67] By Decision of 27 June 2012, the Commission amended its original Decision in order to reinstate fines against the successful applicants before the GC.[68] On 12 September 2012, new actions for annulment were brought against the amending Commission Decision[69] and these are also still pending.

On the national level, the Czech Office for the Protection of Competition (hereinafter 'Office'), which together with its Chairman forms the Czech NCA, initiated proceedings against the same parties on 2 August 2006, i.e., (a) quite some time after accession of the Czech Republic to the EU and (b) after the Commission had started its investigation[70] but (c) before the Commission issued a decision. The Czech NCA's investigation relied heavily on the findings of the Commission. On 9 February 2007, little more than two weeks after the Commission, the Czech NCA issued a decision imposing fines of ca. EUR 37.2 million on the parties.[71]

On 26 April 2007, the Czech fining decision was changed on appeal by the Chairman of the Office, reducing the fines on two of the parties and upholding the remainder of the decision.[72]

---

64. See *Toshiba* judgment, para. 20.
65. Commission Decision of 24 January 2007, relating to a proceeding under Article 81 of the EC Treaty and Article 53 of the EEA Agreement (Case COMP/F/38.899 – GAS INSULATED SWITCHGEAR), available at http://ec.europa.eu/competition/antitrust/cases/dec_docs/38899/38899_1030_10.pdf., notified under document number C(2006) 6762 final and summarised in the *OJ*, C 5/7, 10 January 2008.
66. See GC, judgment of 12 July 2011, Case T-113/07, *Toshiba Corp v. Commission*, not yet reported, and parallel judgments for the other parties concerned.
67. See e.g. the appeal brought by Toshiba on 27 September 2011, Case C-498/11 P (*OJ*, C 347/18, 26 November 2011), currently pending before the ECJ.
68. *OJ*, C 70/12, 9 March 2013.
69. Action brought on 12 September 2012, Case T-404/12 *Toshiba Corporation v. Commission* and Case T-409/12, *Mitsubishi Electric v. Commission*, currently pending before the GC.
70. It is interesting to note this, as according to the Commission's ideas on what NCAs can do during the Commission's investigations, an NCA should not have the right to investigate when the Commission investigates: see section §18.04[E][2][c] below. Then again, the ECJ agrees that the Czech Republic can benefit from its special situation as a newly acceded Member State.
71. Czech Office for the Protection of Competition, Decision No. S 222/06-3113/2007/710 from 9 February 2007.
72. Czech Office for the Protection of Competition, Decision of the Chairman No. R 059-070, 075-078/2007/01-08115/2007/310 of 27 April 2007.

The fined parties challenged the Chairman's decision before the Regional Court in Brno. On 25 June 2008, the Regional Court annulled both the contested decision and the Office's decision in the first instance.[73]

On 10 April 2009, the Supreme Administrative Court of the Czech Republic (hereinafter 'SAC'), acting on an appeal brought by the Office, annulled the first instance judgment and referred the case back to the Regional Court.[74] It was within the framework of this referral that the Regional Court referred questions for preliminary ruling to the ECJ on 11 December 2009.[75]

AG Kokott delivered her Opinion on 8 September 2011 and the Court pronounced its judgment on 14 February 2012. section §18.04 of this Chapter analyses Opinion and judgment in more detail.

After receiving the answers to its preliminary ruling questions, the Regional Court in Brno delivered its judgment on 14 June 2012.[76] It referred to the ECJ's judgment on *ne bis in idem* but nonetheless quashed the decision of the Office and its Chairman for arbitrariness in applying sanctions to the parties. It referred the case back to the Office.

The Regional Court's judgment was appealed by the Office. As a result, proceedings continued a second time before the SAC. By judgment of 24 April 2013, the SAC dismissed the cassation complaint, so that the case remains with the Office awaiting a new decision in first instance.

It is possible that the SAC judgment effectively brings to an end the attempt by the Czech NCA to fine Toshiba and other companies under Czech national competition law. As the re-instating of fines by the Czech NCA may now be time barred, it is possible that the Czech NCA will at most be able to declare that an infringement occurred, if it can establish sufficient proof for such a finding.

National proceedings will continue on this issue, and appeals and actions for annulment are still pending before the ECJ and the GC. Almost ten years after their initiation (and more than twenty-five years after the alleged entering into of the restrictive agreement), the end of the proceedings concerning the alleged GIS cartel is still not in sight. After the involvement of the Office (at three different stages), its Chairman, the Regional Court in Brno (twice), the SAC (twice), the Czech Constitutional Court,[77] and the ECJ, it now appears unlikely that fines will ever be imposed under Czech national competition law.

73. Regional Court in Brno, Case 62Ca 22/2007-489 of 25 June 2008.
74. Supreme Administrative Court of the Czech Republic, case 2 Afs 93/2008-920 of 10 April 2009. The plaintiffs filed a constitutional complaint with the Czech Constitutional Court against this judgment. They argued that the refusal of the SAC, as a judge in last instance, to refer preliminary ruling questions to the ECJ was unconstitutional. On 7 July 2009, the Constitutional Court ruled that the constitutional complaint was inadmissible because the SAC had not ruled in last instance. This, in turn, allowed the plaintiffs to argue before the Regional Court that the Regional Court was still empowered to refer questions to the ECJ, which the Regional Court did.
75. The first question is cited below, section §18.04[E][1][a]. See also *Toshiba* judgment, para. 36.
76. Regional Court in Brno, case 62Ca 22/2007-2067 of 14 June 2012.
77. Note 74 above.

[B] What Was at Stake in the *Toshiba* Case?

Although *Toshiba* may appear to be a case about enlargement, it is first and foremost a case about *ne bis in idem* in competition law. Its assignment to the ECJ's Grand Chamber, the large number of intervening Member States and the first paragraph of the Opinion of AG Kokott suggest that this was sufficiently clear to all involved:

> How many competition authorities in Europe may deal with one and the same cartel and impose penalties on the participating undertakings? That, in essence, is the question [...]. It is a question which not only raises fundamental issues relating to the delimitation of the respective competences of the European competition authorities but also has to do with some sensitive aspects of the protection of fundamental rights in the European Union, particularly in the light of ... ne bis in idem .... The significance of these issues from the point of view of the functioning of the new system for the implementation of antitrust law, as introduced on 1 May 2004 by Regulation (EC) No 1/2003, is not to be underestimated. The same issues also provide the Court with the opportunity to develop its case-law in Walt Wilhelm, which is over 40 years old.[78]

There were at least five important questions to be answered in the *Toshiba* judgment in my view. The first concerns the relationship between EU and national procedures and, indirectly, the relationship between national procedures. Can *ne bis in idem* be successfully invoked in a case where an NCA starts or ends a procedure under national (and/or EU) competition law after the Commission has started or ended a procedure under EU competition law? The answer, even in the context of accession, could give an indication as to the chances of success of a *ne bis in idem* argument in cases where one NCA starts proceedings after another NCA has already done so, i.e., probably the other most pressing *ne bis in idem* situation in competition law.[79]

A second issue concerns the (lack of) harmonization between ECHR law ('factual idem') and EU law ('legal idem' in competition matters), and between EU law in the Schengen area ('factual idem') and EU competition law ('legal idem'). It is of particular relevance since the entry into force of the Lisbon Treaty, because the TEU now (a) confers binding force on the Charter, (b) states that the Charter should be interpreted in light of the ECHR, and (c) confirms in even stronger words that fundamental rights, as guaranteed the ECHR, constitute general principles of EU law: section §18.03[D] above.

To paraphrase the wording of the ECJ's *Van Esbroeck* judgment (cited in, section §18.03[C] above), is it that the Member States should have more mutual trust in each other's criminal justice systems than in each other's competition law systems? Should it not also be that in competition law cases that Member States (and the Commission)

---

78. Opinion of AG Kokott of 8 September 2011 in Case C-17/10, not yet reported (*Toshiba* Opinion) para. 1. Some of the points below were also made in legal literature before the *Toshiba* judgment was rendered. See G. Di Federico, above, 257-258, hinting at a possible reversal of the *Walt Wilhelm* case law, and F. Louis and G. Accardo, 'Ne Bis in Idem., Part 'Bis'', *World Competition* 2011, (97), 109-110 ('The ... Gas-Insulated Switchgear Cases: A Turning Point?').
79. Not the *Toshiba* judgment but the above-cited *Fransson* judgment is leading as far as the dual application of administrative and criminal sanctions is concerned.

'*each ... recognise the competition law in force in the other Contracting States even when the outcome would be different if its own national law were applied*'?

A third question relates to the impact of the modernisation of EU competition law enforcement since 1 May 2004. Can the old three-prong test (identity of facts, unity of offender and unity of the legal interest protected) survive modernization? See §18.03[A] above.

Fourthly, the judgment would have to clarify whether *ne bis in idem* can become a tool to cope with the proliferation of supervisors applying competition law, as the scope for *ne bis in idem* has never been so large. See section §18.01[A] above.

Finally, one should bear in mind that competition law often acts as a laboratory for legal protection in other areas of EU law, so that the judgment may have an impact on other areas of law where quasi-criminal 'administrative' sanctions may be imposed. *Ne bis in idem* arguments are already frequently raised in e.g., financial law cases where (a) under national law a criminal and an administrative sanction can be imposed for the same behaviour by the same offender (e.g., insider trading – market manipulation) or (b) a Member State authority intends to impose a sanction for the effects of behaviour on its territory after another Member State's authority has already imposed a fine for effects on its territory, on the basis of files with similar or common evidence.

[C] Pleadings

Aware of the fact that no one appears able to win an EU competition law case on the basis of *ne bis in idem*, the legal argument of the fined undertakings (the applicants) was not only, and for some not even primarily, based on that principle. It was also, and for some primarily, based on Regulation 1/2003.

[1] Regulation 1/2003 Argument

The argument consisted of different steps. In a first step, it was stated that the first sentence of Article 11(6) of Regulation 1/2003[80] barred the Czech NCA from starting an investigation under Article 101 TFEU after the Commission had already done so.

To this the Czech NCA could simply have answered that it had not initiated any investigation under Article 101 TFEU, but had investigated exclusively under its national competition law. Therefore, an additional step was required. The applicants referred to Article 3(1) of Regulation 1/2003, according to which an NCA applying national competition law to assess an agreement which may affect trade between Member States (as was clearly the case in the agreement fined by the Commission) must also apply EU competition law. However, since the Czech NCA was relieved of its power to apply EU competition law (first step, above), it was also relieved of its power

80. '*The initiation by the Commission of proceedings for the adoption of a decision under Chapter III shall relieve the competition authorities of the Member States of their competence to apply Articles [101] and [102] of the Treaty.*'

to apply national competition law, and as a consequence, so it was argued, the Czech NCA could not fine under national law.

This argument was presented as in line with Recital 18 and Article 13 of Regulation 1/2003 which indicated that the drafters of Regulation 1/2003 prefer that of all competent authorities in the EU one best placed ('*most appropriate*') authority deals with an infringement.

The particularities of the *Toshiba* case (i.e., accession of the Czech Republic to the EU during the infringement but before the NCA started proceedings) required one extra step to support the above reasoning: the applicants had to show that EU competition law, in particular Regulation 1/2003, applied to the Czech NCA when it started proceedings.

Before the ECJ, the Czech NCA and Government argued that Regulation 1/2003 can never have applied to an infringement having an impact on the Czech market before 1 May 2004. The applicants argued that Regulation 1/2003 can probably not be said to be entirely procedural or entirely substantive in nature but that:

(a) to the extent that Regulation 1/2003 is of a procedural nature, it applies with immediate effect to pending cases as from accession – and *a fortiori* to cases where proceedings are started after accession;
(b) to the extent that Regulation 1/2003 is substantive in nature it should apply to the case at hand under the principle of the retroactive application of the more lenient penalty (*lex mitius*), recognized as a general principle of EU law in the ECJ's *Berlusconi* judgment.[81]

The Czech NCA and Government further argued that before accession the Czech Republic was '*like any third country, such as the United States or Canada.*' The applicants countered that the Europe Agreement and privileged contacts between Czech and EU authorities proved that there was at least a common competition culture between the Czech Republic and the EU, even before accession.

According to the Czech government, the new Member States have only gained competences through accession but have not lost any competences. Accession would not have changed anything regarding the application of national competition law. The applicants replied that Article 3(2) of Regulation 1/2003 proves that the new Member States have not only gained competencies after accession but have also lost some competences, such as the competence to prohibit under national law what is allowed under EU competition law.

[2] Ne Bis in Idem Argument

The applicants, with unexpected support from the EFTA Surveillance Authority, urged the ECJ to align its *ne bis in idem* case law in competition law with its *ne bis in idem*

81. ECJ 3 May 2005, Joined Cases C-387/02, C-391/02 and C-403/02, *Criminal proceedings against Silvio Berlusconi* [2005] ECR I-3565, in particular paras 68-69.

case law in other areas, notably Schengen cases, and with the ECtHR's case law as set out above. They also stressed that in accordance with ECtHR case law (section §18.02[A] above), *ne bis in idem* covers not only fining decisions but also investigations.

A very important factual point in the applicants' argument was that according to the applicants the Commission did in fact investigate the effects of the alleged infringement in the Czech Republic: section §18.04[E][1][b] below.

[D] Judgment (and Opinion Where It Substantially Deviates from the Judgment)

All the arguments of the plaintiffs were rejected. In the *Toshiba* judgment the ECJ reaffirms the three-prong test for *ne bis in idem* to apply in competition law cases.

The structure of the pleadings (Regulation 1/2003 argument – *ne bis in idem* argument) is absent in the judgment. The ECJ appears to answer to the different elements of the two pleas in a somewhat random order, which can be explained by the way in which the preliminary ruling questions are formulated.

For the sake of consistency, the points made by the ECJ are reassembled in the order of the pleadings set out above. This is not entirely possible, as the ECJ begins its reasoning with 'Preliminary observations'.

[1] 'Preliminary Observations' by the ECJ[82]

The ECJ finds that the referring court and the applicants assumed that (i) the infringement was single and continuous until after accession and (ii) the Commission's decision penalized the conduct of the applicants in the Czech Republic.[83]

'However',[84] as per the ECJ:

(i) according to the order for reference, the Commission informed the Czech NCA that '*the procedure brought by it would concern only the activities of the cartel carried out in the territory of the Union, as it existed before the enlargement*';[85]

(ii) the Commission stated in its written observations '*that its decision does not penalise the effects of the collusive conduct which materialised in Czech territory before 1 May 2004*';[86] and

(iii) it appears from the information by the referring court itself that the Czech NCA's decision only concerns the period before accession.[87]

82. *Toshiba* judgment, paras 37-43.
83. *Ibid.*, paras 37-39.
84. *Ibid.*, para. 40. The wording suggests that the ECJ rejects the position of the applicants and of the referring court, but this is not made more explicit.
85. *Ibid.*, para. 40.
86. *Ibid.*, para. 41.
87. *Ibid.*, para. 42.

The ECJ does not draw any specific conclusion from these observations. The ECJ does e.g., not take position as to the end date of the infringement, confirming that there was *no* single and continuous infringement until after accession. The ECJ merely states: '*It is therefore in the light of those preliminary considerations that the questions referred are to be examined.*'[88]

[2] Regulation 1/2003 Argument

The ECJ appears to subscribe to the argument to the extent that, through a combination of Articles 11(6) and 3(1) of Regulation 1/2003, NCAs indeed lose the power not only to apply Articles 101 and 102 TFEU but also their national competition law if the Commission initiates proceedings.[89]

However, the ECJ rules that NCAs lose the powers to apply EU and national law only temporarily. Their power is restored once the proceedings initiated by the Commission are concluded.[90]

According to the ECJ this appears from Article 16(2) of Regulation 1/2003[91] which '*establishes that the national authorities may intervene after the Commission, but prohibits them from contradicting a previous decision of the Commission.*'[92] The wording of Article 16(2) '*appears to envisage only the application of EU law by the [NCAs]*' but '*the same rules must apply a fortiori where the NCAs intend to apply national competition law*', provided they do not contradict a Commission decision.[93] Therefore, Article 16(2) does not have the limited scope (national decision after finding of inapplicability by the Commission) that the applicants and the referring court want to read into it.[94]

The temporary character of the loss of power of NCAs is also evident from the explicit choice, made by the drafters of Regulation 1/2003, for the continued parallel application of national and EU competition laws. A proposal to bring restrictive practices which may affect trade between Member States under the scope of EU competition law alone, to the exclusion of national competition law, was rejected. This proves (so I understand paragraph 83 of the judgment) that Member States consciously opted for parallel application of EU and national competition law.[95]

Essential for maintaining the *status quo* on *ne bis in idem* are paragraphs 81–82 of the judgment:

> 81. In accordance with settled case-law, EU law and national law on competition apply in parallel (Wilhelm and Others, ...). Competition rules at European and at

88. *Ibid.*, para. 43.
89. *Ibid.*, paras 70 and 72–78.
90. *Ibid.*, paras 79-80.
91. '*When competition authorities of the Member States rule on agreements, decisions or practices under Article 81 or Article 82 of the Treaty which are already the subject of a Commisison decision, they cannot take decisions which would run counter to the decision adopted by the Commission.*'
92. *Ibid.*, paras 84–85.
93. *Ibid.*, para. 86.
94. *Ibid.*, para. 87.
95. *Ibid.*, para. 83.

national level view restrictions on competition from different angles (Wilhelm, ...) and their areas of application do not coincide (...).
82. That situation has not been changed by the enactment of Regulation 1/2003.

The ECJ holds that Recital 18 in the Preamble to Regulation 1/2003 does not counter this, as Recital 18 relates to Article 13 of Regulation 1/2003 and not to Article 11(6).[96] Recital 18 and Article 13 create a possibility, but do not impose any obligation as to exclusive application of EU law.

The ECJ stresses in its answer to the first question '*that account must be taken, as to the interpretation and application of Article 81 EC and Regulation 1/2003, of the particular situation*' of the Czech Republic as a newly acceded Member State.[97] The ECJ confirms the immediate effect of procedural rules[98] and the mixed procedural-substantive character of Regulation 1/2003.[99] However, '*[s]uch substantive rules cannot in principle be applied retroactively, irrespective of whether such application might produce favourable or unfavourable effects for the persons concerned.*'[100] The applicants' references to *Dow Chemical Ibérica, Saldanha* and the Europe Agreement were all rejected.[101]

Interestingly, the ECJ confirms the principle of the retroactive application of the more lenient penalty and does not appear to object in principle to the application of this principle in other than criminal matters. However, the applicants invoke the principle '*not [to] advocate the application of a more lenient penalty for the period before 1 May 2004*' but to challenge the power of the NCA to impose any fine at all. '*Such a question is linked to the interpretation of Article 11(6) ... and to the principle of ne bis in idem, which will be examined in the context of the second question, and not to the principle of retroactive application of the more lenient penalty.*'[102]

This last argument, made by the applicants as a Regulation 1/2003 argument, is thus referred to the *ne bis in idem* part and is not really dealt with by the Court. However, it is submitted that, implicitly at least, and as in the *Spector* case on insider trading,[103] the AG and the ECJ refuse to treat 'no penalty' as a 'more lenient penalty' which can benefit from the *lex mitius* principle.

96. *Ibid.*, paras 88-90.
97. *Ibid.*, para. 45.
98. *Ibid.*, para. 47.
99. *Ibid.*, para. 48.
100. *Ibid.*, para. 50.
101. *Ibid.*, paras 54–62.
102. *Ibid.*, para. 66.
103. ECJ 23 December 2009, Case C-45/08, *Spector and others v. CBFA* [2009] ECR I-12073.

[3] Ne Bis in Idem Argument

In paragraphs 94–102 of the judgment, the ECJ reiterates the existing principles, including the three-prong test (unity of facts, unity of offender, unity of legal interest protected), as if nothing has changed.[104]

However, the rejection of the plaintiffs' *ne bis in idem* argument is not based on lack of the same interest protected (i.e., the most controversial of the three criteria) but on the lack of unity of facts.[105] As the Commission did not penalize behaviour on Czech territory before accession and the decision of the Czech NCA only penalized behaviour on Czech territory before accession, the ECJ finds no identity of facts:

> 102. It must therefore be concluded that the Commission's decision does not cover any anti-competitive consequences of the said cartel in the territory of the Czech Republic in the period prior to 1 May 2004, whereas, according to the information supplied by the national court, the decision of the Úřad pro ochranu hospodářské soutěže imposed fines only in relation to that territory and that period.
> *103. Having regard to the above, the answer to the second part of the second question is that the ne bis in idem principle does not preclude penalties which the national competition authority of the Member State concerned imposes on undertakings participating in a cartel on account of the anti-competitive effects to which the cartel gave rise in the territory of that Member State prior to its accession to the European Union, where the fines imposed on the same cartel members by a Commission decision taken before the decision of the said national competition authority was adopted were not designed to penalise the said effects.*[106]

It appears from the above-cited paragraphs that the judgment is very much based on what the ECJ already set out in the preliminary observations (section §18.04[A] above), i.e., the absence of overlap between the Commission Decision and the decision of the Czech NCA. The ECJ presents the case as a specific, accession-related case.[107]

The idea to introduce the duration and territory of the infringement as elements of the 'identity of facts' is based on the Opinion: section §18.04[D][4] below.

104. *Ibid.*, para. 97, referring to para. 338 of the above-cited *Aalborg Portland and Others v. Commission* judgment.
105. *Ibid.*, para. 98.
106. See *ibid.*, paras 98 and 100-103.
107. Along these lines, the ECJ clarifies the temporal applicability to *ne bis in idem* in accession situations: '*It is of little importance that the decision whereby the said authority imposed fines relates to a period prior to the accession of the Czech Republic to the Union. The temporal applicability of the ne bis in idem principle in the context of EU law depends not on the date on which the facts being prosecuted were committed, but, in a situation such as that at issue in the main proceedings, falling under competition law, on that on which the proceeding for the imposition of a penalty was opened. On 2 August 2006, when the Úřad pro ochranu hospodářské souteže opened the proceeding at issue in the main proceedings, the Czech Republic was already a Member State of the Union, with the result that that authority was required to comply with that principle.*' *Ibid.*, para. 95.

[4] Differences and Similarities between the Judgment and the Opinion of AG Kokott

There are two main differences and one major resemblance between the judgment and the Opinion in the *Toshiba* case.

A first major difference in approach is that contrary to the ECJ, the AG did accept that the traditional three-prong test should be abandoned in EU competition law. In the view of the AG, 'identity of the interest protected' should be deleted as a criterion for application of *ne bis in idem,* in order to ensure coherence with ECJ case law in other areas and with ECHR case law.[108]

As for the AG, 'unity of the offender' is included in 'identity of the facts' she proposes that 'identity of the facts' be the sole criterion for establishing an '*idem*'.[109]

A second major difference between the Opinion and judgment is the continued reliance of the AG on the ECHR. Whereas the judgment abandons the pre-existing reference to the ECHR, the AG advocates homogeneity between ECHR and Charter, whereby the ECHR sets a '*minimum standard*':

> That close proximity to the ECHR is indicated not only by the Explanations on Article 50 of the Charter of Fundamental Rights, which must be duly taken into account by the courts of the [EU] and of the Member States, but also by the previous case-law of the [ECJ] concerning the general EU-law principle of ne bis in idem.
>
> *The requirement of homogeneity is therefore applicable.*[110]

As fundamental as the differences is the following major resemblance between the Opinion and the judgment: both apply a 'legal idem' rather than a 'factual idem' which would solely focus on the conduct of the offender.

That the judgment applies a 'legal factum' becomes clear from its continued reliance on a three-prong test, including the legal interest protected. The Opinion is more subtle but arrives at exactly the same conclusion as the judgment, i.e., that one and the same cartel behaviour can lead to sanctions by more than one competition

---

108. '*There is no objective reason why the conditions to which the ne bis in idem principle is subject in competition matters should be any different from those applicable to it elsewhere. For, in the same way as, within the context of Article 54 of the CISA, that principle serves to guarantee the free movement of EU citizens in EU territory as a 'single area of freedom, security and justice', so, in the field of competition law, it helps to improve and facilitate the business activities of undertakings in the internal market and, ultimately, to create uniform conditions of competition (a 'level playing field') throughout the EEA.*'. *Ibid.*, para. 118.
109. *Ibid.*, para. 122.
110. '*It follows from that requirement that rights contained in the Charter which correspond to rights guaranteed by the ECHR are to have the same meaning and scope as those laid down by the ECHR. In other words, Article 4(1) of Protocol No 7 to the ECHR, as interpreted by the European Court of Human Rights (ECtHR), describes the minimum standard that must be guaranteed in the interpretation and application of the ne bis in idem principle in EU law*'. *Ibid.*, last sentence of para. 119 and para. 120. Footnotes are not reproduced here.

authority or court if it results in restrictions of competition in different territories[111] (e.g., different Member States) or during different periods are sanctioned:

> This has nothing to do with the legal interest protected or the legal characterisation of the facts. Rather, the actual or potential effects of a cartel are an indispensable component of the facts on account of which the undertakings participating in the cartel are prosecuted by a competition authority and cannot thereafter be prosecuted for a second time (ne bis in idem).[112]

Although the AG probably sees things differently (*'This has nothing to do with …'*), it is submitted that she too refuses to apply a 'factual idem' to the extent that for the AG not solely the conduct of the cartel offender is decisive (section §18.01[B] above) but also, or even predominantly, the *effects* of the offender's conduct.[113] The multiple investigations and finings that are possible under the ECJ's three-prong test are still possible under the AG's single criterion test, but now because the effect (e.g., effect on the territory of Member State A versus effect on the territory of Member State B) or the duration (e.g., conduct lasted longer according to NCA in Member State A than according to NCA in Member State B) of the conduct is different.[114]

The underlying reason for the 'disguised three-prong test' used by the AG to determine whether there is *idem* in *ne bis in idem*, is the fear that cartel offences might go partially unpunished, i.e., the fear of under-enforcement:[115]

> The ne bis in idem principle is intended to ensure that undertakings are not prosecuted more than once and, where appropriate, punished more than once for the anti-competitive consequences – whether by object or by effect – of their collusive conduct. It is not meant to have the effect of leaving the anti-competitive consequences of such conduct in a particular territory and during a particular period of time unpenalised.[116]

111. Comp. the discussion of 'the territoriality criterion' in M. Petr, 'The ne bis in idem principle in competition law', ECLR, 2008, (392), at 393-394 and E. Paulis and C. Gauer, 'Le règlement n° 1/2003 et le principe du *ne bis in idem*', *Concurrences – RDLC*, 2005, (32), 37.
112. *Toshiba* Opinion, para. 130.
113. Comp. W. Wils, note 10 above, 108: *'I personally do not believe that the applicability of Article 50 CFR can be avoided by arguing that the second prosecution would not be for the same offence, given that the first prosecution only took into account the effects of the violation of Article 81 EC on the territory of the Member State of the national authority which prosecuted first. … The principle of ne bis in idem prohibits multiple prosecution or punishments for the same offence, not merely for the same effects of an offence.'*.
114. *'The ne bis in idem principle does not in any way prohibit more than one competition authority or court from penalising restrictions of competition – by object or by effect – resulting from one and the same cartel in different territories or during different periods of time within the European Economic Area.' Toshiba* Opinion, para. 131, last sentence.
115. *'Conceivably, the material acts could always be said to be identical where two decisions adopted by competition authorities relate to the same cartel. This would seem to be the very broad understanding of idem that the referring court and some of the parties to the proceedings have in mind.' Toshiba* Opinion, para. 126.
116. *Toshiba* Opinion, para. 133.

[E] Critical Appraisal

[1] Is the Toshiba Judgment Based on a False Premise?

The entire judgment is built on the premise that there is no overlap between the fining decisions of the Commission and the Czech NCA.

The absence of overlap enables the ECJ to reject the plaintiffs' arguments based on Regulation 1/2003 and on *ne bis in idem*. As discussed, the ECJ rejects the *ne bis in idem* argument on the grounds that there is no overlap and therefore no identity of facts (section §18.04[D][3] above). Similarly, as there is no overlap and the infringement on Czech territory is held to have ended before accession, the substantive provisions of Regulation 1/2003 are found not to apply and the plaintiffs' argument based on that Regulation fails.[117]

The absence of overlap further enables the ECJ to present the case as a mere confirmation of the case law on *ne bis in idem* in relation to third countries. In paragraph 60 of the judgment, the ECJ confirms that the infringement ended before accession, at a time when the Czech Republic was indeed still a third country.

According to the ECJ, the reason for there being no overlap between the Commission and national fining decision is that (a) the Commission investigated and fined only in relation to EU territory before accession (section §18.04[E][1][b] below), whereas (b) the Czech NCA only investigated and fined for its territory and for the period before accession. The judgment does not make it clear whether (b) implies that according to the ECJ the infringement ended before accession, or rather that the ECJ finds that even if the infringement ended after accession, a single and continuous infringement can be split up for fining purposes (section §18.04[E][1][a] below).

In reality, both reasons for finding no overlap are problematic. Instead of presenting them as 'Preliminary observations' the ECJ could have examined and motivated them more thoroughly.

[a] Discussion as to the End Date of the Infringement on Czech Territory (before or after Accession?): Material Error in the Judgment

Throughout the procedure and before the ECJ, there was much discussion on the exact end date of the infringement on Czech territory: did the infringement end before or after

117. The situation might be a whole lot less straightforward if the end date was set after accession. Comp. Saulius Lukas Kaleda, 'Immediate Effect of Community Law in the New Member States: Is there a Place for a Consistent Doctrine?', *European Law Journal*, 2004, (102), 112. After having discussed at length the ECJ's judgments in *Data Delectra, Saldanha, Konle, Beck* and other cases, the author writes: *'It seems more appropriate to accept that the Court of Justice allowed for the application of Community law, since the factual situations forming the background of the cases had not yet been established on the date of accession. ... Advocate General La Pergola suggested a similar interpretaition of Saldanha, remarking in Beck that 'the Court ... stated that Community law was applicable even to events arising prior to Austria's accession, provided that the effects of such previously existing situations persist (and continue) after accession'.'* Exactly this would be the case if it were found that the single and continuous infringement had ended only after accession.

accession to the EU? According to the Office and its Chairman, the alleged cartel had ended on 3 March 2004, i.e., prior to the accession of the Czech Republic in the EU. The referring court, the Regional Court in Brno concluded that the alleged infringement had ended not earlier than on 11 May 2004, i.e., after accession. The SAC agreed in principle but ruled that accession itself had ended the infringement, so that it had ended on 1 May 2004.

The applicants feared that the Office might have manipulated the date so as to set it before accession. They argued – but this is not visible from the judgment – that the finding in the Commission Decision of 2007 that the global cartel ended after accession, was binding on the Czech NCA when it prepared and adopted its investigation, also in 2007. This flows in their view from the doctrine of supremacy of EU law, especially since the Commission finding had been made after accession and the Czech NCA started its investigation also after accession.

The position of the ECJ is ambiguous to say the least. At the beginning of the judgment, the ECJ confirms that there is disagreement about the exact end date. Furthermore, the ECJ states that according to the information given at the hearing by the agent of the Czech Republic and by the representative of the Office, Czech competition law uses different assessment criteria for determining the end of a cartel than the Commission does.[118] The ECJ does not specifically deal with (a) the division of the alleged infringement into two parts (one prior to, and one after, accession) or (b) a possible manipulation of the end date by the Office.

However, in paragraph 60 of the judgment, and under reference to paragraph 42 of its judgment, the ECJ rules that (a) the infringement ended before accession and (b) that the order for reference confirms that the infringement ended before accession:

> As has been found in paragraph 42 of this judgment, *according to the order for reference, the case* in the main proceedings *concerns an infringement* of the legislation of the Czech Republic on competition *which ended before the accession* of that State to the Union. (emphasis added)

The opposite is true: as the ECJ correctly sets out paragraph 31 of the same judgment, the referring court was of the opinion that the infringement ended *after* accession:

> The [Regional Court in Brno] ... based its reasoning on the Commission's decision to conclude that the [Czech NCA] had wrongly concluded that the infringement had ended on 3 March 2004. The latter *continued until 11 May 2004*, that is to say after the accession ... and after the entry into force of Regulation 1/2003. It should therefore be regarded as having been committed under the 'new law', namely Article 81 EC and Regulation No 1/2003. (emphasis added)

If the ECJ had any doubt as to the position of the national judge, it would have sufficed to read the first preliminary ruling question (which however the ECJ chose to rephrase (section §18.04[E][3] below):

> Must Article 81 of the EC Treaty [...] and Council Regulation (EC) No 1/2003 [...] be interpreted to mean that that legislation must be applied (in proceedings

118. *Toshiba* judgment, para. 27 and 31.

brought after 1.5.2004) to the whole period of operation of the cartel, which commenced in the Czech Republic before that state's entry to the [EU] (that is, before 1.5.2004) and continued and *ended after the Czech Republic's entry to the [EU]*? (emphasis added)

The ECJ's reference to paragraph 42 is also materially incorrect, as appears from the text of that paragraph 42.[119] Contrary to what paragraph 60 claims, the (incorrect) statement in paragraph 60 is not the same as the (correct) statement in paragraph 42.

The material error in paragraph 60 of the judgment does not, as one might believe at first sight, result from a translation error. The different language versions are consistent on this point.

The actual *dictum* of the judgment does not refer to the end date of the infringement at all, but only to the effects of the alleged cartel infringement that are fined nationally. Implicitly but certainly, therefore, the ECJ appears to be of the opinion that the end date is not decisive. It would seem that as long as a national decision only fines the *effects* of an alleged cartel that occurred prior to accession, the ECJ is willing to allow the national fining decision, even if it concerns an alleged infringement which ended after accession. However, if that is correct, the ECJ may in the process have split up one single and continuous infringement into one infringement ending at accession (and which the NCA can still fine) and another infringement after accession (which the NCA cannot fine if the Commission has fined). This division of one single and continuous infringement into different infringements for fining purposes is problematic in itself: section §18.04[E][4] below.

[b] Did the Commission Decision Investigate and/or Fine Behaviour in the Czech Republic?

The Opinion and the judgment answer in the negative. They rely heavily on statements made by the Commission to the ECJ[120] and on a letter, dated 30 September 2004, which the Commission is said to have sent to the Czech NCA. The letter is said to have indicated that the Commission investigation would not cover the Czech Republic. The Commission letter and the Commission statements suffice for the ECJ to rephrase the preliminary ruling questions of the Regional Court in Brno (even though that court was supposedly well aware of the letter).

However, there is no trace of this letter in the Commission Decision and the description in the judgment does not make it clear whether the letter indicated that the

119. '*Finally, it is apparent from the information provided by the referring court itself that the decision of the Úřad pro ochranu hospodářské souteže at issue in the main proceedings takes into account only the anti-competitive effects produced, in Czech territory, by the cartel between the undertakings concerned, before 1 May 2004. That decision thus concerns only the period before the accession of the Czech Republic to the Union.*'

120. The fact that the ECJ considers 'the Commission's word' as an element of proof that there was no overlap between the EU and national fining decision, is remarkable. Whereas in preliminary ruling cases the Commission normally brings an objective third party view on the legal issues involved, things were different in this case. Although *formally* not a party to the dispute, the applicants directly attacked the Commission's fining Decision in a parallel procedure before the GC.

Commission would not *investigate* behaviour in the Czech Republic or would not *fine* it.[121] That difference is, nevertheless, of the essence for the application of *ne bis in idem*, which does not only apply to double fining but also to double investigation. When stressing, ever so often,[122] that the Commission Decision has not *penalized* behaviour in the Czech Republic,[123] the *Toshiba* judgment denies that *ne bis in idem* should also apply to double investigation, not only to double sanctioning.

As set out above, the applicants were of the opinion that the Commission, although it did not fine behaviour on Czech territory, did investigate behaviour on Czech territory and even based its decision on that investigation. Their argument was that several paragraphs in the Commission fining Decision dealt with the inclusion of Central and Eastern Europe in the territorial scope of the alleged cartel, and that the Commission actually invoked the discussions on this inclusion as proof that the Japanese companies participating in the 'global' cartel must have been aware of the restrictive agreement concerning Europe. Paragraphs 116,[124] 127,[125] 128,[126] 256,[127]

121. '*The Commission indicated in that letter that the anti-competitive conduct under examination had taken place, in large part, before 1 May 2004 and that, taking account of the difficulty posed by the imposition of a fine as regards only the final days of that conduct (from 1 May to 11 May 2004), the procedure before it would concern only the activities of that cartel carried out in the territory of the European Union before the enlargement of the latter on 1 May 2004. According to the Commission, it was thus unlikely that it would initiate a proceeding concerning the Czech Republic.*' Judgment, para. 20; emphasis added.

122. If the Commission and national procedure really were '*addressing different periods during which the cartel was in operation*' the problem would not be one of *ne bis in idem* but one of parallel procedures which can be solved under the *Anrechnungsprinzip*, according to B. van Bockel, 'The *ne bis in idem* principle in the European Union legal order: between scope and substance', *ERA Forum*, 2012, (325), 339. The reference to the Commission not penalizing behaviour in the Czech Republic could then be explained, but the reference to *ne bis in idem* would no longer be correct. Moreover, the absence of overlap (in terms of end date, as well as in terms of investigations) is doubtful, it is submitted in this Section.

123. *Toshiba* judgment, paras 39, 41, 101 (2x) and 103, and *dictum*.

124. '[...] *There existed a common understanding between the two groups that the Japanese companies would not bid in Europe. References to 'Europe' must be understood in this context as reference to 'Western Europe' at the initial stages of the cartel, while at a later stage it must be understood as covering also other European countries from Central and Eastern Europe as they progressively became open to market economy.* [...].'

125. '*Allocation to Japanese companies was not excluded with regard to [business secret]. The fact that some Central and Eastern European countries were initially open to Japanese members, became controversial over time and, at least as from 2002, the European cartel participants feared that contestation of the Central and Eastern European markets put at risk the price levels charged in the European area traditionally protected by the 'common understanding', i.e. in Western Europe. In a context where the integration of those markets in the Community could be anticipated, the European cartel members perceived Central and Eastern Europe as theirs. The Japanese members were aware that their European counterparts considered those countries as their territory and during the discussions regarding the adjustments of the cartel in 2002, this issue came up, without it being discussed again thereafter.*'

126. '*Despite the alleged rejection by Hitachi/JAEPS of the proposal to include Central and Eastern Europe under the 'common understanding' already covering Western Europe, the Commission file contains evidence that, in fact, the European cartel members allocated amongst themselves the relevant European projects, including, from 2002 onwards, projects in Eastern Europe.*'

127. '*For the reasons stated in recital (127) above, the proposal made in July 2002 by the European companies to consider Central and Eastern Europe as their market can only be interpreted as a proposal to extend the protection of the 'common understanding' beyond Western Europe.* [...]'

316,[128] ..., of the non-confidential version[129] of the Commission Decision may indicate that Central and Eastern Europe, including the Czech Republic, were indeed included in the Commission investigation.

Unfortunately this argument is simply not reproduced, let alone answered, in the judgment. Instead the ECJ presents as (the sole) argument of the parties '*that the Commission speaks of a worldwide cartel and did not expressly exclude the Czech Republic from the scope of its decision.*'[130] It is submitted that this selective presentation of legal argument is regrettable.

In paragraph 101 of the judgment, the ECJ lists three reasons for concluding that the Commission did not investigate cartel behaviour in the Czech Republic:

- 'the Commission's decision refers specifically, in many of its passages, to the consequences of the cartel [...] within the European Community and the EEA, referring expressly to the "Member States of the time" and the States 'which are contracting parties' to the EEA Agreement.'
- the Commission Decision 'does not penalise the possible anti-competitive effects produced by that cartel in the territory of the Czech Republic during the period prior to accession'; and that
- 'it is apparent from the methods of calculation of the fines that [...] the Commission did not take account of the States which acceded to the Union on 1 May 2004.'

It is submitted that the second and third reason are irrelevant, to the extent that they concern fining, whereas *ne bis in idem* does not only prohibit double fining but also double investigation. It has been argued elsewhere that the first reason is irrelevant as well.[131]

Furthermore, the first reason is not only irrelevant but also inconclusive: the fact that '*many passages*' (without further reference) in the Commission Decision refer to the Member States pre-accession does not exclude the fact that the Commission has investigated cartel behaviour in the Czech Republic. It has been argued that, in reality,

128. '*[...] for a long time, allocation to Japanese companies was not excluded regarding Eastern Europe. As already mentioned, the lists [business secret] reflecting the projects discussed with the Japanese companies include GIS projects outside the European countries listed as excluded in the GQ-Agreement and outside the EEA (at the time): projects in [business secret].*'
129. It is obviously not possible to expand here on the confidential version. Suffice it to say that the ECJ always has access or can ask access to the confidential version of the Commission's fining Decision.
130. *Toshiba* judgment, para. 100.
131. See S. Brammer, 'Judgment of the Court of 14 February 2012 in Case C-17/10 Toshiba Corporation and *Others v. Úřad* pro ochranu hospodářské soutěže (Czech Competition Authority)', *Revue de la concurrence belge* 2013, 4-13, at 11: '*However, the effects of an anticompetitive conduct are not a constitutive element of an infringement under Article 101 TFEU where the relevant agreement or practice has the object of restricting competition. Arguably, therefore, the effects of the cartel are irrelevant for the finding of an infringement in the present case ....*' According to Brammer, the effects are not '*an indispensable component of the facts*' but rather a factor to determine the gravity of the infringement, and '*[t]he Court thus was wrong in basing itself on the (alleged) effects of the illegal conduct in order [to] determine the territorial reach of the decision*'.

there are not so '*many passages.*'[132] Moreover, as indicated above, the '*many passages*' are offset by many other passages of the Commission Decision which do refer to non-Member States, in particular to states in Central and Eastern Europe.

Finally, the third reason is not only irrelevant but also not entirely correct, to the extent that the Commission, in paragraph 481 of its Decision,[133] takes into account worldwide sales figures in order to differentiate between cartel participants when setting the starting amount for the fine.[134] Even if the third reason were relevant and correct, which would imply that the Commission did not take into account the new Member States when calculating the fines, the fact remains that the Commission may have taken into account the new Member States for something much more important than the calculation of fines: the establishment of the infringement itself (section §18.04[E][1][b] above).

[c] Summary

The premise on which the entire judgment hinges, i.e., that there was no overlap between the Commission and the NCA fining decisions, may or may not be correct but cannot be founded on the grounds listed in the judgment. The judgment is somewhat flawed by a material error and the selective presentation of legal argument. A more thorough motivation would have been welcome, especially in view of the referring judge's conviction that there *was* an overlap between the two fining decisions.

[2] Status Quo or Step Back?

By presenting the Czech Republic as a third country, the ECJ presents the judgment as a *status quo* judgment, merely confirming earlier case law on *ne bis in idem* in relation to third countries.

A closer analysis reveals that the judgment may not mark a *status quo*, but rather a step back in the possible application of *ne bis in idem* in competition matters, in three respects.

132. S. Brammer, above, 11-12.
133. '*Given the global character of the cartel arrangements, the worldwide sales figures give the most appropriate picture of the participating undertakings' capacity to cause significant damage .... [T]he worldwide turnover of any given party to the cartel also gives an indication of its contribution to the effectiveness of the cartel .... The comparison is made on the basis of the worldwide product turnover in the last full year of the infringement for each undertaking.*'
134. Comp. S. Brammer, above, at 12 who concludes, on several grounds, that the argument is '*not very convincing*' and that '*[t]he two references to the 2003 EEA turnover can therefore hardly be regarded as the criterion defining the territorial scope of the Commission decision*'.

[a] *The End of Consistent Interpretation of Ne Bis in Idem in Different Areas of EU Law*

Toshiba confirms that the interpretation of *ne bis in idem* in competition law is based on a 'legal idem' at a time when the EU has introduced a 'factual idem' in other areas of EU law. As a consequence, it is now certain that *ne bis in idem* is applied differently in different areas of EU law.

[b] *The End of Consistent Interpretation of EU and ECHR Law*

Contrary to its earlier case law, where the ECJ systematically referred to Article 4 of Protocol No. 7 to the ECHR (section §18.02[B] above), and contrary to the Opinion which insisted on the need for homogeneous interpretation of EU and ECHR law (section §18.04[D][4] above), the ECJ has dropped the reference to the ECHR in its *Toshiba* judgment.

The explanation for the deletion of the reference to the ECHR cannot possibly be a desire to 'update' fundamental rights protection from the ECHR to the Charter as indeed any mention of Article 50 of the Charter is equally lacking in the *Toshiba* judgment. The Charter is mentioned in relation to the *lex mitius* principle,[135] which makes its absence in relation to *ne bis in idem* even more striking.

Some may have believed that the deletion of a reference to the ECHR was a one-time '*accident de parcours*'. However, the recent *Fransson* judgment of the ECJ proves otherwise. It confirms – unfortunately again only implicitly – that the deletion of a reference to the ECHR very much translates as a deliberate choice of the ECJ (section §18.05[A] below): the ECJ is no longer willing to interpret the EU *ne bis in idem* requirement in Article 50 of the Charter in conformity with the ECHR's *ne bis in idem* requirement as interpreted in *Zolotukhin*. From now on, it seems, the EU and ECHR *ne bis in idem* principles will diverge in large areas of the law:

- One single ECHR *ne bis in idem* principle will apply in a similar fashion to all ECHR cases. It is based on a 'factual idem' and may prohibit the imposition of criminal sanctions after the imposition of administrative sanctions which fulfil the *Engel* criteria.
- Several EU law *ne bis in idem* principles will apply (one in the Charter, one outside the Charter, with or without reference to the Charter, with or without reference to the ECHR) and they will be applied differently in different sectors. Moreover, *ne bis in idem* continues to be based on a 'legal idem' in competition matters and does not prevent the imposition of criminal sanctions after the imposition of administrative sanctions which fulfil the *Engel/Bonda* criteria.[136]

---

135. *Toshiba* judgment, para. 64.
136. ECJ 5 June 2012, Case C-489/10, *Łukasz Marcin Bonda*, not yet reported, paras 36 et seq.

[c] *Will Proceedings Take Even Longer in the Future? The Powers of NCAs During a Commission Investigation*

Although one finds little trace of it in the judgment, there was vigorous discussion before the ECJ (also between representatives of national governments and the Commission) about the question as to what NCAs can still do while the Commission is investigating a case. Does Article 11(6) of Regulation 1/2003 temporarily relieve NCAs of their power to *decide* under EU and/or national competition law, or also of their power to *continue to investigate* cartel behaviour with a view to adopting a decision soon after the Commission has decided?

According to certain governments appearing before the ECJ, as soon as Article 11(6) of Regulation 1/2003 applies, NCAs are freed of the obligation under Article 3(1) and can continue to apply national law because EU law and national law protect different interests. This position appears to have been rejected, and rightly so it is submitted, as it is untenable. National and EU competition law do not protect different interests (section §18.03[A] above). Furthermore, by closing their investigation and imposing a fine before the Commission does so, NCAs could not only try to influence a future Commission decision based on EU law but could also effectively deprive the first sentence of Article 3(2) of Regulation 1/2003 of all *effet utile*. Under that provision, national competition law must not prohibit what is allowed under EU competition law. The provision confirms that in the opinion of the drafters of Regulation 1/2003, the interests protected under national competition law are not entirely independent of the interests protected under EU competition law, but interact therewith.

The Commission defended the position that NCAs are relieved of their competence not only to decide but also to investigate under national law as long as the Commission investigates under EU law, and regain their powers thereafter. It would appear that the Commission is followed on this point by the AG and the ECJ.[137] Under this position, what NCAs can do with the powers they regain will depend on what the Commission has decided in each individual case.

Although this position does not seem unreasonable, one should be aware of the risks it entails.[138]

Firstly, there is the risk of this approach leading to a case-by-case analysis. If each decision or measure of the Commission on the termination of proceedings has to be assessed individually, this risks to lead to legal uncertainty and unpredictability for NCAs and undertakings alike, and may prove to be a source of endless disputes on the exact effects of individual Commission decisions.

137. See paras 79-80 of the judgment: '*Regulation No 1/2003 does not, however, indicate that the opening of a proceeding by the Commission permanently and definitively removes the national competition authorities' power to apply national legislation on competition matters. 80. As the Commission argues in its written observations, the power of the national competition authorities is restored once the proceeding initiated by the Commission is concluded.*'

138. Comp. the very critical analysis of M. Botta, 'Testing the decentralization of competition law enforcement: comment on Toshiba', *E.L. Rev.*, 2013, 107-117. According to the author the ECJ's '*narrowing down the scope of application of Art. 11(6) of Regulation 1/2003*' and its position on *ne bis in idem* '*has eroded two pillars which have so far safeguarded the stability of the multilevel competition policy enforcement system in the [EU].*'

Secondly, this position implies that undertakings may still be subject to 27 (soon 28) + 1 different procedures, which I continue to find difficult to reconcile with the whole idea of modernization and the Commission's own stated intention of having one best placed ('*most appropriate*') authority deal with each case.

Thirdly, this position risks to considerably extend the number and duration of proceedings in comparison to the already suboptimal situation today. It may lead to one big tangle of proceedings of an even longer total duration than persisting at present. The *Toshiba* case illustrates this very well: almost ten years after their initiation the end of proceedings is not in sight (section §18.04[A] above). Allowing NCAs to continue to investigate while the Commission has initiated proceedings is less straightforward but may at least speed up decision-making by NCAs after the Commission has decided.

[3] Distrust of the Referring Judge

A certain distrust of the national judge is identified in the *Toshiba* Opinion and judgment. To begin, the national judge's preliminary questions are rephrased in a way which appears somewhat suggestive at times. For example, the referring court's first question, cited in (section §18.04[E][1][a] above), is rephrased as follows:

> By its first question, the referring court asks in essence whether, in a Member State which acceded to the EU on 1 May 2004, Article 81 EC and Article 3(1) of Regulation No 1/2003 are applicable to periods of time prior to the date of accession.[139]

Thus rephrased, one very important element of the question is left out: the existence, in the referring court's view, of a single and continuous infringement continuing until after accession. Moreover, the preliminary ruling question referred as much to Article 11(6) of Regulation 1/2003 as to Article 3(1). The first preliminary ruling question could really be summarized as follows:

> In case of a single and continuous infringement starting before accession and ending thereafter [and when an investigation into this infringement starts after accession], does Regulation 1/2003 apply to the whole infringement or not?

It is submitted that the answer might have been less predictable.

Secondly, contrary to the ECJ's normal attitude in *ne bis in idem* cases (also in competition matters), the AG and ECJ do not entrust the national judge to review, on the basis of criteria set by the ECJ, whether an *idem* is present. The AG and ECJ prefer to interpret the Commission Decision themselves and to conclude from it that no *idem* is present, leaving no margin of appreciation to the national judge.[140]

Under the circumstances, one could have forgiven the referring court for having lived under the impression that the ECJ answered a question which it had not asked (application of *ne bis in idem* to a case without overlap between NCA and Commission

139. *Toshiba* Opinion, para. 37.
140. *Toshiba* Opinion, para. 135-146. *Toshiba* judgment, paras 98-102.

fining) and did not answer the question it had asked (application of *ne bis in idem* to a case where an NCA and Commission fining decision overlap).[141] In the end, the referring court quashed the Czech NCA's fining decision on different grounds: section §18.04[A] above.

[4] Other

There is clearly tension between (a) the relative ease with which EU competition law currently qualifies cartel infringements as 'single and continuous' for fining purposes, and (b) the ease with which these same infringements are subsequently split up again to avoid the application of *ne bis in idem* in EU-national relations.[142] The ECJ approach, already applied in earlier case law,[143] has been severely criticized on this point.[144]

Finally, it is remarkable that in the entire proceedings on *ne bis in idem* in the *Toshiba* case (and in most annotations of the judgment) the 'bis' element has not come up. One could obviously not expect the fined undertakings to make this point but can a Commission fining Decision, which was (and continues to be: section §18.04[A] above) vigorously attacked before the EU courts, really be said to have been 'final' at the time of the Czech investigations and fining? According to the established case law,[145] the answer appears to be negative.[146]

141. 'Rephrasing' a referring court's questions may help avoid controversial issues and may make for apparently convincing judgments, but it may also reduce the practical impact of the ECJ's ruling. If the purpose of the preliminary ruling procedure is to interact closely with the national judge and help her solve cases, the ECJ may want to stick as closely as possible to the preliminary ruling questions asked, for no dialogue is possible between the national court and the ECJ on the rephrasing of questions.
142. See also section §18.04[E][1][a] abovepara. . The tension becomes most clear in para. 46 of the *Toshiba* Opinion: '*The cartel at issue may well be a single and continuous infringement but its anti-competitive consequences are subject to different rules of law depending on whether they arose before or after the Czech Republic's accession to the European Union.*'
143. F. Louis and G. Accardo, above, 102 ('*fictitio iuris*').
144. '*This approach* [i.e. the finding of a single and continuous infringement, *note of the author*] *notably implies that the facts which form the basis of the Commission decision are inextricably linked together by their subject-matter ... so as to make up an inseparable whole. On this basis, it seems artificial, if not impossible, to cut off the acts relating to the territory of a specific Member State and consider them as a separate infringement which is based on different facts.*' S. Brammer, above, 12, according to whom such fragmentation '*should be precluded*'.
145. Comp. the definition of 'final' in the Explanatory Report on Protocol No 7, above, section §18.02[A]. See for a discussion of the element 'final' in the case law of ECtHR, ECJ and other (supreme) courts N. Neagu, above, 962-965.
146. Comp. B. van Bockel, *The ne bis in idem Principle in EU Law*, Kluwer Law International, 2010, 338-339 who reaches the same conclusion.

§18.05 TENTATIVE CONCLUSIONS

[A] Continued Legal Uncertainty

It may have become clear from the foregoing that *ne bis in idem* in EU competition law continues to be very controversial, even among European institutions[147] (e.g., in *Toshiba* the EFTA Surveillance Authority pleaded fervently in favour of aligning *ne bis in idem* in competition cases with *ne bis in idem* in Schengen cases and with the ECHR case law[148] whereas the Commission tried every argument to avoid its application[149]).

The ECJ's recent *Toshiba* and, albeit to a lesser extent, *Fransson* judgment have clarified some elements. Most importantly, we now know that the five major evolutions of the law discussed in this chapter have not (yet) significantly altered the application of *ne bis in idem* in EU competition law. This application is still not based on a true 'factual idem'. The AG refers to 'effects', while the ECJ continues to apply a three-prong test (unity of facts, unity of offender, unity of interest protected).

As a consequence, we also know that, for now at least, the application of *ne bis in idem* in competition cases differs from (a) ECHR case law since *Zolotukhin* and (b) certain other areas of EU law, notably Schengen cases.

As to Regulation 1/2003, the ECJ has clarified that the loss of powers of NCAs under Article 11(6) is only temporary.

Much, if not everything else, is still open to interpretation. As the *dictum* in *Toshiba* is carefully limited to accession situations, it remains unclear if and to what extent it would also apply in situations where the national competition law of 'third country' was not involved, but that of a Member State.[150] Furthermore, in its reasoning on *ne bis in idem*, the ECJ does not refer to Article 50 of the Charter and also not, as it did in earlier case law, to the ECHR. This creates additional legal uncertainty on the following issues:

- Does Article 50 of the Charter apply to *ne bis in idem* in EU competition law? The Commission argued in *Toshiba* that it did not, because the Czech NCA was not 'implementing EU law' under Article 51 of the Charter.[151] The AG rejects this argument and holds that Article 50 does apply.[152] The ECJ gives

147. Also within individual Member States, there is controversy. See e.g. on the divergent legal opinion of the Cour de Cassation and the Conseil d'Etat in Belgium D. Renders, M. Joassart, G. Pijcke and F. Piret, 'Le régime juridique de la sanction administrative', in *Les sanctions administratives*, Brussels, Bruylant, 2007, (155), 190-195.
148. *Toshiba* Opinion, para. 117.
149. Note 166 below.
150. Comp. P. Oliver and T. Bombois, note 8 above, 271. G. Oosterhuis and A.M. Huijts, 'Arrest Toshiba: toepassing ne bis in idem-beginsel in kartelzaken', *NtEr* 2012, (301), 305-306 point to the risk that after the *Toshiba* judgment, the Commission could, on purpose or not, limit the fining of an EU wide cartel to a selection of Member States. Authorities of other Member States (e.g. chosen in function of strength of NCA or record of judges controlling NCAs, or not chosen on purpose) would then be free to start additional actions sanctioning the effects of the cartel on their national territory, possibly in part on the basis of the Commission Decision.
151. *Toshiba* Opinion, para. 102.
152. *Toshiba* Opinion, para 103–106.

no indication, but does not mention Article 50 (section §18.04[E][2][b] above). In *Fransson*, the AG argues that Article 50 does not apply in a (VAT, not competition) case where criminal proceedings are commenced after an administrative penalty has already been imposed.[153] However, in that case the ECJ rules that Article 50 can apply.[154]

- Does Article 50 of the Charter have to be interpreted in conformity with Article 4 Protocol No. 7 ECHR? In *Toshiba*, the AG answers in the affirmative.[155] In *Fransson*, the AG answers in the negative, mainly on the grounds that Article 4 of Protocol No. 7 is not sufficiently unanimously accepted by Member States.[156] The ECJ does not explicitly answer but in both *Toshiba* (sections §18.04[D][4] and §18.04[E][2][b] above) and *Fransson*[157] the ECJ deletes the reference to the ECHR. I therefore assume that the answer to this question is negative, for now.

A degree of uncertainty also continues to surround the following questions:

- What can NCAs still do during a Commission investigation (18.04[E][2][c] above)? The ECJ states in *Toshiba* that an NCA '*can no longer apply … EU competition law*'[158] and '*loses the possibility of applying provisions of national law prohibiting cartels*'[159] when Article 11(6) applies. From those statements I derive that NCAs cannot continue investigations while proceedings before the Commission are in progress (section §18.04[E][2][c] above) but a more explicit confirmation would be welcome.
- If *ne bis in idem* does not prevent overlapping sanctions, does then another general principle apply, which requires that the second sanction is reduced in order to take account of the first one? The ECJ in *Walt Wilhelm* and the AG in *Fransson* appear to affirm, but in different wording (section §18.01[A] above). The ECJ and the AG in *Toshiba* are less outspoken.

[B] Taking both Under-enforcement and Over-enforcement Seriously: Where to Go Next?

The concern to fight the possible under-enforcement of competition law is evident from the ECJ's case law on *ne bis in idem* in competition matters in general, and from the Opinion and judgment in *Toshiba* in particular. One can only share this concern. In

153. *Fransson* Opinion, paras 27–64. According to the referring court, the national provisions applied were not adopted in order to transpose EU law.
154. See the *Fransson* judgment, esp. the Sections on 'Jurisdiction of the Court' (paras 16–31), 'Questions 2, 3 and 4' (paras 32–37) and the *dictum*, sub 1. The fact the national provisions applied were not adopted in order to transpose EU law does not alter this conclusion: para. 28.
155. See above, section §18.04[D][4].
156. *Fransson* Opinion, para. 70 and 81–87. See also note 53 above.
157. Any reference to Article 4 of Protocol No 7 is absent in the ECJ's own substantive analysis starting at para. 16 of the *Fransson* judgment.
158. *Toshiba* judgment, para. 75.
159. *Ibid.*, 78.

conformity with ECJ case law, real and sufficiently deterrent punishment should be applied against unwanted cartel behaviour.

However, concerns of over-enforcement (‘*How much is too much?*’[160]) and disproportionate sanctioning, as well as concerns for the excessive societal cost of enforcement proceedings should be taken equally seriously. This does not currently appear to be the case. In *Toshiba* for example, the AG makes reference to the risk of leaving anti-competitive behaviour unsanctioned as against each of the arguments raised by the applicants, i.e., against the argument based on Article 11(6) of Regulation 1/2003,[161] against the *lex mitius* argument[162] and against the *ne bis in idem* argument.[163] This could create the impression that the mere risk that behaviour would go unpunished is enough to reject legal argument, even if that legal argument is based on general principles of law. Referring to Vice-President Tulkens of the ECHR (cited in section §18.01[B] above) the AG and ECJ risk to become one-sidedly concerned with ‘*the interests of repression and administration of justice.*’

Similarly, to the degree that *Toshiba* is to be interpreted to mean that (a) NCAs are relieved not only from the power to decide when the Commission has started investigations but also from the power to investigate, but (b) regain their full powers afterwards, the duration of proceedings may increase even further.

A correct balance may be difficult to reach. This raises the question as to how *ne bis in idem* should be developed further in competition law; in particular, in situations of combined application of EU law, not with the law of a third country but with the law of one or more Member States, and in situations of combined application of different national competition law regimes. At least the following alternatives are open:

(a) continued application of the existing case law, including the continued refusal of a ‘factual idem’ and continued reliance on a three-prong test, also in situations which EU competition law has not yet dealt with;[164] possibility of a reference to the Charter but not to the ECHR;
(b) introduction of a ‘disguised three-prong test’ (section §18.04[D][4] above), as proposed by the AG in *Toshiba,* with unity of facts serving as the sole criterion, encompassing unity of offender as well as territory and duration of behaviour;

160. J. Terzaken and P. Huizing, above, at 56 point out that over-enforcement may lead to over-deterrence ‘*where businesses become too cautious and refrain from undertaking competitive activity because of fear that the activity may be deemed anticompetitive*’. They propose a set of guiding principles, to be adopted by authorities globally and on the basis of reciprocity.
161. See *Toshiba* Opinion, para. 39: ‘*In essence, the undertakings participating in the cartel hope that the application of those provisions of EU law will ensure that they are not penalised by the Czech competition authority altogether.*’
162. *Toshiba* Opinion, para. 59: ‘*Hitachi's real objective in relying on the principle of lex mitius appears to be quite different. What that undertaking would like to secure in relation to the period before 1 May 2004 is not a more lenient decision but no decision at all by the Czech competition authority.*’
163. See *Toshiba* Opinion, para. 133, cited above, section §18.04[D][4].
164. Given the current aversion of both the ECtHR and ECJ of even creating an impression of conflict between their respective case laws, the ECtHR may not object.

(c) continued application of the current three-prong test or of a disguised three-prong test but with the systematic addition that the EU principles of proportionality or '*the principle of the prohibition of arbitrariness, which is inseparable from the rule of law (Article 2 TEU)*' require national courts and authorities to take into account the prior existence of a first sanction for the purposes of mitigating the second sanction;

(d) reversal of, or addition to, the current case law leading to the introduction of a true 'factual idem' in EU competition law in conformity with ECtHR and Schengen case law; the link with Article 4 of Protocol No. 7 ECHR, broken since the ECJ *Toshiba* and *Fransson* judgments, could then be restored;

(e) legislative intervention, including the possibility of introduction of asymmetrical *ne bis in idem* rules (e.g., no possibility for an NCA to fine after the Commission has fined, but possibility for the Commission to fine conduct which has already been fined in a Member State on condition that the Commission takes the national fine into account) and rules to deal with fining in one Member State after another Member State has already imposed fines.[165]

Although my preferences may have become clear,[166] I consider it too early to advocate in favour of one particular solution. However, an open and transparent debate is urgently needed.

[C] Differentiated Application of General Principles of EU Law: How General Should General Principles Be?

One of the few certainties after *Toshiba* and *Fransson* is that many different variants of *ne bis in idem* are currently applied in parallel in EU law:[167]

- *Ne bis in idem* in competition law differs from *ne bis in idem* in other areas.
- *Ne bis in idem* in EU competition law but also in other areas of EU law differs from *ne bis in idem* in the ECHR as interpreted in *Zolotukhin*.
- Without motivation and on an ad hoc basis, the ECJ applies the *ne bis in idem* principle in EU law either (a) with (*Fransson*) or without (*Toshiba*)

165. See for a concrete idea as to what legislative intervention might look like (amendment of Article 3 of Regulation 1/2003) G. Di Federico, above, 258-260.

166. I would certainly not plead in favour of two other routes, not even mentioned here. In *Toshiba* the Commission argued that (a) the ECJ had no competence to apply the Charter when a Member State applies national competition law after the Commission has applied EU law, on the grounds that the Member State concerned is then not '*implementing EU law*' and (b) that Article 4 Protocol 7 ECHR could not be applied because *ratione loci* it envisages national and not cross-border situations. The arguments were not successful and the ECJ, not following its AG on this point, has rejected an argument similar to (a) in *Fransson* above, section §18.05[A].

167. The diversity of interpretations already struck J. Vervaele in 2005 (above, 117). He noted at the time that '*the Union legislator is finding it enormously difficult to give shape and substance to transnational legal principles and this is also true in the case of the ne bis in idem principle*' (above, 118). The *Toshiba* and *Fransson* judgments make it clear that the exercise is certainly not less difficult for the Union courts.

reference to the Charter, (b) with (older case law) or without (*Toshiba, Fransson*) reference to the ECHR, or (c) as an independent general principle, without reference to either the Charter or the ECHR (*Toshiba*). This creates the impression that the content of *ne bis in idem* as a general principle of EU law is different from the content of that same principle under the Charter and the ECHR.

Is such differentiation desirable or even legal? AG Kokott in *Toshiba* is very much opposed to it:

> To interpret and apply the ne bis in idem principle so differently depending on the area of law concerned is detrimental to the unity of the EU legal order. The crucial importance of the ne bis in idem principle as a founding principle of EU law which enjoys the status of a fundamental right means that its content must not be substantially different depending on which area of law is concerned. [...] [T]he same criteria should apply in all areas of EU law.[168]

It is submitted that the unity of the EU legal order indeed requires that general principles of EU law be applied similarly throughout different areas of EU law in the absence of compelling reasons to do otherwise. Furthermore, the current proliferation of *ne bis in idem* principles (as a general principle of EU law, as a principle in the Charter, as a principle in the ECHR) must end.[169]

The ECJ's case law on non-contractual liability comes to mind. The ECJ ruled that the conditions for Member State liability for damage caused to individuals '*cannot, in the absence of particular justification, differ from those governing the liability of the Community in like circumstances*'.[170] It is submitted that, in line with this approach, deviations from the principle of uniform application of general principles also require, at the very least, a '*particular justification*', for which the burden of proof rests on the party or institution wishing to deviate from the principled uniform application.

It is my distinct impression that to the mind of some academics, officials and judges, there are two possible '*particular justifications*' for applying a lower *ne bis in idem* standard in competition matters: (a) the idea that competition law is not 'hard core criminal law', so that a lower standard of protection is acceptable and/or (b) the idea that fundamental rights risk to be trivialized if granted too generously to commercial undertakings instead of only to natural persons.

168. *Toshiba* Opinion, para. 117. In a footnote the AG refers to the Opinion of AG Sharpston of 15 June 2006 in Case C-467/04 *Gasparini and Others* [2006] ECR I-9199, para. 156.
169. See in this sense also P. Oliver and T. Bombois, note 8 above, at 272.
170. '*The protection of the rights which individuals derive from Community law cannot vary depending on whether a national authority or a Community authority is responsible for the damage*'. ECJ 5 March 1996, Joined Cases C-46/93 and C-48/93, *Brasserie du Pêcheur and Factortame* [1996] ECR I-1029, para. 42; ECJ 4 July 2000, Case C-352/98 P, *Bergaderm* [2000] ECR I-5291, para. 41.

It is unfortunate that these concerns are not made more explicit by those who share them.[171] Opaque language does not do justice to these valid concerns: a judgment's message should not be deduced from words which are omitted (*in casu*, a reference to the ECHR and/or to the Charter) but from the sound motivation of the *dictum*.

A clear ruling by the ECJ as to whether, and if so why, (a) *ne bis in idem* can or should be applied differently in EU competition law and other areas of EU law, and (b) the ECtHR's interpretation of *ne bis in idem* should (not) be followed in EU law in general and EU competition law in particular would, therefore, be well received. The impression of a two-speed ECJ – active and innovative in institutional and citizenship matters but conservative and undecided in traditional substantive EU law matters – is to be avoided at all costs.

171. With some laudable exceptions. See e.g. P. Oliver and T. Bombois, note 8 above, at 270 and 272 (on both concerns) and M. Emberland, *The Human Rights of Companies. Exploring the Structure of ECHR Protection*, Oxford, OUP, 2006, Chapter 2 and p. 208 (on the second concern).

Table of Cases

European Court of Justice

Case 26/62, *Van Gend en Loos* [1963] ECR 1, 88, 92, 202, 257, 336
Case 6/64, *Flaminio Costa v. E.N.E.L,* [1964] ECR 585, 257, 336, 375
Cases 56 and 58/64, *Consten & Grundig,* [1966] ECR 299, 100, 356
Joined Cases 18 and 35/65, *Max Gutmann v. Commission of the European Communities,* [1966] ECR 103 and [1967] ECR 1961, 376
Case 14/68, *Walt Wilhelm* [1969] ECR 1, 403, 409
Case C-29/69 *Erich Stauder v. City of Ulm-Sozialamt,* 128, 376
Case 59/70 *Netherlands v. Commission* [1971] ECR 639, 204
Cases 80/70, *Defrenne v. Belgian State* [1971] ECR 445, 204
Case 4/73, *Nold v. Commission,* [1974] ECR 491, 128, 283, 286
Case 8/74, *Dassonville,* [1974] ECR 837, 251
Case 36/74, *B.N.O. Walrave and L.J.N. Koch v. Association Union cycliste internationale, Koninklijke Nederlandsche Wielren Unie and Federación Española Ciclismo* [1974] ECR 1405, 72, 174, 214, 256, 258, 331
Case 43/75, *Gabrielle Defrenne v. Société anonyme belge de navigation aérienne Sabena* [1974] ECR 455, 174
Case 127/73, *BRT v. SABAM* [1974] ECR 313, 337, 344
Case 45/76 *Comet* [1976] ECR 2043 302
Case 13/76, *Donà* [1976] ECR I-1333, 256, 331
Case 33/76, *Rewe Central Finanz* [1976] ECR 1989 302
Case 43/75, *Defrenne v. Sabena,* [1976] ECR 455, 72, 75, 202, 203, 206, 214, 260
Case 10/78, *Belbouab* [1978] ECR 1915 204
Case 106/77, *Simmentahl* [1978] ECR 629, 97, 221, 337, 393
Case 112/77, *Töpfer*[(1978] ECR 1019 204
Case 98/78, *Racke* [1979] ECR 69 204
Case 120/78, *Cassis de Dijon* [1979] ECR 649, 251
Case 230/78, *SpA Eridiana and others* [1979] ECR 2749 286
Case 44/79 *Liselotte Hauer v. Land Rheinland-Pfalz,* 128
Case 58/80, *Dansk Supermarked v. Imerco* [1981] ECR 181, 17, 81, 95, 229, 262, 274
Case 60/81, *IBM v. Commission* [1981] ECR 2639, 351
Case 102/81, *Nordsee v. Reederei Mond,* [1982] ECR 1095, 103

Case C-411/98, *Ferlini* [2000] ECR I-8081, 72, 75, 260
Case 437/97 *Evangelischer Krankenhausverein Wien* [2000]) ECR I-1157, 203
Case C-443/98, *Unilever Italia,* [2000] ECR I-7535, 83, 194, 196
Case C-456/98, *Centrosfeel v. Adipol,* [2000] ECR I-6007, 72
Joined Case C-240-244/98 *Océano Grupo ed. V. Quintero et al.* [2000] ECR I-4941, 312
Joined Cases C-51/96 and C- 197/97 *Deliège* [2000] ECR I-2549, 253, 331
Case C-195/98 *Öst. Gewerkschaftsbund, Gewerkschaft öffentlicher Dienst/Republik Österreich,* [2000] ECR I-10497 325
Case C-144/99, *Commission v. Netherlands* [2001] I-3541 308
Case C-274/99, *Connolly v. Commission* [2001] ECR I-1611 161
Case C-405/98, *Gourmet International* [2001] ECR I-1795, 251
Case C-453/99, *Courage Crehan* [2001] ECR I-6297, 79, 88, 267, 304, 332, 336
Case C-459/00, P(R) *Commission v. Trenker* [2001] ECR I-2823, 360
Case C-481/99, *Heininger v. Bayr. Hypo und Vereinsbank* [2001] ECR I-9945, 318
Case C-60/00, *Mary Carpenter v. Secretary of State for the Home Department* [2002] ECR I-6279, 50
Case C-94/00, *Roquette Frères* [2002] ECR I-9011, 391, 397
Case C-159/00, *Sapod Audic* [2002] ECR I-5031, 254–255, 262
Case C-168/00, *Simone Leitner v. TUI Deutschland* [2002] ECR I-2631, 311
Case C-253/00, *Munoz v. Frumar* [2002] ECR I-7289, 81, 111, 333, 334
Case C-309/99, *Wouters v. Nederlandse Orde van Advocaten,* [2002] ECR I-1577 72, 254–255, 259, 331
Case 515/99 *Reisch v. Salzburg* [2002] ECR I-2157, 299
Joined Cases C-238/99 P, C-244/99 P, C-245/99 P, C-247/99 P, C-250/99 P to C-252/99 P and C-254/99 P *Limburgse Vinyl Maatschappij and Others v. Commission* [2002] ECR I-8375, 389, 408
Cases C-6/01, *Anomar v. Portugal* [2003] ECR I-8621, 299
Case C-20/00 *Booker Aquaculture* [2003] ECR I-7411, 298
Case C-112/00 , *Eugen Schmidberger, Internationale Transporte und Planzüge v. Republik Österreich,* [2003] ECR I-5659, 16, 50, 86, 102, 115,134, 195, 232, 254, 265, 275, 276, 332
Case C-129/00, *Commission v. Italy,* [2003] ECR I-14637, 89
Case C-176/99, *ARBED v. Commission* [2003] ECR I-2737, 397
Case 187/01 and C-385/01, *Criminal proceedings against Hüseyin Gözütok and Klaus Brügge* [2003] ECR I-1345, 408
Case C-194/99, P *Thyssen Stahl v. Commission* [2003] ECR I-10821, 389
Case C-198/01, *CIF* [2003] ECR I-8055, 256
Case C-224/01, *Köbler* [2003] ECR I-10239, 253
Case C-243/01, *Gambelli,* [2003] ECR I-13031, 98
Case 300/01 *Salzmann* [2003] ECR I-4899, 299
Case C-36/02, *Omega Spielhallen,* [2004] ECR I-9609, 16, 50, 69, 134, 175, 265
Case C-71/02, *Karner* [2004] ECR I-3025, 332
Case C-72/03, *Carbonati Apuani* [2004] ECR I-8027, 298
Case 184/02 and C-223/02 *Spain and Finland v. European Parliament and Council* [2004] ECR I-7789, 137, 289, 296

Court of First Instance/General Court

European Court of Human Rights

EFTA Court

European Commission

Germany

Sweden

Konkurrensverket v. AstraZeneca, Stockholm City Court Case Ä 20087-10, 392

United Kingdom

Case C-l88/89, *Foster and Others v. British Gas plc,* Preliminary Reference under Article 177 EEC by the House of Lords, Decision of the European Court of Justice of 12 July 1990, 27 CMLRev. 859, 867(1990), 258

Ian Edgar (Liverpool) Ltd v. United Kingdom judgment of 25 January 2000, 281–282

Paul and Audrey Edwards v. United Kingdom, judgment of 14 March 2002, 232

R. v. Chief Constable of Sussex, ex parte International Traders' Ferry, [1999] 2 A.C. 418, 86, 102

R. (Morgan Grenfell & Co Ltd) v. Special Commissioners of Income Tax [2003] 1 AC 563 at 606, 100

Stanford v. United Kingdom (1994) Series A, No. 282-A, 349

*Stec v. United Kingdom,*judgment of 12 April 2006 GC, 282

United States

Abrams v. US, 1919, 250 US, 616, 630, 46

Shelley v. Kraemer, 334 U.S. 1 (1948), 17, 228

EUROPEAN MONOGRAPH SERIES

1. Lammy Betten (ed.), *The Future of European Social Policy,* 1991 (ISBN 90-654-4585-4).
2. Annemarie Loman, Kamiel Mortelmans, Harry H.G. Post & Stewart Watson, *Culture and Common Law: Before and After Maastricht,* 1992 (ISBN 90-654-4638-9).
3. John A.E. Vervaele, *Fraud against the Community: The Need for European Fraud Legislation,* 1994 (ISBN 90-654-4634-6).
4. Philip Raworth, *The Legislative Process in the European Community,* 1993 (ISBN 90-654-4690-7).
5. Jules Stuyck, *Financial and Monetary Integration in the European Economic Community,* 1993 (ISBN 90-654-4718-0).
6. Jules Stuyck & A.J. Vossestein (eds), *State Entrepreneurship, National Monopolies and European Community Law,* 1993 (ISBN 90-654-4773-3).
7. Jules Stuyck & A. Looijestijn-Clearie (eds), *The European Economic Area EC-EFTA,* 1994 (ISBN 90-654-4815-2).
8. Rosita B. Bouterse, *Competition and Integration: What Goals Count?,* 1995 (ISBN 90-654-4816-0).
9. René Barents, *The Agricultural Law of the EC: An Inquiry into the Administrative Law,* 1994 (ISBN 90-654-4867-5).
10. Nicholas Emiliou, *Principles of Proportionality in European Law: A Comparative Study,* 1996 (ISBN 90-411-0866-1).
11. Eivind Smith, *National Parliaments as Cornerstones of European Integration,* 1996 (ISBN 90-411-0898-X).
12. Jan H. Jans, *European Environmental Law,* 1996 (ISBN 90-411-0877-7).
13. Síofra O'Leary, *The Evolving Concept of Community Citizenship: From the Free Movement of Persons to Union Citizenship,* 1997 (ISBN 90-411-0878-5).
14. Laurence W. Gormley (ed.), *Current and Future Perspectives on EC Competition Law,* 1983 (ISBN 90-411-0691-X).
15. Simone White, *Protection of the Financial Interests of the European Communities: The Fight against Fraud and Corruption,* 1998 (ISBN 90-411-9647-1).
16. Morten P. Broberg, *Broberg on the European Commission's Jurisdiction to Scrutinise Mergers*, 4th Edition, 2013 (ISBN 978-90-411-3339-7).
17. Doris Hildebrand, *The Role of Economic Analysis in the EC Competition Rules: The European School,* 2nd Edition, 2002 (ISBN 90-411-1706-7).
18. Christof R.A. Swaak, *European Community Law and the Automobile Industry,* 1999 (ISBN 90-411-1140-9).

19. Dorthe Dahlgaard Dingel, *Public Procurement: A Harmonization of the National Judicial Review of the Application of European Community Law,* 1999 (ISBN 90-411-1161-1).
20. John A.E. Vervaele (ed.), *Compliance and Enforcement of European Community Law,* 1999 (ISBN 90-411-1151-4).
21. Martin Trybus, *European Defence Procurement Law: International and National Procurement Systems as Models for a Liberalized Defence Procurement Market in Europe,* 1999 (ISBN 90-411-1167-0).
22. Helen Staples, *The Legal Status of Third Country Nationals Resident in the European Union,* 1999 (ISBN 90-411-1277-4).
23. Damien Geradin (ed.), *The Liberalization of State Monopolies in the European Union and Beyond,* 1999 (ISBN 90-411-1264-2).
24. Katja Heede, *European Ombudsman: Redress and Control at Union Level,* 2000 (ISBN 90-411-1413-0).
25. Ulf Bernitz & Joakim Nergelius (eds), *General Principles of European Community Law,* 2000 (ISBN 90-411-1402-5).
26. Michaela Drahos, *Convergence of Competition Laws and Policies in the European Community,* 2002 (ISBN 90-411-1562-5).
27. Damien Geradin (ed.), *The Liberalization of Electricity and Natural Gas in the European Union,* 2001 (ISBN 90-411-1560-9).
28. Gisella Gori, *Towards an EU Right to Education,* 2001 (ISBN 90-411-1670-2).
29. Brendan P.G. Smith, *Constitution Building in the European Union,* 2001 (ISBN 90-411-1695-8).
30. Friedl Weiss & Frank Wooldridge, *Free Movement of Persons within the European Community,* 2nd Edition, 2007 (ISBN 978-90-411-2545-3).
31. Ingrid Boccardi, *Europe and Refugees: Towards an EU Asylum Policy,* 2002 (ISBN 90-411-1709-1).
32. John A.E. Vervaele & André Klip (eds), *European Cooperation Between Tax, Customs and Judicial Authorities,* 2001 (ISBN 90-411-1747-4).
33. Wouter P.J. Wils, *The Optimal Enforcement of EC Antitrust Law: Essays in Law and Economics,* 2002 (ISBN 90-411-1757-1).
34. Damien Geradin (ed.), *The Liberalization of Postal Services in the European Union,* 2002 (ISBN 90-411-1780-6).
35. Nick Bernard, *Multilevel Governance in the European Union,* 2002 (ISBN 90-411-1812-8).
36. Jill Wakefield, *Judicial Protection through the Use of Article 288(2) EC,* 2002 (ISBN 90-411-1823-3).
37. Sebastiaan Princen, *EU Regulation and Transatlantic Trade,* 2002 (ISBN 90-411-1871-3).

38. Amaryllis Verhoeven, *The European Union in Search of a Democratic and Constitutional Theory,* 2002 (ISBN 90-411-1872-1).
39. Paul L.C. Torremans, *Cross Border Insolvencies in EU, English and Belgian Law,* 2002 (ISBN 90-411-1888-8).
40. Malcolm Anderson & Joanna Apap (eds), *Police and Justice Cooperation and the New European Borders,* 2002 (ISBN 90-411-1893-4).
41. Christin M. Forstinger, *Takeover Law in EU and USA: A Comparative Analysis,* 2002 (ISBN 90-411-1919-1).
42. Antonio Bavasso, *Communications in EU Antitrust Law: Market Power and Public Interest,* 2003 (ISBN 90-411-1974-4).
43. Fiona G. Wishlade, *Regional State Aid and Competition Policy in the European Union,* 2003 (ISBN 90-411-1975-2).
44. Gareth Davies, *Nationality Discrimination in the European Internal Market,* 2003 (ISBN 90-411-1998-1).
45. René Barents, *The Autonomy of Community Law,* 2003 (ISBN 90-411-2251-6).
46. Gerhard Dannecker & Oswald Jansen (eds), *Competition Law Sanctioning in the European Union,* 2004 (ISBN 90-411-2100-5).
47. Nauta Dutilh (ed.), *Dealing with Dominance: The Experience of National Competition Authorities,* 2004 (ISBN 90-411-2211-7).
48. Stefaan van den Bogaert, *Practical Regulation of the Mobility of Sportsmen in the EU Post Bosman,* 2005 (ISBN 90-411-2327-X).
49. Katalin Judit Cseres, *Competition Law and Consumer Protection,* 2005 (ISBN 90-411-2380-6).
50. Philipp Kiiver, *The National Parliaments in the European Union: A Critical View on EU Constitution Building,* 2006 (ISBN 978-90-411-2452-4).
51. Alexander Turk, *The Concept of Legislation in European Community Law,* 2006 (ISBN 978-90-411-2472-2).
52. Dimitrios Sinaniotis, *The Interim Protection of Individuals before the European and National Courts,* 2006 (ISBN 978-90-411-2498-2).
53. M. Holoubek & D. Damjanovic, M. Traimer (eds), *Regulating Content: The European Regulatory Framework for the Media and Related Creative Sectors,* 2006 (ISBN 978-90-411-2597-2).
54. Anneli Albi & Jacques Ziller (eds), *The European Constitution and National Constitutions: Ratification and Beyond,* 2006 (ISBN 978-90-411-2524-8).
55. Gustavo E. Luengo, *Regulation of Subsidies and State Aids in WTO and EC Law: Conflicts in International Trade Law,* 2007 (ISBN 978-90-411-2547-7).
56. Eniko Horvath, *Mandating Identity: Citizenship, Kinship Laws and Plural Nationality in the European Union,* 2007 (ISBN 978-90-411-2662-7).

57. Rass Holdgaard, *External Relations Law of the European Community: Legal Reasoning and Legal Discourses,* 2007 (ISBN 978-90-411-2604-7).
58. Jill Wakefield, *The Right to Good Administration,* 2007 (ISBN 978-90-411-2697-9).
59. Dimitry Kochenov, *EU Enlargement and the Failure of Conditionality: Pre- accession Conditionality in the Fields of Democracy and the Rule of Law,* 2008 (ISBN 978-90-411-2696-2).
60. Despina Mavromati, *The Law of Payment Services in the EU: The EC Directive on Payment Services in the Internal Market,* 2008 (ISBN 978-90-411-2700-6).
61. Anne Meuwese, *Impact Assessment in EU Lawmaking,* 2008 (ISBN 978-90-411-2720-4).
62. Ulf Bernitz, Joakim Nergelius & Cecilia Cardner (eds), *General Principles of EC Law in a Process of Development,* 2008 (ISBN 978-90-411-2705-1).
63. Johan van de Gronden (ed.), *The EU and WTO Law on Services: Limits to the Realisation of General Interest Policies within the Services Markets?,* 2008 (ISBN 978-90-411-2809-6).
64. Alina Tryfonidou, *Reverse Discrimination in EC Law,* 2009 (ISBN 978-90-411-2751-8).
65. Mikael Berglund, *Cross-Border Enforcement of Claims in the EU: History Present Time and Future,* 2009 (ISBN 978-90-411-2861-4).
66. Theodore Konstadinides, *Division of Powers in European Union Law: The Delimitation of Internal Competence between the EU and the Member States,* 2009 (ISBN 978-90-411-2615-3).
67. Mattias Derlén, *Multilingual Interpretation of European Union Law,* 2009 (ISBN 978-90-411-2853-9).
68. René Barents, *Directory of EU Case Law on the Preliminary Ruling Procedure,* 2009 (ISBN 978-90-411-3150-8).
69. Yan Luo, *Anti-dumping in the WTO, the EU and China: The Rise of Legalization in the Trade Regime and its Consequences,* 2010 (ISBN 978-90-411-3207-9).
70. Patrick Birkinshaw & Mike Varney (eds), *The European Union Legal Order after Lisbon,* 2010 (ISBN 978-90-411-3152-2).
71. Thomas Gr. Papadopoulos, *EU Law and Harmonization of Takeovers in the Internal Market,* 2010 (978-90-411-3340-3).
72. Bas van Bockel, *The* Ne Bis In Idem *Principle in EU Law,* 2010 (978-90-411-3156-0).
73. Veljko Milutinović, *The 'Right to Damages' under EU Competition Law: From* Courage v. Crehan *to the White Paper and Beyond,* 2010 (978-90-411-3235-2).

74. Amandine Garde, *EU Law and Obesity Prevention*, 2010 (978-90-411-2706-8).
75. Leonard Besselink, Frans Pennings & Sacha Prechal (eds), *The Eclipse of the Legality Principle in the European Union*, 2011 (978-90-411-3262-8).
76. Sacha Garben, *EU Higher Education Law: The Bologna Process and Harmonization by Stealth*, 2011 (978-90-411-3365-6).
77. Dimitry Kochenov (ed.), *EU Law of the Overseas: Outermost Regions, Associated Overseas Countries and Territories, Territories Sui Generis*, 2011 (978-90-411-3445-5).
78. Pablo Ibáñez Colomo, *European Communications Law and Technological Convergence: Deregulation, Re-regulation and Regulatory Convergence in Television and Telecommunications*, 2012 (978-90-411-3829-3).
79. Elise Muir, *EU Regulation of Access to Labour Markets: A Case Study of EU Constraints on Member State Competences*, 2012 (978-90-411-3823-1).
80. Tim Corthaut, *EU Ordre Public*, 2012 (978-90-411-3232-1).
81. Oana Ştefan, *Soft Law in Court: Competition Law, State Aid and the Court of Justice of the European Union*, 2013 (978-90-411-3997-9).
82. Francesco Rossi dal Pozzo, *Citizenship Rights and Freedom of Movement in the European Union*, 2013 (978-90-411-4660-1).
83. Jens Hartig Danielsen, *EU Agricultural Law*, 2013 (978-90-411-3280-2).
84. Ulf Bernitz, Xavier Groussot & Felix Schulyok (eds), *General Principles of EU Law and European Private Law*, 2013 (978-90-411-4683-0).